Advance praise for *Unheroic Conduct*:

"Few commentators on the vexed issue of Jud
as much passion, courage, and audacity to
Boyarin to his. None combines these virtue
mastery of contemporary theory, and ebulli
her religious and sexual identity, the reader
not fail to be touched by the explosive power
ishly calls 'Jewissance.' " —Martin Jay, author
Denigration of Vision in Twentieth-Century Fre Thought

"Daniel Boyarin's work has been instrumental in opening a way for
me into Jewish thinking, Jewish history, and Judaism itself. The obsta-
cles and barricades presented by reactionary dogma, deadweight un-
thinking orthodoxy, and bewildering, centuries-old Otherness
Boyarin masterfully, delightfully, movingly transforms into sites of
rich controversy, into sources of meaning: in which inclusion becomes possible, in which a place can be found in the suddenly surprisingly roomy, surprisingly complex, contrary Tradition for the utopian
expectations of Diasporan Jewish, modernist (politically progressive)
culture. Boyarin's is a thoroughly dazzling intellect: he is a scholar, a
critical and political thinker, a wit, and a wonderful, passionate
writer. His new book surveys and explores Jewish masculinity with
astonishing acuity, with an encyclopedic grasp of not only nineteenth-
century and modernist but very recent literature on the subject, and
with a playfulness and honesty appropriately unashamed of subjec-
tive experience —full of vitality, both emotional and intellectual, a
reckless and rigorous diving deep after truth. Boyarin's readings of
'two of the most fateful movements of modern times, psychoanalysis
and Zionism,' illuminate our current crises in such a way as to suggest, and it is a very Jewish suggestion, that such slim hope as exists
for transformation and redemption can only be found through a
countenancing and a settling of accounts with the past." —Tony
Kushner, author of *Angels in America*

"Daniel Boyarin has written a bold and learned book on Jewish gender identities. In rabbinical commentary and modern history, he has
found the sources for a Jewish definition of masculinity—a flexible alternative to the western macho hero, but rigid and unjust in its exclusion of women from the high duties of religious study. Boyarin proposes another model, one in which Talmud and the study of the Law

are sustained by women and men in full equality. Whether citing the ancient Sage Johanon, taking issue with the Zionist Theodor Herzl, or approving the feminist Bertha Pappenheim, Boyarin invites his readers into a lively, generous, and often humorous debate. Here Orthodox Judaism is both celebrated and transformed." —Natalie Zemon Davis, author of *Women on the Margins*

"The innovative and startling theses of this book command attention. It fills a blank space in our analysis of modern Jewish history inasmuch as it sees concepts of manhood as the central facts which determine the attitudes of Jewish men toward themselves and toward women. The book is stimulating and controversial; it forces us to face its challenging thesis." —George L. Mosse, author of *The Image of Man: The Creation of Modern Masculinity*

"Daniel Boyarin forges a complex network of connections among attitudes to gender, anti-Semitism, and East European orthodox Judaism at the end of the last century to offer new reflections on alternative modes of thinking about all three questions today. Using Talmudic studies, psychoanalytical theory, and historical research, Boyarin's wide-ranging scholarship underpins a truly unusual political openness. It is exciting to read a book marked by optimism of the intellect as well as of the will." —Juliet Mitchell, author of *Psychoanalysis and Feminism*

"This wide-ranging and exciting book has a least three projects. One, as Boyarin says, is to allow him to find himself in history as the Jewish-valorized soft man. Another is to place him in a tradition that makes possible the active interventions of women into history, in spite of the oppressive aspects of the tradition. And a third is to try to locate Freud as a pivotal figure, pivotal because while he is the son of an Eastern European Jew, he also helps to create modern bourgeois Western Europe. . . . This book will create enormous controversy, not least because of its frontal attack on the Zionist image of the 'muscle-Jew'; but it is intellectually alive, full on new readings and thrilling interconnections. Contentious without being arrogant, argumentative without being self-righteous, the book will reach far beyond scholarly audiences." —Natalie Boymel Kampen, editor of *Sexuality in Ancient Art*

Unheroic Conduct

Contraversions
Critical Studies in Jewish Literature, Culture, and Society
Daniel Boyarin and Chana Kronfeld, General Editors

1. *A Radical Jew: Paul and the Politics of Identity,* by Daniel Boyarin

2. *On the Margins of Modernism: Decentering Literary Dynamics,* by
Chana Kronfeld

3. *The Two Shores of Yabbok: Sickness and Death in Ashkenazy Judaism,*
by Sylvie-Anne Goldberg, translated by Carol Cosman

4. *Foregone Conclusions: Against Apocalyptic History,* by Michael André
Bernstein

5. *Founder of Hasidism: A Quest for the Historical Ba'al Shem Tov,* by
Moshe Rosman

6. *Embroideries: My Conversations with Dvora Baron, 1990–1991,* by
Amia Lieblich, translated by Naomi Seidman, edited by Chana Kronfeld and
Naomi Seidman

7. *A Marriage Made in Heaven: The Sexual Politics of Hebrew and Yiddish,*
by Naomi Seidman

8. *Unheroic Conduct: The Rise of Heterosexuality and the Invention of the
Jewish Man,* by Daniel Boyarin

Unheroic Conduct

The Rise of Heterosexuality
and the Invention of the Jewish Man

Daniel Boyarin

UNIVERSITY OF CALIFORNIA PRESS

Berkeley • *Los Angeles* • *London*

University of California Press
Berkeley and Los Angeles, California

University of California Press, Ltd.
London, England

© 1997 by
The Regents of the University of California

Library of Congress Cataloging-in-Publication
Data

Boyarin, Daniel.
    Unheroic conduct : the rise of heterosexuality
and the invention of the Jewish man / Daniel
Boyarin.
        p.   cm. — (Contraversions ; 8)
    Includes bibliographical references and index.
    ISBN 0-520-21050-6 (pbk.: alk. paper)
    1. Sex—Religious aspects—Judaism.   2. Man
(Jewish theology)   3. Heterosexuality.   4. Judaism
and psychoanalysis.   I. Title.   II. Series.
BM720.S4B69   1997
296.3'878343—dc20   96-46047
                                            CIP

Printed in the United States of America

08   07   06   05   04   03   02   01   00

9   8   7   6   5   4   3   2

For Shamma and Yishai נ״י

To reclaim cultural traditions without getting bogged down in the mire of traditional constraints, to attack stereotypes without falling prey to their binary opposites, to chart new topographies for manliness and womanliness, will surely demand genuine heroism.

—King-Kok Cheung

Contents

Elaborate Acknowledgments ix

Prologue: Justify My Love xiii

Introduction 1

PART ONE: MEN WHO ROAM WITH THE SHEEP:
 DIASPORA AND THE IMAGE OF THE JEWISH MAN 31

1. *Goyim Naches;*
 Or, the *Mentsh* and the Jewish Critique of Romance 33
2. Jewish Masochism:
 On Penises and Politics, Power and Pain 81
3. Rabbis and Their Pals:
 Rabbinic Homosociality and the Lives of Women 127
4. Femminization and Its Discontents:
 Torah Study as a System for the Domination of Women 151

PART TWO: THE RISE OF HETEROSEXUALITY AND
 THE INVENTION OF THE MODERN JEW 187

5. Freud's Baby, Fliess's Maybe;
 Or, Male Hysteria, Homophobia, and the
 Invention of the Jewish Man 189
6. "You May Not Tell the Boys":
 The Diaspora Politics of a Bitextual Jew 221
7. The Colonial Drag: Zionism, Gender, and Mimicry 271
8. Retelling the Story of O.;
 Or, Bertha Pappenheim, My Hero 313

Works Cited 361

Index 387

Elaborate Acknowledgments

*(because a book is not the product
of the author's subjectivity)*

For the past four years (at this writing) I have had the privilege of teaching at Berkeley, where I have been conducting graduate seminars in talmudic sexuality and gender. This teaching has been a constant source of learning and self-disclosure for me on many levels, "intellectual" as well as "emotional." (I scare-quote this distinction, because it is hard for me to make it; the intellectual so clearly shot through with desire and desire so clearly inscribed by theory.) As originally planned, this was to be a study of the construction of gender through descriptions of the female body in the Talmud. While we were studying the material in the seminars, however, my students made me sharply aware of the political—for me a synonym of ethical—impossibility of the project as conceived that way. A project that explicitly set out to be feminist in its politics was clearly, inescapably reinscribing the very relations of dominance that it desired and claimed to criticize. This insight about scholarship is not new; what is new is that it was made clear to me before the book was published or even written, thanks to the courage, integrity, and passion of my junior colleagues—male and female.

After a semester of reading the talmudic materials relating to the female body, and at the insistence of these students, we began to read the (more meager) materials that discuss male sexual physiology. Reading texts about penises and ejaculations, I discovered, exposed myself to myself (and to others), and it exposed men to female gaze in ways that were intensely generative of the present project. Suddenly the question was not: How can I/we do something about the "situation" of women in Judaism, but: What does it mean to be a Jewish man? What kind of a man am I, and what kind of a man do I want to be—if I want to be a man at all? From that interactive mutual reading (of text and "self") the present project evolved, one in which the original proposal is subsumed into a different context that, I hope, involves it in a different politics of male feminism.

Homi K. Bhabha and Juliet Mitchell are simply the most generous and constructively critical teachers a scholar could hope to have, and both of them read and critiqued several of the chapters (some of them several times). This book would have been impossible without the courses that I followed with them at the School of Criticism and Theory at Dartmouth College in summer 1993.

The following have been exceedingly generous and helpful readers of parts or all of this text in various forms: Fawzia Afzal-Khan, Gil Anidjar, Shuli Barzilai, Yariv Ben-Aharon, David Biale, Alice Boyarin, Jonathan Boyarin, Sidney Boyarin, Natalie Zemon Davis, Howard Eilberg-Schwartz, Yaakov Elman, Sidra Dekoven Ezrahi, Yaron Ezrahi, Schlomo Fischer, Charlotte Fonrobert, Diana Fuss, Catherine Gallagher, Jay Geller, Michael Gluzman, Stephen Greenblatt, Samuel Haber, Nonna Verna E. F. Harrison, Galit Hasan-Rokem, Judith Hauptman, Hanan Hever, Marianne Hirsch, Martin Jay, Marc Kaminsky, Madeline Kochen, Chana Kronfeld, Christopher Lane, Laura Levitt, Natan Margalit, Chaim Milikowsky, Donald Moss, Adi Ophir, Ann Pellegrini, Miriam Peskowitz, Jennifer Ring, Michael Rogin, Eric Santner, Jonathan Schorsch, Naomi Seidman, Kalpana Seshadri-Crooks, Susan Shapiro, H. Aram Veeser, Steven Zipperstein, and especially Ruth Stein, who read the book and helped write the author. I want to express special gratitude to feminist friends who have seen me as an ally even when I have gone drastically wrong, and who helped me to both raise my consciousness and correct my errors through trenchant and sometimes angry criticism for the sake of heaven.

Thomas J. Luxon's reading of the entire manuscript at an early and critical stage of its existence was enormously helpful, and many of his comments have been incorporated nearly verbatim in the text. One of the characteristics of my "authorial" style is a constant dialogue with others as I am writing. My bibliography for this book is populated with perhaps an unusual number of "letters to the author," written in response to drafts sent to various close and distant colleagues. The occasional epistolary style of the text reflects their collegiality and critical generosity, and I am grateful to them all.

I would like also to forthrightly acknowledge that I am not a classicist, and, although I have tried to inform myself as well as I can from the best of classical scholarship, there is an obvious difference between knowing a culture through its texts and through what scholars have written about those texts. Friends and colleagues among professionals in the field have been invaluable in "keeping me honest." Among these unsparing—in both senses—critics I would like to thank Carlin Barton, Chava Boyarin, Erich Gruen, David M. Halperin, Natalie Boymel Kampen, Molly Levine, Amy Richlin, and Brent Shaw. Froma Zeitlin has over and over again inspired me and kept me from making things too easy for myself, and I am very grateful for her friendship and collaboration. I have tried my best to observe the learned counsel of these people, but none of them has read the entire text, and so no one but I am responsible for such errors as remain.

I especially thank Virginia Burrus for being a true pal. Since discovering how closely related our two current projects are—almost like fraternal twins—we have been exchanging drafts and conversations. The book and my life have been immeasurably enriched by our growing friendship. Much of this book is hers.

I would also like to acknowledge the input of many interlocutors at the School of Criticism and Theory, SUNY Buffalo, Syracuse University, Duke University, the University of Wisconsin, Princeton University, Johns Hopkins University, Columbia University, and Maʿayan (a Jewish feminist research group in New York) for invaluable discussions of various chapters of the book in earlier forms, and I would especially like to acknowledge the formal respondents at the last-mentioned occasion: Dawn Rose and Ann Golomb Hoffman.

A reading for the University of California Press by Muriel Dimen provided important critical comments and missed bibliographical items which I have been happy to add to my reading for final revisions.

A special debt of gratitude must be repaid to Paul Breines, who with great generosity of spirit appreciated the manuscript (as a reader for the Press) in spite of the fact that I had not read (nor, obviously, cited) his very apposite and admirable book, *Tough Jews*. I have since redressed that serious lapse in my reading and wish to couple my project to his, for I, too, "have tried to write on behalf of the victims of modern politics and in the service of gentleness" (Breines, *Tough Jews*, xii).

I owe special thanks to the donors of the Taubman Chair of Talmudic Culture, the President's Research Fellowship in the Humanities of the University of California, the Committee on Research of the College of Letters and Sciences at the University of California at Berkeley, the Leo Baeck Institute, the Memorial Foundation for Jewish Culture, and the John Simon Guggenheim Foundation for crucial support of my research during the preparation of this book. I would like to mark as well the enthusiastic and erudite help of Renata Stein of the Leo Baeck Institute particularly in helping me locate the images that (I hope) "bring home" several of the points made in the book. Ms. Stein also provided me with excellent translations of some of the texts of Bertha Pappenheim discussed in the book.

I would also like to express a special debt of gratitude to the unsung heroes of publishing, my editors: Bud Bynack, Scott Norton, and always Doris Kretschmer.

Several parts of the book have been previously published in earlier forms. A version of chapter 1 has appeared in *Modernity, Culture and "The Jew,"* edited by Bryan Cheyette (Stanford University Press); versions of chapter 2 in *American Imago;* of chapter 3 in *differences;* of chapter 5 in *GLQ: A Journal of Lesbian and Gay Studies;* and of chapter 6 in *Queer Diasporas,* edited by Cindy Patton and Benigno Sánchez-Eppler (Duke University Press). I thank all these editors, journals, and presses for permission to revise and reprint my work.

A note to the "nonacademic" readers who—I hope—will find this book: I have tried to make my writing here as clear and readable as I can, but there are aspects of my style that will undoubtedly be strange to readers unaccustomed to reading this kind of text, in particular the extensive citation and discussion of others' work. The purpose of this is not, as folklore would have it, to give the appearance of erudition, to make the text difficult for those not in the "guild" to read, or to bolster my arguments, but rather to signal the intellectual debts that I have and to indicate how any project of thought takes place in a community of thinkers and is part of a social process. The references should also help readers who wish to follow further any particular aspects of the argument or the materials under discussion to find their way to other writers and, furthermore, to help them to dispute and argue against me when they so wish. It is rather the text that just "tells its story" that insists on its own authority, while an "academic" text gives ample room and provides equipment for others to contend with it and contest it. I have thought long and hard about ways to make this citation as unintrusive as possible, and if it still annoys, consider please the alternatives and the losses they would entail.

Prologue

Justify My Love

As I reflect on my coming of age in New Jersey, I realize that I had always been in some sense more of a "girl" than a "boy." A sissy who did not like sports, whose mother used to urge me, stop reading and go out and play, in fifth grade I went out for—ballet. (Of course I explained to the guys that it was a kind of sophisticated bodybuilding.) This in itself is rather a familiar story, a story of inexplicable gender dysphoria, but one that had for me, even then, a rather happy ending. I didn't think of myself so much as girlish but rather as Jewish.

I start with what I think is a widespread sensibility that being Jewish in our culture renders a boy effeminate. Rather than producing in me a desire to "pass" and to become a "man," this sensibility resulted in my desire to remain a Jew, where being a sissy was all right. To be sure, this meant being marginal, and it has left me with a persistent sense of being on the outside of something, with my nose pressed to the glass looking in, but the cultural and communal place that a sissy occupied in my social world was not one that enforced rage and self-contempt. In a quite similar account another male American Jew of my generation, Harry Brod, writes: "I found the feminist critique of mainstream masculinity personally empowering rather than threatening. As a child and adolescent, I did not fit the mainstream male image. I was an outsider, not an athlete but an intellectual, fat, shy and with a stutter for many years. The feminist critique of mainstream masculinity allowed me to convert my envy of those who fit the approved model to con-

tempt. It converted males previously my superiors on the traditional
scale to males below me on the new scale, for I had obviously shown
premature insight and sensitivity in rejecting the old male mode. I could
pretend that others' rejection of me had really been my rejection of
them. Of course, I could not have admitted this at the time. To do so
would have seemed effeminate, and confirming of my fears of others'
worst judgments of me." Brod moves on to a critique of this sensibility,
referring to it as a "shield against other men." While I share his concern
about the self-serving (and triumphant) countenance of the "use of my
Jewishness to avoid being categorized as a 'real' man, 'real' understood
as a term of critique rather than praise,"[1] I want to use the sissy, the
Jewish male femme as a location and a critical practice.

I am interested right now in investigating what critical force might
still be left in a culture and a cultural memory within which "real men"
were sissies. The vector of my theoretical-political work, accordingly, is
not to deny as antisemitic fantasy but to reclaim the nineteenth-century
notion of the feminized Jewish male, to argue for his reality as one Jewish ideal going back to the Babylonian Talmud. I desire also to find a
model for a gentle, nurturing masculinity in the traditional Jewish male
ideal—without making claims as to how often realized this ideal was—
a male who could be so comfortable with his little, fleshy penis that he
would not have to grow it into "The Phallus," a sort of Velvet John. He
whom a past dominant culture (as well as those Jews who internalized
its values) considers contemptible, the feminized Jewish (colonized)
male, may be useful today, for "he" may help us precisely today in our
attempts to construct an alternative masculine subjectivity, one that
will not have to rediscover such cultural archetypes as Iron Johns,
knights, hairy men, and warriors within.

I am increasingly called upon to clarify something that I have never
quite been able to explain until now, namely, the grounds for, and possibility of, a dual commitment to radical reclamation of traditional Jewish cultural life/practice/study and to radical reconstruction of the
organization of gendered and sexual practices within our society (including necessarily the Jewish subculture). The first commitment is generated out of a sense of cultural/religious continuity as a value in itself
and of Judaism as a rich, sustaining, and fulfilling way of life; the second derives from a deeply held conviction (and the affective stance) that

1. Brod, *Mensch*, 7, 8.

Jewish practices have been oppressive to people in ways that I cannot stomach.

I have learned these dual commitments through living experience. Growing up in a way typical of most American Jews of my generation (the 1960s), I experienced Judaism as a vaguely attractive, sometimes silly, sometimes obnoxious set of occasional intrusions in my life, called Rosh Hashana, Yom Kippur, and Pesah. On the positive side, it represented for me a compelling passion for social justice which led me in high school to (almost) join the Communist Party of America. I finally turned, again like many American Jews of my time to Far Eastern mysticism as a mode of escape from the arid, nonspiritual microclimate that the synagogue had become and the equally arid possibilities and promises of a life without spirit at all.

Chance encounters—with a lulav-wielding Lubavitcher, with a therapist who gave me an English translation of the Zohar, with a young disciple of Zalman Schachter—began to hint that there might be more to Judaism than I had been misled to believe by American liberal Judaism. One night, in my second year in college, I dreamed that I was in Israel, and so came to spend my third year of college in Israel thinking that I was destined for a life as a kabbalist. I wasn't.

The Talmud tempted me away from kabbala. Most American Jews don't have an inkling even of what the Talmud is. I certainly didn't. Sometimes I think I imagined it as a sort of commentary on the Torah (confusing it, I suppose, with midrash); sometimes as something like Euclid's geometry applied to precisely what I couldn't imagine, since my image of Jewish "Law" was that it was something unambiguous and found in a book called the *Shulkhan Arukh*. I had never seen even the outside binding of the Talmud, let alone the *Shulkhan Arukh*.

My friend, the aforementioned disciple of Shachter, had said to me: "Before you can understand Zohar, you have to know Talmud," so at the Hebrew University I signed up for the preparatory course in reading the Talmud and was charmed—in the full antique sense of the word— from almost the first sentence we read. Here was a world so strange and rich, so colorful and exciting, with myths and legends, challenges to the intellect, and, most of all, personalities rendered so vital that they seemed living men, men, moreover, who devoted their lives to the elaboration of what it means to live correctly, as a Jew. And this was all "mine." I became Orthodox for love of the Talmud. I admit freely, if ruefully, that it was so absorbing that I hardly noticed they *were* all men, or that the text was primarily addressed to me just because I was a Jewish *man*—I didn't recognize the exclusions and oppressions that those facts encode and mystify.

I believe there is no textual product of human culture that is quite like the jumbled, carnivalesque, raucous, bawdy, vital, exciting Talmud, nor is there anything quite like the practices of study that characterize it and the whole way of life that it subtends.[2] These are not, of course, the adjectives that have been traditionally used, either from within or from without, to describe the talmudic life. I make it sound, and indeed I experience it, as if it were almost Rabelaisian. When after a year and a half of study I came upon a text that described the death of Rav, I underwent an emotional experience akin to hearing of the death of a beloved teacher. It had become, I realized, almost unimaginable to me that Rav was not alive, because he was so alive in the text—alive I would add because not idealized, because the Talmud was as open to the flawed humanity of its heroes as the Bible had been to its. I have discovered that I am not alone: there are many people, including many women and lesbigay people, who are just as entranced by the Talmud as I have been and just as passionate about devoting their lives to it.

I deeply love and feel connected to rabbinic texts and culture, and even more to the Rabbis themselves, but there is much within them that I find deeply disturbing as well, and much of that has to do with the oppression of women.

This awareness also came to me from significant encounters. In the late 1980s I attended the School of Criticism and Theory at Dartmouth College, and for reasons that I cannot now quite remember or reconstruct, I joined a feminist reading group, as one of two men in the group among approximately twenty women. This little community provided me with my first direct experience of feminism as theory and the experiences that had produced it as practice. Although very different from the affect that had compelled me to devote a life to the study and practice of Talmud, this experience was no less compelling. At the end of the summer I could no longer describe myself only as an Orthodox Jew; I had now to say (for a long time only to myself) that being a male feminist was constitutive and definitive of my experience of self. The

---

2. Astonishingly to me, I know not why, Eve Kosofsky Sedgwick has captured perfectly my sensibility when she writes of "Talmudic desires, to reproduce or unfold the text and to giggle" (*Epistemology*, 240). I am grateful for that sentence, as for much else in her work. In contrast to this, I wonder at Christine Delphy's repeated use of "talmudic" as a pejorative for the discourse of false feminists. This remains a stumbling block for me in my appreciation of her otherwise quite wonderful work.

contradictions seemed so ungappable that I just endeavored to live with them for a number of years until I could no longer do so. Unable, however, to let go or even diminish either one of these fundamental components of my self, I discovered that I had to find ways to theorize a rapprochement (or at least to make the contradictions creative).

My endeavor is to justify my love, that is, both to explain it and to make it just. I explain my devotion in part by showing that Judaism provides exempla for another kind of masculinity, one in which men do not manifest "a deeply rooted concern about the possible meanings of dependence on other males,"[3] and thus one within which "feminization" is not experienced as a threat or a danger. I cannot, however, paper over, ignore, explain away, or apologize for the oppressions of women and lesbigay people that this culture has practiced, and therefore I endeavor as well to render it just by presenting a way of reading the tradition that may help it surmount or expunge—in time—that which I and many others can no longer live with.

In this dual aspect of resistance to pressure from without and critique from within, my project is homologous to other political, cultural acts of resistance in the face of colonialisms. For some three hundred years now, Jews have been the target of the civilizing mission in Europe. In her recent dissertation, Laura Levitt makes palpably clear the homologies between the "liberal" colonizing impulse directed toward those Others within Europe and toward the colonized outside of Europe insofar as for both it is constituted by a demand that their sexual practices be "reformed" to conform to the liberal bourgeois regime.[4] One of the most common of liberal justifications for the extension of colonial control over a given people and for the maintenance of the civilizing mission is the imputed barbarity of the treatment of women within the culture under attack.[5] The civilizing mission, and its Jewish agents among "the Enlighteners," considered the fact that Jewish women behaved in ways interpreted as masculine by European bourgeois society to be simply monstrous.[6] Modern Jewish culture, liberal

3. Edelman, "Redeeming," 50.
4. Levitt, *Reconfiguring,* 152–73.
5. Butler, *Gender,* 3; Geller, "Of Mice"; Hyams, "Weininger"; Sharpe, "Unspeakable Limits."
6. In an earlier version I had written: "its Jewish agents, the 'Enlighteners,'" but as Naomi Seidman has correctly admonished me, this was not entirely fair, since there was a genuine feminist impulse animating a not insignificant component of the Jewish Enlightenment as well. Nor am I prepared, of course, to entirely disavow the Enlightenment project as part of who I am. Nevertheless, the insistence of the Jewish Enlightenment that

and bourgeois in its aspirations and its preferred patterns of gendered
life, has been the result of this civilizing mission. As Paula Hyman has
recently demonstrated, the very Jewish religiosity of the modern bourgeois Jewish family is an assimilating mimicry of Protestant middle-
class piety, not least in its portrayal of proper womanhood.[7] The richness of Jewish life and difference has been largely lost, and the gains for
Jewish women were largely illusory.[8] This having been said, however,
the Jewish anticolonial project—like any other—cannot refrain from a
trenchant, unflinching, and unapologetic internal critique of the harsh
oppressions within the very traditional culture that it seeks to protect
from destruction from without, namely, the structure of systematic exclusion of women from the practices that the culture most highly regards and especially the study of Torah. This exclusion has been a
breeding ground of contempt—sometimes quite extreme—for women
and a perpetrator of second-class status within Jewish law.

I repeat that I deeply love and feel connected to rabbinic texts and
culture, but there is much within them that I find deeply disturbing as
well. If Jewish culture has been a place of safety for a sissy, it has
hardly—to understate the case—provided such felicitous conditions for
Jewish women. This is a feminist project, at least to the extent that it
owes its life to feminism and the work of feminist critics. Male self-
fashioning has consequences for women. I feel an inner mandate to see
to it that a project of reclamation of Judaic culture from the depredations of the civilizing, colonializing onslaught to which it has been subject does not interfere with (even perhaps contributes something to) the
ongoing project of feminist critique of that same traditional culture
from within—to see to it, as best I can, that is, that my practice,
whether or not it is part of the solution, is not part of the problem. I
thus try to meet the challenge implicit in Tania Modleski's observation

only an eradication of the "talmudic spirit" could fit the Jews for civilization is an unre-
mittingly colonialist project. As my student Abe Socher has pointed out: "Jewish Enlighteners (*Maskilim*) even identified the mortifying 'jargon' of Yiddish with the Aramaic of
the Talmud. Just as Yiddish was a corruption of the pure language of German and, as
such, an impossible vehicle for anything but *unbildung*, so too was Aramaic a corruption
of the pure Hebrew of the Bible. This equation between the two pure languages of biblical
Hebrew and eighteenth-century German was epitomized in Mendelssohn's *Biur,* a Hebrew Bible with a running translation into High German, rendered in Hebrew letters.
Almost a century later, the great nineteenth-century historian Heinrich Graetz summed
up the *Maskilic* attitude when he wrote of the eastern European Talmudists' love of 'twist-
ing, distorting, ingenious quibbling,' which has 'reduced the language of German Jews to
a repulsive stammer'" (Socher, "Magus")—QED. See also Aschheim, *Brothers,* 14–15.
    7. Hyman, *Gender,* 26–27.
    8. Magnes, "Pauline."

that male critique of masculinity is feminist when "it analyzes male power, male hegemony, with a concern for the effects of this power *on the female subject* and with an awareness of how frequently male subjectivity works to appropriate 'femininity' while oppressing women."[9] The dual movement of the political project, to resist the delegitimization of Judaic culture from without, while supporting the feminist critique from within, dictates the structure of my work.

Thinking about the sissy body of the "Jewish man," I think simultaneously about another discourse and practice—possibly but not necessarily liberatory—that constructs the male body in a very different way. The "gay male gym body" is an example of another male body constructed as an alternative to the heterosexual male body. David Halperin (following in part D. A. Miller) has recently given us a brilliant and moving rejoinder to "straight, liberal" attacks on gay male bodybuilding by arguing for an absolute, total differentiation between the "macho straight male body" and "the gay male gym body": "What distinguishes the gay male gym body, then, in addition to its spectacular beauty, is the way it advertises itself as an object of desire. Gay muscles do not signify power." He further makes the impeccable point that the (ideal) gay male body does not look like at all like the straight macho body

> they [gay male bodies] are explicitly designed to be an erotic turn-on, and in their very solicitation of desire they deliberately flaunt the visual norms of straight masculinity, which impose discretion on masculine self-display and require that straight male beauty exhibit itself only casually or inadvertently, that it refuse to acknowledge its own strategies. If, as Foucault hypothesized in *Discipline and Punish,* those whom modern disciplinary society would destroy it first makes visible, then gay male body-builders, in visibly inscribing their erotic desires on the surfaces of their bodies, have not only exposed themselves to considerable social risks in the course of pursuing their ethical projects but have also performed a valuable political service on behalf of everyone, insofar as they have issued a challenge of defiance to the very mechanisms of modern discipline.[10]

This is inarguable—and I am hardly insensible to the attraction of that "spectacular beauty"—but it nevertheless remains the case that the very standard for male beauty that is being prescribed is one of a certain form of muscular development that emphasizes the dimorphism of the gendered body and thus participates, to this extent, in the general cul-

---

9. Modleski, *Feminism,* 7.
10. Halperin, *Saint Foucault,* 117.

tural standard of masculinity rather than resisting it.[11] The pale, limp, and semiotically unaggressive "nelly" or sissy male body is not seen within this construct as beautiful or erotic at all, but this exclusion as well can be shown to be culturally specific and limited.

Lori Lefkovitz makes the point that Joseph in the midrash is described as having a body that is explicitly designed to be an erotic turn-on, but it is not at all the body of a Muscle-Jew. He penciled his eyes, curled his hair, and lifted his heels, and, moreover, his was a beauty like that of his mother Rachel—and it was *this* beauty that so attracted Potiphar's wife and indeed all the noblewomen of Egypt![12] Thus, on one hand I think that Halperin clearly is right that "the hypermasculine look of gay clones is deceiving. What the new styles of gay virility represent, paradoxically, is a strategy for valorizing various practices of devirilization under the sign of masculinity, thereby forging a new association between masculinity and sexual receptivity or penetrability, while detaching male homosexuality from its phobic association with 'femininity' (conceived in phallic terms as 'passivity' or as an absence of phallic aggressivity)."[13] On the other hand, I fear that this strategy backfires insofar as it continues to register only one kind of male body as desirable, thus "clonedom" (and I do not claim, of course, that this is true for all gay male culture). Thus, in addition to the dislodging of sexual receptivity from "femininity"—conceived of as lack, castration, and the negatively encoded "passivity"—that the gay male gym body enacts, there also has to be a parallel dislodging of the penetrating penis—gay or straight—from masculinity, conceived as "phallic aggressivity," as well as from the ways that, as Foucault has pointed out, such "topness" is still valorized over receptivity in nearly all sectors of our sexual culture.[14]

One place to find the eroticized sissy is at a reading of the rabbinic textual tradition. On one hand, this tradition clearly privileges—to understate again—sexual connections between men and women[15] and also clearly prescribes social domination of men over women; at the

---

11. Put another way, and granting once more the plausibility of Halperin's construction, is there not at least the possible danger of misreading—not only by "straight, male liberals"—this "devirilizing" performance as being complicit with an earlier, peculiarly Teutonic reading of the homosexual male body as the quintessence of virility? For the latter, see Sedgwick, *Epistemology,* 134 and, especially now, Mosse, *Image,* 32.

12. Lefkowitz, "Coats," 6.

13. Halperin, *Saint Foucault,* 90.

14. Kritzman, *Michel,* 300.

15. But see D. Boyarin, "Are There Any Jews?"

same time, it does not privilege "masculinity" over "femininity"—
"tops" over "bottoms"—nor stigmatize "femininity" in anything like
the ways that hegemonic European culture has come to do particularly
since the nineteenth century. In part, Jewish culture demystifies European gender ideologies by reversing their terms, which is not, I hasten
to emphasize, a liberatory process in itself but can be mobilized—stra-
tegically—for liberation. In any case, the modern Jewish abandonment
of our sissy heritage has been a noxious force in modern Jewish culture,
an ill wind that has brought no one good. As Paul Breines has written,
"[T]he cult of the tough Jew as an alternative to Jewish timidity and
gentleness rests on ideals of 'masculine beauty,' health, and normalcy
that are conceived *as if their validity were obvious and natural.* They
[Muscle-Jews] have, in other words, internalized unquestioningly the
physical and psychological ideals of their respective dominating cultures. In doing so they forget that, far from being self-evident cultural
universals, those ideals are predicated on a series of exclusions and era-
sures—of effeminate men, pacifism, Arabs, gentleness, women, homosexuals, and far from least, Jews."[16] For a member of several of these
intersecting categories, the politics of this recovery work has, then, a
sharp urgency.

The politics of my project to reclaim the eroticized Jewish male sissy
has, however, two faces. The traditional valorization of "effeminism"
for Jewish men hardly secured good news for Jewish women. There is
no question that women were disenfranchised in many ways in traditional Jewish culture. The culture authorized, even if it did not mandate, efflorescences of misogyny. If the ideal Jewish male femme has
some critical force vis-à-vis general European models of manliness, at
the same time a critique must be mounted against "him" for his oppression of Jewish women—and indeed, frequently enough, for his class-
based oppression of other Jewish men as well, namely, the ignorant who
were sometimes characterized as being "like women."[17] Any attempt at
a feminist rereading of Jewish tradition must come to terms with this
material fact and the legacies of pain that it has left behind. My goal is
not to preserve rabbinic Judaism "as we know it," but to reconstruct a
rabbinic Judaism that will be quite different in some ways from the one
we know and yet be and feel credibly grounded in the tradition of the
Rabbis. My work is one of changing ethos and culture and I hope it

16. Breines, *Tough Jews*, 167.
17. Weissler, "For Women."

joins with a stream of feminist work on rabbinic Judaism that includes
the research of Judith Baskin, Judith Hauptman, Miriam Peskowitz,
Laura Levitt, Susan Shapiro, and others.

As significant as the different gendering of Jewish men was, so was
there a significant difference in the gendering of Jewish women. While
their men were sitting indoors and studying Torah, speaking only a
Jewish language, and withdrawn from the world, women of the same
class were speaking, reading, and writing the vernacular, maintaining
businesses large and small, and dealing with the wide world of tax col-
lectors and irate customers. In short, they were engaging in what must
have seemed to many in the larger culture as masculine activities, and
if the men were read as sissies, the women were read often enough as
phallic monsters. In certain apologies for Judaism, the fact of women's
economic activity in traditional Jewish culture has been used as an alibi
for the entire system of oppression of women. This economic power,
however real, was a double-edged sword. Iris Parush has captured
something of this paradoxical double charge of gender politics in early
modern European Jewry: "Over the years, the lifestyle which crystal-
lized in Jewish society caused the men to cluster under the sacred tent
of Torah study, and the women to stand at the front line of the daily
confrontation with the outside world. . . . An interesting combination
of weakness and power—of inferiority in terms of the traditional Jewish perspective, and superiority in terms of the trends of Europeaniza-
tion—opened the 'door of opportunity,' so to speak, for certain circles
of the female population."[18]

The "fact" then that Jewish women (of certain classes) had opportunities in the secular world and access to education and economic power
and autonomy beyond that of their husbands must not be permitted to
erase the fact that, nevertheless, within Jewish culture these roles were
genuinely less valued than those of men. The time for the apologetic
strategy of pointing to "positive" structures or ideals and allowing
them to excuse whole systems of repression has passed, and I have no
desire to return to it, for it is a fundamentally reactionary strategy. My

---

18. Parush, "Women." Pappenheim makes this point herself in quite similar terms:
"Particularly the indifference with which everything women and girls learned was treated
(at the time of early marriages 'girlhood' as we understand it hardly existed) compared to
what men and boys were to learn and know, introduced a continuous current into the
women's world. . . . Particularly among the Jewish women a thirst for education clearly
marked by German culture grew that made new cultural elements accessible to the bilin-
gual, often trilingual (if French was added) women of the higher classes" (Pappenheim,
"Jewish Woman").

desire is not to discount, excuse, or pretend that there was not powerful oppression of women but rather to displace that oppression by arguing that such abuse is a product of a particular reading of the past and its canonical texts. This reading, while not "inauthentic" or "invalid," is nevertheless not the only one possible, nor even a uniquely compelling reading of the tradition. I hope, then, to be making a very different discursive move here, one that maintains the passion of critique of what has been and yet seeks to mobilize that same past for a different future by reinterpreting it.

What I want is to produce a discursive catachresis, not a quick fix by a halakhic committee but a new thing in the world, the horizon of possibility for a militant, feminist, nonhomophobic, traditionalist—Orthodox—Judaism. The reasons for Jewish conservatism are not essential but accidental. The force of my writing is to avow not that traditional Judaism does not need radical change but rather that it can accommodate radical change and still remain viable if the terms of the change themselves can be seen as rooted in the documents, traditions, texts of the Rabbis. The only reason—other than divine mandate—for seeking this accommodation is that such practice brings to many men and women an extraordinary richness of experience and a powerful sense of being rooted somewhere in the world, in a world of memory, intimacy, and connectedness, a pleasure that I call *Jewissance*. Note that I am *not* arguing for a continuation of Judaism on the grounds that it makes people better, although in some sense my justification for indulging in the extreme pleasures of Jewishness is the assumption that it does have something to contribute to the world as well. I treasure in principle and with deep emotion cultural difference per se—not only my own—and for me the disappearance of a cultural form is attended with a pathos and pain not unlike that experienced by many people when a species of bird goes out of the world. The demand for cultural sameness, universalism, has done much harm and violence in the world, but cultural difference as well has to work hard to do no harm; to participate in this work is the calling of the scholar.

My role model for this kind of scholarship is Bertha Pappenheim, cohort of such giants of Jewish scholarship as Shmuel Krauss and, among her many accomplishments, teacher in Rosenzweig and Buber's *Lehrhaus*. I want to claim Bertha Pappenheim here as a model for an alternative to the pseudo-objectivity of *Wissenschaft*. Although I can barely stake out my claim here, I would suggest that it was her first-wave feminism that fueled her achievements in Judaic scholarship, just as it is second-wave feminism that has empowered engaged, politically frank scholarship and critique in our generation. Let her become the foremother of another genealogy for Jewish cultural studies, one that enacts passionate love for the culture and devotion to its continued creative and vital existence without losing sight for a moment of the necessity for equally passionate critique.

Daniel Boyarin, October 21, 1995

Introduction

EMBODYING RABBIS

In a recent review of my earlier work, Miriam Peskowitz has recorded her students' images of traditional Jewish males, imagined as ancient rabbis:

> In the imagination of my students, the Rabbis of Roman Palestine and Sassanian Babylonia are 'little old Jewish guys,' 'nice, sweet,' 'kind of grandfatherly.' They are 'bearded' and 'balding.' . . . Rabbis are imaged as 'sitting, studying,' 'hunched over,' and 'slight of frame.' They 'would have worn glasses, had they been invented.' My students' ancient 'Rabbis' do not pole vault across the Jordan River to engage a bathing woman who turns out to be a man, and Rabbi Yohanan at that, as in b. Baba Metzia 84a. Nor do they contemplate sexual desires and trade hints about sexual techniques for the marital bedroom (b. Nedarim 20a–b), or hide beneath their teacher's bed to listen to and analyze the sounds of sexual intercourse (b. Hagiga 5b). Invariably, my students think ancient 'Rabbis' are 'very unattractive,' if their bodies can be imagined at all.[1]

Peskowitz's students know something about the Rabbis, but there is something else they clearly do not get. In early modern eastern Europe, the ideal Jewish male, the Rabbi or talmudic student, was indeed characterized by qualities that made him very different from, in fact almost

---

1. Peskowitz, "Imagining," 288.

the exact opposite of, the "knight in shining armor" heartthrob of our romantic culture. The East European Jewish ideal of a gentle, timid, and studious male—*Edelkayt*—moreover, does have origins that are very deeply rooted in traditional Jewish culture, going back at least in part to the Babylonian Talmud. These characteristics, however, were not supposed to render the male even slightly unappealing, let alone "very unattractive." For Peskowitz's American students, even American Jews, the gentleness of the rabbinic male can only be imagined as sex-lessness, encoded as unattractiveness, because these students (like most of us) have been molded so thoroughly by the "dominant fiction"[2] of gender that our culture maintains. A gentle, studious, sweet man can only be imagined as old and nearsighted (i.e., castrated?) and could not possibly be attractive sexually. In the readings that follow this introduction, we will see that such a man is interpreted as anything but sexless within rabbinic texts; indeed, he is represented as the paramount desir-ing male subject and object of female desire.

The dominant strain within European culture, in contrast, continues to this day to interpret activity, domination, and aggressiveness as "manly" and gentleness and passivity as emasculate or effeminate. In this book, I will argue that the early modern Ashkenazic traditional ideal Jewish male, "unmanned" but not desexualized, has something compelling to offer us in our current moment of search for a feminist reconstruction of male subjectivity (while being ever mindful, at the same time, of the absolute necessity for an equally trenchant critique of that culture for its *own* systems of oppression of women).

As a recent critic, Carole Siegel, has written about the fin de siècle English sexologist Havelock Ellis, one of the consequences of the domi-nant fiction of gender in our culture involves the patronizing assump-tion that "men whose deepest sexual desire does not involve dominance of women [i.e., rape] must be in some way physically deficient."[3] Ellis considers "the hymen an anatomical expression of that admiration of force which marks the female in her choice of a mate."[4] Psychoanalyst Frederick Lane continues to reflect this ideology of maleness by assum-ing confidently that "strength, assertiveness, activity, stoicism, courage, and so forth" are "gender syntonic" for men.[5] In this, he perpetuates

2. This very useful term is Kaja Silverman's: see *Male Subjectivity.*
3. Siegel, *Male*, 59.
4. Quoted in Craft, *Another Kind*, 90.
5. Lane, "Genital," 147.

the commonly held wisdom of a culture within which nineteenth-century novelist Grant Allen could write:

> Hermenia was now beginning to be so far influenced by Alan's personality that she yielded the point with reluctance to his masculine judgement. It must always be so. The man must needs retain for many years to come the personal hegemony he has usurped over the woman; and the woman who once accepts him as lover or as husband must give way in the end, even in matters of principle, to his virile self-assertion. She would be less a woman, he less a man, were any other result possible. Deep down in the very roots of the idea of sex we come on that prime antithesis—the male, active and aggressive; the female, sedentary, passive, and receptive.[6]

And as that consummate representative of Victorian culture, John Ruskin, wrote, "The man's power is active, progressive, defensive. He is eminently the doer, the creator, the discoverer, the defender. His intellect is for speculation and invention; his energy for adventure, for war, and for conquest." Women, in contrast, "must be enduringly, incorruptibly, good; instinctively, infallibly wise—wise, not for self-development, but for self-renunciation . . . wise, not with the narrowness of insolent and loveless pride, but with the passionate gentleness of an infinitely variable, because infinitely applicable, modesty of service."[7] While this description of "woman" could almost serve as a job description for a traditional rabbi, the application of such norms to male comportment and the rejection of the "masculine" ones by traditional Judaism, as well as the cultivation of activity and even aggressivity in dealing with the outside world for women, led, of course, to a stereotyping of Jews (male and female) as outside the realm of normal sexuality, as queer, as sexually predatory, or as entirely sexless. As Camille Spiess, a French writer of the 1920s opined, Jews were "at best, 'half men, half women.' "[8]

A central claim in this book is that there is something correct—although seriously misvalued—in the persistent European representation of the Jewish man as a sort of woman. More than just an antisemitic

---

6. Grant Allen, quoted in Reynolds and Humble, *Victorian Heroines*, 41. Note that there is actually tension within this text between indications that the situation of male dominance is natural and that it is historical: "It must always be so," followed immediately by "for many years to come"; but finally we come to something that is "deep down in the very roots of the idea of sex."

7. Quoted in Craft, *Another Kind*, 73. On Ruskin see Dellamora, *Masculine Desire*, 117–29.

8. Quoted in Mosse, *Image*, 73.

stereotype, the Jewish ideal male as countertype to "manliness" is an assertive historical product of Jewish culture. This assertion constitutes the central new point of this book, in contrast to the consensus view, according to which "[the] ideal of masculinity, indeed modern society as a whole, needed an image against which it could define itself. Those who stood outside or were marginalized by society provided a countertype that reflected, as in a convex mirror, the reverse of the social norm. Such outsiders were either those whose origins, religion, or language was different from the rest of the population or those who were perceived as asocial because they failed to conform to the social norms. For those so marginalized, the search for an identity proved difficult and painful. However, not all outsiders faced the same problems, though basically their options were limited to a denial of their identity or its co-optation by the acceptable norm, until—in the last decades of the nineteenth century—these choices were increased by acts of self-emancipation."[9]

For Jews, male Jews at any rate, one can neatly reverse this picture. Jewish society needed an image against which to define itself and produced the "goy"—the hypermale—as its countertype, as a reverse of its social norm, and its self-identity was hardly difficult or painful (except, of course, for the pain of being mistreated physically). This form of Jewish stereotyping of the gentile Other had enormous historical tenacity. Emblematic, perhaps, of this relationship is the fact that in early modern Europe, the little finger was referred to by gentiles in certain places as "the Jew," while the thumb is called in Yiddish "the goy"! In other words, rather than thinking of the stereotype as a one-way process of domination, we must begin to consider processes of complex mutual specular relations. Premodern Jewish culture, I will argue, frequently represented ideal Jewish men as femminized[10] through various

---

9. Mosse, *Image,* 56.

10. I write this way to indicate clearly that I am not ascribing some form of actual or essential femininity to certain behaviors or practices, as to a Jungian anima. For the toxic effects of that ideology, see Connell, *Masculinities,* 12–15; and cf., now especially, Garber, *Vice-versa,* 211–14. (I anticipate returning to this critique in a future work, D. V.) I am rather marking these performances as "femme" within the context of a particular culture's performatives, and particularly as it intersects with other cultural formations. The point then is not to reify and celebrate the "feminine" but to dislodge the term. "Phallus" and the "feminine" (and in only a slightly different register, "Jew") are fatally equivocal terms in Western discourse, insisting on their disconnection from real human beings of particular groups—men, women, Jews—at the same time that they inescapably declare their connection with these groups. Weininger goes through contortions to insist that everyone is "Jewish" but Jews only more so, and that there can be Jews (such as

discursive means. This is not, moreover, a representation that carries with it any hint of internalized contempt or self-hatred. Quite the opposite; it was through this mode of conscious alternative gendering that Jewish culture frequently asserted its identity over-against its surroundings. If anything, as we shall see, it was the process of "Emancipation" of the late nineteenth century that produced both the pain and the difficulty of Jewish (male) identity.

By suggesting that the Jewish man was in Europe a sort of "woman," I am thus not claiming a set of characteristics, traits, behaviors that are essentially female but a set of performances that are read as nonmale within a given historical culture.[11] This culture can be very broadly described as Roman in its origins and as European in its scope and later history.[12] It is the culture of romance that, while always contested—in large part by "feminized" Christian religious men—maintained hegemony as a male ideal, ever gaining intensity through the nineteenth century and beyond.[13]

Bernadette Brooten has described well the Roman origins of this culture: "Active and passive constitute foundational categories for Roman-period culture; they are gender coded as masculine and feminine respectively. In their presentations of a wide range of sexual behaviors and orientations, astrologers often categorized an active sexual role as masculine and a passive sexual role as feminine; for this reason they described passive men as effeminate and active women as masculine."[14]

Weininger) who escape being Jewish; by doing so he provides only one dramatic example of this aporia. For the coinage itself, compare Ed Cohen's " 'fem'-men-ists" (E. Cohen, "Are," 174). I had, in fact, for a long time considered "femmenize" but worried that it would be read as a pun on "men" and not on "femme." My usage further distinguishes the cultural processes that I am describing from those referred to when one speaks of the "feminization of the synagogue," by which is meant the fact that in certain "assimilating" communities only women typically attended the synagogues (at the same time that Protestant churches were being feminized in the same sense). This phenomenon, discussed most recently and cogently by Paula Hyman, is not what I am talking about here (Hyman, Gender, 24–25).

11. The project has nothing to do with men "getting in touch with their feminine sides" or the anima or "androgynous Judaism" but rather with unsettling and destabilizing the cultural model(s) of gender that such formulations and movements underwrite and reinforce for our culture (Garber, Vice-versa, 223–26).

12. Veyne, "Homosexuality."

13. More accurately, as pointed out by George Mosse, the romanticism of the nineteenth century involved a fantasized revival of medieval romance (Mosse, Nationalism, 8). In his newest book, Mosse provides a much more detailed and nuanced account of what elements are retained or reappropriated from early ideals—Roman martial ones and medieval chivalrous ones—and what are wholly transformed in the production of modern manliness (Image).

14. Brooten, Early Christian.

This paradigm can be asserted as the dominant fiction of Roman cultural engendering.

Like any dominant fiction, this one does not necessarily represent the "real" experience of Roman subjectivity. It was, moreover, vulnerable to breakdown under conditions of historical pressure.[15] The early Rabbis constitute an instance of opposition to the representation of masculinity as activity and dominance, just as their later analogs in modern Europe would resist romantic ideas of masculinity like those of Ellis and Ruskin. Rabbinic culture was originally formed at a moment of great ferment within Roman society, in the period known as the Second Sophistic (approximately the second century C.E.), within which new gender paradigms were forming throughout the Empire and Jews and Christians were playing important roles in such formations. Both early rabbinic Jews and early Christians resisted the Roman imperial power structure through "gender bending," thus marking their own understanding that gender itself is implicated in the maintenance of political power.[16] Various symbolic enactments of "femaleness," as constructed within a particular system of genders—among them asceticism, submissiveness, retiring to private spaces, and interpretation of circumcision in a particular way—were adopted variously by Christians or Jews as acts of resistance against the Roman culture of masculinist power wielding. This point is made by Virginia Burrus about early Christianity: "For men, the pursuit of Christian ascesis entailed the rejection of public life and therefore of the hierarchies of office and gender; in this respect, their opponents were not far off the mark when they insinuated that male ascetics were 'feminized' through their rejection of the most basic cultural expressions of male identity."[17]

Judith Perkins has described the situation thus: "Societies are char-

---

15. In her recent work, Carlin Barton is engaged more and more in documenting the interruption of the fictions of masculinity—under circumstances not entirely unlike those that attended the crisis in the dominant fiction in the United States after World War II, as demonstrated by Silverman—in Roman culture (Barton, "Savage Miracles"; "All Things").

16. In other words, the "ambivalent cultural space" that Garber speaks of (*Vested Interests*, 229) is constituted at least in part, and very early on within Jewish culture, out of a fraught attraction/resistance to the dominant cultural models of gender and its relation to the public/private opposition. In *Making*, Burrus includes very important reflections on the question of the cultural universality or specific historicality of this very distinction which, as we see also from the rabbinic material analyzed here, is so implicated in constructions of gender as well.

17. Burrus, *Making*, 14. The similarities with the Rabbis are obvious. The difference, which is equally striking, is that for the Rabbis this feminization was not coeval with asceticism, a point that I shall be making throughout this book.

acterized by competing relations of power, but, distanced by history, cultures often appear univocal. Either only the discourse produced by the dominant culture is left or, dulled by time, our ears are not keen enough to overhear the competing strains. Such a situation adversely affects the understanding and tracing of social change over time. It is by good fortune, therefore, that, from the social body known as the Roman empire, narratives remain that embody the voices—the values and the passions—of alienated groups at the brink of momentous change."[18] The Rabbis were only one of such alienated groups within the Roman political and cultural sphere. Early Christians were another, and there were yet others neither Christian nor Jewish.

The Greek romances also first appear on the scene during this period of ferment in the construction of gender and especially masculinity. Perkins has pointed out that "until recently, the Greek-ideal romance found few admirers; one of the genre's perceived flaws was its heroes' characterization. Commentators faulted the heroes for being weak, passive, and overly prone to threaten or seek suicide. The romance protagonists did not conform, it appears, to contemporary expectations of behavior proper for the male lead."[19] Paradoxically it seems, the heroes of these romances were not romantic heroes or even "real men." There is a wonderful moment in Achilles Tatius's novel *Leucippe and Cleitophon* in which our hero is being beaten and not fighting back. After a while, the hero and first-person narrator declares that his opponent "grew tired of thumping me and I of philosophizing."[20] "Philosophizing" is thus equated with passivity, with not thumping back. But as Perkins herself notes, "Even as it has been in the modern period, in antiquity such mildness [as that of the Stoic or the hero of the novel] could be misconstrued as cowardice."[21] That same "philosophizing," how-

18. Perkins, *Suffering Self,* 124.
19. Perkins, *Suffering Self,* 90.
20. (5.23.7); see Goldhill, *Foucault's,* 95.
21. Perkins, *Suffering Self,* 91. In demonstrating the shifts in sensibility within Hellenistic/Roman culture at the time of the Rabbis (not the periodization that she uses), Perkins adduces the difference between a scene in one of the Hellenistic romances and its Homeric intertext. When Hector is beseeched by his mother, exposing her breasts, to remain in Troy, he does the "manly" thing and goes off, nevertheless, to war. In contrast, in Chariton's *Charaeas and Callirhoe,* the hero, faced with exactly the same plea and action in support of the plea, attempts suicide (Perkins, *Suffering Self,* 100). Perkins quite convincingly explains this (and other actions of the romances) as instantiations of a new Stoic ethic. Epictetus explicitly cites the heroes of epic and tragedy as "anti-models" because they imagine that "great things" reside in "wars and deaths and the destruction of cities" rather than in self-control (101). While clearly there are enormous differences between the Rabbis and the Stoics—for the former suicide was never an option—there yet

ever, is associated (as nonphallic Christian maleness is as well) with asexuality. In the same text we read an incredulous response to a claim of virginity on the part of the heroine who had been captured by robbers and pirates: "You a virgin? Were the robbers eunuchs? Was it a pirate den of philosophers?!"[22] The Rabbis, I repeat, provide a uniquely different exemplum of this oppositional form of masculinity in that they, like "philosophers," did not regard violence as enhancing or definitional for masculinity; for them, being philosophers (i.e., students of Torah) did not entail entering into a eunuchlike state by any means. Rabbis had—indeed were—bodies, as the texts referred to by Peskowitz, among many others, would clearly establish.

However, and quite paradoxically, it is also this very insistence on embodiedness that marks the male Jew as being female, for maleness in European culture has frequently carried a sense of not-being-a-body, while the body has been inscribed as feminine. A medievalist, Clare Kinney, has recently written of another definitive moment in European cultural history: "Real men—that is, representative Arthurian heroes—don't have bodies."[23] If this "not-having-a-body" is defined as manliness, then Jewish men were not "real men" at all, for they quite decisively were bodies, were defined by their bodies. This idealization of the male body and its reinscription as spirit with no body reached its apotheosis in the nineteenth century. As George Mosse has observed, "Above all, in the first decades of the nineteenth century, male beauty symbolized timeless order."[24] The Lacanian distinction between the phallus and the penis reinscribes the identical dualism that privileges "male" incorporeality over "female" embodiedness.[25] This cultural motive, which goes back at least to the pre-Socratics in Greek culture,

---

remain to be fully explored the ways in which rabbinic care of the self is part of the new techniques of the self being developing in their world. Thus, if the supreme ethic for Stoics was to be willing to die when hope of success at one's task had been lost, leading to the athlete's/martyr's choice of death rather than defeat, for the Rabbis, staying alive at *almost* any price was a fundamental value. Presumably this would have rendered a Rabbi even more "feminized" than a gentle Stoic sage. I hope to treat these questions more fully in a work-in-progress. For another fascinating parallel between the Romances and early Christian sensibilities, see Shaw, "Passion," 9.

22. (6.21). See Goldhill, *Foucault's,* 116.

23. Kinney, "(Dis)embodied Hero," 49. For quite a different—but not entirely irreconcilable—reading of the same text, see Dinshaw, "Kiss."

24. Mosse, *Nationalism,* 31.

25. An earlier version of this introduction included an extensive discussion of the Lacanian phallus. At the urging of good critical friends, I have decided to make that discussion into a separate paper which will appear elsewhere, D. V.

privileges the ideal over the real, the homogeneous over the heterogeneous, and thence the phallus (as an ideal abstraction from the penis) over
the female body, the sex that is not one.[26] Insofar as the penis of flesh—
as opposed to the phallus, which is a platonic idea of the penis—is paradoxically feminine in the European Imaginary because it is body,[27] it is
this insistence on the penis that inscribes the Jewish male as forever carnal and thus female. Another way of making the same point would be
to avow that for rabbinic culture, femminization is not equivalent to
castration precisely because masculinity was not defined by possession
of the phallus. To resist this sort of patterning, rabbinic thought must
be antidualistic.

It seems highly significant that nowhere in rabbinic literature is there
a representation, for instance, that would have the body of the embryo
supplied by the mother while the spirit is provided by the father, nor, a
fortiori, one in which the father supplies the form and the mother the
raw matter. Indeed, the standard and explicit myth of conception in
rabbinic texts is a partnership of three in that the father supplies the
white parts of the body: bones, teeth, the white of the eye, brain matter;
the mother the red parts: blood, muscle, hair, the pupil of the eye; and
God supplies the intelligence, the spirit, the soul, eyesight, motion of
the limbs, and the radiance of the face (Nidda 31a).[28] In other words
that which in many of the surrounding Greco-Roman cultures was be-
stowed by the father is provided here by God. For rabbinic Judaism, the
father and mother provide the matter—the white and the pupil—of the
eye, and only God provides spirit, the capacity of the eye to see. The
father and the mother provide the muscle and sinew; only God provides
the spirit, the active motor capacity.

Lacanians will immediately object, of course, that according to
their theory no one, in fact, has the phallus. And that is certainly true.
Jacques Lacan obviously escapes one crude and vulgar possible (and actual) reading of Freud, the "penis envy" tradition, which projects men
as the possessors of the phallus that women desire and can achieve only

26. This sort of patterning presumes an allegorical metaphysics, and in its crudest
naturalizations, an allegorical physics, as well. Woman is man's signifier. As such, she may
never be the thing signified, but allegorical discourse allows her to be *taken for* the signified as a kind of reading procedure. And man is God's signifier in much the same way.

27. Montrelay, "Why Did You."

28. This is based, of course, on a notion of menstrual blood as being the female equivalent of semen (Satlow, "Wasted Seed," 158–62). Here again, as Satlow points out, rabbinic conceptions are quite different from the ones of the more Hellenized, Greek-writing
Jews, whose views were Aristotelian.

through possessing a man as an "appendage to the penis" (in Freud's
charming formulation) or by giving birth to men. For Lacan, castration
consists specifically of the recognition by all subjects, male and female,
that they can never possess the phallus. It nevertheless remains the case
that for Lacan, to have the phallus remains the *desire* of all people always and everywhere, male and female, even if "having the phallus" is
only an imaginary phenomenon.[29] The phallus is for Lacan a psychic
universal, while I avow that the "phallus" is not even so "real" an entity
as a psychic universal, however imaginary or symbolic, but a culturally
specific representation of human desire and fulfillment, one belonging
to the dominant strand of European culture but resisted and refused
(albeit not entirely successfully) by a subaltern culture that subsisted
within the dominant one, namely, the culture of rabbinic Judaism. I
shall argue that the phallus, for which universal status is claimed by
Freudian and Lacanian psychoanalysis, is in fact not a universal but a
culturally specific representation of sexual difference and of human
adequation. Freud and Lacan were misled by the pressures of their own
cultural situation, not in the sense that this "charge" is usually made—
that Freud was simply a Victorian or simply a Jewish male—but rather
that Freud's and Lacan's ideas on this matter were formed by the entire
tradition of Western culture going back to the Greeks. The only way to
dislodge this representation, then, is to find an Archimedean point "outside of" European phallogocentric culture, something that will not be
easy to do, given the historical relations between that culture and its
interlocutors, in our case the ways that Judaism is from its very beginning both a part of and apart from Hellenistic/Roman/European culture.

   Though hardly feminist, rabbinic Jewish culture thus refuses prevailing modes through which the surrounding cultures represent maleness
as active spirit, femaleness as passive matter, a representation that has
dominated much (if certainly not all) of European cultural imagination
and practice. Maleness is every bit as corporeal as femaleness in this
patriarchal culture. This refusal provides a partial explanation for how
Jewish cultural imaginings could conceive of a valued masculinity as
being femminized in the terms of the dominant Roman culture. When
Europe has sought female equality and autonomy, this has been
achieved through dis-embodying the female;[30] we have, rather, to em-

---

29. Lacan, "Meaning," 83–84.
30. D. Boyarin, *Carnal Israel.*

body men, to take away the phallus and leave only the penis behind. Only a new cultural theme—not a mere transformation of the old one—could re-embody the male. We critically require a historicizing relativization of the psychoanalytic account of the phallus, via what might be called an ethnography of male subjectivity. This book is intended as one small chapter in such an ethnography,[31] a chapter on rabbinic Jewish maleness. I am not claiming an antiphallic location for an essentialized and dehistoricized Jewish culture but rather something much more complex—and, I dare hope, more convincing—to wit the elaboration, at certain moments of Jewish cultural history and within particular political conditions, of the possibility of an embodied male who fully within the order of sexuality and even paternity, is nevertheless not "masculine" or "manly" in the terms of the dominant fiction and thus inscribes the possibility of male subjects who refuse to be men. In a sense then my argument is congruent with those, particularly Zionists, such as most recently Aviva Cantor, who see Jewish masculinity as being different owing to a peculiar political situation.[32] The difference is that whereas they pathologize this difference and seek only to end it, I critically celebrate it and seek to retrieve it as an Archimedean lever to help move the world of the Western phallocentric culture.

In the antisemitic imaginary of Christian Europe (and perhaps Muslim Africa and Asia as well), male Jews have been represented traditionally as female,[33] but as Sheila Briggs points out with reference to the latest forms of this representation, this obtained only with respect to "the negative sense of the feminine."[34] There is, however, a positive signification to "feminization" as well. In a cultural system within which there are only two genders, the only way to symbolize "refusing to be a man"[35] may be an assertion that one is, in some sense, a woman. This represents then, at least potentially, a positive oppositional identity to "manliness" that is neither "castrated" nor emasculate, because it does not read femininity as lack. To make a point early that I hope will become clearer throughout, it is not the identification with women that bears here the "feminist" potential but the "refusal to be a man." The identification with women is an epiphenomenon of resisting manliness, but not one that implies "castrated" status for either the unmanly man

31. Cf. Gilmore, *Manhood*, and Eilberg-Schwartz, *God's*.
32. Cantor, *Jewish Women*.
33. Mirrer, "Representing," 181.
34. Briggs, "Images," 256.
35. Stoltenberg, *Refusing*.

or the woman.[36] Traditionally many Jewish men identified *themselves* as femminized, beginning with the Talmud and through an opposition to "Roman" ideals of the male, and understood that femminization as a positive aspect of their cultural identity. Accordingly, while not feminist, rabbinic culture might yet prove a resource in the radical reconstruction of male subjectivities that feminism calls for.

Lest this appear an idyllic picture, I must introduce at this juncture some less than idyllic images, powerful moments within which early rabbinic discourse is not resistant to Roman representations of masculinity and violent exercise of sexual power but fully complicit with them. Michael Satlow has demonstrated that Palestinian rabbinic culture in the Roman period did not eschew representations of penetration as a mark of status. The most dramatic example of this is a text that Satlow cites from the Palestinian Talmud: "'May the house of Yoab never be without someone suffering from a discharge or an eruption, or a male who handles the spindle, or one slain by the sword, or one lacking bread' [2 Sam. 3:29]. 'A male who handles the spindle'—this is Yoash, 'they inflicted punishments on Yoash' [2 Chr. 24:24]. Taught Rabbi Ishmael: This teaches that they appointed over him cruel guards who had never known woman, and they abused him as a man abuses a woman."[37] For this text, then, punishment consists of being anally penetrated—a "castration" that renders the man a woman, that is, "a male who handles the spindle." Satlow writes, "The language and superficial topics under discussion by Palestinian rabbis of the third and fourth centuries might be biblical, but their assumptions about homoeroticism certainly are not. Underneath these few and scattered traditions lurks the same complex attitude toward the pathic as exhibited in Roman sources. For a man to allow himself to be penetrated was tantamount to him 'effeminizing' himself, a prospect viewed with loathing by (at least) the male elite of antiquity." As Satlow emphasizes, however, "this same concern with the penetrated male did not exist in Babylonia."[38] The point is thus not to marginalize as "foreign," and clearly not to deny, the existence of such representations within rabbinic Jew-

36. See the very interesting discussion in Dellamora, *Masculine Desire*, 141–46.

37. Palestinian Talmud Qiddushin 1:7, 61a; translation in Satlow, "They Abused," 14, slightly modified.

38. Satlow, "They Abused," 11, 15. As we will see in chapter 3, it is Babylonian Rabbis who represent themselves positively as femminized, while in Palestinian versions of the same story (the legend of Resh Lakish) this motif does not appear. In Palestine, Resh Lakish remains a military hero even after his conversion to the study of Torah, while in Babylonia within seconds after the conversion, his lance no longer works.

ish culture of the talmudic period, still less to conjure up some ahistorical Jewish essence that would resist them always and everywhere, but rather to ferret out the evidence for an equally significant discourse that is resistant to the dominant fiction of an inexorable association of male gender and sexuality with power and violence and of female gender—that is, being penetrated—with humiliation.

I am not arguing for the absence of certain voices and patterns of meaning within rabbinic culture but rather for the presence of other voices within the somewhat discordant chorus that makes up the multivocality of rabbinic discourse on the body, gender, and sex. I could make a case as well for the dominance of these other voices at certain junctures of rabbinic textuality with the material conditions of Jewish lives, but I don't need to argue for such dominance in order for my text to do its work. In my eyes, my book will have succeeded if it does no more than convince readers that the discourse I have sought is one valid among the multiple discourses of Jewish cultural life, materialized on the one hand as a highly valued text for study, the Talmud, and, on the other, in the particular practices (or better, some of the particular practices) of Jewish cultural life at a distinctive moment in its history on the cusp of European modernity.

It hardly needs saying yet again that the official discourse of this culture was certainly sympathetic neither to women nor to homoeroticism, and yet it is important that I say it here lest I be perceived (once more) as denying these nearly self-evident facts. Modern Jewish "Orthodoxy" is marked by pervasive (though not ubiquitous) misogyny and by nearly ubiquitous homophobia. Clearly the seedbed for extremely violent discourses of gender and sexuality is well prepared within rabbinic textuality; my task here is not to deny the existence of these seedbeds but to cultivate other ones that are equally "there" in the texts, even if not highly regarded or even noted by the current social institutions within which rabbinic Judaism is (mostly) lived.

JEWISH CULTURE AND THE "RISE OF HETEROSEXUALITY"

I find it necessary at this point to clarify some terms of art that I will be using—some of them fairly idiosyncratically—throughout this book. I shall begin with my notion of "queer" and then move on to "heterosexual" and "homophobia." Since the term "queer," its extension, and its political valence are highly contested I wish to explain my usage of "queer" and "queer theory." I understand this to be an investigation that systematically puts into question any praxis, theoretical or political, of the "natural" in sexuality, praxes that historically in our culture have naturalized heterosexuality, enforcing heteronormativity.[39] Queer theory is theory that recognizes that human desire—that is, even desire for "straight sex"—is queer, excessive, not teleological or natural, and is that for which the refusal of heteronormativity on the part of gays, lesbians, bisexuals, and others provides a privileged but not exclusive model.[40] The conformations of desire are a cultural construction, and traditional Judaic culture, for all its well-known abhorrence of a certain homosexual act, male anal intercourse, and its near-universal inducement of marriage and procreation,[41] was *not* a "heterosexual" culture—because "heterosexuality" had not yet been "invented." As Michael Satlow has recently pointed out, "The rabbis [of the talmudic period] considered male sexual attraction to other males to be unexceptional,"[42] and "no evidence suggests that the rabbis defined people by the gender of the object of their sexual desire" (24).

Heterosexuality is a peculiar institution of contemporary Euro-American culture. It has been best defined by David M. Halperin as "the production of a population of human males who are (supposedly) incapable of being sexually excited by a person of their own sex *under any circumstances*" and has been referred to by him as "a cultural event without, so far as I know, either precedent or parallel."[43] Neither the assumption that some (even most) people prefer to have sex with people who have different genitals than they do, nor even the tabooing of certain or all same-sex genital acts, constitutes heterosexuality.[44] Only the premise that same-sex desire is *abnormal*, that it constitutes, in Foucault's words, a separate species of human being, creates this category. There is an enormous gap between the earlier condemnation of one

39. Freud, despite his somewhat tarnished reputation in this regard owing, in part, to the American Ego psychologists' reading of his texts, can plausibly be identified as the originator of queer theory (Freud, "Three Essays"). Bersani (*Freudian Body*) and Dean ("On the Eve") explicate Freud in this regard.
40. Others (and indeed, I, in other contexts) use the term differently as a theoretical approach to identity formation and not a theory of sexuality. The two usages are complexly related in ways that go far beyond the scope of this introduction. In "On the Eve," 124, Dean has very interesting things to say about this motive.
41. D. Boyarin, "Are There Any Jews?"
42. Satlow, "They," 18.
43. Halperin, *One Hundred Years*, 44.
44. In his latest book, Halperin has expanded on this point compellingly (*Saint Foucault*, 44).

who pursues certain forms of pleasure as a sinner, on the same order as one who eats forbidden foods, for instance, and the modern placing of that person into a special taxon as an abnormal human being. This is not to say, of course, that the earlier formation was more benign to those who engaged in same-sex practices than the latter; but the production of the heterosexual as the normal type of human being has powerful effects that ripple throughout the projects of constructing gender within a social formation such as our modern one. And as Satlow has concluded, "Penetration, not same-sex desire was problematic for the rabbis."[45]

The "normal" male in our social formation, and especially the adolescent, is engaged in a constant project of demonstrating to himself that he is not queer, that he does not desire other men. This is quite different, I hypothesize, from socialization in a society where it is assumed that men do desire other men but it is forbidden to do anything (or some things) about that desire, that is, a culture without heterosexuality. There is accordingly a necessary connection between heterosexuality and homophobia. Homophobia is not an accidental or facultative adjunct of heterosexuality but its enabling condition.

One of the richest and most evocative descriptions of the actual psychic workings of homophobia in the American adolescent male is one by Larry Bush:

> No one called me faggot, but I was *younger* than all of them—admitted to school at four and a half, hanging around with my brother's friends, always the aspiring innocent, always the willing victim. Gentle but slow with girls. Quick to cry. Thank God I had a great outside jump shot in basketball and could handle a bad hop like Brooks Robinson. So the misconceived jokes ("Take Bromo, homo, and wake up feeling yourself") and careless exclamations ("You suck") were rarely aimed at me.
>
> Yet now, as a dry-boned adult, I walk the streets, ride the subways, meet my public, with the fear of being considered homosexual shaping my posture, wardrobe and facial expressions. I'll carry a dirty canvas shoulder bag rather than a nice leather one—better to be considered an overage hippie than a queer. If I cross my legs (knee to knee) on the subway, I'll be sure to match it with a sober, "masculine" look on my face. . . .
>
> Whatever happened to the joy of being a boy who loved other boys, who giggled himself to near insensibility with boyfriends . . . ? How is it that the subtle warnings about being effeminate have completely overwhelmed the warmth and pleasure of same-sex bonding?[46]

45. Satlow, "They," 24.
46. Bush, "To Be," 34.

Crucial in Bush's account is the ratio between the necessity to demonstrate that one is not effeminate and the rejection of intimacy between men, both driven by the exigency to certify "straight" status, that one is a certifiable heterosexual. In other words, homosexual panic and the consequent homophobia that it generates become the source of a violent impulse, verbal or physical or both. This violence, I suggest, is directed toward both women and gay men alike in the effort to prove (to oneself) that one is not queer. Gay-bashing and wife-beating are close companions.[47]

Homophobia in this exact sense is a product of the modern culture of heterosexuality,[48] in which male sexual desire for men or any effeminate behavior threatens to reveal and expose that the man is essentially not straight but queer.[49] Without a doubt, and to somewhat understate the case, male-female sexual relationships were nearly exclusively prized within traditional Jewish culture. In that sense, one could surely claim that rabbinic Jewish culture has always been heteronormative, even if not heterosexual, that is, homophobic. The absence of heterosexuality permits a much greater scope for forms of male intimacy, eroticized and otherwise: "Who is a friend?" a midrash asks. "He that one eats with, drinks with, reads with, studies with, sleeps with, and reveals to him all of his secrets—the secrets of Torah and the secrets of the way of the world."[50] "Sleeps with" does *not* have the euphemistic value that it has in English or German, but the text is certainly reaching for a very intense and passionate level of male-male physical intimacy here. The "way of the world" is a somewhat ambiguous metaphorical term that can refer to several areas of worldly life, including business,

47. Sedgwick, *Between Men*, 88–89; *Epistemology* 186; D. A. Miller, "Cage," 112.

48. Jonathan Ned Katz, *Invention*, 33–55. This chapter of Katz's is one of the most convincing demonstrations and exemplifications of Foucault's hypothesis about the invention of sexuality that I have yet seen. Unfortunately this fine book is marred by a cynical and vicious foreword by Gore Vidal that demonstrates only that he had not even read the book when he wrote the foreword.

49. Note the difference between this account and a superficially similar one that treats the man policing "himself for traces of femininity" as thereby victimized (Lentricchia, "Patriarchy," 743) or that elides the difference between "teaching men who will not conform how to alienate and despise themselves"—and "even men who do conform" (774–75)! For discussion, see Edelman, "Redeeming." I am not commiserating here with the "poor" male who "submits" to heterosexuality by dominating others, but with the victims of this practice. Lentricchia's discourse is reminiscent of those Israeli liberals, like Golda Meir, who are most angry at the Palestinians because the latter have "forced them to be oppressors."

50. Shechter Aboth, chapter 10.

but especially sex.[51] Male intimacy, it seems, for the talmudic culture includes the physical contact of being in bed together while sharing verbally the most intimate of experiences, a pattern not unknown in other cultures. The image of two men in bed together talking of their sexual experiences with women is reminiscent of ethnographic descriptions of Barasana (Colombian) tribesmen, lying in hammocks, fondling each other and talking about sex with women.[52] Thus, while we cannot draw conclusions about the sexual practices of rabbinic men from such a passage, we can certainly, it seems to me, argue that it bespeaks a lack of "homosexual panic" such as that necessitated by the modern formation known as "heterosexuality." The absence of homosexual panic in premodern Jewish culture permitted a much greater scope of behavior coded as "feminine," within the larger cultural context, to be normative in male performance in general and in affective relations between men. As we shall see in chapter 4, this very structure for the production of gentler, antimacho men was not thereby rendered empowering for women. If anything, this "kinder, gentler" form of patriarchy may have solidified certain forms of male power.

I am convinced that homophobia is a significant tool of misogyny, or, better, that homophobia and misogyny are intimately imbricated with each other, as Larry Bush's paradigmatic account richly suggests. This alone should make clear the urgent need for antihomophobic (or even better, queer) cultural criticism to be directed as forcefully as possible against misogyny. This does not mean, unfortunately, that no gay man or lesbian is misogynist or that no feminist is homophobic. Wayne Koestenbaum has written of his own work: "I pursue these slant readings because I believe that I am drawing on a system comprehensive enough to unravel a range of perplexities. This system is, in essence, feminist: it questions heterosexuality's privilege and forces masculine writing to take seriously the threat of 'queerness.' "[53] I would seriously

---

51. As indicated by the following text among others: "When his wife died, Rabbi Tarfon said to her sister during the mourning period: Marry me and raise your sister's children. And even though he married her, he did not behave with her according to the way of the world until after thirty days." (Kohellet Rabba, 9. See also Bereshit Rabba, 22.) Now although the sexual meaning is not the most frequent one for this collocation, it is certainly a readily available one. Thus while it is a meaningless claim (because unfalsifiable) that this is what the author of this text "intended," it is hard to escape concluding that the sexual connotation would have been present for any recipient of this text.

52. Greenberg, *Construction*, 71.

53. Koestenbaum, *Double Talk*, 5.

question, however, whether all critique that calls itself feminist questions the privilege of heterosexuality.[54] Similarly, I find Koestenbaum's declaration that "when men are sexually engaged with each other they are acting against and not in accord with the wishes of patriarchy" curiously unhistorical. Is there only one patriarchy, pristine, timeless, changeless? Have there not been patriarchies (e.g., Greece of the fifth century B.C.E.) in which the sexual engagement of men with men was in accord with the wishes of patriarchy, further enacting the thoroughgoing marginalization of women and the age- and class-related systems of male domination that marked those cultures as patriarchal?

Alan Bray has, for instance, explicitly considered "the ways in which sexual activity between men, far from being an adversarial practice, can merely repeat prevailing patterns of dominance and subordination in cultures characterized by gender polarity."[55] Of course I am not claiming that the "political dreams of a feminist and of a gay man [necessarily] have nothing in common," only resisting the implication that they *necessarily* (naturally?) have something in common.[56] At the same time I insist that they ought to have (nearly) everything in common, for there is no partial liberation. I share Koestenbaum's vision of a criticism antipatriarchal, feminist, and queer but am less certain (than he was when he wrote the book, at any rate) that it is so easily reachable. In fine, the question of how focusing on the historical constructions of masculinity, a project in which both the subject and object of discourse is male, can remain feminist and not be a more sophisticated reinstatement of androcentrism remains for me a problem and an open question.

An intentionally feminist endeavor, my project is, nevertheless, a venture in the description of male subjectivity, its formation, regulation, and construction. I do not wish this to be taken as, or worse, to *be,* complicit with a project or a politics that is beside the point of or even hostile to feminism—as a lot of "men's studies" or gender studies seem to be.[57] Much of *that* endeavor seems to end up conniving, in fact, with reinvestments and reinforcements of *heterosexuality,* with what Chris Craft has called "the excruciating acoustics of the so-called men's movement (heady jamborees at The Tom-Tom Club, itself something of

54. Edwards, *Erotics,* 10–11.
55. Dellamora, *Masculine Desire,* 3.
56. Edwards, *Erotics,* 44.
57. Modleski, *Feminism.*

a traveling circus), the major impetus behind which seems to be to dis-
pel a circumambient sissy-boy anxiety by forging fashionably dysfunctional males into iron men and warrior dads."[58] In contrast to a men's
studies that would be collusive with such a men's movement, this study
is engaged not in dispelling sissy-boy anxiety but in revalorizing and
reeroticizing the sissy. I believe, then, that feminism needs to liberate
not only women but also femininity, *not* because "femininity" is the
natural state of women but because the "repudiation of femininity" has
played a central role in the oppression of women within European culture.[59] Jewish culture has something to teach us about the liberation,
the raising up of femininity, and while the feminist return will not be
direct because of the ways that Jewish culture itself has been oppressive
of women, it is nonetheless a real potentiality.[60]

Donald Hall has recently referred to Stephen Heath's claim that
"men's writing, male discourse, will simply be the same again; there is
no politically progressive project that can work through that idea [of
writing the male body] (unless perhaps in and from areas of gay men's
experience, in a literature for that)." As Hall correctly observes, Heath
ignores differences *within* the male body, other than those of sexuality,
notably differences of race and class: "I submit that during and around
the [nineteenth century], the caricatured bodies of lower-class, Irish,
and non-European men provided remarkably similar sites [similar to
the bodies of women and gay men] for the play of classist, racist, and
imperialist beliefs."[61] Certainly for at least the nineteenth and much of
the twentieth centuries, the caricatured bodies of Jewish men also provided such a site (see Plate 1); however, my argument is not only that
the oppressed male body is a site of discourse for his (male) oppressors

---

58. Craft, *Another Kind*, 15.
59. A very concrete example of this can be found in Susan Estrich's *Real Rape*.
Estrich shows how the traditional rule requiring the "reasonable woman" to have engaged in actual physical combat in order to argue that she was raped renders her "not a
woman at all. Their [the judges'] version of a reasonable person is one who does not scare
easily, one who does not feel vulnerable, one who is not passive, one who fights back, not
cries. The reasonable woman, it seems, is not a schoolboy 'sissy'; she is a real man" (65).
One does not by any means have to be an essentialist in order to see how the masculinist
value system that despises sissies oppresses female subjects here just as it oppresses deviant
male subjects.
60. Contrast the approach of Barbara Breitman, who, though sympathetic, considers
the "affective program" of rabbinic Jewish maleness pathological and proposes a whole-
sale adoption of Robert Bly's "Tom-Tom Club" in order to "liberate the energy" (Breitman, "Lifting Up" 107).
61. D. E. Hall, "Muscular Christianity," 5–6.

Plate 1.   The Caricatured Body of the Male Jew. Cartoon of a Jew falling
off a bicycle, by H. Mayr, 1890. (Courtesy of the Leo Baeck Institute, New
York.)

but that the submissive, dominated male body is also a site of knowledge.[62] Surely what defines all of the cited groups over-against the male
body that cannot write itself progressively is that they are all not in
power over (all) others. This is almost tangibly the case for ancient Ath-
ens, within which adult citizen males penetrate all other bodies and may
not be penetrated by them, thus an almost literal phallocracy. In other
words, I suggest that the very fact of being politically dominant, of hav-

62. An analogous point is made by Lori Lefkovitz when she argues that the subversion of the pattern of primogeniture for which Genesis is famous is to be explained "perhaps because they [i.e., the ancient Israelites] may have been a relatively small, militarily
weak, and young people" ("Coats," 19). Satlow also makes an analogous point: "Romans saw the individual citizen male as primarily responsible for sexual self-control; according to the rabbis, it is God, whose words are revealed through rabbinic interpretation,
who sets sexual limits. This difference, in turn, might well have arisen from the differing
political conditions between Romans and Jews. For the (wealthy) adult male Roman citizen, sexual penetration, as well as sexual restraint, were political acts, assertions of one's
power over others and oneself. That is, for the Roman, the subjugated Jews would have
been linked, on some level, to those who were penetrated, an idea that clearly would have
made the Jews uncomfortable. For the rabbis (who were juridically virtually powerless)
and the Jews (who were politically dominated by Rome) of late antiquity, sexual penetration and self-control were not understood politically" ("They," 24).

ing empires, produces mystification of the male body.[63] As an instructive example, I offer a brief case study from the work of Virginia Burrus on the shift in Christian discourse of gender from the period before Christianity became imperial to the time after its domination of the Roman Empire.

In a series of recent articles, Burrus has been analyzing the transformation of the gendered effects of early Christian discourses of martyrdom as Christianity became dominant within the Empire. Burrus provides the following schematic account: "It was a favorite story in the post-Constantinian church, when the days of imperial persecution were for most Christians long past: a trembling young girl, brought before the magistrate, courageously defies her male oppressors; shattering expectations of age and sex, she manages against all odds to preserve both her virginity and her faith, an audacious act of self-assertion finalized by the welcomed death of the executioner's sword."[64] Burrus shows through her intertextual reading that the meaning of female martyrdom has been refocused by this period via the increasing emphasis on a different Roman cultural model specifically for virtuous women, one that reinforces female passivity. In the second century, we find Perpetua, who is marked as a Christian resister to the Roman culture of gender by her "ability to stare directly back into the faces of her persecutors, not with the elusive demeanour of a proper *matrona*," an ability that "broke with the normative body language in a way that signalled an aggressiveness that was not one of conventional femininity." And slightly before her lived Blandina, whose "fortitude and endurance were compared to those of a victorious male athlete."[65] By the fourth century, we have the trembling Agnes. No longer the victorious, valorous, virilized gladiator, the virgin martyr is now modeled on such types of passive, female virtue as Lucretia or Polyxena. Burrus traces the discursive modes through which is achieved "the literary transformation of would-be 'manly' women—*viragines*—into femininely docile *virgines*."[66]

The most important aspect of the revision from Perpetua to Agnes is the transformation of the martyr from victorious gladiator to "Bride of Christ," that is, from a figuration that bends gender to one that reinforces its hierarchies while nevertheless subtly shifting their mean-

63. For a fascinating exploration of connections between imperial power and representations of gender, see Joshel, "Female Desire."
64. Burrus, "Reading."
65. Shaw, "Passion," 4, 19.
66. Burrus, "Reading."

ings. Indeed, we find the beginnings of this transformation already in the work of the male editor of Perpetua's account.[67] Thus in Prudentius' version of the story of the martyrdom of St. Agnes, the girl understands her impending execution as being just short of literal sexual intercourse: "This is my lover, I confess, / A man who pleases me at last! / I shall rush to meet his steps / So I don't delay his hot desires. / I shall greet his blade's full length / Within my breast; and I shall draw / The force of sword to bosom's depth. / As bride of Christ."[68] However, there is more, for as Burrus shows, this active expression of female desire is transformed within Prudentius' text into something that confirms gender expectations much more powerfully, a passive surrender of the girl's neck to executioner's sword. Instead of Christ's lover, she ends up being merely his suppliant: "She bent her head / She worshipped Christ as suppliant / That her sinking neck, more readily / Might endure the threatened wound." This is a highly charged displacement. In the classical models which served the well-educated Prudentius, women die by the neck, not by the breast. In what may be the most important proximate intertext, Euripides' *Hecuba*, exactly the same alternatives are offered; Polyxena offers her executioner either her breast *or* her neck, and Burrus writes: "May not the virgin Polyxena claim the virile death of a sword plunged into a defiantly bared chest? But the tragedian entertains the possibility of boundary transgression only to reassert gender distinctions more firmly; in the end, Euripides' Polyxena, like Prudentius' Agnes, dies of a wound not to breast but to neck. . . . Prudentius provides Agnes with the place of death which for him, as for ancient Greek tragedy, reestablishes her essential femininity in sexualized subjugation."[69]

By the fourth century, the masculine discourse of the Church triumphant no longer wanted Mary to be made male, as the early Christians did. One way to think of this is that with temporal power becoming an increasingly important element of Christianity's praxis, the gender hierarchy of male and female became an important symbolic structure for naturalizing that power; whereas before, the subversion of that hierarchy was a tool for neutralizing, denaturalizing imperial power. "Orthodox" Christianity was no longer involved in a subversion of all the hier-

67. Shaw, "Passion," 32.
68. Quoted in Burrus, "Reading."
69. Burrus, "Reading." See her complex and nuanced further discussion.

archies of empire, having become imperial itself.[70] Pre-imperial Christianity thus provides an elegant example of the knowledge of gender that powerlessness makes available.

At the same time, it cannot be argued that lower-class, Irish, non-European, Jewish, pre-Constantine Christian, colonized, or gay men have not oppressed women. This is not to say nor even to suggest or hint—in fact I wish to expressly deny—that we find some sort of nonpatriarchal paradise in Jewish or any other colonized society. Gender and hierarchies do not cease to be a problem in these subaltern formations—indeed they may be exacerbated—but we do end up with a very different sense of how gender and the symbolization of the sexed body function within these subcultures, one of which I will study here.

THE FLOW OF THE ARGUMENT

The flux of the book is as follows. Part 1 is a critical presentation of the construction of the femminized Jewish male ideal. In the first chapter I present a series of texts intended to show that traditional Ashkenazi Jewish culture produced a model of masculinity that was openly resistant to and critical of the prevailing ideology of "manliness" dominant in Europe. The alternative Jewish form of maleness was known as *Edelkayt* (literally, "nobility," but in Yiddish "gentleness and delicacy"!); its ideal subject was the *Yeshiva-Bokhur* (the man devoting his life to the study of Torah) and his secularized younger brother, the *Mentsh*.

Within traditional Ashkenazi Jewish culture,[71] as I said earlier, the soft man was the central and dominant cultural ideal, not a marginalized alternative. In contrast to a certain tradition in Jewish historiography that has also recognized this reality, I do not consider this ideal as the desperate product of an abnormal situation but as one possible (and for me highly desirable) realization of talmudic culture. Talmudic culture means, in my parlance, the series of different cultural entities that

---

70. Yuval Rotman has recently argued that the earliest clear official Christian condemnations of self-castration are also from the fourth century, and that this shift in Christian discourse is also related to the imperialization of Christianity (Rotman, *Attitude*).

71. I want to make clear that by emphasizing "Ashkenazi" here my intent is not to imply that Sefaradic (Spanish and Eastern) Jews do not manifest these readings of talmudic culture and the cultural constructs of gender that they lead to, but only that my research and knowledge have focused almost exclusively on northern Europe. Not to mark this would be precisely to subsume Sefaradic Jews under an undifferentiated rubric of the universal Jew and thus erase their specificity and difference.

are in large part and in constantly changing ways crucially informed by the centrality of the reading of the Talmud in their practice. The Talmud was the most valued text (indeed virtually the only valued text, the Bible not excepted) of Ashkenazi culture, and constant study of it by the male elite—with all the trickle-down effects that such centrality implies—is one of the most important material facts of the culture. Indeed, one of the names that this culture had for itself was "the way of the Talmud," דרך הש"ס. I argue that the scholarly ideal male found in the text had a profound effect on the production of this ideal in Ashkenaz in a Jewish culture that, like that of the Babylonian Rabbis, sought explicitly to produce its ideals in opposition to and dissimilation from the ideals of the circumambient dominant culture.

Accordingly, in the second and third chapters I discuss talmudic texts in which such an ideal countermale is articulated as an alternative, subaltern fiction. In making this appeal to the talmudic texts, I am decidedly not arguing for some essential, continuous Jewish countergendering, a working out of some national spirit or even cultural continuity that persists down through the ages through all the vicissitudes of Jewish history. Such romantic historiography runs contrary to my cardinal ideas and commitments.[72] Rather than seeing the culture of the Babylonian Rabbis as an antecedent of Ashkenazi culture, implying a continuous essential Jewishness, I proffer the Talmud text as the most relevant intertextual matrix in the production of traditional Jewish cultures. Judith Perkins has recently described well the "Foucauldian" perspective that informs my work as well as hers: "My focus is writing itself as a historical agent as it enabled the institutional formation . . . and not on historical events or figures as such."[73]

The cultural theme that I am recovering in rabbinic Jewish culture can easily be countered by citing contradictory texts. This very theme has not always been dominant within the tonality of even Diaspora Jewish culture. In the Middle Ages, there were prominent rabbinic figures who were, at the same time, generals in the armies of Spain, and of course they were just as Jewish as the *Yeshiva-Bokhur* "sissies" with whom I identify. As David Biale writes: "Perhaps the best-known Jewish military figure of the Middle Ages was the poet and communal leader, Samuel HaNagid, who led the armies of Granada in the early

---

72. The recent analysis by David Myers (*Re-inventing,* 142–44) of such trends and their location in modern Jewish political life will immediately show why.

73. Perkins, *Suffering Self,* 9–10.

eleventh century. He left an array of military poems describing his exploits in battle."[74] Not surprisingly, this Spanish Jewish culture picks
up on other themes and moments in rabbinic literature and, moreover,
places much more emphasis on the Bible and classical Hebrew cultural
models than does its contemporary Ashkenazi adjunct. German-speaking Jews of the late nineteenth century, such as Theodor Herzl, not infrequently affected Sefaradic ancestry as part of their assimilationist
projects.[75] I am not claiming an essentialist, pure (and utopian) construction of masculinity in the Talmud or in later Jewish cultural practice but am instead focusing on a particular theme that attracts me,
owing to my own particular set of identifications and desires, both
political and erotic. Audre Lorde has written, "Our visions begin with
our desires." I am tracing a cultural theme, an overtone, or a voice
in the polyphony that I wish to isolate and amplify.[76]

Christian culture also presents an array of male exemplars and models, from the knight on one hand to a gentle, passive St. Francis on the
other. What it does not imagine, at least not until modernity perhaps,
is a fully sexualized male who is not active, powerful, and aggressive.[77]
One might well ask at this point: If this discourse was contested, however, from within Jewish culture, and if within the history of European
Christian culture there has been pervasive opposition to its dominant
fictions of masculinity, what then constitutes the basis for any claim for

74. D. Biale, *Power*, 76. He was also one of the exceptional rabbis who recommended beating a disobedient wife! On this, see chapter 4 below. Biale has done a wonderful job of dislodging ahistorical notions of eternal Jewish powerlessness in Diaspora.

75. Aschheim, *Brothers*, 28.

76. I want to take this opportunity to correct a methodological error in my previous
work, *Carnal Israel*. Although I was clear then as well that the (nonmisogynist) strains of
tradition that I was isolating were not the only ones that were there, I still had some
conception of a possibility of identifying dominant and subordinate ideologies. This was
a mistake. There is no method, neither statistical nor other, that enables such weighing of
authority. The contrary (but identical) mistake is made by Judith Baskin who comes to
the exact opposite conclusion from mine. For her, the misogynist strain is dominant, and
the antimisogynist one a "minority voice."

With reference to my current project, I am not, therefore, claiming for the vision of
gender that I am exploring, dominance, exclusivity, or authenticity over others that are
equally "Jewish." I am asserting that this particular voice can be found in the texts and
saying that I like it and wish to strengthen its presence and influence in the current Jewish
(and general) society. This is a strategy different from the one of *Carnal Israel* and, I hope,
one that avoids its apologetic pitfalls.

77. This is not contradicted by the notion, prevalent from Roman times, that what
characterizes true masculinity is control of self, as so brilliantly documented in Foucault's
Care and the work of many classicists. As Pateman describes Rousseau's theories of gender (which are, I think, quite typical): "Men are the active and aggressive sex and are
'controlled by nature' [i.e., they naturally control themselves]; passive and defensive
women have only the control of modesty" (*Disorder*, 21).

difference on the part of Judaism? I shall attempt to show through textual readings that within Judaism, in contrast to much of Christianity,
femminized men were not read as emasculated or desexualized. They
thus occupied a space in the erotic economy of Jewish culture that
monks, quite obviously, never could (at least openly) within Christianity. Another way of putting this would be to state that since the
monk within Christian culture has a binary opposite in the knight, the
former can be removed from the category of "real men" within Christianity and stand as an oppositional force to it. Monks, then, effectively
form a distinct gender within Christian society, one that is removed
from the paternal and sexual order. Within the Jewish culture that I am
describing, however, the opposition is not between different men so
much as between Jewish men and non-Jewish men, with Torah the primary marker of the difference.[78] Although rabbinic Judaism also provides an array of male ideals and modalities, it fell to Ashkenazic Judaism to furnish European culture with the possibility of a male who is
sexually and procreationally functioning but otherwise gendered as if
"female" within the European economy of gender.[79] The Jewish men
obviously remain within the sexual order, since they do not form a
separate gender within the Jewish cultural system. Seen however from
the point of view of the larger cultural system, they appear similar to
monks and thus femminized. This appearance as femminized, from the
perspective of the surrounding culture, can then be mobilized as a signifier in Jewish culture as well—for good and ill.

I have, however, attempted to show that some of the very talmudic
texts that play this theme also are aware of its problems and contradictions, even its misappropriations of female capacities. Second, in the
very instances in which I find a utopian alternative to the dominant fiction in talmudic culture, I also try to show how even that utopian instant itself contains pitfalls, especially for women. I must constantly
reckon, indeed struggle, with the ways that "utopian" analysis can slip
from a hermeneutics of recovery connoting that a wish and hope for
something vastly new and better show through a cultural product into

78. Since these are the primary terms of gendered difference, Jewish men who *do not*
have Torah are occasionally marked as being "like women" (Weissler, "For Women"),
but these are the Jewish men who will appear most "manly" to the non-Jewish world, as
will become apparent in the next chapter of this book.

79. I emphasize "ideally" to make clear that I am not claiming that Jewish men necessarily behaved differently from other men, but that there were different cultural ideals
at work, which sometimes may even have had a referent in "reality." For the continuity
between medieval and classical ideas about maleness, see Bullough, "On Being," 31.

a hermeneutics of conservation, in which that wish and hope are taken for *the already existing reality* and thus are used as an alibi for a fundamentally conservative, even reactionary position. These considerations should serve as a caution against any essentializing or totalizing statements about Jewish culture that I do not, in fact, claim to be making.

Following the analysis of these talmudic texts, accordingly, there will be a chapter in which I strive to articulate a theory of the rabbinic domination of women. In this fourth chapter, I carry out what I hope is a more incisive critical analysis of the structure of male domination within rabbinic culture and its functions than I have done heretofore in this or other work. I open the chapter by presenting some of the women's voices that, raised in protest against the exclusion of women from Torah, enabled the foundation of a feminism for traditional ("Orthodox") Jewish women. As in so much else, second-wave feminists here are highly indebted to our mothers of the first wave, and the debt should be paid in part through recovering their voices and honoring them. In this chapter, two diverse realizations of talmudic culture are contrasted: one that absolutely condemned male violence toward wives and another that did not. This serves two purposes. The first is to exemplify how different social possibilities can be founded on the same textual base, making clear that the claim for a talmudic culture does not constitute an essentialism. The other purpose is to clarify the structural defects of an important aspect of halakha, namely, paternalistic male control of women, which even at its most benevolent, can easily be turned to its malevolent opposite, just because women were excluded from real power. My goal is to delineate this oppression in sufficient specificity that the description will be an effective diagnostic tool in the search for therapies for this cultural ill and, moreover, to ensure that the culture will survive the therapy. I could not possibly undertake to perform a full-scale and detailed analysis of rabbinic "patriarchy" in the context of this book, and in any case such work is well under way by other scholars (Baskin, Hauptman, Levitt, Peskowitz, Wegner). But I do want to look at the structurally "negative" consequences of that very moment within the culture that I am recovering as "positive."

The second half of the book describes the reconstruction of Jewish gendering under the pressure of the rise of heterosexuality, especially in Vienna at the fin de siècle. The fifth, sixth, and seventh chapters focus largely on two crucial figures in the invention of the modern Jewish man as an undoing of the tradition of the effeminate Jewish male:

Sigmund Freud and Theodor Herzl. Although the interconnections of these two have been explored by critics before, I think the full measure of the implications of their two cultural projects, psychoanalysis and Zionism, for the invention of the modern Jewish man has not yet been taken. One of the major purposes of this book will be to understand what happened to Jewish culture as the regime of heterosexuality increasingly impinged on it in the nineteenth century. Much of my argument turns upon the claim that psychoanalysis and Zionism were two specifically Jewish cultural answers to the rise of heterosexuality at the fin de siècle. The "hero" of this part of the book, however (and mine), is a Jewish woman who successfully diagnosed and resisted these projects: Anna O. (Bertha Pappenheim).

The extent to which the heterosexualization of Jewish culture implied a loss for Jewish women has not been fully realized. The final chapter provides, then, a positive model for Jewish modernity in the guise of Bertha Pappenheim, once Anna O. (the first psychoanalytic patient), grown to be the militant leader of Jewish feminism in Germany. Pappenheim remained an Orthodox Jew all her life and thus, for me, is the prototype of a radical critic who yet remains within (and not outside of) the traditional culture. She also criticized bourgeois culture and its effect on the female subject by identifying with traditional Jewish alternatives and models for women's lives, notably Glikl of Hameln, an early modern female Jewish memoirist who will be discussed below.[80] Pappenheim empowered herself by reclaiming the "deviant"—that is, deviant from the bourgeois heterosexual ideal—gendering of traditional Jewish women as her own and using this alternative gendering as a tool in the struggle for women within and outside of Judaism. I seek to do the same, to save myself and also contribute something to others, through a parallel (not identical) reclamation of the Jewish sissy. Pappenheim teaches that the struggle against oppression within Jewish culture need not lose sight of the critical force that Jewish culture can bring to bear on models of gender that were developed within romantic European culture. I hope herein to continue her work.

Talmudic culture is the culture that is crucially informed by a pivotal practice of reading the Talmud as its most valued book. Actual cultural forms are mediated through a complex set of social, economic, historical, and cultural conditions, which frequently include the nature of the

---

80. In referring to Glikl here I shall use the Yiddish spelling that she would have adopted, and not the German "Glückel."

cultural practice of the societies within which Jews found themselves in different times and climes. Not a history, my book attempts to understand one Jewish social formation, Ashkenaz on the cusp of modernity, as one such realization of the cultural possibilities that a certain strain of talmudic discourse made possible. Another way to describe how this text differs from a history would be to say that I am not trying to recover the "truth" of Jewish culture but rather the "best" of what Jewish culture has offered in the past, and I want to suggest what it can be in the future. This "best" is, of course, a value judgment, one that many will not share, and the judgment grows out of who I am, where I come from, and where I have been in my life. *Unheroic Conduct* also constitutes a narrative of how I take myself to be a Jew and to be a product of my love for the Talmud and my feelings of commitment to its authority, as well as my commitment to certain ethical norms, including most prominently my feminism and my identification with gay, lesbian, and bisexual Jews (and the Queer Nation as a whole).[81]

81. I would like to express that the spaces in which I have felt most accepted and validated as an "out" Orthodox Jew in America, yarmulke, beard, and all, have been such queer environments as Pride parades and gay, lesbian, and bisexual studies conferences.

Men Who Roam with the Sheep

Diaspora and the Image of the Jewish Man

Given the dedication of the strong to a narrative which invents their strength, it is possible for the weak to refuse the necessity of this strength by telling a different story, posing different roles for human beings to inhabit. This might, indeed, be a questionable, metaphysical story about a disembodied, characterless soul always free to choose, but it could also be a story which simply changed the metaphors: which, for example, proposed a humanity becoming sheep-like, pastoral.

—John Milbank, *Theology*, 283

Goyim Naches

Or, the Mentsh
and the Jewish Critique of Romance

Long live war. Long live love. Let sorrow be banished
from the Earth. —Giuseppe Verdi, *The Sicilian Vespers*

I begin with a story, indeed one of the initiatory stories of modernity.
In *The Interpretation of Dreams,* Sigmund Freud reports the following
event from his early childhood:

> At that point I was brought up against the event in my youth whose power
> was still being shown in all these emotions and dreams. I may have been ten
> or twelve years old, when my father began to take me with him on his walks
> and reveal to me in his talk his views upon things in the world we live in.
> Thus it was, on one such occasion, that he told me a story to show how much
> better things were now than they had been in his days. "When I was a young
> man," he said, "I went for a walk one Saturday in the streets of your birth-
> place; I was well dressed, and had a new fur cap on my head. A Christian
> came up to me and with a single blow knocked off my cap and shouted: 'Jew!
> get off the pavement!'" "And what did you do?" I asked. "I went into the
> roadway and picked up my cap," was his quiet reply. This struck me as un-
> heroic conduct on the part of the big, strong man who was holding the little
> boy by the hand. I contrasted this situation with another which fitted my
> feelings better: the scene in which Hannibal's father, Hamilcar Barca, made
> his boy swear before the household altar to take vengeance on the Romans.
> Ever since that time Hannibal had had a place in my phantasies.[1]

With all that has been written about this text connecting it with
Freud's individual psychology, I think it has not been sufficiently em-

---

1. Freud, *Interpretation,* 197.

phasized how emblematic the story is of a historical moment, the parallel shift of Jews from "traditional" to "modern" and "eastern" to "western," and the ways that both are intimately implicated in questions of male gender. Freud's anecdote is, accordingly, not merely autobiographical but historiographical, and it will serve as the specimen text for this disquisition.

The historical shifts are, with Freud's characteristic rhetorical brilliance, indicated with deft and subtle strokes in the text. First of all, there is the signal that a historical shift is at stake in the father's declaration that he is about to tell a story that will indicate how much "better things are now." Second, there is the indication of the shift in space. The incident took place in "the streets of Freud's birthplace," that is, in the eastern place from which the Freuds had come to Vienna. Third, there is the indication that Freud's father had been, at that time, a very traditional Jew. He was wearing the *shtreimel*, the Sabbath fur hat of the East European Hasid, an emblem in Freud's world of the unreconstructed primitive *Ostjude*, the eastern or, particularly, Polish Jew[2] (see Plate 2). All of these cultural forces are explicitly concatenated with issues of masculinity within the text. Freud's father, "a big, strong man," behaves in a way that Freud experiences as shameful, and Freud seems to know, although he does not explicitly say, that this "passivity" had to do with his father's Jewishness. The specificities of the incident reported by Freud are highly significant as well. The hat was certainly for him a symbol of the phallus. In at least two places in *The Interpretation of Dreams,* in which this story is reported, Freud writes as much explicitly.[3] Thus, whether or not it is "true" that the hat symbolizes male genitalia, for Freud it was certainly the case. He would have interpreted this incident, then, as sexually as well as politically emasculating—castrating—for his father, the paradigmatic traditional Jewish male.[4]

In fact, as Martin Bergmann has noted, the "feminine" response of Freud's father in this incident was not "unheroic" but antiheroic and indeed traditionally Jewish: "A Jew was expected to be able to control his anger, not to be provoked; his feelings of inner dignity were sustained by a belief in his own spiritual superiority which a ruffian and a

---

2. This point had been earlier remarked by Ernst Simon and otherwise ignored (and obscured by Freud himself) in the quite voluminous literature on this moment in Freud's texts (Simon, "Sigmund," 271).

3. Freud, *Interpretation,* 355–56, 360–62.

4. McGrath, *Freud's,* 64.

Plate 2.   Jew Wearing the Traditional Fur Hat. *Selbstbildnis*, 1920, by Lazar Krestin. (Courtesy of the Leo Baeck Institute, New York.)

'Goy' can in no way touch."[5] For traditional Jewry there were both alternative civilities, *Edelkayt,* and alternative paradigms of "manliness"
that could be summed up in the relatively modern term *mentsh.*[6] *Edelkayt,* which means "nobility," was a counter-ideal to many of the markers
of the noble in romantic culture, in that its primary determinants within
the culture were delicacy and gentleness, not bravery and courtliness.[7]

    The behavior of Freud's father in the hat incident is the quintessence
of *Edelkayt.* Marc Kaminsky has isolated two aspects in the construction of the *mentsh.* These two aspects, which to a certain extent pull in
different directions, are both nevertheless significant and need equal attention:

> *Mentsh,* as cultural ideal, proposes an ideal of person that is purportedly
> genderless, a norm to which both genders have to adhere. Now, we are ac-
> customed to thinking of such ideals as erasures of difference, in which
> women were subordinated. No doubt this is an important line of analysis to
> follow and work through. But to let this monological concept monopolize
> interpretation would be a mistake. There are two points to be made. Within
> a certain ongoingness of tradition, exalted gender-free ideals are a starting
> point upon which conventional notions of the differences between genders
> are set to work in a scale of values that subordinates women. But the second
> point is more important for your project. The concept of *mentsh* in modern

    5. Bergmann, "Moses," 12.
    6. Marc Kaminsky argues that this term functions as a secularization and universali-
zation of the traditional term—Jew ("Discourse," 298–99)! For a relatively early usage
of the term in a religious context, one could cite the following statement of the late nineteenth-century Lithuanian Rabbi Israel Salanter: "The Maharal of Prague, of blessed
memory, created a golem. It is a great wonder, but it is far more wondrous to transmute
the nature of the materiality of Man and to make out of it a *mentsh*" (Goldberg, *Israel,*
210). (Throughout this book, I shall be using Yiddishistic transcriptions of Yiddish
words, such as *mentsh,* not *Mentsch; Edelkayt,* not *Edelkeit,* etc.) In a book that appeared
too late to be integrated in any serious way into the present work, George L. Mosse has
discussed the peculiar development of the "manliness" ideal since the first half of the
eighteenth century, that is, the development that was ultimately to put so much pressure
on the ideal of *Edelkayt* (Mosse, *Image*).
    7. At the same time, I should emphasize (following remarks to me by Marc Kamin-
sky) that this semiotics, while reversing the definition of noble masculinity current in the
European culture, nevertheless, maintains the class coding of the term. In other words
what this culture takes to be noble may have shifted, but there is still a hierarchy whereby
a privileged class gets to embody the cultural ideal. Furthermore, it should be added very
clearly that, once more, while the cultural ideal is a reversal and contestation of European
notions of the manly, it also explicitly leaves gender hierarchy in place, since the ignorant,
virile, strong, and economically active male is frequently derided as being like a woman
[*Yiddene!*] in this culture (Weissler, "For Women"). In a future project, I hope to delineate Jewish responses to the chivalrous ideology at three crucial historical points: Rome
and its ideals of *andreia,* the medieval period and chivalry proper, and the neochivalry of
modern European manliness, for which see Mosse, *Image,* 18, 23, and throughout. For
softness and delicacy as effeminate, see Mosse, 9.

Yiddish culture exalts an ethics of the household, of the extended family, of the sphere of the domestic, and, from the purview of the masculinist ideals of the alien cultures in which [Ashkenazi] Jews lived, refigured the feminization of Jewish men in ways that secular Jewish men had to be conscious of.[8]

Without vitiating critique of the subordination of women that Kaminsky as a feminist male properly emphasizes, he is correct, moreover, to maintain that we need to spotlight at the same time the consequence of the second, the ways in which *Yiddishkayt,* that is, Ashkenazi secular culture, exalts for men an "ethics of the household and a sphere of the domestic" as a secular continuation of the rabbinic opposition to European romantic "masculinism." The paradoxical role of Yiddish can be read as exemplary of this dual movement, for on one hand Yiddish was explicitly marked as the language of female spaces—the kitchen and the marketplace[9]—but on the other hand, it was the vernacular of the quintessentially male space of the Study-House. The texts were in "masculine" Hebrew, but the language of study was in the "feminine" Yiddish, thus marking the intimate connection between the *Yeshiva-Bokhur* male ideal (the later *mentsh*) and the domestic and female.[10]

The Westernization process for Jews, clearly then not to be simply identified with modernization *tout court,*[11] was one in which *mentsh* as Jewish male ideal became largely abandoned for a dawning ideal of the "New Jewish Man," "the Muscle-Jew," a figure almost identical to his "Aryan" confreres and especially the "Muscular Christian," also born at about this time.[12] Reversing the cultural process by which the late antique Jewish male and the Christian religious male got their self-definition in opposition to prevailing imperial modes of masculinity, in the Victorian era both of these groups sought to conflate their masculinity with that of "real men."[13] I shall be concentrating here, of course, on

---

8. Kaminsky, letter.

9. Parush, "Readers," 5; Seidman, *Marriage,* 80.

10. While I have emphasized here Yiddishkayt, that is, Ashkenazi secular culture, it should not be understood as if I intended to exclude modern Sefaradic or Eastern Jewish culture. These simply must be made the object of study in their own right from this historical and theoretical perspective before any similar conclusions can be drawn.

11. Pace Cuddihy, as discussed below.

12. D. E. Hall, *Muscular Christianity;* Nordau, *"Muskeljudentum."*

13. See Mosse, *Image,* 49, and literature cited there for the problems that Evangelical Christians had with manliness, including being vilified as effeminates. This was the background to the formation of "Muscular Christianity" just as the description of Jewish men as effeminates was to inspire "Muscle-Judaism." See also Garber, *Vested Interests,* 211–14. For an extraordinary reading of Thomas Heywood's *A Woman Killed with Kindness* as a Christian rewriting of *Othello,* see Fletcher, *Gender,* 109–12.

the Jewish side of this history, on the process that I refer to as "the invention of the Jewish man." Central to the concerns of this chapter as a whole is the notion of *goyim naches,* which might be translated as "games goyim play," a sometimes "racist" term of opprobrium for European Christian culture and its "masculine" values such as war-making, dueling, and adulterous courtly love affairs that end in *Liebestod.*[14]

IS LOVE *GOYIM NACHES?*

RUDOLPH: Mud head to foot. Cut your hand open. Lockjaw.
               They make you kaput, Leopoldlebkhen. You watch
               them chaps.

  BLOOM: (*Weakly.*) They challenged me to a sprint. It was
               muddy. I slipped.

RUDOLPH: (*With contempt.*) *Goïm nachez.*

                                 —James Joyce, *Ulysses*

In what I take as the most brilliant moment of a brilliant and highly influential (if disturbing) book, John Murray Cuddihy has also contributed to our understanding of the significance of the "hat incident" for Freud's thinking.[15] This formative moment involved a father who was

14. For an eloquent discussion of some of these cultural entailments, see Kopelson, *Love's,* 20–27.
15. Cuddihy, *Ordeal,* 50–57. For a lengthier consideration of Cuddihy's book, see D. Boyarin, "*Épater.*" Other writers also simply assume western European bourgeois social patterns as a norm against which others are seen as anomalous. In a very revealing moment, Madelon Sprengnether writes: "Looking at Freud's own preoedipal phase in Freiberg, for instance, we find a family structure that differs significantly from the one that characterized his subsequent years of development in Vienna. Freud appears to favor *the latter, more conventional model*—a preference that has the effect of displacing or repressing questions regarding his mother's desire" (*Spectral Mother,* 13; emphasis added). This formulation is typical of a whole series of statements about Freud's parents in the critical literature that treats his family as an anomaly. The Viennese bourgeois nuclear family structure—dominant father, passive mother—is depicted as "the more conventional" in contrast to a traditional East European Jewish family structure—active mother, passive father—which is marked then as "unconventional" with seemingly no questioning of who gets to own "convention." Furthermore, we will have to interrogate the very terms "active" or "dominant" and "passive" in this context, for they themselves represent a reading of Jewish family life from a European perspective. Robert Holt also, in an otherwise stimulating paper, refers to Jakob and Amalie Freud as "an atypical couple in that their actual personalities reversed a number of *standard* sex-typed expectations. In certain key ways, Freud did share his parents' characteristics, probably on the basis of fantasied incorporation or identification. Yet his conscious, verbalized ideas about what was male, what female, are transparently derived from *general cultural* sources and bear little relation to the traits of his own parents" (Holt, "Freud's" 1, emphasis added). Since the contrast drawn is between the seemingly singular characteristics of Freud's parents and "gen-

forced off the road because he would not stand his ground like a man.[16] In the story that becomes foundational for Freud's thinking of gender, the Oedipus story, a father who refuses to be dislodged from a road is the center of action. By imagining himself as Oedipus, then, Freud gained a father he could respect, Laius, who stood his ground like a man and was killed for it. Laius, the "Aryan," even more than Hamilcar, the "Jew," was ultimately the father that Freud would have had.[17]

Cuddihy, however, writes from a position that fully accepts the mystifying European notion that there is only one civilization and only one civility, that of Protestant Europe.[18] Knowing nothing of eastern European Jewish literature or "high" culture, of *Edelkayt* or the *mentsh*, he

---

eral culture," there is apparently no recognition that this "standard" and "general" set of expectations is itself culturally specific and culturally constructed. Kaminsky implicitly answers such writers when he describes his project as an attempt to "link the psychological and cultural formation of East European Jews in a description that translated the experience-near norms and terms of 'the cultural other' into 'our' experience-distant concepts without losing cultural difference in the translation; that is, without subtly stigmatizing and pathologizing alien ways of being, thinking, and acting, but rather taking them as the ground for a shift in evaluative perspective that crucially entailed renouncing the claim to universality of Western psychological ideas" ("Discourse," 294–95). Kaminsky's work is, moreover, a beautiful demonstration of the capacity of a psychoanalytic theory of the psyche to grow beyond its universalistic (and scientistic) origins—appropriate in its nineteenth-century provenience—and comprehend cultural diversity as an essential, intertwined, part and parcel of self-formation. Cf. also Hoberman, who writes, "This mutually critical dialogue between male groups would be better known if the traditional historiographical emphasis on German and Austrian opinions about Jewish deficiencies had not obscured contemporary Jewish critiques of the Germanic male type" ("Otto," 147). But of course, this "obscuring" is typical of the occlusion of the critique of colonizers by the colonized.

16. Marc Kaminsky has drawn my attention to the topical character of this encounter, the scrimmage in the street between one who in the past had the right to force others into the gutter and an antagonist who will no longer suffer this, and thus paradigmatic for modernization *tout court*. Berman (*All That Is Solid,* 217–19, a reference I owe to Kaminsky) has provided some marvelous discussion of this topos as it appears in an obscure Russian novel of 1863. Even more striking is the example from Dostoyevsky's *The Underground Man,* discussed by Berman (221–28), wherein what is crucial in marking the Underground Man as a " 'new man,' a 'man of the sixties,' is his desire for a head-on clash, an explosive encounter—even if he turns out to be the victim of the encounter." Dostoyevsky (and Berman) raise this virtual cliche to the status of "primal modern scene" (Berman, 229), as it functions for Freud.

17. For Hannibal as a Jew in Freud's mind, see *Interpretation,* 196. Sprengnether's reference to the period of Freud's life in Freiberg as "preoedipal" takes on new meanings and new ironies as well. (See also Pellegrini, "*Without* You," for some more fascinating evidence linking Freud's developmental narratives with cultural differences of East—Jews—and West.) For the "Aryanness" of the Oedipus complex, see no less an authority than Bronislaw Malinowsky who writes: "The complex exclusively known to the Freudian school, and assumed by them to be universal, I mean the Oedipus complex, corresponds essentially to our patrilineal Aryan family with the developed *patria potestas,* buttressed by Roman law and Christian morals, and accentuated by the modern economic conditions of the well-to-do bourgeoisie" (quoted by Walton, "Re-placing," 777).

18. Cuddihy, *Ordeal,* 99.

imagines an *Ostjude* constructed more or less in the image known from the Borscht Belt. He thus accepts Freud's arraignment of his father as dishonorable and, moreover, produces an account of Freud's whole life as an attempt to escape the "coarseness" of the traditional Jewish culture. He sets up a stark binary opposition between the "modern" which is civil and the premodern which is then necessarily uncivil. In 1908 Freud wrote a letter to Karl Abraham in which he imparted that he had been in Berlin for twenty-four hours and been unable to see him and wished him not to misunderstand this as a sign of disfavor. Cuddihy glosses this passage by saying, "[T]o make oneself accountable for one's appearances before strangers is the first step to social modernization."[19] Cuddihy finds it impossible, apparently, to imagine that an East European Jew (which he interprets Freud to have been) would have had "native" traditions of thoughtfulness to draw on. The Galician Jew, as a member of a "primitive" culture, could not possibly have cared that an associate might have been hurt through a misunderstanding.

What Cuddihy seems unable to imagine is that the conflict is not between the uncivil and the civil but between alternative and different civilities, that the cultures of the "East" and the past maintained their own civilities. One of the clearest instances of Cuddihy's "Orientalism" involves someone who will be the "heroine" of the final chapter of this book, the first psychoanalytic patient, "Anna O." Cuddihy describes Anna O.'s reticence on certain occasions as a result of the fact that "she *wanted* to be polite" (emphasis added) and then explicitly characterizes this as "a far cry from *being* polite."[20] True politeness is clearly in his view something only a civilized person (read "Protestant") is capable of. Bertha Pappenheim (Anna O.), like Freud in the Abraham incident, only desires to appear polite. She and he could not possibly be sincerely motivated here, as the Protestant would be, by her "interiority and internalization."

The grand irony of Cuddihy's writing, and the reason it is finally so revealing, is that he naively (or perhaps not so naively) accepts the evaluation of East European Jewish culture that was current among the "evolved" Jews of western Europe (not to mention West European non-

---

19. Cuddihy, *Ordeal*, 42.
20. His own situation as an Irish Catholic lends a certain (partly represented) pathos and irony to the discourse. For a trenchant analysis of the complicity between the Parsonian sociology that Cuddihy espouses and the "liberal Protestant narrative" cum Spencerian racist evolutionism, see Milbank, *Theology*, esp. 126 and passim.

Jews), assumes its complete accuracy, and then interprets the discomfort of the West European Jews as a reasonable reaction to their "genuine" East European origins. This analysis provides the basic term for Cuddihy's account of Freud's theories of sexuality, which are summed up by his outrageous "the id of the 'Yid' is hid under the lid of Western decorum (the 'superego')."[21] Hid under the lid of this droll formulation is a doubly Orientalist fantasy: the Jew as Oriental and eastern Europe itself as the Orient, the site of Dracula and his brethren: "Dracula may not officially have been one of those horrid inbred Jews everyone was worrying about at the time Stoker wrote his novel, but he came close, for he was very emphatically eastern European, and hence, like du Maurier's 'filthy black Hebrew,' Svengali (Trilby, du Maurier, 52) a creature who had crawled 'out of the mysterious East! The poisonous East—birthplace and home of an ill wind that blows nobody good.'"[22]

All of the theoretical problems of his (and their) bizarrely reified notions of traditional premodern, shtetl Jewish life show up in the following crucial representation of Cuddihy's, in which Jews, like women, manage to be both crude animals and "puritans" at the same time:

> Freud paid scant attention to sexual foreplay. It either maneuvered the partners toward orgasm, or it was perversion. To Freud's shtetl puritanism, forepleasure—like courtship, essentially, or courtesy—was a form of roundaboutness, of euphemism. To play with sexual stimulation, to postpone the intense endpleasure of orgasm, was a form of *goyim naches,* of games goyim play, endlessly refining themselves. Freud had a choice here. If the rules of that game genuinely transformed the old coarse "fuck" into something "rare and strange," then he, Freud was missing out on something. "They" were *experiencing* something he wasn't. He, most of the time, bore a grudge against their claim.[23]

There is something truly grotesque in Cuddihy's claim that "[i]n bourgeois-Western lovemaking, foreplay—'love play'—foreshortens the ritual of courtly love into the space-time requirements of the bourgeois bedroom," from which it follows, according to him, that if "Freud and his psychoanalytical heirs make short shrift of the 'rules' of courtly love," and Judaism has no patience for these rules either, then this ade-

21. Cuddihy, *Ordeal,* 29.
22. Dijkstra, *Idols,* 343, and see also 335.
23. Cuddihy, *Ordeal,* 70.

quately explains an alleged Freudian disdain for foreplay.[24] This "ritual of courtly love," however, was essentially a prescription for adultery, that is, for a sexual ideology that understood "love" to be the polar opposite of the intimacies of the coupled life. Is there, in fact, any evidence that Austrian gentiles engaged in more or different foreplay than Galician Jews did?[25] The term *goyim naches* refers to violent physical activity, such as hunting, dueling, or wars—all of which Jews traditionally despised, for which they in turn were despised—and to the association of violence with male attractiveness and with sex itself, not to foreplay.

Thomas Luxon has reminded me of several examples from English literature within which images of warfare, and rape, are central to valorized descriptions of male "love," such as Phillip Sidney's "Astrophil and Stella" and John Donne's "Batter My Heart." As Luxon stunningly remarks, "Violence *is* foreplay in the misogynist imaginary."[26] High European culture indeed invented romantic and courtly love, essentially misogynist formations,[27] but not foreplay, if the latter we understand to be simply techniques used by partners to excite each other in preparation for intercourse, and *not* a reduced bourgeois form of courtly love. Thus, just for example, we find the following bit of talmudic advice to wives—a father is speaking to his daughter: "When he takes the pearl in one hand and the furnace in the other, show him the pearl and not the furnace, until you [plural] are suffering, and then show it to him," which Rashi, the eleventh-century French talmudic commentator, forthrightly glosses as: "When your husband is caressing you to get ex-

---

24. Cuddihy, *Ordeal*, 72.

25. Has Cuddihy made any attempt to learn *anything* at all about the prescriptions for foreplay that Jewish culture insists on, going back to the Talmud? The Talmud even explicitly permits oral and anal intercourse between husbands and wives, acts that Freud would presumably regard as "perversions," operating as he is, in part at least, with the teleological assumptions about sexuality that were current in his day. For the talmudic material and its ambivalences, see my *Carnal Israel*, 109–22.

26. Luxon, letter. For romance as mystification of rape, see Gravdal, *Ravishing*, 42–71. Once more, I refer to Havelock Ellis, who, according to Siegel, held that "men whose deepest sexual desire does not involve dominance of women must be in some way physically deficient" (Siegel, *Male*, 59). And as Anthony Fletcher remarks (following David Turner), "[M]en were described as aggressive, hunting creatures, lions and greyhounds, while women are described as prey to be hunted, as deers [*sic*] or hares, or to be tamed and used in men's service as horses." And even more significantly, "Studies of church court records are revealing male sexual behaviour which is entirely consonant with all this material" (*Gender*, 94). Discourse is significant!

27. Fletcher, *Gender*, 92–93; R. H. Bloch, *Medieval Misogyny*; Gravdal, *Ravishing*, 11–12.

cited for intercourse, and he holds your breast in one hand, and your vulva in the other, give him access to your breast, in order that his passion will be great, and not quickly to your vulva, in order that his passion and affection will be great, and he will feel suffering, and then give him access to it" (Babylonian Talmud Shabbath 140b). It is interesting to note the sexist shift in the axis of the discourse from the Talmud to Rashi—in the former the desire sought is mutual, in the latter only the husband's is relevant—but it is certain that neither the Talmud nor this French Jewish contemporary of courtly lovers was ignorant or disdainful of foreplay and even of its "sweet suffering."[28]

To be sure, courtly love with its conventions (honored in the breach perhaps?) of chaste adultery would have seemed silly and immoral to Jews like Rashi, just as romantic notions of "love at first sight" did to their nineteenth-century descendants.[29] In the process of "modernization," Westernization, and embourgeoisement, the "inability" of Jews to appreciate romance was considered a mark of the great deficiency of their culture. As John M. Hoberman so perspicaciously puts it with reference to typical Viennese thinking of the fin de siècle: "Why, for example should the Jews' abstention from violent crime be a liability? How could their devotion to family life be a defect of character? What is implied in the claim that Jews are estranged from nature? Why does [Otto] Weininger allege that the Jews lack 'vibrancy'?"[30] An antisemite wrote in 1911 that "[t]he Jews' whole being is opposed to all that is

---

28. For other relevant texts, see D. Boyarin, *Carnal Israel,* 122–25.

29. Efron (*Defenders,* 66) cites the Jewish anthropologist Joseph Jacobs who explains the high incidence of cousin-marriages among Jews as being the product of "the absence of any ideal of pre-nuptial love." This is not a claim about all Jews everywhere, of course, but about the dominant, hegemonic strains of Jewish culture. For intriguing evidence of Jewish awareness of the discourse of romantic, courtly love and even the possibility of its impact on traditional medieval Jewish life, see D. Biale, *Eros,* 63–67 and notes there. Particularly fascinating is a text that Biale cites (72–73) from the medieval pietistic work, *Sefer Hasidim,* which seems to be partially imitative of the discourse of courtly love. It is significant, however, that even there, the practice is cited only to condemn it. There was at least one later Jew, moreover, who engaged in practices somewhat similar in form (although different in ethos) to "courtly love." Leib Melamed was a radical mystical figure of eighteenth-century Poland who reported of himself that he was alone with a naked woman lying on a bed, who wanted him to sleep with her, but that he only contemplated her beauty until a "spirit of holiness came upon him." The mystic concluded that "therefore it is proper for a man when he sees a woman to have great desire for her, but nevertheless not to have intercourse with her, but rather to contemplate her and look at her intensely and he will pass the test and rise to great heights" (D. Biale, 126). I think I would be justified in referring to this as an exception that proves the rule. Even the radical pietists of the Hasidic movement were opposed to figures such as Leib Melamed (D. Biale, 130).

30. Hoberman, "Otto," 143.

usually understood by chivalry, to all sentimentality, knight-errantry, feudalism, *patriarchalism.*"[31] In light of contemporary demystifications of the ideology of "romantic love," not to mention "knight-errantry, feudalism, patriarchalism," and in light of feminist demonstrations of its extreme misogyny incognito as regard for women—of the defining moment of romance being "the cultural habit of conceptualizing male violence against women as a positive expression of love"[32]—we need no longer continue such misrecognition of an asset as a defect.

Far from being a continuation of courtly love, there is much in post-Reformation European companionate marriage[33]—as opposed to the medieval Christian forms of marriage that predated it—that is similar to, and maybe even partly dependent on, for good or ill, talmudic marriage ideology as lived in medieval and early modern Judaism, in marriages such as Glikl's (see below). In this context, it is important to emphasize the growing Protestant condemnation of wife-beating in the seventeenth century and after.[34] This similarity includes the estimation of foreplay, a practice entirely *unlike* the pseudocourtesies of courtly love, and one designed, after all, to increase mutual pleasure in the actual consummation of normatively married love, not in its deferral. (It is not for nothing that even today marriage is frequently represented as the end—i.e., destruction, not *telos*—of romance.)[35] If we look for the successors to "courtly love," we find them perhaps in the modern rituals of adultery, as well as in the notion that married partners must inevitably ultimately find sex with each other unexciting. These are not "facts of nature" but inheritances of the culture of romance. Official Judaism indeed had no room for such "refinements"—although the story of unofficial interactions of Jews and romance, as a genre and a culture from the Middle Ages on, remains to be told.

Cuddihy quotes Ernest van den Haag: "Love as 'an aesthetic exhilaration and as a romantic feeling' . . . never made much of a dent on Jewish attitudes towards the body or towards the opposite sex. Love as

---

31. Werner Sombart, quoted in Hoberman, "Otto," 147, emphasis added.
32. Gravdal, *Ravishing,* 20.
33. Fletcher, *Gender,* 154–72.
34. Fletcher, *Gender,* 118; but see the rather harrowing material cited there as well; see also chapter 4.
35. Oscar Wilde's *The Importance of Being Earnest* includes a telling reference to this topos: "ALGERNON. I really don't see anything romantic in proposing. It is very romantic to be in love. But there is nothing romantic about a definite proposal. Why, one may be accepted. One usually is, I believe. Then the excitement is all over" (Wilde, *Importance,* 3).

'sweet suffering' was too irrational. If you want her, get her."[36] The quotation from van den Haag represents perhaps the silliest statement ever made about traditional Jewish culture. What on earth could "If you want her, get her" mean? Per chance: "Hit her over the head with your club and drag her to your cave"?[37] In traditional Jewish upper-class culture the process of finding a spouse involved the efforts of a matchmaker who sought to discover a suitable pairing. Both members of the potential couple, after having met the "intended" or even "fated" one, had the absolute right to refuse the match. God himself was understood in Jewish folklore to pick out appropriate partners for people even before birth; indeed, according to the Talmud this is what God does for a full third of his time. How does such a pattern, only sketched out here, get translated into "if you want her, get her" *as an imputed Jewish cultural ideal?* As far back as the Bible, we are informed that after Isaac's father had picked out a wife for him, "[h]e took her into his tent and he loved her."[38]

A much truer generalization would be that traditional Jewish culture did not make the dualistic split between the body and the spirit that enabled such culturally peculiar practices as the adoration of unconsummated loves between men and women. Love is understood to be profoundly connected with and enhanced by the physical intimacy of the (always married, of course) lovers as well, including both the intimacies of living together and of intercourse.[39] It is not love that is *goyim*

---

36. Cuddihy, *Ordeal,* 72.

37. Altogether, the idea of serious scholarly works turning to a vulgar popularization such as van den Haag's as a major source of information on traditional Jewish culture is simply staggering. As an example of the level of this book, I quote the following: " 'Jewish girls are the world's most boring women,' a friend of mine who is something of a Don Juan recently remarked to me. 'They keep telling me that I'm not interested in their minds. They have a point, but when I tell them I'm interested in them as women, they burst into tears. Why don't they want to be women? Why do they want to be less than a woman? That's what a mind is, only part of a woman.' " The whole book—at least the chapter on sex—is basically one long, humorless, JAP joke presented as pop sociology. Van den Haag's values, as, in many ways, those of Cuddihy, are the values anatomized (and anathematized) in Dijkstra's book. Referring to the misogynist writers of the fin de siècle, Dijkstra writes, "They discovered the glories of the 'gratuitous act' as evidence of their power" (*Idols,* 204). Van den Haag notes, "Like a river that is regulated to avoid floods or drying up, love and even sex, carefully and usefully regulated, lose their wild, spontaneous, impractical beauty" (149). I suggest that this "impractical beauty" of which van den Haag speaks owes much to the "glories of the 'gratuitous act,' " that is, to the aesthetics of fascism.

38. On the biblical "patriarchs" as antithetical to "manliness," see Feldman, "And Rebecca."

39. D. Boyarin, *Carnal Israel,* 53.

naches but courtly, romantic love that would have been so stigmatized by traditional Jews.[40]

This point is rendered highly significant if we attend to the gender politics of romantic love as they have been analyzed by several recent writers, especially in their late nineteenth-century version. As Bram Dijkstra has made only too clear, much of the sexual imagining of "Anglicism" in this period involved fantasies of women ripe and available for rape at any time, and this was typically expressed in representations of primitives of one sort or another: cavemen, barbarians whose cultures allegedly permitted such "free" sexual behavior.[41] Particularly telling is Dijkstra's summation of this ideology: "Many middle-class men dreamed of those simple times when the sight of a male was enough to make a woman cringe, *and when, if you wanted a woman, you simply reached out and took her.*"[42] Whose fantasies are being played out then when van den Haag describes East European traditional Jewish sexual ethics as "if you want her, get her" and Cuddihy repeats this nonsense? This seems an almost embarrassingly classical case of racist projection. There is, of course, something seductively beautiful in romance, but it is far too late in the day for western European culture to still be granted its self-avowed superiority over traditional cultures in its treatment of women. Too often and too clearly has this false claim been adduced in support of colonialist projects. And especially the Western ideology and practices known as courtly and romantic love can no longer be read as "good for women" in any sense.[43]

It is astonishing to me how much recent writing is still firmly en-

40. Estelle Roith's critique of the androcentrism of traditional Judaism seems generally on the mark. There may be no doubt at all, of course, that women were extremely disenfranchised in traditional Jewish culture. But she correctly observes also that "contrary to some feminist opinion, assumptions that women's status has been generally lower in Judaism than in other religious and social systems, is without much foundation" (*Riddle*, 90).

41. Dijkstra, *Idols*, 109–18. Dijkstra's exhaustive documentation of European fin de siècle images of women in both discourse and visual arts demonstrates eloquently how unnecessary is the hypothesis of any direct influence of Jewish gender ideologies on Freud's theories of femininity.

42. Dijkstra, *Idols*, 111, emphasis added.

43. Recent writers have written eloquently of the virulent misogyny of the cultures of bourgeois romantic love. Among the most cogent on the subject are R. Howard Bloch and Bram Dijkstra. Bloch has particularly investigated the historical genesis of this ideology in certain Christian ideals of sexual purity: "The principled deferral of satisfaction synonymous with courtliness represents a striving for spiritual purity that is deeply beholden to a Christian notion of love, the poetic expression of a desire deferred in this world because it is deflected toward the next" (*Medieval Misogyny*, 113–14). At the same time, Bloch shows how this poetic expression is deeply structurally wedded to misogyny: "The discourses of courtliness and misogyny conspire with each other" (114).

sconced within the Orientalist Whig tradition of perceiving Protestant male culture as some sort of ideal to which mankind [*sic*] is progressing. This extends even to approbation of the violent performances of European masculinity. Thus, a recent Jewish commentator on Freud, Estelle Roith, manages to write: "*Shtetl* values held that physical superiority was appropriate only for *goyim* but even the far more sophisticated Berlin Jews, according to Theodor Reik, regarded military honours cynically as '*Goyim Naches*' (Reik 1962: 61)."[44] Roith is at least more accurate than Cuddihy in her identification of "*goyim naches.*" Violence was, indeed, not particularly highly regarded in traditional Jewish culture. What is remarkable is her uncritical valorization of the opposing value-system of the Protestant bourgeoisie who saw fighting (e.g., dueling) as fundamental to manly honor. Thus she is surprised that "sophisticated" Berlin Jews are still "cynical" about military honors. Presumably she would not be so cynical. Her analysis, far from demystifying Freud's contempt for his "shtetl" father who refused to battle with the "goy," simply reproduces the terms of the malaise of the Jew in between.[45]

We begin to sense the ways in which the problem of male gender in the modernizing process of the Jews involves complex reformations of Jewish practices with respect to both sexuality and violence. Rather than see these effects as they do—as the products of an inevitable and

44. Roith, *Riddle,* 132.
45. If Roith has fully assimilated the ideology of war as manliness and sophistication, then it is not at all surprising that she has also fully assimilated the ideological mystification that romantic love (even courtly love) are somehow more respectful of women than traditional cultures—nearly all—in which sexuality is understood as a matter of fulfilling—not sublimating—physical desire and love, the product of such mutual fulfillment and other joint effort and activity. It is only thus that she can get to formulations such as the following: "On the other hand, the Jewish sexual ethos has been described by Max Weber as being characterized by 'the marked diminution of secular lyricism and especially of the erotic sublimation of sexuality' (Weber 1964: 257), whose basis he finds in *the 'naturalism of the Jewish ethical treatment of sexuality.'* This, I suggest, is closely related to the ancient Jewish perception of women as spiritually and intellectually inferior*" (Riddle,* 5, emphasis added). Unpacking Roith's comment a bit, we perceive that she is describing Weber's "naturalism of the Jewish ethical treatment of sexuality" as misogyny, presumably because it does not put women on a pedestal and represent them as angelic creatures above such "naturalistic," unsublimated forces as actual unlyrical sexual desire. One has to be peculiarly besotted by and with European romantic culture and totally oblivious to the feminist critique of the ideology of the "angel in the house" to imagine that it is less misogynistic than traditional Jewish "naturalism" around the sexual body, whatever the flaws of the latter formation—which I do not, of course, downplay. While it may be open to question whether Judaism as a whole perceived women as "spiritually and intellectually inferior" to men, it may be asserted with confidence that traditional Judaism never fell into the misogynistic trap of perceiving women as *superior* to men.

desirable evolutionary process—I would argue that these oppositions reproduce the terms of difference already set up for European culture at the outset of the split between Judaism and Christianity. As Charles Mopsik has written, "*Modern* societies tend more and more to separate the body that reproduces, a link in an immemorial genealogical adventure, from the body that desires, a lonely object, a consumer of briefly gratifying encounters. Thus, *modern* man has two distinct bodies, using one or the other as he pleases. This caesura is perhaps merely the persistence of a split opened two millennia ago by the ideological victory over one part of the inhabited world of the Christian conception of carnal relation—and of carnal filiation—as separate from spiritual life and devalued in relation to it."[46]

Bloch astutely argues that virginity is an Idea, and the loss of virginity then "seems closest to what the medievals conceived as the loss of the universality of an Idea through its expression."[47] This relationship of the universality of the Idea to the particularity of its expression is, of course, the very relation between Christianity and the Jews with their particularist insistence on physical practices and disdain for mere spiritual faith.[48] No wonder, then, that traditional Jewish culture had little use for merely spiritual loves between men and women as well.[49] Traditional Jewish culture may not have had room for romance (and was cynical about it when encountered in either its medieval or modern forms), but it was *not* cynical about love between married couples: "Our Rabbis have taught: One who loves his wife as he loves his own body and honors her more than he honors his body and raises his children in the upright fashion and marries them soon after sexual maturity, of him it is said, 'And you shall know that your tent is at peace' " (Babylonian Talmud, Yevamoth 62b).

The imputed cynicism of Jews toward romantic love, the aspersion that it is *goyim naches*, needs, then, to be revalued in the context of the serious critique of that formation that has been mounted from feminist (and other critical) quarters. Rather than reading it as misogynist disdain for women, it should be taken as disdain for a cultural ideal that

46. Mopsik, "Body," 49, emphases added.
47. R. H. Bloch, *Medieval*, 114.
48. Briggs, "Images."
49. I have pursued this argument in various ways through my *Carnal Israel*, as well as *mutatis mutandis* through *Radical Jew*. To return to the argument of this book, the relation between virginity as Idea and sexual experience as loss of the universality of the idea is the relationship between the phallus and the penis and thus, paradoxically, between the masculine and the feminine.

was so uncomfortable with women that they had to be transformed into angels before men could imagine living with them. This transformation, however, was to be crucial in the production of the "modern" Jew.[50]

East European Jewish culture, far from being "primitive" and mono-vocal, was full of conflict and contention—like, in fact, all other cultures.[51] We must be allowed to hear the voice of the traditional Jew[52] himself or, when we can, herself.[53] The real point that needs to be made is that nineteenth-century East European Jewry was not a morally degenerate *people,* as Cuddihy seems to simply assume, thus reproducing, rather than criticizing, the cultural forces that he seeks to account for.[54] As in any other human group, there were different forces and tendencies within this community—I am not proposing *Fiddler on the Roof* idealization—and much misery and degradation, of which widespread

50. For the reaction of one modern Jewish woman—Anna O./Bertha Pappenheim—to *embourgeoisement* and her analysis of its relation to traditional Jewish gender culture, see the final chapter.

51. David Biale is very good on this. Thus he notes that eighteenth-century Hasidism had developed in some of its disciple circles views of sexuality that were very similar to those of the ascetic church fathers. For these groups, he notes, "sexuality as a whole might be seen as feminine, since the feminine is connected to the material, while the masculine represents transcendence of the material—that is, celibacy. While some Jewish Hellenists as well as early Christians sometimes advanced such an equivalence between men and renunciation of sexuality, one searches in vain for such an extreme position in any rabbinic or medieval Jewish text" (*Eros,* 137). As Biale shows, it was within these Hasidic circles that it first became possible for a woman to be "made male" in a Jewish society—since the first century! We have then an exception that again proves the rule and, at the same time, makes it impossible to isolate any one strain as the authentic Jewish tradition. Hannah Rokhel, the "Maid of Ludmir," as described by Biale resembles nothing so much as a nineteenth-century Jewish Thecla. The strategy of my writing is to frankly admit such heterogeneity as Jewish and then seek to amplify those strains that I find most congruous in the service of a particular construction of a Judaism firmly rooted in tradition but more ethically compelling (in my view) than some other such constructions of modern traditional Judaisms. Note for the record that this does not comprehend picking and choosing parts of the Torah to accept or reject but rather choosing between particular interpretations of the Torah that subsist within the traditional sources of rabbinic Judaism.

52. See above, n. 51. By this, of course, I do not mean "the single, essential traditional Jew" but the many voices of different premodern Jews. I use the singular, because I can think of no other effective way to emphasize the gender imbalance of our access to such voices.

53. Michael Berkowitz makes the point of how surprised German Jewish soldiers were to discover "the intelligence, and depth and breadth of education" of East European Jewish women in comparison with the bourgeois Jewish women of the west, and "several soldiers' memoirs imply that the attention they received, and the level of intellectual engagement with the Russian and Polish Jewish women was beyond that to which they were accustomed at home with the Jewish women in their cohort" (*Western Jewry,* chapter 1). At the same time, Berkowitz does not fail to emphasize the degradation of this community as manifest in the widespread prostitution of Jewish women, even by their own, sometimes formally religious, families. Both are true, and this is the precise point of my comment.

54. Cuddihy, *Ordeal,* passim.

Jewish pandering and prostitution was only the most outstanding symptom,[55] but this was also a time of the highest religious cultural creativity for East European Jews, both in the rationalist wing of Lithuania[56] and in the mystical-literary wing of Galicia, Hungary, and farther east, as well as a time of widespread secular cultural production from poetry to politics.

Particularly telling is a comparison of the notions of modernity as the product of "differentiation," which Cuddihy emphasizes following Talcott Parsons,[57] and the racist social Darwinism of a Herbert Spencer, as discussed by Dijkstra: "There is a clear correlation, for instance, between the notion that with the progress of evolution men and women had become more *un*like and Herbert Spencer's famous dictum, in *First Principles*, that 'evolution is definable as a change from an incoherent homogeneity to a coherent heterogeneity.'"[58] Note also the affinities with Otto Weininger—an association that I am sure would repel Cuddihy—for whom, according to Dijkstra, "women [and Jews] were, in essence, human parasites. They could not live without men or without each other. In a sense they were interchangeable, undifferentiated beings, for the capacity to differentiate was a characteristic of the intellect, of genius. True genius yearned for true individualism and stood sternly and ruggedly alone, . . . all of which served to show that regressive, materialistic anti-individualistic political philosophies such as communism were basically the weak conceptions of benighted men who, like Karl Marx, were suffering from terminal cases of effeminacy."[59]

I do not, of course, mean to associate Cuddihy with Weininger's misogyny or Spencer's racism, only to show how deeply problematic the ideas of social evolution and "differentiation" to which he subscribes truly are. I would rather propose that it is, as we have seen, the colonizing eye that perceives "incoherent homogeneity" in the culture of the colonized, just as misogynists produce such incoherent homogeneity in their descriptions of women. Rabbi Ḥayyim of Volozhin (like my grandmother) was just as capable of making differentiations—although to be sure different ones—as the "modernized" people described by the sociologist are: "Differentiation on the level of the cultural system is the power to make *distinctions* between previously fused—*confused*—

55. Berkowitz, *Western Jewry*, chapter 1; M. A. Kaplan, *Jewish Feminist Movement*.
56. Etkes, *Lita*; Dijkstra, *Idols*.
57. Cuddihy, *Ordeal*, 10.
58. Dijkstra, *Idols*, 165–66 and 170 ff., esp. 171.
59. Dijkstra, *Idols*, 219–20.

ideas, values, variables, concepts."[60] There was a "native" tradition of "civility" among East European Jewish cultural elites that Cuddihy is totally incapable of realizing.[61] The "ordeal" was not the product of conflict between coarseness and civility but between two different cultures of gendering, an ordeal, if you will, of virility.

EDELKAYT; OR, THE CIVILITY OF THE OSTJUDE

In the present section, I wish to depict with some broad strokes what the masculine ideal of traditional European Jewry in the nineteenth century looked like, through both positive self-representations of the *mentsh* and his ideal characteristic of *Edelkayt* (nobility) and, somewhat more corrosively, through an exploration of the pejorative *goyim naches*, as a salient Jewish critique of European "manliness." As Paul Lawrence Rose has remarked in a related context, "To contest these unspoken [antisemitic] assumptions, which governed the attitudes even of those who were friendly to the Jews, required an acquaintance with subtle and difficult categories of Jewish thinking not easily accessible to most observers—Jewish as well as Christian—brought up in western Christian culture."[62]

The oppositions between the knight and the sage as respectively abjected and valued stereotypes of maleness remained alive in European Jewish culture throughout the Middle Ages and into the early modern period. In the early Middle Ages, in glossing a passage that speaks of a "skillful knight [*Reiter*]," Rashi feels that he has to inform the reader that this man was a Jew, in spite of the fact that this is entirely obvious from the context, precisely because it was so counterintuitive to Jews that there would be a Jewish knight (Rashi ad Yevamot 121b). As late as 1823, in a Haggada [the home liturgy for Passover eve] published in Vienna, the "righteous son" is depicted as a Middle Eastern scholar wearing a robe and carrying a scroll, while the "wicked son" is a sort of Roman soldier, with a long sword attached to his belt (see Plate 3). The iconographic tradition thus represents the continuity of the stereo-

60. Cuddihy, *Ordeal*, 11 (his emphases).

61. Justin Miller squarely diagnoses this fatal weakness in Cuddihy's book: "Among the many questionable points in Cuddihy's argument is the accuracy of his understanding of *shtetl* culture which had its own sense of social propriety reflecting a socially stratified structure of which Cuddihy appears to have been unaware" ("Interpretation," 368). It is difficult to recommend most of the rest of this rather weak article.

62. Rose, *Wagner*, 19.

Plate 3. Illustration of the Four Sons from Vienna, 1823. In the traditional Haggada, the wicked son is always signified by possession of a weapon. (Collection of the author.)

typing of the bad Jew as one who imitates the martial ideals of the prototypical "goy," the Roman, while the good Jew is a scholar, in dress
more like an abbot than any other European male type.

In general, medieval and early modern Haggadas illustrate the
wicked son as some form of martial figure, almost always, in fact, a
knight in shining armor (see Plate 4).[63] This, of course, establishes a
direct and explicit contrast between the Jewish ideal and the models of
"manliness" that the circumambient culture had developed. As George
Mosse has remarked of nineteenth-century western Europe, "Manliness
drew upon the aristocratic ideal of knighthood as a pattern of virtue in
a changing world and a model for some of its behavior."[64] As we have
seen, however, for traditional Jewish iconography it was the ideal of
knighthood that represented the negative ideal, the "wicked son," the
antithesis of a pattern of virtue. For such traditional Jews the knight
and all that he represented both on the field of battle and in the bedroom of courtly and romantic love were the essence of *goyim naches*. In
a less caustic vein, this contrast could be brought out by citing the following contrast between the masculine ideal of Freud and that of a near
contemporary *Ostjude*. The great Lithuanian rabbi and psychologist
Israel Salanter had written that the ideal man is sensitive and the cure
for a lack of sensitivity is "to revive emotion and to arouse [in oneself]
constant concern and care,"[65] while Freud for his part was to describe
"the essence of great men" as "above all the autonomy and independence of the great man, his divine unconcern which may grow into
ruthlessness."[66]

GLIKL'S *MENTSH;*
OR, "THE PERFECT PATTERN OF A PIOUS JEW"

In the seventeenth century, a Jewish wife describes her husband:

> However much my husband toiled, and truly the whole day he ran about
> upon his business, still he never failed to set aside a fixed time to study his
> daily Torah. He fasted, too, a great part of every day the Torah was read
> forth in the synagogue [Mondays and Thursdays], at least until he began to

63. Metzger, *Haggada*, 152–56. See the insightful remarks by David Biale, who
makes the excellent point that if the wicked Jewish son could be depicted as an armed
figure, there must indeed have been Jews who bore arms (*Power*, 73).
64. Mosse, *Nationalism*, 23.
65. Goldberg, *Israel*, 278.
66. Freud, *Moses*, 109–10.

Plate 4.   The Wicked Son as "Knight in Shining Armor." From a medieval Haggada manuscript. [London Ms. Add. 14762; fol. 9 recto]. Courtesy of the British Library.

make his long business journeys, with the result that even in his youth he became sickly and needed much doctoring. Yet, for all that, he never spared himself, and shirked no pains to provide his wife and children a decent livelihood.

So good and true a father one seldom finds, and he loved his wife and children beyond all measure. His modesty had no like, throughout his life he never once gave thought to holding public office; on the contrary, he would not so much as hear of it, and he was wont to laugh at people who hankered after such things. In brief, he was the perfect pattern of a pious Jew, as were his father and brothers.

Even among the great rabbis, I knew but few who prayed with his fervour. If he were praying in his room, and someone came to fetch him forth where something could be bought up cheap, neither I nor any servant in my whole house would have the heart to go to him and speak of it. Indeed, he once missed a bargain in this way, to the loss of several hundred thalers. He never regarded these things, but served God faithfully and called upon Him with diligence; and He repaid him for all, two and threefold over. A man so meek and patient as my beloved husband will not be found again. All that he had to contend with, and often, from friends and strangers, he bore in patience.[67]

Glikl of Hameln, who wrote this description, was a woman of the Jewish trading class of Hamburg and Altona.[68] Her life spanned the second half of the seventeenth century. In her description of her young husband as the ideal male Jew of her time, she emphasizes his inwardness, piety, and especially "meekness." Her book is suffused with descriptions, tender and delicately erotic, of her love for this man who forms in a sense the prototypical *mentsh* as husband, devoted, reliable, gentle, and emotionally warm (see Plate 5). These were not the characteristics of a "knight in shining armor." Indeed many of these traits—meekness, patience, long suffering—would be more likely to fit the damsel in distress or an anchorite friar than a husband and man of the world. Glikl herself, moreover, was mightily empowered in this marriage in the classic terms of socioeconomic autonomy and power. She will be playing an important supporting role in the drama of the last chapter of this book as well.

PIOUS EROS: HASIDISM AND THE MODERN JEWISH MAN

Analyzing a fascinating Jewish text of the nineteenth century brings many of these conflicts between the traditional Jewish culture of gender

67. Lowenthal, *Memoirs,* 34–35.
68. N. Z. Davis, *Women,* 5–62.

Plate 5. "The Perfect Pattern of a Pious Jew." The painting *Sabbath Rest,*
eighteenth century, by Moritz Oppenheim. (Courtesy of the Leo Baeck Institute, New York.)

and its European context to light.[69] This analysis will have the perhaps
surprising result of revealing Hasidism as a movement of at least partial
accommodation of Jewish culture to romantic culture.[70]

At the beginning of the volume of legends and sayings of "the Besht,"
Rabbi Israel of the Good Name, who founded Hasidism, the modern
Jewish Pietistic movement, there is a remarkable legendary account of
the origins of this figure, covering his birth, childhood, and marriage
up until the point when he "revealed" himself to the world. Moshe Ros-

69. In the general German society at this same time, "[f]or a boy to establish himself
as a man meant engaging fully in a youth culture where manhood was learnt by drinking,
fighting, and sex" (Roper, *Oedipus,* 107; see also Fletcher, *Gender,* 92).

70. For an illuminating account of closely related ways that Hasidism involves ac-
commodations of the sexual ideology of European Christian culture, see D. Biale, *Eros,*
121–48.

man has argued quite persuasively that this text represents a move in a nineteenth-century controversy among different Hasidim to establish different models of leadership and authority within the movement.[71] Paradoxically, this very "defect" of the text as a historical source about the founding of Hasidism magnifies its significance for my purposes, for the text seeks to "reduce" the subversiveness of the image of the Besht and to make him over in the image of the classical Talmud scholar.[72] In other words, there is tension within the text itself between two "redactional" levels that can be read as sociocultural conflict within the communities that produced the composite text, one in which traditional Jewish masculinity was being reformed by Hasidism and one in which it was being reinstated. I am not suggesting by this, however, that lives as they were lived necessarily actually followed these models, but the models themselves are a significant cultural fact. Moreover, since the Besht was for much of eastern European Jewry in the nineteenth century a hegemonic figure, to the extent that this text was accepted as canonical (and it was), it would have been effective in reproducing certain gendered roles, whether or not those roles had been actually practiced before. Exploring this text carefully gives us, then, some insight into the effectiveness, the materiality, of the talmudic model in informing the gender practices of early modern traditional Jews.

The text begins with a fantastic narrative of the birth of the hero, elements of which will be entirely familiar to many readers. The father of the Besht was captured by pirates who took him away to another country where there were no Jews and sold him. Rabbi Eliezer, the father, served his master so well that the latter appointed him overseer of his house, allowing him to keep the Sabbath. Afterward, Eliezer was given as a gift to the viceroy of the kingdom. The only task that the

71. Rosman, *Founder,* chapters 9 and 12.
72. For this shift toward a more conservative, mainstream rabbinism within Hasidism, see D. Biale, *Eros,* 122. Rosman for his part has thoroughly demystified the legendary and popular accounts of Hasidism and shown that within his own context the Besht was hardly subversive. The very contrast between the eighteenth-century "reality" exposed by Rosman's careful research and the images in the later legendary text only enhances the value of the latter as a historical source for cultural conflict in the later period. Rosman remarks, "As primarily ideological reifications, most descriptions of the Baal Shem Tov [Besht] over the past two hundred years or so tell relatively little about him, but very much about the issues confronting Jewish culture in the Western world beginning at the end of the eighteenth century. . . . With continual re-invention, the Baal Shem Tov can authoritatively epitomize or serve as a counterpoint to one cultural trend or another." My analysis here would have been impossible without his prior work, and I am grateful to him for sharing it with me prior to publication.

slave had was to wash the master's feet when he came home. Otherwise he spent all of his time studying Torah and praying in his special chamber. At a later date, the viceroy was unable to help the king in a matter of military strategy until his Jewish slave (whom he did not know was Jewish) dreamed the appropriate advice. The king forced the viceroy to reveal whence his information had come, and upon hearing the truth elevated the slave to battle commander. According to the story, "[h]e won every battle that the king sent him to fight."[73] The king gave him the viceroy's daughter as a wife, but he did not touch her, finally revealing to her that he was a Jew, in spite of the fact that in that country all Jews were immediately put to death. She gave him gold and silver and helped him escape, but on the way home all was stolen from him. He arrived home and found his wife still alive, and "[t]he Besht was born to them, when both of them were close to a hundred."[74]

Aside from the obvious elements of biblical intertextuality—Eliezer is a combination of Joseph, Moses, and Abraham—this story has other meanings for a politics of Jewish maleness. It is a sort of allegorical wish-fulfillment fantasy of threatened Jews.[75] Like the biblical Joseph, Eliezer is able to arrive at political power through dreams afforded to him by God. He also manages to keep his Jewishness in a world which is the limit case of hostile gentile society: no other Jews and Jewishness punishable by death. Moreover, as in the case of Joseph, this retention

73. Ben-Amos and Mintz, *In Praise*, 10.
74. Ben-Amos and Mintz, *In Praise*, 11.
75. In another sequence of the same cycle, which will not be treated here, an antisemite puts his hand into his pocket and pulls it out covered with excrement. He is informed by a Jewish mystic that his hand will not become clean unless it is urinated on by a Jew: "When he put his hand in his pocket, he dirtied his hand, and he took it out filthy with human dung. There was a terrible stink and the kaiser ordered him to be removed. He washed his hand with water, but it did not do any good, and he appealed for mercy to Rabbi Adam. Rabbi Adam said to him: 'If you swear never to be a Jew hater it will be all right. If not, your hands will be filthy all your life.' He swore, and Rabbi Adam told him: 'There is only one remedy for you—a Jew must urinate on your hands. You will wash in it and this will help you.' And so it happened" (Ben-Amos and Mintz, *In Praise*, 14). One of the most interesting aspects of this entire sequence of the Besht's training in mystical matters by "Rabbi Adam" is that it is almost impossible to imagine such a figure actually existing, not least because Adam is a name almost never (if ever) used by Jews. For discussion of the scholarly literature on "Rabbi Adam" and possible identifications with a heretical Jewish mystic of the seventeenth century, see Ben-Amos and Mintz, *In Praise*, 309–10.
As will be seen throughout this discussion, the text is exploring the boundaries of Jew and gentile at the same time that it is treating gendered boundaries as well—and this is not accidental. For a much earlier version of such Jewish wish fulfillment, compare the texts discussed in chapter 3 below.

of Jewishness is signified in part by his avoidance of sexual intercourse with a non-Jew. He thus achieves wealth, power, and sexual access to a princess, all of the signifiers of gentile masculine success, but he refuses all of them. He returns to his humble Jewish existence poor, weak, and married to a poor old Jewish woman.[76] This is how he achieves his true vocation as father of a great mystic. This true Jewish existence had been maintained throughout in the domestic, private, "female" space of his own room, where he engaged in the nonmanly, quintessentially Jewish pursuit of the study of Torah.[77] At the same time, the story signals that his passion for this inner, "passive" space is owed not to his inability to perform in the world of manliness but to his commitment to the alternative values of Jewish male gendering.[78] There is, accordingly, nothing radical or even critical in this sequence vis-à-vis the traditions of Jewish masculinity.[79]

This will begin to change in the continuation. The gendered overtones of this narrative become palpable in the next sequence, where we

76. This text functions, then, as a virtual counter-romance, rejecting the values of a society within which, as Perkins emphasizes for a much earlier period, beauty and power were equated with virtue (Perkins, *Suffering,* 54–55). This is, of course, not simply a contrast between Jewish and Christian, for there are many such Christian counter-romantic texts as well. Early Christianity is itself, as Perkins's book demonstrates, entirely an oppositional movement to Hellenistic romance culture. The complex of relations between romance, Jewish, and Christian culture in Europe remains to be fully explored.

77. The text signals some of this as well through a curious statement cited in the name of the Besht himself that "it had been impossible for his father to draw his soul from heaven until he had lost his sexual desire" (Ben-Amos and Mintz, 11). David Biale has discussed this notion of procreation without desire as typical of Hasidism (D. Biale, *Eros,* 130). This comment seems almost readable as a justification for the practice of young Hasidic married men spending years away from their wives until their sexual desire was overcome and then returning home to "produce offspring, fulfilling this commandment of their Creator just like any other, filled with love of God and with nothing extraneous," an almost Augustinian vision of sexuality. The quotation is from Menachem Nachum of Tschernobyl, one of the most important of the early Hasidic masters.

78. Contrast the view of Cantor, who maintains that "the downgrading of providing was thus not the result of an authentic belief in its inappropriateness as a male activity. This is borne out, for instance, by the haste with which East European men who immigrated to America reestablished themselves on the work turf once they saw its doors open to them" (*Jewish Women,* 112). This argument is clearly invalid, since by its lights one would come to the conclusion that eating pork was also not "the result of an authentic belief in its inappropriateness," since that prohibition was also abandoned with great haste upon arriving in America. Second, is there any reason to believe that it would have been harder in Europe for Jewish men than for women to work?

79. The great opponent of the Hasidim, the Vilna Gaon, wrote that "true heroes are men of noble heart with the fullest trust in God, constantly doing mitzvoth and meditating on the Torah day and night even though their home be without bread and clothing" (Vilna, *Commentary* on Prov. 23:30, "Who is a hero? He who conquers his desire."). See also Etkes, "Marriage," 154.

find explicit textual marking of its intertextuality, of the cultural heterogeneity that has produced the text:

> The boy grew up and was weaned. The time came for his father to die, and he took his son in his arms and he said, "I see that you will light my candle, and I will not enjoy the pleasure of raising you. My beloved son, remember this all your days: God is with you. Do not fear anything." (In the name of *Admor,* I heard that it is natural for a son and a father to be closely bound, for as our sages, God bless their memory, have said: "The talk of the child in the market place is either that of his father or of his mother" [Sukka 56b]. How much closer then are ties between parents and children who are born to them in their old age. For example, Jacob loved Joseph because he was born to him in his old age, and the ties between them were very great, as it is said in the holy Zohar. And it was true here. Although the Besht was a small child, because of the intensity and sincerity of the tie, the words were fixed in his heart.)[80]

This is actually quite an extraordinary passage, the meaning of which is not entirely obvious at first glance. The editor/compiler of the legends about the founder of Hasidism has received a tradition within which the father spoke to the child upon the former's impending death, holding him in his arms and describing raising the child as a pleasure, and he provides a gloss explaining this tradition. The gloss marks the site, I would surmise, of a cultural gap between the textual source and the editor of the text, that is, presumably between an eighteenth-century Ukrainian source and a nineteenth-century Lithuanian editor, although I do not know whether the chronological or the geographical parameter is the important one.

The gloss, apparently, functions as a justification for what the redactor expected would seem as strangely intimate behavior of a father toward his son. This interpretation is further borne out by the citation from the Talmud. The talmudic text, after all, does not indicate that sons are particularly close to their fathers; rather it indicates equal intimacy between children and either of their parents. Its function here, then, must be to support the point that sons are intimate with their fathers as well as with their mothers, and especially when the son is born to the father in his old age. I derive from this two sorts of information. One is that, at least in the cultural world of this editor—early nineteenth-century Lithuanian Hasidism—fathers were not necessarily physically and emotionally close to their children. The passage also in-

---

80. Ben-Amos and Mintz, *In Praise,* 11.

dicates that such intimacy was being promoted by the rabbinical leaders, at any rate by the highly significant Rabbi Shneur Zalman of Ladi,
the founder of Ḥabad Hasidism (*Admor* in the text), and, moreover,
supports this norm by citing the Talmud. The explicit rupture in the
passage marked by the parenthetical gloss provides a key to the stresses
within the representations of gender in the narrative as a whole.

The sense of conflict around the role of the Jewish male continues in
the next section of the text as well:

> AFTER THE DEATH OF HIS FATHER THE CHILD GREW up. Because the people
> of the town revered the memory of his father, they favored the child and sent
> him to study with a melamed [Hebrew teacher for children]. And he suc-
> ceeded in his studies. But it was his way to study for a few days and then to
> run away from school. They would search for him and find him sitting alone
> in the forest. They would attribute this to his being an orphan. There was
> no one to look after him and he was a footloose child. Though they brought
> him again and again to the melamed, he would run away to the forest to be
> in solitude. In the course of time they gave up in despair and no longer re-
> turned him to the melamed. He did not grow up in the accustomed way
> [11–12].

The curious contradiction between "and he succeeded in his studies"
and the immediately following running away to the forest marks, once
more, the site of a tension within this text between two norms. It would
seem that the tradition that the redactor has received is invested in
a Besht who was not a student of Talmud in the classical sense but a
nature-mystic, one who ran away from school and spent time alone in
the forest like a Ukrainian Pietist.[81] We should note the thematization
of the opposition between the indoor space of traditional Jewish piety
versus the (gentile) outdoors of this radically idiosyncratic figure.[82] In a
sense, the "original" text seems to represent a significant breech of the
inner cultural boundaries that separate Jew from gentile. A new form
of pietistic, nature-oriented, antischolarly, outdoors-oriented Jewish
leadership is being produced. Our redactor, however, apparently a devo-
tee of the Besht but at the same time a member of the unique Lithuanian, scholarly branch of Hasidism (whose members other Hasidim
considered not true Hasidim because of their devotion to study), cannot

81. Some have speculated, indeed, that Hasidism is in significant fashion a product
of the "influence" of Ukrainian Pietism on Judaism at this time (D. Biale, *Eros*, 124). This
would explain the identity of the Besht's teacher, Rabbi Adam. (See above n. 74.)

82. For the outdoors as the realm of the "Other" in quite a different but related context, see D. Biale, *Eros*, 67.

imagine a Jewish religious leader who would not be a scholar, so the child Besht becomes a successful student who nevertheless runs away from school—undoubtedly, as the continuation will certify, for reasons of modesty.

In any case, it is the conservative, talmudically oriented revisionist wing of Hasidism that I am interested in here specifically because it is closer to what might be called, for want of a better term, the normative traditional Judaism of nineteenth-century East Europe. In the continuation of the narrative, which describes the further adventures of the Besht's youth, we see the same conflicts being played out:

> He hired himself out as the melamed's assistant, to take the children to school and to the synagogue, to teach them to say in a pleasant voice, "Amen, let His great name be blessed forever and to all eternity, kedushah, and amen." This was his work—holy work with school children whose conversations are without sin. While he walked with the children he would sing with them enthusiastically in a pleasant voice that could be heard far away. His prayers were elevated higher and higher, and there was great satisfaction above, as there was with the songs that the Levites had sung in the Temple. And it was time of rejoicing in heaven. And Satan came also among them. Since Satan understood what must come to pass, he was afraid that the time was approaching when he would disappear from the earth. He transformed himself into a sorcerer. Once while the Besht was walking with the children, singing enthusiastically with pleasure, the sorcerer transformed himself into a beast, a werewolf. He attacked and frightened them, and they ran away. Some of them became sick, heaven help us, and, could not continue their studies. Afterwards, the Besht recalled the words of his father, God bless his memory, not to fear anything since God is with him. He took strength in the Lord, his God, and went to the householders of the community, the fathers of the children, and urged them to return the children to his care. He would fight with the beast and kill it in the name of God. "Should school children go idle when idleness is a great sin?" They were convinced by his words. He took a good sturdy club with him. While he walked with the children, singing pleasantly, chanting with joy, this beast attacked them. He ran toward it, hit it on its forehead, and killed it. The corpse of the gentile sorcerer was found lying on the ground. After that the Besht became the watchman of the Beth-hamidrash. This was his way: while all people of the house of study were awake, he slept and while they slept, he was awake, doing his pure works of study and prayer until the time came when people would awaken. Then he would go back to sleep. They thought that he slept from the beginning until the end of the night.[83]

---

83. Ben-Amos and Mintz, *In Praise*, 11–13.

As above, the text here manifests a powerful cognizance of the tension between its valorization of "Diasporic" models of Jewish masculinity and the inability of such men to "protect" Jewish children from antisemitic violence. The Jewish boy who did not grow up like other Jewish boys is able to protect the children from the gentile sorcerer who wishes to eat them up. The "original" level of the text thus promotes a revisionist model of masculinity, one closer in certain of its parameters—protecting dependents[84]—to the chivalric, romantic ideal of manliness than to the scholarly ideal of the Yeshiva-Bokhur. However, within the scholarly community that is promulgating this particular version of his life, it is not this ability that brings him praise but, once more an endeavor in which he resembles his father, his secret studies of Torah. In other words, while the original Hasidic text emphasizes the overturning of traditional Jewish norms of masculinity in the Hasidic movement, the revised version of the text wishes to preserve those very norms through the same text and the same exemplary figure. A delicate semiotic code opposing indoors to outdoors is mobilized throughout this text. Indoors is the place of the (Jewish) male, while outdoors symbolizes the world of gentiles with its threats and practices. The unusual, subversive (but also protective) aspects of the Besht are all placed in the outdoors, but his true nature as a Jew is revealed in the secret activities that he carries on in the Beth-hamidrash. The message is clearly that on the surface he is somehow more like "them," but truly he was a real Jew.

Moreover, and for my purposes most significant, it is not his prowess in battle against antisemitic demons that will win him a wife, as would be predicted by versions of chivalric culture, but again his devotion to the indoor pursuit of Torah study: "When the people of the community saw that our teacher Israel was studying with Rabbi Adam's son, they said that it was probably on account of Israel's father that Rabbi Adam's son came here to care for Israel. It seemed to them that Israel was behaving in the right way. And so they gave him a wife."[85] The very qualifications that would render a young man fit to be a monk within European Christian culture—scholarliness, quietism, modesty, and a spiritual aptitude—are those that qualify him to be a husband in this Jewish culture. This is almost explicitly contrasted with the qualities

84. Bullough, "On Being," 34.
85. Ben-Amos and Mintz, *In Praise*, 17.

that certified his father as appropriate spouse for the daughter of the gentile viceroy in the sequence discussed above. There, of course, it was winning battles that made him a desirable husband, as was more typical of early modern European narratives of love, such as the chapbook version of St. George, in which "the noble hero never failed of carrying the prize at tilts and tournaments, quelled monsters, overcame giants and slaughtered beasts," and then ended up with a "happy-ever-after marriage with the Egyptian princess he rescued."[86] The point is not that Christian cultures lacked similar valorized models of femminized masculinity, but that they assigned this male type an entirely different place within the erotic economy of the society.[87] In Christian culture, speaking very broadly, the feminized male was de-eroticized, while in Jewish culture he was projected as the husband par excellence, and even, as we shall see in the next section, as favored object of female desire. Indeed, a major part of the "biography" of the holy Rabbi is devoted to making an appropriate match for him.

This point will be borne out further in analyzing the detailed account of the Besht's marriage that follows:

> Our master, Rabbi Gershon of Kuty, was head of the rabbinical court in the holy community of Brody. His father, our master Abraham, had a law-suit to settle with one of the people in the community where the Besht was staying, so he went there. He asked his opponent to travel with him to the holy community of Brody to settle the issue between them according to the law of the Torah. But the man said to him: "There is with us here a teacher, eminent in the knowledge of Torah, who is a righteous judge. Whenever a case is brought before him both sides agree completely with his decision because he clearly explains the verdict. Let us go to him and present our arguments, and, sir, if you are not satisfied with his decision, then I will go with you to the holy community of Brody." He accepted his advice and they went to him. When our master and rabbi, Rabbi Abraham, came before the Besht, he immediately was inspired with the holy spirit *and perceived that his daughter was to be the future wife of the Besht*. At that time it was the custom of great scholars that when a worthy guest came he would give an explanation of a difficult passage. And the Besht clarified a complex point in the *Rambam* with great subtlety. He continued to do so until Abraham's soul became attracted to the Besht's soul and their souls were in accord [19, emphasis added].

---

86. Fletcher, *Gender*, 88.
87. This parallels my reading of late antiquity as well, within which the Christian ascetic demasculinized male is also desexualized and rewarded with saintliness, while the femminized Rabbi is rewarded with a wife, as we shall see in chapter 2.

The narrative goes on to relate how the Besht returned such a just decision in the case that had been brought before him that once more, as in the past, both sides went away satisfied. His future father-in-law had so fallen in love with him, moreover, that he offered him the hand of his daughter, which the Besht accepted on condition that he not be revealed in Brody as the great scholar that he was. For all its apparent subversiveness, this narrative is characterized by the remarkable continuity between its norms of masculinity and ones that go back as far in Jewish culture as the Babylonian Talmud itself, as will be brought out in the next two chapters.

The sequence that follows is almost a direct reversal of romance, in that the daughter keeps insisting that she will follow her father's wishes in the marriage plot, however surprising they may seem. The question is never whether she will be willing to marry the intended but whether her brother will fall in love with him as her father had. The father, having died in the meantime, has left behind a document indicating that his daughter is to marry someone named Israel, without background or family lineage. His son, the brother of the prospective bride, is shocked, but the daughter says, "If our father thought the match was proper, we shouldn't doubt his decision" (21).

The Besht, of course, as is his way, exacerbates the situation by showing up to claim his bride in "clothes like those worn by loafers. He put on a short coat and a broad belt, *he changed his demeanour* and manner of speech" (21). The short coat signifies two things, both encompassed in the term "*baṭ lanim*," translated "loafers"; it indicates modernity and aping of gentile fashions. The appropriate clothing would be a long robe more similar to the robe of a Christian monk than to the short coat of a doctor, soldier, or businessman.[88] Once more, we have the near topos of the Besht as openly disdainful of traditional Jewish social norms but secretly in full harmony with them. The daughter, notwithstanding the fact that according to Jewish law she has every right to refuse a match, chooses once more to follow her father's desire. He reveals himself in secret to the bride and swears her to secrecy as well. They are married and her brother, who is also a great rabbinic scholar,

---

88. The ironies of this term in this context are fabulous. People who work as doctors or businessmen are called "loafers," while those who spend their time in study are not. However, in talmudic times the term is used for those who devote their entire lives to study and prayer, but it is there a positively coded signifier. We see the multilayered heterogeneity (class-inflected) of any given term of cultural discourse, and the same is true for gendered terms.

endeavors to teach his brother-in-law Torah. But the latter pretends both ignorance and inability to learn, whereupon the brother drives both the sister and her husband away. After several years of living as a semi-hermit in the mountains, digging clay that his wife sells in town, the Besht returns with his wife to the town of the brother, where the brother takes pity on his sister.

The following description of their lives follows:

> AFTER THAT OUR MASTER AND RABBI, RABBI GERSHON, rented a place for the Besht in a certain village where he would be able to earn a living. And there he achieved perfection. He built a house of seclusion in the forest. He prayed and studied there all day and all night every day of the week, and he returned home only on the Sabbath. He also kept there white garments for the Sabbath. He also had a bathhouse and a mikveh. His wife was occupied with earning a living, and God blessed the deeds of her hand and she was successful. They were hospitable to guests: they gave them food and drink with great respect. When a guest came she sent for the Besht and he returned and served him. The guest never knew about the Besht [27].

The points do not need belaboring. First of all, as was frequently the case in eastern European elite (and ideal) Jewish culture at this time, a wife is working successfully at some trade or business in order to support a husband's religious and scholarly activities.[89] This issues in a reversal of the topoi of public and private that encode male and female within European culture. Although, to be sure, those topoi are themselves seriously open to question, they are nevertheless active as commonplaces and as norms, and much of upper-class Jewish culture reverses them exactly, offering the private spaces of study and prayer as most appropriate to the male and the public spaces of getting and spending to the female.[90] In some traditional communities, men even

89. Of course, this pattern was (and could be) only a minority pattern and an ideal model, since in most families both members of the couple worked to support the family. Similarly, the commonly held picture of very early marriages among East European Jews of the nineteenth century has been contested on demographic and archival grounds (Stampfer, "Gender"); however, it remains the case that this was the common pattern for the scholarly elite. It is this elite that represents the discourse of ideal masculinity that I am studying in this book.

90. The class stratification is, of course, highly important, and were I intending to discuss social history, it would be crucial. However, it is the play of elite cultural models—understood as social practice in their own right—with which I am concerned here. It must not be forgotten, nevertheless, how problematic the connections between these representations and "reality" are.

did housework while their wives supported them by working outside the home or by maintaining a business.[91]

Once more, we observe within this short paragraph the contradictions that mark this text as a site of conflict over these ideals. In the first sentence, we are informed that the Besht was installed in a village where he was to be able to earn a living, but then it turns out that what he was really doing was praying and studying, while only pretending to be a householder. It was his wife who was entirely supporting him economically. Thus where early Hasidism seems to have been anxious to recreate an economically productive male ideal, as well as resisting the disdain for such men within elite Ashkenazi culture,[92] the redactor's level of the text reinstates this ideal as such. This is indicative of a virtual reversal in the traditional Ashkenazi ideal of gendered positions vis-à-vis the general culture, except, of course, for monks.[93] The most remarkable aspect of this narrative however is simply that it is a story of a "married monk," a story, I repeat, within which a man fit to be a celibate religious according to European Christian mores is married.[94] It seems, then, that while we can learn very little of the history of the founding of Hasidism in the eighteenth century from such a clearly legendary text, we can derive some knowledge of social norms and ideals that informed its authorship in the nineteenth. This bears out anthropologist Percy Cohen's observation, cited and discussed below, that "the values and status inhering in the physically passive, scholar idea safeguarded the pre-emancipation Jew's sense of masculinity." The Besht finally "reveals" himself as an appropriate marriage object for his

---

91. Stampfer, "Gender," 85.

92. Kaminsky, "Discourse," 302.

93. Cf. the distinctly negative reading given this reversal by one "enlightened" nineteenth-century Jew who describes his sexual problems upon early marriage as having been exacerbated by the fact that he was a "feminine male" while his bride was a "masculine female" (Mordecai Aaron Guenzburg, quoted in D. Biale, *Eros*, 155). One wonders whether this was his judgment at the time or only after extensive exposure to "European" culture. One hint that the latter might be true is Guenzburg's further praise of "the customs of countries where men work and women stay at home" (D. Biale, 160), which suggests that having adopted the gender ideology of the European bourgeois he was bound to see traditional Jewish gender practice as a reversal of the proper and natural order. This is obviously not a definitive argument but seems to me suggestive, nevertheless.

94. The sense of this term is reversed from the sense in which I used it in *Carnal Israel*. There it indicated a married man who is away from home for years to study Torah, while here it represents a mystic adept who remains living at home (at least on Sabbaths) with his wife and certainly sleeps with her as well. At any rate, they have children later on.

brother-in-law, that is, as scholar and mystic, as he had done earlier for his father-in-law and all is peaceful once he takes on his mantle of leader of the Hasidim, the sect of the pious.

"GIVE ME A BRIDEGROOM SLENDER AND PALE":
THE "EFFEMINATE" TALMUDIST AS EROTIC OBJECT FOR WOMEN

In order to construct my proposition, however, that the passive, pale, gentle, and physically weak *Yeshiva-Bokhur* was an object of erotic desire, I shall have to show him as desirable to female subjects as well, not only to fathers and brothers. Otherwise it is too easy to "demystify" the eroticism of the homosocial attachment as being a mere effect of the seeking of cultural capital on the part of the male "lovers" of the scholar and not a truly affective, erotic attachment, in spite of the phraseology of "souls loving souls" that the texts embrace. Two genres of Yiddish folk literature, however, represent the pale, gentle scholar as favored love-object for women as well, not only for their fathers and brothers. One genre consists of legends, lullabies, and songs representing the desire of the young woman to be married and whom she chooses as her ideal partner. The other genre is memoirs of nineteenth-century Ashkenazic life.

Not atypical of these folk texts is the following:

I sit on a stone
and think and cry:
All the girls have become brides,
And I remain alone.
If my mother were a good one,
She would have found me a match,
She would have traveled to Wolkemir;
and brought a little bride-groom for me,
With black hair and blue eyes,
Let him be fit for Torah.
And Torah as the Torah prescribes,
He must learn day and night;
let him write me a little letter,
Let him remain a good little Jew.[95]

This is clearly a folk text and not the production of a learned elite— one can hardly imagine old bearded Rabbis singing such songs—and if

95. Ginzburg and Marek, *Yiddish Folksongs*, 198.

it does not definitively represent a woman's voice in its production (although it plausibly does), it is certainly the type of song that young Jewish girls in *Lite* (roughly Lithuania, Latvia, Beloruss) would have been singing in the nineteenth century. Another such song from the same collection plaintively imparts that:

I am certainly a pretty girl,
I spin red thread,
I certainly have a rich father,—
Today what do I still lack?
Poppa, Poppa, go to the *Ben-sochor*[96]
And pick me there a beautiful *bokhur,*
With long side-curls, with black eyes,
For Holy Torah he must be fit.[97]

In yet another of these texts, a girl asks her father specifically for a Rabbi to marry.[98] Moreover, these texts clearly inscribe the young man as an object of desire for the young woman: in addition to his scholarliness, we find his black (or blue) eyes, his beauty, his black hair, his long side-curls (see Plate 6). There is, it seems, sufficient evidence to make it plain that the notion of the pale, thin, side-curled, studious *Yeshiva-Bokhur* as erotic object for young women is not a mere nostalgic construction à la *Fiddler on the Roof.*[99] "For Holy Torah he must be fit" is thus the structural equivalent in these romantic narratives of female desire that would be played by deeds of derring-do in another culture. As we will see, such a "reversal of values" in the construction of the male object has its precedents in the Babylonian Talmud, the very "Torah" for which these young heartthrobs were entreated to be fit.

A semidocumentary text, taken from the autobiography of a Polish Jew, Yehiel Yeshayahu Trunk (1887–1961) and relating the story of the marriage of his great-great-grandmother at the beginning of the nineteenth century, is highly evocative.[100] This story is all the more revealing

96. This is a very rare Yiddish expression borrowed from Hebrew. In the Hebrew its literal meaning is "boy-child." I believe that in the local dialect of Yiddish in which this song is written, it refers to a men's party to celebrate the birth of a male infant, known in other communities as a "Sholom Zokhor"—"Welcoming the male." The daughter is suggesting that her father look over the young men at such a party and choose one for her.

97. Ginzburg and Marek, *Yiddish Folksongs,* 199.

98. Ginzburg and Marek, *Yiddish Folksongs,* 202.

99. I am grateful to Galit Hasan-Rokem and Dov Noy for helping me to find this material.

100. For information on Trunk and his great work, see Roskies, *Bridge,* 312–18.

in that it reveals the desire of a socially and economically independent
woman:

> His mother, Devora, was a poor and simple orphan, who came from Plotsk.
> She had a stall in the market, and from this labor supported herself. When
> she had gathered an amount of money from her standing in the market for
> long days in sweltering heat and freezing cold—and she had for some time
> been sexually mature—she came to the local Rabbi, Rabbi Leibush the Bril-
> liant, showed him the fund of gold coins that she had gathered through her
> toil, and requested that he, Rabbi Leibush the Brilliant, would provide for
> her a husband who was a Talmudic scholar. Rabbi Leibush answered her
> that he knew in Plotsk a Jew, somewhat advanced in age, who was a great
> Talmudic scholar, and who was supporting himself through teaching chil-
> dren. The man was poor and destitute, but an outstanding sage. . . .
>
> The damsel Devora asked Rabbi Leibush the Brilliant: "Is this poor
> schoolmaster truly a great Talmudic scholar?"
>
> "Yes, my daughter," answered her Rabbi Leibush, "he is an outstanding
> Talmudic sage."
>
> "If so," said the orphan Devora, "I agree."
>
> From this union was born only one son, he was Rabbi Yehoshuale Kut-
> ner.[101]

This is truly a remarkable story in many ways and paradigmatic
of rabbinic culture. We have here several reversals of the gendered expectations of bourgeois European culture. First of all, the dominant,
desiring subject is clearly the female one. It is she who seeks to find a
husband. It is important to emphasize, moreover, that she is totally independent of father and brother and any other male who could directly
control her desire. To be sure, her desire is constructed by her cultural
formation, but then so is all desire. The point of my research is to inquire as to what sort of desire this culture constructed or sought to construct. Second, in order to find the sort of husband that she desires, she
must be economically well established. She accomplishes this task, presumably starting from nothing, through great effort.

The prospective bridegroom, on the other hand, is working as the
Jewish equivalent of a governess. I do not mean, of course, to imply that
he is doing women's work from the point of view of Jewish culture; he
is not. However, in terms of a western European marriage plot, it would
be a young woman who would be supporting herself through the honorable but somewhat humble work of taking care of others' children
until an economically established man would come along to rescue her

101. Trunk, *Polin*, 6–7.

Plate 6. A Groom Fit for Torah. *The Zaddik's Son,* 1912, painting of a young Yeshiva-Bokhur, by Lazar Krestin. (Courtesy of the Leo Baeck Institute, New York.)

with marriage. Although the text does not make this explicit, we should understand that from now on the husband will devote himself entirely to study, no longer forced to waste his time on the teaching of children and no longer oppressed by grinding poverty. He now has a proper wife to support him. At least for the narrative's purposes, it is simply assumed that he would agree. Finally, the story has a happy end, because

although only one child was born of the union, he was a very famous
talmudic sage and rabbi in his own right, the eminent Rabbi Yehoshuale
Kutner. In a sense, that is the whole point of the story, to narrate the
birth of the hero. Also important, this same Rabbi Yehoshuale's wife
came from a similar family structure. As Trunk describes his other
great-great-grandmother, "Ratza was the central figure in the manage-
ment of the business and the household. Her name appears in the place
of honor in the family history. Her husband, Grandpa Haim, remained
obscure."[102] To be sure this is also a story that has been filtered through
a male textuality, yet it is not entirely imaginary that within this cultural formation such a man, a slightly aging, economically ineffective
but brilliant talmudic scholar would be desired as an object for marriage on the part of a young, nubile, and independent girl.[103]

Nothing could be more directly in opposition to the ideals of masculinity of romantic, "civilized" society. What we observe here is not,
however, a "primitive" unawareness of the evolved norms of western
European culture but a principled and deliberate reversal and rejection
of those norms. Not so, however, for the "emancipated" Jew of Vienna,
the Jew living a life "in between," to adopt the evocative terminology
of Leo Spitzer (the younger). For the emancipated Jew this representation would have been transvalued into something negative and shameful, especially as two discourses were intensifying at the fin de siècle,
the discourses of misogyny and homophobia.[104] These two discourses

---

102. Trunk, *Polin*, 7.

103. For a sensitive and nuanced account of the problem of writing Jewish women's
history on the basis of the autobiographical accounts of male relatives, see Parush, "Readers," and especially the following: "Most of the testimonies about female personalities
come from male members of the family. Only toward the turn of the century do we begin
to find memoirs and autobiographies portraying women born in the second half of the
nineteenth century from a feminine point of view. Regrettably few of these contain evidence from a firsthand source. Perusal of such books can indeed yield valuable tidbits of
information about the education and reading habits of these women, and perchance even
something about their outlook on life. But rarely do they offer a glimpse of their inner
world" (2-3). The same promise and problem attend my own project (which depends, in
part, on the same texts as Parush's).

104. E. Cohen, *Talk*; Senelick, "Homosexual." Estelle Roith has also sensed how
decolonization and modernization produced a crisis in Jewish masculinity in the fin de
siècle but also seems to assume "enlightened" Protestant culture as a norm to which Jews
needed to accede: "It has been suggested that the whole question of masculine gender
identity is likely to be problematic in populations and communities that have become
marginal and that the traditional Jewish emphasis on scholarship and prayer might have
posed additional and specific problems for the emancipating Jewish male. Percy S. Cohen
has proposed that the emphasis on the 'culture of learning' enabled Jewish males to sus-
tain a cultural identity as well as permitting a sense of superiority that effectively comple-
mented and compensated for their sense of vulnerability. Thus the values and status in-

were, moreover, profoundly related at this time, owing to the associations of male homosexuality with passivity, that is, with femaleness; hatred of femaleness was raised to a fever pitch seemingly unknown before this time.[105] It is no surprise then to discover that a "New Jewish Man" was being invented within this sociocultural matrix and under the pressure of these developments. The strange phenomenon known as Jewish Wagnerism and its undeclared and surprising connections with other Jewish cultural developments were symptoms of this disorder among Jews, so a brief look at one aspect of this phenomenon will provide a precis of the narrative of this book.[106]

TANNHÄUSER; OR, THE APOTHEOSIS OF *GOYIM NACHES*

My only recreation was listening to Wagner's music in the
evening, particularly to *Tannhäuser,* an opera which I attended as often as it was produced. Only on the evening
when there was no opera did I have any doubts as to the
truth of my ideas.[107]

—Theodor Herzl

Among the most prominent avatars of romantic manhood that Europe produced in the nineteenth century, Richard Wagner was certainly representative. That paragon of the "New Jewish Man," Theodor Herzl, has provided us with extremely precious information on the cultural/psychological condition of the Jews among whom "the invention of the Jewish man" took place. He has invited us to see Wagner and

---

hering in the physically passive, scholar ideal safeguarded the pre-emancipation Jew's sense of masculinity (P. S. Cohen, 1979, personal interview)" (*Riddle,* 10). She has further argued that "[t]he Jew aiming at citizenship of the world outside ghetto and *shtetl,* however, found that he lacked a tradition or cultural stereotype for the model of masculinity employed by that world" (10). Roith here describes Jewish masculinity in terms similar to those which Freud would employ to describe femininity, that is, as a lack and a response to a lack, whereas I have been trying to account for this form of male subjectivity as the positive production of a cultural knowledge that obtains under certain conditions, namely the status of being politically nondominant. Although, then, Roith herself is strangely uncritical (even this is an understatement) of the "model of masculinity" that "the Jew aiming at citizenship of the world" was forced to adopt, this account itself has much merit.

105. Dijkstra, *Idols;* Showalter, *Sexual Anarchy.*

106. For an analysis of the most recent forms of this cultural phenomenon, see Mass, *Confessions.*

107. Herzl, *Zionist Writings,* 17, on the writing of his book *The Jewish State.* See also Elon, *Herzl,* 3. I thank Jonathan Boyarin for reminding me of this passage.

especially the *Tannhäuser* as the most relevant of intertexts for his
thought. To corroborate this point and indicate that it was not a passing
fancy, I adduce the fact that at the Second Zionist Congress, Herzl ordered the music of *Tannhäuser* to be played.[108]

Steven Beller has recently produced a compelling reading of *Tannhäuser* as Zionist allegory, as Herzl might have experienced it, thus accounting for its effect on him. After carefully allowing for the possibility that it was just the glorious music that inspired Herzl, Beller
suggests that for him there was more there, that Tannhäuser himself is
a symbol of "the Jew" who has spent "a long time in the arms of Venus
in her grotto. Now he wants to be freed from the grotto (ghetto) and
achieves his wish, reentering human society."[109] Unfortunately, the fact
that he has been released from the ghetto has not freed our hero from
his moral faults; he remains a Jew, caught within the walls of the new
(spiritual) ghetto.[110] He goes to Rome in an attempt to achieve absolu-
tion and thus final assimilation back into German Christian society.
Beller stunningly associates this moment with Herzl's former plan to go
to the Pope and offer to convert all of the Jews in return for his aid
against the antisemites. Coming back from Rome, having failed in his
attempt to win acceptance from the Pope, the Jew seeks to return to his
grotto/ghetto of sensuous, material, effeminate indulgence and corruption; however he is saved by that figure of pure womanhood, Elizabeth,
who translates him into another world—Zion. Beller concludes:
"*Tannhäuser* can thus be seen as a great acting out of the redemption
of the Jews from their own degeneracy and from their rejection by
Western society. Whether or not one believes that they were degenerate
[but Herzl did], the fact remains that it was quite possible for Herzl to
be inspired by Wagner's *Tannhäuser* in a way quite in keeping with his
newfound Zionist faith. . . . "[111]

108. Beller, "Herzl," 128. The contortions that Steven Beller puts himself through in
apologizing for his exploration of the palpable ideological connection between Wagner's
antisemitism and Herzl's are arresting (Beller, "Herzl," 27–28). The general adoration of
Herzl borders on idolatry. It is characteristic that Beller refers to Herzl as being "the man
who gave Jews back their pride," assuming that Jews in general were ashamed of their
Jewishness and that getting back their pride was of value to them. For most East European
Jews who eventually followed the Zionists, it was not pride but survival that motivated
them. Similarly, Ernst Simon, usually a sober and balanced analyst, suddenly decided that
Herzl's plan for all of the Jews to convert to Catholicism (see chapter 7 below) "causes
no dishonour to him" (Simon, "Sigmund," 278).
    109. Beller, "Herzl," 150.
    110. For the term "The New Ghetto," the title of Herzl's most famous play, see dis-
cussion of this text in chapter 7.
    111. Beller, "Herzl," 150.

Beller's reading can be corroborated from a source that he apparently did not see, namely, Wagner himself, for as Paul Lawrence Rose has pointed out, "Wagner himself referred to the Flying Dutchman as an 'Ahasverus of the Ocean', while the parallelism of Tannhäuser and the Wandering Jew would have been impressed on him by his friend and mentor in German myth, the Dresden librarian J. G. Grasse, who recognized the correspondences between the Tannhäuser and Ahasverus legends."[112] As ambivalent as the Wandering Jew is vis-à-vis "real" Jews, this association could certainly have impressed itself on a Jew such as Herzl in a way that would further the Zionist reading of the opera, particularly insofar as Heinrich Heine and Byron for instance had used the Ahasverus myth as a symbol for Jewish vitality.[113]

Beller, however, both ignores and explicitly discounts the gendered aspects of this appropriation of the Tannhäuser myth as an allegory of Zionism. This text represents a distillation of German Romantic ideals of masculinity and thus, in the eyes of Jews (and others) who would be critical of such ideals, manifests itself as the apotheosis of *goyim naches*. Let me begin with a moment that Beller discounts openly, the fact that Tannhäuser's redemption is bought at the price of his death.[114] Yet in *The New Ghetto*, the very play of Herzl's that Beller invokes as a source for his interpretation of Herzl's feeling for Wagner, this ideology of redemption through death is clearly promoted. As I shall claim in chapter 7, this was of a piece with other aspects of Herzl's thought, both "prezionist" and Zionist. Second, *Tannhäuser* certainly promulgates that very notion of love as more spiritual than sexual, of sweet sorrows and extended, if not permanent, deferment of gratification that Cuddihy and Roith define as the very soul of civility. We should remember at this point R. Howard Bloch's analysis of this very discourse, which found it deeply, structurally misogynist in character. Third, and perhaps most relevant, the specific human activity that Tannhäuser wishes to return to, his reason for desperately wanting to escape the grotto/ghetto, is war-making, to be readmitted to the homoerotic world of the martial *Männerbund*, Band of Men.[115] It was especially through violence—dueling—that Herzl imagined that the "honor" of the Jews would be restored (see chapter 7 below). It is really no wonder

112. Rose, *Wagner*, 37.
113. Rose, *Wagner*, 33.
114. Beller, "Herzl," 151–52.
115. Cf. also Berkowitz, *Zionist Culture*, 137, on the mythic or symbolic aspect of the friendship of Herzl and Nordau.

at all that *Tannhäuser,* as no other text, inspired him to write *The Jewish State.*

Beller argues: "Given that we know Wagner saw the present world of 'life and art' as controlled by 'modern Jews,' whose 'sensual' forms of (linguistic) expression disgusted him, it can well be argued that the world that Wagner, the Ahasverian artist, is trying to escape in *Tannhäuser* is precisely the perverse world of 'Jews in music.' Elizabeth, 'the woman who, as a heavenly star, leads Tannhäuser up from the hedonistic den of the Venusberg,' is in effect redeeming Wagner from an Ahasverian existence in a Jewish world."[116] Perceptively reading the nexus between Herzl's adoration of this text and his Zionism, Beller argues for a threefold Wagnerian analysis of the "Jewish Question" that was identical to Herzl's: (1) the Jewish problem was caused by the fact that there were Jews, that is, in Beller's language, by "an insufficiently thorough, perhaps impossible, integration"; (2) mixtures of German and Jewish culture were "pernicious"; and (3) the only solutions were either the complete disappearance (*Untergang!*) of the Jews through total assimilation or their exit from Europe to somewhere else. Beller writes: "From our perspective this might appear quite horrendous, but, with a few very minor changes, this was also the diagnosis and prescribed remedy that Herzl proposed in 1895, except that by then he had come to the conclusion that the only true remedy was not complete assimilation but rather Wagner's other option, the exit or emigration of the Jews — in Herzl's version, to the 'Promised Land.' "[117] It is not clear to me how Herzl, having adopted such a view, would make it appear any less horrendous, and, moreover, the bit of intended amelioration at the end is hardly valid, since Herzl in 1895 was not dreaming of any Promised Land at all but only of a Wagnerian exit of the Jews from Europe — to Africa, in point of fact. Careful study of Herzl's writings will show how thoroughly he, like other half-assimilated Jews of the fin de siècle, was possessed of the ideology of "manliness" that, as the crescendo of a millennia-old European gender ideology, had overrun European culture at that time.[118]

It is well known that Max Nordau, the second in command of the Zionist movement in the early decades, longed for the creation of

116. Beller, "Herzl," 138.
117. Beller, "Herzl," 139.
118. Dijkstra, *Idols;* Showalter, *Sexual Anarchy.* Beller's attempt to rewrite Herzl's repugnance for traditional *Ostjuden* as cultural critique of assimilated bourgeois Jews is totally unconvincing to me. In chapter 7 below, I shall discuss Herzl at length.

שאינו
יודע לשׁאול   תם   רשׁע   חכם

Aki kérdezni se tud   Együgyü   Gonosz   Bölcs

Plate 7. The Wicked Son as Muscle-Jew. This image is from a Budapest Haggada, 1938. (Collection of the author.)

Muscle-Jews, the very antithesis of the Jewish ideal that I have just been describing.[119] As late as 1938, in a Haggada published in Budapest, such a Muscle-Jew is portrayed as the "Wicked Son" (see Plate 7). Now it is fascinating to note that there is no attempt to render this figure as non-Jewish or even as nonreligious. He clearly has a yarmulke on his head. What marks him as the "wicked son," is only one composite characteristic, the muscularity of his body and his "modern" clothing.[120] Such bodily development is deployed in this icon as the virtual equivalent of

119. How delicious the irony that the "scientists" invoked by Stoker to confirm the criminality of the visage of Dracula the crypto-Jew (Dijkstra, *Idols,* 343), namely, Lombroso and Nordau, were themselves Jews, a fact discreetly left unmentioned by Dijkstra. (On Nordau, see Baldwin, "Liberalism," and George Mosse's introduction to Nordau, *Degeneration;* on Lombroso, see Harrowitz, "Lombroso.") *Degeneration* was dedicated to Lombroso, and Freud expressed pride in the fact that Lombroso was a fellow Jew. This irony, though delicious, was not rare. As Mosse remarks, "[Nordau's] concepts of degeneration and manliness were taken up by European racism" (Mosse, *Nationalism,* 36). About Lombroso, Mosse says: "Lombrosian psychology, elaborated chiefly during the 1860s, made the accusation of Jewish criminality still more meaningful" (147). This should not be mistaken for a "backshadowing" claim that would make Nordau or Lombroso *responsible* for racism.

120. Charlotte Fonrobert has emphasized this to me. Cf. the "short coat" in which the Besht dressed to hide his holy identity as discussed above in this chapter.

the martial knightliness of the earlier symbols of a dystopian Jewish masculinity, as an epitome of *goyim naches*.[121] *Goyim naches* can now be defined as the contemptuous Jewish term for those characteristics that in European culture have defined a man as manly: physical strength, martial activity and aggressiveness, and contempt for and fear of the female body.

Significantly, then, we see that this is not a racist representation, however contemptuous of the surrounding "goyish" culture. Another very rich passage from Trunk's memoirs describes in detail the ways of a Jew who represented the antithesis of the Talmud scholar as male ideal. Trunk's grandmother rented for a time an apartment of a Jewish farmer, a certain Simcha Geige. Here is how the man is described:

> As I remember him, Simcha Geige walked around all day, in the manner of peasants, in an undershirt and trousers. He would get up with the goyim and the chickens. An odor of the barn was exuded from him. Simcha Geige was friendly with the peasants and used to curse them in accord with their custom. His language was authentically peasant-like and the company of peasants was more pleasant to him than the intimacy of the Rabbi of Strikev. Simcha Geige was never separated from the pistol in his pocket and used to have a wild pleasure when he was shooting a few rounds among the trees. The echo of the shots in the wood, the voice of the cuckoo all around, the lowing of the cattle, the calls of the chickens and the geese, the mysterious humming of the ancient and massive oaks in the forests of Laginsky, the song of wind and rain, aroused in the crude and primitive heart of Simcha Geige, a sweeter echo than the delicate and fragile sighs of the study-tables of the righteous to which grandpa Baruch used to drag him on occasion. Similarly to the peasants, Simcha Geige had a certain contempt for the delicate and pale city-Jews. . . . His wife, Sore-Bina, a small and corpulent Jewish woman with an old-fashioned yellow wig, was deathly afraid of him, and thus, in trembling terror, became pregnant by him and bore him his sons, who were like him, crude and healthy of body.[122]

Such is the romantic hero in the eyes of the elite Jewish culture of eastern Europe of the nineteenth century. Many of the features of this Simcha Geige are in fact endemic to that romantic tradition, wild pleasure in physicality, love of weapons, fierce attachment to nature and to locale, healthy body, and hard work. All of these features are encoded within the Jewish text, however, as features that mark him not as an

---

121. A recent haggada put out by very traditionalist groups in Palestine/Israel shows the wicked son as a soccer player!

122. Trunk, *Polin*, 20–21.

example of a high form of masculine humanity but as a very low, crude, primitive, violent, and cruel one—a Jew who, like gentiles, has contempt for the effeminately marked scholars and for his wife whom he terrorizes as well.[123]

In the romantic ideology of manliness that Wagner promulgates in texts like *Tristan und Isolde* and *Tannhäuser* we can discover the ultimate development of what Jews had derisively called *goyim naches*. At the fin de siècle, and especially in the Viennese milieu, many Jews were desperately seeking their own *naches* (peace, as well as satisfaction) in becoming just as male and just as Aryan as Tannhäuser himself and his creator. Herzlian Zionism is only one of the manifestations of this transformation in the gender of the Jew—male and female. Although it is perhaps easy to "exonerate" Jews who, in the early part of this century, considered these deformations of Jewish masculinity—the substitution of Muscle-Jew for *mentsh*—as an ideal, it is much harder to do so in the second half of that same century and particularly after such writers as Dijkstra and Klaus Theweleit have demonstrated the near direct connections between these masculinist ideologies and Nazi genocide.[124] This does not, I stress, constitute a hideous accusation of complicity with or responsibility for a not-yet-born Nazism, any more than would, for instance, pointing out the use of the swastika as emblem by Jewish followers of Stefan George. It implies rather that with hindsight we can see the dangers of a certain line of ideology and practice whose horrors were, of course, unforeseeable at the time, and we can emphasize, moreover, the imbrications of misogynist masculinism with racism against Jews. *Goyim naches* can be interpreted now not as a primitive

123. Natalie Kampen has pointed out to me what should certainly have been obvious, namely, the class dimensions of these representations. This is the view of a Jewish peasant from the perspective of another class, but the question I would raise is: from the perspective of precisely *what* other class? In a social system within which penurious scholars supported by their wives are the elite, and wealthy peasants are the "underclass," some form of class analysis other than the one appropriate for European industrial society seems necessary. Very tentatively I wish to suggest that the most salient two classes of rabbinic society are "men" and "women," and that Simcha Geige belongs to the class of "women" within rabbinic society! See chapter 4 below. David Roskies has discussed the emergence of this social and economic Jewish type, the *baal guf*, or physical Jew, as a new kind of hero—one who can defend other Jews—in modern Jewish literature at around the time that the real Simcha Geige was alive (*Against the Apocalypse*, 141–43). I have already discussed the story of the Besht as being an early, ambivalent reflex of this cultural development. The stories analyzed by Roskies do emphasize the distinction as one of economic class in the Marxian sense. See also the discussion by Paul Breines, *Tough Jews*, 133–34.
124. Theweleit, *Male*.

inability to perceive the virtues of Western civilization so much as a sign
of prescient awareness of the devastating defects and effects of that cultural formation—even if, of course, the crematoria could hardly be
foreshadowed. [125]

   In the next two chapters, I am going to jump back in time a millennium and a half to the Talmud, the reading of which was the most valued practice of rabbinic Jewish culture, in search of a textual genealogy
for the *mentsh* as the ideal type of male Jew.

   125. I emphasize this last point in order to avoid the epistemological error of backshadowing so shrewdly exposed by Michael Andre Bernstein.

CHAPTER II

Jewish Masochism

On Penises and Politics,
Power and Pain

To make oneself an object, to make oneself passive, is a very different thing from being a passive object. —Simone de Beauvoir

Empires were exceedingly masculine affairs. —George L. Mosse

The next two chapters will consist of an extended reading of one highly
significant passage in the Talmud in which the ideal male is the central
theme. The point of this exercise is to counter two prevailing notions
of the femminization of Jewish men: first, that it is a mere canard of
antisemites and has no basis in reality; and second, that it is a real phenomenon but a mere pathology and not a desired trait on the part of
the culture. I shall try to demonstrate that the image of the ideal male
as nonaggressive, not strong, not physically active is a positive product
of the self-fashioning of rabbinic masculinity in a certain, very central,
textual product of the culture, the Babylonian Talmud. Far from being
a desperate grab for some kind of self-esteem in a powerless situation,
this development, as I see it, is the product of a kind of knowledge perhaps available only to the (relatively) powerless.

At the same time, let me say what I am not claiming: I am not suggesting that even in the Talmud this was the only representation of an
ideal masculinity; indeed, in some of the material below I shall point
out contestation and conflict over models for ideal male behavior. It follows that I am also not arguing for a direct genetic line between the
society that produced the Talmud and the *Edelkayt* of nineteenth-century eastern European traditional Judaism or proposing the *mentsh* as
the only type of male Jew. I am concerned rather with the Talmud
as discourse within Ashkenazic culture, that is, as "writing itself as a

historical agent as it enabled the institutional formation."[1] As Judith
Perkins has argued, "A society's subjects come to understand themselves
through all the self-representations their society offered them. But writings like Epictetus' had the overt purpose of teaching people how to conduct themselves properly. They were explicitly designed to help people
to reform and refashion themselves to a particular cultural ideal."[2] The
Talmud, as *the* canonical text of Ashkenazic culture—novel and philosophy all rolled into one—provided the cultural models and resources
around which the self-representation of a gentle, recessive, nonviolent
masculinity could crystallize under specific material and historical conditions. At the same time, these remarkable, legendary texts will provide us with an autocritique that the Talmud already mobilizes against
its own social structure, suggesting powerfully how the exclusions and
dominations of women and the appropriations of "femaleness" engaged in the production of their male ideal formed a fatal fly in the
unguent of femminized antiphallic masculinity.

    In the introduction, I denoted that some men in late antiquity, Chris-
tian and Jewish, resisted the modes of masculinity most succinctly symbolized as the imperial phallus. One type of such resistance involved
various symbolizations of males "becoming female," of femminization.
In European culture, from nearly its origins until the development of
psychoanalytic thought, a "natural" masochism has been attributed to
women. One of the latest and clearest expressions of this representation is in the work of Helene Deutsch, who in 1930 defined femininity
as "the feminine, passive-masochistic disposition in the mental life of
women,"[3] treating "passive-masochistic" as a virtual synonym for
"feminine." In this chapter I wish to focus on one practice of femminization, one that might be defined as cultural masochism, the seeking of
pain and passivity, as both an acting out of male envy of and desire for
"femaleness" as well as a "shattering" abnegation of the "phallus"[4]
and thus a politically significant form of resistance to phallic imagina-
tions of maleness and imperial power.[5] Like much radical cultural ac-

    1. Perkins, *Suffering,* 9–10.
    2. Perkins, *Suffering,* 89.
    3. Deutsch, "Significance," 412.
    4. Cf. Bersani, "Is."
    5. Judith Perkins has approached this issue (vis-à-vis early Christianity) from exactly
the opposite perspective: how a discourse of suffering enabled the construction of institutions and power in Christianity, indeed, that became Christianity. As she argues, "Christian discourse in the early empire worked to construct a particular subject, a particular

tion, masochism both subverts and asserts the dominant order of society at the same time. As Paul Smith has recently put it, "Male masochism is at first a way of not having to submit to the law, but, equally important, it turns out to be a way of not breaking (with) the law, either. Masochism might well bespeak a desire to be both sexes at once, but it depends upon the definitional parameters of masculinity and femininity that undergird our current cultural contexts."[6]

Robin Morgan has totally rejected any possible political promise from such a practice of resistance: "In patriarchy men have power. In patriarchy women are powerless. These are facts. It is also a fact, though perhaps a less evident one, that he who has power can do what he likes, *including playing at powerlessness* in a manner never available to the powerless. For him it can be an experiment, a game, a fad, a fake (or even genuine) attempt to divest himself of his power, or a mere kicky new experience."[7] My interest is in the possibility, marginalized by Morgan through parenthesis, that here and there amidst appropriation we may find a genuine attempt on the part of men to divest themselves of power over women, an attempt born in part of their own experience of being dominated and the understanding of domination that it furnishes.[8] Even Morgan's parenthetical concession, however, is obliterated in her next comments: "Some politically co-optive men even have claimed their masochistic identification is 'woman-identification' and that it is meant as evidence of sympathy with feminism—which shows how abysmal is their understanding of women *and* feminism. But that any men should *wish* to experience what they *think* women experience—this is old news, as old as Pentheus' curiosity (and is rooted, I think, in envy). Men who see themselves as relatedly masochistic, 'femme,' feminine, etc., obviously are insulting the female (in person and in principle)." I am staking this book (and to a certain extent my life) on the assumption that there is more to the story than Morgan

---

self-understanding: namely, the Christian as sufferer" (*Suffering,* 24). Did rabbinic Judaism construct a similar subject, the Jew as sufferer, at the same time? Was it as central a moment in rabbinic culture as in early Christianity? The answers to these questions will have to await future research.

6. Smith, "Eastwood," 91.

7. Morgan, "Politics," 117.

8. Barton, in "All Things," has provided from Roman culture a stunning confirmation of Morgan's hypothesis stating: "That men should sometimes fantasize themselves as masochists therefore strikes me as ironic but not surprising (perhaps it is merely a novel break from the real-life sadism patriarchy both requires and permits of them)" (117).

would allow, that she is largely but not entirely or always or inevitably correct in her uncompromising judgment.[9]

The talmudic text that I will read in this chapter seems to me both to demonstrate the essential justice and precision of Morgan's perception as well as to provide some counterforce to its monolithic complexion. In part it does so via a constant wavering or dialectic between two modes of response to male envy of female capacities. These two alternatives have been sharply defined by Sarah Lee Caldwell: "Either the female power is invoked in an abstract form, separated from women, and incorporated into men; or female power is denied and repressed, and masculine power is exaggerated and elaborated. Either way, such rituals manage simultaneous envy of female power and fear of identification with that female power."[10] While it is clearly true, and made palpable (I hope) by everything said so far in this book, that the first option does not represent any more than the second a true valuing of women, nevertheless men who incorporate female reproductive powers are different from those who deny and repress them. Moreover, even the incorporation itself, the couvade, can be differently inflected and have different meanings and associated social practices in different cultures. One might be described as a fetishistic (and very familiar) insistence on male superiority and might be characterized accordingly as a phallic response, that is, there is nothing that women have or can do that we want; we have the phallus. The other would be best described as an envious mimesis of femaleness in order to appropriate for men *as well* what are seen *by men* as the positive, desirable characteristics and potentialities of femaleness. This response is counterphallic, which of course does not yet make it feminist, but that evident fact does not empty it of political significance, even for feminism. In fact, one of the most fascinating aspects of this talmudic text is its seeming awareness

9. Morgan, "Politics," 117. I always allow for the possibility that Morgan is simply right and that I, among others, understand nothing of feminism, that everything I write is an "insult to the female (in person and in principle)." But even Morgan refers positively to the "effeminist movement" and its credo that "strong women and gentle men are a real threat to masculine domination" (122 n. 7). Morgan's reading of sadomasochistic fantasies in women as an appropriation of power in a near desperate situation is moving and convincing (117–20). What she misses, I think, is the possibility that masochistic fantasies in men might be (sometimes) an equally powerful, last resort, symbolic challenge to patriarchal privilege. I obviously am not making this claim for masochism in general but arguing that our only hope lies in finding chinks in the armor of patriarchy that let in rays of light.

10. Caldwell, *Begotten*, 10.

of the imbrication of the politics of gender with the politics of imperial power and resistance.

Eric Santner has articulated the following helpful reflection: "The effectiveness of a model is ultimately based on the fact that *it never in fact works*. Models function not so much as programs for consistent constructions as strategies of disavowing the inconsistencies of constructions. Indeed, I would define the *phallus* as the entitlement to engage in just such a disavowal. Non-phallic masculinity would then be a masculinity that *knows* of and perhaps even *enjoys* its heterogeneous, inconsistent make-up. Perhaps the images of the body's 'porousness' in rabbinic texts could be conceived as a performance not so much of femininity as of this inconsistency of masculinity. It might of course be that men can't help but imagine their inconsistency *as femininity*. The difference between masculinities would be the extent to which they are capable of claiming this dimension of (fantasmatic) femininity as their own."[11] I want here to suggest with fear and trembling a theoretical-political scenario within which mimesis of culturally constructed femaleness may not be *only* appropriation as in theft but *also* appropriation as in hermeneutical appropriation, and that desirable political and ethical consequences are recognized along with the political perils of such appropriation.[12]

In his genealogy, Nietzsche wrote: "It was the Jews, who rejecting the aristocratic value equation (good = noble = powerful = beautiful = happy = blessed) ventured with awe-inspiring consistency, to bring about a reversal . . . saying, 'Only those who suffer are good, only the poor, the powerless, the lowly are good; the suffering, the deprived, the sick, the ugly, are the only pious people, the only ones saved, salvation is for them alone.' "[13] A rich and strange talmudic legend of male desire

11. Santner, letter.

12. This provides another and different parallel between the askesis of late antiquity (Jewish or Christian) and the modern askesis of gay life as expounded most compellingly by David Halperin in his recent exegesis of Foucault (*Saint Foucault,* 88).

13. For an eloquent, and very early, critical Jewish response to Nietzsche's "transvaluation of values," see Achad Ha῾am [Asher Ginsburg], "Transvaluation." Ginsburg wittily suggests that one might accept Nietzsche's principle that "the end of moral good is not the uplifting of the human race in general, but the raising of the human type in its highest manifestations above the general level"; however, "Nietzsche, if his taste had been Hebraic, might still have changed the moral standard, and made the Superman an end in himself, but would in that case have attributed to his Superman quite different characteristics—the expansion of moral power, the subjugation of the bestial instincts, the striving after truth and righteousness in thought and deed, the eternal warfare against falsehood and wickedness; in a word, that moral ideal which Judaism has impressed on us"

and pain provides—perhaps in its most extreme Jewish (i.e., non-Christian) formulation—the "inversion of aristocratic value equations" that Nietzsche so despised.[14] The inversion is thematized in terms of gender reversals, or femminizations, and explicitly in terms of the response of the politically weak "Jews" to the politically strong "Romans."

Amy Richlin has made the interesting claim that "though the structure remains fixed, the identity of each position can change much more readily for imperialism than for gender: Etruria-owns-Rome becomes Rome-owns-Etruria, while the bottom position in a model for gender *qua* gender is female. . . . In Rome, as in other imperialist cultures, an upper-class woman could own a male slave or far outrank a lower-class male; for class, as for empire, the bottom position would tend to be feminized."[15] The question that needs to be asked, however, is: From whose point of view? Did those men "on the bottom" see themselves as feminized? And if and when they did, what was the value placed on femminization by those men? I can begin to suggest through discussion of early Christian and Jewish texts at least a tentative and partial answer to this question, namely, that even for those men "on the bottom," being there was indeed interpreted as femminization, but femminization itself was transvalued and received at least some positive significance.

COPS AND RABBIS

The following text begins on a purely political note that seems hardly to have anything to do with gender:[16]

> Rabbi Elʿazar the son of Rabbi Shimʿon found a certain officer of the king who used to catch thieves. He [the Rabbi] asked him [the officer], "How do you prevail over them? Aren't they compared to animals, as it is written 'at night tramp all the animals of the forest' (Psalms 104:20)?" *There are those*

(162–63). In other words, Ginsburg argues that the "transvaluation of values" is more Christian than Jewish, and he himself ends up with a rather nasty sort of near-racist reverse Nietzscheanism whereby the Jews become the Super-race. The text we are about to read and my current analysis suggest that much finer discrimination between rabbinic and Christian Judaisms is necessary in this regard.

14. Nietzsche, *On the Genealogy,* 19.

15. Richlin, *Garden,* xviii.

16. This portion of my text is a rereading of a talmudic narrative that I have treated before ("Great Fat Massacre"). My reading here partially overlaps with and partially corrects (or supplements) my earlier treatment.

who say that he said it to him from the following verse: "He will ambush
from a hiding place like a lion in a thicket" (Psalms 10:9). Said he to him,
"Perhaps you are taking the innocent and leaving the guilty."

He [the officer] said to him, "How shall I do it?"

He [the Rabbi] said to him, "Come I will teach you how to do it. Go in
the first four hours of the morning to the wine-bar. If you see someone
drinking wine and falling asleep, ask of him what his profession is. If he is
a rabbinical student, he has arisen early for study. If he is a day-laborer, he
has arisen early to his labor. If he worked at night, [find out] perhaps it is
metal smelting [a silent form of work], and if not, then he is a thief and seize
him."

The rumor reached the king's house, and he [the king] said, "Let him who
read the proclamation be the one to execute it." They brought Rabbi Elʿazar
the son of Rabbi Shimʿon, and he began to catch thieves. He met Rabbi Yehoshua, the Bald, who said to him, "Vinegar son of Wine: how long will you
persist in sending the people of our God to death?!"

He [Rabbi Elʿazar] said to him, "I am removing thorns from the vineyard."

He [Rabbi Yehoshua] said to him, "Let the Owner of the vineyard come
and remove the thorns" (Baba Metsiaʿ 83b).

This brief story is about resistance to and collaboration with "Roman" domination. It thematizes, as well, blatant abuse of power. It is
therefore a text that teaches us much about rabbinic ideologies of power
and resistance. I have argued elsewhere that such ideologies are intimately involved with models of gender.[17] The text assumes the subjugated status of the Jews to Roman rule, a status that strains the legitimacy of the internal leadership by the Rabbis of the Jewish polity. Our
hero himself moves within the context of the story "from mocking
challenge to collaborative submission."[18]

The story begins by assuming that thieves are necessarily stronger
than those who seek to catch them. The Rabbi cannot believe that the
officer of the king is successfully catching thieves, since they are compared to animals, and on the physical plane it is understood that animals will always defeat human beings. Therefore his statement "Perhaps you are taking the innocent and leaving the guilty" is itself less

17. See for the nonce D. Boyarin, "Tricksters," and the forthcoming *Powers of Diaspora* (J. Boyarin and D. Boyarin). In the following paragraphs I am occasionally indebted
to insights into this text by my student Helen Choi, who participated in my undergraduate
women's studies seminar on "constructions of gender in late antique Judaism and Christianity" in spring 1995 at Berkeley. Much of Choi's analysis involves a Kristevan reading
of the text which I have not adopted but I hope will be published soon.

18. The phrase is Choi's.

than innocent, the "perhaps" only a bit of self-protection. What he is saying is surely you are taking the innocent and leaving the guilty.

A certain orientation toward physicality is already being projected here. Thieves are analogized to animals, and animals are associated with strength. The opposite of this proposition would be that humans, that is, being human (what later Judaism would call being a *mentsh*) is defined by physical weakness. The Rabbi assumes that if the officer is indeed catching somebody, it must be innocent people, since otherwise how could he, a *mentsh* and weak, be successful against them who are bestial and strong? In other words the semiotics of this text at its very beginning set up the paradigm of valorized weakness versus a denigrated physical strength. Moreover, the "text-critical" gloss that offers an alternative verse specifies what the animal in question was, a lion. If the villains of the piece are compared to lions, the heroes must be, of course, the lambs.

This imagery, not only Christian, was continued throughout the Jewish Middle Ages. Thus we find in a medieval Hebrew prayer for the Atonement Season: "*Through my guilt I am likened to and resemble a lion in the forest*, my utterance is foolish, my language is unintelligible! . . . Faint, banished, and despised, I am shaken and tossed about, drunken and intoxicated with wormwood, I am become full of sorrow and grief and oppressed by masters, to whom I was sold for naught; yet when my soul fainted within me, I remembered the Lord. I remembered thy kindness and love which were as a banner over me; they removed my guilt and made me thy treasure; *thy lambs now accustom themselves to prayers and entreaty*, the poorest among men exult in the Holy One of Israel."[19] There is, of course, much to be said about this text and cognates which cannot be said here, but it is worth emphasizing that lionlike is clearly not what the speaker desires to be: being like a lion describes his guilt, while being a lamb is the attribute of his probity. It would not be entirely unwarranted to compare this text with the Sermon on the Mount. This imagery was, of course, totally reversed in modern Zionist imagination. In a fascinating account, Yael Zerubavel has shown how a "myth" about Bar Kochba defeating, and then befriending, a lion was invented in the 1920s by Zionist educators and gradually accepted as if an ancient legend and an explicit figure of contrast to the Jews of Europe who were "led like sheep to the slaughter."[20]

19. Rosenfeld, *Authorised Selichot*, 66; emphasis mine.
20. Zerubavel, *Recovered Roots*, 105–7.

In place of power, Rabbi El'azar proposes stealth as a tool to defeat power. It is as if the text says, neither the brute physical power of the animal-like thieves nor even the more rational and controlled power of the Roman government but only the cultural knowledge and cunning (compare the Greek Metis, a goddess) will in the end prevail. Since he has given this "good" advice, the Rabbi has established that he sees the fate of the Jews as tied to the good order that the Romans can provide. He is accordingly recruited by the Roman authorities as a collaborator who turns over Jewish thieves to the Roman authorities.

This behavior is roundly condemned by the narrative. Another rabbinic voice within the text calls Rabbi El'azar, "Vinegar son of Wine" (i.e., Wicked One Son of a Saint) and asks, "How long will you persist in sending the people of our God to death?" Although the capture and punishment of thieves would normally be accepted practice, in a colonial situation what appears as a judicial act is an act of treachery. While rabbinic Judaism in general thematizes staying alive at (virtually) all costs in order that the People and the Torah would continue, here we have the slip into collaboration which threatens the life of the People, and hero becomes villain.[21] It is feigned collaboration as resistance, of course, that is valued as colonial ethic, not real collaboration. The story thematizes, therefore, communal solidarity and resistance under conditions of domination (and it resonates in interesting ways with modern contentions about the role of the *Judenrat* during the Nazi genocide, but these resonations I will not pursue here directly). As long as the Rabbi's "advice" to the Roman policeman consisted of techniques for preventing the capture of innocents, his behavior was satisfactory. But as soon as he himself began to engage in capturing thieves—even guilty ones[22]—and turning them over to the Romans, he was condemned.

The narrative goes on to elaborate further the consequences of collaboration, or rather of deployment of physical political power altogether:

One day a certain laundry man met him, and called him, "Vinegar son of Wine." He said, "Since he is so brazen, one can assume that he is wicked." He said, "Seize him." They seized him. After he had settled down, he went in to release him, but he could not. He applied to him the verse, "One who guards his mouth and his tongue, guards himself from troubles" (Proverbs

---

21. See D. Boyarin, "Tricksters."
22. It is important to note that according to Jewish law, thieves are never executed but only required to make restitution with a fine.

21:23). They hung him. He stood under the hanged man and cried. Someone said to him, "Be not troubled; he and his son both had intercourse with an engaged girl on *Yom Kippur*." In that minute, he placed his hands on his guts, and said, "Be joyful, O my guts, be joyful! If it is thus when you are doubtful, when you are certain even more so. I am confident that rot and worms cannot prevail over you."

But even so, he was not calmed. They gave him a sleeping potion and took him into a marble room and ripped open his stomach and were taking out baskets of fat and placing it in the July sun and it did not stink. . . . He applied to himself the verse, "even my flesh will remain preserved" (Psalms 16:8–9).

In a fit of anger, our hero uses his imperial (and imperious) power to condemn to death a Jew who has opposed him. He immediately, however, realizes what a terrible thing he has done and tries to retrieve it, but cannot. Applying to himself (or to the dead man) the verse from Proverbs regarding the terrible power of speech, he is desolate. Upon being reassured that indeed the dead man eminently deserved death by Jewish law, he at first affirms the value of his "gut" reaction but still remains doubtful as to the righteousness of his own actions. The Rabbi performs a bizarre test on himself for righteousness. In order to demonstrate that his actions with regard to the Jew that he sent to his death were blameless ones, he attempts to prove (to himself) that his body is indeed impermeable — that is, that he possesses the "classical" phallic body, the body that, at least since Plato, has been associated *by male culture* with the male, unlike the open, permeable, porous, embodied body considered "female." The connection of this impermeable body with political power has recently been underscored once again by Carole Pateman: "The body of the 'individual' is very different from women's bodies. His body is tightly enclosed within boundaries, but women's bodies are permeable, their contours change shape and they are subject to cyclical processes. All these differences are summed up in the natural bodily process of birth. Physical birth symbolizes everything that makes women incapable of entering the original contract and transforming themselves into the civil individuals who uphold its terms. Women lack neither strength nor ability in a general sense, but, according to the classic contract theorists, they are naturally deficient in a specifically *political* capacity, the capacity to create and maintain political right."[23]

23. Pateman, *Sexual Contract*, 96.

It is here that the contradictory enactments of "male envy" reveal their different political and ethical possibilities, for a strategy that deals with male envy by denying value to bodily creation and appropriating all creativity to thought and political power is very different from one within which men enact a desire for femaleness via the subversion of the impermeability of their own bodies. In other words, the Rabbi's efforts to gain "the phallus" will be thematized as having effects directly opposite his later efforts to renounce the phallus by mimesis of femaleness. Both are male strategies for dealing with sexual difference and neither has much to do with (or promise for) women, but they nevertheless have quite different political and ethical effects. As Pateman has argued, classical liberal feminism is grounded in the argument that women have the same capabilities as men (because classical patriarchal theory grounded itself in the argument that they do not), but "struggle over this terrain presupposes that there is no political significance in the fact that women have an ability that men lack."[24] In other words, rather than an acknowledgment of male envy of female ability, "the phallus" and all of the political theory that it entails is a massive mystification and disavowal of that envy. Without claiming any utopian (or even protofeminist) moment for rabbinic and early Christian culture through this analysis, I would nevertheless suggest that the challenge to the phallic, classical body that texts such as ours enact (however—or *because* it is—riddled with self-contradiction) provides an Archimedean point for critique.

Our "hero" problematizes that "phallic" understanding of masculinity paradoxically through his own attempts to substantiate it. He begins by making the claim that since he is so certain that he is righteous, he is equally sure that his body will be impervious to the depredations of worms after his death. That is, he imagines himself as the classic impermeable body, the body which is pristine and closed off from the outside world—"Even my flesh will remain preserved." Ironically, however, the test that the Rabbi devises in order to prove his self image is one that undermines it. He has the integrity of his body violated in the bizarre operation of removing basketfuls of fat from his stomach and having them placed in the sun to see if they will indeed be immune from rotting. We have then, an incredible moment of self-destruction of the very models of masculinity that are being both proposed and defeated at the same time.

24. Pateman, *Sexual Contract*, 95.

As Mikhail Bakhtin has pointed out, the image of the body part grown out of all proportion is "actually a picture of dismemberment, of separate areas of the body enlarged to gigantic dimensions."[25] The Rabbi is clearly grotesquely obese if several basketfuls of fat could be removed from his body. The topoi of exaggerated size, detachable organs, the emphasis on the orifices, and stories of dismemberment are all representations of the body as interacting with the world, not self-enclosed as the classical body. Moreover, the association of the coherent, impermeable body with imperial power is thematized directly in the story as well. When the Rabbi acted in consonance with imperial power, he was attacked by the text. However, when the Rabbi allows his body to be dismembered, to be made grotesque in a process that is almost parodic of birth as well as castration, then he is validated by the text.[26] The talmudic text bears out Bakhtin's remarkable insight by combining in one moment the monstrous belly that "hides the normal members of the body" and the actual dismemberment of that monstrous organ. Indeed, the image of what is done to the body of the Rabbi is almost a mad cesarean section, a parodic appropriation of female fecundity. In other words, this operation is a form of critique of male power through a mimesis of femaleness. The logic of referring to it as appropriation grows out of the very fact that it uses the female body as its metaphor for critique of modes of male hegemony. I do not discount the critique of male power or its usefulness if, at the same time, I pay skeptical attention to the fact that it "shifts the gaze away from the physical suffering of the female body to the . . . dilemmas of men."[27]

If we imaginatively think through what it was that this Rabbi was feeling guilty for, namely, collaboration with the violence of the "Roman" authorities, then this particular response, femminizing his body and rendering it grotesque, makes perfect sense. If the violence of Rome was experienced as a peculiarly male imposition, then correction of having participated in this violence would require a self-femminization. This representation, that is of the necessity to become female in order to renounce and repent for violence, is iterated within the talmudic text

25. Bakhtin, *Rabelais*, 328.
26. This pattern repeats itself in Babylonian rabbinic literature. It is not, therefore, a sport. See D. Boyarin, "Great Fat Massacre."
27. Gravdal, *Ravishing*, 15.

at several junctures and will be explicitly doubled in a later sequence of this very narrative. This response, moreover, has "positive" meanings as well—and not only corrective or reactive ones—just as and just because the grotesque body itself is suffused with creative power, as Bakhtin saw: "All these convexities and orifices have a common characteristic; it is within them that the confines between bodies and between the body and the world are overcome: there is an interchange and an interorientation."[28] This body can be taken, then, as an ideal representation of Jewish culture in Diaspora as a site where the confines between the body of Jewish culture and other social bodies are overcome,[29] not forgetting, of course, the frequently violent response from many of those other bodies. Paradoxically, however, this diasporazation of the body is also a pursuit of purity, of a moral pristineness that engagement with power seemingly would preclude. This paradox of Diaspora as the site of purity and cultural interchange is inherent in postbiblical Jewish culture. No wonder, then, that the Rabbi's body is both purified and violated in the same operation, rendered classical through precisely that which marks it as grotesque.

The dismembered, "castrated" male body is also deterritorialized, as the text troubles to relate to us in its continuation. Another of the Rabbis, put into exactly the same situation of either collaboration with Roman tyranny or probably dangerous resistance, is urged to simply run away: "To Rabbi Ishmaᶜel the son of Yose there also occurred a similar situation. Eliahu (the Prophet Elijah) met him and said to him, 'How long will you persist in sending the people of our God to death?!' He said to him, 'What can I do; it is the king's order?' He said to him, 'Your father ran away to Asia-Minor; you run away to Lydia.'"

The appropriate form of resistance that the Talmud recommends for Jews in this place is evasion. The arts of colonized peoples of dissimulation and dodging are thematized here as actually running away, the very opposite of such "masculine" pursuits as "standing one's ground." The central Babylonian talmudic myth of the foundation of rabbinic

28. Bakhtin, *Rabelais*, 317.

29. I am mobilizing Mary Douglas's formative insight here as to the homology between practices relating to the individual body and the cultural and social problems relating to the body of the group (Douglas, *Purity*). Whereas she, however, was primarily concerned with such practices that defend the body, and thus the body-politic, from impurity, I find here a set of symbolic representations that at least partially overcome the limits between the Jewish body and the world.

Judaism involves such an act of evasion and trickery, the "grotesque" escape in a coffin of Rabbi Yoḥanan ben Zakkai from besieged Jerusalem, which the Rabbis portray as the very antithesis of the military resistance of the Zealots who wanted to fight to the very last man and preserve their honor.[30] Here we find the same political theory—"Get out of there!"—adumbrated in a much less direct way but one that is all the more rich in its overtones for that. The text designates "diaspora" modes of resistance—deterritorialization; the grotesque; symbolically (not actually, this is not about martyrdom) dismembered, dephallicized male body—resistance not as the attempt to gain power and dominance but as resistance *to* the assumption of dominance: "Run away to Lydia." This prescription is put into the mouth of one of the most authoritative oracles that rabbinic culture has produced, Elijah the Prophet. Nor is this recommendation unique in rabbinic texts. As the Palestinian Talmud recommends, "If they propose that you be a member of the *boule,* let the Jordan be your border" (Mo‘ed Katan 2:3, 81b and Sanhedrin 8:2, 26b).[31] Even though a case can be made that the Diaspora modes of ideal masculinity are more pronounced in Babylonia than in Palestine of the talmudic period, this distinction is only relative. In Palestine, as well, the Jews of this time were in Diaspora. The tenacity that is valorized by these texts is the tenacity that enables continued Jewish existence, not the tenacity of defending sovereignty unto death.

While I emphasize the syntonic aspects of the rabbinic self-representation as female or femminized, there can be no doubt that the Rabbis were sensitive to the dystonic aspects of this representation as well—or at least to some of them, a fact the talmudic narrative will expose. Not surprisingly for the ancient (and for that matter, the modern) world, the political quickly shades into the sexual. This narrative, which seems to be almost as uncensored as a dream, sports unusually graphic and explicit representations of maleness and the question of maleness as figured through the body:

> When Rabbi Ishma‘el the son of Yose and Rabbi El‘azar the son of Rabbi Shim‘on used to meet each other, an ox could walk between them and not touch them. A certain matron said to them, "Your children are not yours." They said, "Theirs are greater than ours." "If that is the case, even more so!"

---

30. See Zerubavel, *Recovered Roots,* 200 ff. and D. Boyarin, "Tricksters."

31. In other words, if you are called to serve as an official of the Roman government, leave town!

There are those who say that thus they said to her: "As the man, so is his virility." And there are those who say that thus did they say to her: "Love compresses the flesh.". . .

Said Rabbi Yoḥanan, "Rabbi Ishmaᶜel the son of Yose's member was like a wineskin of nine *kav*; Rabbi Elᶜazar the son of Rabbi Shimᶜon's member was like a wineskin of seven *kav*." Rav Papa said, "Rabbi Yoḥanan's member was like a wineskin of three *kav*." And there are those who say: like a wineskin of five *kav*. Rav Papa himself had a member which was like the baskets of Hipparenum.[32]

I would like to suggest here that the connection between the first part of the story and this sequel, within which the "virility" of this same Rabbi is impugned, is not accidental, not by any means. The solution that the Rabbi has been offered to the problem of Roman domination and collaboration is a femminizing one. He is not counseled to "stand up and fight" but rather to run away.[33] From the point of view

32. That "an ox can walk between them and not touch them" is made possible by the fact that they are giants. The ox walks under the bridge, which is wide enough because the rabbis are so fat. Rav Papa is also a legendary fat rabbi, as is known from several other Babylonian talmudic intertexts.

33. Note that this counsel provides almost a direct antithesis to the Greek (and Roman) ideal of *andreia,* manliness. The whole question of *andreia* (and its Roman equivalent, *virtus*) has to be thought through with reference to rabbinic texts. As Zeitlin has phrased it: "What is manliness, the quality the Greeks call *andreia,* a word that is synonymous with virile courage, as even we understand it, and requires a willingness to face danger, to risk one's life, and to maintain control over self and others? Continuing the epic values of heroic renown (*kleos*) and in pursuit of an everlasting name and glory in a city ruled by democratic principles as well as by protocols of honor and shame, the Athenian male in this competitive, agonistic society faces problems of collective identity and responsibility along with a growing sense of individual selfhood that will develop into a full-fledged concern in later antiquity." The question that I am addressing is: What about Jews and Christians in this picture of a manliness defined in these ways? How do the Jewish and Christian branches of Hellenistic-Roman culture accept, reject, modify, resist, and collaborate with such notions of manliness? Here it is apposite, however, to point out that the motif of "self-control" or "restraint" as determinative of *andreia*—in its modern form: "Real men don't cry"—is not the same thing as renunciation or submissiveness, the more typical ideals of the early Christians and Jews. Such self-control is, indeed, one of the trappings of the powerful (J. C. Scott, *Domination,* 50–51). As Catherine Edwards notes, "Cicero, defining *continentia,* writes that it consists in avoiding behaviour which is unmanly—*parum virile* (De fin. 2.47)" (*Politics,* 78).

An effective ground to this figure of a valorized submissiveness, of an emotional dependence of men on men, can be garnered from Roman texts. When Cicero wishes to attack Antony, he first accuses him of having been a prostitute and then says to him, "[B]ut soon Curio turned up, drew you away from your meretricious trade and, as if he had given you a matron's robe, established you in lasting and stable matrimony. No boy bought for sexual gratification was ever so much in the power of his master as you were in Curio's" (Cic. Phil. 2.44–45, quoted in C. Edwards, *Politics,* 64). Edwards, in citing this passage, makes the excellent point that what offends here is not primarily the sexual practice, for as she says, "Cicero contrives to make a stable, lasting relationship sound far more reprehensible than prostitution," and this because "Antony's emotional attachment to Curio, he implies, reduced him to a position of slave-like dependence" (64–65). Rather

of Roman culture, such behavior would be heinously cowardly and feminizing.[34] This, plus their enormous abdomens, apparently signified impotence to that stereotypical figure of Roman culture in Babylonian rabbinic literature, the *matrona,* who mocks our heroes in time-honored Mediterranean terms by impugning the legitimacy of their wives' children, in effect calling the rabbis cuckolds.[35]

What follows next is a deliciously humorous bit of linguistic byplay. The rabbis, exhibiting for once the stereotypical male pride in the penis, understand that the matron is obliquely "complimenting" them that they are so enormous that they could not possibly fit into their wives' vaginas. They accordingly answer her cryptically, "Theirs are bigger than ours." The matron, however, apparently was referring to their abdomens and not to any conjectures about the sizes of their penises. She, misunderstanding in turn their answer and thinking that they are claiming that their wives' abdomens are even larger than the husbands',

---

it was the dependence of one man on another, emotionally and materially, that was considered shameful and not their sexual practices. We have here the founding moments of a culture characterized recently by Lee Edelman as one in which there is "a deeply rooted concern about the possible meanings of dependence on other males" ("Redeeming," 50). However, for slaves it seems, it was dependence on other males that was honored. Slaves have something to teach us about demystifying masculinist ideologies. Dale Martin has derived some fascinating evidence to this effect from inscriptions: "The very names of slaves and freedpersons and the epithets they accepted for themselves demonstrate their acceptance of patronal ideology: many slaves were named Philodespotos, 'master-lover,' and one freedman is complimented as being a master-loving man in spite of the fact that this very term occurs in literary sources as an insult similar to 'slavish.' Several slaves honored a deceased fellow slave by saying he was a real lord-lover (*philokyrios*). They bear, *probably without shame,* names that bespeak servitude, for example, Hope-bearer, Pilot, Gain, Well-wed, and Changeable" (Martin, *Slavery,* 28–29, emphasis added; for a counterexample, see Martin, 43). Before rushing to dub such data as mere evidence of false consciousness, we would do well to examine our own ideological investments, investments which still, as in Greek times, validate "tops" over "bottoms" (Kritzman, *Michel,* 300; quoted in Bersani, "Foucault," 14). It is fascinating to note that, as Mosse points out, immorality, weakness, and *servility* were defined in modern times as the antithesis to true manliness (Mosse, *Image,* 6).

34. Barton, "Moment." Brent Shaw has commented to me: "This was a *professed* part of a dominant ideology, but it was, even as such, constantly under debate. See, for example, in its extreme form, the Livian stuff (which is already Augustan ideology) on Quintus Fabius Maximus, who constantly ran away from Hannibal as his main military tactic. The fact is that the political domination of the Principate, and even earlier (as Carlin Barton sees with respect to the civil wars), the implosion of violence internally upon Roman society, compelled free citizen Romans to elevate and accept more peaceable and passive values" (Shaw, letter). This is an important qualification. As such, it becomes possible to read Christian and Jewish resistance as one part of a growing internal cultural contestation of the "dominant" Roman ideology thus further disrupting any essentialization of Jewishness and Romanness, even at the cultural level.

35. Ilan, *Jewish Women,* 200–204.

retorts, "If your wives are even fatter than you are, then all the more reason that you could not have intercourse." At this point the obese rabbis finally understand the matron's concern and answer—according to one tradition that the size of a man's genitals is in keeping with the size of the rest of his body, and according to the other, that desire overcomes obesity.

It is at this moment of anxiety about paternity in the text that the account of the gargantuan phalloi of the Rabbis is mustered, not altogether different from Roman sexual humor, in which, according to Amy Richlin, "[t]he central persona or protagonist or narrator is a strong male of extreme virility, occasionally even ithyphallic (as in the Priapus poems)." The function of this figure is to be anxious "to defend himself by adducing his strength, virility, and (in general) all traits that are considered normal—and this is the appeal of the joke teller to his audience, as if both are confirming and checking with each other that they are all right,"[36] phallically well endowed. The text here is, on my reading, thematizing one possible response to the classic Levantine charge of "effeminacy"—"Your children aren't yours"—that is, cocky machismo insistence on virility.[37]

Given the way that the situation of being dominated would insistently have been read (by the dominators) as femminizing with the inevitable leakage of such affect into the consciousnesses of the dominated males as well—there being no domination completely without hegemony—and the explicitly female modes of resistance that rabbinic culture developed, in opposition to the honored modes of resistance current among the Romans, it is no wonder that Rabbis sometimes felt it especially necessary to adduce their strength and virility in order to confirm with each other that they were all right and that indeed their children were theirs.[38] I shall be arguing throughout this book that it is this counterphobic rejection of the charge of effeminacy that produces the most toxic political (gender and sexual) effects within dominated male populations, as opposed to its alternative, enjoyment of femminization. This text represents that "female" mode of resistance,

36. Richlin, *Garden*, 58.
37. Brandes, *Metaphors*.
38. Cf. the moralizing interpretation of the מהרש"א, Maharsha R. Shmael Idelis explaining why rabbinic penis size is religiously significant. It is very interesting to note that until the Maharsha in the sixteenth century, the commentatorial tradition had been anxious to interpret the "members" discussed here as anything but the *membrum virile*.

renunciation of the phallus, as being the highly honored option, for after all, there is no greater voice of authority within these texts than the
voice of Elijah the Prophet.

In other words, what I am postulating is that within the culture the
"weapons of the weak" were valued, not despised. While there is anxiety expressed within the text about consequences for the virility of men
when "feminine" arts of survival are employed, these anxieties have
more to do perhaps with what the outside world will say than with inner cultural gender patterning. After all, it is the Roman matron who
is portrayed by the text as querying the potency of our heroes. Yet the
text clearly thematizes as well the negative moment in the response of
oppressed men to their representation as not-male: machismo with all
its violent and repressive consequences toward the women of their own
community. Barbara Gottfried has remarked about quite a different era
in the history of Judaism: "In effect, Alex [Portnoy] experiences one
cultural system of gender in conflict with another; and what his 'complaint' underscores is both the anxiety this conflict produces vis à vis
gender identity, and the appropriative and destructive force that displaced anxiety has for those others, especially women, who come into
contact with it."[39] While this particular defensive-aggressive move of
certifying manhood through phallic swaggering and misogyny seems to
have been generally resisted within rabbinic Judaism, it is obviously not
absent and clearly satirized here.[40]

This is a significant point, for it illustrates the enormous complexity of the play of gender in cultural interactions and self-definition.
On one hand, it is clear that the behaviors that the Rabbis portray as
ideal for themselves are understood as proper male demeanor within
their own system of cultural values, particularly as gender dimorphism
and separation of roles obviously were crucial to them. They therefore
reject representations that would despise such practices as "effeminate." At the same time, they live within and are an integral part of
a larger cultural world, within which those very valorized rabbinic
practices are often stigmatized as "female," and the Rabbis seem sometimes to have been willing and able to take that representation in and
transvalue it into a positive self-representation as female or fem-

39. Gottfried, "What *Do* Men?" 41.
40. There is an enormous difference in the meaning of this text, depending on
whether we read it as satirizing machismo or as asserting it.

minized. This moment will be cranked up dramatically in intensity in the sequel.

THE PANGS OF LOVE

The talmudic narrative continues:

> And even so, Rabbi El'azar the son of Shim'on did not trust himself, perhaps God forbid, such an incident would befall him again. He solicited painful disease upon himself. In the evening, they used to fold under him sixty felt mats, and in the morning they would find under him sixty vessels full of blood and pus. His wife made him sixty kinds of relishes and he ate them. His wife would not let him go to the study-house, in order that the Rabbis would not reject him. In the evening, he said, "My brothers and lovers, come!" In the morning, he said, "My brothers and lovers depart!"
>
> One day his wife heard him saying this. She said, "You bring them upon you. You have decimated the inheritance of my father's house." She rebelled and went to her family home. Sixty sailors came up from the sea and came to him carrying sixty purses and they made him sixty relishes, and he ate them. One day she said to her daughter, "Go see what your father is doing." He said to her, "Ours is greater than yours." He applied to himself the verse, "From afar she will bring her bread" (Proverbs 31:14).
>
> One day he went to the study-house. They brought before him sixty kinds of blood, and he declared all of them pure. The Rabbis murmured about him, saying is it possible that there is not even one doubtful case among those? He said, "If I am right, let all of the children be boys, and if not, let there be one girl among them." All of them were boys. They were all named after Rabbi El'azar. Our Rabbi said, "How much procreation did that wicked woman prevent from Israel!"

༄༄༄

> [After Rabbi El'azar's death] Our Rabbi sent to her to propose to her. She said, "A vessel which has functioned for the holy, shall it function for the profane?!" *There [i.e., in Palestine] they say, "In the place where the master hangs his battle-ax, shall the shepherd hang his stick?!"*[41] He sent to her, "Indeed in Torah he was greater than me, but was he greater than me in deeds?" She sent to him, "As for Torah, I know nothing; you have told me, but as for deeds, I know, for he accepted pain upon himself."

---

41. Note the thematic inconsistency of the text that is explicitly marked here as Other. If over and over again in our Babylonian rabbinic text it is the weapon that is despised, here suddenly the weapon is valorized over the shepherd's stick, and this antithetical version is referred to as from Palestine.

Rabbi said: "Sufferings are desirable!" He solicited on himself thirteen years of sufferings; six of gall stones and seven of toothache. The stable-master of the House of Rabbi was richer than King Shapur.[42] When he used to throw hay to the animals, the sound would be heard for three miles. He used to devise that he would throw [the food to the animals] when Rabbi went into the toilet, and even so his voice was louder than theirs, and the sailors in the sea would hear it.

And even so, the pains of Rabbi Elʿazar the son of Rabbi Shimʿon are preferable to those of Rabbi, for those of Rabbi Elʿazar the son of Rabbi Shimʿon came because of love and departed because of love, whereas those of Rabbi came because of an incident and departed because of an incident.[43]

What is this [incident]? A certain calf was being taken out to be slaughtered. It went and hid its head in the hem of Rabbi's garment [a gesture of supplication], and it was crying. He said, "Go, for this you have been created!" They said, "Because he was not merciful, let pains come upon him." And by means of an incident they departed. One day, the servant woman of the house of Rabbi was sweeping the house. There were baby rats there, and she was sweeping them. He said to her, "Let them be. It is written 'His mercy extends to all of His creatures' [Psalms 145:9]." They said, "Since he is merciful, let us be merciful to him"[44] (Babylonian Talmud, Baba Metsiaʿ 88a).

The overall theme of the passage itself as well as its surrounding context—it continues after all the discussion of rabbinic penises—is maleness. What is the function of pain in that same discourse of masculinity? It is clear that one of the most significant moments in this text has to do with the intersection between pain and eroticism. As I shall argue,

42. The Persian emperor.

43. Some insight into this distinction, I think, can be won by comparing it to the valuation of self-sacrifice among the Romans that Carlin Barton so subtly investigates in her "Savage Miracles." The same act of suffering is variously valued in accord with the emotion (presumed or known) of the sufferer: for instance, whether she suffers voluntarily or under duress; that is, even bravely accepted suffering is valued less if it can be understood as having been undertaken without volition (Barton, "Savage Miracles," 50–52). However, there is a great deal of ambivalence within this text as to the nature of Rabbi's suffering; in fact, the text is remarkably split within itself into a story of suffering that is voluntarily undertaken because "sufferings are desirable" (itself an ambivalent formulation), and one in which the suffering is a punishment for hybris and a cause for learning mercy. But finally, the rabbinic text is distinguished from the Roman at one crucial point. For the Roman, "any act could be the act of a hero or a coward! One needed and wanted desperately to demonstrate that one was not motivated by desire for life" (Barton, "Savage Miracles," 52–53). However, for the Rabbis surely desire for life (at *almost* any price) was the very apex and sine qua non of humanness.

44. This structure wherein Rabbi becomes "female" after a deed of cruelty and then is restored to his "maleness" after a different act seems almost to echo the story of Tiresias becoming a woman after striking copulating snakes. The latter, however, is restored after attacking another pair of snakes (Loraux, *Experiences*, 11).

the construct of masochism provides a useful rubric within which to analyze this material, particularly insofar as it is directly associated with desire and pleasure. In Theodor Reik's classic study of masochism, however, what we might call cultural masochism is explicitly associated with celibacy, with renunciation of sexuality (see below). But here we find an unambiguous complicity between male (moral) masochism and male sexuality and even paternity.

Let us begin with the most obvious marker of the relay between suffering and sex here. After the death of his rival,[45] Rabbi El'azar the son of Rabbi Shim'on, Rabbi comes to seek the hand of his widow, who rejects him using sexualized imagery that is almost shocking in its directness. She says to him: "Shall a vessel that served for the holy now serve for the profane?" referring to her own body or, in the "Palestinian" version: "In the place where the master hangs his battle-ax, shall the shepherd hang his stick?" referring to the body of the male.

The narrative does not leave us long in suspense as to what made Rabbi El'azar the son of Rabbi Shim'on such a superior erotic object. Indeed Rabbi himself lets us know part of the story, namely, that his rival was greater than him in the study of Torah. The widow immediately discounts knowledge of this realm—as a good rabbinic wife would be expected to do—but cites her husband's greater performance of "deeds" as the reason for finding Rabbi an unsuitable successor to him. There is very little doubt in my mind that the use of the term "deeds" involves a kind of cultural irony. In the Greco-Roman world, the deeds that would render a man a suitable erotic object would have been phallic deeds par excellence, deeds of valor of one sort of another, while for the Rabbi these deeds are antiphallic, masochistic challenges to the coherence and impermeability of the male body. Paradoxically, it is the penetrated body that constructs the penile ideal. Where the Roman had to show that he had a phallus to win a woman, the Rabbi has to show he has none![46]

Rabbi, according to the story, "gets the message." Desiring the woman and realizing that "sufferings are desirable," he also prays for and invites upon himself extremely painful disease. This male subject, at any rate, is called upon and learns to recognize himself through fe-

45. The larger context includes stories of their rivalry as schoolchildren and the competition between their fathers as well. See for the nonce D. Boyarin, "Great Fat Massacre."

46. Compare the story of Resh Lakish in the next chapter who had to give up his "phallus" in order to win a wife.

male desire, not through an image of "unimpaired masculinity," but through an image of masculinity as impairment, as what would be interpreted in another culture as castration.

The details of the account of Rabbi El'azar's disease are exceedingly revealing as well. They repeatedly reconfigure his body as "female." The first hint of such a configuration is in the description of his symptoms. "In the evening, they used to fold under him sixty felt mats, and in the morning they would find under him sixty vessels full of blood and pus." If this depiction were not graphic enough, the text provides us with other clues for reading its significance. The number "sixty" provides one such, for at another juncture in the larger narrative of which this is a part we are told, "One day he went to the study-house. They brought before him sixty kinds of blood, and he declared all of them pure." According to rabbinic practice, when a woman has a discharge, if it is certainly menstrual blood, then she and her husband are forbidden to have sex until after the period and a purification ritual. However, if it is doubtful as to whether the discharge is menstrual or not, a stain is shown to a rabbi who makes a judgment based on his expertise.

I have interpreted the details of this episode in another place and here wish merely to emphasize that wherever the number sixty appears in our narrative, it functions as a kind of leitmotif signaling a moment of gendered instability.[47] In this case the reference to exactly sixty specimens of female blood strongly amplifies the association that the placing of felt mats under a body and their filling with blood would have with femaleness in any case. Rabbi's disease also has femminizing elements. The image of him at the toilet screaming in pain cannot be separated from representations of women giving birth screaming while sitting on a birth stool. Moreover, metaphorical confusions of excrement and babies occur in fantasies of male birthing at many points in our culture.[48]

47. I have no idea as yet whether the number itself is significant intertextually but am using it here as a subtext in the Riffaterrian sense of a recurring linguistic moment within a narrative that points to the cultural paradigm with which the narrative is concerned.

48. Modleski, *Feminism*, 79–82 provides a particularly instructive analysis of a recent version of this fantasy. Modleski, however, adopts (strangely) a rigidly psychoanalytic view here, claiming that "the regressive phantasy involving babies and bowels in no way precludes castration anxiety, but, on the contrary, exacerbates it: it is, in fact, a prototype of it. 'Feces,' 'child,' and 'penis,' writes Freud, 'form a unity, an unconscious concept ... —the concept, namely, of a little thing that can become separated from one's body'" (81). But if we do not identify the child with the phallus, assuming this as a universal psychic condition, then isn't it possible that the relations between fantasies of birthgiving (via defecation) and their coordinated images might have different meanings, different relations to "castration" in different times and different places, and indeed, in different individuals? Another, perhaps simpler, way of making this point would be to

Finally, it is important to note that for Roman culture as well the acceptance of pain was crucial in the definition of the masculine. However, this moment in the text distinguishes it sharply from that formation, for within Roman culture the undergoing of the ordeal required a "manly" bearing of the pain with fortitude, hardly the stance of our text with its grotesque hero sitting on the toilet and screaming like a woman in labor.[49] A comparison of this image of the Rabbi with Laocoön's dignified and classical self-control in the face of great pain will make the point eloquently.[50] It is hard, once more, not to read the talmudic text as an almost deliberate reversal of that cultural ideal. Nietzsche, in short, knew what he was talking about.

However, an even more outlandish moment in this text provides a striking symptom of this thematic motive, as well as the means to a tentative interpretation. At one point in the narrative Rabbi Elʿazar is abandoned by his wife because, upon understanding that his suffering is voluntary, she becomes angry. She realizes that the expensive delicacies that she has fed him to keep him healthy while she believed that he was "naturally" sick—or at any rate, sick against his will—are in effect wasting her inheritance to feed his guilt and ego. "She said, 'You bring

argue that Freud's assumption that "castration anxiety may coexist with 'an identification with women by means of the bowel'" depends on his prior assumption that women are indeed castrates in the psyche. But what if that were not so, what if Schreber's *Entmannung* is (as it seems to be) a gain and not a loss? Then the "contradiction" would disappear.

49. This is again quite distinct from the masculine bearing of pain with fortitude and joy that was so exalted by Romans of nearly the same period. Thus in the typical narrative of the time, the sublimity of the spirit (i.e., its masculinity) is demonstrated by the calm or even majestic endurance of pain, and the desired result is a lifting up or exaltation of the spirit—"self-realization, an expansion of the self" (Barton, "Savage Miracles," 55)—while here the pain is suffered with grotesque screaming in the toilet, and the desired telos is a reduction of the spirit and empathy for the lowest of creatures: baby rats. Neither should this be confused with the paradoxical cultural events that Carlin Barton exposes in a particular moment in Roman cultural history within which proper "masculine" behavior, having been experienced as a burden, "[t]hose who would proclaim their freedom had now to do it with behavior traditionally associated with servility and femininity" ("All Things," 90). It is, to be sure, somewhat more difficult to articulate why I claim that what is happening in the rabbinic text is quite disparate from this. One way of making sense of this difference would be through the projected reactions of (fictional) women. Whereas in the story of Hercules's mimesis of femininity, his wife is appalled ("All Things," 92), in the rabbinic text the fictional wife reads the mimesis as erotically attractive, as that which makes a man fit to be her husband. Second, it would be hard indeed to describe the femminization of these Rabbis as "delighting in the freedom of playing a slave and a woman," as in Barton's description there. The latter is more reminiscent of some modern femminizations so devastatingly anatomized in Tania Modleski's *Feminism without Women*.

50. On the Laocoön and its reception in the eighteenth century, see Mosse, *Image*, 32–35.

them upon you. You have decimated the inheritance of my father's
house.' She rebelled and went to her family home. Sixty sailors came up
from the sea and came to him carrying sixty purses and they made him
sixty relishes, and he ate them. One day she said to her daughter, 'Go
see what your father is doing.' He said to her, 'Ours is greater than
yours.' He applied to *himself* the verse, '[*She* is like the ships of Tar-
shish;] from afar she will bring her bread' (Proverbs 31:14)."

In accordance with the generalization that I have made above about
the number sixty in this text, here also we have a marked moment of
gender crossing. Beginning at the end, as I have emphasized in my citation, the verse that he applies to himself is a verse that refers to women.
However, there is more to this, for the verse comes from the very passage of Proverbs that describes the "woman of valor," the ideal wife.[51]
It is as if Rabbi El'azar is insisting that he is a better wife (to himself?)
than the woman is. On the other hand, in thematizing the wife's rebellion, the text is indicating at least a nascent awareness that the Rabbi's
(Rabbis') self-femminizing is not necessarily welcome to his (their) female intimates or to women in general, that indeed, it may be, in Robin
Morgan's words, "insulting the female (in person and in principle)."

If we move upward in the text then from this clue, we will find further detail to support and further "flesh out" this reading. First of all,
let us note that the sailors provide Rabbi El'azar with the same food
(both type and amount, sixty kinds of relish) that his wife had formerly
provided. Second, there is the very curious reply that the rabbi gives his
daughter when she comes to inquire after his situation. He responds by
claiming that "ours is greater than yours," a seemingly opaque, even
meaningless, statement. This occult remark is rendered further obscure
when compared with a seeming echo from earlier in the same narrative

51. Not so incidentally this very attribute, from the root that means strength and
soldier, also marks a set of gender attributes different from the ones familiar to "our"
culture. The persistence of these differences was brought home in a graphic, if unpleasant,
context recently when the mayor of Jerusalem was quoted as saying: "This is a Jewish
city. I think that having more Arabs is calling for trouble. I have to show who is the
balabusta." Clyde Haberman, the *New York Times* reporter who cited this then wrote,
"That Yiddish word means master of the house," but, of course, it doesn't; it means
"housewife"! Even in the masculinist world of Zionist conquest, then, the traditional
form of thinking of power as female and representing temporal power via the wife and
not the husband remains alive for some Jews for whom the traditional culture is not completely dead. "Housewife" would hardly have carried that meaning in English, so Haberman has to perform an "f"-to-"m" transexualization of the mayor's racist metaphor
(Haberman, "Israeli Seizures").

in the passage discussed above. There the bodies of Rabbi Elʿazar and a compatriot and those of their wives—either the genitals or the abdomens—are being compared, and the rabbis claim: "Theirs are greater than ours." Since that passage is clearly dealing with sexual (and procreative) matters—whether genitals or abdomens are being referred to, the subject is explicitly sex—the use of the identical phrase here strongly suggests a sexual meaning as well. It is as if the rabbi (the text) is saying that men have no reason to be jealous of the greater sexual, procreative, nutritive capacities of women; men can appropriate those capacities for themselves, even through appropriating bleeding and corporeal pain, the pain of childbirth, as well. If previously the rabbi conceded that his wife's was greater than his, now he commands his daughter: Tell her, ours is greater than hers. If the first represents the anxiety, the second represents a way of reducing that anxiety.

This interpretation is supported as well by another moment in the text already referred to above: "One day he went to the study-house. They brought before him sixty kinds of blood, and he declared all of them pure. The Rabbis murmured about him, saying is it possible that there is not even one doubtful case among those? He said, 'If I am right, let all of the children be boys, and if not, let there be one girl among them.' All of them were boys. They were all named after Rabbi Elʿazar. Our Rabbi said, 'How much procreation did that wicked woman prevent from Israel!' "

It seems to me that this passage also provides significant clues to the concern of the text as a whole. In the arrogation of the procreative function indicated by the Name-of-the-Father (here transferred from the biological father to males in general), the text is once again repeating its underlying paradigm of maleness as lack. There is an extraordinary reversal here. On one hand, the "blame" for the prevention of procreation is displaced onto the poor wife of Rabbi Elʿazar because she kept her husband from going to the study-house, where he would have disagreed with the other rabbis who were, after all, the ones preventing the wives from having sex, not she.[52] On the other hand, Rabbi Elʿazar himself symbolically takes the credit for the bearing of these children by having them all end up named after him. The paternal function here simply absorbs into itself the maternal one, suggesting that one of the

---

52. Note the irony: the "Our Rabbi" who blames her is the same one who seeks her hand after her husband's death.

motivations for this text is to "restore" the lack occasioned in the male psyche by inability to bear children—"Ours are greater than theirs."[53] This suggestion will make it possible to interpret the function of male corporeal pain and its eroticization in this text as well.[54]

One of the strikingly equivocal features of the talmudic narrative is that for both of its heroes it offers two incompatible explanations for their masochism, and thus for the cultural/psychic functions of masochism itself. One could suggest that in each case both an erotic explanation and a "political" explanation for the masochism are offered. Thus for Rabbi Elʿazar, one explanation given within the text has him in an erotic relationship to his pain, "My brothers and lovers, come!" and his suffering is explicitly called by the text suffering brought on by love. The other explanation, however, indicates that the pain came on him—however voluntarily—as punishment for his defection and collaboration in sending an innocent Jew to his death. Rabbi, on the other hand, is presented as taking on his suffering because he sees that suffering is desirable, that is, the suffering man is desirable to the female erotic object/subject, but, on the other hand, his pains are explicitly located (and devalued) as a punishment as well for his moral obtuseness regarding the consequences of power. The two are in a kind of chiastic relationship. Rabbi Elʿazar invites his pains for moral reasons and then they are eroticized, while Rabbi invites his pains for erotic reasons and then they are provided with a moral explanation.

It would be thus an easy temptation to simply heal the tension within the talmudic text at the level of the psyche and argue that what is being acted out here is the attempt of the psyche to disguise erotogenic masochism in moral masochism, to camouflage erotic pleasure in playing the woman as the achievement of some high political and moral purpose. This would be consistent, after all, with Freud's very interpretation of moral masochism. He demystifies "moral" masochism as a mask for masochism per se. The moral masochist is identified as merely hiding further—as self abnegation for higher purposes—the erotic scenario underlying his pleasure in pain.[55] By temporarily asserting this prospect, I would emphasize once more that the pursuit of the shattered—

53. Cf. Pardes, *Countertraditions*, 48, where naming and female power are thematized.

54. Referring to quite a different cultural context, Carol Siegel writes of "masochism that allows man glorious suffering in resistance to society only at the expense of his colonization of woman" (*Male*, 38). The phraseology seems queerly apt for the present context as well.

55. Cf. also Reik, *Masochism*, 15.

"dephallicized"—body is a source of pleasure which much in our cultural formation, with its clear hierarchy of "tops" over "bottoms," nearly prohibits us from seeing.[56]

This is, however, too easy and will not allow us to see the differences between cultural formations within which such psychic positions for males are pathologized—with names like "masochism"—those in which they are the province of celibate saints, as in early Christianity, and those in which they are valorized models for normative, paternal masculinity, as in early rabbinic Judaism. In other words, moving exclusively in this psychoanalytic direction seemingly annuls the possibility of reading masochism politically as a form of resistance. These rabbis, for all their masochism, that is for all of their femminization when perceived from the standpoint of the European myth of the phallus, are not, when seen from within the culture's texts, unmanned.[57] The distinctive structure of Jewish masochism thus has a particular cultural and historical valence. Comparing the structures of "Christian masochism" and these examples of rabbinic masochists will help us see this point.

CHRISTIAN MASOCHISM: THEODOR REIK

> The old problem of suffering, which had occupied the ancient philosophers for so long, had been subjected to a new attempt at solution in late Judaism and early Christianity. Suffering was affirmed, even glorified, and its value was acknowledged, for it opened the gates of paradise. Did Jesus not say: "Be of good cheer. I have overcome the world"? The dying Savior had found a new way of enjoyment. The steps of suffering became rungs of the ladder to heaven. The warrior-ideal is by and by replaced by the ideal of the saint or martyr. The late Jewish prophets and the Christian faith bring the glorification of masochism. But behind the pleasure of the suffering there appears the triumph. The greatest of all sufferers, who drank the cup of sorrow, who was humiliated and crucified, was the one to conquer the world.[58]

It is perhaps symptomatic that Reik here refers to "late Judaism" and "early Christianity," that his Judaism ends with the Prophets, and that

56. Bersani, *Freudian Body*. This issue will be followed more extensively in chapter 5 in connection with the *Entmannung* of Daniel Paul Schreber, which Freud read as "castration" or "emasculation," while Schreber himself interpreted it as an achievement and a gain, symbolized by the possibility of giving birth—not an emasculation but a femminization.

57. Geller, "Unmanning."

58. Reik, *Masochism*, 342.

he, a Jew, refers to Jesus as the "greatest of all sufferers," for what is missing in his account is a differentiation of Jewish from Christian masochism. This suggests as well the necessity for a more nuanced account of practices of self-mortification than a mere binary opposition of ascetic versus anti-ascetic practice, particularly insofar as asceticism has come, through Christianity, to be associated with celibacy. We have in this text an account of extreme self-mortification that is not only compliant with sexual life and procreation but understood as somehow a promotion of them. The Talmud seems to be anticipating an insight that, according to Carol Siegel, would be repeated by another thinker on Jews and gender: "[James] Joyce seems to be suggesting that submissiveness, even masochism, far from presenting an impediment to procreation, can be a way to express virile passion."[59] I am suggesting, *very* diffidently and somewhat paradoxically, that in the Jewish psychoanalyst's exclusive turn to Christianity for his models he missed a highly significant theme that the "Catholic" novelist realized through his reading of Jewishness!

For Reik a paradigmatic case of Christian masochism is the story of Francis of Assisi, who upon feeling intense sexual desire went outside and rolled himself in the snow and in a bush of wild roses, thus explicitly attacking the "thorn in his flesh" with thorns in his flesh.[60] As Reik correctly interprets: "In the experience of Saint Francis the pain serves as defense against the sinful desire."[61] The question remains, however, why sexual desire is sinful. Here we have, in a sense, the crux of my argument that there is a particularly Jewish pattern of masochism represented in these talmudic stories that is significantly different from Christian masochism. Without intending this to be an inclusive or exclusive explanation, I would like to suggest that the "masochism" of the Christian saints and martyrs is integrally and necessarily connected with the rejection of sexuality, just because masochism (for men) is an attempted renunciation of the phallic order.[62] However, since Christian

---

59. Siegel, *Male*, 67.

60. Incidentally, Christian tradition notwithstanding, there seems little reason to understand the "thorn in my flesh" of 2 Corinthians 12:7 as referring to sexual desire. Everything in the context suggests that it is Paul's physical infirmity or deformity that he is citing.

61. Reik, *Masochism*, 350.

62. Paradoxically, it is possible that for women martyrs and ascetics, "masochism" has the opposite and complementary political value, namely *resistance* to the phallic order. This claim is not based on an essentialist difference between genders but on a con-

culture had fully accepted the myth of the phallus—the fantasmic equation of the phallus to the penis—renunciation of the phallic order could be read only as renunciation of the penis. Hence, the necessity for "castration," for celibacy.[63] This provides, I suggest, one of the fundamental differences between rabbinic Jewish and Christian cultures.

Christianity, for all its post-Constantine temporal success, did continue to seek to produce radical reform of the empire. As Burrus has put it, "To state the thesis in general terms: post-Constantinian Christianity lays claim to the power of classical male speech; yet at the same time late ancient Christian discourse continues to locate itself in paradoxical relation to classical discourse through a stance of feminizing ascesis that renounces public speech."[64] This shift does not, then, connote that even later antique Christianity simply became complicit with the discourse of the imperial phallus. There is not an absolute binary opposition between episcopal leaders and "ascetic scholars." As Burrus's work reveals, within the late-fourth-century discourse of Ambrose and Prudentius, which serves to reinstate strict gender differentiation in the Christian context, there are elements of resistance to the dominant (Roman) discourse of masculinity and masculine sexuality in particular. This resistance is achieved partly through an ambiguity of gender that the virgin martyr reaches for—as Burrus puts it, "female audacity was first . . . entertained and then firmly restrained"[65]—even as it is being suppressed in the texts of this period.

Thus, for example, in Ambrose's *On Virgins*, we find such countermasculinity thematized and symbolized. In one crucial episode, Thecla, the apocryphal female associate of Paul, has entered the martyrological ring. She is the proverbial Christian who has been thrown to the lions.

---

sideration of the different political positions of male and female subjects with respect to sexuality in a given culture.

63. See also Mitchell, *Psychoanalysis,* 124, and Ramas, "Freud's," 499, on the immaculate conception as an attempt to resist the phallus. I wrote "attempt" to imply failed, because to the extent that male celibacy is a further dis-embodying move it can at the same time be a renunciation of the phallic order of activity, penetration, and power and a bolstering of its meanings of coherence, univocity, and spirituality (as opposed to corporeality), just because it is still functioning within the binary opposition of phallus and castration. In other words, this "castration," by reinforcing the separation of the phallus from the penis and thus the myth of the phallus per se, can in fact be at the same time a personal renunciation that is a social edification of the phallic order. Just as in our culture "straight men need gay men" (Miller, "Anal Rope," 135), one could argue that in medieval Christian culture knights needed monks.

64. Burrus, "Reading"; see also Foucault, "Subject," 214.
65. Burrus, "Reading."

As Ambrose structures his recounting of this episode, the lion "initially represents the sexual violence signaled by both the 'rage' of Thecla's would-be husband and the 'immodest eyes' of the male onlookers who gaze upon the spectacle of her nakedness."[66] The would-be martyr, Thecla, voluntarily presents to the lion her "vital parts," an obvious eroticized displacement of the offer of her sexual parts to her rejected fiancé. Having intercourse is figured for the woman as being devoured. This lion, however, undergoes a miraculous transformation (in addition to his pluralization, duly noted by Burrus): "The lions taught a lesson in chastity when they did nothing but kiss the virgin's feet, with their eyes turned to the ground, as though bashful, lest any male, even a beast, should see the virgin naked."[67] Burrus sums up her reading of this passage by remarking that "the subjugating force of male sexual violence has not been defeated so much as sublimated. On one reading at least, the lion's averted, feminized gaze continues paradoxically to restrain the virgin; the very gesture of honoring her—indeed of freely mirroring her feminine subjugation—becomes itself the vehicle of her constraint."[68] I would unpack this conclusion in the following manner: Even in the era of "imperial Christianity," the resistance to male sexuality, understood as "naturally" violent because of its cultural construction within the dominant Roman formation to which most Christians

66. Burrus, "Reading."

67. *De virg.* 2.7, quoted by Burrus, "Reading." Interestingly enough, the Rabbis also use the lion as a symbol for a violent male sexuality, saying that "the ignorant man is like the lion who tramples and then devours its prey," while the courting routine of the rooster is taken as a positive example of the husband who plays with, dallies with, and arouses his wife before intercourse. For the lion as an image of violent male sexuality in Roman literature, see the text of Martial cited by Richlin, *Garden,* 137. For the persistence of the lion in this guise, see James Joyce's *Ulysses,* in which Bloom remarks "the lion reek of all the male brutes that have possessed [a prostitute]" (409).

68. Burrus, "Reading." Compare the fascinating discussion of Ramakrishna's exhortation to his disciples to "become woman" in order to transcend their own sexual desire to be with women! "A man can change his nature by imitating another's character. By transposing on to yourself the attributes of woman, you gradually destroy lust and the other sensual drives. You begin to behave like women" (quoted in Roy, *Indian Traffic,* 175). As Parama Roy remarks, "This feminine identification was quite compatible with a marked gynophobia [sic]" (Roy, *Indian Traffic*). Alice Jardine also reminds us that Daniel Schreber's desire to become woman was an attempt to transcend sexual desire. Schreber wrote: "When I speak of my duty to go deeper into voluptuous pleasures, I never mean by that sexual desires towards other human beings (women) and even less sexual commerce, but I imagine myself man and woman in one person in the process of making love to myself," upon which Jardine comments, "The desire to be both woman and spirit . . . may be the only way to avoid becoming the *object* of the *Other's* (female's) desire" (Jardine, *Gynesis,* 98–99). The text discussed above in this chapter makes eminently clear that something like the exact opposite (desire to be desired by the female Other) is at least partly what is at stake in rabbinic self-femminization.

had belonged, remained an important part of Christian male self-construction, but it could no longer accommodate such resistance through figurations of female "achievement" of maleness. Gender hierarchy now had to be preserved, but not at the cost of reinstating an ideal of invasive phallic maleness. The point was to "sublimate" it; subjugation was to be retained but without violence. It is not, then, primarily female virginity that is the issue but male renunciation of sexuality (figured through the lions' "example") that becomes crucial, because it is only by renouncing sexuality entirely that *male* sexuality, understood as "naturally" violent, just as the Romans had read it, can be gotten rid of or sublimated. The female virgin still remained a highly charged symbol, owing to her subversions of sexuality, but she functioned now most readily as an example for the male ascetic, as *virgo*, not *virago*. She is no longer a figure for the viraginized female but rather for the feminized male, the male who upon perceiving her, like the lion, is inspired to—which is not to say that he achieves—a complete renunciation of his "naturally" violent, leonine, male sexuality.

The Talmud also uses the rapacity of a hungry lion to represent male sexuality. But in contrast to at least this Christian text, the lion is not male sexuality *tout court* but a particular social and individual configuration of male desire, one that can and must be denied, without, however, giving up sexuality entirely and becoming celibate.[69] Jewish culture, then, contrary to its current reputation, may have something rich and utopian to offer present-day feminist projects that undertake the reconstruction of male subjectivity.[70]

MASOCHISM AND FECUNDITY

In contrast to Christian representations, the rabbinic masochists represented in the story here are clearly not celibate. The story is embedded

69. Rabbi Me'ir used to say: "One who marries his daughter to an ignorant man, it is as if he tied her up and placed her before a lion. Just as a lion kills and eats and has no shame, so an ignorant man hits and has intercourse and has no shame" [Pesahim 49b].

70. Because I know how easy it is to misconstrue the politics of such comparative study, let me repeat once more what my intention is. I am not trying to portray rabbinic Judaism as feminist and as "triumphing over hopeless misogynist Helleno-Christianity" (pace Burton Visotsky) but trying to indicate ways in which talmudic, rabbinic culture has some theoretical, political contribution to make to both common and culturally specific projects of social change. At the same time, I am convinced that Christianity (and other cultures as well) have vital contributions to make to the reconstruction of Jewish culture in our time (see my *Radical Jew*). Obliterating the differences between cultures erases their power to provide mutual cultural critique.

in a context in which it is the rabbis' conjugal lives that are the issue, and they are represented in the larger context as having children. Indeed, the issue of progeny is the central theme of the text.[71] If it were not already marked enough, the fact that Rabbi undertakes his masochistic passage in order to win the heart and hand of a woman makes this painfully clear. All this suggests to me that refusal of the phallus—even this may be granting too much "realness" to the phallus—does not necessarily entail giving up the penis; it is not equivalent to castration in Jewish culture.[72] We find this brought out explicitly in another text of the Babylonian Talmud which deals with the issue of voluntary suffering:

> Rava said [and some say it was Rav Ḥisda]: If a man sees that physical suffering is coming upon him, let him examine his ways, as it says, "We will examine our ways, and research them, and repent unto the Lord" [Lamentations 3:40]. If he examines but finds no [fault], then he should assume it is because of slackness in the study of Torah, for it says, "Blessed is the person whom God makes suffer and to whom He teaches Torah" [Psalms 94:12]. But if he assumes so, but cannot discover any slackness in the study of Torah, then it is known that these are the sufferings of love, as it says, "He whom God loves, He will chastise" [Proverbs 3:12]. Rava said that Rav Seḥora said that Rav Huna said: Anyone whom God desires, He will cause him physical sufferings, as it says, "[Whom] God desires—disease oppresses!" [Isaiah 53:10]. It could be even if he did not receive them [the pains] lovingly, but it says, "And if he makes himself a sin-offering" [Isaiah 53:10]—just as the sin-offering is brought willingly, so the sufferings must be willing. *But if he accepted them [lovingly], then what is his reward? "He will see offspring and live a long life" [Isaiah 53:10]*, and not only this, but his studies of Torah will succeed, for it says, "He whom God desires, he will cause to succeed" [Isaiah 53:10] [Babylonian Talmud, Berakhot 8a].

The ascetic, or living martyr, who lovingly accepts the pains, even devastating ones, that God *in His desire and love* causes the loved object, what is his reward? The supremely noncelibate satisfactions of fa-

---

71. D. Boyarin, "Great Fat Massacre."
72. To put a point on this, as it were, I argue that the Roman horror of Jewish circumcision derives from the inability to distinguish between the penis and the phallus, such that circumcision becomes—explicitly—merged with castration! The point has been frequently made by scholars that the Roman prohibition on circumcision was not directed against the Jewish practice per se (indeed at one point Jews were exempted from the prohibition) but that circumcision and castration were understood as identical under the Roman *Lex Cornelia de sicariis* (Schürer, *History*). This conflation has had inordinate tenaciousness in our cultural history as well.

therhood. In other words, the very representation of fatherhood inscribed and valorized within rabbinic Judaism (at least within this
strand) is explicitly figured as embodied in the way that motherhood is
embodied, and the male body is apprehended as just as physically physical as the female one, in contrast to the recurrent, almost endemic
theme of Western representations in which—to quote Butler—the male
body is written as "as a disembodied universality and the feminine
get[s] constructed as a disavowed corporeality."[73] We see here then a
psychocultural pattern different from the one that issued in what Reik
calls Christian masochism.[74] Whatever the mechanisms are that produce this Jewish cultural pattern, they are not apparently connected
with a disavowal of the sexually reproductive body.

This text not only supports the previous interpretation of talmudic
masochism, it provides an important dimension that the earlier text
was lacking. The psychic structure that I have hypothesized as underlying "feminine" masochism is male mimesis of the "female" position,
owing to birth envy and a genuinely subversive (if ambivalent) relation
to phallic power. Observing the specifics of the descriptions of the pain
in the talmudic stories, I have, of course very tentatively, suggested as
well that the desire for pain involves a form of couvade, an acting out
of birth pains themselves. The last-cited text enables me to add another
dimension, however. Desire for pain need not be explicable in only one

73. Butler, *Gender*, 12. I thus directly disagree with Paul Smith, who, like Robin
Morgan, sees ultimately only recuperation of male power in masochism: "Male masochism might, finally, be seen as another way for the male subject to temporarily challenge
his desire for the father and to subvert the phallic law, and as ultimately another step in
the way (might one even say the puerile way?) of guaranteeing the male subject to be the
origin of the production of meanings. Indeed, it might be said that male masochism is a
kind of laboratory for experimenting with those meanings to which ultimately we accede.
The rules of masochism are, then, primarily metaphorical, and the game is a game played
out unquestioningly in the thrall of the symbolic; crucially, the lessons of masochism do
not last, they come and are gone, forgotten as part of the subject's history of struggle in
learning how to triumphantly reach symbolic empowerment. Masochism, grasped in this
way, would be a closed space where masculinity sets the terms and expounds the conditions of a kind of struggle with itself—not a struggle necessarily for closure, but a struggle
to maintain in a pleasurable tension the stages of a symbolic relation to the father—*a
struggle in which, ironically, the body becomes forgotten*" ("Eastwood," 91 [emphasis
added]). Further along, on p. 95, Smith produces what I take to be a much more nuanced
account, in which even Clint Eastwood's later films "are not, ultimately, moves that will
encourage any radically new male subjectivities, but written across them, in the shape of
Eastwood's hysterical body, are the silent signs of what might best be described as a coming out."
74. It is certainly not insignificant that the rabbinic proof-text repeatedly cited here
is Isaiah 53, in Christian tradition is interpreted as referring to the sufferings of Jesus.

way. As Dr. Ruth Stein has remarked to me, the psychoanalytic experience affords evidence of "conspicuous, painful and abhorrent personal
experiences generative of what later becomes a masochistic personality." Even more to the point, she observes "the abuse, humiliation, de-
spair, and the terrible no-exit dependency on a powerful, malevolent or
opaque other."[75]

We discover this element here at the psychosocial level, where God
has apparently sent suffering without cause, that is, we find here such a
no-exit dependency on an opaque Other, and the response is—as in
clinical masochism—eroticization of the pain itself. Without denying in
any way the clinical reality of certain pathological kinds of masochism—in the sense that the people who inhabit them are miserably
unhappy—I would not want to discount the pragmatic evidence for
"happy" masochism as well,[76] for an orientation to bodily pain that
works to disintegrate phallic mastery and configure a different kind of
masculinity with a different orientation toward power and nurturance.
The difference, finally, between a Lacanian account and mine would be
the difference between a subjectivity that knows of its heterogeneousness but still conceives of it as lack and a male subjectivity that knows
of its heterogeneousness and summons it, symbolized in our talmudic
text by the summoning of that which penetrates the body—that is the
difference between a translation of Daniel Schreber's *Entmannung* as
"castration" (Freud) or as femminization (see chapter 5 below)! We
come closer and closer to Leo Bersani here.

This eroticized pain is expressly thematized in yet another place in
the Talmud, where it is given the explicit name, "the sufferings of love."
Jessica Benjamin remarks that "current psychoanalytic theory appreci-
ates that pain is a route to pleasure only when it involves submission to
an idealized figure."[77] Here we have a literal rendition of this thesis, for
the *already existing* pain is transformed into pleasure through interpreting it and experiencing it as submission to an idealized figure. Thus if
"anyone whom God desires, He will cause them physical sufferings,"
then it follows that anyone to whom God causes physical sufferings, He
desires.[78] This is yet another aspect of masochism as identification with

75. Stein, letter; cf. Brennan, *Interpretation*, 197.
76. Bersani, "Foucault."
77. Benjamin, *Bonds*, 60–61.
78. I think that this interpretation (and thus this text) provides strong support for
Freud's contention that "the erotization of pain allows a sense of mastery by converting

the Mother, as the one who seeks and finds recognition through the Father.[79] We thus see the mimesis of the "feminine" doubled and over-determined. On one hand, it is an acting out of couvade, of desire to bear the father's baby, and on the other, a more general psychosocial demand for recognition from the Father.[80] Thus, according to my speculation, we have two sources for the eroticization of pain which converge in a mimesis of femininity: identification with the mother and desire to bear the father's child and a mimetic, painful enactment of childbirth; and an acting out of "female" demand for recognition from the male Other, God, once more through an acceptance of, even a desire for, pain.

In this respect therefore Christian and Jewish masochism are very similar, even identical. The point of the cultural specificity of Christian masochism and of its relation to the phallus can, however, be seen further in a subtle comparison of Jewish and early Christian martyrologies. The rabbinic discourse of martyrdom itself shares many of the features of the Christian discourse, including willingness, even eagerness, to die for love of God. One might, indeed, in both cases refer to the discourse of martyrdom as an eroticization of pain and death. That is to say, at one level—shall we call it the psychoanalytic?—masochistic behavior in the individual and in cultural representations is "about" gender, but at another level it also has particular political and social functions that are inflected from culture to culture.[81]

At this level, there is an enormous difference between Jewish and early Christian martyrologies. The Jewish martyrs, of which Rabbi Akiva is the ideal type,[82] are all within the paternal order. Every single one of them was married and a parent. According to the tradition, Rabbi Akiva, the paradigm, undergoes his martyrdom at the age of 101, that is, he is the sort of prototype of the sufferer rewarded with progeny and long life. All of this suggests a different relationship between asceticism-martyrdom—understood under the sign of masochism—and the phallus.

---

pain into pleasure," against Benjamin's puzzling assertion that "this is true only for the master" (*Bonds*, 61).

79. Lacoue-Labarthe and Nancy, "Unconscious," 196.
80. Benjamin, *Bonds*, 60.
81. It is fascinating to compare here the Roman practice of the *devotio*, described in Barton, *Sorrows*, 40–46.
82. D. Boyarin, "Language."

These rabbinic male ideals, then, provide a representation of a third term, the bodied penis that mediates between the plenitude and lack, a "good enough" father who needs not have the phallus in order not to be castrated. The metaphor of the stick/ax used by Rabbi Elʿazar's wife is seemingly a phallic image par excellence, and, of course, it cannot be denied that there is one aspect of the phallus that is retained here, namely, its use as an image of penetration.[83] However, in this context, where that which renders the ax so effective and desirable is the drastic pain and disease that the rabbi has taken on himself, this is hardly a representation of the unimpaired and unimpairable bodily envelope, of the coherence and plenitude that the phallus is taken to mean. Two things that ought not to be combinable have conjoined in the figures of these rabbis; on one hand a male subjectivity that refuses the dominant fiction, that refuses, if you will, to be a representation of wholeness, coherence, and impenetrability; on the other, sexual and procreative competence. These men have no phallus, but their penises remain intact. It is this structure that I am referring to as Jewish masochism.[84]

It is impossible of course to ignore a dark and sinister moment in this text. I have already spoken of the paternal function simply absorbing the maternal one. We do not have, therefore, in this "couvade" a pure celebration of femaleness, not by any means, but rather an attempt (as

83. It is, however, striking that it is explicitly marked in the text as belonging to *them,* that is, the rival Palestinians. There are other texts in the Babylonian Talmud as well that mark the Palestinians as supermales, vis-à-vis "us," the Babylonians.

84. As in other related issues, in his discussion of "male masochism" Freud more faithfully represents the "Christian" sensibility than the rabbinic one. Thus for him, masochism is a frustration of procreative instincts (Freud, "Economic," 161–62; see also Siegel, *Male,* 53–54, for an illuminating discussion and critique of the assumption by many critics that masochism is incompatible with a male role as husband and father.). As Siegel emphasizes, Freud himself was well aware that masochistic performance could be foreplay for penile-vaginal intercourse with ejaculation and thus was not "actually" incompatible with biological fatherhood. It is the symbolic dimension, therefore, of feminization that Freud (and Western culture in general) have understood as sterilizing for men. In order to impregnate, a man must perform in a manly fashion, that is, be physical, aggressive, and active, the opposite of a masochistic "feminizing" performance. Siegel makes clear that for Freud, as for much of the theory of male sexuality which the "dominant European fiction" produced, sadism is merely a minor exaggeration of what is normal and gender syntonic for men anyway (55): it is masochism—male submissiveness and receptivity— that is perverse and incompatible with the normal sexual functioning of men. From this source stems one line of representations of Jewish men as sexually inadequate, impotent, and sterile (the other line, of course, reads them as the exact opposite, that is, as hyper-sexed predators of Christian females). Out of sheer pleasure, I cannot refrain from quoting Siegel's deliciously wicked account of sexologists' offering "analyses of male masochism in order to help men like Savarin/Sacher-Masoch overcome 'compulsions' to behave in ways that the analysts themselves would prefer not to" (57).

in most forms of couvade) to appropriate and control completely the reproductive function. Envy always has the potential for grave violence toward the envied person, and womb envy is no exception. I very tentatively suggest that it is the motivating force for much of the violent practice toward women in general, that is, cross-culturally. In effect, in this text, at the moment in which procreation is arrogated by the House of Study with the birth of sixty boys owing, as it were, to the activity of Torah, the text and culture seem to be straining for an all-male parthenogenetic ideal, one that would simply erase women.[85] This is thematized in two ways: by the very locus of the annunciation to these women that they will become pregnant (of course, I do not mean to deny that their pregnancies will take place in the "natural" fashion) and by the insistence that a whole generation of children born will all be male.

This theme is carried out as well in the implicit contrast between the blood that the Rabbi sheds which is, as we have seen, a symbolic female blood and the blood that he controls through the ritual of the blood examination to determine the "purity" of the women.[86] The latter is the realm of Torah, as opposed to the realm of "deeds." We seem to have, then, a representation and celebration of the all-male world of Torah in which women function only as necessary biological instruments to produce more men. The creation and maintenance of such homosocial communities produced practices (or at any rate discourses) of erasure of female desire and even cruelty toward women, as has been well documented by feminist critics and as will be brought more clearly into focus in the next two chapters.

The point that is often missed in critical analyses of the material is that the Talmud itself is self-critical with regard to these practices.[87] The world of the House of Study is presented in this text as a place of danger and competition. The Rabbi's wife does not want him to go back because she fears danger to her husband there. Moreover, much of the narrative context deals with the jealousies and rivalries of the House of

85. Cf. the material cited in Showalter (*Sexual Anarchy*, 77–78), but, once more, keep in mind the enormous caveat that the men of whom she speaks (late Victorian Englishmen) all believed in celibacy as an ideal.

86. Fonrobert engages this practice and associated discourses in the Talmud from a critical feminist and anthropological perspective (*Women's*).

87. Cf. also chapter 3 for a similar structure of self-critique built into a "utopian" text.

Study, and in one passage such rivalries even have deadly effect.[88] I think, therefore, that here the text itself exposes us to the dark side of its own, valued homosociality, that the text itself indicates the violence and distortions of the community in which "all the children are boys," and it proposes a version of masochism, of mimesis of femaleness, that will be not only an appropriation of the female but an attempt to celebrate female/maternal, nonviolent behavior and thus approach an "antiphallic" masculinity, one that incorporates "femaleness" without stealing it.

Nicole Loraux has remarked similar moments in Greek culture: "The Greek male dreams of the penetrating pain (*odunē*), of the rending of labor (*ōdis*), and not simply, as has been said and as I myself have argued, in order to 'dispense with women in the bearing of children'—unless it is understood that one dispenses with women only to incorporate their femininity. . . . In the same way, the *anēr* [man] adopts maternal qualities." I would go further with reference to the particular Jewish culture that I am studying and insist that there is no fantasy of dispensing with women implied at all, but only of an incorporation of femininity. Moreover, this femininity is one that does not serve to "increase their [men's] virility to its highest pitch" because "childbirth, not war, is the cause of the most intense pain,"[89] but rather because of the moral transformations that such pain and pity (symbolized here by Rabbi's newly won compassion for the infant rats) were understood to confer. Virility itself takes on a different cast here. The text clearly indicates (perhaps more openly than any other in the Talmud) what it expects the motivators of female desire to be: valor in the study of Torah and in lust for pain. The desiring male, Rabbi Yehuda, simply sets off to meet the woman's criteria of desirability, not to reform them.

About a similar moment in the cultural production of fin de siècle Europe, Siegel has remarked: "*Ulysses* appeared at a crucial historical moment when the homophobia which, as Eve Kosofsky Sedgwick has shown, had been increasingly deployed in literary, legal, and medical texts to regulate all relations between men was extended, by pseudoscientific psychological theorizing, to radically constrict possibilities in men's romantic [*sic*] relations with women, as well. Allied with Ellis and against Ellis's precursor Krafft-Ebing and his successor Freud,

88. Cf. again chapter 3.
89. Loraux, *Experiences*, 12.

Joyce offers an alternative reading of the male masochist as a man well suited to act heterosexually, marry, beget and raise children. Idealizing male masochism on these grounds is hardly synonymous with championing the cause of women's liberation. Still it creates a model for marriage that offers women more space to voice their own concerns than exists in the male-dominated marriage that psychoanalytic theory would describe as healthier and more normal. And it challenges psychoanalysis's implicit categorization of gentle, yielding husbands as gynophobic latent homosexuals."[90] Is it possible that rabbinic culture, about the actual living practice of which we know next to nothing, enacted this model of marriage, a "reading of the male masochist as a man well suited to act heterosexually, marry, beget and raise children" and not the male-dominant one that its current reputation would suggest? After all, as Rav Papa remarked in the fourth century: "If your wife is short, bend down and whisper to her" (Baba Metsiaᶜ 59a)?! Arnold Cooper has written that "all cultures value most those achievements that are fired in pain. . . . The hero is someone who has suffered."[91] Following this logic, one concludes that nurturing is an achievement most valued by talmudic culture and that rabbinic culture as well challenges (some of) psychoanalysis's implicit categorization of gentle, yielding husbands as "latent homosexuals" and inadequate men.

A reading of the end of the story will help, perhaps, to bring this conformation into better focus. Rabbi Yehuda in this tale is Rabbi Yehuda the Prince, the political leader of Palestinian Jewry and a good friend (according to legend) of the Roman emperor, Antoninus. It is this man, the most powerful Jew in Palestine, who has to undergo decades of humiliating disease and pain to learn how to be a real man, that is, to have compassion for baby rats. It is impossible to read his masochism, then, as a form of political resistance in quite the fashion that Christians' or Girondins' martyrdom has been read.[92] What then is the

90. Siegel, *Male,* 76. As Nancy Chodorow has recently argued, in much of psychoanalytic theory "heterosexual erotism" is explained "by embedding it in male dominance—and in so doing implicates in normal heterosexuality not just gender but gender inequality as well. Heterosexuality either definitionally requires and means acceptance of such inequality, or it developmentally seems to entail such dominance and submission" (Chodorow, *Femininities,* 51). We must recognize, however (as Chodorow does), the existence of other psychoanalytic models as well. For Silverman, masochism is always about defeating the paternal order (*Male,* 211). See also Smith, "Eastwood," 87, for a somewhat different account of the relationship of masochism to paternity.

91. Cooper, "Masochism," quoted in Siegel, *Male,* 33.

92. Sacher-Masoch, "Venus," 212.

purpose of his pain? Both the context of the story and the details suggest that it is not political resistance at stake here but cultural resistance. A way, then, is suggested for drawing together the two themes of
Jewish masochism that I have been speculating about. The general problem of (male) masochism is how to be a man. In a cultural world in
which masculinity is associated with the phallus, the question becomes:
What is a male who has no phallus? Is he a woman or a eunuch? The
answers that the text offers refuse in a sense both options by suggesting
that the nonphallic male, the male who individually or culturally resists
or renounces the myth of bodily coherence, power, singularity, and un-
impairability symbolized by the phallus can nevertheless be a good-
enough male, good enough, that is, to be a father. Indeed, such renunciation is demanded by this culture in its representation of ideal
masculinity.

This structure is doubled as well in the story of Rabbi Elʿazar that
has been discussed at length above. The result of his actions, condemned within the text by Rabbi Yehoshua the Bald, is the death of an
apparently innocent man. Although the text retrieves Rabbi Elʿazar's
own innocence by emphasizing that the executed laundryman was not
so innocent himself, nevertheless Rabbi Elʿazar is seized with guilt for
his violent behavior. The very recovery of innocence here is problematic, because it leaves Rabbi Elʿazar in collaboration with the "phallic"
Roman authority. The story virtually guarantees, as Thomas Luxon has
pointed out to me,[93] that his intuition serves the Romans without running explicitly counter to the halakha, and indeed the condemned
behavior of the laundryman is itself doubly coded. It is formally an
egregious violation of halakha, but it is also intensely phallic in its content—after all, why not have the laundryman eating pork on Yom Kippur, rather than engaging in what is effectively a father-son "gang
bang"? We end up with a spectrum of behavior in which the laundryman is closer than the Rabbi to the condemned phallic extreme, but the
latter, because of his association with "Roman" power, is not free of
contamination either. While Rabbi Elʿazar stays just this side of the
halakha, he nevertheless has behaved, in his own eyes according to
the text, in an inadmissible fashion through his service to Roman
power.

The punishment that he takes on himself is first of all the painful

93. Luxon, letter.

operation of having basketfuls of fat removed from his stomach—another grotesque violation of the envelope of the body and perhaps also a symbolic representation of childbirth—and then the acceptance of the painful disease that involved the bleeding discussed above. We find, doubled, therefore, the relationship between masochism as punishment and masochism as the acting out of birth envy that we have already seen in the story of Rabbi. Because the fault is read as phallic, as behaving in the fashion of and in collaboration with "Roman" masculinity, its redemption is antiphallic. *Entmannung*, as in the case of Daniel Schreber,[94] is both a loss of the posture of maleness ("castration") as well as achievement and appropriation of the status of femaleness.

This feature finally provides us with an opportunity to understand the culturally distinct connection between the "feminine" masochism of these rabbinic texts and the dimension of "moral" masochism involved in them as well. If the desire to be female, to be fecund and nutritive, is *not* symbolized as a castration, simply because masculinity is not symbolized as the phallus in the sense of plenitude and perfection, then the appropriation or incorporation of "maternal" characteristics is not a loss of the male capability to generate. Both the word for love in Aramaic and the word for mercy in Hebrew are identical in root with the word for womb: רחם. Without the phallus, birth envy need not turn into repudiation of femininity but can be its opposite. If you wish a womb, the text seems to suggest, become loving and merciful.[95] Rabbi is taught here twice. He learns that the suffering male is desirable, to women and to God, and that therefore bodily pain—impairment—is to be desired by the male. If he begins as the arrogant phallic ruler who tells the calf that she is to die because that is her destiny, in the end he has learned to have compassion on the infant rats; you don't have to be a Mother (i.e., a woman) in order to be "maternal."[96]

94. Geller, "Unmanning."

95. This figure should be carefully compared to the patterns of Greek tragic drama within which, according to Froma Zeitlin, the "playing of the other," that is, the enactment by men of female roles, enables the male citizen to open himself "to the often banished emotions of terror and pity" ("Playing," 80).

96. Benjamin, *Bonds*, 172; for Roman culture, see C. Edwards, *Politics*, 79–80. Cf. on this Burrus, "Fecund," and see also P. C. Miller, "Devil's," 54. An interesting point is made by Sarah Caldwell who argues that "in metaphorical ritual expressions of the birth process, it is *power* and ultimate responsibility for life, far more than cooperation and nurturing, which most capture the male imagination and fire envy, and least engage the interest of women" (*Begotten*, 9). I would suggest that at least this particular text is an

As Bersani shows, surprisingly, "MacKinnon, Dworkin, and Foucault are all saying that a man lying on top of a woman assumes that
what excites her is the idea of her body being invaded by a phallic master."[97] Assuming that this claim is true, what is the ethical meaning of
a man becoming excited through the mimesis and appropriation of that
which he assumes (and the assumption is presumably fallacious) to be
the situation of excitement and pleasure of women? Christine Delphy
has claimed: "The relationships which exist between men and women
are *power* relationships, and no understanding of gender, sexuality or
sexual orientation can be divorced from this for an instant. To 'revalue'
femininity within our existing society is therefore to celebrate masochism."[98] If this claim is true, then does it not make sense that masochism *for men* involves, at least potentially, an upsetting of those power
relationships, as for example in the case of Daniel Schreber? On one
hand, it is clear that he is just acting out a male fantasy of femaleness
and one, moreover, that has served in various ways to oppress women.
But on the other hand, by taking that position on himself, he is at the
same time subverting the seemingly natural associations between maleness and being on top, being a top together, at least potentially, with the
privileges of domination and violence that attend on such topness. "If
Schreber could not step into his father's shoes," John O'Neill remarks,
"it was because the father trampled upon his little children; not because
Schreber is pleading for another beating."[99]

---

exception to this general rule. In other words, I submit that *sometimes* couvade may represent a desire to have what women have *without* taking it away from women. Interestingly enough, rabbinic (and even biblical) culture, contrary to one's immediate assumption, are characterized by an absence of male puberty initiatory ritual. And as Caldwell
would suggest (15), such rituals are characteristic of "phallic" cultures, as opposed to
"couvade" cultures. Circumcision has been removed to infancy with a concomitantly entirely different set of meanings, certainly in the psychoanalytic context, since the child is
not physically removed from the mother at that time, and the *Bar Mitzva* is, of course, a
much later historical development. Moreover, following Caldwell's typologies, it is cultures within which the child is entirely with the mother in early childhood and separated
from the father—with sexual taboos between the parents of a year or more after childbirth—that lead to "hypermasculine" cultures (15), and Judaism—neither biblical nor
talmudic—would not conform to that picture. In contrast to the generally held image, in
Jewish culture the Father God is as likely to be *Tate,* "Daddy," *Abba* (cf. Gal. 3), the
loving intimate father, as the punishing castrating one. Other aspects of Jewish culture
conform obviously to the phallic type, suggesting the need for a more nuanced continuum
taxonomy rather than a binary opposition.

97. Bersani, "Is," 214.
98. Leonard, "Preface," in Delphy, *Close,* 5.
99. O'Neill, "Law," 245.

Let me make perfectly clear that I am not speaking of the putative "terrible burden of masculinity," which is relieved through mimesis of a male fantasy of the feminine, but of a genuinely subversive and renunciatory resistance to male dominance, violence, and privilege for moral reasons, because I do not want to be that kind of a human being. I am, in John Stoltenberg's memorable formulation, refusing to be a man.[100] Even if this "refusal" be the acting out of a male fantasy of femaleness and thus both appropriative and oppressive of women in some ways, it may yet be "good for women" in ways that we have not yet even begun to imagine.

Self-psychologist Heinz Kohut is perhaps the only one within the psychoanalytic tradition who would be in full sympathy with this project:

> I do not believe that the castration threat (the male's repudiation of passivity vis-à-vis another male; the female's repudiation of her femininity) is the bedrock beyond which analysis cannot penetrate. The bedrock is a threat that to my mind is more serious than the threat to physical survival and to the penis and to male dominance: it is the threat of the destruction of the nuclear self. . . . If the self-objects' selective responses have not laid down the *usual* nuclear self in the boy or girl, but have led to the acquisition of nuclear ambitions and ideals that are not characterized by the primacy of phallic-exhibitionistic physical survival and triumphant active dominance, then even death and martyred passivity can be tolerated with a glow of fulfillment. And, in the reverse, survival and social dominance can be bought at the price of the abandonment of the core of the self and lead, despite seeming victory, to a sense of meaninglessness and despair.[101]

There is however a problem even here. The problem is the "usual" one. Is Kohut's "usual" statistical or normative, and if the former, is it ahistorical or culture specific? Even the enormously expansive Kohut—and even at the point where he is being expansive—falls prey perhaps to a discourse of the transhistorical normative. Is it possible that the usual is, in fact, unusual and that phallic exhibition and triumphant active dominance are not the données of a usual subjectivity? Finally it seems that there is an enormous gap between all of these European versions of dephallicized masculinity and Jewish masochism in that they all represent a loss of self as well. That is to say, I think that selfhood

100. Stoltenberg, *Refusing.*
101. Kohut, *Restoration,* 117 (emphasis added).

or subjectivity itself has been so thoroughly identified with the masculine within the European imaginary that renunciation of the phallus can be imagined only as loss of self, as Georges Bataille claims in his *Eroticism*. In the rabbinic tradition the incoherence of the project of masculinity is recognized, summoned, perhaps even enjoyed—and not correlated with loss of self or even with loss of maleness.

RESISTING THE DOMINANT FICTION; OR, IS THE VAGINA A GRAVE?

For Kaja Silverman, "history" is the trauma that temporarily disrupts the phallic imaginary. I would rather treat "history" as the set of processes that produces the phallus as a defense against male envy, as a form of couvade. The material analyzed here suggests that there are cultural formations wherein masculinity itself is not identified with the phallus.[102] If my hypothesis—namely, that the phallus itself is a defense mechanism against male envy of femaleness—has any explanatory value, it would predict that there would be cultures that enact (and defend against) this envy differently and that do not, therefore, "need" the phallus, allowing the female body to take up directly (and not by reversed privation) its function of signifying sexual difference. While this may indeed not be any "better for women," as Marianne Hirsch has ruefully remarked to me, it does involve a very different configuration of gender and set of performances of gender.

If nothing else, the way, it seems, that our talmudic story valorizes male envy of femaleness is by, in effect, exhorting men to be more like women, specifically by taking on nurturing functions and behaviors. The whole point of these stories would seem then to be to provide an alternative masculinity to the dominant fiction that the Romans were busily imposing all over the Mediterranean region and the rest of Europe, an alternative masculinity not unlike the Christian alternative ideal of the gentle, humble, compassionate, "maternal" male.[103] Christian culture, however, ascribed such qualities to celibates in contrast to

---

102. Silverman could, of course, argue that these were examples rather of traumatized male subjects in the kind of historical crisis that temporarily disrupts the phallic relation, that is, to accept the prevailing "Zionist" reading of Jewish Diaspora culture as pathological, owing to the "unmanliness" of Diaspora Jewish men. Given her (gender) politics, however, I hardly think that she would wish to promulgate such a view.

103. Bynum, *Jesus*.

the other masculine models of hero and warrior. Talmudic culture, by refusing the phallus myth, made possible the production of another type of dominant fiction and thus another kind of male subjectivity. Bersani has written with his characteristic thoughtfulness, "I want . . . to argue that a gravely dysfunctional aspect of what is, after all, the healthy pleasure we take in the operation of a coordinated and strong physical organism is the temptation to deny the perhaps equally strong appeal of powerlessness, of the loss of control. Phallocentrism is exactly that: not primarily the denial of power to women (although it has obviously also led to that, everywhere and at all times), but above all the denial of the *value* of powerlessness in both men and women. I don't mean the value of gentleness, or nonaggressiveness, or even of passivity, but rather of a more radical disintegration and humiliation of the self."[104] As the Talmud charges its predominantly male readers: "The heart of the matter is: Be one of the persecuted and not one of the persecutors; one of the insulted and not the insultors" (Bava Kamma 93a and passim)—a signally "unmanly" sentiment. And even more explicitly it states: "Our Rabbis have taught: The insulted who do not insult in return; those who hear their dishonor and do not answer; those who perform with love and are joyful with pain, of these the verse says 'His lovers are like the rising of the sun in its heroism' (Judges 5:31)" (Yoma 23a). This admonition is one of the most frequently quoted in all of later Jewish ethical literature, and it deliberately reverses the definition of heroism that the dominant fiction would recognize.

In a recent collection of traditional "ethical wills," testaments that Jewish men (and sometimes women) left for their children enjoining behavior and practices, we find this maxim cited frequently in these documents from nineteenth-century Europe. The author of the second cited of these wills, Benjamin Roth (1854, Hechenberg, Württemburg), moreover explicitly enjoins a "feminine" ideal and model for his sons: "Be meek and patient, and seek to acquire the character and patience of your mother. Through many years of continual suffering and pain she showed herself, in this manner, to be a true angel of patience. Be, as she was, forgiving when injustice or misfortune seeks you out; and strive in this to emulate your all-forgiving God."[105] Such appropriation of "female" ideals and models *for men* is by no means disingenuous nor

104. Bersani, "Is," 23, 217.
105. Riemer and Stampfer, *So That Your Values*, 10, 22, 28.

misogynist in impulse, as it is when imposed on women. At the same time, as already has been observed, it is also by no means altogether good for "real" women and sometimes distinctly rotten for them. Unpacking and bearing out this observation will form the burden of the next two chapters.

CHAPTER III

Rabbis and Their Pals

Rabbinic Homosociality and the Lives of Women

That famous school of fighting... where athletes dispute
Best in Babylon...
Did their intellectual tilting.[1]   —Heinrich Heine

Although the Talmud imagines an alternative to phallic, aggressive, machismo as a definition of manliness, it seems aware (at times) of the deeply flawed character of its own ideals, practices, and institutions, including, strikingly enough, the evils of the erasure of female agency, desire, and subjectivity from its homotopic world of Torah study. The text that I will read in this chapter presents a Rabbi who had been like "Romans" but became a "proper" Jewish man, a Rabbi. Since the end of the story is tragic, however, and violent, we see that at the same moment that the narrative presents the rabbinic male ideal it contests its own presentation and questions the validity of its own ideals:

> One day, Rabbi Yoḥanan was bathing in the Jordan. Resh Lakish saw him and thought he was a woman. He crossed the Jordan after him by placing his lance in the Jordan and vaulting to the other side. When Rabbi Yoḥanan saw Rabbi Shimᶜon the son of Lakish [Resh Lakish], he said to him, "Your strength for Torah!" He replied, "Your beauty for women!" He said to him, "If you repent, I will give you my sister who is more beautiful than I am." [Resh Lakish] agreed. [Resh Lakish] wanted to cross back to take his clothes but he couldn't. [Rabbi Yoḥanan] taught [Resh Lakish] Mishna and Talmud and made him into a great man.
>
> Once they were disputing in the Study-House: "The sword and the lance and the dagger, from whence can they become impure?"[2] Rabbi Yoḥanan

1. Heinrich Heine, quoted in Cantor, *Jewish Women*, 92.
2. Raw materials are not subject to ritual impurity, but finished implements or vessels are. The question, then, that this text asks is: what constitutes the completion of production for these various weapons?

said, "From the time they are forged in the fire." Resh Lakish said, "From the time they are polished in the water." Rabbi Yoḥanan said, "A brigand is an expert in brigandry" [i.e., sarcastically: You should know of what you speak; after all, weapons are your métier]. [Resh Lakish] said to [Rabbi Yoḥanan], "What have you profited me? There they called me Rabbi and here they call me Rabbi!" [Rabbi Yoḥanan] became angry, and Resh Lakish became ill [owing to a curse put on him by Rabbi Yoḥanan]. His sister [Rabbi Yoḥanan's sister; Resh Lakish's wife] came to him [Rabbi Yoḥanan] and cried before him. She said, "Look at me!" He did not pay attention to her. "Look at the orphans!" He said to her, "Leave your orphans, I will give life" (Jeremiah 49:11). "For the sake of my widowhood!" He said, "Place your widows' trust in me" (loc. cit.). Resh Lakish died, and Rabbi Yoḥanan was greatly mournful over him. The Rabbis said, "What can we do to comfort him? Let us bring Rabbi Elᶜazar the son of Padat whose traditions are brilliant, and put him before [Rabbi Yoḥanan]." They brought Rabbi Elᶜazar the son of Padat and put him before him. Every point that he would make, he said, "there is a tradition which supports you." [Rabbi Yoḥanan] said, "Do I need this one?! The son of Lakish used to raise twenty-four objections to every point that I made, and I used to supply twenty-four refutations, until the matter became completely clear, and all you can say is that there is a tradition which supports me?! Don't I already know that I say good things?" He used to go and cry out at the gates, "Son of Lakish, where are you?" until he became mad. The Rabbis prayed for him and he died [Baba Metsiaᶜ 84a].

I propose to read this legend as a paradigmatic story of the formation of the Jewish male subject and to focus on the issue of male intimacy that it encodes and problematizes especially with respect to its consequences for women.

Resh Lakish, although "ethnically" Jewish, is clearly in the beginning of the narrative stereotyped as a follower of Roman cultural paradigms. The term used to describe him at this stage in his life is *listes* [in Greek, *lêstês*], brigand, but he seems here to have been as much a soldier or gladiator as a thief, and a sexual libertine as well.[3] Indeed, by the

3. For Resh Lakish as a gladiator, see Babylonian Talmud Gittin 47a, where it is related that Resh Lakish sold himself as a gladiator (*ludaʾa* from *ludus*, which means games). An adroit literary use of this tradition can be found in the Palestinian Talmud Kilʾaim 27a. Resh Lakish has delivered himself of the pronouncement: "Everywhere that it says 'according to its kind' [Gen. 1:25–26 and passim], the laws of forbidden mixtures apply." Rav Kahana answers with the reductio ad absurdum that then it would follow that the laws of forbidden mixtures apply to fish as well, which is ridiculous since fish obviously dwell together. Rabbi Yosi the son of Rabbi Bun remarks: "Here Rav Kahana spread his net over Resh Lakish and caught him!" This quip is doubly significant. First of all, since the hook was fish, the fishing metaphor is appropriate, but I think that I am not over-reading if I see here as well a reference to the *retiarius*, the gladiator who fights with a trident and a net and defeats his opponent by throwing the net over his head and im-

time that this story is being told, and in the eastern reaches of the Sassanian Empire *where* it is being told, these figures would probably have been conflated in the cultural imagination into a single image of violent, sexually aggressive masculinity.[4] There is, accordingly, a thematization of rape at the very beginning of the story. Resh Lakish, the quintessential "goy," vaults over the river with clear and aggressive sexual intent. Kathryn Gravdal has recently demonstrated how the semantics of one successor language to Latin, Old French, builds rape into its very definition of masculinity by using as its prime term for rape the "euphemistic" paraphrase, "to force a woman," while otherwise retaining the lexeme "force" as its main defining feature of manliness: "Within this chivalric rubric of admirable strength and heroic efforts appears, also in the late twelfth century, the word *esforcement,* denoting effort, power, military force, bravura, and rape. From the notion of strength, manliness, and bravery, we move to the knight's striving after heroism, and then to the idea of forced coitus. This specifically medieval *glissement* suggests that rape is part of the feudal hegemony, built into the military culture in which force is applauded in most of its forms."[5] The talmudic text, four hundred years earlier than the *Chanson de Roland,* seems to be burlesquing this very Roman(ce) male ideal of force and rape.

Rabbi Yoḥanan, the object of this sexual aggression, is the quintessential symbol of rabbinic Jewish maleness, and he has already been introduced to us within the immediate context in highly erotic or even sexualized imagery as both extravagantly beautiful and androgynous or effeminate in appearance:

> Said Rabbi Yoḥanan, "I have survived from the beautiful of Jerusalem." One who wishes to see the beauty of Rabbi Yoḥanan should bring a brand new silver cup and fill it with the red seeds of the pomegranate and place around its rim a garland of red roses, and let him place it at the place where the sun meets the shade, and that radiance is something like the beauty of Rabbi Yoḥanan.
>
> Is that true?! But haven't we been taught by our master that, "The beauty of Rabbi Kahana is like the beauty of Rabbi Abbahu. The beauty of Rabbi Abbahu is like the beauty of our father Jacob. The beauty of our father Jacob

mobilizing him. For a similar play—with, however, quite different import—on the activity of the *retiarius,* see Wiedemann, *Emperors,* 26.

4. Barton, *Sorrows,* 12–15, 48.

5. Gravdal, *Ravishing,* 3.

is like the beauty of Adam," and that of Rabbi Yoḥanan is not mentioned. *Rabbi Yoḥanan did not have a beard [literally, splendor of face].*[6]

Rabbi Yoḥanan's beauty is described as an almost angelic beauty, a beauty marked however by his effeminate appearance. But he is left off the list of the most beautiful men in history because his face does not bear the mark of "true" masculine beauty, the gray beard of an aged sage.[7] While from the perspective of "Jewish" values Rabbi Yoḥanan's remarked lack of a beard explicitly marks him as less beautiful, it seems also calculated to inscribe him (from the perspective of "Roman" culture) as the appropriate object of Resh Lakish's desire, signified in the text by the explicit statement that Resh Lakish thought that Rabbi Yoḥanan was a woman.[8] Since Rabbi Yoḥanan is arguably one of the two or three most central rabbinic heroes and models within talmudic literature, his presentation as androgynous is highly significant. Here we can locate almost explicit evidence for my claim that certain textual/ideological strands, particularly within the Babylonian Talmud, were at pains to construct their ideal male figures as androgynes or as femminized men.

6. Emphasis added. The derivation of this metaphor is via the verse: "Thou shalt give splendor to the face of an elder" (Lev. 19:32), understood as an injunction to give splendor to one's own face by growing a beard. Gleason points out: "In Clement's view, to depilate one's beard and body while coifing one's head was to announce a preference for unnatural acts. Clement feels entitled to take this reading of the effeminate's body language because the beard is agreed to be the distinctive mark of a man (*to andros to sunthēma*). It serves as a symbol of Adam's superior nature (*sumbolon tēs kreittonos phuseōs*, 19.1). Hairiness in general is the mark of a manly nature (19.3)" (*Making*, 68; the parenthetical references are to chapter and line in Clement's *Paidagogos*). We see from here that the resolution offered by the Talmud, to wit that Rabbi Yoḥanan was not mentioned owing to his lack of a beard, is not as arbitrary as might first appear.

7. In the Roman culture of the second Sophistic as well, the beard was an important positive signifier: "Philosophers, as well as sophists, were interested parties in the struggle, and some of them used the beards that were a traditional component of the philosophical costume to claim high ground" (Gleason, *Making*, 73). Once more, we are reminded of the complexity and multiple ironies of the stereotyping texts of self-fashioning. Gleason is, however, careful to point out the corresponding ambiguities built into Roman culture as well. Thus, "[a]fter all, these mannerisms—from depilation to ingratiating inflections of the voice—were refinements aimed at translating the ideal of beardless ephebic beauty into adult life, and as such might appeal to women and boys" (74). It is easy to see how the tensions and partial self-contradictions of our talmudic text fit into such a cultural matrix.

8. There is a manuscript tradition that leaves out the statement that Resh Lakish interpreted the object of his desire as a female, suggesting that he read him as the appropriate object of a pederastic desire. See Dover, *Greek*, 68–81, for consideration of this issue with respect to differing historical periods of Greek culture. For Roman culture: "Still, the general rule appears to be that the more the boy seems like an adult without development of body hair, the more attractive he is" (Richlin, *Garden*, 37). See also C. Edwards, *Politics*, 69, and Gleason, *Making*, 74 n. 84, for the same point.

After vaulting over the river, leaving his clothes—but not his lance—behind, Resh Lakish is in for a surprise. The nature of the surprise is however left tantalizingly inexplicit, particularly according to the version of the text that does not explicitly claim that Resh Lakish thought he was pursuing a "real" female. The talmudic academy consists of an all-male grouping structured around intensely eroticized relations to the object of study, the Torah imagined as female, and to each other.[9] The sexual meanings of such erotic male-male desire and its relation to learning were, I suggest, no less an issue for the Talmud than they are for Plato's *Symposium*.[10] Our text and its larger context provide us with a reflection on this subject through one of talmudic culture's favorite media for such thinking, the biographical legend. Instead of rabbis thinking, we have a sort of "thinking with rabbis." The questions being considered in this passage have to do with rabbinic, that is, ideal Jewish maleness and its relationship to homosocial desire, to women, and especially to the phallus as a definition of masculinity. I shall suggest that whatever else is going on here, the questions of *philia* and the phallus, and the understanding of "proper" manhood and proper male intimacy and their consequences for women, are central to the text, and that the text is about Jewish collective male self-fashioning in the context of a dominant Greco-Roman culture, a culture which this text projects as its other.

Rabbi Yoḥanan invites Resh Lakish to join him in the fellowship of "real men," those who devote themselves to the service of the female Torah—"Your strength," the virility of the lance with which you vaulted the Jordan, "for Torah." Such manhood is wasted in the pursuit of mere physical sex objects. Resh Lakish in turn answers with the ambiguous, "Your beauty for women."[11] For both characters there is a powerful element of identification and envy in their utterances.[12] By desiring Resh Lakish's strength for Torah, Rabbi Yoḥanan is also expressing desire to have that strength himself. By desiring Rabbi Yoḥanan's

---

9. See also Sedgwick, *Epistemology*, 110, on all-male social spaces and their cultural meanings.

10. See the interesting discussion of Lacan's reading of Plato in Reinhard, "Kant." I hope to develop this comparison in a forthcoming essay.

11. Cf. Dover, *Greek*, 172: "[T]he attributes which made a young male attractive to *erastai* [male lovers] were assumed to make him no less attractive to women; Pentheus, sneering at Dionysos in Eur. *Bacchae*, 453–59, treats his good looks, long hair ('full of desire') and fair skin as particularly captivating to women."

12. For the lineaments of such a conformation, see Sedgwick's stunning reading of *The Beast in the Jungle* (*Epistemology*, 211).

beauty for women, Resh Lakish speaks his envy of that beauty. The envy will remain throughout the story, as we shall yet see. Rabbi Yoḥa-nan's appeal is: Bring that virility to me, share it with me in a love that will be mediated through our erotic attachment to the Torah. For Resh Lakish, initially resisting Rabbi Yoḥanan's invitation, it is: Bring that beauty to me, share it with me in the love that will be mediated through our common pursuit of women. These two possibilities—mediation of male erotics through "female" texts or women—seem to reproduce the twin foundations of a by-now model pattern of homosocial desire.[13]

The narrative has set up two alternative homosocial communities, both having exactly the same erotic economy: an all-male hierarchical society—as we will see, Rabbi Yoḥanan is the dominant male in his, Resh Lakish in his—structured around close male attachments with fe-male figures "between" the men. Rabbi Yoḥanan's next rejoinder to Resh Lakish proves to be disingenuous—at best—as we will immedi-ately see. He says to him: You can have it all, both the spiritual female, the Torah, and an embodied female as well, one who, moreover, has exactly the same carnal characteristics that attracted you to me.[14] "I will give you my sister": In this imagined world of homosociality, the human female has as little to say about her fate as does the Torah about her own. When the female is only a symbolic function of displaced ho-moeroticism, then her will or subjectivity is hardly relevant: "Reign-ing everywhere, although prohibited in practice, hom(m)o-sexuality is played out through the bodies of women, matter, or sign, and hetero-sexuality has been up to now just an alibi for the smooth working of man's relation with himself, of relations among men."[15] The structure

13. Sedgwick, *Between Men*, 2. Wayne Koestenbaum describes "male collaborative writing as an intercourse carried out through the exchange of women or of texts that take on 'feminine' properties" (3), thus anticipating the two alternatives proposed for their friendship by Resh Lakish and Rabbi Yoḥanan respectively. Rabbi Yoḥanan, of course, ends up by offering both—a pattern also not unknown within European homosocial for-mations. (R. Howard Bloch is working on such relationships within the community of French medievalists of the last century.)

14. For tension between the female Torah and a human wife as lover as a perennial problematic of rabbinic culture, see D. Boyarin, *Carnal Israel*, 134–66.

15. Irigaray, *This Sex*, 171. I am not insensitive to a possible critique of Irigaray as "homophobic" and thus implicitly to a critique of my invocation of her (Edelman, "Re-deeming," 42–43). I think, however, that this critique issues in part from a misrecognition of her "hom(m)osexuality," which is not "homosexuality," but, if anything, its opposite, that is, homophobia! There are ways in which the American literary rituals of male-bond-ing are both deeply misogynistic as well as homophobic. In other words, I suggest that it is fallacious to conflate Irigaray's "hom(m)osexual" with Lentricchia's "in some sense homosexual," but that Irigaray would agree precisely with Edelman (pace Edelman him-self, "Redeeming," 296 n. 29) that "the scene of phallic empowerment, the enabling sei-

that is set up is a perfect synecdoche of rabbinic homosociality, a structure of intense homosocial, even homoerotic, connections between the male denizens of the Study-House, channeled through and partly displaced via their focus on two types of "female" objects: the Torah that they study and their wives.

In replacing Resh Lakish's unsanctioned desire for coerced sex (with Yohanan—whether he knows him to be male or not) with a sanctioned, but apparently no less coerced sexual relationship, marriage, the narrative is both offering the latter as a better alternative to the former and raising the suspicion in our minds that they are not all that different. Illegitimate rape is replaced by legitimate marriage, setting up a dual hermeneutic within which the latter is represented as the proper substitute for the former but also suggested as its virtual equivalent. In other words, the text proposes a marriage within which the subjectivity, desire, and agency of the female partner are effectively ignored as being the virtual moral equivalent of a leap over a river to rape an attractive nude bather.[16] Lest it seem to readers that I am tendentiously conveying or even smuggling modern ideas into this text, I offer that this suggestion of a suspicious reading by the text of its own social formation is borne out dramatically in the continuation wherein we see that the erasure of female desire, subjectivity, and agency is the fatal flaw that brings the hero down in a denouement best described as tragic.

Interestingly enough, according to talmudic law what Rabbi Yohanan did here was impossible. There is no way that he could betroth his

zure or rape of one male by another" is determinedly heterosexual ("Redeeming," 49), as clearly laid bare in the talmudic story analyzed here.

16. Thus, to the best of my knowledge, we find nowhere in rabbinic literature a notion that women like to be raped, nothing analogous to the text that Gravdal cites from Old French within which it is asserted that "[a] maiden ravished has great joy; no matter what she says" (*Ravishing*, 5). The Talmud recognizes and abhors all rape as violence, including rape of wives, as opposed to canon law which "disallowed the punishment of forced coitus in marriage, since consent was given at the time of marriage" (9). Talmudic culture is generally much less sensitive, however, to the subtler (and therefore arguably more insidious) ways that its own assumptions about women, (for example, that they always prefer to be married [to almost anyone] than alone [Yevamot 18b and parallels]) institutionalize a comparable legalized erasure of female erotic agency—the right to say no—that is, less explosive but ultimately just as violent as rape. Furthermore, some Rabbis in the Talmud do assume that sometimes a woman who is being raped may end up enjoying herself and is to be treated legally as one who had sex willingly (Ketubboth 51b). Even within that passage itself, however, this view is rejected and the strong view of Rava is maintained that even if a raped woman had an orgasm, she is still legally considered as having been raped. In any case, even the repugnant minority view that sometimes women end up enjoying a situation that begins as rape and that in such cases they are not considered as having been raped is not equivalent to the proposition that women desire to be "ravished, . . . no matter what she says."

sister without her consent. However, the story as story represents the
actual social situation perhaps in ways that a statement of the law cannot, for in a society in which the disparities in power are as great as
they were between men and women in rabbinic culture, even requiring
consent or assent to marriage arguably does not mean a great deal.[17]
Read this way, the story is a *mise-en-abîme* of the entire rabbinic structure of gender relations that I have theorized in chapter 4. On one
hand, this is a text (and synecdoche of a culture) that clearly considers
desiring a woman compatible for men with the highest of intellectual
and spiritual striving and indeed with the most intense of homosocial
bonds. The text, moreover, almost explicitly inscribes a kinder, gentler
male, via the femminization of Resh Lakish, who can no longer vault
on his lance from the moment he accepts Torah; that is, Only if your
lance no longer works will you be fit to marry my sister. And this renunciation of "the phallus" is, moreover, not a surrender of male sexuality at all, nor a transcendence of the body. Nothing of the sort. The
whole point of it is to win the hand of (though no one asks about the
heart of) a woman. And this is the self-critical fatal flaw in the cultural
narrative that generates the tragedy of the story. Even if the formal, institutional arrangements exclude sexual and other violence against
women, this is analogous to the situation in rape cultures within which
an individual man (and even most) may totally avoid such violence
and be repelled by it but still benefit from it. In a sense, the very condemnation of male violence against women is arbitrary within a system
in which women have no voice, so the threat of such violent domination
is always there.[18] This, by itself, is not so startling a revelation; what
seems astonishing here is the extent to which it is the text itself that
produces (as opposed to merely being subjected to) this critique.

At first all seems to be going well between Rabbis. Rabbi Yoḥanan
introduces Resh Lakish fully into the world of Torah. One might say

17. In her very subtle analysis, Gravdal shows that medieval laws against "rape" may
have sometimes functioned precisely to efface female subjectivity, insofar as they were
directed toward securing the woman's body for her father's purposes. In other words, an
elopement of a daughter with a lover for purposes of consensual marriage was legally
raptus, as opposed to a legal marriage to a man of her father's choosing against her will
(*Ravishing*, 8). Rabbinic texts, however, treated in other parts of the present book represent women taking a highly active role in determining whom they will (or will not) marry,
including one woman's refusal to marry the very Patriarch of the Jews of Palestine himself,
Rabbi, author of the Mishna (and friend of the Roman emperor, whom we met above).
Roman law also required mutual consent for a valid marriage to be contracted. This principle was later abrogated in European law (7).

18. For further analysis and exemplification of this argument, see chapter 4.

that the *shiddukh* (match) that he makes between the new ephebe and the two female figures is highly successful. He produces Resh Lakish as an adult, rabbinic male, a great "man," and apparently as an adequate husband as well, if we may judge by the wife's distress at the prospect of losing him. The two Rabbis are imagined as a sort of Jewish answer to such archetypical pairs as Achilles and Patroclus on one hand and David and Jonathan on the other.[19] Both of these couples and their associated meanings would have been available in the rabbinic sociolect, the biblical one obviously but the Homeric one very likely as well. As Halperin has said of such alliances, "whatever [their] sentimental qualities, [they] always [have] an outward focus, a purpose beyond itself in action, in the accomplishment of glorious deeds or the achievement of political ends. Each of the . . . friends, accordingly, is an exceptionally valiant warrior: we are dealing not with an instance of some neutral or universal sociological category called 'friendship,' then, but with a specific cultural formation, a type of heroic friendship which is better captured by terms like comrades-in-arms, boon companions, and the like."[20]

Within this text of rabbinic self-fashioning over-against their fantasies of Roman culture—explicitly signified by the "ethnically" Jewish but culturally "Roman" gladiator, Resh Lakish—the valor of war-making is replaced by the valor of Torah study, metaphorically realized as a sort of battle. The dialectics of the Rabbis are frequently referred to with metaphors of gladiatorial combat or battle. The Rabbis themselves are called in the Talmud "the shield-bearers," that is, hoplites.[21] (I shall suggest below that the positive significance of this substitution is being both asserted and contested within the text at one and the same time.) Following this reading of the narrative as being constructed within the Mediterranean paradigm of heroes and their pals, the ending fits as

---

19. Patroclus's concubine is a gift from Achilles (Halperin, *One Hundred Years*, 77). Note, moreover, that David's first wife was also Jonathan's sister. Although Halperin analyzes the composite story as two narratives and reads the David and Jonathan friendship sequence as a later substitution for the David and Michal conjugal sequence, for the text "as we have it" the structure is that David is married to his pal's sister—just like Resh Lakish. Halperin is, of course, arguing for the historico-cultural archaism of the hero and pal pattern (87); nevertheless, in some ways the model was still alive into the Hellenistic period, however inflected through later sexual paradigms.

20. Halperin, *One Hundred Years*, 77; and see the entire essay: 75–87.

21. Within Roman culture itself such metaphors were also used, demonstrating that there is no contradiction between describing intellectual life as agon and in terms drawn from the arena and the simultaneous valorization of physical combat (Gleason, *Making*, 123).

well. The exquisite portrayal of Rabbi Yoḥanan's bereavement—we see him going from door to door, a wanderer in the city, crying out for his lost love—strongly supports the reading as well. This sentence is the literary equivalent of David's lament for Jonathan: "I am pained for you my brother Jonathan. You were exceedingly pleasant to me. Your love was wonderful beyond the love of women. How have the heroes fallen, and the weapons of war are lost" (II Samuel 1:26–27).

Traditional interpretations have sought to reduce the unsettling nature of this moment by insisting that its pathos is Rabbi Yoḥanan's consciousness of the sinfulness of his behavior. They thus both recuperate Rabbi Yoḥanan as hero via his "repentance" and eliminate the homoerotic desire from the text. The text, however, gives no indication that the pain suffered by Rabbi Yoḥanan was caused by a sense of sinfulness on his part. This story would not fit into a folktale type of the sinner redeemed. It depicts rather a man desperately missing the man he has killed, fitting, if you will, into the folktale type of lover killed in jealousy and then bitterly mourned. The rabbis sought fruitlessly to comfort him with another friend and his crying is not of self-contempt or repentance but of loss and desire: "Son of Lakish, where are you? Son of Lakish, where are you?"—not, "I am a sinner. I am a murderer."

There are several indications in this text that the anxiety which inhabits it is not anxiety about sexuality so much as anxiety about gender and the boundaries of gendered performance.[22] Rabbi Yoḥanan's gender is uncertain from the beginning of the story. Before the narrative even begins we are ceremoniously informed by the Talmud that the reason Rabbi Yoḥanan was omitted from the list of the most beautiful men was his lack of a beard.[23] Now this is the feature, it would seem, that recommended him as sexual object to Resh Lakish, whether or not the latter "knew the truth" of his gender. The latter point, indeed, is a moment of undecidability between manuscripts. One manuscript tradition leaves it quite uncertain as to whether he thought he was pursuing a woman, or a man who was attractive just because he had the physical attributes of a woman.[24] In the version of the narrative that I have re-

22. Cf. C. Edwards, *Politics*, 78, and especially 87–88.

23. The congenital eunuch rhetor of the second century, Favorinus, is described by Philostratus as "born double-sexed, both male and female, as his appearance made plain: his face remained beardless even into old age" (quoted in Gleason, *Making*, 6).

24. See Halperin, *One Hundred Years*, 35 n. This represents a moment of incoherence in the formation of masculinity within the rabbinic culture, not entirely different from the incoherence involved in the figure of Jesus for Christians, so beautifully evoked by Eve Kosofsky Sedgwick in *Epistemology*, 141–43; see also Bynum, *Jesus*, and Silverman,

produced here, drawing on another manuscript tradition,[25] this point is made almost superfluously obvious by indicating that Resh Lakish actually thought that Rabbi Yoḥanan *was* a woman.[26] On one hand, this renders the sexual theme more explicit and might have been censored out for this reason; on the other hand, it reduces the homoerotic subtext and might, therefore, have been added at a time when such anxiety was more powerful. In any case, the conflict between the two manuscript traditions points up the fact that the question of gender undecidability is in the "unconscious" of this text.

A second point of undecidability in the narrative has to do with the repartee between the two Rabbis once Resh Lakish arrives at the scene. Yoḥanan's immediate response to Resh Lakish's "virility" is "Your strength for Torah," that is, Physical prowess is wasted on the pursuit of carnal objects of desire—like me—; instead of seeking to seduce [rape?] me, you should be joining me in lusting after learning. Although Yoḥanan's invitation is not without its ironies, it is, however, Resh Lakish's response—"Your beauty for women"—that holds the greater potential for multiple readings. In the text above, I have preferred the reading that contextually makes the most sense, namely, that beauty is wasted on the pursuit of spiritual objects of desire; join me in seeking women.[27] The phrase itself can also mean, of course: That beauty is wasted on a man; why aren't you a woman? Once more the blurred status of Yoḥanan's gender is what is at stake here; at some level, the entire narrative is engendered by the confusion that his body represents: Is he male or female?[28]

Male, 102–6. In a sense, the ambiguity within the European tradition as to whether male beauty is more or less like female beauty—paralleled, perhaps, by the problematic of whether same-sex desire is more masculine or feminizing—is reproduced here in the extravagant description of Rabbi Yoḥanan's supreme beauty followed by its qualification in that he is not listed in the lists of the most beautiful men because he has no beard! In important segments of our own cultural tradition, it is the man who is attracted to women who is figured as effeminate. On the other hand, if the remark in the manuscript that Resh Lakish thought Rabbi Yoḥanan a woman is a secondary gloss, it might have had an apologetic intent, that is, rendering it impossible to imagine that Resh Lakish, himself to end up a culture-hero, "really" vaulted a river to get at a man, even one as beautiful and effeminate as Rabbi Yoḥanan.

25. The famous Hamburg 19 manuscript, the "dean" of talmudic witnesses.

26. Compare the dreams in which Gilgamesh imagines Enkidu as a woman before actually meeting him, as discussed by Halperin, *One Hundred Years,* 81.

27. For "effeminate" beauty as appealing to women in Rome, see C. Edwards, *Politics,* 82–83.

28. Edwards remarks that frequently in Roman literature, as in patriarchal societies in general, "it is not uncommon for men to compare to women other men they wish to humiliate" (65). Interestingly enough, I can think of very few, if any, such comparisons

A final hint of the underlying cultural disquietude of this text has to
do with the curious detail about Resh Lakish's attempted return to take
his clothes. This is a highly overdetermined moment in the text. He will
no longer be wearing the clothes that he wore before, the masculine
clothes of a Roman man—presumably the *toga virilis*[29]—he will now
be wearing the robes of a scholar of the Talmud. This change is doubled
in the text by the failure of Resh Lakish's lance as a means of propulsion
back to the masculine signifiers of his clothing. His lance no longer
works. He is dephallicized (but not castrated or emasculated—a crucial
distinction).[30] I am not, of course, invoking some putative Freudian notion of a phallic symbol here. I am suggesting, rather, that the text itself
is animating such a symbolism—knowingly. A narrative that has a man
vault over a river on his lance, undergo a spiritual transformation in
which gender is explicitly thematized and then be unable to vault back
on the same lance, seems clearly to be symbolizing masculinity through
the working or nonworking of the lance. Bram Dijkstra has made the
point that painters of the nineteenth century frequently used snakes as
a symbol of male sexuality, not because they were under thrall to psychological symbolism that they could not control (and that Freud
would diagnose), but because this symbolism was culturally available
to them (as it was, indeed, to Freud as well).[31] I am making a similar
claim about the symbolism of the lance here, not imagining that it is a
psychically universal "phallic symbol" but rather that this text has
summoned it as a symbol of a repudiated active, violent, thrusting masculinity.[32]

---

in talmudic literature. Men whom other men wish to humiliate in the Talmud are more
likely to be accused of crudity than effeminacy. I realize that this is a very risky claim to
make, as well as an argument from silence. If my observation is borne out, however, it
may have some significance.

29. Of course, no Jew or brigand actually would have been wearing this garment. We
are dealing with symbolic, fictional representations here, so I allow myself this speculation
as to the reference about the clothes that Resh Lakish cannot reclaim, paralleling the lance
that no longer works. For the gendered significance of the changing of clothes, see C.
Edwards, *Politics*, 64, and the passage from Cicero quoted above.

30. The confusion between these two processes, endemic to Western culture and
most explicitly realized in Freud's reading of the Schreber case (Geller, "Freud"), has been
crucial to the modern misunderstanding of Jewish gendering.

31. Dijkstra, *Idols*.

32. This represents a possibly consistent and significant difference between the Palestinian and Babylonian Rabbis, for in Palestinian sources, Resh Lakish does not give up
his physical strength by becoming a student of Torah. Indeed, this very prowess is turned
to the study of Torah and the defense of Torah, as in the story in the Palestinian Talmud,
Sanhedrin 25b, where Resh Lakish strikes a "Samaritan" who blasphemes, or Palestinian

Nor were such representations of masculinity entirely foreign to actual Roman cultural productions. Roman sexual discourse was pervaded with images of violence. The penis itself was most commonly figured as a weapon. Amy Richlin has given abundant examples to support the Roman cultural identification of the phallus as a weapon,[33] and this is, according to her, considered by the Romans a "positive" representation: "All these patterns depend on a scale of values in which the Priapus figure is top or best and the other figures are subordinate; *militat omnis amans*, [Every lover a soldier] with a big gun. The image of the phallus as weapon is a common one."[34] A nice, and relatively decorous, example can be cited from Ovid, who after a bout of impotence was moved to write:

> Why do you lie there full of modesty, o worst part of me?
> So I have been taken in by your promises before.
> You're cheating your master; caught weaponless because of you [*per te deprensus inermis*].[35]

Altogether, Richlin makes the excellent point that (at least following Suetonius), sexual activity and potency were considered homologous with political effectivity. The weak emperors had inactive sexual lives

---

Talmud Sanhedrin 19a, where he defies the authority of the Patriarch, the Jewish representative of Roman authority who sends bailiffs to capture him. See also Palestinian Talmud Terumot 46a, where Resh Lakish is presented as physically defending the rabbinic community against Roman tyranny. It would seem from these texts alone that there was a significant difference between the "totally" diasporized Babylonian rabbinic community and the only partially diasporized Palestinian community in relation to the issue of masculinity and power, a conclusion that would strongly support the general thesis of this book. Further research is required, however, to substantiate this suggestive point, for which (as well as for these references and much else) I am grateful to Yariv Ben-Aharon and to his colleagues in the Beth-Hamidrash at Oranim. For the nonce, it is interesting to compare the differential narratives about Rabbi Yohanan ben Zakkai (not the same as Rabbi Yohanan of the story in the present chapter), who, in Babylonian versions, opposed the revolt against Rome, made a separate peace with Vespasian, and required as his reward only the town of Yavne for a Yeshiva (D. Boyarin, "Trickster"). In contrast, according to Palestinian sources, he was militant, he supported the war against Rome until it was clear that it was hopeless, and he made Yavne a sort of internment camp (D. Biale, *Power*, 23)! Once again, I emphasize that the issue is not the truth or falsity of these respective myths of origin but what we can learn about the discourses of the respective rabbinic cultures that circulated them. In both cases we find the Palestinian Rabbis much less enamored of renunciation of physical power than the Babylonian ones.

33. Cat. 67.21; *Pr.* 9.2, 11.3, 20.1, 25.7, 31.3, 43.1, 55.4; Diehl 1103; Mart. 11.78.6 (Richlin, *Garden*, 26).

34. Richlin, *Garden*, 59; see also C. Edwards, *Politics*, 73, on penetration as "stabbing," and Goldhill, *Foucault's*, 51 on intercourse as fighting.

35. *Am.* 3.7.69–71, cited in Richlin, *Garden*, 118.

and were cuckolds; the powerful emperors had active sexual lives and cuckolded others.[36] Catherine Edwards also makes clear the connection between seducing other men's wives and political power.[37] According to at least one poem by Martial, moreover, an unsatisfactory husband, a "*cinaedus*" is described as "unwarlike [*imbelles*]" and "soft [*molles*]," and as Richlin comments, this refers "both to their lovemaking and their way of life."[38] Clearly the implication is that a satisfying male sexuality will be "warlike."[39]

It is important at this point to emphasize that I am sure that actual sexual life and discourse in Rome was much more complex and heterogeneous than this picture would allow. There is no more reason to doubt tender, sexual love between some husbands and wives, women and their lovers (male or female), or *kinaidoi* (men who desire to be penetrated) and their lovers in Rome than anywhere else.[40] The important issue here is what face Roman culture presented to its others, especially to those it subjugated, and that it was a face of violence, of a male sexuality suffused with brutality and domination. This image would have been received through a variety of discourses, ranging from graffiti to the poetry of such canonical figures as Catullus, Martial, and Ovid—although these actually subvert the paradigm through parodic appropriation of it, as pointed out to me by Molly M. Levine—to the gladiatorial arena, paradigmatic of Roman culture for the Rabbis.[41]

36. Richlin, *Garden,* 88–89.
37. C. Edwards, *Politics,* 47–48.
38. Richlin, *Garden,* 139.
39. It should be pointed out, however, that Edwards's description is somewhat less categorical than Richlin's. She points to counterexamples as well, where the adulterer was considered "effeminate." Moreover, according to Gleason, a man who sought to please women sexually (rather than be pleased himself) was also called a *cinaedus,* a pathic, in the same category as a man who wished to be penetrated by other men (Gleason, *Making,* 65). It is "passivity" per se that is feminized, according to this view.
40. It should, of course, not be forgotten that *within* Greco-Roman culture there were strong currents of opposition to the equation of male sexuality with violence, and if I were writing about the Romans, it would be important to pay attention to these currents. Plutarch's *Advice to Bride and Groom,* with its much more tender understandings of heterosex, certainly belongs in this category.
41. To a great extent, they were also paradigmatic for Romans themselves. As Thomas Wiedemann has remarked: "Although the popular image of the Roman mob spending most of the year looking on from its comfortable seats in the Colosseum while men killed each other and killed or were killed by wild beasts in the arena is a considerable distortion, the investment of time, wealth, and emotion into the games was nevertheless enormous. Attending the games was one of the practices that went with being a Roman" (*Emperors,* 1)—and, for the Rabbis, at any rate, it defined, not surprisingly, what a Roman was. Significant also is Wiedemann's comment—supported of course by evidence—that the gladiatorial contests "played a major role in the way people arranged their private experience" (23).

Violence, brutality, and domination were, to a great extent, the "public" meanings of maleness.

Another way of saying this is to emphasize that every society has elements of violence within it (and perhaps every individual has as well). The question, therefore, concerns not the existence of such matter within a culture but its placement in a particular system of values. One could even imagine a Jewish cultural complex (Rabbinic Judaism) as itself a part of Roman culture in the broadest sense, and as such allied (willy-nilly, perhaps even unwittingly) with forces within Latin culture that were counterhegemonic with respect to the dominant gender fictions, thus further breaking the binary opposition between Roman and Jew. It nevertheless remains the case that for the purposes of its self-presentation, the Jewish text dramatizes those aspects of Rome qua Rome that were most in opposition to their own values either for rhetorical purpose or because these were, as I have said, the face of Rome that they most obviously encountered. On the other hand, I emphasize again, virtually all of the texts that I am reading here focus on transformations between Jew and Roman that interrupt the ethnicity of the stereotypes at the same time that they promote strongly a peculiar set of values, antithetical to the "official" and dominant discourse of the Roman ruling elite.

Since the text that I am analyzing here projects it as belonging to the "Other," this forms a comment on the fancied antiphallicism of the projecting culture—a self-critical and ironic one, as it turns out. The traditionally definitive talmudic commentator Rashi suggests this interpretation when he glosses the nonworking lance as "his strength had been sapped [like that of a woman]."[42] For Romans, according to Edwards, it was rather "sexual indulgence" that "sapped a man's strength and made him like a woman."[43] With a certain irony, however, the text indicts that Rabbi Yohanan taught him Torah and Mishna and made him a "great *man*."[44]

Resh Lakish's lance is replaced by his speech.[45] Note that the metaphor of gladiatorial activity for Torah study is marked at least twice in

42. My completion of the phrase is based on its topical usage throughout talmudic literature.

43. C. Edwards, *Politics*, 86.

44. See now Gleason for an illuminating exposition of the ways that rhetorical excellence and competition "made men" in the Roman Second Sophistic, that is, in the very period within which our legend is set!

45. For a fascinating discussion of the relation of virility to voice, see Rousselle, *Parole;* C. Edwards, *Politics*, 86; and Gleason, *Making*, 122–30.

the text: once in the dialogue between Resh Lakish and Rabbi Yoḥanan
in the beginning and once more when the former bitterly complains:
There they called me Rabbi and here they call me Rabbi. Resh Lakish,
deprived of the "phallus," nevertheless is not castrated. He marries and
fathers children.[46] The same difference obtains between the nonphallic
monk (or the transvestite female saint) of European culture and Jewish
talmudic scholars. These former achieve the status of "third sex" by
escaping sex (and sexuality) altogether;[47] not so the Rabbi. I read the
(first part of the) story, therefore, as a utopian fantasy about the production of a normative, nonphallic Jewish male subjectivity. It is also a
story in which same-sex desire and homoerotic intimacy can be com-
prehended within a context of fulfilling paternal functioning.

Given the larger cultural context within which they worked, the
Rabbis who devoted themselves exclusively to study were femminized
vis-à-vis the larger cultural world, explicitly figured in our text by the
pre-Torah Resh Lakish. For the Romans—at least as they were imagined by Jews and presumably for many Jews themselves—a man who
did not have a weapon was not a man at all.[48] He was castrated, but
from within the rabbinic Jewish perspective he is merely circumcised.
In other words, those practices and performances that defined the rabbi
as femminized from the point of view of the dominant culture were
those that constituted masculinity within the dominated culture—although here too the dominated men understood themselves in part, and
in a positive sense, as femminized as well. As I emphasize throughout
this book, however, such perceptions of men as femminized whether
by self or others are hardly subversive of gendered hierarchies or necessarily good for female subjects.

Rabbinic masculinity is significantly like Roman femininity in certain ways. This is not to deny, of course, the presence of valorized exemplars and even models of contemplative masculinity within Roman
culture as well. However, as Brent Shaw has pointed out to me, even
such highly marked contemplatives as Marcus Aurelius and Seneca in
their public faces felt it necessary to approbate Roman violence as cul-

46. The previous chapter explored a renunciation of the phallus signified by extreme
masochistic behavior on the part of Rabbis, whose reward is the promise of progeny, thus
producing a parallel structure of giving up the phallus and retaining the penis. That text
forms a thematic doublet of this one.

47. Warner, *Joan*, 146.

48. For the Romans themselves, as David Halperin reminds me, it was frequently the
toga virilis that signified masculinity and not a weapon, but see also C. Edwards, *Politics*,
77. For the Greeks, see Halperin, *One Hundred Years*, 37.

tural/social practice. In fact, Marcus Aurelius the stoic contemplative
was not even known until the Middle Ages. As Shaw strikingly puts it:
"The fragmentary quasi-Nietzschean meanderings of his *Eis Heauton*
(the "Meditations") were *not* widely known at the time. Marcus Aurelius would have been 'known' by public monuments like his great col-
umn at Rome (just about as phallic an image as one would wish to get)
which publicly celebrates his near-genocidal extermination of 'others'
along the Danube frontier."[49] Studying Torah is a kind of cross-dressing, marked by Resh Lakish's crossing of the river and doubly marked
by his inability to cross back on his masculine lance to take up again
his masculine clothing.[50] The issue is more complex than this, however,
for studying Torah within rabbinic culture is obviously primarily the
definitive performance of male gendering. Men studying Torah are not
cross-dressed from within the culture's own norms and models; rather,
it is women studying Torah who would be "cross-dressing." The modern text, "Yentl, the Yeshiva-Bokhur," which many will know from the
Barbra Streisand film, exemplifies this point elegantly. On one hand, it
is clear that the one who is cross-dressed is the girl, Yentl, who dresses
as a boy in order to study in the Yeshiva; her very study is cross-dressing
as well. On the other hand, the fact that she is indistinguishable as a
girl dressed as a boy owes something to the effeminate or cross-dressed
nature of the boys vis-à-vis European norms of manliness in the Yeshiva
as well. The slippage of two cultural norms one over the other, almost
emblematic of a diaspora culture (a culture of doubled-consciousness),
is that which produces a positive sense of self-femminization within
rabbinic representations.

The study of Torah is the quintessential performance of rabbinic
Jewish maleness. In other words, precisely the stylized repetitions that
produced gender differentiation (and thus cultural as well as sexual reproduction) within classical Jewish praxis were the repetitive performances of the House of Study, including the homosocial bonding. At
the structural(ist) level the specific performances themselves are irrelevant; what is culturally significant is the very inscription of sex through
any gender-differentiating practice. The House of Study was thus the
rabbinic Jewish equivalent of the locker room, barracks, or warship;
compare the historically similar taboos against the presence of women

49. Shaw, letter.
50. For Torah study as cross-dressing, see Garber, *Vested Interests*, 224–33, especially 227.

in those environments. On the level of cross-cultural contact, however, gaps between the gendered performances of one culture and another become exceedingly consequential. In this case, the performance of maleness through study became particularly fraught because this performance was read as female in the cultural environment within which European Jews lived from the Roman period onward.

The ambivalence is also, however, fully internal to Jewish culture itself. The "tent" is the prototypical space of the female; of Ya'el it is said: "She is blessed more than all of the women in the tent" (Judg. 5:24), glossed by the midrash as more blessed than the Mothers, Sarah, Rebecca, Leah, and Rachel, of whom it is said that they occupied the tent.[51] But on the other hand, Jacob, the ideal male of rabbinic culture is also "[a]n innocent, a dweller in tents" (Gen. 25:27), glossed by the midrash as the tents in which Torah study is carried out.[52] Since the "tent" is the epitome of private and "female" space and "the common thread [of late antique political philosophy] was the insistence on the subordination of the private to the public sphere and of the female to the male,"[53] once the House of Study is figured as a "tent," the gender of its inhabitants becomes extremely equivocal even in their own estimation as well in as that of others. The political subordination of the Jew to the Roman worked perfectly with this patterning as well. If study of Torah is the singular performative that determines the Jewish man as gendered male, then we can understand—which is not the same thing, of course, as accept—the basis for a cultural taboo against women entering that space and engaging in that performance.[54] The easy contrast between the female inside and the male outside having been breached, and males (ideally) now occupying an inside space as well, set up the tension that produced the extreme exclusion of women

---

51. See Genesis Rabbah, section 48. Yael is, of course, a singularly "phallic" female herself, who, within her very tent, drove a peg into the head of a tyrant and saved Israel.

52. Genesis Rabbah, section 63 and passim.

53. Burrus, *Making*, 8.

54. Cantor, *Jewish Women*, 105. As Chava Boyarin has remarked to me, to a certain extent this is a pseudoproblem because in most ancient and medieval cultures (if not all) learning was restricted to men. It does seem to me, however, that the acuteness of this restriction was greater in Jewish culture than in, for example, Christianity, where, if learned women were not common, neither were they rare. Finally, it should be recognized that there is evidence for many more women who did manage to study a great deal of Torah also in early medieval times even though in public discourse they were not recognized as learned. This point supports the argument that I am offering here that there was no essential difficulty with women coming in contact with Torah, but a structural necessity to restrict Torah study "officially" to men. See the next chapter.

from the practice of the study of Torah, thus generating from within the very solution the flaw that brought the system (in the allegorical guise of Resh Lakish) down.

Interestingly enough, but not entirely surprisingly by now, some Christian men at the same period were also entering into traditionally female spaces. The resistance to Roman models and ideals was common to these Christians and the Rabbis. While in some aspects, however, this rejection was similar to that of the Rabbis, its ultimate meanings were quite different. Scholars of early Christianity, among them prominently Verna Harrison, have discussed the uses in Christian imagery of the female body as an entirely *valorized* metaphor for Christian spirituality.[55] More appositely to our present context, Virginia Burrus writes of an early fifth-century contemporary of the talmudic Rabbis: "Sulpicius' asceticism is, I propose, explicitly *'anti-public'* and as such represents a conscious expression of political and cultural alienation which separates him from more traditional aristocratic Christian contemporaries like Ausonius. This preliminary thesis leads me to another: we may, I think, anticipate a certain destabilization of gender identity in the writings of an aristocrat who voluntarily retires from the uniquely male sphere of public life and withdraws to a sphere commonly associated with women and female influence."[56]

On one hand, Sulpicius's conversion is, as Burrus remarks, "a radical rejection of power," and in this respect one could find abundant parallels in rabbinic texts as well; moreover, as she argues, at least in this case, we do not have a simple transfer of enjoyment of power from the secular to the episcopal realm. Indeed, Sulpicius's total retirement is an affront to the public life of bishops in the Gallic Church of his time. Most suggestive for my purposes is, however, the fact that Sulpicius explicitly remarks women and especially virginal women as his models for the ascetic life of retirement and withdrawal from public exposure and activity. Burrus concludes, quite stunningly, that "Sulpicius puts forth the radical suggestion that the male must indeed 'become female' through his ascetic renunciation of public life." The most powerful parallel, however, to my interpretation of rabbinic culture is that Sulpicius proposes "feminine" characteristics as ideals for the life of the Christian, and yet, or rather because of this, "reintroduces, first, the classical

55. Harrison, "Receptacle," "Male," and "Gender."
56. Burrus, "Male Ascetic," and see Burrus, *Making,* 146.

topos of the separation and subordination of women and, second, the traditional rhetoric of negative womanly influence":

> Let not a woman enter the camp of men, but let the line of soldiers remain separate, and let the females, dwelling in their own tent, be remote from that of men. For this renders an army ridiculous, if a female crowd is mixed with the regiments of men. Let the soldier occupy the line, let the soldier fight in the plain, but let the woman keep herself within the protection of the walls.[57]

Now, the "camp of men" here is the individual solitude of a single, near hermetic male ascetic, and the point of this admonition is that he must separate from his also converted, celibate wife. The historical meanings of the gendered roles have been thus thoroughly undermined by these men also for whom the imperial phallus has become odious. As Burrus shrewdly interprets, the point is that the intentional, valorized, self-feminization of the Christian male ascetic produced gender anxiety for those same men at the same time, and they reasserted their maleness through reinforcements of traditional gender roles transposed to a new metaphorical key. Christians were ultimately to create new literal female spaces in the form of female monastic communities, separate and (nearly) equal to those of men. Owing to the absolute commitment to marriage and communal life of the Rabbis, the structures of their practice were entirely different. Nevertheless, I think this counterpart situation in contemporary Christianity serves to help us diagnose the kinds of gender anxiety produced by the males "dwelling in their own tents" and their available "solutions" via forms of segregation and exclusion of women. It is this cultural narrative that our story of Rabbi Yoḥanan and Resh Lakish retells as well.

One of the remarkable aspects of narrative as cultural discourse is, however, its haunting ability to tell a hegemonic story and contest it at the same time. I have read this story as a one of Jewish male subjectivity, a subjectivity explicitly figured here as at the margin of, not a dehistoricized masculinity but the Roman cultural Empire. Using for the moment psychoanalytical terms, traditional Jewish culture cuts the "phallus" down to size, demonstrating that the choice is not between a phallus and castration, and that a man can have a working penis even if he has "taken off" his phallus—or never had one to begin with.

The continuation of the story thus directly contests the idealized and utopian picture of masculine subjectivity that the beginning constructs.

---

57. Sulpicius, *Martinian Dialogues*, 2.11, quoted in Burrus, *Making*, 146.

Resh Lakish bitterly complains to Rabbi Yoḥanan: "What have you profited me? There they called me Rabbi and here they call me Rabbi!" You offered me a masculinity that would be resistant to that of the dominant culture, one that would not depend for its adequation on the violence of male rivalry and cruelty to women, but this substitute, this resistant male subjectivity turns out to be just as brutal—claims Resh Lakish—as that which I left behind me. At one moment the text insists that Jewish masculinity is different, less violent; at the next, with a hermeneutics of sharp suspicion, it suggests that nothing is really different after all. At one moment the text argues, as it were, that the gladiatorial combat of Torah study is somehow finer, less cruel, more sublimated than the gladiatorial combats that "they" engage in, but then the text seems to suggest with its deadly ending that perhaps our vocal combat is not so different from theirs after all.[58] They kill with the spear, but we kill with the voice. The renunciation of the weapon turns out to be merely the substitute of the vocal weapon for the physical one. In this reading of the narrative, it essays a far-reaching critique of the implicit violence of the institutionalized male competitiveness in Torah study. In addition to this, in the heartfelt representation of the pain of the wife-sister and the extreme arrogance of her brother, represented via his quotations from Jeremiah as arrogating to himself the place of God, there is a powerful and salient critique of the indifference to the subjectivity, pain, and desire of women that rabbinic homosociality could promote as well.[59] Her subjecthood is represented through the powerful demand of her brother that he *see* her, and his refusal to do so (eliminated from the printed editions) speaks volumes of his callousness in rivalrous rage and wounded male pride.

It is, of course, no accident that the incident that precipitates this epiphany is a controversy having to do with weapons. With its remark-

58. Maud Gleason has recently described Roman society during the Antonine age as one "where an intensely competitive ethos made it difficult to grant another man success. The relationship between performers was definitely a zero-sum game" (*Making*, xxiii). Sister Verna Harrison informs me that at about the same time, the Desert Fathers used the metaphor of athletic competition to describe their vying with each other in ascetic prowess. According to them, just as *eros* could be turned to good effect rather than being suppressed, so could *thymos*. It is that very possibility that is being simultaneously advanced and contested in our talmudic text. See above, n. 21.

59. For a similar critique of rabbinic callousness to women, from *within* the Talmud, see D. Boyarin, *Carnal Israel*, 146–50. Now the question might very well be raised: Is Boyarin reading here "against the grain," or perhaps even worse, simply importing modern ideological concerns into the Talmud? And the answer: I don't know. This is what I see in this text. For discussion of the theoretical issues in a very similar context, see Winkler, *Constraints*, 126; and Goldhill, *Foucault's*, 42–43.

able self-consciousness, then, this text serves as a point of origin for both a Jewish antiphallus and for an inner Jewish critique of the real achievement of such a utopian moment in masculinity. One of the weapons mentioned in the Mishna about which the fictional discussion between the Rabbis is constructed is that very lance that Resh Lakish had renounced. On one hand, the story seems to be saying, we do not use weapons, we talk about them, but at the same time it suggests that very talk may be as evil—and even as deadly—as their gladiatorial combats.[60] Although the text tries to recover a utopian vision of rabbinic combat in Rabbi Yoḥanan's rejection of the irenic Rabbi Elʿazar for the pugnacious Resh Lakish, the critique of the danger and violence of such verbal competitiveness is not erased.[61] We can regret them, but just as Resh Lakish cannot be brought back from the dead, so also destructiveness can never be entirely expunged from rabbinic male rivalry, as long as its homosocial and thus willy-nilly masculinist base is maintained.[62]

The inner critique that this text projects of its own utopian vision of a shattering of the phallus can be understood in two ways—both very important for the discussion at hand. It could be understood as a statement of recognition that violence—or at any rate, aggression—is inherent in the psyche of the human being (or at any rate, the human male?) and that, therefore, any attempt to repress it will result in its return in some other, perhaps more deadly, form. Such a view is adopted—not with respect, however, to this text—by neo-Jungian analyst Barbara Breitman who argues that it is the attempt of traditional Jewish culture to produce gentle men that results in violence, because of its suppression of what she terms "healthy aggression," which she sees as "vital life energy," thus completely adopting the very ideology that Judaism in our text sets out to combat.[63]

I see little evidence, however, in traditional Jewish culture for "the healthy aggression of growth" being "fused with rage" or of "vital life energy [being] lost." These seem to me to be exactly the sort of inter-

---

60. When I presented this text orally on several occasions listeners proposed that there ought to be a symbolic connection between Resh Lakish's statement that the weapon is completed by being plunged into water and his own history as revealed in the story, but I have not ever been able to work out such an analogy in a way that makes sense to me.

61. For a very interesting discussion of the specific ideological function of the figure of Rabbi Elʿazar here, see Kalmin, *Sages*, 28–29.

62. The Palestinian Talmud, in the text referred to above, n. 32, presents a much more sanguine view of rabbinic "combat." There, in the temporary absence of Resh Lakish, Rabbi Yoḥanan himself describes himself as "one hand clapping."

63. Breitman, *Lifting*, 107.

nalization of antisemitic stereotypes that Breitman diagnoses so clearly and sensitively in Freud. Adopting the biases and essentialism of a neo-Jungian will scarcely cure anything at all. Finally, Breitman describes a pattern of Jewish men identifying with their oppressors and seeing Jewish women as the enemy, as "the dominating, emasculating, persecutor."[64] While this claim can surely be documented for the nineteenth and twentieth centuries, it has virtually nothing to stand behind it before that. This does not deny in any way the systemic oppression of Jewish women within traditional Jewish culture, but I categorically reject the notion that aggression is "natural" to men and that, therefore, the oppression of women in rabbinic culture is a derivative of the very attempt to produce gentle men, that is, that because it is a repression of "natural" aggression it produces rage that "must" then burst out somewhere. This is the "repressive hypothesis" with a vengeance—literally.

I would like to suggest instead another interpretation, one that does not appeal to transhistorical hydraulic claims about the psyche but to historical, material conditions of human societies. The problematic, on this view, is not one of biological aggression built into the species or the gender but rather a fully social and cultural one. Until the coming of the Messiah takes place, it seems, there will always be hierarchy within human societies, symbolized in this case by the patriarchal hierarchies within the House of Study—There they called me Rabbi and here they call me Rabbi—as well as the hierarchy of relations between the House of Study, coded male, and the home, coded female. The text proposes a dismantling of hierarchy, then, at the same time that it raises the danger of such a (necessarily imaginary) overturn, as if to point up the pitfalls of a symbolic renunciation of power for a group which retains actual power, such as men clearly did within rabbinic society.

As Robin Morgan and Tania Modleski among others have made palpably clear (in texts cited in the last chapter), even sincere male renunciation of "the phallus" contributes to the oppression of women when men remain dominant. Even a society that renounces power vis-à-vis its "outside" and raises to ideal the situation of being out of power, as I read *this* talmudic text to be doing, nevertheless will have its own internal structures of power differential, and the very renunciation of power as a value may lead to deadly abuse of that power. This danger is even more palpable when the same group enacting opposition to and renunciation of power becomes the dominant source of power within a soci-

64. Breitman, *Lifting,* 108.

ety, as Christians did after the Constantine revolution and Jews much more recently. Then, as Virginia Burrus has put it: "Christian bishops and scholars must constantly reinvent the fiction of their own 'persecution' (not least by borrowing the imagined body of the virgin martyr—who significantly turns out to be more ferocious than even her executioner), again and again they must force a construction of paradox on a power that is thereby not so much renounced as veiled. At some level, there is something feigned and deceptive (though not purely so, not at all) about the male ascetic resistance."[65]

The fatal flaw, then, within the cultural system itself—represented almost allegorically within our story as a literally fatal flaw in its hero, Rabbi Yoḥanan—is in its nonrecognition of the fact that any resistance to power and masculinist constructions of the phallus must be accompanied by a revolution in the power relations between men and women as well, if it is to be material and critical.[66] It is the reinscription of male dominance within the text itself that causes the crisis that leads to its catastrophic and tragic end. The next chapter will consist of a more detailed analysis of how the very mechanism for the production of femminized men, the study of Torah, provided the means for the systematic maintenance of gender hierarchy within talmudic culture just as surely as the economic and physical methods of control that were promoted by the European dominant fiction.

---

65. Burrus, letter.

66. As Aviva Cantor points out, this same tragic flaw was to accompany another Jewish social revolution millennia later: "The kibbutz, despite its incorporation of female values [sic], was patriarchal, all mythos to the contrary. . . . Unfortunately, the kibbutz men had one grievous flaw: their sexism. . . . The men, whose revolutionary and egalitarian ethos precluded advancing an ideological rationale for excluding women from agricultural labor, fell back on claiming that women were incapable of it. Mostly they engaged in passive resistance, on a case-by-case basis, to those women who tried it. Although the men initially knew as little about farming as the women, they did not seem to find anything illogical in arguing that women would not be able to extract milk from a cow or wheat from a field—just as the Talmudic sages had argued that women are incapable of fathoming the subtle intricacies of scholarly learning (and, in both cases, acted to prevent women from engaging in these activities to avoid being proven wrong)" (Jewish Women, 182, 183).

CHAPTER IV

Femminization
and Its Discontents

Torah Study as a System
for the Domination of Women

One has to learn to move like a gendered human body.
—Maud W. Gleason[1]

In direct contrast to the firm handshake approved (for men and businesswomen) in our culture, a *Yeshiva-Bokhur,* until this day, extends the right hand with limp wrist for a mere touch of the other's hand. If the handshake is, as frequently said, originally a knightly custom, the counter-handshake of the ideal Jewish male elegantly bears out my thesis of the *Yeshiva-Bokhur* (and his secular grandson, the *mentsh*) as antithesis to the knight of romance. Indeed, one of the things that most repelled the Victorian journalist Frank Harris upon meeting Oscar Wilde was that "he shook hands in a limp way that I disliked"[2]—presumably owing to its "effeminacy." The very handshake of the ideal male Jew encoded him as femminized in the eyes of European heterosexual culture, but that handshake constituted as well a mode of resistance to the models of manliness of the dominant fiction.

Torah study itself was associated with a whole range of deportment, of manners of standing, sitting, walking, and speaking, an entire habitus in Bordieu's terminology, a set of techniques of the body. As most recently powerfully documented by the work of Naomi Seidman, the study of Torah was what marked the early modern Ashkenazi Jewish male as male, over-against the female for whom this enterprise was a forbidden asset.[3] This is not to say that all male Ashkenazi Jews actually

1. Gleason, *Making,* xxvi.
2. Sinfield, *Wilde,* 2.
3. Seidman, *Marriage,* 85–86 and passim. Again, I emphasize that my qualification of my discourse as being about Ashkenazi Jews does not serve to make an exception of

studied Torah, any more than all medieval German men were knights, but this social marker was what defined the ideal male, indeed defined maleness itself. Torah study was, for these Jews, a tertiary sexual characteristic, defined by Maud Gleason as "the tilt of the pelvis, the gestures of the hand, even certain movements of the eyes—all these function as a conventional language through which gender identity may be claimed and decoded."[4]

If study defined the rabbinic male, then the exclusion of women was the practice that constructed gender differentiation and hierarchy within that society. The typical explanations given by most feminists for this segregation are unconvincing. One is that women were considered essentially and always contaminated and contaminating and that contact with the Holy Torah had to be prohibited on those grounds. This assumption simply does not hold water. First, there is very little evidence in rabbinic Jewish literature that women were so regarded. Indeed one of the characteristics of the rabbinic movement is the ways that it set itself up in opposition to older, more Hellenized Judaisms, in which such ideas—including extreme misogyny and antisexuality—were rampant.[5] Simply conflating these different Judaisms misses the point entirely, as does the collapsing of all systems of male domination into an undifferentiated unhistoricized "patriarchy," often referred to as "the patriarchy."[6] Second, there is no evidence, and indeed counterevidence, that the Torah had to be protected from impurity. The standard phrase in halakhic literature is: "The words of Torah are not susceptible to impurity"; and it was not until the early medieval period that women were considered contaminating entities in the context of Torah.[7] The formal halakhic level of the texts suggests strongly that there were no bars to women studying Torah, but nevertheless, even in talmudic times it seems to have been practically unknown and later there is a positive horror of it.[8] Third, since even at its medieval worst the exclusion from

Sefaradic and eastern Jews but the opposite: to indicate that Ashkenazim are not the only Jews in existence but are the only ones that I have studied (for the modern period). It would be fascinating to find out whether or not these characteristics and gender practices are common to the whole Jewish people at given periods of time.

4. Gleason, *Making,* xxvi. For a quite different usage of the term "tertiary sexual character," see Weininger, *Sex,* 195.
5. D. Boyarin, *Carnal Israel.*
6. Pateman, *Sexual Contract,* 29–30.
7. Cohen, "Menstruants."
8. D. Boyarin, *Carnal Israel,* 167–96.

study of Torah did not, paradoxically, include the most holy book, the Bible itself, but only the culturally more valued practice of study of Talmud, the explanation that women contaminate the holy text is incoherent. In rejecting this explanation as genetically unconvincing, however, I am not denying the degree to which it has functioned synchronically since the end of late antiquity as the means for the production of an ideology of women as contaminated and contaminating, which men disseminated and women internalized. Exclusion from the study of Torah was not caused by the belief that women were polluting agents; rather, the belief was an effect of that exclusion. Whether or not it is a "correct" interpretation of the Talmud, it is thus nonetheless certain that women have been made in historical Judaism to experience themselves as impure, dangerous, and devalued through these exclusions. It is virtually impossible to overemphasize the intensity of affliction and humiliation that this systematic ritual expression of inferiority has caused for many Jewish women.

A second explanation has it that the presence of women within the sites of the study of Torah would be too disturbing a factor, at least distracting and probably worse. This seems to me much closer to the mark: Torah study was understood to have a powerful erotic charge which would indeed have been very "dangerous" if men and women were to do it together. But it does not explain the apparent impossibility of separate spaces within which women could study Torah, just as there were separate spaces within which they could participate in the prayer. There has to be a fuller, sharper structural cultural necessity for such an extreme pattern of exclusion.

I propose that for rabbinic patriarchy the central moment in the construction of gender and thus of the subjection of women is the exclusion of women from the study of Torah and that this exclusion fulfills the functions that in other patriarchies are fulfilled in the realm of economic activity (work) and sanctioned physical domination of women by men (*patria potestas* in its most extreme version).[9] Talmudic discourse (halakha and aggada) provides a frame of social and cultural

---

9. Cantor, *Jewish*, 5. Interestingly enough, Leopold von Sacher-Masoch, whom we met in chapter 2, seems also to have understood this point. In one of his "Jewish tales," the liberation of a wife from domination by her husband (and her accession to dominance) is signified by her acquisition of talmudic knowledge (D. Biale, "Masochism," 315; see also Aschheim, *Brothers*, 25)! As Biale demonstrates, Sacher-Masoch's knowledge of *Ostjudische* life was by no means superficial or drawn from books alone.

theory that is an important material fact in the production of rabbinic
Jewish cultures, although the social realizations of the structural possibilities afforded by the 'theory' vary in accord with different economic,
social, and political conditions. Actual cultural forms are mediated
through a complex set of social, economic, historical, cultural conditions, including frequently the nature of the cultural practice of the
societies within which Jews found themselves in different times. Thus,
I am not claiming either that Jewish culture as it was actually lived
"on the ground" conformed to the norms of the talmudic discourse,
or that Christian culture, as it was lived, was structured according to
the theories of gender that Carole Pateman, among others, has described. I cannot, however, escape the sense that these differing theories
both respond to and structure at least somewhat different sets of social
practices as well.

I theorize that the exclusion of women from the study of Torah subtended the rabbinic Jewish gender hierarchy in two closely related ways,
via the construction of a "fraternity" and via the production of a social
system within which a group of men (the Rabbis) held power over the
actual practices and pleasures of female bodies. It is here, I emphasize
once more, that the point of sharpest feminist critique must be aimed:
at this generally compassionate and humane (but absolute) control of
female subjects through maintaining them in virtual ignorance of the
practices that enable ritual decision making.

As to the first category, I suggest that the rabbinic phratry was substantially similar in its gendered structure and engendering function
to such analogs as the guild or shop in Western economic and social
practice. As Carole Pateman has put it (depending in this instance on
Cynthia Cockburn), "The workplace and the trades unions are orga-
nized as fraternal territory, where 'it was unthinkable' that a girl could
be part of an apprenticeship system so clearly 'designed to produce a
free *man*,' where 'skilled' work is the work done by men, and where
manhood is tested and confirmed every day."[10] The same function is
performed for rabbinic Jews (once again, at least ideally) in the Bes-
Hamidrash (House of Study), while Jewish women are to be found in
the workplace. It is similarly unthinkable for a girl to be part of the
homotopic space of the Study-House. Manhood is tested and confirmed
(and I would add constructed) every day precisely in the House of Study,

10. Pateman, *Sexual Contract*, 141.

and the workplace becomes the relatively devalued site that the "private sphere" is in bourgeois society.

The second way that rabbinic Jewish culture produced a hierarchy of genders through the study of Torah was in its actual construction of the meaning of femaleness through this exclusion. In this respect it is similar in substance to the modes of production of gendered difference and gendered subjection endemic within Western society in general. Another of Pateman's formulations seems to capture the meanings of men's exclusive access to Torah: "Women's relations to the social world must always be mediated through men's reason; women's bodies must always be subject to men's reason and judgements if order is not to be threatened."[11] Analogously, for rabbinic Judaism, women's relations to the sacred world are mediated through men's reason in the practice of the study of Torah. Finally, a question must be raised—and I do genuinely raise it as a question—whether the frequent discussion of sexuality and female bodies that took place in the talmudic academy, which we can guess at from the text, did not function (הבדלות אלף להבדיל) as sexual banter does in the all-male workplace, from composing room to locker room, as a means of asserting male sex-right as well?[12]

What is common to both of these modalities is that they steer toward the judgment that it is not appropriate to ask, with respect to classical rabbinic culture, whether or not a pre-given entity, the class of women, is or is not permitted to study the Torah, but rather to see that it is study of Torah as a gendered activity that produces the hierarchically ordered categories of men and women.[13] As Delphy has observed: "The concept of class starts from the idea of social construction and specifies the implications of it. Groups are no longer *sui generis*, constituted before coming into relation with one another. On the contrary, it is their relationship which constitutes them as such. It is therefore a question of discovering the social practices, the social relations, which, in constituting the division of gender, create the groups of gender (called 'of sex')."[14] Men are those human beings of whom it is expected that they "study Torah." Men, as the dominant class of traditional Judaism, are precisely

---

11. Pateman, *Sexual Contract*, 101.
12. Pateman, *Sexual Contract*, 141–42.
13. For the clarity of this formulation I am indebted to Peskowitz, "Engendering."
14. Delphy, *Close to Home*, 26.

those who are obligated to study Torah as well as to perform the entire panoply of positive commandments.

Rabbinic Judaism as a discourse was, to borrow Laura Levitt's terms from another context, primarily detrimental to women's agency but not to their physical welfare.[15] By saying this, I do not minimize the effect of psychic pain, of the constant insult and denial of value and autonomy that the system produced and enforced. To put it in James Scott's terms, it is in the exclusion from study of Torah that we find the clearest structural, ritual expression of an inferiority of women "in rituals or etiquette regulating public contact between strata"[16] (see Plate 8).

Gender, in short, in rabbinic culture and thus gender domination are forged via the construction of the ideal male as Torah scholar. Torah study is the functional modality by which male dominance over women is secured in rabbinic discourse, thus fulfilling the functions that physical domination secures in various other cultural formations. Male power remains secure, insofar, at least, as the Rabbis, an all-male group, held power over Jewish women.[17]

I propose that the tertiary sexual characteristics of Jewish men render them readable as pseudowomen within the habitus of the larger cultural context, and that Jews from the Babylonian talmudic period and its cultural descendants were frequently aware of this "linguistic" slippage, responding to it differently in different times and places. The stylized repetitions that produce gender differentiation within Jewish praxis were the performances of Torah study. However, at the same time that these techniques of the body and, especially, the praxis of Torah-learning that they supported and were supported by produced (ideally) gentle, passive, emotional men, they also formed the tech-

15. Levitt, *Reconfiguring*, 235.

16. J. C. Scott, *Domination*, xi.

17. It remains secure only in theory. An important point to realize is that until quite late in the talmudic period, the Rabbis themselves exercised very little power over Jewish communities. It was only late in the third century C.E. that their political power increased, and even then only over a relatively small part of the Jewish population at large (Levine, *Rabbinic Class*). For the implications of this point vis-à-vis the specific question of female power, see Brooten, *Women*. I emphasize here what I have stated in the introduction: In studying the classical rabbinic literature, we are not studying social history but looking at the construction of an ideal Jewish society through the eyes of one Jewish sect. This "constitution"—with all of its heterogeneity and contentions intact—became one vitally significant material fact in the production of Jewish cultures in later periods. It is not inapposite, therefore, to compare rabbinic theories of the sexual contract with those of the philosophers studied by Pateman.

Plate 8.   The Exclusion of Women from the Beth Hamidrash. Painting of women watching men studying Torah, *Andacht in der Franensynagoge,* by Tadensz Popiel. (Courtesy of the Leo Baeck Institute, New York.)

nology through which the domination of women was carried out in this culture.

Male self-fashioning has consequences for women.

THE "KINDER, GENTLER" PATRIARCHY

In this section of the chapter, I wish to show how the rabbinic social system provided for the domination of women by men precisely through its technologies for the production of gentle men. Certain aspects of this system have been portrayed by apologists as recommending rabbinic culture as "good for women." Careful analysis shows, however, that while there may have been some ways in which the lives of Jewish women were more satisfying and less vulnerable than those of their non-Jewish contemporary sisters, this did not result in a social system any more (or less) egalitarian than those of the coexistent Christian subcultures.

To be sure, at least in theory, Jewish husbands do not have automatic sexual access to their wives, and even their economic rights in their wives' labor are limited by law. In contrast to western legal systems, in rabbinic law, wives continued to own their own property. The significance of this point is that the doctrine of coverture, the legal disappearance of a wife into her husband's person, which was active in European legal systems until the nineteenth century,[18] did not obtain in classical Jewish law. As Levitt writes, "In the late 18th century, when Jewish women entered into this legal system, they ironically became even less able to act on their own behalf."[19]

Rabbinic wives are just as subordinated, however differently, as other women. Moreover, it is very important to emphasize that while economic and sexual coverture do not obtain for rabbinic culture, something that we might best style spiritual coverture does. Because of the system of commandments within which significance and value are placed on the fulfillment of a commandment which one is obligated to perform, and since women were "exempted" from the fulfillment of many commandments, they were understood as being able to achieve spiritual merit only through the enabling of their husbands to perform these commandments. Women only could gain, on this system, a religious identity through being married and through their support of their husbands' religious lives. The import of this structure of subordination of women's spiritual value to that of their husbands should not be underestimated nor underemphasized, precisely at the moment that the greater autonomy and significance of women in the economic realm is being articulated. Since, for this culture, the greatest value was placed specifically on the economically "useless" practice of Torah study, which many women enabled through their labor and business acumen, the notion of women as an exploited class of economic actors is not inapposite. At the same time, neither should we ignore the potentially greater satisfactions of a life of economic autonomy, activity, and usefulness vis-à-vis life in the "doll's house" of the bourgeoisie. Moreover, this economic autonomy at certain times has led to potentially greater scope for women's religious roles as well. With regard to medieval Jewish women of France and Germany, David Biale writes, "In fact, women in the French and German Jewish communities of the High Middle

18. Pateman, *Sexual Contract*, passim, esp. 90–100.
19. Levitt, *Reconfiguring*, 130–31.

Ages appear to have enjoyed rather astonishing freedom, probably a result of their active role in business and other public professions. Women
may have also demanded a greater liturgical role, for lively debates were
carried on in legal circles about the place of women in the synagogue
and in talmudic study."[20] It is only, for instance, in this chronotope
of Jewish history that in some communities women were counted for
the minyan, the public quorum for prayer. Louis Finkelstein proposes
that this increased participation—which he calls a "movement toward
'women's rights,'" with authorities permitting women to act as judges
in religious courts, to be counted for a quorum for grace, and to be
called to the Torah, as well as with shifts toward equality in marriage
and divorce laws—"had its origin and compelling force largely in the
fact that women began to occupy a prominent position in the economic
world."[21]

   Not atypical for early modern Jewish women, *in terms of her economic status,* is the famous Glikl. Glikl had been a full partner in
her husband's successful business while he was alive and sole proprie-
tor after his death. When contracts needed to be drawn for the business, it was she who drafted the document and pursued the negotia-
tion. She relates that she and her sisters were "taught in religious and
worldly things." Perhaps more surprising, this study was moreover not
at home but in the regular religious Jewish school, the *Cheder.* Finally, she was highly educated in German culture of the day as well.
She traveled to fairs all over Germany, bought and sold on the Exchange, and ran a factory. In a quite matter-of-fact way she describes
another such woman as "a woman of virtues [*Esches Chajil*]" because
"she carried on the business and saw to her husband and children in
a handsome way," clearly seeing nothing aberrant in a wife as breadwinner.[22]

   It is crucial to realize that Glikl's exceptionality consists primarily in
the fact of her writing; there is no reason to assume that the other aspects of her life were *sui generis,* neither her education, the partnership
of her marriage, nor her business and public-service life. As Natalie
Zemon Davis points out, Glikl herself had good role models in her

20. Biale, *Eros and the Jews,* 74; Marcus, "Mothers."
21. Finkelstein, Jewish *Self-Government,* 378–79.
22. Abrahams, *Memoirs,* 13, 14, 42, 61, 92.

mother and grandmother.[23] Glikl writes of one Jewish woman who "understood business well and supported the household. She went regularly to the fairs." Of another pious Jewish girl she writes that she "knew French perfectly,"[24] and this same girl knew Hebrew fluently as well.[25] Early in the seventeenth century, the Jews negotiated with the city of Breslau to allow women to attend that city's commercial fair, because otherwise the Jewish business would have been seriously impaired.[26] Glikl of Hameln had in many ways the kind of marriage that Mary Wollstonecraft describes as a nearly utopian vision. Her life was the antithesis of the *höhere Töchter* (bourgeois daughter) and "the angel in the house."[27] Her society, and traditional European Jewish society in general, well into the nineteenth century, hardly instantiated Hegel's typical and banal view that "[t]he husband has the 'prerogative to go out and work for the [family's] living, to attend to its needs, and to control and administer its capital.' "[28]

This economic power may have resulted in greater autonomy and satisfaction for Jewish women of this period, certainly vis-à-vis their bourgeois granddaughters.[29] Nevertheless, male domination of women was firmly in place. Pateman argues that "the civil sphere gains its uni-

---

23. N. Z. Davis, *Women,* 14. For that matter, as Davis makes clear, even her writing of an autobiography in the form of an "ethical will" may not have been as unusual as previously thought (20).

24. Abrahams, *Memoirs,* 17. This, to be sure, is more like the accomplishments of the later bourgeois *höhere Töchter.*

25. Abrahams, *Memoirs,* 19–20.

26. D. Biale, *Eros,* 68.

27. On the significance of this point, see chapter 8. It is important to emphasize, however, that there were many Protestant women in western Europe—and especially England—who were leading lives quite similar in outlines, *mutatis mutandis,* to that of Glikl as well (Fletcher, *Gender,* 173–91). My point is hardly, then, to argue for some particular superiority of Jewish-European culture over others. My claim is rather that in its significantly different ideas about gender, Jewish culture may have provided some tools for resistance to the more severely constricted lives for women that embourgeoisement/heterosexuality provided.

28. Quoted in Pateman, *Sexual Contract,* 177.

29. M. Kaplan, *Making,* 52. See also Shepherd (*Price,* 6–7), who shows the effect of this greater autonomy on mustering the participation of Jewish women in radical movements, and who disputes the unsupported view of Richard Stites that the reason for the greater participation of Jewish women in such movements was owing to the "greater despotism" of the Jewish family. In direct contrast, Shepherd argues that it was the encouragement that these women received from their fathers to seek education, along with their partial (if fraught) identification with their fathers, that prodded their radicalism. Shepherd is clearly correct and supports her conclusions with hard data. Knee-jerk prejudices about Jewish society being systematically worse for women than any others die hard. Of course, as Shepherd makes clear, the pull to radical movements was, at the same time, in large part a form of rebellion against the disabilities that women did suffer under traditional Jewish culture.

versal meaning in opposition to the private sphere of natural subjection
and womanly capacities. The 'civil individual' is constituted within the
sexual division of social life created through the original contract. The
civil individual and the public realm appear universal only in relation
to and in opposition to the private sphere, the natural foundation of
civil life."[30] At first glance, this would seem not to apply to rabbinic
society, precisely because women are not removed from the eminently
public realm of commerce, but in fact all we have to do is substitute the
House of Study (or even the space of study of Torah in the home) for
the "public realm" in order to see that for this rabbinic cultural system,
commerce simply shifts into the structural equivalent of the "private
sphere." In other words, technologies of domination have to be interpreted within their own systemic structure, and within the structure of
rabbinic Judaism it is the "indoor," somewhat private realm of the
House of Study that defines the social prestige and power of men over
women, and not the estate of getting and spending, of economic power,
that produces such distinction in bourgeois society. Indeed, the commitment of "men" to indoor, seemingly private pursuits of study in
Ashkenazi culture was certainly one of the factors that inscribed them
as femminized in the eyes of the Others. The hierarchy in Judaism, by
valorizing the "private" over the "public," exploits gender as yet another modality by which the Jewish People in Diaspora valorizes itself
over those very Others. As Virginia Burrus has remarked, "If in some
sense it is Judaism's 'colonization' that forces it into a purely (even exag-
geratedly) private sphere after the fall of the Temple and thus inscribes
its men as 'femminized,' then the response of the resistant subculture of
audaciously marking the private as 'high' (in value) and the public as
'low' and then sending its women out to deal with the public is eye-
opening indeed" (letter). This seems to me a valid insight, but we must
be careful not to allow it to become another version of a Nietzschean

30. Pateman, *Sexual Contract,* 113–14. See Pateman, *Disorder,* 118–40, for extensive critique of the notion of public/private as a transhistorical dichotomy. Especially relevant is her discussion of the separation of production from the household and the development of the theory of a public/private separation (123). In contrast, see the insightful
remarks of Virginia Burrus: "Indeed, as terms of 'ordinary discourse' evoking 'unreflec-
tively held notions and concepts' that shape day-to-day lives, 'public' and 'private' may
not appear in need of interpretation at all, but it is doubtful whether the dichotomous
categories with which so many operate are in fact either as universal or as transparently
'commonsensical' as is sometimes claimed. Indeed, I would suggest that the public-private
distinction is most fruitfully applied to the study of the Priscillianist controversy precisely
because it is an artifact of the very Mediterranean cultures that shaped the terms of the
late-ancient controversy" (Burrus, *Making,* 7).

ressentiment argument that then loses the critical force of the reversal of values that nevertheless has taken place, while still attending to the ways that within the culture itself gender hierarchy has revealed once more its resilience and persistence even in these altered situations. In other words, the relevant distinction is not between public and private at all but between the most valued and less valued practices of the culture, so within the culture itself, the ascriptions of maleness and femaleness are almost reversed.[31] For this reason, men ignorant of Torah who "support their women" through working and selling, and who thus are more like "real men" and Iron Johns, may be described by this society as men who are "like women."

THE CASE OF "WIFE-BEATING"

Rabbinic culture, then, defined ideal men as gentle, peaceful, and nuturing. It is here that we find the origin of the notion that Jewish men do not beat their wives. This old nostrum is not a "true fact," but it also is not just an apologetic myth. Substantial segments of the rabbinic tradition delineated the essence of the rabbinic Jewish male as he who does not beat his wife, as opposed to "them," for whom such practice was normative. Although in the early middle ages (from the ninth to eleventh centuries) there was a great deal of equivocation on the part of Babylonian halakhic authorities (the *geonim*) as to the permissibility of hitting one's wife in order to "educate" her,[32] at the crest of the medieval period the Ashkenazic tradition was nearly unanimous, unequivocal, and very compelling in condemning all violence by husbands to-

---

31. Weissler, "For Women." A moment like this brings into brilliant focus the value of Christine Delphy's analysis of gender as a class-system within which "[i]t may be (and this remains to be proven) that women are (also) females, and that men are (also) males" (Delphy, *Close to Home*, 24–26). It should not, however, be forgotten that there were economic class differences within Jewish society as well, a point shortchanged in this book. Thus, for example, a man who was an excellent businessman and also learned in Torah had status every bit as high as (or perhaps higher than) that of the man who failed in business and was a great Torah scholar. Glikl's husband as described by her in chapter 1 above, fits this former model, but later on, in the nineteenth century, the distinction between scholars and businessmen was, I believe, more sharply drawn—with some notable exceptions: R. Shmuel Strasson, for example, a very wealthy businessman whose commentaries appear in a prominent place in every modern Talmud print. In any case, it seems that status (for men) was determined primarily by learning, such that the ignorant but wealthy man would definitely be in a class lower than that of the learned poor man. A full analysis of the class structure of Ashkenazi Jewry (informed, as well, by feminist theory) remains a desideratum. (I am grateful to Natalie Zemon Davis, Todd Endelman, and Natalie Kampen for comments that led to the above reflections.)
32. Grossman, "Violence," 189.

ward wives under any circumstances whatever. This fact hardly defines the culure as affording an egalitarian status to women; indeed, the very terms within which this self-definition was promulgated are evocative of male privilege and domination.

Wife-beating provides me with a very elegant case study with which to exemplify the thesis of this book, namely, that being out-of-power can provide a location for important ethical knowledge at the same time that it undermines the very knowledge it has produced. Ironically, the same textual and legal moments that express "compassion" for women and condemn male violence against them are those that most clearly indicate male "possession" of women.

There is an apparent difference between two medieval rabbinic cultures with respect to the discourse surrounding wife-beating. While the great Ashkenazi rabbis condemned violent chastisement of wives for any reason virtually unanimously and unequivocally, Maimonides notoriously held quite different ideas. Maimonides permitted (recommended) scourging a wife with a rod if she refused to perform her duties (Nashim 21:10).[33] Most of the standard and hegemonic commentators on Maimonides' code immediately dissented from his ruling, one writing that "I have never heard that [it is permitted] to chastise women with whips."[34] The definitive code of Jewish Law, the *Shulkhan Arukh*, which normally follows the views of Maimonides, pointedly leaves out this sentence in which he permits physical chastising of the wife.[35] Hauptman demonstrates, moreover, that the author of this sixteenth-century work, R. Joseph Caro, of Turkey and Palestine, in several places in his writings makes particularly strong statements against domestic violence of any type, including in his commentary on the Maimonidean text. Others apparently accepted Maimonides' authority, however: according to Grossman, not even one of the Ashkenazic halakhic authorities endorsed this position of Maimonides, while of the major rabbinic codifiers of Spanish Jewry, only Ramban and Rashba seemingly followed him.[36] These are, it should be emphasized, pillars of the Sefaradic

33. As Avraham Grossman points out, however, it is not entirely clear from Maimonides' wording whether the husband or the court is to do the hitting ("Violence," 193).

34. Rabbi Avraham ben David of Posquières, the Raʾabad *ad loc;* and see Grossman, "Violence," 193.

35. The Shulkhan Arukh does, however, permit the use of modes of "force" other than physical violence, thus explicitly making the point that there is violence in the system even where beating is prohibited.

36. Grossman, "Violence," 193–95.

[Spanish] halakhic tradition.[37] Grossman hypothesizes that this position on the part of Maimonides and those Spanish rabbis who follow him owes to the "influence of the situation in the surrounding Moslem culture."[38]

I find this a less than convincing explanation, however, since the culture surrounding the Ashkenazim had legally institutionalized violence against wives that was, if anything, more extreme than that of Islam at the time. The laws of many medieval European cities institutionalized, for instance, any sort of nonlethal violence by husbands against wives, even sometimes recommending that a husband may "cut pieces of his wife's body from the sole of her foot to her head and warm his feet in her blood."[39] I tentatively suggest that the difference between the position of the Sefaradic and Ashkenazic rabbis had to do with their different sociopolitical conditions. Maimonides and many of the other Sefaradic Rabbis were socially dominant and close to the ruling circles and courts of their homes. Maimonides was court physician to the Sultan, and Shmuel Hanagid who had written that men should not give their wives a chance to "raise their heads" and should beat them if they do, was the commander in chief of the Grenadan army. The Ashkenazic Rabbis, on the other hand, were for the most part relatively marginalized when they were not dominated, despised, and persecuted by the prevailing culture.[40] I hypothesize that this would have led the Sefaradic

37. Other texts of both of these authorities, however, seem to contradict this claim. Responsa of Rashba, Part 7, Responsum 477: "A husband may not beat his wife, because she was given for life and not to cause her to suffer." Note that in this text a distinction is drawn between a husband beating his wife "for no reason" and one who is hitting her because she "curses him incessantly for no reason," but in both cases he is forced to divorce her. The only question is whether or not he must pay her the divorce settlement. This seems similar, moreover, to the language of the Ramban cited at Tur Bet Yossef EH 74. Thus, according to these texts it is difficult to say that even these two authorities followed Maimonides' ruling. For discussion of this passage in the Rashba, see below.

38. Grossman, "Violence," 195. This is an example of a prevalent scholarly position that seeks to glorify Ashkenazic culture by associating it with the "white" European culture while subtly denigrating Sefaradic culture as "Moslem," thus hitching a ride, as it were, on the current hegemony of Europe. I am not accusing Grossman, of course, of any overt or conscious racism.

39. Law of Aardenburg, fourteenth century, quoted in Grossman, "Violence," 185.

40. As preeminent Jewish historian Jacob Katz has argued, "In the older corporate structure, there had been a group of intellectuals attached to each estate: writers and lawyers served at the courts of kings: priests and teachers provided for the needs of the commonalty; and Talmudic scholars did the same for the corresponding niche in Jewish society" (Tradition, 220). So much for Ashkenaz, but in Sefarad, Jewish writers and lawyers (who were also the talmudic scholars) served at the courts of the kings. Generally, we have had research on the "positive" aspects of this cultural situation: the Hebrew poetry, philosophy, and medical science that it produced. This is referred to as the Golden Age of Jewish culture. I am pointing out here some possible "negative" consequences: that this

leaders, who were important government officials,[41] to identify with the local culture, for good and for ill, including the masculinism and misogyny that such power promotes, while the Ashkenazic Jews were busy identifying themselves as the "opposite" of that which surrounded them, and had, moreover, potentially greater reason for empathy with the victims of violence. This would be, then, a historical reenactment of the story of Rabbi that we read in chapter 2, who had to take on himself overwhelming suffering in order to learn compassion and nonviolence. This hypothesis avoids two kinds of potentially invidious conclusions — one, that Jews are somehow better than others, and two, that Ashkenazim (in the Christian world) are somehow better than Sefaradim (in the Moslem world) — by suggesting that the material conditions of power versus powerlessness are the significant factor in generating discourses that promote or disdain male violence against women. This hypothesis would provide also an explanation for why a postexpulsion Sefaradic Rabbi such as Rabbi Caro would so thoroughly and decisively reject the authoritative tradition that he normally embodies.

In Ashkenaz, there was a tendency to mark off Jewish practice overagainst its neighbors' mores, wherein even extreme violence against wives was encoded into law. Thus, a definitive thirteenth-century halakhic authority, the Mordekhai, writes that Jewish men, unlike the men of other cultures, are not in the habit of beating their wives.[42] Slightly later, Rabbi Meʾir of Rothenberg, arguably the dominant halakhic authority of medieval Ashkenazic Jewry, defines wife-beating as a legally institutionalized gentile practice, which, of course it was, and thus differentiates Judaism as the privation of such a usage. Rabbi Meʾir writes: "It is the way of the Gentiles to behave thus, but God forbid and God forfend for a son of the Covenant to behave thus."[43] He goes on to

---

was not only a position of cultural integration but of social power and political dominance as well. David Biale correctly points out that both Sefaradic and Ashkenazic Jews considered their rabbinical leaders as the internal equivalent of kings, but vis-à-vis the general power structure they obviously held very different positions. Thus, as he himself makes clear, the local descriptions of figures like the Nagid draw on Arabic models, while the Ashkenazi descriptions of rabbis as kings draw on biblical models (D. Biale, *Power*, 44). Again, it seems highly significant that the Nagid, who was the leader of Spanish Jewry, was, as Biale remarks, "a leader without any sacred ancestry, usually rising to his post from a position as a court financier or physician" (46). Biale sums up: "We may generalize that individual Jews achieved greater political power under Islam, while the Jewish community as a whole enjoyed, if sporadically, a better status under Christianity" (69).

41. D. Biale, *Power*, 70.
42. Hauptman, "Traditional Jewish Texts."
43. Rothenberg, Responsa, no. 81.

recommend cutting off the hand of the repeat offender. Without, of
course, accepting the descriptive validity of these statements—indeed
the necessity for such language indicates that the problem was rampant—we must nevertheless reckon with their normative functioning.[44]
It should be carefully noted, however, that Jewish feminists have shown
how such "apologetic" statements can work to prevent the correction
of abuse as well as function to reduce incidences of abuse. When a community refuses to recognize, or denies the existence of, a problem, silence can equal death.[45]

Instead of allowing ourselves to exonerate traditional Jewish culture
by referring to the fact that Jewish men do not (normatively) maintain
power through physical violence, we have to interrogate the ways that
hierarchy and power imbalance were and are maintained within traditional Jewish culture without the exercise of violence or, precisely, with
the participation of men who are *not* violent—analogous to the ways

44. Graetz, "Rejection," 14. Grossman formulates it well: "We ought not to be misled by the principled opposition to hitting of women which is found in the words of the
Sages of Israel and to conclude that the phenomenon was rare. This is highly important
opposition from a theoretical point of view, and one may hypothesize that it gave the wife
a certain measure of protection at the time of complaints before the courts. However,
from these sources it becomes clear that the phenomenon of violence toward women was
prevalent in all of the communities of Israel. We do not intend to make light of the trenchant opposition of most of the Sages of Israel in the Middle Ages to the beating of wives,
but we must see the matters in the correct proportion and to make a clear distinction
between their normative decisions and the situation in reality" ("Violence," 201, my
translation). The prevailing unconditional opposition of medieval rabbis to wife-beating
should be contrasted with contemporary non-Jewish legal discourses in Europe that almost universally permitted and promoted it (Fletcher, *Gender,* 192). The rabbinic view
can be contrasted with the situation in England, where, according to Margaret Hunt,
"relatively few men or women in early modern England thought wives had an absolute
right not to be beaten" ("Wife," 24). To put a point on it, it has never been the case
within rabbinic law that "a man could do what he liked inside his own home, that his
wife was his sexual and physical property" (Fletcher, *Gender,* 196). Of course, I emphasize yet again, as Grossman does, this is not equivalent to a descriptive/apologetic claim
that Jewish men do not beat their wives—far from it. Wife-beating was made a crime in
Calvin's Geneva and by Puritans in England at the beginning of the seventeenth century,
as it was by English Baptists several decades later (Fletcher, 198–99). See also next note.
45. I thus concur with Levitt that denial of wife abuse has been a serious problem in
modern Jewish society. I quite dissent, however, from her diagnosis of the reasons for this.
She argues that "the power inequities built into the ketubbah exacerbate this problem.
They gave a husband unlimited legal power over his wife while the contract did not provide her with any way of addressing this kind of abuse" (*Reconfiguring,* 103). I, however,
would suggest that the situation is almost the exact opposite of this description. Jewish
law did not give a husband unlimited legal power over his wife, and the *ketubba* was
largely oriented to protecting her from him. The problem is, rather, that in the narcissistic
assumption that rabbinic Judaism had succeeded in protecting wives from abuse, the traditional culture became incapable of acknowledging its failure and thus perpetuated,
through denial, the violence that it would not recognize within itself.

that even the nonrapist gains power over women (including sexual access) in a social system in which rape is represented as normative for men.[46] As Susan Estrich has put it, "[F]orce is the power that [a man] need not use (at least physically)."[47]

The very terms within which the condemnations of violence against wives occur in rabbinic literature demonstrate how that condemnation served as a technology for the control of women by men. Thus the foundational argument that a husband is forbidden (by the Torah) to hit his wife, that to do so is a sin, is derived from a talmudic statement that since Eve is "the mother of all living," "she is given for life; she is not given for causing pain to her" (Ketubboth 61a). The Talmud itself derives from this reasoning that a husband may not prevent his wife from breastfeeding (and hire a wet nurse), since this causes her pain, and the early and later medieval rabbis, both Sefaradic and Ashkenazi, base on this source their strong condemnations of striking a wife. This argument is found in such definitive authorities as Nachmanides of thirteenth-century Spain; the Rashba of thirteenth- and fourteenth-century Spain; and Rabbi Me'ir (Maharam) of thirteenth-century Rothenberg, Germany. Perhaps the strongest of all of these statements is to be found in the Responsa of Rabbi Binyamin Ze'ev, a Greek Rabbi of the early sixteenth century, who writes:

> With every blow, he violates the Torah's law "Do not add" [Deut. 25:3],[48] and his punishment is greater than that for one who hits his fellow, for she dwells with him in trust [i.e., she trusts that she is safe with him].[49] ... We force him to divorce her even by means of Gentiles (i.e., we [the court] hire Gentiles to beat him until he agrees to divorce her). ... And even Shmuel who said in the Talmud: "[If he refuses to support her], rather than force him to divorce her, force him to feed her," that only applies in a case where he refuses to support her, for there we have a solution. We enter his property and seize it, but here where she is in his hands, and we have no solution, even Shmuel would agree that we force him to divorce her [Responsum 88].

For all this clear execration of male sexual violence against women, it is absolutely patent that only men have the power to condemn or per-

46. Cf. also Delphy, *Close to Home,* 114-15.
47. Estrich, *Real Rape,* 67.
48. This is a very interesting argument in its own right. The verse is speaking of the hitting of a criminal and indicates that one may hit him no more than thirty-nine times; more constitutes a sin. The rabbi's argument is that if one hits one's wife even once, this same sin is already being committed.
49. This language follows the ancient German Ashkenazic tradition (Grossman, "Violence," 201).

mit such violence. This point is made, moreover, at the very site of the origin of the condemnation: "she is given [to him] for life; she is not given [to him] for causing pain to her." While this statement clearly constrains the power of the husband over his wife, indicating that he may not behave toward her or demand of her anything that causes her pain, it nevertheless also indicates that she is "given" to him in some sense and for some purpose, whatever the normative constraints on his power over her.[50] At least one early modern rabbi, Rabbi David ibn Zimra of sixteenth-century Egypt, came to the conclusion from this argument that while it is absolutely forbidden for a husband to hit his wife for refusing to serve him, if he can prove that he hits her because she "violates the Torah," he may do so, "because she is his property."[51]

Thus even for those rabbis who recoil in disgust and horror from the idea of physical violence toward women/wives, the systemic violence and psychic violence remain. While it is certainly not irrelevant to point to the fact that the virtually unanimous voice of the Ashkenazic tradition is to condemn wife-beating in no uncertain terms, what is finally invidious is the very fact that a male power structure has the right even to discuss the issue, that it assumes this kind of (benevolently) despotic control over women and their lives. It is this that ultimately provides the soil within which violence against women can germinate, and in contemporary Israel, for instance, flourish without the rabbis there hindering it at all. As the one lone Ashkenazi voice who does permit wife-beating as a means of preventing wives from performing egregious sins had already written, "Anyone who is under the authority of someone else [children, slaves, wives], and he sees that the person is committing sins, he may hit him in order to keep him from sinning" [*Terumot Hadeshen,* part 1, Responsum 218]. In other words, taking his words as descriptive and not prescriptive, the point is that any system of domination contains the potential for systematic violence as well. In this

---

50. In support of this reading of the term "given," I would offer the following parallel. In Nidda 47a, Shmuel has a slave woman undergo a physical examination that involves exposing her breasts in order to learn something that he needs to know about female anatomy. He indemnifies her for her shame, saying "They [slaves] are given for work; they are not given for shaming." For discussion of this passage, see Fonrobert, *Women's.*

51. Radbaz, Part III, Responsum 447. Radbaz, it should be mentioned, absolutely condemns striking a wife because she does not meet his own personal needs, whatever these are, even when these are mandated by Torah or custom and, moreover, puts the burden of proof that he has hit her because of her violations of Torah, squarely on him. He thus dissents in part from the extreme patriarchalism of the Maimonidean ruling. From a modern perspective this hardly ameliorates the situation.

sense, the dominant rabbinic culture, which absolutely and resolutely condemns *any* physical violence to women, nevertheless maintains its authority and power, as it were, precisely to allow or forbid, and thus the very veto on violence is at bottom a threat of violence and it perpetrates the male power monopoly. While protecting women from some of the threats and danger to their physical well-being that were rampant within certain versions of the surrounding society, the Rabbis nevertheless maintained women in a state of permanent and painful second-class citizenship through their exclusion from the Torah as the most valued practice of the society.

THE RABBINIC SEXUAL CONTRACT

Another example within which male power is secured precisely through the production of a kindler, gentler discourse has to do with male sex-right within marriage. The classical European sexual contract does not recognize the right of a wife ever to refuse sex with her husband. The husband who "protects" her from other men is afforded unlimited access to her body in return. Within this system, as has been observed, not only are her protector and the one from whom she is being protected often indistinguishable, but that from which she is being protected and the "right" afforded to the protector are identical. A very explicit and revealing example of this structure is produced by Chrétien in his *Lancelot*, as analyzed by Kathryn Gravdal. In this sequence, a certain maiden has a mock rape of herself staged by her knights, from which Lancelot is intended to rescue her. She explains her action by referring to a certain imaginary "law of Logres" that utterly forbids rape of a woman found alone by a knight but permits him to "do with her as he will" if he "rescues" her from another man.[52] In other words, in exchange for protecting her from rape, her "protector" is permitted to rape her! While the "law of Logres" is, as Gravdal emphasizes, make-believe, the structure of a marriage contract in which in exchange for physical protection a husband is permitted to rape and beat his wife is the same as that legal fiction. Indeed, one could argue that the romance tradition is, in great measure, a conspiracy to make women believe that they want to be raped. As I have already mentioned, the English sexologist Havelock Ellis held that "men whose deepest sexual desire does not involve dominance of women [i.e., rape] must be in some way physically

52. Gravdal, *Ravishing*, 66–67.

deficient."[53] Ellis considers "the hymen an anatomical expression of that admiration of force which marks the female in her choice of a mate."[54]

The rabbinic sexual contract never permits a husband to rape his wife and never promulgates a notion that women desire to be ravished. This did not, however, ultimately weaken the exercise of male sex-right within rabbinic Judaism. It is necessary to identify, accordingly, the modalities by which the male power structure of the society nevertheless maintains control over women and protects male sex-right.

Discursive practices related to female desire that appear in the Talmud and Midrash constitute a structure that functions as an equivalent to the "conjugal right" of European legal discourse in terms of the ordering of sexual relations between the genders, even as the structure does so without sanctioning physical force or economic coercion. The hegemonic rabbinic discourse provides for male sex-right paradoxically through a mystifying construction of women as being needy for sex and of men as being primarily service providers to their wives.

Although, once more, in the context of this argument, I cannot provide a full analysis of the discourse, a partial discussion will indicate the direction of my thinking here as well. The Babylonian Talmud on Eruvin 100b includes the following discussion:

> Rami bar Ḥama said in the name of Rav Assi: a man may not force his wife to have sex with him. . . . [55]
>
> Rabbi Shmuel the son of Naḥmani said in the name of Rabbi Yoḥanan: Any woman who requests sex from her husband will have children such as were not seen even in the generation of Moses. . . .

It is not accidental that the prohibition on wife-rape and the endorsement of the open expression of female desire are juxtaposed so closely in the Talmud, because the second fulfills a cultural function rendered unfulfilled by the prohibition on wife-rape that the first encodes so unambiguously, namely the securing of male access to female bodies. In other words, the furnishing of a strong religious, cultural incentive (the provision of children of a certain preferred type) for women to desire

53. Siegel, *Male,* 59.
54. Quoted in Craft, *Another Kind,* 90.
55. For the full text and a discussion, see D. Boyarin, *Carnal Israel,* 114–15. My purpose here is to add a critical dimension that is absent in that discussion.

sex, and, according to this view, to express their desire, obviates the
need for *patria potestas*.[56]

This argument is supported by the continuation of the text that proposes, in contradistinction to the cited view of Rabbi Yoḥanan, that it
was the curse of Eve to desire her husband when he is about to go on a
journey but to express her desire only through signs of various types
and not to openly request sex. This is, moreover, to the best of my
knowledge, the only interpretation of the verse "To your husband will
be your desire, and he will rule over you" within classical rabbinic texts.
A verse that is taken in other, nonrabbinic, Jewish traditions (and much
Christian writing as well) to endorse wife-rape is understood by the
Rabbis to enjoin on husbands a particular "attentiveness" to their
wives' sexual needs, as a sort of *noblesse oblige*. Thus although the wife
has the right in principle to refuse sex on any occasion, her consent can
be understood through silence and necessarily ambiguous signs.[57]

As feminists (including, especially for the Jewish context, Laura
Levitt) have pointed out, any consent through silence works seriously to
reduce its significance as real power and autonomy for women. Moreover, the Talmud has already informed the husband that under certain
circumstances, for instance when he is about to depart for a journey,
his wife needs him to have sex with her. In other words, through the
construction of sexuality as a form of the husband taking care of the
wife's needs and through the construction of her needs as both compelling and in part inexpressible, virtually the same effect in terms of the
differential political meanings of women's and men's bodies is achieved
as that which Pateman has discussed for the Western sexual contract,
with one enormous difference: it is accomplished without physical violence—indeed with a strong execration of any violence in association
with sex—on one hand, and with the absolute right in principle of the
wife to say no strongly encoded in law on the other.[58]

56. Cf. Christine Delphy's analysis of the way that men secure "monopoly of a prized
commodity," wine, in rural France through the folk-saying: *"femme de vin, femme de
rien."* As Delphy remarks, "[the saying] completely masks the repressive aspect, since it
leaves those concerned to be 'worthless' and passes in silence over the anticipated benefit
of such repression, i.e. the monopoly of a prized commodity" (*Close to Home,* 47–48).
The rabbinic passing in silence over the anticipated benefit to men of their caring for their
wives' sexual needs is both like and unlike the case described by Delphy, in that there is
here, after all, the provision of what must be, at least fairly often, that which is a benefit
(and not a deprivation) for the wife as well.
57. See also Pateman, *Disorder,* 76.
58. This argument could be drawn out via an analysis of the laws of ʿōna, always
described in terms of the man's sexual obligation to his wife. In other words, once more

This oppressive social structure as institutionalized by the rabbinic textual system has produced a methodical configuration of affronts to women that has replaced the need for both economic and physical domination as a technology for maintaining control of the subordinated class, women. Indeed, one might ask whether the male ideal of rabbinic culture should not be figured as control of women through the more subtle forms of thought-manipulation, without effacing the fact that Rabbis' wives probably did get raped and beaten less frequently than the wives of knights. As Scott has put it, "Perhaps one vital distinction to draw between forms of domination lies in the kinds of indignities the exercise of power routinely produces."[59] Ultimately it is the indignity of being the object of a discourse and not the subject of it that is the source of the greatest injury for women within rabbinic Judaism. In other words, even though the text above and many others could be cited to indicate that normative rabbinic Judaism is at least as much about protecting women from male exploitation as it is about institutionalizing exploitation,[60] nevertheless it remains a system within which men are empowered virtually exclusively to make decisions about the lives of women. Even when the male text condemns male violence toward women, it is still assuming and arrogating to itself the power to condemn or approve of such violence and thus, in effect, merely displacing the domination from the personal to the political level and the violence from the physical to the psychic.

The pain of this status has been eloquently recorded by two nineteenth-century women, Reina Batya and Bertha Pappenheim, in trenchant analyses of the function of the study of Torah in the oppression of Jewish women.

ORTHODOX FEMINISTS: REINA BATYA AND BERTHA PAPPENHEIM

In the nineteenth century we begin to hear the voices of Jewish women reacting to and reflecting upon their situation within the cultural/religious system. In fact, one could begin to trace such a genealogy back to the eighteenth century in the person of Sarah Rebecca Rachel Leah,

---

by coding male sexuality as a form of service to women, a mystifying protection of male access to women's bodies is secured.

59. J. C. Scott, *Domination*, 7.

60. Shepherd, *Price*, 27–28, 35. For exemplification of rabbinic efforts to improve the legal and economic status of women vis-à-vis biblical law, see Ilan, *Jewish Women*, 167–72, and especially Hauptman, "Women."

daughter of Yukl Horowitz. She was learned in Hebrew and Aramaic and who wrote women's prayers in which she protested against the marginalization of women in Ashkenazic religious life.[61] Later in the nineteenth century (and in the twentieth century even more so) these voices are increasingly those of women such as Devora Baron[62] or Puah Rakowski and Ita Kalish,[63] who have "left the fold" of traditional Judaism. For the purposes of this book I will discuss women who can be said to have remained within (in their own perceptions and desires) the traditional community and system of values while registering pain and strong protest against the ways that that system marginalizes, excludes, disempowers, and oppresses them. The longing for study of Torah and the recognition of the pain of exclusion are reflected in the Yiddish books of religion for women from the early modern period that indicate that the reward for female piety in this world is learning Torah "just like men" in the next.[64] These explicit nineteenth-century female voices go beyond this longing and begin to articulate the clear understanding that it is the exclusion from Torah study that subtends the whole system of domination of women. From the early modern period on, we are not confined (as we are for much of earlier Jewish history) to projections of female voices as imagined by men. I hope now to begin a nascent genealogy for a critique of the exclusion of women from Torah study from within traditional Judaism, by attending to significant female voices of protest that were raised in the first wave of European feminism.

REINA BATYA, THE WIFE OF THE *NATZIV,* AND HER PROTEST

A remarkable memoir written in the early twentieth century provides evidence of women's protests against the system of exclusion at the very Parnassus of the Yeshiva world.[65] The woman, Reina Batya of Volozhin, was the daughter of a rabbinical leader of Lithuanian Jewry in the gen-

---

61. Weissler, "Women's," 40–42. I part from Weissler's views expressed in this remarkable essay only in disagreeing with her statement to the effect that "[w]hatever Leah had to say on this topic, and on the others she takes up in the introduction, her voice was effectively silenced, or perhaps it would be more precise to say that there was no audience who could hear her" (41). I would suggest that she is at the beginning of a groundswell that finds its full force a century later, a groundswell empowered precisely by learned women like her.

62. Seidman, *Marriage,* 252.

63. Hyman, *Gender,* 57–58, 62–64.

64. Weissler, "Religion," 93; "Women in Paradise."

65. I wish to thank my friend Yaakov Elman for pointing me to this text.

eration before her and the wife of Lithuanian Jewry's greatest talmudic and religious authority of her generation, the *Natziv*, Rabbi Naftali Tzvi Berlin. Although the text unfortunately, once again, preserves the woman's voice only as filtered through a male amanuensis, a nephew, I believe that in this case its evidence is no less precious, for reasons that should become clear below. The conversation reported would have taken place in the last quarter of the nineteenth century. Since the text has never been published in full in English and is difficult to find even in Hebrew, I shall provide here a fairly long extract:[66]

> I frequently heard her complaining and protesting, in pain and distress, with angry heart and bitter spirit, about the bitter fate and meager portion of women in the life of the world, because they deprived them of the fulfillment of time-bound commandments such as phylacteries and fringes, sitting in the Sukkah and waving the lulav, and much much more.
>
> And in the midst of this protest, there used to shine through a tacit complaint and envy of men who had received everything, "who had (as she expressed it) 248 positive commandments, while to the abject and humiliated women, only three were given."

Although within the Ashkenazi tradition women had been "allowed" to perform the commandments that Reina Batya mentions, their participation had been considered as voluntary, as supererogatory and therefore as less significant than that of men. In contrast to a Protestant religious sensibility in which it would be precisely the free, unobligated performance of works that would be considered "higher," within Judaism it is the fulfillment of that which is "forced" upon one that is read as the most consequential and therefore socially prestigious. Reina Batya's interpretation of the exemption of women from positive commandments as abjection and humiliation is thus entirely on point, and apologists who refer to "permission" for women to perform commandments have missed the point. The text continues:

> Even more than this, she was worried and vexed about the defiled honour of the women and their lowly status due to the fact that the Rabbis forbid teaching them Torah. One time she told me that if Eve (meaning the female sex) was cursed with ten curses, this curse, [the prohibition] of learning Torah, is equivalent to all the curses, and is even more than all of them. There was no end to the grief.
>
> One time, while she was speaking with great feeling on this subject, I said to her, "But my aunt, you women are blaming the men for this prohibition

66. Shaul Stampfer published a briefer extract (Stampfer, "Gender").

when they are not at fault. You yourselves caused this and you are guilty in the matter," and I explained my words. Our Sages said (at the end of the second chapter of *Avot de Rabbi Natan* [an early midrash]) that Torah should only be taught to a humble person. About women, our Sages decided in *Yerushalmi Shabbat* [i.e., the Palestinian Talmud], Chapter 6, that "they [women] are jaunty" [*šaḥṣaniot*, a rare Aramaic term] meaning that they are proud. If so, isn't it forbidden to teach them Torah because of their character traits, and who is to blame if not they themselves, and why do they complain?

. . .

She said to me: "I am not clearly convinced of the meaning of the word 'jaunty,' whether it in fact refers to pride, and from where do you know this?"

I said to her: "I also did not understand this word, but that is the way that the scholars understand it, and the only other source that I know for it is Rashi's commentary on Tractate Shabbat (62b), for with respect to what it says there that 'the people of Jerusalem are people of *šaḥaṣ*,' Rashi interpreted that they speak in a prideful manner, and similarly with this interpretation one can explain the words of Tosafot on Pesaḥim. . . . "

She said to me: "When I have free time I will do research on the word and find out the exact meaning. In the meantime bring me *Avot de Rabbi Natan* and I will investigate the text that you cited." I went and brought—and fell right into the trap!

For in *Avot de Rabbi Natan* the wording is as follows: "Bet Shammai says: 'A person shall only teach to one who is clever, humble and rich' and Bet Hillel says: 'We teach to everyone, because there were many sinners in Israel and they started learning the Torah and became righteous, observant men.' "

As she finished reading these words, she raised her voice in anger and said, "How did you do this evil thing, or was it because you wanted to trick me that you took the opinion of Bet Shammai as the basis for your word? Every boy who has studied even a little Talmud, and even one who is only learning in elementary school, knows that when there is a disagreement between Bet Shammai and Bet Hillel, the law is in accordance with Bet Hillel, and here Bet Hillel permits teaching Torah to everyone!!"

And I told her the truth that I am not guilty in the matter, for the words that I had cited I did not know from their original source, from the text of *Avot de Rabbi Natan*, but from one of the books in which it was quoted, and there *they only cited the words of Bet Shammai* [emphasis in the original]!

As she was in good spirits at her victory, she was no longer angry with me, and when she saw that I was somewhat upset, she was sorry, and she comforted me and said to me: "You are released, you are forgiven, for this sort of deception is not a new thing in the hands of the scholars and the authors, and such it was always, but in the future be more careful about it!"[67]

67. Epstein, *Mekor*, 1950–1952.

This document provides us with a subtle but clear articulation of the problems of authority and voice in the matter of control of women regarding the study of Torah. At an earlier point in the conversation, not reproduced here, Reina Batya had already rebuked the nephew for citing a text that he had not read in the original, and here she demonstrates to him the inadequacy, indeed the falsehood of his argument against her, owing to the same "deception." He has produced an argument for the prohibition of women from the study of Torah based on an interpretation of a text from the Palestinian Talmud, which he had not seen in the original either, and a text from the midrash, *Avot de Rabbi Natan,* which, as it turns out, he misquotes in a crucial way. Reina Batya contests his interpretation on two grounds: first of all that it is dependent on a virtually unsupported interpretation of a word that is nearly a *hapax legomenon,* and second that once the full text of the *Avot de Rabbi Natan* is read, its conclusion turns out to be the exact opposite from what was claimed. The interpretation of the rare word that the nephew had relied upon is cited in the name of "the scholars," that is, the contemporary community of talmudists, and the truncated text that he had cited came also from a contemporary secondary source. The net effect of these two interventions on Reina Batya's part is to demonstrate fully that the "prohibition" of women studying Torah is an artifact of the exercise of hermeneutic authority on the part of the later tradition, which by selectively interpreting and quoting the rabbinic sources—just as the nephew has done—produces this very prohibition. Reina Batya's voice represents a plea for scholarly standards, for a virtually "modern" critical attention to "original sources" and contexts, indeed for historical criticism over-against the naive ahistorical method of the nephew, which represents the style of scholarship of the Yeshiva—more dependent on blind authority (at least in this issue) than critical text analysis. It is not only, then, that she "wins" the argument, but that she does so through demonstrating the superiority of her learning to that of the very man (men) contesting her right and obligation to study.

Reina Batya goes on to cite positive examples of learned women in support of her claim that the "prohibition" is an arbitrary imposition by a male power structure of a system of insults to women and not something that is mandated by the Torah:

And in a continuation of the discussion and with intent to lend force to her protest, she accounted and mentioned the names of many learned women:

Beruria, the wife of Rabbi Meʾir, Yalta, the wife of Rav Naḥman, and the daughter of Rabbi Ḥanina the son of Təradion, the mother of the author of the Səmaᶜ [a central early modern halakhic work], and the sister of Rabbi Yeshaya Berlin Pik, and then she finished by asking, "And what wrong did they [the Rabbis] find in them that they had learned Torah?" And in no wise was she willing to acquiesce in the terrible shame to women and this violation of their dignity in this exclusion of them from the study of Torah.

I remember that when she mentioned the name of Beruria, the wife of Rabbi Meʾir, I told her that a wrongdoing was found against her—that she mocked the words of our Sages, for "women are light-headed." In the end she herself was guilty of light-headedness, as is brought out in the story of Rashi on Avoda Zara 18b.

She answered me, "In truth, I know of this legend, but did our Sages find all men guilty because of the sin of Aḥer, who left the right way (Hagiga 15a)? Furthermore, Beruria did not mock with contempt and derision. She only thought that our Sages did not fully understand the rationality of women. According to her view, women are also strong-minded. This was the entire incident and nothing more."[68]

This is an extraordinary text that can be taken as a representation of an actual woman's protest. I am fully cognizant of the ways that male self-presentation as defeated can provide complex rhetorical advantages in contestations with other men.[69] Indeed, it is conceivable in this case that the issue is precisely conflict over canons of scholarly criticism, and that our author is covertly attacking (almost caricaturing) the standards of the mediocre practices of scholarship that were all too common in the Yeshiva. (Given his position as a scion of a particularly acute scholarly and critical family, this would make a great deal of sense.) Nevertheless, this does not preclude the possibility—even the plausibility—of the conversation having happened, and the loss of our ability to recover a feminist grandmother (for me, almost literally a grandmother) here seems a price too high to pay for hyper-suspiciousness. My great-grandmother Miriam, of approximately the same generation as Reina Batya and the same status and class, is famous to this day for her Bible scholarship and for knowing the entire Bible, with traditional commentaries, by heart. (My other great-grandmother, more the Glikl type, ran a lumberyard and supported her family in style while her husband studied Torah.) The discursive force of this powerful text, mediated from male interlocutor (nephew) to this male feminist writer (the "grandson"), is clearly both a *cri de coeur* and a highly sophisticated

68. Epstein, *Mekor*, 1953.
69. Cooper, *Virgin*, 19.

protest. Both aspects are significant—both the depth of the anger and
pain and the perspicacity of the feminist and critical analysis.

First of all, let me emphasize that which is crucial to my argument.
This is a protest from within the very nerve center of rabbinic Judaism
in the nineteenth century. This woman was married to the dominant
spiritual, practical, and intellectual leader of the Lithuanian Jews of
that time and thus of the Ashkenazic (non-Hasidic) world. There is no
sign, moreover, in this text, that she wished to be anything else, although here the fact that we have a secondhand report might indeed
raise some questions. There are, however, no indications from outside
this text that Reina Batya was disaffected about Judaism in general. She
did, however, protest strenuously against the domination of and insult
to women that was produced, as she correctly perceived, by the exclusion of women from the study of Torah. In a move prescient of much
later stratagems to reclaim Lilith or Dora, moreover, she turns Beruria,
a figure of the medieval tale designed to protect the boundaries of male
privilege, into a protofeminist. Although indirectly, she is in effect contesting the very assertion that the Rabbis have the right to determine the
nature and status of women, "to establish that women are 'jaunty.'"
Beruria wished only to explain to the sages the rationality of women,
which they did not understand, and, by implication, continue not to
understand.

Notably material, moreover, is the fact that this woman is clearly
highly learned by any standards. The nephew describes her as spending
all of her time winter and summer sitting at a table in the dining hall
of the house with the Bible, the Mishna, various midrashic texts, other
religious literatures, and traditional historiographies before her, studying day and night. He describes her as "righteous, wise, modest, and
outstandingly learned, equal [in learning] to exemplary men."[70] She is
not only familiar with the contents of the arguments that her scholarly
nephew provides, but she can counter them with examples and arguments that disprove their validity. She is competent, likewise, to seek
out the text, a classical Hebrew/Aramaic rabbinic text, that he cites and
confute his interpretation, indeed to argue for a certain bad faith on his
part since he violated, albeit through carelessness, the usual canons of
authority in preferring Bet Shammai's view over that of Bet Hillel. Finally, she indicates that she intends to do further lexicographical work
on the meaning of a technical term in rabbinic Hebrew that is critical

70. Epstein, *Mekor,* 1949.

for determining the Rabbis' true position on women learning Torah. In spite of her obvious erudition in Torah, this exceedingly learned woman bitterly (and seemingly paradoxically) protests her exclusion from the learning of Torah and the cruel sense of indignity that it produces for her and her sisters.

What we must conclude from this argument is that the exclusion of women from Torah was not intended to keep them in ignorance, nor was it the product of a sense that women were contaminated and contaminating, as some scholars have erroneously interpreted it, but it was purely and simply a means for the maintenance of a male power-structure via the symbolic exclusion of women from the single practice most valued in the culture, the study of Talmud. It is study of Talmud alone, the "Oral Torah," to which is ascribed the dignity of the title "Torah study," over and against, then, study of the actual "Written Torah," the Five Books of Moses itself or its commentaries. Women of the learned classes were encouraged to become competent scholars of everything *except the Talmud itself.* My great-grandmother's prodigious Bible-learning, for all the respect that it earned her, would have been considered eccentric at best in a man, who ought to have been spending his time studying Torah, which certainly means for this community the Talmud and its commentaries. This text thus strongly supports the stance that I and others have maintained to the effect that the exclusion of women from the study of Torah, that is, Talmud, is not a religiously necessary principle but a sociological development that subtended the entire system of male domination of women within the society, what Reina Batya calls the "defiled honour of the women and their lowly status," and it is here, as well understood by Reina Batya, that pressure must be put on the system (and indeed can be put on the system) if that domination is to end.[71] Insofar, then, as Beruria represents a structural

---

71. It should be remarked that even this exclusion was not as total as is sometimes imagined. In an apparent memoir, couched as a short story, Rebecca Goldstein writes: "So both my father and my mother taught the Jewish subjects to Gideon and me. There was no gender discrimination in what they taught us. My father studied Talmud with me just as hard and as long as with Gideon. I know that Orthodox Jews are rumored to be sexist. Hell, it's no rumor. One sage wrote that it was better for the sacred books to be burned before they were taught to Jewish daughters. And the Vilna Gaon warned, in a letter to his daughters, that women should stay away from the synagogue, since they're likely to engage there in nothing more uplifting than malicious gossip, which is a fairly serious sin in Judaism.

"My family wasn't at all tainted by this kind of bigotry. . . .

"I've read some of the angry literature that's been put out recently by Jewish feminists. And truly there seems to be a lot there to be angry about. All I can say is that the kind of mindless dismissal of girls that seems to typify certain parts of the Orthodox Jewish world

possibility, nascently actualized in contemporary Orthodox Jewish life, that female subjects will engage fully in the study of Torah, there is also the prospect of a revolution in gender within current Jewish life as well. In my mind, the important question is whether or not such a revolution will require a loss of the useful and positively marked categories of traditional Jewish gendering as well, namely the construction of maleness as gentle, receptive, and nurturing, femaleness as powerful and competent. The critical project is to see that it does not.

BERTHA PAPPENHEIM AND "THE JEWISH WOMAN"

If there will be justice in the world to come, women will be
lawgivers, and men have to have babies.
                                    —Bertha Pappenheim[72]

Another nineteenth- (and early twentieth-) century Jewish woman who strenuously protested the exclusion of women from Torah while retaining her allegiance to Jewish traditional culture and religion itself was Bertha Pappenheim (whose own story will be the subject of the last chapter below). In her essay, "The Jewish Woman," Pappenheim documents "a cultural dichotomy in the life of the Jewish woman, as was demonstrated in the widely held view that women were to 'be Jewish,' but were not allowed to learn."[73] "Learn" is, indeed, the proper translation here and not "study," because Pappenheim is referring accurately to the religious practice known as "learning Torah," that is, study of the Talmud. Pappenheim continues with her strong voice of protest: "The People of the Book closed the entry way to Jewish spiritual life, to its fountainheads, to women; only piecemeal and cropped were they to have faith and act, without knowing why. No Bes-Jakob School, no continuing education can repair how the souls of Jewish women—and thus Judaism in its entirety—have been sinned against, by withholding the Jewish meaning of life from the unknown Jewish woman, harnessing just her physical strength to the man. The wife of the Jew was allowed to carry the building blocks of family life as a beast of burden; in numb-

---

simply wasn't my experience at all" (Goldstein, *Strange,* 205–6). Quite obviously the perceptions of Judaism among women in those "certain parts of the Orthodox Jewish world" and in Telz (Lithuania), where this "memoirist's" family (and mine) came from, will be quite different.
    72. Bertha Pappenheim (Edinger, *Bertha,* 95).
    73. Pappenheim, "Jewish."

ness is she to keep in step. But how she was praised and lauded, the *eshes hayil* (*Minnesang* with gefilte fish), how much the male-human interpretations of the law turned against her, whose spirit was certainly receptive and ready!" In this brilliantly bitter moment, Pappenheim presents a sophisticated feminist analysis of the gender system of rabbinic Judaism and its version of control of women through a combination of exaltation and exclusion. There is both a caustic protest against the "sin against the souls of Jewish women," reminiscent in tone to that of Reina Batya, and the sarcastic reference to the song (from Proverbs) that is sung in praise of the Jewish wife every Friday night at the dinner table, just before she serves the gefilte fish.

But, it must nevertheless be noted, that the tone and purpose of Pappenheim's critique, however bitter, is to ensure that traditional Jewish life be reformed so that it could continue with vitality and justice. As evidence of her ongoing allegiance to Orthodoxy, I offer the following quotation: "Naturally the women went to the Temple on the High Holidays, the older ones also on Saturday, but they could not follow the services properly. Here the fracture, leading to the Liberal and Reform liturgy in later decades, already begins. Wouldn't it have been more reasonable to educate the women—and of course not the women alone—of the congregation to understand the service, rather than building a service that unhistorically and without tradition conforms to the failing understanding of the congregation?"[74] It is clear from this citation, in the very heart of her feminist protest, Pappenheim remained convinced that the historical and traditional form of the culture and its practices was what held vitality and a future, and that that future was crucial for her.[75]

Something of the complexity and nuance of Pappenheim's perceptions of traditional Judaism may be garnered from the following letter that she wrote on one of her trips to Galicia, as part of a series of letters that she wrote to the members of her women's group, eventually published under the title, *The Work of Sisyphus* (1912):

I was yesterday with Frau B. at the Wonder Rabbi's, a visit most interesting in thousands of details. Frau B. is German, from Silesia, highly respected all

74. Pappenheim, "Jewish."
75. I would also note that her account of the origins of Reform as due to the forced ignorance of the women is a compelling early example of the insight that accrues when a feminist perspective is brought to bear on Jewish history. This is at least as convincing a thesis as the more famous one of Scholem, who attributes Reform Judaism to the aftermath of the Sabbatai Zevi false Messiah convulsion of the seventeenth century.

over; specially since she still lives strictly orthodox. It was quite doubtful whether the rabbi would receive us, but a Frau D. who lives in B.'s house, is the rabbi's sister, and she introduced us.

This woman is a true living Glückel von Hameln. It's just wonderful of what and how she talks, her faith, her common sense, her naivete. I hope I remember the story she told me as a parallel to the exposure of Moses. But since it took at least half an hour to tell, I cannot possibly write it down. She asked about my business, of course. She grasped, with incredible speed, when I explained what I wanted to achieve. She looked at me with doubt-fully raised eyebrows, and said, "A swallow wants to drain the *Yam* (sea)? *Rebbaun schel aulom* (the Lord) may help, but since it is done in purity to the Lord's praise, my brother, the rabbi, may he live, will also help." Isn't that the true Glückel? She introduced us to her dear sister-in-law, the rabbi's wife. Then I told her about the women's movement, and she told me right away how she talks to young wives, and to husbands, too. We spoke about the illegitimate children, the *Mamser* [the child of an illicit union who can never marry except for another *mamser*] and much more—she just could not finish spitting [to ward off the evil eye]. Finally, audience at the rabbi's. We had waited for two hours. Piously, he turned his back to me. I gave a vivid lecture. He called my endeavor a great *Mitzvah* (religious commandment); he will warn people in his own circle [of the dangers of the procurers of girls]. I am to write down all I told him. And he helped; I think it was good and important and right to have been at the Alexandrover's. Respect for the rabbi is such that there is complete silence in his house—only if one knows how Hasidic Jews behave, can one understand what this does mean.[76]

We learn much from this rich document that has been nearly ignored until now in the readings of Bertha Pappenheim. In the very heat of her struggle against fearful effective collusion of Jewish society in the forced prostitution of young Jewish girls, she finds time and energy to sing the praises of a vital, learned Jewish woman she meets, calling her a true Glückel. All of her writings suggest that she wanted to cure a "sick patient," not to kill it. As Marion Kaplan has written, "Her con-victions as a religious Jew were as intense as her feminist beliefs. While her feminism was often incompatible with Jewish tradition, bringing her into conflict with the Jewish establishment, she insisted that only greater participation by women in their community would prevent Ju-daism's decline."[77]

More interesting than the behavior of the "Wonder Rabbi" [miracle-working Hasidic leader] is the practice of his sister, who is both clearly

76. Pappenheim, *Sisyphus-Arbeit*, 149–50; English translation in Edinger, *Bertha,* 46.
77. M. Kaplan, "Anna," 102.

learned in rabbinic lore and a religious leader in her own right.[78] The
Polish Wonder Rabbi's wife counsels not only the young women but
also their young husbands, and this in one of the most traditional possible of all European Jewish communities. In the context, since this
statement that she speaks to the young husbands follows immediately
after "I told her about the women's movement," the suggestion is that
the content of the rabbi's sister's address to the couples was "feminist"
as well. Pappenheim compares these powerful Jewish women with Glikl
of Hameln, the seventeenth-century Jewish businesswoman and Yiddish
memoirist, Pappenheim's ancestor, whose work she translated and with
whom she identified.[79] Glikl of Hameln was the first great female literary voice in Jewish history (since Miriam and Deborah in the Bible).
Her text is thoroughly informed by the Old Yiddish literary tradition,
including prayers for women, a translation and classic commentary on
the Bible, and books of legends and moral instruction.[80] As rich a literary life as these works provided,[81] however, by the nineteenth century
we can meet pious ("Orthodox") Jewish women in both eastern and
central Europe for whom the women's literary tradition is not sufficient,
because they recognize the spiritual and cultural power that full access
to the most fully canonical rabbinic tradition offers.

Interestingly enough, at the same time that these women are strenuously protesting the exclusion of women from the study of Torah, it is
their access to the Yiddish literary canon that provides them with the
terms and the power, as well in certain measure with the animus, with
which to protest. I emphasize this factor, because it will be of some importance in the denouement of my narrative in the final chapter. It is in
this letter that Pappenheim most clearly articulates her identification of
Glikl as a role model for Jewish women and suggests that this powerful,

78. On the Jewish learning of women in the nineteenth century, see the important
paper of Shaul Stampfer ("Gender"), who argues that the projected image of women's
ignorance was at variance with the actual reality and served, in fact, explicit ideological
purposes. Where I dissent from Stampfer is in his assumption that women were happy and
pleased with the system of exclusion from Torah learning because it was functional. There
is sufficient evidence to the contrary (including some presented here, some of which is
presented in Stampfer's article as well) even within the inner sancta of traditional East
European Jewish life.

79. For the clue that got me going in this direction, as for much else, I am grateful to
Juliet Mitchell. For the significance of this identification in the interpretation of "The Case
of Anna O.," see the final chapter.

80. Lowenthal, *Memoirs,* xiv–xv.

81. Weissler, "Religion."

capable type of woman is not unknown among the *Ostjuden* of her day. This text bears out, then, my claim that Bertha Pappenheim is at one and the same time a militant critic and passionate defender of traditional Jewish life, a critic of the subordination of women in the religious sphere and advocate of their traditional economic and social power. She, moreover, desires reform of the religious sphere precisely so that its traditional form ("Orthodoxy") may continue and not be replaced by what she herself perceives are debased imitations of Protestant culture. This dual critique and redemption provide the most important model for me in my own work on rabbinic Judaism.

These first-wave Orthodox feminist analyses support the thesis to which the analysis of this chapter has been pointing. While traditionally European Jewish women maintained a great deal of economic autonomy and power together with the respect and prestige that these conferred and, moreover, were *normatively* protected by the culture from both exploitation and violence—as opposed to a legal system surrounding them that enfranchised men to exploit and brutalize "their" women at will—this does not in any way forestall or weaken a feminist critique of the rabbinic Jewish social system. Indeed, it may be that rabbinic patriarchy is a partial anticipation of the "kinder, gentler patriarchy"—what Aviva Cantor calls a "reformed patriarchy"[82]—that in some quarters is seen as being in the birthing today, an even more powerful and astute domination of women by men to secure their (male) desires than the gross physical dominations, namely, permission to beat, rape, and sell, encoded by European custom and common law. Nevertheless, as Bertha Pappenheim clearly saw, the way forward into a feminist modernity for rabbinic culture does not necessitate an abandonment of the culture *tout court* but rather the recovery and retention of the (relative) power for women that it did maintain as well as the virtues of alternative and oppositional male socialization that it produced, while investing full participation of women in the power- and prestige-producing central practice of Torah study.

Unfortunately, at the fin de siècle much of Jewish culture was moving in exactly the opposite direction. Under the pressure of the developing ideology of heterosexuality and the extreme exigencies that it produced to enforce male/female psychosocial (and physical) dimorphism ever more stringently, the "modernizing" Jews of central Europe

82. Cantor, *Jewish Women*.

abandoned that which was valuable in traditional Jewish gender culture, enforcing "manliness" for men and "femininity" for women.
Documenting this process and the cataclysmic cultural effects that
it produced (not only for Jews!) is the task of the second half of this
book.

PART II

The Rise of Heterosexuality and the Invention of the Modern Jew

Freud's Baby, Fliess's Maybe

*Or, Male Hysteria, Homophobia, and the
Invention of the Jewish Man*

Something happened around 1890, something that John C. Fout has called "a 'new,' historically specific stage in the history of sexuality."[1] Our reading of what exactly happened will be contingent in large measure on our assessment of Freud's "discovery" of the Oedipus complex, and thus of psychoanalysis, just at this time. How to interpret this foundational event, however, is less clear. According to the "official" accounts endorsed by the psychoanalytic establishment, what happened was simply that Freud's attainment of psychological maturity—marked not least by the "overcoming" of homoerotic desire—led to an advance in the theory of sexuality that made possible a great scientific discovery.[2] According to critiques of Freud that currently enjoy hegemony, however, the story is one of betrayal and abuse.[3] According to this revisionist version, Freud originally asserted that abuse of girls by adult male relatives (usually fathers) is the cause of later hysteria in women, but he abandoned this correct understanding in favor of a theory of infantile sexual desire and fantasy because the "true" account was threatening to patriarchal privilege. Neither of these extremes will do, neither Saint Sigmund nor Freud the fraud. There is something that hagiographers and demonologists of Freud alike have left out of accounts of this

1. Fout, "Sexual," 389.
2. Kris, *Origins.*
3. Masson, *Assault.*

stage in the history of sexuality: the ways in which the foundations of psychoanalysis and the Oedipus complex are specifically embroiled in the homophobic–antisemitic movement of the fin de siècle.

THE COMPLEXITIES OF OEDIPUS

I must begin by delineating as precisely as possible the shift in Freud's thinking that I am setting out to explain. As is quite well known by now, there are two Freudian theories of the psyche, an earlier one, of which the dominating trope is hysteria, and a later one, in which hysteria was largely set aside in favor of the diagnosis and investigation of the neuroses. Moreover, the fundamental account of psychic development also shifted epochally, from traumas of infantile sexual abuse that cause later disturbances leading to hysteria in certain people to unresolved fantasies of sexual desire for parents that produce neurotic symptoms in almost everybody: the Oedipus complex, with its aide-de-camp, the castration complex. These two aspects of the reversal are also well known, although the first is frequently ignored in favor of the more sensational second one. This latter is, moreover, read by Jeffrey Masson and his followers simply as a misogynist refusal on Freud's part to take seriously accounts by female patients of being raped as children. However, there is an even greater shift that seems hardly to get noticed at all. The first model is gendered as paradigmatically feminine, while the second one is gendered as normatively and exclusively masculine.

In a recent essay, Martha Noel Evans has paid explicit attention to the incongruity of this shift in the apparent object of the scientific theory: "What is strange in Freud's shift from the seduction theory to the theoretical assertion of sexual drives in young children is the uncanny substitution that takes place: at the center of the seduction theory is a young girl seduced by the father; at the center of the Oedipus complex, there is a young boy constructing erotic fantasies about his mother." Evans notes as well how odd it is that in *The Studies in Hysteria* Freud has virtually nothing to say about male hysteria since nothing in his theory precludes it and previously he had published several papers on male hysterics. Her explanation, however, seems less compelling. It depends on the stereotype of "the fantasy of a feminine patient and a masculine authority figure,"[4] in other words on another version of the fa-

---

4. Evans, "Hysteria," 80, 75.

miliar story of "the misogyny of male physicians and the persecution of female deviants in witch-hunts."[5]

The presupposition of the currently canonical account is that "Freud succumbed to the popular, medical and legal prejudices of his time: respectable men wouldn't commit such acts; hysterical women are liars."[6] Against this account we must place two historical considerations: (1) there were men—Freud's brother and Freud himself—among the victims, and (2) there were women among the abusers.[7] It follows that the interpretation that Freud was just defending the privilege of men against the imprecations of women does not hold water.

Moreover, in the current version of events, it seems obvious that Freud's new model should also have explained the etiology of neurosis in women, or at least dealt with the sexuality and sexual development of women. Another way of saying this is that we can't both "accuse" Freud of dealing only with women in the first theory because of the age-old androcentric theme of male scientist and female patient and, at the same time, account for his dealing only with men in the second as a product of simple androcentrism in which men are the only object of interest. Such theories end up explaining everything and consequently explain nothing. If indeed, on Evans's account, "Freud's new theory can be seen as a symptom at once symbolically reenacting and concealing the abuse of young women,"[8] why does it have so little to do with young women? Evans has seen the problem and has given what I take to be a correct answer as far as it goes: "What was denied along with the stories of childhood sexual abuse and then returns symptomatically in the second theory is the (for Freud) devastating knowledge that a boy—perhaps himself—might experience sexual seduction in the passive mode of a female; that, to state it more radically, a boy might be treated like a girl. The theory of childhood sexual fantasies which sup-

---

5. Showalter, "Hysteria," 287. When I delivered this chapter at the School of Criticism and Theory, Prof. Showalter pointed out that other psychiatrists in Freud's time publicly suppressed an awareness of male hysteria that they recognized in private. The famous story of Meynert's "confession" to Freud of his own male hysteria, after having opposed him in public, would be a case in point. The question remains: Why was a thinker who was in many ways willing and able to break the paradigms of his culture, here seemingly unable to do so?

6. Brenkman, *Straight Male*, 96.

7. "Today I am able to add that one of the cases gave me what I expected (sexual shock—that is, infantile abuse in male hysteria!)" (Garner, "Freud and Fliess," 149). Of recent writers, only Sprengnether (*Spectral Mother*, 37) has emphasized this point. For the ways that my reading converges and diverges from hers, see below.

8. Evans, "Hysteria," 76.

plants the seduction theory very precisely protects against this indeter-
minacy of the sexes by positing a law of heterosexuality" (80–81).

Hysteria, in short, while gendered as paradigmatically feminine, is
not exclusively about women but involves both women and "feminized" men. Evans, however, situates this insight in a timeless narrative
of male self-protection against loss of male privilege and power: "Denied in these instances is first, fear of being feminized by seduction, and
second, fear of losing control of knowledge, with concomitant fear of
the sexual autonomy and power of women." Madelon Sprengnether
also clearly perceives the fact that Freud avoids putting himself into a
"feminized" position, but like Evans she does not locate this within a
specific historical cultural/political scenario. She writes: "Feminine
identification for Freud seems to threaten loss of power for the male and
a corresponding gain (through refusal) for the female." She thus locates
Freud's resistance to identification with female positions in an apparently ageless "war of the sexes" rather than in the struggles of a disempowered political, social, and cultural male subject.[9]

Elaine Showalter, however, proposes the notion of hysteria as a "disease of the powerless and silenced," as an *alternative* to the conclusion
that hysteria is about "women's questions." In a recent paper she has
written that "although male hysteria has been documented since the
seventeenth century, feminist critics have ignored its clinical manifestations, writing as though 'hysterical questions' about sexual identity are
only women's questions."[10] Hysteria is indeed about femaleness but not,
therefore, exclusively about "women." The feminist critics that I have

---

9. Evans, "Hysteria," 82; Sprengnether, *Spectral Mother,* 53. See for instance how
this trenchant avoidance of historicizing interpretation impacts on her correct understanding of Freud's avoidance of anything that appears to put him into a "feminine" position.
A good example of this is Sprengnether's insight that in the Dora case, Freud "produces
a fantasy of an impotent father, whose daughter not only nurses him in a conventional
sense but who also wishes to 'nurse,' or suck at his penis. Superimposed on this fantasy
of ambiguous sexual identification, however, in which the father plays a passive, quasi-
maternal role, Freud offers a more stereotyped image, that of a virile, phallic male who
pursues a young girl in spite of her resistance. Gradually, his fascination with the fortunes
of Herr K. appears to overtake his interest in the more threatening and volatile scene of
father-daughter incest." After this acute insight, however, the best that Sprengnether can
offer in explanation is the claim that "the subject Freud avoids in this instance is his own
vulnerability, his implicitly feminine role in relation to his daughter" (*Spectral Mother,*
175), even though this was decades before the fact of any such role for Freud with respect
to his daughter. It is not inapposite to point to the fact that neither the word "Jew" nor
"Judaism" appears in the index to Sprengnether's book.
    10. Showalter, "Hysteria," 288.

been citing have captured a highly compelling insight. In order to maintain both the perceptions of the "feminist critics" (I hardly think that Showalter is taking herself out of this category, nor am I) and also to take more seriously the connections of hysteria to the oppression of male subjects, we will have to reconceive the category of gender itself in directions that the most sophisticated current feminist theory is already taking us.

The opposition itself between hysteria being about "women's questions" and hysteria as the "disease of the powerless and silenced" is an artifact of the false binary between race and gender. Insofar as gender is a set of cultural expectations and performances, usually but not determinately mapped onto the "anatomical differences between the sexes," it becomes impossible to assume constant genderings in cross-cultural comparison. As Christine Delphy has written, "It may be (and this remains to be proven) that women are (also) females, and that men are (also) males."[11] Thus genders, like races, are classes—not anatomical phenomena—classes that are mystified through mapping them onto more or less arbitrary physical differences, such as alleged physical strength versus weakness, hormonal differences, skin color . . . or ability to gestate. If being gendered "man" in our culture is having power and speech—phallus and logos—the silenced and powerless subject is "woman," whatever her anatomical construction.[12] As I have observed in the previous chapter, the status of working men, who are referred to as being "like women" in East European Jewish culture, provides an example of this point. "Hysteria" itself—a woman's malady, as feminist historians have properly registered—provides another elegant demonstration of this thesis, because hysteria was not exclusive to anatomical women but to women and certain racially marked men. This recognition, indebted to Hortense Spillers's claim that "there is no such thing as a black woman," will give us a clue to a fresh reading of the great shift in Freud's thinking.

The key to understanding the development of Freud's oedipal model

11. Delphy, *Close to Home*, 24–26; see also Butler, *Gender*, 62.

12. J. W. Scott, *Gender*, 42. Obviously this does not preclude further gender differences within cultural groups; power, powerlessness, speech, and silencing are all relative, not absolute conditions. Cf. Reynolds and Humble's observation that "[p]erhaps more contentiously, all orphans are nominated 'she' because, whatever the designated gender of the fictional orphan, orphanhood as a condition operates to highlight dependency, and dependency in the Victorian separation of sex roles is the domain of the female" (Reynolds and Humble, *Victorian Heroines*, 26).

is indeed that his hysteria theory is about such men, as well as about women. Freud said as much openly.[13] It is well known that what most aroused the ire of the Viennese medical audience that heard Freud's first lecture upon his return from Charcot was the fact that it was about *male* hysteria. In his first model, Freud reconstructed (or invented) memories of child abuse not only for female patients but for boys as well—including his brother—as a means of accounting for his own male hysteria. Six out of the eighteen cases mentioned in the paper on which the seduction theory is based, "The Aetiology of Hysteria" (1896), are cases of boys, not of girls.[14] In one of the most famous of his letters to his friend Wilhelm Fliess, Freud writes: "Unfortunately my own father was one of these perverts and is responsible for the hysteria of my brother (all of whose symptoms are identification) and those of several younger sisters."[15]

This theory implicated Freud himself quite directly, a point that enables me to propose an explanation for otherwise quite startling developments. Freud adopted the language of Oedipus as a self-diagnosed hysteric, a representation that further configured him as female and thus, according to the "inversion" model then current, as queer. This transpires clearly in his letter to Fliess of October 3, 1897, where he refers to "resolving my own hysteria."[16] Interestingly enough, this diagnosis was current in the psychoanalytic establishment itself, albeit discreetly so. In 1951 James Strachey wrote to Ernest Jones, "I was very much interested by your account of the suppressed passages in the Fliess letters. It is really a complete instance of *folie à deux*, with Freud in the unexpected role of hysterical partner to a paranoiac."[17] This is easily decoded as "with Freud in the unexpected role of female partner to a

13. Showalter, "Hysteria," 315.

14. Robinson, *Freud,* 160. Sabine Hake, writing in 1993, still asserts with reference to this essay: "At the center of this reading formation stands the female body, which is always the hysterical body and which brings together seemingly disparate elements: the woman as archaeological site, archaeology as the paradigm of interpretation, and the problem of femininity as the test case of psychoanalysis" (Hake, "Saxa Loquuntur," 148). The second and third points stand, in my opinion; the first does not—quite. Hence my dissociation of femininity from the female body in what follows.

15. Masson, *Complete Letters,* 230-31; see also 264.

16. Masson, *Complete Letters,* 269. Freud's apparent renunciation of all sexual contact early in his forties takes on a new meaning in this light. He would not be the first married man not meant to be the marrying kind for whom celibacy ends up being the only psychologically tolerable solution. His famous fainting incident with Jung in 1912 was interpreted by Freud himself in a famous letter to Jones as powerful evidence for continuing homoerotic desire on Freud's own part (Jones, *Young Freud,* 317).

17. Quoted in Masson, *Assault,* 216.

male," hysteria naming the characteristically female neurosis, while paranoia represents the characteristic male (homosexual) neurosis.[18] This diagnosis in the letters was, moreover, explicitly associated both by Strachey and by Jones with Freud's "bisexuality," by which they, writing in the 1950s, meant not the theory of androgyny but what we mean by this word, sexual desire for both male and female objects.

Very soon after the letter in which he identifies his father as a "pervert," simply and only on the basis of the symptomatology of his siblings, Freud writes, "The point that escaped me in the solution of hysteria lies in a different source, from which a new element of the product of the unconscious arises. What I have in mind are hysterical fantasies which regularly, as I see it, go back to things that children overhear at an early age."[19] In short, Freud was already beginning to abandon (or better, complicate) the "seduction" theory in early April 1897, only two months after indicting his father as child abuser. The explanation that Freud abandoned the (absurdly named) seduction theory because he became convinced that it is impossible to assume the existence of such an incredibly enormous number of paternal child abusers accounts for the abandonment of the theory that sexual abuse lies at the origin of every hysteria, but it does not explain the Oedipus theory that "replaced" it. Freud could, after all, simply have substituted childhood fantasies of and desires for seduction for the actual events and otherwise maintained the structure of his "neurotica."

Only a month later we find him writing, "It is to be supposed that the element essentially responsible for repression is always what is feminine. . . . What men essentially repress is the pederastic element."[20] In spite of the odd use of "pederastic" here, or perhaps because of it, it seems that Freud means that men always repress their desire to be penetrated. Else, how could he call it "the feminine"?[21] And indeed, Freud's

18. I accordingly disagree with Downing, *Myths,* 19, who claims that Strachey and Jones are denying or ignoring here the evidence for Freud's homoeroticism. I think they are directly recognizing it.

19. Masson, *Complete Letters,* 234; and see 239. Right after Freud's most famous letter, in which he abandons his *neurotica* (264) and indicates his reason as incredulity at the fact that so many fathers including his own were "perverts," he is still pursuing child abuse, albeit not by the father, as the etiology of his own hysteria (268), and three months later is still producing evidence for the "paternal etiology" (286). This is clearly not consistent with a man abandoning a theory that he knows to be true because he fears the reactions of his surroundings, but rather with a man in a conflicted and ambivalent state produced by the implications of his thinking.

20. Masson, *Complete Letters,* 246.

21. Shuli Barzilai called my attention to the oddness of the term "pederast" here.

oedipal theory reenacts the repression of the pederastic element of which he himself speaks. Because it has not been actually replaced with an alternative, the seduction theory remains like a repressed memory in Freud's thought, a sort of phantom, a revenant, reappearing only considerably later (especially in the Wolf Man text)[22] as the so-called Negative Oedipus, the desire on the part of the son to be penetrated by the father. More than the possibility of seduction (that is, child-rape), which Freud never, in fact, denied, it is the fantasy and desire of the boy child for the father that is repressed in the oedipal theory.[23]

Two questions concerning the invention of the oedipal theory occur as a result of recognizing that Freud's hysteria theory was also about men. Why was the role of desire for the father so threatening to Freud? Equally shocking desires are given their due by Freud, but the role of the "Negative Oedipus" remains a black sheep of the family, never quite acknowledged although not, to be sure, entirely rejected.[24] Second, why did hysteria practically disappear from the scene of Freud's writing at this time, and, especially, whatever happened to the male hysteric?[25] If we forget that he existed, this is surely because Freud wanted us to. What, in short, was at stake?

FREUD'S HYSTERIA AND THE SEDUCTION THEORY

The first step toward answering these questions is easily taken. It is striking to me how many scholars and interpreters of Freud have recently been talking about the powerful homoerotic content in some of Freud's early writings, notably in his letters to Fliess and in the text produced at about the same time, *The Interpretation of Dreams*. The association of homoerotic desire with the "feminized" men included in

22. R. H. Davis, *Freud's*, 65–71.
23. Cf. the quite different way of formulating this issue by Borch-Jacobsen: "Freud, in his diverse presentations of the Oedipus complex, almost always privileges the example of the positive complex of the young boy. In that case, in fact, the desire object is clearly objectal and heterosexual" (Borch-Jacobsen, "Oedipus," 269). For all the differences in approach, Borch-Jacobsen and I have identified the same problem. The difference between my approach and Borch-Jacobsen's is that where he (like Brenkman) sees the point as the construction of the heterosexual male, on my reading the point is the invention of the male Jew — Freud — as heterosexual. These two motifs are entirely compatible, even conspiratorial, with each other. I am trying to identify more of the historical pressures that led to Freud's particular collaboration with the political project of heterosexuality, that is, with his own domination.
24. Montrelay, "Why Did You?" 222.
25. My attention was focused on this question by Juliet Mitchell. It will be a major theme of her forthcoming book.

the category of hysterics was a commonplace of fin de siècle culture. That the "seduction" theory disclosed Freud's own homoerotic inclinations becomes clear if we look more deeply into his understanding of the hysteria that the Oedipus model effaces and represses—the hysteria that Freud had diagnosed in himself.

To begin with, it is increasingly being recognized that the parental seductions Freud reports in his early case histories of hysterics were indeed very likely fantasies—not, however, fantasies of the patients but of Freud himself.[26] In Freud's own description (before "abandoning" the theory): "The fact is that these patients never repeat these stories spontaneously, nor do they ever in the course of treatment suddenly present the physician with the complete recollections of a scene of this kind. *One only succeeds in awakening the psychical trace of a precocious sexual event under the most energetic pressure of the analytic procedure and against enormous resistance. Moreover, the memory must be extracted piece by piece.*"[27] The Fliess correspondence provides an excellent example of how Freud led some of his patients to "remember" parental abuse:

> *Habemus papam!*
> When I *thrust the explanation at her,* she was at first won over; then she committed the folly of questioning the old man himself, who at the very first intimation exclaimed indignantly, "Are you implying that I was the one?" and swore a holy oath to his innocence.
> She is now in the throes of the most vehement resistance, claims to believe him, but attests to her identification with him by having become dishonest and swearing false oaths. *I have threatened to send her away and in the process convinced myself that she has already gained a good deal of certainty which she is reluctant to acknowledge.*
> She has never felt as well as on the day when I made the disclosure to her. In order to facilitate the work, I am hoping she will feel miserable again.
> The pain in her leg appears to have come from her mother.[28]

The patients reported symptoms; it was Freud who translated the symptoms into narratives of child abuse. Here is Freud describing his method: "Having diagnosed a case of neurasthenic neurosis with cer-

26. Robinson, *Freud,* 165.

27. SE III:153, emphasis added. Freud never denied the possibility of real child abuse nor minimized its traumatic effects. (See below, n. 33.) What he abandoned was a theory that located virtually all neurosis in such abuse, a theory that he very likely had generally imposed on the patients.

28. Masson, *Complete Letters,* 220–21, emphases added.

tainty and having classified its symptoms correctly, we are in a position to translate the symptomatology into aetiology."[29]

In contrast to other writers who have pointed out these texts, I see here, however, no defect in either Freud's procedure or in his honesty.[30] What, after all, is the procedure of any diagnosis but reasoning from symptomatology to etiology? This recognition does, however, force us to reevaluate both the standard interpretation of the discovery of psychoanalysis in the "recognition that the seduction stories told by the patients were fantasies," as well as the indictment that Freud chose to disbelieve true stories of child abuse. Both equally depend on the assumption that the patients actually produced such accounts, but as he himself wrote, even after he revealed the secret to the patients, "they have no feeling of remembering the scenes." Freud later revised these forced, in every sense of the word, interpretations of his—not the memories of his patients—into narratives of childhood desires and fantasies of seduction by the parent.[31] Let me make myself absolutely clear: the issue here is not belief or disbelief of patients but rather the almost violent imposition ("thrust") of a theory on the patients, through threats, against their "most vehement resistance." In contrast, in December 1897, months after the letter in which he "abandoned my *neurotica*," Freud writes of "the intrinsic authenticity of infantile trauma" and of a father who "belongs to the category of *men who stab women*, for whom bloody injuries are an erotic need. When she was two years old, he brutally deflowered her."[32] The end of this same letter reads: "A new motto: 'What has been done to you, you poor child?'"[33]

29. SE III:269.

30. In this regard, I agree with the facts as given in Esterson, *Seductive Mirage*, 17–21, and in Crews, "Unknown Freud," 62. Our judgments as to the consequences of these facts for an evaluation of Freud could not be more different, however. See also Fish, "Withholding," especially 552–53; and below n. 33. It must be admitted that the question of integrity will come up when Freud's later accounts of the discovery of psychoanalysis, in which he insists that the patients had indeed reported rapes and seductions, are contrasted with these contemporaneous ones which seem so much more frank (Esterson, 22–23). Explanations other than deliberate attempts to mislead are, however, adduceable for this discrepancy (cf. Esterson, 24, who allows that Freud may have "come to believe his own story"). Since being Freud's "defense attorney" is not my mission, I can leave the matter here.

31. SE III:204. I am, of course, not denying even now the possibility that this particular patient, or any other, was indeed abused.

32. Masson, *Complete Letters*, 288, emphasis in original.

33. In 1917, in his introductory lectures, Freud stated, "You must not suppose that sexual abuse of a child by its nearest male relatives belongs entirely to the realm of phantasy. Most analysts will have treated cases in which such events were real and could be unimpeachably established." In 1924 Freud added a note to the Katharina case in *Studies*

Freud never chose to systematically disbelieve women; he abandoned a theory whereby all hysteria was to be explained by child abuse, whether remembered or not. The question, then, is not why did Freud revise his theory, but why was it necessary in the first place for him to assume childhood sexual abuse as the universal etiology of hysteria? Why, in short, did Freud force these narratives on (at least some of) his patients, male and female? If we assume as a hermeneutical principle that Freud thought what he thought and wrote what he wrote in good faith, then there was some reason within him—psychological or socio-cultural—that led him to read those symptoms as narratives of seduction by the father. Here, as well, the most plausible interpretation is that these were projections of Freud's own fantasies and desires (or memories of childhood seduction) onto his patients. This need not be read as unconscious projection but could simply have been the product of a strong heuristic principle that Freud employed even much later to generalize from his own experience and assume its universality.[34] Such seduction, moreover, according to Freud's own theories, as we shall see, would have led as well to homosexuality.

It should not be understood that the hysterogenic sexual event was necessarily homosexual. Indeed, as it is eminently clear, in the cases of male hysteria including Freud's own, there was often a female sexual abuser.[35] Sprengnether focuses on this aspect of the issue and arrives at the interesting hypothesis that Freud was primarily motivated by a need to erase the desiring mother from his theory: "Because of its strategic function in this regard, Freud's focus on Oedipal masculinity effectively obscures his vision of the preoedipal mother." Sprengnether writes of Freud's interpretation of an incident in which the Wolf Man's sister had played with his penis: "Freud's comment on this episode reveals the extent to which he associates it with the kind of sexual humiliation he had

in Hysteria, in which he wrote that Katharina had fallen ill as a result of paternal sexual abuse (Robinson, Freud, 168). This is simply not consistent with the picture of Freud as the big-bad-wolf doctor who thinks girls are liars and only patriarchs tell the truth. Nor does it support the Massonic construction of a Freud who knows and admits the truth but hides his knowledge out of cowardice. In fact, Freud gets attacked coming and going. His other great Berkeley-based antagonist, Frederick Crews, holds him responsible for exactly the opposite crime: not for causing disbelief of girls who were abused but for causing false accusations of fathers and child-care workers who are innocent victims (Crews, "Unknown Freud," 65)! Catch-22. If Freud finally disbelieved true stories, then he is an abuser of women, but if he had previously believed untrue ones (or rather, as I agree, induced them—I think in good faith), then he is a traducer of men. How could Freud possibly escape from being a moral monster with antagonists like these?

34. Cf. Mahony, Cries.

35. Masson, Complete Letters, 268; see also Sprengnether, Spectral Mother, 36–37.

experienced at the hands of his own nannie. He characterized the Wolf Man's memory of this event as 'offensive to the patient's self-esteem,' and one that elicits a counterfantasy in which he takes the aggressive role." It is the sexual passivity of the male that feminizes (and paradoxically homosexualizes), not the gender of the active subject.[36] As Freud wrote to Fliess about his childhood nurse, "[S]he had been my teacher in sexual matters," and she laid the foundation for "my neurotic impotence."[37] This transfer takes place within Freud's reading of the Wolf Man. The reality (or fantasy) of female sexual aggression directed at the boy is translated into a "feminine" desire directed at his father. Freud writes: "The boy had travelled, without considering the difference of sex, from his Nanya to his father,"[38] the same journey that Freud took in his own psyche, from the nanny to the father, representing for us via the Wolf Man his own feminized and thus homosexual desire.

Let us follow the sequence of thoughts that are produced in Freud's crucial letters of late September to early October 1897. In the first, he claims to abandon the theory of hysteria that he has been so laboriously developing because it would imply that an incredible number of fathers (including his own) would have had to be sexual abusers to produce the numbers of hysterics that there were, and he cannot believe that. A few days later, however, he still seems to believe the "seduction" theory and, in the case of his brothers and sisters, that his father is responsible. He writes: "I can only indicate that in my case the 'prime originator' was an ugly, elderly, but clever woman," apparently indicating that in the case of his siblings the "prime originator" was the original suspect.[39] Moreover, in the very next sentence, Freud is already referring to an entirely hypothetical outburst of desire directed toward his mother after seeing her nude on a train trip at the age of two to two and a half years. Finally, less than two weeks later, Freud for the very first time

---

36. Sprengnether, *Spectral Mother*, 38, 50, 72. It should be carefully noted here that the terms "active" and "passive" and their correlations with masculine and feminine and notions of inversion invoked throughout this text are Freud's—not mine. In fact, they are not even Freud's but a general aspect of his sociolect. The best study of this issue belongs to Davis. In this context it is worth noting that my account is in at least one regard directly contrary to Davis's. He claims that "the active oedipal aim, 'I want to copulate with my mother,' by reversal and turning round becomes the passive aim, 'I want to be copulated with by my father'" (R. H. Davis, *Freud's*, 97). I am, of course, suggesting the exact opposite.

37. Masson, *Complete Letters*, 269.

38. SE XVII:46.

39. Masson, *Complete Letters*, 268.

refers to Oedipus and to "everyone in the audience" having been "a budding Oedipus in fantasy."[40] Following the reasoning that Freud produced in the Wolf Man, the logical conclusion would be that the sexual stimulation provided by the nurse, which put the boy in the passive (feminized) position, would have been translated into passive desires directed at Freud's father. The immediate shift to the (again I emphasize quite "fictional") account of having seen his mother naked and the accompanying "awakening of libido toward *matrem*," as well as the rapid discovery of Oedipus, suggests strongly that something indeed is being repressed here: passive desire for the father. Because of its strategic function in this regard, Freud's focus on oedipal masculinity effectively obscures his experience as the passively desiring male.[41]

Psychoanalytic historian Samuel Slipp has remarked that "Freud's early oedipal experience with a dominant mother and a passive father probably led him to the conclusion that male homosexuality was due to lack of resolution of the Oedipus complex and failure to identify with the father."[42] What seems to be missing from his account is the obvious logical conclusion to which it inexorably leads, namely, that Freud himself identified as "a homosexual." That is the only way that Freud's experience could have "led him" to such a "conclusion."[43]

FREUD AND FLIESS AS LOVERS

I am looking forward to our congress as to the slaking of
hunger and thirst. I bring nothing but two open ears and one
temporal lobe lubricated for reception.[44]

The various interpreters of Freud who have been at the same time focusing on the homoerotic content of Freud's early writings complement each other and together yield the possibility of a powerful hypothesis with regard to the question of the origins of the Oedipus complex. Freud was engaged in what can only be described as a highly erotic relationship with his friend. They exchanged the most intimate of letters

40. Masson, *Complete Letters*, 272.
41. See also Davis, who has written, "Freud, it seems, feared certain forms of passivity and tried to avoid it through a phallic stance: being on top of it, subduing it" (R. H. Davis, *Freud's*, 13).
42. Slipp, *Freudian Mystique*, 6.
43. Perhaps Slipp was merely being delicate, leaving it to the reader to draw her own "conclusion."
44. Masson, *Complete Letters*, 193.

and had "congresses."[45] The next sentence of the letter quoted above includes a reference to "male and female menstruation in the same individual," that is, to the bisexuality theory. The association seems hardly coincidental.

This element was first paid attention to by Peter Heller,[46] even though he was limited to the "censored" version of the Freud-Fliess correspondence published by Ernst Kris. Shirley Garner has remarked that when she first read the full edition of the letters, "[W]hat was most apparent—and surprising—to me about them was that they are love letters. Careful rereadings have not changed my mind."[47] One example will do beautifully to illustrate her point: "If there now are two people, one of whom can say what life is, and the other can say (almost) what the mind is—and furthermore the two are very fond of each other—it is only right that they should see and talk to each other more frequently."[48] Didier Anzieu makes the even more startlingly pungent observation that Freud's love letters to his fiancée Martha were "a kind of dress rehearsal for his later correspondence with Fliess," and indeed the tone of these two bodies of correspondence is remarkably alike. Freud had written to Martha, "The sweet girl . . . came towards me [and] strengthened the faith in my own value and gave me new hope and energy to work when I needed it most."[49] Later he was to write to Fliess, "When I think of the many weeks when I felt uncertain about my life, my need to be with you increases greatly."[50]

In addition to the elements of homoeroticism in the letters of Freud to Fliess, or rather intimately bound up with them, are manifold symptoms of fantasies of pregnancy by Fliess. Erik Erikson has already cited evidence for Freud's self-feminization in the relationship in a justly famous 1954 paper. During the course of this liaison Freud repeatedly figures his own creativity as the product of his congress with Fliess; he fantasizes (consciously?) that he is bearing Fliess's child.[51] "In his 12

45. To be sure, as Jay Geller notes, the word *Kongress* in German does not have the sexual meaning that it can have in English. The erotic nature of these tête-à-têtes does not depend on the semantics of "congress," however.

46. Heller, "Quarrel," 95.

47. Garner, "Freud and Fliess," 86; see also Koestenbaum, *Double Talk*, 19; Garber, *Vice-versa*, 185.

48. Masson, *Complete Letters*, 287.

49. Anzieu, *Freud's*, 22.

50. Masson, *Complete Letters*, 89.

51. Erikson, "Dream," 33.

June 1895 letter to Fliess, Freud states that 'Reporting on [the psychological construction of defense] now would be like sending a six-month
fetus of a girl to a ball.'" In 1897 Freud writes, "[A]fter the frightful
labor pains of the last few weeks, I gave birth to a new piece of knowledge."[52] Were it not for all of the other evidence, one might be inclined
to take these as "mere (and conventional) metaphors." The other evidence, however, suggests much more—and indeed is suggestive as to the
ultimate origin of these conventional modes of expression themselves.

Jay Geller interprets Freud's and Fliess's theoretical speculations on
the connections between noses and genitals, and especially between
nose bleeds and menstruation, accordingly: "The reference to the *Na-
senmuscheln* also evokes one other intrinsically 'feminine' body process:
birthing. Again, according to Fliess, these 'genital spots' were intimately related to the birthing process." Geller further notes that "the
process of conception is alluded to at both the beginning and end of the
'Irma' dream. When the dream opens, Freud and his wife are receiving
guests. The German term for 'receive,' '*empfangen,*' is rife with associations to conception; for example, the '*unbefleckte Empfängnis*' is the
Immaculate Conception." Geller also observes that "Freud would later
write to Fliess that birthing—or miscarrying—is dirty, diarrhetic:
'everything related to birth, miscarriage, period goes back to the toilet
via the word *Abort* [toilet] (*Abortus* [abortion])' (288; letter of 22 December 1897). And the cause of the conception, the unclean syringe, is
a dirty squirter or penis [*Spritze nicht rein*]. These images of befouled
or failed birth conflict with Freud's desire to create. His works are his
creations, his children with Fliess."[53]

In an unpublished paper, Gerard F. Beritela has augmented Geller's
reading of this letter, noting that Freud refers to "making" and "making more" and boasts to make more shit as the "new Midas." This shit
is clearly connected with birth in Freud's own explicit and conscious
expression "via the word *Abort*." According to Beritela, "Freud is thus
bragging about his own anal fertility, as if trying to entice Fliess into
'making more' with him." From here Freud segues into a description of
anal rape, and then: "The last paragraph of the letter speaks of censor-

---

52. The notion of male lovers' bearing spiritual children to each other was a topos of
homosexual discourse at this time, drawn from readings of Plato's *Symposium*. See Showalter, *Sexual Anarchy,* 174–76.
53. Geller, "(G)nos(e)ology," 260.

ship and repression as if to signal that what has gone before is indeed the remnant of a highly censored communication. Read this way, the letter begins with Freud's desire to be passive in the upcoming congress with Fliess. It continues with a description of Freud's anal fertility and a crypto-pornographic description of anal rape."[54] Freud's own comments in the letter just before this about "keeping one's own mouth shut about the most intimate things" certainly buttress this reading.

For Freud's own associations between shit and creation, the letter of February 23, 1893, is significant;[55] Freud refers in this letter to "depositing his novelties" in his *Dreckologisch Report*, or "DR." Masson translates this as "collection of filth," interpreting *Dreck* in its German sense, while to me it is clear that Freud is using the term in the Yiddish sense to mean shit. Freud thus deposits his novellae in the place for shit; the novelties are shit. And on March 5 Freud writes, "The DR have been interrupted, since I no longer write them for you"![56] Consider, as well, two key passages from the *Wolf Man*. In the first, Freud is explaining the Wolf Man's obsessive concern with blood in his stool and writes: "Under the influence of the primal scene he came to the conclusion that his mother had been made ill by what his father had done to her; and his dread of having blood in his stool, of being as ill as his mother, was his repudiation of being identified with her in this sexual scene. . . . But the dread was also a proof that in his later elaboration of the primal scene he had put himself in his mother's place and envied her this relation with his father. The organ by which his identification with women, his passive homosexual attitude to men, was able to express itself was the anal zone."[57]

In another passage of the same text, Freud writes, as explicitly as possible, that "the stool was the child," and then continues:

> The necessary condition of his re-birth was that he should have an enema administered to him by a man. . . . This can only have meant that he had identified himself with his mother, that the man was acting as his father, and that the enema was repeating the act of copulation, as the fruit of which the excrement-baby . . . would be born. The phantasy of re-birth was therefore bound up closely with the necessary condition of sexual satisfaction from a man. So that the translation now runs to this effect: only on condition that he took the woman's place and substituted himself for his mother, and thus

54. Geller, "(G)nos(e)ology," 265–66.
55. See also Koestenbaum, *Double Talk*, 36–37.
56. Geller, "(G)nos(e)ology," 300.
57. Masson, *Assault*, 293, 301.

let himself be sexually satisfied by his father and bore him a child—only on that condition would his illness leave him.[58]

We are entitled to interpret excrement in Freud's writing as having to do with birth, then, not because this association is a universal of the psyche, but because, on the evidence of Freud's own texts, Freud made this association himself. The association between the anus, anal penetration, shit, and birth-giving seems to be well established on the overt intertextual level within which Freud worked and can thus be legitimately read in his own letters as well. Freud here provides the key for reading his fantasies of being pregnant with Fliess's child when he implicates "excrement babies" with "the necessary condition of sexual satisfaction from a man."

When all of these data and interpretations are put together, a reading emerges. What is at stake in the suppression of the male hysteric and of the desire for the father in the shift to the oedipal theory is the suppression of Freud's own homoeroticism. Freud was motivated in his relationships with men, and especially with Fliess, by acknowledged homoerotic desires, associated as they were at the time with both fantasies of "inversion" and of all-male procreation. To what extent these desires found physical satisfaction, we will never know,[59] although the possibility that he fulfilled them at all seems rather improbable.[60] The Oedipus complex is an inexorably heterosexual, even heterosexist concept.[61] The concept was gradually unfolding itself and its full heteronormative purport, moreover, approximately at the same time as the rift with Fliess was opening and then widening, finally resulting in what Freud later refers to as an overcoming of Fliess as well as an overcoming of "a bit of unruly homosexual investment."[62] As Davis has acutely noted, "Those who think that Freud's understanding of the nature, importance, and prevalence of the Oedipus complex was complete following his self-analysis and his subsequent publication in 1900 of *The Interpretation of Dreams* may be surprised to learn that Freud's first published use of the term did not occur until 1910 in a paper called 'A Special Type of Choice of Object Made by Men.'" Nineteen ten is a

58. SE XVII:78.
59. SE XVII:100.
60. Heller, "Quarrel," 95.
61. Cf. Freud's similar remarks anent the possibility of Leonardo's having had homosexual relationships with his pupils (Freud, "Leonardo," 73).
62. Brenkman, in *Straight Male*, is excellent on the heteronormative enforcement that the Oedipus complex enacts.

crucial year—as crucial as 1897. In 1910, as we shall see, Freud was claiming (in letters to his disciple, Sandor Ferenczi) that he had been recently "occupied with overcoming Fliess,"[63] that is with repressing his own homoerotic desire. And in 1910 he was writing the Schreber text. An adequate explanation of these developments will, therefore, necessitate an understanding of how they are imbricated in each other.[64] Moreover, since I am not psychoanalyzing Freud but historicizing him, the explanation will have to go beyond the biographical details of Freud's life and intellectual development.[65]

Freud was apparently aware of the homoerotic dimensions of his attachment to Fliess from the beginning, as Shirley Garner effectively argues.[66] He almost explicitly described his relationship with Fliess as one in which he adopted a passive, that is, "feminine," role, in *The Interpretation of Dreams*, chapter 6: "A little girl asked me the way to a particular street, and I was obliged to confess that I did not know; and I remarked to my friend: 'It is to be hoped that when she grows up that little girl will show more discrimination in her choice of the people she gets to direct her.' "[67] Anzieu notes "Freud's female/passive identification (he is the little girl who chooses the wrong person to direct her) vis-à-vis the male/active Fliess," and concludes that "Freud's interest, now enthusiastic, now hesitant, in the notion of bisexuality is directly connected with a 'transference effect' of a homosexual nature. Freud still had a long way to go before he was able to realize the latent submission and homosexuality that bound him to Fliess. It was only after Freud had shaken off that bond that psychoanalysis became an independent science."[68]

According to Anzieu's reading, then, the invention of psychoanalysis was intimately connected with Freud's repudiation of his "homosexu-

63. Freud and Ferenczi, *1908–1914,* 221. The friendship was largely over by August 1901 (Garner, "Freud and Fliess," 447), although it could be plausibly argued that at that point it was Fliess who was motivated by homosexual panic to separate from Freud and not the other way around. Freud still seems in this period to be affirming the value of homoeroticism; it is only in the next decade that he will finally claim to "overcome" it. R. Davis, *Freud's,* 54, 221.

64. See now also the important discussion in Eilberg-Schwartz, *God's,* 40–42, and below, n. 108.

65. Cf. R. H. Davis, *Freud's,* 130–36, for an example of the precise obverse of my practice. For Davis, Freud's repudiation of passive aims is totally explicable as a function of inner psychic conflicts having to do with death. Freud could have lived anywhere and anytime and been anyman (i.e., not Jewish) and have produced his symptoms and theories.

66. Garner, "Freud and Fliess," 95–96.

67. Freud, *Interpretation,* SE.

68. Anzieu, *Freud's,* 259.

ality." Anzieu—like Max Schur and William McGrath—understands this event, however, as a deliverance of Freud from Fliess's pernicious influence so that he would be free to develop his own theories. I question the inexorability of this explanation. Once it is questioned, other possibilities arise almost of themselves. Listen to Freud explaining his breakup with his early friend and mentor, Josef Breuer, in a letter to Fliess: "If Breuer's masculine inclination were not so odd, so faint-hearted, so contradictory, as is everything emotional in him, he would be a beautiful example of the kinds of achievements to which the androphile current in men can be sublimated."[69] What Freud is saying here, astonishingly, is that if Breuer had been more open and direct about his homoerotic nature, he would have been a worthier friend for Freud to hang onto. Can there be much doubt that a message is being sent to Fliess as well, just as Freud is acknowledging the unbridgeable rift between them?[70] Freud never quite got over his love for Fliess, even according to Jones. Why did Freud feel comfortable with (sublimated) homoeroticism early in the 1890s but later feel that he had to "overcome [repress]" it, "overcome" Fliess, and produce a theory in which repudiation of passivity—of femininity—is projected as the "bedrock" of the psyche?

The "official" view of the link between Freud's break with Fliess and his discovery of Oedipus is summed up by Schur: "He recognized that his patients' fantasies rather than early seductions were the most frequent etiological factor of their hysteria; he uncovered the ubiquitous role of infantile sexuality and especially the oedipal conflict in normal and abnormal development. He now knew that he had solved one of the great riddles of nature. With this conviction he also achieved an inner independence. Simultaneously the critical part of him reasserted itself in relation to Fliess."[71]

I am turning this picture upside down. Freud indeed abandoned the seduction theory/trauma theory of hysteria (the fantasy of his own "seduction") at the same time he was beginning to separate from Fliess. In the letter that first announces Oedipus there is already a strong—if indirect and ironic—indication of the skepticism about Fliess's theories that would eventually be one of the major causes of their break.[72] Schur

69. Anzieu, *Freud's,* 447.
70. August 7, 1901.
71. Schur, *Freud,* 139.
72. Schur, *Freud,* 273.

and McGrath both date the beginnings of the "collision course" to Fall 1897.[73] The final breakup was, of course, not until 1900. But during this period, when Freud struggled with his growing ambivalence about Fliess and Fliess's theories and about his own theories of seduction and the oedipal complex, what was constantly at work was the tension between a theory of sexuality that would heterosexualize him via the repression of homoeroticism and a theory of sexuality that implicated him homoerotically and that was mapped over a heartfelt (if unconsummated) homoerotic relationship.

In short, not only was the new theory of psychoanalysis essentially an act of repression/overcoming, but the Oedipus model itself ought to be interpreted as a repression of homoerotic desire. In Freud, the fundamental ideas of human sexual development are a sort of screen or supervalent thought for a deeper but very threatening psychic constituent that Freud had found in his own hysteria but that had then panicked him: the desire for "femaleness," for passivity, to be the object of another man's desire, even to bear the child of another man. The analysand in whom Freud came to disbelieve was thus himself.

MALE HYSTERICS AND THE RACE OF MENSTRUATING MEN

The real question underlying the invention of the heteronormatizing Oedipus model is: What was the source of this panic? I suggest that it was occasioned by a nexus of historical forces that included the pathologizing of the "homosexual," an appellation that had only recently become available, and the racialization of the Jews, which Freud also remarks as happening in his own lifetime. "I found that I was expected to feel myself inferior and an alien because I was a Jew. I refused absolutely to do the first of these things. I have never been able to see why I should feel ashamed of my descent or, as people were beginning to say, of my 'race.' "[74] In spite of the sanguine tone of this reminiscence—or perhaps because of it—I hypothesize that in the 1890s Freud panicked at the discursive configuration imposed on him by three deeply intertwined cultural events: the racialization/gendering of antisemitism, the fin de siècle production of sexualities, including the "homosexual," and the sharp increase in contemporary Christian homophobic discourse

73. Schur, *Freud,* 138–39, and McGrath, *Freud's,* 234.
74. Freud, *An Autobiographical Study.*

(the "Christian Values" movement).[75] These discourses produced a perfect and synergistic match between homophobia and antisemitism. By identifying himself as hysterical and as Fliess's *erōmenos* (object of pederastic desire), Freud had been putting himself into the very categories that the antisemitic discourse of the nineteenth century would put him in: feminized, pathic, queer—Jewish.[76]

Stewart suggested in 1976 that among the factors that led Freud to abandon Charcot's heredity theory were its connotations of racism, which meant at that time antisemitism. It is important to emphasize that this factor need not be read reductively to the effect that Freud abandoned and created theories in order to protect himself against racism and that the theories, themselves, therefore have no value. I could as easily interpret this to mean that because of his sensitivity as a victim of the racist implications of the theory, he was led to think further and more deeply and critically about the problem itself. With reference to a case in which a man who was sexually abused by another man as a child then abused his sister, whereupon both became hysterical, Freud writes to Fliess: "You may gather from this how a neurosis escalates to a psychosis in the next generation—which is called degeneracy—simply because someone of more tender age is drawn in. Here, by the way, is the heredity of this case."[77] That the word "degeneracy" is used ironically by Freud—as is "heredity"—provides evidence for this interpretation. And in the same ironic tone Freud writes in his *Studies:* "We should do well to distinguish between the concepts of 'disposition' and 'degeneration' as applied to people; otherwise we shall find ourselves forced to admit that humanity owes a large proportion of its great achievements

75. Fout, "Moral Purity Movement" and "Sexual Politics"; Davidson, "Sex"; E. Cohen, *Talk*. In an important and fascinating article, Siobhan Somerville has argued for the correlation of the "inventions" of race and sexuality in the American context, relating them to Plessy v. Ferguson of 1896 (Somerville, "Scientific Racism," 244–45). Freud also writes that the term "race" was coming into use in Europe to refer to Jews at precisely the same moment. This only underlines once more how powerfully analogous are the discourses of American antiblack racism and European antisemitism, for which see Gilroy, *Black Atlantic,* 212–17.

76. There was, of course, another description of male homosexuality also available in Freud's time, figuring it as hypermasculinity. This turn, however, appealed precisely to the Aryan, the Greek, the Dionysiac, and it condemned the Jewish homosexual rights activist, Magnus Hirschfeld (for instance), as the ultimate queer. It is no accident that Hirschfeld's greatest enemy, Benedikt Friedländer, the founder of a hypermale homosexual movement, was a converted Jew and virulent antisemite. For a homoerotic excoriation of effeminacy, see Sedgwick's discussion of Nietzsche in *Epistemology,* 134; and for its connections with the "Christian," see there 136–41. On Friedländer, see Steakley, *Homosexual Emancipation,* 54. See also n. 92 below.

77. Stewart, "Freud," 221, 222.

to the efforts of 'degenerates,' " that is, Jews and homosexuals.[78] It was at the same point that Freud stopped writing about male hysterics.

In the second half of the 1890s, Freud realized (consciously or not) the deeply problematic implications of his position.[79] Charcot had, of course, referred to the special propensity of Polish Jews to hysteria.[80] An American Jewish doctor of the time wrote: "The Jewish population of [Warsaw] alone is almost exclusively the inexhaustible source for the supply of specimens of hysterical humanity, particularly the hysteria in the male, for all the clinics of Europe."[81] Sander L. Gilman shows that this view, which resulted from a misquotation, became the standard view in German psychiatric circles. By focusing on hysteria, especially in light of his own self-diagnosed hysteria, Freud was fashioning a self-representation that collaborated with one of the most tenacious of antisemitic topoi—that male Jews are a third sex: men who menstruate.

The topos of the Jewish man as a sort of woman is a venerable one going back at least to the thirteenth century in Europe, where it was widely maintained that Jewish men menstruate.[82] As the fourteenth-century Italian astrologer Cecci d'Ascoli writes: "After the death of Christ all Jewish men, like women, suffer menstruation."[83] As Peter Biller has shown, melancholia and sexual excess (attributes later assigned to both women and homosexuals) were already given in the thirteenth century as among the major factors that produced Jewish male menstruation. The explanation of this myth is to be found in the consistent representation of male Jews in European culture as female, largely because of their circumcision, which was interpreted as feminiz-

78. Freud, *Studies,* 104.

79. Although I am dependent on Gilman's rich scholarship, it will be noted that my interpretation is quite different from his. For Gilman, already in the late 1880s Freud had rejected those views of hysteria—Charcot's heredity theory—that put the Jew at risk (Gilman, "Image," 416). While I agree, of course, that Gilman is correct on this point, his interpretation does not pay attention in my view to the extent to which the trauma theory was also putting Jews at risk. Any theory of male hysteria had that potential simply because of the prevailing myth, which Gilman himself has documented, that male hysterics are almost always Jews.

80. Mosse, *Nationalism,* 142; Jan Goldstein, "Wandering Jew," 536, and especially 540–41.

81. Maurice Fishberg, quoted in Gilman, "Image," 405.

82. Biller, "Views," 192–93, 196; Efron, *Defenders,* 6.

83. Biller, "Views," 199. I thank my student, Willis Johnson for calling this text to my attention. Gilman, somewhat bizarrely in my opinion, theorizes a factual, historical basis for the myth of Jewish male menstruation, referring to a parasite that does cause genital bleeding in men around the time of puberty (Gilman, "Struggle" 304 n. 32). There does not seem to be any evidence that Jews in particular ever suffered from this disease.

ing.[84] In the Viennese slang of Freud's time, the clitoris was called "the Jew" and female masturbation was "playing with the Jew."[85] If Jewish men are a kind of women, or even women *simpliciter*, then it is hardly surprising that they menstruate; moreover, if a primary cause of the theory of their femaleness is their circumcision, an operation which causes genital bleeding and within which the bleeding is in fact a primary motif, then the base for myths of Jewish male menstruation seems clear.

This ambivalent gendering was the reason that male Jews were particularly prone to hysteria in the medical imaginary of the nineteenth century: they were gendered as Victorian women. According to Thomas Sydenham, a mid-seventeenth-century English medical writer, the prime candidates for (male) hysteria were "such male subjects as lead a sedentary or studious life, and grow pale over their books and papers."[86] These men were enacting a male equivalent of the "female" pursuits of embroidery, tatting, and such, in short—although Sydenham surely did not realize it—almost a perfect portrait of the ideal Jewish male of eastern Europe, the pale, sedentary, studious *Yeshiva-Bokhur,* whose wife (and he did always end up with one) was ideally robust, energetic, and economically active. If, as Freud writes after discovering the heteronormativizing power of Oedipus, the etiology of homosexuality is "masculine women, women with energetic traits of character, who were able to push the father out of his proper place,"[87] then we describe, it seems, exactly the sort of mother Freud had, as well as a father who had indeed been pushed out of his "proper place." More to the point, Galician Jewish culture in general had such mothers and fathers.

The representation of the ideal male Jew as female thus was not only an external one, one that originated in the fantasies of antisemites, but also an internal one that represented a genuine Jewish cultural difference. It is, moreover, while not untroubled, also not negative in its tra-

84. Geller, "Paleontological View"; see also Garber, *Vested Interests.* Indeed, circumcision was often read in European culture as a partial castration. Roman law forbade it under the same rubrics as castration. Interestingly enough, even authors who denied that male Jews menstruate credited the notion that they bleed, attributing it to hemorrhoids caused by melancholia, thus another "female" attribute (Dahan, *Intellectuels,* 529).
    85. Gilman, *Freud,* 38–39.
    86. Quoted in Veith, *Hysteria,* 141. Catherine Gallagher cites evidence that as early as classical Greece, being a writer was sometimes associated with emasculation ("George," 125).
    87. SE XI:99.

ditional cultural manifestations. In fact, as we have seen throughout
this entire discussion up till now, this sense of self-femminization was
one of the traditional ways in which male Jews defined themselves over
and against the gentile world. Within traditional rabbinic Jewish culture, the femminization of the male, in part symbolized (or effected?)
through truncation of the penis, was experienced as a positive phenomenon, as a positive sense of self-identification and differentiation
from the Romans (and their descendants). The shift in Freud's thinking
records the subjectivity of a person living and experiencing the invention of heterosexuality in his lifetime, and he invented himself as that
new type of man, the heterosexual, by repressing his own homoerotic
desire.[88] "Heterosexuality," as its tenets have been ventriloquized by
David Halperin, involves the strange idea that a "normal" man will
never feel desire for another man.[89] Two particular events of the fin de
siècle may very well have been instrumental in focusing Freud's attention on the dangers that his own theories posed to him: the Oscar Wilde
trials in 1895 and the discourse of and around Otto Weininger with his
claim that Jewishness is essentially female.[90] In 1902 and 1906 there
were sensational "homosexual" scandals in Germany as well.[91] Traditional Jewish male passivity—associated with queerness—would have
become problematic in such an environment.[92]

88. See also Breines, *Tough Jews,* 36. In the light of Breines's observation that "the
blossoming of tough imagery among American Jews during the past two decades is also
bound up with male concerns about a perceived threat of emasculation provoked in part
by contemporary feminism" (37), I wonder if at least some of the anticircumcision fervor
among contemporary males is generated not by a feminist impulse but is precisely the
product of such a phobic response to feminism. Its approbation by such figures as Sam
Keene (on the cover of Howard Eilberg-Schwartz's *God's*) suggests as much.

89. Halperin, *One Hundred Years,* 44.

90. The timing seems slightly off on this latter suggestion, since Weininger's book
was published in 1903; but Freud had read it in manuscript before and undoubtedly was
aware of Weininger's thinking even before that. Freud was, in fact, the first reader of
Weininger's manuscript, probably sometime late in 1900 (Heller, "Quarrel," 99 and passim). Since I am not arguing for a one-time sudden development but a complex process
within Freud's thinking—from the first mention of Oedipus in 1897 to the hardening of
the developmental theories into their fully heterosexist form in the first decade of the
twentieth century—Weininger could have been a factor. Even more to the point, the sort
of ideas that Weininger was spouting were very likely in some sense "in the air." The
Oscar Wilde trials would certainly have been a factor, for they had enormous impact in
Germany as well (Showalter, *Sexual Anarchy,* 172). It should also not be ignored that the
Dreyfus case was at its climax in the crucial year 1897 (cf. Garner, "Freud and Fliess,"
299), when, moreover, the antisemitic Karl Lueger finally became mayor of Vienna.

91. Mosse, *Nationalism,* 88, 105.

92. There was even an antisemitic homoerotic movement in Germany, Hans Blüher's
Bund, which promoted an ideal of the homosexual as supermanly, not degenerate and
effeminate like the queer Jew (Mosse, *Nationalism,* 87). As Garber has written, "Here,

Gilman connects Fliess's fantastic theories of male periodicity associated with bleeding from the nose with antisemitic fantasies of male
menstruation and argues that by generalizing these as theories of maleness, Fliess was attempting to deflect the marginalizing effect of such
representations of Jewish men. Freud's apparent assent to such ideas, at
least at first, indicates his similar concern about the situation of the
Jewish male physician. It is at least as plausible to assume that Freud's
persistent expressed fantasies of his own menstruation are rather a reflection than a deflection of his femminization.[93] Such an interpretation
would be more consistent with Freud's apparently quite self-conscious
production of homoerotic fantasy about Fliess, his open references to
"a special—let us say feminine—side" of his personality,[94] which certainly, for Freud, means the presence of "passive" homoerotic sexual
aims,[95] and his persistent use of birthing imagery for the relationship.
It also gives us a powerful explanation for his fainting—a performance
of femaleness in his culture—when Emma Eckstein hemorrhages from
the nose. *Madame Eckstein, ç'est moi.*[96] As Sprengnether has written,
"The dramatic scene attended by Freud in which Eckstein nearly bled
to death elicited in him a mirror response—'I felt sick.' The real terror
of this moment may consist not only in the castration fantasy hovering

---

too, definitions of 'homosexuality' cross with stereotypes of Jewish male identity, for the
'homosexual' could be either super-male, especially manly and virile, and therefore associating only with other men (rather than with polluting and 'effeminizing' women), or, on
the other hand, a 'degenerate' 'aesthete,' blurring the boundaries of male and female"
(*Vested Interests*, 227). See also Mosse, *Nationalism*, 201 n. 83, who notes that Benedikt
Friedländer, a Jewish homosexual rights advocate, was careful to claim that all of the
"effeminate" homosexuals were in the other movement, that of Magnus Hirschfeld.
Friedländer was associated as well with the most vicious of antisemitic racists (Mosse, 41).
It would not be entirely wrong to suggest that it was passivity and effeminacy that were
more problematic at this period than homoeroticism itself—that is, homophobia is, *at this
time,* almost subsumed under misogyny, to which antisemitism bears a strong family connection as well. See also n. 60 above.

93. Masson, *Complete Letters*, 256, 270. On 10 March 1898, Freud declared that
his and Fliess's periods had become synchronized (Masson, *Complete Letters*, 301). See
also Koestenbaum, who, overlooking the historical career of Jewish male menstruation,
interprets this fantasy somewhat differently, as being a "figure for the distressing anal
bleeding that would have been the likely consequence of their intercourse—if we postulate the existence of a symbolic anal hymen, broken upon first penetration" (Koestenbaum, *Double Talk*, 74–75). Interestingly enough, I think that the two explanations can
converge in one overdetermined moment.

94. Masson, *Complete Letters*, 412.

95. R. H. Davis, *Freud's*, 52, citing SE IX:250.

96. Note how my intervention here contests the claim of Hélène Cixous that of the
three male writers whom she privileges as modes of access to protofeminist consciousness,
only Flaubert and Michelet are accorded the status of "most 'feminine'" of men, while
Freud is explicitly denied that designation (Cixous and Clément, *Newly Born*, 6).

on the edges of Freud's description but also in the collapse of sexual difference which it implies. To be like Eckstein, a victim of Fliess's bungled operation, is not only analogous to being a victim of sexual violation; it is also to be a woman."[97] And I add, for Freud, bleeding from the nose was particularly redolent with images of Jewish male menstruation. Freud reports easily, almost with pride, Eckstein's taunt: "So this is the strong sex!"[98]

In other words, for Freud at least, the early acceptance of these seemingly bizarre representations and notions was a signifier of his initial self-construction as homoerotic, as femminized. But as Jewish difference became configurable not only as feminine but also as homosexual, and as "homosexual" solidified into an identity toward the end of the century, Freud would have been even more at pains to deny and repress anything that would seem to cast him as the bent Jew, the queer.

Gilman has provided a vitally important piece of information by observing how thoroughly Jewishness was constructed as queer in fin de siècle central Europe: "Moses Julius Gutmann observes that 'all of the comments about the supposed stronger sexual drive among Jews have no basis in fact; most frequently they are sexual neurasthenics. Above all the number of Jewish homosexuals is extraordinarily high.' This view is echoed by Alexander Pilcz, Freud's colleague in the Department of Psychiatry at the University of Vienna, who noted that 'there is a

---

97. Sprengnether, *Spectral Mother,* 31. Past this point, however, I find myself in disagreement with Sprengnether. She writes: "First he absolves Fliess of culpability by interpreting Eckstein's bleeding as hysterically motivated, while affirming his renewed faith in Fliess's medical diagnoses in regard to his own symptoms. The latent contradiction in this position gives rise, in turn, to a thesis concerning infantile eroticism, which has the double advantage of emphasizing the boy's active desire for his mother and further absolving adult male figures of blame" (*Spectral Mother,* 37). By thus acceding to the canonical interpretation of the gender politics here, namely, that exoneration of male adults is what is at stake for Freud and that this is fully analogous with and indeed provoked by his desire to exonerate Fliess, another male adult, Sprengnether almost loses sight for the moment of the radicality of her recognition that adult females and immature males were just as much at issue in the "seduction" theory as adult males and juvenile females. Sprengnether argues (like Masson, *Assault*) that Freud's *defense* of Fliess "prepares the path for his subsequent exoneration of fathers (including himself and his own) of the charge of sexual violation of their children" (33). But surely by the time that Freud had (even according to the view that he had) fully "exonerated" the fathers, he had broken with Fliess and admitted his guilt. In contrast, I would interpret Freud's initial desperate attempts to exonerate Fliess as whistling in the dark as he increasingly realized the implications of his passive dependence on Fliess and what it implied about his own gendering. My interpretation of this point is, then, more similar to Schur's ("Some Additional 'Day Residues'") than to Masson's or Sprengnether's, and it is, to be sure, a matter of interpretative protocols and tact.
98. Masson, *Complete Letters,* 117.

relatively high incidence of homosexuality among the Jews.' "[99] The literary locus classicus for this association is, of course, Proust, for whom both Jews and homosexuals are the "accursed race." Both of these conditions constitute, for Proust, "incurable diseases."[100] All the features that construct the figure of the homosexual construct the Jew as well, namely, hypersexuality, melancholia, and passivity. It was this factor and the hysterization of the *Ostjude* that led to Freud's relative abandonment of hysteria together with its etiology in childhood seductions, that is, fantasies of seduction of the son by the father, and to the production of the inexorably heteronormative Oedipus narrative.[101] "To say to a man 'You are hysterical' became under these conditions a form of saying to him 'You are not a man.'"[102] Since within this culture, male hysteria and homosexuality are both symptoms and products of gender inversion, there is a slippage between them: the Jew was queer and hysterical—and therefore, not a man. In response, the normatively straight Jewish Man was invented to replace the bent *Ostjude*, and his hysteria—his alternative gendering—was the first victim: "All psychoanalytic theory was born from hysteria, but the mother died during the birth."[103] The Oedipus complex is Freud's family romance of escape from Jewish queerdom into gentile, phallic heterosexuality.

With the shift in the discourse of sexuality in the 1890s—with homosexuality identified as a Jewish problem, not least via Magnus Hirschfeld's prominence,[104] and with the growing homophobia and antisemitism, indeed with the virtual identity of these two discourses in the Christian Values movement documented by John Fout—Freud needed desperately to hide this dimension of his personality. As Fout has observed of one of the leading exponents of this "moral purity" (family values) movement in Germany, "Adolf Stoecker was a rabid anti-Semite, and many of the moral purity attacks on Hirschfeld were of a fundamentally anti-Semitic character—homosexuals were always depicted as outside the bounds of society."[105] Freud had good reason to

99. Gilman, "Sigmund," 59–60. Mosse, however, argues that in Germany (as opposed to Austria?) the Jew was not so much identified as homosexual himself but as seeking to spread homosexuality among the population as part of a plot to take over Germany (*Nationalism*, 140).

100. Proust, *Sodom*, 22.

101. Brenkman, *Straight Male*.

102. Showalter, "Hysteria," 291.

103. Etienne Trillat, quoted in Showalter, "Hysteria," 291.

104. For the ways that Hirschfeld was experienced as threatening by Jews (and especially gay Jews), see Garber, *Vested Interests*, 227–28.

105. Fout, "Moral Purity Movement," 405.

be scared: the persistent association of Jews with homosexuals and homosexuals with Jews was to turn not half a century later into the most
murderous practice against both that the world has ever known. In
1928 a typical Nazi newspaper referred to the "indissoluble joining of
Marxism, pederasty, and systematic Jewish contamination,"[106] and in
1930 Wilhelm Frick, soon to be Minister of the Interior of the Nazi
government, called for the castration of homosexuals, "that Jewish pes-
tilence."[107] The Oedipus complex, the fantasy of a masculinity rendered
virile through both of its moments, the desire for the mother (not the
father) and violent hostility toward the father, provided Freud with the
cultural/psychosocial cover for his dread.

FREUD AS SCHREBER

A look at Freud's analysis of the Schreber case shows the difference this
reading of the epochal event during the 1890s makes for our understanding of Freud.[108] My argument here depends on the perspicacious
analyses of Freud's texts by Geller, who nevertheless does not draw the
conclusions from his readings that I do. A core term within the text is
the *Entmannung,* the unmanning, that Schreber fantasizes himself undergoing. Geller points out that this core term is equivocal. In Freud's
usage, and especially as translated in the *Standard Edition,* it comes out
as emasculation, "physical and figurative castration." " 'Emasculation'
evokes the castration complex, the matrix of childhood phantasies and
theories which leads to the recognition of sexual difference and the
interpellation of the child into normative structures of symbolic differences." Macalpine and Hunter, however, in their translation of Schreber's original text, emphasize the attainment of femaleness that *Entmannung* implies. As Geller notes: "The choice of 'unmanning,' by
privileging women's necessary activity, here the female-specific capacity

106. *Völkischer Beobachter,* quoted in Moeller, "Homosexual Man," 400.
107. Mosse, *Nationalism,* 158.
108. My initial thinking about the Schreber text was stimulated by reading a draft of
Howard Eilberg-Schwartz's *God's.* I wish to thank him for sharing that work with me
prior to publication. In general, there is only one area of major theoretical disagreement
between my work and Eilberg-Schwartz's. He reads biblical religion as condemning "homosexuality" per se, while I would argue that it is only male anal intercourse that is ma-
ligned there as a form of "cross-dressing," and not homoeroticism or even other homosexual practices—male or female—thus my view is consistent with the Foucauldian view,
directly opposed by Eilberg-Schwartz (*God's,* 243 n. 3)—which sees "heterosexuality" as the exclusive invention of modern Western culture (D. Boyarin, "Are There Any
Jews?").

to reproduce, questions the authority of castration as the determinant of difference. The 'unmanned' Schreber, for Macalpine and Hunter, is a pregnant Redeemer. 'Emasculation' and 'unmanning' converge on *Entmannung* in Schreber's text."[109] Geller's argument hinges, as he says, on an ambiguity in the word *Entmannung* itself. It may mean "emasculation," that is, castration, or it may mean exiting from the category of men and entering into the category of women. For Freud, strangely enough, the two are explicitly equated in the later oedipal theory. However, they are most definitely not the same thing, and their lack of equivalence comes to the fore in Schreber's text where emasculation would have meant sterility while "unmanning" as feminization means the exact opposite, the attainment of female superfecundity. Freud's elision of the positive desire in *Entmannung* is of a piece with his reading of femininity as castration. They both constitute an attempt to deny his own desires and fantasies of feminization, his own hysteria.

Geller elegantly argues that "Freud's deployment of *Entmannung* in 'Psychoanalytic Notes,' particularly his separation of Schreber's 'emasculation' from his pregnancy phantasies, endeavors both to constrain the overdetermination of the term and to elide the mixture of personal concerns and competing theories betrayed by that polysemy."[110] What were those personal concerns of which Geller speaks that led Freud at this time, about 1910, to deny completely the positive aspects of Schreber's fantasies?[111] Geller himself "suggests a relationship between the 'emasculated' Schreber's problems with his sexual identity and the circumcised Freud's own concerns about his ethnic identity. *Entmannung* reproduces a Jewish difference Freud would disavow." I might put it in the following fashion: *Verjudung* is equivalent to *Entmannung*.[112] This

---

109. Geller, "Freud," 181.

110. Geller, "Freud," 182.

111. Eilberg-Schwartz points out as well how in Freud's account of monotheism in *Moses* the positive aspects of God's love for humans are completely elided, and he suggests that there, too, it is homoerotic implications that are being denied—once again a marginalization of the so-called negative Oedipus complex.

112. Cf. Walton's discussion of a 1917 psychoanalytic account of women with the "masculinity complex," who fantasized that they had "Hottentot nymphae," the supposedly hypertrophied genitalia of the black woman. Walton reads this as a refusal on the part of these women to accept the gendered designation "masculinized" through identification with a racial Other who was not a "woman": "It is as though van Opuijsen's patients sought to assert sexual and gender identities that would challenge and contradict the strictly (white) feminine one that had hitherto been culturally prescribed (and was about to become psychoanalytically codified) in terms of passivity, receptivity to the 'active' male, and de-emphasis of the pleasures of the clitoris. Since it had become probable by the 1910s that defiance of the feminine role would inevitably be 'diagnosed' as a 'mas-

relationship becomes particularly clear because Schreber imagines himself as the Eternal Jew, and this Jewish identity constitutes the unmanning that makes it possible for him to reproduce as a female. As Geller notes, where for Schreber himself the unmanning is an epiphenomenon of becoming a woman, for Freud the opposite is true: becoming a woman is a mere side effect of castration.[113]

Geller suggests as well the connection between Freud's curious ostracism of *Entmannung* and "his lingering homosexual affect for Fliess."[114] We can go further than Geller in analyzing this motive, however, for the *Entmannung* of the Schreber text recalls (in both senses) the overcoming of Freud's homosexual investments of which he writes in a letter to Ferenczi, composed at the same time that he was working on the Schreber text.[115] It was just about at this time, moreover, that Freud "discovered" the negative (or inverted) Oedipus complex and thoroughly pathologized it.[116] Freud's concern was not only with his Jewish difference but with the particular way that difference configured him at the fin de siècle as feminized and especially as queer. His "overcoming" was thus an attempt to conquer the unmanning that all Jewish males suffer in confrontation with a heteronormative gentile culture. Weininger is very important here, for it was he who wrote obsessively of the necessity to overcome the Jewish spirit, that abject female element within everyone,[117] but especially in Jews. As I shall argue at length in the next chapter, Freud had much more in common with Weininger than he was prepared to admit.

Freud's comment to Ferenczi about "Fliess's case, with the overcoming of which you *recently* saw me occupied . . . "[118] lets us know that just about the time he was writing about Schreber he was also involved

culinity complex' (that is, if you do not wish to be 'feminine,' you must wish to be 'masculine'), these women would seem to have sought an alternative means of asserting a gendered identity that both was and was not officially 'feminine.' Drawing from the kinds of clinical or anthropological depictions of the genitals of African women that would doubtless have been circulating in the early twentieth century, they found images of themselves in a mirror that was striking for its racialized, not its masculine-gendered, depiction of sexual difference" ("Re-placing," 788–89). Schreber's identification with a racial Other who is not a man, also owing to a "deformation" of the genitals, would be cut of the same cloth!

113. Geller, "Freud," 182, 184.
114. Geller, "Freud," 198.
115. Jones, *Life,* II:92–93.
116. R. H. Davis, *Freud's,* 10.
117. Heller, "Quarrel," 101.
118. Letter dated October 6, 1910 (Freud and Ferenczi, *1908–1914,* 221, emphasis added).

with his "overcoming" of Fliess. He continues in the same letter: "A part of homosexual investment has been withdrawn and made use of to enlarge my own ego. I have succeeded where the paranoiac fails." At the end of the letter he writes, "I surely have not yet written that I have worked through the Schreber once, that I have found the core of our paranoia hypotheses corroborated." The "paranoiac" is accordingly Fliess, but also Daniel Schreber. For Freud, recognition of the positive attraction that femaleness and being transformed into a female held for Schreber would have involved the psychological necessity for him to face again his own unresolved desires for femaleness, which in his culturally conditioned eyes was equivalent to homosexuality.[119] Both of these, feminization and homosexuality, were "Jewish diseases" that Freud was anxious to overcome, and, once overcome, they could be safely pathologized.

This connection between the texts (of Freud's "life" and his interpretation of the Schreber case) suggests, moreover, another powerful intertextual nexus.[120] In perhaps the most famous passage of that text, Freud writes that in a homophobic regime, the sentence, "I (a man) *love* him (a man)" must be transformed in the following ways: "First, 'I do not *love* him—I *hate* him'; second, 'I do not love *him*, I love *her*'; third, '*I* do not love him; *she* loves him.'"[121] Note what a perfect analogy this provides to the shift from the negative Oedipus to the positive Oedipus complexes. The so-called negative homoerotic desire, "I wish to be penetrated by my father and have his baby" is replaced by "I do not love him (my father); I love my mother and hate my father, even to the point of desiring to kill him, because, after all, it is he whom my mother loves and he who threatens me with castration"—in short, replaced by paranoia![122] In describing the etiology of Schreber's paranoia in homosexuality—or better, as clearly pointed out by Kendall Thomas in internalized homophobia[123]—Freud was writing, consciously or unconsciously, another chapter of his psychosexual-intellectual autobiography. As

119. See also the powerful argument of O'Neill, "Law."

120. Note again how completely different my model of such a nexus is from that of Freudian interpreters of Freud who connect "the content of his theory and the dynamics of his self-analysis" (R. H. Davis, *Freud's*, 84). Davis himself regards his work as "psychohistory" and justifies it by referring to Freud's own psychohistories of Leonardo, Dostoyevsky, and Schreber.

121. Freud, *Psycho-analytic Notes*.

122. For an argument similar in structure, see Kazanjian, "Notarizing," 110–12.

123. Thomas, "Corpus," 34; see also Sedgwick, *Epistemology*, 187; Craft, *Another Kind*, 101.

O'Neill has quite stunningly remarked, "In his struggle to reduce Schreber's divinity, Freud for once was prepared to make himself sound perfectly boring—indeed, to crackle like the miracled-up voices, everything belongs to the Father, the father is behind everything, behind God, behind Fleschig, behind your bum!"[124]

If Freud was not able to cure himself of his desire for the passive, "feminine," hysterical role of male birth-giver, however, he was able to cure his theory, the part of himself that he showed the world. In that discourse, he shifted the main male protagonist from hysteric to paranoiac, from what was gendered female, bent, and Jewish in his fin de siècle world, to what was gendered male, straight, and Aryan. After the 1890s, no longer would a femminized male, father-desiring, pathic, hysterical Jewish queer be at the center of his thinking but an active, phallic, mother-desiring, father-killing, "normal" man.

Freud's invention of the Oedipus complex was not, therefore, a product of his own private psychological development but part of a larger sociohistorical history, one that I have dubbed "the invention of the Jewish man." In the next chapter, I hope to further illuminate this process by reading other central Freudian texts in its light.

124. O'Neill, "Law," 243.

"You May Not Tell the Boys"

The Diaspora Politics of a Bitextual Jew

Psychoanalysis is the Rashi-commentary on the present generation
of Jews. —Franz Kafka

OUTING FREUD'S ZIONISM

On January 5, 1898, Sigmund Freud went to the theater.[1] The play was
Theodor Herzl's *Das neue Ghetto* (*The New Ghetto*). Very soon after—
if not that very night—he dreamed the dream that he later called "My
Son the Myops."[2] Until now the significance of this marvelous conjunction of texts has been "exploited" primarily in readings of Freud's individual psychobiography. But its significance is much broader. The intertextual meeting of Freud and Herzl in Freud's dream constitutes a
singularly illuminating moment in that multifold psychopolitical phenomenon known as the "Emancipation of the Jews," and the event is
crucial for understanding not just that phenomenon but also psychoanalysis and Zionism as materially implicated in the history of sexuality, indeed in the invention of sexuality at the fin de siècle.[3]

Freud recorded his dream as follows:

> On account of certain events which had occurred in the city of Rome, it had
> become necessary to remove the children to safety, and this was done. The

1. Masson, *Complete Letters*, 293.
2. The dream was given this name owing to a passage within it that I will not include
here. There is a great deal of unclarity about whether or not Freud dreamed the dream
after seeing the play or perhaps even before seeing it (McGrath, *Freud's*, 236). He could
have heard about it, or even read it, for it was published in Vienna in 1897. For my
argument this does not matter at all, since I am reading the two texts as elements in a
certain discourse, as synchronic intertexts. It makes a better opening anecdote, however,
if we assume that Freud saw the play and then dreamed the dream.
3. Davidson, "Sex."

scene was then in front of a gateway, double doors in the ancient style (the
'Porta Romana' at Siena, as I was aware during the dream itself). I was sitting on the edge of a fountain and was greatly depressed and almost in tears.
A female figure—an attendant or nun—brought two boys out and handed
them over to their father, who was not myself. The elder of the two was clearly
my eldest son. I did not see the other one's face. The woman who brought
out the boy asked him to kiss her good-bye. She was noticeable for having a
red nose. The boy refused to kiss her, but, holding out his hand in farewell,
said 'AUF GESERES' to her, and then 'AUF UNGESERES' to the two of us
(or to one of us). I had a notion that the last phrase denoted a preference.[4]

One of the most significant aspects of the "My Son the Myops"
dream is the way that it produces a conjunction of political and sexual
meanings. Freud's dream of a safe haven clearly thematizes a positive
affect for Zionism,[5] but Zionism for Freud, and indeed for Herzl, was
not simply a political program.[6] It was not even an alternative to assimilation with the culture of western Europe, but rather a fulfillment of the
project of assimilation, as I shall argue in the next chapter. Assimilation
for these Jews was a sexual and gendered enterprise, an overcoming of
the political and cultural characteristics that marked Jewish men as a
"third sex," as queer in their world. For Freud, Zionism was motivated
as much by the Oscar Wilde trials as by the Dreyfus trial.[7] It was a
return to Phallustine, not to Palestine. Freud's sexualized politics is not
so much about freedom from oppression as about passing. It is impossible to separate the question of Jewishness from the question of homosexuality in Freud's symbolic, textual world. In that world, passing, for
Jews, entailed homosexual panic, internalized homophobia, and, ultimately, aggression. The aggression, however, was turned in a surprising
direction, as we shall see via a reading of Freud's most explicit text of
Jewish politics, *Moses and Monotheism*.[8]

4. Freud, *Interpretation*, 269.
5. Frieden, *Freud's*, 120.
6. Loewenberg, followed by McGrath, detects in this dream a "hidden Zionist
theme." The main evidence for this interpretation lies in the phrase in Freud's commentary about "one's children, to whom one cannot give a country of their own." In fact,
there is a great deal of ambiguity in this interpretative move itself, since for Loewenberg
it would seem the dream represents "a latent attraction to, and envy of, the world of
Jewish salvation through politics" ("Hidden Zionist," 132), while for McGrath, the
dream constitutes an assertion that "directly dismissed Herzl's new cause" (*Freud's*, 237).
7. The latter itself was, moreover, as we learn clearly from Proust (and might have
surmised anyway), as much a matter of Jewish manliness as of Jewish safety. The appropriate response to the Dreyfus affair was to fight duels with antisemites (Proust, *Sodom*,
11, 20–21). This point will take on more resonance in the next chapter.
8. In the course of completing this argument I came across Jacques Le Rider's *Mo-*

The political meanings of the "Myops" dream are explicitly thematized in Freud's associations to it. After noting the connection with Herzl's play, Freud writes: "The Jewish problem, concern about the future of one's children, to whom one cannot give a country of their own, concern about educating them in such a way that they can move freely across frontiers."[9] The phrase that provides the clearest associations with Herzl's play is "concern about educating them [the children] in such a way that they can move freely across frontiers."[10] The play is explicitly founded on the premise that although physical walls have broken down between Jew and German, spiritual, cultural, and social walls are still in place. The "double doors in the ancient style," can be taken to refer to Jewish life in the ancient style, since, after all, Freud's word for *doors* is *Tore*, that is, via a typical dream-work pun, *Torah*. This verbal association would be strengthened by a visual connection with the double doors of the Holy Ark within which the Torah is kept in the synagogue.

The dual doors, the Torah, are the gates of the new ghetto, the ghetto without walls in Herzl's play, from which they must be able to escape. The phrase reflects Freud's conflicted desire to educate his children in such a way that the borders between them and the gentiles would be broken down, that they would be able to freely cross that frontier—whether by conversion or, more likely, by assimilation. Freud,

---

dernity, in which the same set of contexts is mobilized for reading *Moses* with, interestingly enough, quite different results (Le Rider, 217–27).

9. Freud, *Interpretation*, 573.

10. The "standard" psychoanalytical readings of this sentence all seem inadequate to me. The best that Grinstein can offer, for example, is that "[i]t will be recalled how many of Freud's references in *The Interpretation of Dreams* deal with his wish to attain the rank of Professor and with the antisemitic prejudices to which he was constantly exposed. Quite understandably he wanted to spare his children this kind of treatment and wanted to move to another country, such as England, where his children and he himself could enjoy greater freedom and tolerance" (*Sigmund*, 321). This seems to me hardly an adequate gloss for "educating the children in such a way that they can freely move across frontiers." The emphasis here is surely on the mode of the children's education and not on the freedom or intolerance of the place in which they are being educated. Still less is it obvious to conclude that the meaning of this sentence has to do with Freud's dream of being a professor and its frustration at the hands of antisemites. McGrath accepts Grinstein's reading, similarly ignoring the fact that Freud's concern is not with the crossing of frontiers but of educating the children so that they could cross frontiers (*Freud's*, 243). Anzieu's only allusion to this sentence is part of a denial, when he writes, "Nothing in this dream justifies the interpretation formulated by Maylan (1930), who, writing from an anti-Semitic point of view, claims that Freud's neurosis was the result of a repressed wish to be converted to Christianity" (Anzieu, *Freud's*, 261). I find Maylan's view compelling.

like Herzl, at a deep level wished to be recognized as a complete and authentic member of German *Kultur,* in no way different from others. At the same time, though, like Herzl he wished to remain Jewish while abandoning Judaism—not only the religion itself but all the cultural practices that divide Jews from gentiles.

Such a wish is, of course, a highly ambivalent one, and it is no wonder that "My Son the Myops" is a highly ambivalent dream. The most obvious site (literally) of ambivalence in the dream is the role of "Rome" in it. "On account of certain events which had occurred in the city of Rome, it had become necessary to remove the children to safety, and this was done. The scene was then in front of a gateway, double doors in the ancient style (the 'Porta Romana' at Siena, as I was aware during the dream itself). I was sitting on the edge of a fountain and was greatly depressed and almost in tears." To this part of the dream, Freud contributes the association: "By the waters of Babylon, there we sat down, and there we wept when we remembered Zion." This verse from Psalm 137 refers to the exile from Jerusalem, and it is clearly this association that provides the occasion of sitting by the fountain and weeping. But Jerusalem has been "converted" in Freud's dream wishes into Rome. The waters of Babylon are the fountain at Siena, at the Porta Romana, the gates that lead to Rome. By the waters of Siena, there we sat down, and there we wept, when we remembered Roma. It is Rome that is the object of desire here. Freud's next associations to his desire to educate the children so that they can freely cross frontiers would mean, then, to educate them so that they can return to Rome, the locale of the gentile oppressor as well. It is, after all, not surprising that Rome should function in this way for Freud, given the role that classical learning, *Bildung,* played in his cultural aspirations and achievements, as in those of most Viennese Jews. The salvation of the Jews will come when they are no longer distinguishable as Jews.

There is more evidence for this conflation of Jerusalem and Rome in Freud's thoughts, that is, for his desire for a Jewishness that would be indistinguishable from gentility. In the dream, Freud refers to taking the children to safety, and through one set of associations to "GESERES" / "UNGESERES," via *ungesäurt,* unleavened bread, to the flight to safety from Egypt. But in his interpretative associations, Freud supplies a reference to another threat to the safety of children. He writes that he and Fliess had passed the door of a physician called Dr. Herodes, and Freud had jokingly remarked, "Let us hope that our

colleague does not happen to be a children's doctor."[11] In the Gospel of
Matthew, Joseph saw in a dream that Herod was going to kill the baby
Jesus, and fled *into* Egypt. Herod flew into a rage, and had all of the
male children in the region of Bethlehem killed, and thus "was fulfilled
what was spoken by the prophet Jeremiah: 'A voice was heard in
Ramah, wailing and loud lamentation'" (Matt. 2:13–18). Obviously,
the Matthew pericope is itself a Christian typological reading of the
slaughter of the innocents in Egypt by Pharaoh, and the threat to the
Christ child by the ambiguously Jewish king and a flight into Egypt
from Palestine are a typological, reversed rewriting of that story. (For
Matthew in general, as is well known, Jesus is a Moses antitype.) Freud
himself refers to the etymology of *GESERES,* from the Hebrew/Yid-
dish *goiser,* "to decree evil." Pharaoh's determination to kill all the male
Israelite infants is named by this verb in the Pesach liturgy, and this
returns as well in the Matthew allusion, for *GESERES,* as Freud himself reveals, was (Viennese? Galician?) Yiddish slang for weeping and
wailing.

It is however of a piece with the rest of the evidence brought forward
here that for Freud, the Christian version and the "Jewish" version of
the salvation of children through flight, through crossing borders, are
completely conflated, paralleling the conflation of Rome and Jerusalem.
This assimilation of Jewish to Christian allusions is, moreover, doubled
by Freud's repeated reference to Pesach as Easter in his text: "In their
flight out of Egypt the Children of Israel had not time to allow their
dough to rise and, in memory of this, they eat unleavened bread to this
day *at Easter.*"[12] Freud's famous parapractic confusion of when his
meeting with Fliess had taken place, whether at Christmas or Easter,
seems also related to his confounding of the Exodus flight from Egypt
at Pesach/Easter with the Gospel flight into Egypt at Christmas.

It is no wonder that such dream thoughts were stimulated by a day
residue of Herzl's play.[13] As Jacques Kornberg has written: "Herzl experienced intense Jewish self-disdain and feelings of inferiority, but he was
also animated by feelings of Jewish pride, loyalty, and solidarity. In this

---

11. Freud, *Interpretation,* 574.

12. Freud, *Interpretation,* 574; emphasis added; cf. Frieden, *Freud's,* 124–25. To the
best of my knowledge, garnered from native informants, Viennese Jews did not refer to
Pesaḥ as "Easter."

13. This is so, on Freud's own account, whether he had actually seen the play then
or read it or even read a plot summary of it. See above, n. 2.

sense the contempt for Jews Herzl was struggling with was, not least, his own. That he struggled with it instead of succumbing to it makes the term *ambivalence* the operative one in describing Herzl's attitude."[14]

The ambivalence underlying wishes for Jewish assimilation, like other performances of colonial mimicry, is deeply embedded in issues of both gender and sexuality. Pressures to assimilate were exacerbated in the case of the fin de siècle Jews by the invention of heterosexuality, and thus of homosexual panic, that was proceeding in just that chronotope. Gerard Beritela, accordingly, reads the "Myops" dream as about conflicted homoeroticism. Going to Rome represents Freud's desire directed originally toward his nephew John, whom Freud explicitly identifies with his "martial ideals" and Hannibal fantasies,[15] and then toward Fliess.[16] Strong support for Beritela's argument is offered by a different dream reported in another of the Fliess letters, written several months before the "Myops" dream, in which Freud writes quite explicitly:

> The dream had fulfilled my wish to meet you in Rome rather than in Prague. My longing for Rome is, by the way, deeply neurotic. It is connected with my high-school hero worship of the Semitic Hannibal, and this year in fact I did not reach Rome any more than he did from Lake Trasimeno. Since I have been studying the unconscious, I have become so interesting to myself. A pity that one always keeps one's mouth shut about the most intimate things.
>
> Das Beste was Du weisst,
> Darfst Du den *Buben doch nicht sagen*
>
> [The best that you know, you may not tell the boys.][17]

This "*meshugene* letter," as Freud dubbed it, is riveting. Freud recognizes that his dream of meeting Fliess in Rome is based in some deep and hidden range of his psyche. He connects it with Hannibal's desire for Rome and with his own identification with Hannibal. Hannibal is explicitly marked as a figure for the Jew (Semitic) in the text, and his desire (like Freud's) is to possess—and perhaps destroy—Rome, the gentile.[18] Rome thus occupies a highly equivocal position within the economy of desires that this letter projects, the ambivalence of possessing and being possessed that is eroticism itself.

14. Kornberg, *Theodor*, 2.
15. Freud, *Interpretation*, 196–97.
16. Beritela, "Wish."
17. Masson, *Complete Letters*, 285.
18. Freud, *Interpretation*, 196.

Finally, we have the revealing segue into the quotation from Goethe, an allusion to an explicitly pederastic context; the speaker is Mephistopheles, "that old pederast."[19] The secret then that Freud cannot reveal, that most intimate thing, seems very likely to be the secret of his desire for Fliess. This interpretation is further confirmed by Freud's own reflections in *The Interpretation of Dreams,* where he writes that his Hannibal fantasies were traceable back to the very early relationship with his nephew John, an attraction whose erotic dimensions Freud himself remarked and that he connected with his later need to have "an intimate friend and a hated enemy," which ideally "come together in a single individual."[20] The "official" oedipal interpretation of Alexander Grinstein[21] rewrites the homoerotic components of the Rome ambivalence, identifying them as screens for desire for the mother, thus, like Freud himself, repressing his homoerotic desire. Furthermore, Jones, anticipating Eve Sedgwick,[22] already realized that the "hunting in couples" aspect of Freud's connection with John is homoerotic in nature; the two of them used to engage in mutual sex play with John's sister Pauline.[23] Finally, as McGrath sagely remarks, the Hannibal story itself has a well-known homosexual component in the guise of a Livian story of homosexual relationships between Hannibal and Hasdrubal.[24]

Late in the "Myops" dream, two boys are presented by a female figure. Freud writes: "[She] handed them over to their father, who was not myself. The elder of the two was clearly my eldest son."[25] Freud is not their father but at least one of them is Freud's son. The simplest resolution of this paradox is that Freud is their mother. The denial represents, then, an assertion. These boys have two male parents. As Beritela notes, this proposition is doubled at the end of the dream, when Freud writes that the boy greets "the two of us (or the one of us)." Since a child cannot—both "in reality" and because of censorship—have two male parents, the two have to be collapsed into one "who was not myself/or the one of us." Beritela explains the otherwise unexplained association with Fliess in the text, one that Freud himself refers to as a "sudden association":[26] "I remembered how, during the previous Easter, my Ber-

19. Heller, "Quarrel," 95.
20. Freud, *Interpretation,* 198, 483.
21. Grinstein, *Sigmund,* 90–91.
22. Sedgwick, *Between Men.*
23. Jones, *Life,* I:11.
24. McGrath, *Freud's,* 66.
25. Freud, *Interpretation,* 441.
26. Freud, *Interpretation,* 443.

lin friend and I had been walking through the streets of Breslau." It is thus Fliess who is the unnamed father of Freud's child in the Rome dream, which also takes place at "Easter."

But of course we must once more pay attention to Freud's famous confounding of Easter and Christmas. The meeting had actually taken place not at Easter at all, but at Christmas. Above I have read this as the product of a conflation of the flight from Egypt—Easter (read Passover)—with the flight into Egypt—Christmas. Under the sign of the sexual interpretation, however, this confusion is further overdetermined. On this reading, it is more to the point that Freud has suppressed "Christmas" than that he has mentioned "Easter."[27] As Thomas Luxon suggests,[28] since Freud's desire is to bear Fliess's baby,[29] then if Easter is a slip for Christmas, Freud has already "sublimated" his desire to have Fliess's baby into a fantasy of bypassing sex with Fliess—of conceiving miraculously. If we read Freud's letter to Fliess, it becomes clear that such a conception would be through the ear, just as the Immaculate Conception of Mary was through the ear: "I am looking forward to our congress as to the slaking of hunger and thirst. I bring nothing but two open ears and one temporal lobe lubricated for reception."[30] Beritela's sexual reading of "My Son the Myops" is very well grounded indeed.

Given the "racialized" construction of sexuality—or is it a sexualized construction of race?—prevalent in fin de siècle central Europe, it is not surprising to find that in Freud's text the sexual and the political are so perfectly superimposed on one another. In the confluence of the erotic and political themes in the "My Son the Myops" dream, the ambivalence about homoeroticism that it manifests is directly and intimately related to the theme of Jewish assimilation that Freud himself read in it.

Beritela argues that Freud's insistence in the dream that the city is both Rome and not-Rome cannot be explained convincingly, as Freud himself explained it by the fact that he had never seen the actual

27. Of course, the two readings do not contradict but supplement each other.
28. Luxon, letter.
29. Geller, "(G)nos(e)ology," 265–66.
30. Masson, *Complete Letters*, 193; cf. Jones, "Madonna's." Luxon suggests: "Maybe Fliess is a Joseph type of father and Freud's 'real' desire is to be 'visited' by a bigger Father?" thus rendering Freud a type of Schreber (Craft, *Another Kind,* 100)! This is suggestive of further support for a point of Freud's identification with, and as, Schreber that I made in chapter 5, namely, an explanation for Freud's own "paranoid" tendencies directed at male lover/rivals, from Fliess to Jung. This should not be read reductively. Even paranoids have real enemies, and Jung, at any rate, was certainly an enemy to Freud (and to his people).

Rome—a city for which a multitude of images existed—but must, in fact, be a screen for ambivalence. And Rome indeed would have carried a whole set of complicated associations for Freud, ranging from the original Roman Empire to the hegemony of Christian culture (the nun in the "Myops" dream) within his life-world.[31]

These signifiers were both objects of enormous desire—culture, learning, *Bildung*—as well as enemies and oppressors. This very nun, moreover, is transparently a figure for the elderly Catholic woman whom Freud claims stimulated him sexually in early childhood and thus, on his own interpretation, made him queer, as I have proposed. Note the ambivalence in the portrait of this nun. On one hand, she is a nurturing figure; on the other, she has the prototypical red nose of the stereotyped drunken gentile of eastern European Jews. She wants to kiss the boy, but he refuses. Rome is thus overdetermined as both the site of desired homoerotic congress and the location of the gentile oppressor. Rome is split into the good, male, "Protestant" Rome (*Bildung*, "the head of a Roman citizen" in Freud's study) and the bad, female, Catholic Rome (the nun).[32]

The situation of the European Diaspora male Jew as politically disempowered produced a sexualized interpretation of him as queer, because political passivity was in Freud's world equated with homosexuality (see Plate 9).[33] As John Fout has written, "The male homosexual was portrayed as sickly, effeminate, perverse, and out of control, just the opposite of the 'normal' male, who was physically strong and active, the head of the family, dominant in the public world of politics at home and abroad, and in complete control of his sexuality and his emotions. The male homosexual only personified female characteristics, such as passivity and physical and emotional weaknesses."[34] These "female characteristics" are also, of course, the very characteristics identified as belonging to the Jew—by antisemites and Zionists. Diaspora is

31. Masson, *Complete Letters*, 449. The insightful comments of Bluma Goldstein are very relevant here (B. Goldstein, *Reinscribing*, 72–74).

32. Torgovnick, *Gone*, 196–97. It seems indeed worth noting that in totally Catholic Vienna, only half of the Jews who converted, converted to that faith, and the rest declared themselves either Protestant or "*konfessionslos*" (Le Rider, *Modernity*, 187–88). For the association of Protestantism with manliness by another Jewish, queer writer in a Catholic country, see Proust, *Sodom*, 31.

33. Wiedemann makes (and illustrates) the point that this stance, knees close together, has been used as a representation of effeminacy since the fifth century B.C.E. Specifically it is the stance of the defeated gladiator in Roman reliefs cited by Wiedemann, *Emperors*, 37.

34. Fout, "Sexual Politics," 413.

Plate 9.   The Male Jew as Effeminate. Sheet music for the antisemitic
"March of the Jewish Militia to Warsaw," by anonymous, n.d. Since Roman
times, the knees-together stance has signified effeminacy. (Courtesy of the
Leo Baeck Institute, New York.)

essentially queer, and an end to Diaspora would be the equivalent of becoming straight. The fact, then, that political Zionism was invented at the time of the invention of heterosexuality is entirely legible. The dominant male of Europe, the "Aryan," is the one who is already "physically strong and active, the head of the family, dominant in the public world of politics at home and abroad" and thus not queer, so an assimilation that would lend the male Jew these characteristics would accomplish the same heterosexualizing project as Zionism. Freud himself seems to conflate these two schemes for inventing straight, male, modern Jews. It is, according to this view, no accident that *Moses and Monotheism* was written at the same moment in Freud's life when he was identifying the "repudiation of femininity" as the "bedrock of psychoanalysis," but I anticipate my argument below. The "Zionist" elements of the dream thus fit perfectly with the homoerotic ones, that is, as their negation. Freud's Zionism outs itself as homophobia.

"UNIVERSALIZING IS A SYMPTOM"; OR, LITTLE HANS WAS JEWISH

As Kafka so tellingly remarked, Freud is indeed the Rashi-commentary on his generation of (male) Jews. There is an absolutely stunning moment in Freud's *Analysis of a Phobia in a Five-Year-Old-Boy: "Little Hans"* in which Freud reveals the imbrications of gender and Jewish difference as the very motivating force of his (and his generation's) male Jewish self-fashioning. At the point where he is presenting Little Hans's castration complex, Freud claims: "The piece of enlightenment which Hans had been given a short time before to the effect that women really do not possess a widdler was bound to have had a shattering effect upon his self-confidence and to have aroused his castration complex.... Could it be that living beings really did exist which did not possess widdlers? If so, it would no longer be so incredible that they could take his own widdler away, and, as it were, make him into a woman."[35]

This is an amazing act of interpretation. Freud had earlier in the text informed us that Hans's mother had threatened him with actual castration if he continued masturbating, and that this was the source of his "castration complex."[36] This is in fact the first time that the term "cas-

35. Freud, *Analysis,* 36.
36. Freud, *Analysis,* 8.

tration complex" appears in Freud's texts.[37] This threat, however, had not produced any symptoms in Hans at the time. In fact, he quite in-souciantly informed her that he would then "widdle with his bottom." The symptoms that Freud wishes to associate with anxiety about hav-ing his penis cut off appear—following the course of *Nachträglich-keit*—only more than a year later. Having been instructed by his father in the difference between men's and women's genitals—his mother does not, in fact, possess a widdler, and his sister's will not grow—Hans, according to Freud, mobilized the anxiety that had been initiated by his mother's threat in deferred action[38] upon his accession to knowledge of sexual difference. This, then, constitutes in somewhat attenuated form the "sighting" of the mother's genitals that arouses the castration com-plex.

Freud, however, at this moment informs us of another etiology for the onset of the castration complex, in addition to the "sight" of the female genitalia, namely, the "hearing" of the little boy about the dam-aged (castrated) penis of the circumcised Jewish male. He writes:

> I cannot interrupt the discussion so far as to demonstrate the typical char-acter of the unconscious train of thought which I think there is here reason for attributing to little Hans. The castration complex is the deepest uncon-scious root of anti-Semitism; for even in the nursery little boys hear that a Jew has something cut off his penis—a piece of his penis, they think—and this gives them the right to despise Jews. And there is no stronger uncon-scious root for the sense of superiority over women. Weininger (the young philosopher who, highly gifted but sexually deranged, committed suicide after producing his remarkable book *Geschlecht und Charakter* [1903]), in a chapter that attracted much attention, treated Jews and women with equal hostility and overwhelmed them with the same insults. Being a neu-rotic, Weininger was completely under the sway of his infantile complexes; and from that standpoint what is common to Jews and women is their rela-tion to the castration complex.[39]

Freud does not wish to interrupt his text to demonstrate what he takes to be Little Hans's "unconscious train of thought," one that is, moreover, qualified as being "typical." He does, however, provide us with the outlines of this train of thought, namely, that Little Hans had heard that Jews have something cut off their "widdlers" when they are infants and that this has provoked (or at any rate contributed to) Hans's

37. Editor's note: *ad loc.*
38. Freud, *Analysis*, 35.
39. Freud, *Analysis*, 198–99.

castration fantasies and fears. What is more, we are informed that this is the deepest root of antisemitism, that knowledge of the Jew's circumcision interacts with the gentile's castration complex.

Freud goes on to write: "And there is no stronger unconscious root for the sense of superiority over women," a highly ambiguous formulation that supports more than one interpretation. What, after all, is the antecedent for the anaphora of this sentence—the subject, here, of "there is"? One quite easy possibility is to read that the sense of superiority over women is engendered by the apparent fact of possession of a penis, just as the sense of contempt for Jews is occasioned by their "lack" of a penis.[40] There is however a much more radical reading hiding within the syntax: that what produces a sense of superiority over women is that little boys hear in the nursery that Jews have something cut off their penises and conclude thereby that they are women who look like men, or perhaps more exactly that they are men who have become like women.[41] This would be the most frightening possibility of all, because it powerfully and directly raises the specter of the man's potential "unmanning."[42] These readings are not really contradictory; the second is the more disturbing (and more revealing) double of the first. Moreover, the association of male Jews and women had a basis in European cultural history, if not (as Freud would have it) in universal psychology. As John Hoberman has put it: "By the time Weininger absorbed it, this intuitive sense of the Jew's deficient masculinity had been germinating for centuries, dating from the Middle Ages."[43]

Freud writes that little (gentile) boys hear in the nursery about Jewish circumcision, and this hearing contributes to their castration anxieties. Moreover it produces in them antisemitic contempt for Jews, which is similar in kind or even identical to the feelings of superiority that men have over women. Weininger was one such "little (gentile) boy"—except for one thing; Weininger was Jewish, a fact that Freud

40. Geller, "Paleontological View," 52.

41. Freud really seems to mean that misogyny is caused by fear of losing the penis. However, since he uses the positive language of "sense of superiority," it is hard to escape the positive language of sense of possession as well.

42. Cf. the similar reading of Geller: "The circumcised Jew seems to question sexual difference" ("Paleontological View," 56). Jonathan Boyarin has proposed an even more disturbing reading that the syntax allows, and even prefers: little boys hear in the nursery about the "castration" of the Jews and learn to feel contempt for them long before they know that women have no penises. The contempt for women is derived from the primary antisemitism, because women are similar to Jews. Antisemitism (including Jewish antisemitism) is then literally the unconscious root of misogyny.

43. Hoberman, "Otto," 143.

chose to conceal. It would certainly have been apposite for Freud to
have emphasized this in a context where it is the "unconscious root of
anti-Semitism" that is at issue; this is no trivial ellipsis.[44] The occlusion
of Weininger's Jewishness is doubled by another, even more significant
occlusion: the fact that "Little Hans" was also Jewish. His real name
was Herbert Graf, and as an adult he became a successful musician.[45]
Hans too did not hear about Jews having something cut off their penises; he, in fact, possessed such a "damaged penis," as did Freud himself.

In presenting "Little Hans" and Weininger as if they were gentiles
gazing, as it were, at the Jewish penis and becoming filled with fear and
loathing, Freud is actually—I want to suggest—representing himself,
or at least an aspect of himself, gazing at his own circumcised penis and
being filled with fear and loathing. Indeed, this interpretation is an ineluctable consequence of the logic of Freud's position. The much ma-
ligned Fritz Wittels seems to have cottoned on to this point, when he
glosses Freud as arguing that "[t]he unconscious thus despises the Jews
because they have been castrated, and at the same time dreads them
because they castrate their children."[46] But there is, of course, only one
unconscious in Freud, and it must be then the unconscious of the Jew
as well as that of the Aryan that so despises and dreads. Wittels has read
Freud well here. Since the fear of castration was, for him, unconscious
and therefore a psychic universal, how, for Freud, could the response to
one's own circumcision be different from the reaction to that of the circumcision of someone else?

In his essay on "The Uncanny," Freud writes of a moment in which
he looks by accident into a mirror and thinks he sees someone else: "I
can still recollect that I thoroughly disliked his appearance. . . . Is it not
possible, though, that our dislike of [the double] was a vestigial trace
of the archaic reaction which feels the 'double' to be something uncanny?"[47] Strangely, no matter how many usages and situations of the

44. Nor can it be objected that he assumed that everyone knew this fact, since he
informs us exactly who Weininger is, leaving out only the fact that he was Jewish.

45. As just another example of the intimacy of the whole situation, I note that Herbert Graf was a colleague of Dora's (Ida Bauer) son, Kurt Adler, also an accomplished
musician and, at the end of his life, music director of my beloved San Francisco Opera
(Appignanesi and Forrester, *Freud's,* 166–67).

46. Wittels, *Sigmund,* 358.

47. Freud, *Uncanny,* 248. Susan Shapiro is now writing a book on the uncanny as a
trope for the Jew.

uncanny have been described or adduced, for Freud it always comes
back to castration. Thus, even Otto Rank's account of the "double"
as producer of the uncanny is immediately connected with dreams in
which castration is represented by "a doubling or multiplication of a
genital symbol."[48] Following example after example of instances of the
uncanny which have nothing to do with castration and none which
does *manifestly,* Freud sums up, "We have now only a few remarks to
add—for animism, magic and sorcery, the omnipotence of thoughts,
man's attitude to death, involuntary repetition and the castration complex comprise practically all the factors which turn something frightening into something uncanny."[49] Something in Freud's world was press-
ing in this direction so insistently. In another text, Freud has written
that circumcision "makes a disagreeable, uncanny impression, which is
to be explained, no doubt by its recalling the dreaded castration."[50] Reversing the terms of Freud's interpretation, I suggest rather that it is castration that recalls the dreaded circumcision, dreaded because it is this
act that cripples a male by turning him into a Jew. If we read these two
"uncanny's" in conjunction with each other, we are led to the conclusion that seeing himself in the mirror produced in Freud the same feeling of uncanniness that he himself claims is produced in the antisemite
who looks at the Jew. It is himself that Freud dislikes. It is the sight of
his Jewishness, a metonymy of his circumcised penis, in the mirror that,
recalling "the dreaded castration," arouses Freud's uncanny feeling, his
"thorough dislike" or misrecognition of himself in the mirror. Accordingly, it would be impossible to maintain that Freud intended this disagreeable, uncanny impression to be only the province of gentiles. The
"appearance" that Freud thoroughly dislikes, on this reading, is the appearance of his own circumcised penis.[51]

Hearing about the circumcision of Jews, Freud claims, would arouse
fears of being castrated, just as knowing about the lack of a penis
in women would arouse similar fears. If both the Jew and the woman
are castrated only from the standpoint of infantile complexes, then it

48. Freud, *Uncanny,* 235. Freud's interpretation of *The Sandman* in *Uncanny* remains just that, a compelling interpretation, hardly, however, an explanation or proof of
the centrality of castration in the uncanny.

49. Freud, *Uncanny,* 243.

50. Freud, *Moses,* 91. For an explanation of the "uncanniness" of this recalling, see
Freud, *Uncanny,* 247–48.

51. Contra Geller, "Paleontological View," 57; Geller, "Glance," 438; cf. Kofman,
Enigma, 32.

would appear from the logic of Freud's position that by the "healthy" adult, neither ought to be perceived as castrated, or, *what is from my perspective the same thing,* each should be re-cognized as equally castrated as all subjects.[52] The "neurotic" Weininger treated women and Jews with equal hostility because neither possess the penis, but both are castrated only "from the standpoint of the infantile complexes," the stage at which Weininger was fixated. However, as the castration complex is "resolved," or "dissolved," these unrealistic fears ought—if the standpoint is no longer to be the "infantile" one of the neurotic Weininger—to give way to a "normal" (non-infantile) appreciation of the equal value of women and Jews.

In Freud's own account, however, the castration fantasy—the assumption that women have something missing and are inferior—remains the unconscious root of misogyny and clearly not only in infants and neurotics, since Freud considers a perception of male superiority as a simple truism in adult males and not a marginal and pathological form. After all, it is the "repudiation of femininity that is the bedrock of psychoanalysis" in Freud's famous 1937 formulation. As Jessica Benjamin has put it, "We might hope that the boy's 'triumphant contempt' for women would dissipate as he grew up—but such contempt was hardly considered pathological."[53] Similarly, the fantasy that Jews have something missing, the lesson learned in the nursery, *remains* the unconscious fantasy that produces antisemitism in adults as well, and no one has argued that antisemitism is only a childhood illness. As John Brenkman has written, "The simple positive Oedipus complex simplifies the child's multifarious attachments to this one heterosexual drama in an attempt to explain how the so-called bisexual male child, filled with contradictory ideas about the salient differences between his parents, uncertain of his own or others' gender, . . . rife[54] with passive and

52. These formulations are ultimately the same because, as I have argued in the introduction to this book, the very positing of the phallus is already an instantiation of the dominant fiction. I know that this statement will be, at best, obnoxious to Lacanians, but it is the nature of my argument to suggest that the very terms phallus and castration, if they are not interrogated historically, lose the symptomatic power that they might have to explain misogyny, homophobia, and antisemitism/racism, and they become, willy-nilly, complicit with those discourses. We must then, with Juliet Mitchell, read Freud not as positing "the phallus" but as positing the *positing* of the phallus (Mitchell, *Psychoanalysis*).

53. Benjamin, *Bonds,* 160.

54. I have elided here two words "pace Freud," because I disagree with them and am appropriating Brenkman's otherwise exact formulation here for my own text. I would

active sexual aims toward both parents, reemerges on the other side of latency and adolescence merely a more or less neurotic heterosexual."[55] Following Brenkman's extension of Freud, then, neither neurosis is ever completely resolved in adulthood.[56] Rather than pathologizing antisemitism, Freud was, in fact, naturalizing it via the castration complex.

We have in Freud's note on Little Hans not only an anatomy of misogyny and of antisemitism—both read as products of the unconscious—but also of Jewish self-contempt, also read as a sort of inevitability. In other words, I am suggesting that Freud essentially *accepts* Weininger's argument, indeed that that is the reason that Freud cites him here, and not as an example of the pathology of antisemitism in gentiles, for which he would be a rather strange example. It should be emphasized, however, this is not an idiosyncrasy on Freud's part. Gerald Stieg has made an analogous point with reference to a similar moment in Kafka: "It is beyond question that such texts are treating something besides the private sphere and that the epoch itself is being heard." And Stieg chillingly continues: "The uncanny part is that in such writings the most dreadful aspects of the political propaganda of National Socialism seem to present themselves in the most private sphere, internalized to the point of self-torture."[57] Thus, it seems, was Freud's self-torture as well. Increasingly scholars are coming to recognize how all-pervasive thinking like Weininger's was and to what extent he simply distilled and concentrated the ordinary thought of his time and place,[58] and this is, of course, his true significance. As Arens notes, "His [Weininger's] work represented a facet of the discussion that *was acceptable to the public curators of science,* not just an isolated stab into the realm of theory; Weininger was not alone, or if his version of the paradigm was deviant, it was at least on the fringe of the public debate in the scientific community. The second way in which Weininger's work entered the public sphere was as a popular science bestseller, suiting the general reader so well that it stayed in print into the Nazi era; it touched a popular chord."[59] Weininger and Freud were symptomatic of a crisis

---

argue, and indeed in the last chapter *have* argued, that Freud is, at least sometimes, brilliantly aware of the "rifeness" of these passive and active aims.
55. Brenkman, *Straight Male,* 123.
56. Brenkman, *Straight Male,* 17.
57. Stieg, "Kafka," 198.
58. Arens, "Characterology," 124–25.
59. Arens, "Characterology," 130. I think that Arens misreads, however, what was at stake in the controversy between Horney and the Freudians. Pace Arens, it was Horney

of male Jews in the German-speaking (and especially Viennese) world of their day.[60]

According to my reading, Freud was more identified with than differentiated from Weininger.[61] Only barely hidden behind the figure of Weininger in Freud's note and even hidden behind the incognito Jew, Little Hans, is Freud, "the specialist on the inner nature of the Jew."[62] Thus Freud effectively reveals one strand of his own complex and conflicted "inner nature" as the "Jewish antisemite."[63] Where Gilman

---

who essentially believed that sexual difference is inborn, Freud who argued that it is made.

60. Hoberman, "Otto," 142. In his reading of this Freudian text, Sander Gilman finesses this enigma by writing as if Freud had revealed precisely that which he concealed, that which he hid in the closet. (See also Pellegrini, "Without You" for a parallel critique.) According to him, Freud cited Otto Weininger as "an example of the problematic relationship of the Jew to his circumcised penis" (Gilman, Freud, 77). Gilman goes on to argue that "Weininger is like the little (non-Jewish) boy in the nursery who hears about the Jews cutting off penises, except that he, of course, knows that it is true. His hatred of the Jew is 'infantile,' according to Freud, since it remains fixed at that moment in all children's development when they learn about the possibility of castration. Jewish neurotics like Weininger focus on the negative difference of their bodies from ones that are 'normal,' and use this difference, like their evocation of the bodies of women, to define themselves" (80). Gilman treats Freud's Weininger as an analysand and Freud as an anatomist of antisemitism: "Freud has evoked the Jewish 'scientist' Otto Weininger as an anti-Semite." Gilman explicitly sequesters Freud—and Herzl!—from "Jewish self-hatred": "He understood himself as a Jew, as different. And this for him (as for Jewish contemporaries such as Theodor Herzl) was in no way negative" (Case, 8). In chapter 7 below, I argue that Freud's affect about his Jewishness was very similar if not identical to Herzl's, and if there is anyone to whom the appellation of Jewish antisemite belongs, it is to the leader of the Zionist movement, as Arthur Schnitzler explicitly and perceptively wrote. Schnitzler has a Jewish character in his novel The Road to the Open say: "I myself have only succeeded up to the present in making the acquaintance of one genuine antisemite. I'm afraid I am bound to admit . . . that it was a well known Zionist leader" (quoted in Kornberg, Theodor, 154). Similarly, Steven Beller excuses Weininger of Jewish self-contempt by comparing his views with Herzl's (Beller, "Otto," 100), rather than drawing the opposite conclusion. It is this contention of Gilman's that I contest here. Where Gilman reads Freud as analyzing Weininger's pathology as if Weininger were an analysand, I read Freud as enlisting Weininger as a fellow analyst. It is interesting that in earlier work, it was Gilman himself who noted similar occlusions in Freud's writings, such as the "masking" of the Jewishness of Bertha Pappenheim ("Anna O.") and Ida Bauer ("Dora") (Gilman, Jew's, 81). In both cases the Jewishness of the subject is arguably less relevant than is Little Hans's, where it is occluded in the context of circumcision and a discussion of its psychic effects.

61. If indeed, as Gilman claims, Freud had not "responded to Weininger's self-hatred as the reflection of his identity crisis" (Jewish Self-Hatred, 251), this would have been a classic example of denial and defense, but I am suggesting that he did respond.

62. Gilman, Jewish Self-Hatred, 242; Simon, "Sigmund," 277.

63. See Gilman, Jewish Self-Hatred, where he writes, "Freud's scientific German, at least when he sits down to write his book on humor, is a language tainted by Weininger's anti-Semitism," a claim that seems to contradict his later argument that Freud pathologized and thus rejected Weininger's antisemitism. In 1986, it seems, Gilman was closer to the perspective on Freud that I am adopting here than he is in his latest work. See also, however, Gilman's most recent essay, "Otto," for further revisions of his thinking on this subject. For a similar case of a "scientist," Cesare Lombroso, obscuring his own Jewish-

reads Freud as responding to the racism directed against Jews by displacing these differences onto the absolute (i.e., universal) difference between men and women, by recoding race *as* gender, I would suggest that Freud accepts the characterization of Jews as differently gendered, as indeed female, and tries to overcome this difference. Freud, moreover, seems at least once to have recognized this component of his personality himself, writing in a letter to Arnold Zweig in 1933: "We defend ourselves against castration in every form, and perhaps a bit of opposition to our own Jewishness is slyly hidden here. Our great leader Moses was, after all, a vigorous antisemite, and he makes no secret of this. Perhaps he was an Egyptian."[64] Given the role, of course, of Freud's Moses-identification—to be explored more fully in the next section—this is a highly symptomatic deposition.

Freud was enacting, at the same time that he was disavowing and denying, the self-contempt of the racially dominated subject. He was discursively closeting his circumcision. What we have here is a sort of psychic epispasm,[65] a wish fulfillment to be uncircumcised—to be a man like all other men, a fetishized whole phallus. Not only of Weininger and Little Hans but of Freud we could say "that he, of course, knows that it is true," that Jews have a piece of the penis cut off. By occluding the fact of Weininger's and Hans's Jewishness, and by obscuring the role of his own here, Freud was hiding a darker claim that Jewish knowledge of his own circumcision must inevitably produce in the Jew a sense of inferiority vis-à-vis the gentile, a sense of inferiority that Freud himself shared. This inferiority, closely allied to the "inferiority complex" that Frantz Fanon identifies in the colonial subject, is what Freud seeks to escape.

As Kalpana Seshadri-Crooks points out: "If [premodern] Jews as a minority loathed their difference, then conversion could be a simple option. But that didn't happen." In fact, for traditional Jewish culture, only the circumcised male was considered as "whole."[66] Circumcision was, for them, not productive of anxiety and self-contempt but rather a mark of resistance and a deliberate (private) setting apart of oneself

---

ness and writing an "objective" account of antisemitism that reveals, in fact, his own feelings of contempt for Jews, see Harrowitz, "Weininger."

64. Quoted in Le Rider, "Otto," 31.

65. "Epispasm" is the operation to restore the foreskin, very popular among Hellenized Jews in antiquity (David Hall, "Epispasm"). In Nordau's (in)famous lecture, "Muscle-Jews," he approbated the ancient epispasm as a metaphorical model for modern Zionists (Nordau, *Muskeljudentum*)!

66. J. Boyarin and D. Boyarin, "Self-Exposure."

from the dominant culture, a version of James Scott's "hidden transcript." Even if premodern Jewish male subjects frequently perceived
themselves as femminized, in part because of their circumcision, this
did not cash out for them as a lack or deprivation but as a gain, insisting that the foreskin is a blemish and that circumcision, far from being
a mutilation, is an adornment of the male body.[67] In the premodern
Jewish descriptions of the uncircumcised penis as ugly, gross, impure,
we find the parodic rejections of the claims of the colonizing culture
that Scott refers to as "hidden transcripts."

Scott argues eloquently against the notion of hegemony, claiming
that the appearance of hegemony is only the "public script" which
serves the purposes of both the colonizer and the colonized in situations
of near total domination: "In this respect, subordinate groups are com-
plicitous in contributing to a sanitized official transcript, for that is one
way they cover their tracks."[68] He further claims that something like
"genuine" hegemony is achieved in situations where the oppressed or
dominated party hopes one day to be the dominator (not, of course,
over their present oppressors but over others), for example, age-graded
systems of domination. I would suggest that the condition of incipient
decolonization, represented for Jews by the transitional emancipation
status of the fin de siècle, is an "expectation that one will eventually be
able to exercise the domination that one endures today" that would be,
according to Scott "a strong incentive serving to legitimate patterns of
domination"[69] and thus canceling the hidden transcript of contempt for
the oppressor and turning into self-contempt. Thus, the moment (or the
incipient moment) of decolonization on the political level ("emancipation" for the Jews) ironically gives rise to hegemony. An early twentieth-century American Jewish professor, Israel Davidson, remarked of
his coreligionists in eastern Europe that their bodies are bound but their
spirits free, while for those of the West it was the opposite, anticipating
this analysis of hegemony.[70]

It is at this moment for the Jewish colonial subject that circumcision
suddenly takes on the aspect of a displaced castration.[71] Freud looking

67. D. Boyarin, "This We."
68. J. C. Scott, *Domination,* 87.
69. J. C. Scott, *Domination,* 82.
70. See also Guha, "Dominance."
71. Geller, "Paleontological View." I would go so far as to offer the transition between Ramakrishna's embrace of femaleness (not, of course, as Parama Roy so poignantly
makes clear, a "feminist" move) and homoeroticism and the aggressively masculinist and
heterosexual subjectivity of his primary disciple, Swami Vivekenanda, as an exact parallel

into the mirror experiences his own circumcision as the "uncanny" and, hidden behind the white mask of the scientist, sets out to explain, almost to justify, antisemitism. To the extent that psychoanalysts reading circumcision in that way were and are Jews, this reading becomes a chronic inscription of their own ambivalent gaze on Jewish male difference, an ambivalence recorded in American culture in such mythic figures of Jewish psychoanalytic discourse as Alexander Portnoy and Woody Allen. Freud is thus a paradigm for this ambivalent subjectivity, and one of the strongest symptoms of it is the frequent but by no means ubiquitous misogyny, racism, and homophobia of his thought.[72] Indeed, the incongruity of this misogyny, homophobia, and racism with the best of Freud's thought leads me to search for a specific etiology for them, as if they constituted a kind of lapse.

The most dramatic example of this particular sociopsychic process in Freud himself is the production of the master complex, the Oedipus/castration complex, the notional infrastructure that is Freud's most conspicuous speech act of misogyny. I return to the Freudian passage: "The castration complex is the deepest unconscious root of anti-Semitism; for even in the nursery little boys hear that a Jew has something cut off his penis—a piece of his penis, they think—and this gives them the right to despise Jews. And there is no stronger unconscious root for the sense of superiority over women." I have already noted the passage's equivocal meaning, arguing that Freud claims that hearing about circumcision is the unconscious root of misogyny, antisemitism, and, at a deeper level, Jewish self-hatred, a Jewish male reaction to outsiders' accusation of "castration" or "feminization." What Gilman understands as the development of normal (male) Jews who "overcome their anxiety about their own bodies by being made to understand that the real difference is not between their circumcised penises and those of uncircum-

---

to this shift. As Roy remarks, "I do not wish of course to assert that Ramakrishna was not hailed by colonialism. I am suggesting, rather, that he probably was hailed by colonialism-and-nationalism (I speak of this here as a single category) in a way distinct from the ways his best-known disciple was hailed. . . . In Vivekenanda, then, Hinduism becomes very specifically an address to colonialism and the 'west,' " and this address is marked in large part, as Roy demonstrates, by a shift in gender representations to match that of the West. "Vivekenanda discovers himself as the swami, as Indian, as Hindu, and as male, and implicitly a heterosexual male, in the 'west,' outside of the Indian nation-space" (Roy, *Indian Traffic* [Berkeley: University of California Press, forthcoming]; see the chapter entitled "As the Master Saw Her: Religious Discipleship and Gender Traffic in Nineteenth-Century India"). Vivekenanda's period of greatest activity was the time of Herzl's and Nordau's Zionist venture and the beginning of Freud's work as well.

72. Gilman, *Freud,* 23.

cised males, but between themselves and castrated females" would determine the misogyny of the colonized Jew.[73]

Freud's universalized developmental theories, all of which centered on the phallus—the Oedipus complex, castration anxiety, and penis envy—function as an elaborate defense against the femminization of Jewish men, and his essentializing of misogyny is a way to appropriate the phallus for himself as a circumcised male. In other words, it allowed Freud to assert that the "real" difference is not between the Jewish and gentile penis but between having a penis at all and having none. The binary opposition phallus/castration conceals the same third term that Freud conceals in his mystification of Little Hans's identity, namely, the circumcised penis. Both the "*idealization* of the phallus, whose integrity is necessary for the edification of the entire psychoanalytical system"[74] and the flight to Greek cultural models and metaphors signal the imbrication of this production in the affect of the colonized person. In psychoanalytic terms, the Oedipus complex is Freud's "family romance," in the exact sense of the term. He is unconsciously fantasizing that he is not the circumcised Schelomo, son of Jakob, but the uncircumcised and virile Greek Oedipus, son of Laius,[75] just as earlier he had consciously fantasized that he was Hannibal, son of the heroic Hamilcar, and not the son of his "unheroic" Jewish father.

At the same time, by diagnosing Weininger's "pathology"—and "his own" as well, "a bit of opposition to our own Jewishness," as in the letter to Zweig just quoted—Freud shows how the liminal racial position that he occupies is a place that generates knowledge as well as unknowing. My historicizing account of the conditions that produced Freud's theories of sex and gender is not reductive. Freud's narrative of sexual differentiation as *nonbiological* in its foundations is more liberatory than, for instance, Karen Horney's contention that people are born already male or female.[76] The castration complex thus represents a theoretical advance over naturalized views of sexual difference. Freud's

---

73. I am of course drawing a distinction here, as everywhere in my work, between the disenfranchisement of women in the social sphere and misogyny per se, that is, expression of contempt and hatred for women. The two are obviously related but, I think, not to be conflated. The former is endemic in Jewish culture; the latter, I argue, sporadic. Moreover, misogyny per se, in the sense defined, grows constantly stronger throughout European Jewish history, reaching its peak in eastern Europe, I would argue, precisely in the moment of modernization (decolonization).

74. Johnson, "Frame," 225.

75. Cf. Anzieu, *Freud's*, 195.

76. Cf. also Ramas, "Freud's," 480–81.

greatest insight, that sexual difference is made and not born, and also his darkest moment of gross misogyny, emerge out of the same point in his discourse, like one of those words that mean both something and its opposite (words to which he was so attracted). If we do not accept crude readings of Freud that caricature him merely as a white male woman-hater, neither can we ignore the gross gender effects of the discourse of castration. The point is certainly not to disqualify Freud's contribution by locating it in a particular social circumstance; rather, the function of an argument such as this is to help contextualize those places where Freud's thesis seems incoherent, unnecessary, or otherwise unhelpful— that is, not to identify its moments of insight but rather its moments of blindness. There is a signal blindness in Freud's unwillingness to see any possibility for figuring sexual difference other than by the phallus. Why was a thinker who was in so many ways willing and able to break the paradigms of his culture seemingly unable to do so here?

It is as if there is a moment of oscillation between looking with contempt at the circumcised nonphallus and then understanding his own contempt for himself as the product of the psychotic,[77] antisemitic imaginary that he cannot escape, an enormous gap between the self-mystification of figuring his affect as defense against castration and the savvy of recognizing it as "a slyly hidden opposition to our own Jewishness." This is then an instance of the doubled consciousness of the colonized subject from which is generated "the divided subject posited by psychoanalytic theory to refute humanism's myth of the unified self,"[78] as well as the misogyny and homophobia of that very subject. We have now a paradigm with which to explain the curious Freudian effect whereby his texts support both the most radical and the most reactionary of sociopolitical projects.

Barnaby B. Barratt and Barrie Ruth Straus have captured well the effect of this division within Freud (without relating it to his doubled "racial" positioning):

> Freud's psychology *both* stands as the apotheosis of modern reason, the heir to enlightenment values grounded in reflective-subjective and scientific-objective practices, . . . *and* it stands as the harbinger of postmodern inspiration, the exemplar of discursive practices that emancipate whatever may be excluded or repressed by the totalization of analytico-referential reason. In

---

77. Lacan, *Psychoses*. See also the elegant discussion of Lacan's reformulation of Freud's theory of psychosis in Reinhard, "Freud."

78. Parry, "Problems," 29.

this sense, the discipline of psychoanalysis occupies a very significant but disconcertingly ambiguous position in relation to the critique of patriarchy. . . . In one frame, psychoanalytic doctrine can be seen as one of the last manifestos of patriarchal legitimation, an ideological structure that systematically rationalizes masculinism [heterosexuality]. In another frame, psychoanalytic method can be seen as an inspiration for feminist [queer] critique, an enigmatic and extraordinary challenge to the hegemonic structuration of masculinist [heterosexual] discursive practices.[79]

My argument suggests that in a very strong sense, it was the division of Freud's social positioning that produced the division within his subject position, resulting in both a Janus-like doubledness of his discourse, radical and reactionary at the same time, and his very understanding of the doubledness of the subject itself. Seen in this light the peculiarly American developments of Ego Psychology that mobilize only the most reactionary side of Freud's thinking on sex and gender can be read as a rather desperate attempt to escape the postcolonial subject position on the part of European Jewish refugees.

"AN IMAGINARY AND DESIRABLE CONVERSE": *MOSES AND MONOTHEISM* AS FAMILY ROMANCE

Freud himself drew the analogy between the sexual and the political, between the situation of the individual, sexually passive, "inverted," humiliated Jew and the Jewish People as a whole—and between himself and the collective status of Jews. Associations between "passivity" and humiliation were all-pervasive in the culture of Europe.[80] In a passage from the *Wolf Man,* already referred to in the previous chapter, Freud describes an incident in which the Wolf Man's sister had played with his penis when he was "still very small." Freud concludes that the patient had developed fantasies of active sexual aggression toward his sister that "were meant to efface the memory of an event which later on seemed offensive to the patient's masculine self-esteem, and they reached this end by putting an imaginary and desirable converse in the place of the historical truth. . . . *These phantasies, therefore, corresponded exactly*

---

79. Barratt and Straus, "Toward Postmodern Masculinities," 38.

80. With respect to the "division of people into 'active' and 'passive' races by Gustav Klemm," Efron writes, "[i]n his *General History of Civilization* (1843) Klemm posited that the active races were masculine, thriving in cold climates, while the passive ones, residing in warm climates, were effeminate" (Efron, *Defenders,* 15).

to the legends by means of which a nation that has become great and proud tries to conceal the insignificance and failure of its beginnings.[81] As Madelon Sprengnether has remarked, "Freud's comment on this episode reveals the extent to which he associates it with the kind of sexual humiliation he had experienced at the hands of his own nannie."[82]

This passage provides the hermeneutic key for a deeper understanding of the cultural/political situation of the Jews within which psychoanalysis was produced: the memory of a situation that seemed offensive to Freud's masculine self-esteem was effaced by putting an imaginary and desirable converse in place of the historical truth. "Feminine" Jewish passivity coded as homosexual and experienced as shameful for "real men" was to be rewritten as an originary, "manly" aggressiveness, an imaginary and desirable converse indeed. And Freud's gratuitous political remark is a perfect precis for *Moses and Monotheism*. This is Freud's Family Romance, writ large as the Family Romance of the Jewish People.

Male was encoded within this culture as spiritual, "abstractly sublime," incorporeal, powerful, and universal, and this is how Freud (and others of his time and place) described the "true" Judaism, directly counter to those representations of it as a feminine religion, primitive, physical, carnal, and weak. One such account of the time, by Rudolph Grau, has it that "Semites are like women in that they lack the Indo-German capacity for philosophy, art, science, warfare, and politics. They nevertheless have a monopoly on one sublime quality: religion, or love of God. This Semitic monism goes hand in hand with a deep commitment to female monogamy. The masculine behavior of the Indo-German, who masters the arts and sciences in order to dominate the natural world, is met with the Semite's feminine response of passivity and receptivity. As the wife is subject to her husband, so the Semites are absolutely permeable to the God who chose them."[83]

The religiosity and spirituality of the "Semite" are depicted here as a female sexuality. Monotheism equals "natural" female monogamy. The early Nazi theologian, Reinhold Seeberg, held similar views, writing of "the essential Semite character in its leaning toward religion, whereas the Indo-Europeans lean more to critical scholarly thought.

81. Freud, *From the History*, 20, emphasis added.
82. Sprengnether, *Spectral Mother*, 72.
83. Olender, *Languages*, 110, paraphrasing Rudolph Friedrich Grau (1835–1893).

The latter would, so to speak, represent the masculine element, the Semites the feminine."[84]

Freud's *Moses and Monotheism* is best read as part of a massive sociocultural attempt by German-speaking Jews in the nineteenth century to rewrite themselves and particularly their masculine selves as Aryans, and especially as Teutons.[85] As Paul Breines has written, "The ideal of the tough Jew that emerges in response to anti-Semitic images is their inversion. The imaginary Jewish body despised by the anti-Semite is rejected by the *fin de siècle* tough Jews as well. The tough Jews go so far as to create an ideal Jewish body imagery that closely resembles the classical Greek and Roman bodily ideals of the anti-Semites themselves. Jewish toughness, like the anti-Semitism it abhors, is literally a body politics, a politics of ideal body images and the moral virtues that supposedly inhere in them: courage, dedication to the national-racial cause, loyalty, self-discipline, readiness for self-sacrifice, robustness, manliness, and so on"[86] (see Plate 10). In order to accomplish this transformation of the male Jewish body, they engaged in a rereading of the biblical and postbiblical past, emphasizing in that past exactly what traditional rabbinic Judaism had deemphasized, namely, its martial aspects.

These Jews were caught in a terrible double bind, most eloquently described by Gilman: "Become like us—abandon your difference—and you may be one with us," but "[t]he more you are like me, the more I know the true value of my power, which you wish to share, and the more I am aware that you are but a shoddy counterfeit."[87] Since they were vilified as female and opportunistic because of their Jewishness, conversion to Christianity was no escape for these Jews; it only confirmed the stereotype of opportunism and lack of manliness. The solution that they hit on was to reconstruct themselves, via a reconstruction of the Jewish past, as virtual Aryans, thus providing the impetus for the mimicry that I have been discussing. An entire Jewish collective—not excepting its Orthodox members—engaged in a project of the assimilation of Jewish culture to *Kultur,* including an assimilation of Judaism

84. Seeberg, quoted in Briggs, "Images," 250. For Seeberg's Nazi-sympathies, see Briggs, 251.
85. Note Freud's comment that the Jews were in Cologne, where he fantasized his own ancestors came from, before the Germans (Freud, *Moses,* 90)!
86. Breines, *Tough Jews,* 127.
87. Gilman, *Jewish Self-Hatred,* 2.

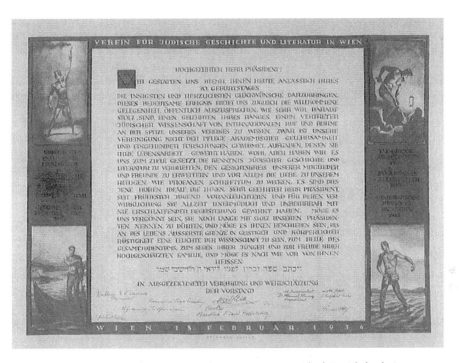

Plate 10.   "The tough Jews go so far as to create an ideal Jewish body imagery that closely resembles the classical Greek and Roman bodily ideals of
the anti-Semites themselves"—Paul Breines. Birthday presentation scroll for
Shmuel Krauss, published by the Vienna Society for Jewish Publications, February 18, 1936. Illustration by Reinhold Pollak. (Courtesy of the Leo Baeck
Institute, New York.)

itself to Protestantism, the sublime faith, and much of this assimilation of Judaism involved the reconstruction of gendered roles.[88] A striking confirmation of this interpretation has recently been provided by Paula E. Hyman, who argues that the retained and even deepening religious loyalty of German Jewish women in comparison to their husbands, was not a counter to assimilation but a form of assimilation, because "[m]en and women alike within Western Jewish communities adopted the dominant middle-class view that women were responsible for inculcating moral and religious consciousness in their children and within the home more generally. According to this view, women were also the primary factor in the formation of their children's Jewish identity. *The conservative role of maternal keeper of the domestic flame of Judaism became a fundamental aspect of the project of assimilation.*" Rather than the conversion of the Jews, the total conversion of Judaism was the solution. As Hyman stunningly concludes, "the Mother in Israel" was but "a Jewish version of the American 'True Woman.' "[89]

Without in any way denying that Jewish culture, like any other, was subject to critique and "modernization," I would categorically assert that the efforts of German-speaking Jews at a "purposeful, even programmatic *dissociation* from traditional Jewish cultural and national moorings" was a form of colonial mimicry, such as best anatomized in Fanon's *Black Skins, White Masks,* and one that was predicated on an "Orientalist" reification of traditional Jewish culture as a mere "social pathology."[90]

As the terms of antisemitism would predict, the conversion of Judaism involved primarily a gendered discourse, a massive attempt to re-

---

88. To be sure, Freud lived in Catholic Vienna, but I think it is not inaccurate to suggest that the kind of religiosity that he admires and constructs as originally "Jewish" in *Moses* is more like German Protestantism than Austrian Catholicism. For discussion, see below.

89. Hyman, *Gender,* 27, emphasis added; 28. Neuda, in *Stunden,* provides an elegant proof-text for her thesis. If one takes away the minimally, specific Jewish content, it could have been produced by any advocate for domesticated bourgeois sentimental religiosity of the period, but it was written by an Orthodox Jewish woman! On Neuda, see Hyman, *Gender,* 34. It should be noted that although this book of prayers for women was translated and published in English, the appendix to which I am referring, which held the pleas for women's education in order that they might more fully perform their "angel in the house" role, was not included in the English version.

90. Aschheim, *Brothers,* 5–6. In other words, I agree completely with Seshadri-Crooks when she writes that "[Freud's] easy condensation of totemic rites as being 'the same thing' as present day neuroses also elides the glib pathologization of non-Western cultures" (Seshadri-Crooks, letter, 192). My intervention is to claim that for Freud the traditional Judaism of the Ostjude is in the same category of the non-Western and primitive as totemic rites and equally as pathologized (see also Aschheim, *Brothers,* 15).

write the Jewish male of the past as indeed a man. Among the traits that Goethe believed the Jew would have to give up in order to be acceptable to German society were "wild [read hysterical] gesticulations," "effeminate movements," and the "queerness of an ancient nonsense."[91] Freud's original title for *Moses and Monotheism* was *The Man Moses and Monotheist Religion,* a title much closer to its cultural import,[92] for Freud's whole point was to argue that Hebrew monotheism was a religion of manliness, self-defense, and self-control, to efface the "effeminate" Jewish difference of Judaism and rewrite it as "manly" Protestantism *avant le lettre.*[93] The analogy between the autobiographical and the political is compelling. Shades of the Wolf Man.[94]

Let us begin as Freud does with Moses himself and his name. Echoing the plausible philological reading of the name as a reflex of the Egyptian *Mose* that forms theophoric names such as Thutmose, and so on, Freud then makes a very strange move. He writes: "Now we should have expected that one of the many people who have recognized that 'Moses' is an Egyptian name would also have drawn the conclusion or would at least have considered the possibility that the person who bore this Egyptian name may himself have been an Egyptian. In relation to modern times we have no hesitation in drawing such conclusions, . . . though a change of name or the adoption of a similar one in fresh circumstances is not beyond possibility."[95] Freud himself bore an "Aryan" name. His name had been changed, to be sure, but the "original," Sigis-

---

91. Aschheim, *Brothers,* 7.

92. Van Herik, *Freud,* 175.

93. I do believe that it was the Protestantism of high German *Kultur,* understood as *Aufhebung* [sublimation] of all previous cultures, that was Freud's model, in spite of his dwelling in Catholic Austria, or perhaps because of it. But again, let me emphasize, Freud's was an assimilationism like Herzl's Zionism (for which, see next chapter) one that sought not to erase the name "Jew" but rather to reconfigure Jews as identical to gentiles and, as such, identical in origin. The "Egyptian" Moses is a perfect figure for this move. Therefore, arguments that Freud was not "ashamed" of his Jewishness or was pugnacious against antisemites are beside the point.

94. Freud returned to this view in his analysis of the Schreber case, in which he argued that Schreber's fantasies of being the Redeemer followed his feminization, *Entmannung.* "For we learn that the idea of being transformed into a woman (that is, of being emasculated) was the primary delusion, that he began by regarding that act as constituting a serious injury and persecution, and that it only became related to his playing the part of Redeemer in a secondary way. There can be no doubt, moreover, that originally he believed that the transformation was to be effected for the purpose of sexual abuse and not so as to serve higher designs. The position may be formulated by saying that a sexual delusion of persecution was later on converted in the patient's mind into a religious delusion of grandeur" (Freud, "Psycho-analytic Notes," 18). The two passages provide striking commentary on each other and together a hermeneutic key for the reading of *Moses.*

95. Freud, *Moses,* 9.

mund, the name of an early modern Polish king known for his friend-
liness toward Jews,[96] was *historically* just as gentile as Sigmund—although in Freud's time it was a stereotypically Jewish name.[97] "In
relation to modern times we have no hesitation in drawing such conclusions," ergo, Sigmund must have been an Aryan. Freud's sublimation of
the Jewish child Moses into the Egyptian prince Mose, via the forgetting of his own name, strongly supports the readings of this text as
Freud's own family novel—he actually called it *ein Roman*—his own
fantasy that he is not the child of the abject Jakob but Oedipus, son of
Laius, or Hannibal, son of Hamilcar. The implication of Freud's own
argument, then, is that he himself "may have been" an Aryan. This
family romance for Freud and for the entire Jewish people is borne out
throughout the work.

Freud's descriptions of biblical religion are tendentious, to say the
least. Thus, near the beginning of the second essay, he writes: "Some of
these differences [between the Jewish religion attributed to Moses and
the religion of Egypt] may easily be derived from the fundamental contrast between a strict monotheism and an unrestricted polytheism. Others are evidently the result of a difference in spiritual and intellectual
[the German word for both is *geistig*] level, since one of these religions
is very close to primitive phases [of development], while the other has
risen to the heights of *sublime abstraction*."[98] It is not often noted how
wildly inappropriate either of these adjectives is when attributed to biblical religion, which was neither a "strict" monotheism, nor had it risen
to the "heights of sublime abstraction."[99] Take for instance the common misapprehensions that the Bible forbids pictorial representation of
any kind and that God is necessarily invisible because wholly spiritual.
Neither of these two popular dogmas corresponds to what we actually
find in biblical text, as a result of which the obvious meaning of that
text is typically revised by its readers.[100]

The rewriting of the history of Judaism, Kantian, Hegelian, and Pla-

96. Klein, *Jewish Origins,* 46.
97. Gilman, *Freud,* 70; see also Pellegrini, "*Without* You."
98. Freud, *Moses,* 19.
99. Freud himself realized how malapropos these descriptions are of actual biblical
religion, but ascribed all of the "primitive" characteristics to the religion of the "Midian-
ite Moses," as opposed to the spiritual religion of the "Egyptian Moses [who] had given
to one portion of the people a more highly spiritualized notion of god, the idea of a single
deity embracing the whole world, who was not less all-loving than all-powerful, who was
averse to all ceremonial and magic and set before men as their highest aim a life in truth
and justice" (Freud, *Moses,* 50). See also Robert Alter, "Freud's."
100. D. Boyarin, "Eye."

tonic-Pauline in its impulses, has been going on for so long and been so successful that we think we recognize Judaism in such descriptions. Thus, typically, Judaism is thought of as the religion of abstract thought and as one indifferent or hostile to aesthetics. Ernst Renan, however, only a little more than a century ago thought differently. For him the "Aryan" was characterized by "abstract metaphysics," while the "Semite" represented poetry; the Aryan scientific reason, the Semite religious feeling; the Aryan philosophy, the Semite music.[101] It is clear how this maps onto Rousseau's and Kant's distinction between the female beautiful and the male sublime.[102] Moreover, as Genevieve Lloyd further remarks (without noticing the theological subtext), for Hegel, "Divine Law" (i.e., the Jew), insofar as it is concerned with "duties and affections towards blood relatives," is the "nether world" and "is also the domain of women."[103] Freud's narrative both accepts and contests this picture. To be sure, the Jews of Freud's day are "atavistic," "fossilized," caught in a world of superstitious ritual, feminized, but it was not always so; once they were as sublime as Aryans, and it is that sublime, Aryan-like, true Mosaic tradition that Freud seeks to recover and revive.

As Eric Santner notes, Weininger had written that "[i]t is, however, this Kantian rationality, this Spirit, which above all appears to be lacking in the Jew and the woman."[104] Weininger, of course, was right. Traditional Judaism has very little to do with Kantianism. The desperation to make this not be so becomes nearly an obsession in the writings of Freud's Jewish contemporaries,[105] as in Jacques Derrida's paraphrase of Hermann Cohen: "Let us go directly, by way of a beginning, to the clearest proposition, the firmest and, for us, the most interesting one: the close, deep internal kinship (*die innerste Verwandschaft*) between Judaism and Kantianism. That is to say also between Judaism and the historical culmination (*geschichtliche Höhepunkt*) of idealism as the essence of German philosophy, namely, the Kantian moment, the inner sanctum (*innerste Heiligtum*) which Kantianism is, with its fundamental concepts (the autonomy of universal law, liberty, and duty)."[106]

Whatever its other parameters, Kant's sublime comprises also the

---

101. Olender, *Languages,* 78.
102. Lloyd, *Man,* 75.
103. Lloyd, *Man,* 81.
104. Weininger, *Sex,* 411.
105. Ellenson, "German," 15.
106. Derrida, "Interpretations," 48–49, 58.

move toward abstraction that Freud would refer to as sublimation and
Lacan as *Aufhebung*.[107] Kant himself had written that the commandment against making graven images or idols (Exod. 20:4) is "the most
sublime passage in the Jews' book of laws."[108] In Kant's definition, the
"sublime is directly concerned with the *unrepresentable*. It calls for de-
tachment from sensibility (from perceptible forms) in order to accede
to the experience of a supersensible faculty within us."[109] But as I—and
others—have shown in earlier work, the prohibition on graven images
of God in biblical religion has little or nothing to do with a putative
unrepresentability of God. If, as Jean-Joseph Goux writes, "nothing
that can be the object of the senses can, strictly speaking, be considered
sublime," then the biblical God, the seeing of Whom is the *summum
bonum* of religious life, can hardly be described as sublime.

Kant may have been in some ways "the Jewish philosopher" as is
sometimes claimed, but his "Jewishness" is only so by virtue of the
Kantianism of German Judaism.[110] One German ultra-Orthodox leader
wrote, "Blessed be God, who in His wisdom created Kant! Every real
Jew who seriously and honestly studies the 'Critique of Pure Reason' is
bound to pronounce his 'Amen' on it."[111] This sublimation of Judaism
is, however, a sort of fetish, recognizing and disavowing at the same
time the connections between Judaism and the religions of "primitives," especially insofar as rites like circumcision are shared among
these.[112] Howard Eilberg-Schwartz, in *The Savage in Judaism*, has both
exposed how inadequate such descriptions of Judaism are and described

107. Lacan, "Meaning," 82.
108. Quoted in Olender, *Languages*, 160. Hegel's description of Judaism as "the religion of the sublime," of which Jay Geller has reminded me, seemingly follows from this
point.
109. Goux, *Symbolic Economies*, 141.
110. Ellenson, "German." This provides quite a different spin on Kant's alleged "in-
nermost affinity with Judaism," as recently discussed by Harpham, "So . . . What *Is*?"
530. The point of the *construction* of such an affinity by figures like Hermann Cohen
would be to *produce* identity between "Judaism" and the German Spirit. Harpham also
quite curiously seems to underplay dramatically Kant's own spectacular expressions of
antisemitism. However, he fathoms acutely that "from serene thoughts of reason it is but
a short step to critical terrorism in the service of revolutionary fantasies of the essential
unity of mankind" (531–32). Harpham explores the contiguities between Inquisition and
Enlightenment; I would locate the sources of the Kantian Universal—with both its light
and dark aspects—further back, in Paul (D. Boyarin, *Radical Jew*). My point is that Enlightenment and Difference are structurally, systemically antithetical, which does not yet
mean that we can do without either Enlightenment or some kind of Universal. For further
articulation of the paradox see Boyarin and Boyarin, "Self-Exposure."
111. Quoted in Ellenson, "German," 23.
112. Cf. Gilman, *Freud*, 188, both for the ways that my reading of *Moses* is similar
to his and for the equally considerable ways that we differ.

the cultural processes by which Judaism came to be so rewritten in modernity.[113] Among their tendentious characteristics, such descriptions of the history of Judaism require an assumption—explicit in the work of Wellhausen—that the "priestly" aspects of the Bible, such as food taboos and purity rituals, were the products of a late degeneration of Israelite religion and not its pure fountainhead.[114] It follows, of course, that Orthodox Jewish adherence to such ritual behavior marks Judaism as both "degenerate" and primitive with respect to Christianity, but this is true only according to these scholars of the "late corrupt form" of Judaism.[115] Freud at once accepts and defends against this Protestant interpretation of Judaism. For him, as for the German Protestant Bible scholars, the "true Jew" was nothing like the priest-ridden ritualist projected in the Torah. Freud's defense of Judaism ends up almost identical to the antisemitic denunciation of it.

Masculine renunciation and its links to the putative triumph of spirituality over the senses is the essence of Freud's argument in *Moses and Monotheism*. It is the sublimation of the sensible penis in the unrepresentable—thus sublime—(veiled; cf. 2 Corinthians 3:13) phallus that is at issue here, and this implies the sublimation of the Jewish people.[116] Where the Jews have been accused of carnality and, therefore, of being like women, Freud (like Philo before him) would demonstrate that they are more spiritual, and more rational, than the Others, and therefore more masculine than the accusers themselves.[117] In other words, Freud did not set out to explain the prohibition on images of God in a psychoanalytical framework; Freud set out to counter antisemitic charges that Jews are not spiritual but carnal, female and not male. Moreover, as I have argued at length, after the turn of the century Freud was very busily, almost frantically, engaged in disavowing his own homosexual desires. This "repression" was produced in the context of the virulent antisemitism and homophobia, which comprised one and the same movement, Adolph Stoecker's "Christian Values" movement, in Ger-

---

113. Eilberg-Schwartz, *Savage*.

114. This view, which was the scholarly consensus about the history of Judaism among German Protestant scholars, is directly evinced in Freud's *Moses* (51). This historiography of Judaism was enshrined in German Reform Judaism as well.

115. It is for this reason that Solomon Shechter referred to the Higher Criticism of the Bible as the Higher Antisemitism.

116. Gilroy, however, remarks the "dangers for both blacks and Jews in accepting their historic and unsought association with sublimity" (*Black Atlantic*, 215–16). See also on this Boyarin and Boyarin, "Self-Exposure."

117. Lloyd, *Man*.

many in his time.[118] The last thing Freud would have wanted to do, at
the onset of the Nazi genocide of Jews and homosexuals,[119] was to confront the feminization/homoeroticization of the male Jew in relation to
God. Eilberg-Schwartz has provided dramatic confirmation for this
reading of Freud's work.[120] He shows that Freud drew back from a conclusion that from his argument seems ineluctable, namely, that monotheism predicts representations of the male worshipper as feminized vis-
à-vis the male God and as a fantasized erotic object for the male God,
thus producing the tension that leads eventually to the de-anthropomor-
phizing—the unmanning, if you will—of the deity. Eilberg-Schwartz
explains Freud's reluctance to come to this conclusion as a product of
his fear that it would amount to representing Jewish men as feminized,
thus playing into the hands of that representation of himself as Jewish
male that he was trying so hard to avoid.

I wish to pursue this reading further. It is not only the case, as
Eilberg-Schwartz has it, that Freud seems to hold back from a conclusion to which his own theory leads him, namely, the avoidance of homoeroticism giving rise to the abstraction of God, but more: there is
an active contradiction within his discourse. Renunciation of the fulfillment of desire, which is encoded in Freud's text as masculine, is occasioned by a submissiveness vis-à-vis a male Other, whether it be the
"great man" Moses or the deity. But that very submissiveness, the mark
of the religious person, was itself feminizing in the terms of nineteenth-
century culture. The "higher," that is, the more "masculine," that Judaism gets, the "lower," that is, the more "feminine," its adherents become. Freud's constant skirting and finessing of this issue are the mark
of the true tension that generates the text.

The Jewish male, having been vilified for hundreds of European
years as feminized, and this no longer—after the rise of heterosexuality—being readable as a mark of resistance and honor by the "emancipated" Jew, set out to reinstate himself as manly in the terms of the
masculinist European culture that had rejected and abused him.[121] He
sought "manliness." And perhaps the most revealing part of *Moses and
Monotheism* is the disquisition on the qualities of the "great man" that
Freud delivers in the third essay.[122] This passage introduces his section

118. Fout, "Sexual Politics," 405; see also Gilman, "Karl," 180.
119. Moeller, "Homosexual."
120. Eilberg-Schwartz, *God's*, 39.
121. Hoberman, "German-Jewish Ideas."
122. Freud, *Moses*, 107–11.

on "The Advance in Intellectuality"—his term for the historical situation of Judaism. In his various attempts to define what it is to be a
"great man," Freud immediately discards chess masters, virtuosi on
musical instruments, distinguished artists, and scientists, but unhesitat-
ingly declares, nevertheless, that Goethe, Leonardo da Vinci, and
Beethoven were great men.[123] He believes that a closer approximation
to the category will be found among "men of action—conquerors, generals, rulers," but ultimately decides that "all the characteristics with
which we equipped the great man are paternal characteristics, and that
the essence of great men for which we vainly searched lies in this con-
formity. The decisiveness of thought, the strength of will, the energy of
action are part of the picture of a father—but above all the autonomy
and independence of the great man, his divine unconcern which may
grow into ruthlessness."[124] Whatever else is going on here, it is precisely
the modes of achievement characteristic of Jews in Freud's world—science, performing music, and chess—that are excluded from those that
define "greatness." Strikingly enough, artists are left out as well, but
somehow the Aryan artists Goethe and Beethoven are in. It would be
very hard, indeed, to imagine a Jewish cultural paradigm within which
"autonomy, independence, and divine unconcern" not to speak of
"ruthlessness" are ideal characteristics of the male.

   In his study of the Schreber case, in a chapter entitled "Schreber's
Jewish Question," Eric Santner has focused on yet another aporia of
Moses and Monotheism. He writes that "for Freud, the ethically oriented monotheism of the Jews and the historical condition of diaspora
are linked by a series of traumatic cuts: of the deity from plastic representation; of spirituality from magic, animism, and sexual excess; of the
passions from their violent enactments; of the people from a territory
conceived as proper to them. These various modalities of loss, separation, and departure, which Freud views as so many forms of the instinctual renunciation [*Triebverzicht*] that undergirds the rule of law in the
most general sense, procure for the Jews what he calls 'their secret treasure,' namely, a sense of self-confidence and superiority with regard to
pagan cultures whose spirituality has remained, as he puts it, 'under the
spell of sensuality' (Freud 1939:115)."[125] Santner points out that Freud

   123. Freud, *Moses*, 108. Cf. Gilman's point that in his discussions of creativity, Freud
never once mentions a Jewish writer or painter (Gilman, "Otto," 119).
   124. Freud, *Moses*, 109–10.
   125. Santner, *My Own Private Germany*, 122.

has a great deal of difficulty, however, in accounting for this "secret treasure," not being able to clearly articulate just why a "set-back to sensuality" should have such a powerful effect in raising the self-regard of individuals or peoples. Freud writes that "[w]e are faced by the phenomenon that in the course of the development of humanity sensuality is gradually overpowered by intellectuality and that men feel proud and exalted by every such advance. *But we are unable to say why this should be so.*"[126] Freud's final response to this aporia is to discover an "uncanny secretion of *jouissance* within the precincts of the moral law,"[127] a sensual ascetic rapture [*In einem neuen Rausch moralischer Askese*] in the very renunciations of sensuality. Santner comments:

> What Freud discovers as a paradoxical kernel of *jouissance* within the domain of an otherwise austere, Kantian moral universe is, as Boyarin has rightly noted, occasioned, *in Freud's narrative,* by submissiveness to a "great man." But that narrative construction was itself generated by an impasse in his argument apropos of the Jewish valuation of *Geistigkeit.* Freud was unable to imagine a resolution of that impasse—the impossibility of accounting for the value of this value—outside the terms of the "father complex." Freud's "great man" fills a gap, a missing link in his argumentation about the emergence of a new cultural value. But to follow Freud here, as I think Boyarin does, is to miss, once more, the encounter with this missing link. To interpret Freud's failure as the avoidance of a homoeroticism implied by his own narrative is to domesticate the impasse on which Freud's interpretation founders, the impasse that called his narrative into being in the first place.

Santner's comment is profoundly cogent, revealing a dimension in the European imaginary of the Jew, the woman, and the queer as an "abjection, the experience of something rotten within" that "signifies a cursed knowledge of *jouissance* which only by way of a kind of secondary revision becomes legible as 'homosexuality,' 'femininity,' or 'Jewishness.'"[128] This "secondary revision," however, is only for Schreber the Aryan, for the one to whom femininity and Jewishness can be put on and taken off. The Jew Freud is mostly too busy trying to get the Aryan phallus, to get "invested" with it to experience such cursed knowledges—except, of course, for the one very significant moment that Santner spotlights, that brief gap when *Jewissance is* glimpsed by Freud.

Freud's impasse is occasioned by his very assumption that Judaism is

126. Freud, *Moses,* 118.
127. Santner, *My Own Private Germany,* 124.
128. Santner, *My Own Private Germany,* 124.

to be characterized as a compelling renunciation of the senses (the mother) for the spirit (the father, phallus, logos), and that this renunciation has generated in the Jew, *from the time of Moses,* a sense of superiority with respect to pagans, that is, a sense of profound well-being in a world which is hostile and threatening to Jews. But there is hardly any reason to think that this was the way ancient Israelites imagined themselves—neither as superior by reason of renunciation nor as particularly threatened. Rather, it is, if anything, a parental or erotic intimacy with God, a perception of being the object of God's desire, that would have described their sense of being special—*Gott der Tatte,* not *Gott der Vater.* In other words, the first point that should be absolutely clear and obvious is that Freud is concerned not at all with Moses or the Bible but with the situation of Jews in his own time.

Freud first has to posit Judaism as "a posture of severe self-control grounded in an endless series of instinctual renunciations," *because he must ward off* Weininger and the latter's argument that "the (masculine/Christian) point of view of Kantian critical philosophy was as foreign to the (feminized) Jewish psychic and moral constitution as was Wagner's *Parsifal* to the Jewish aesthetic sensibility.[129] Freud's very description of Moses's "advances" and the aporia that it produces for him is, in the first instance, a desperate grab for this Spirit (phallus) that Weininger had denied the Jew, a signifier of his profound need to ward off, not so much homoeroticism as in Eilberg-Schwartz's account, but femininity. Freud, having misread biblical Judaism as such an austere, desiccated, incorporeal renunciation of the senses, is then genuinely troubled by the question of why Jews should feel good about it at all, why they should not be denied all *jouissance.* But he knows, of course, that they do feel good, that at least for the *Ostjude* being Jewish is a source of secret joy. He had written to his fiancée, Martha Bernays, "The form wherein the old Jews were happy no longer offers us any shelter."[130] And then through this misprision of the "essence of Judaism," Freud reveals and conceals the secret of abject *jouissance* that Santner saves in Schreber's discourse from Freud's attempt to hide it again. But at the first level, the question remains what it is that occasioned the originary misreading, and I conclude that it is Freud's dire need to be manly, to discover a manliness at the origins of Jewishness, Moses, and the Bible.

129. Santner, *My Own Private Germany,* 124.
130. Freud, *Letters,* 318.

As Jay Geller has put it, "[Freud's] crucial problem was to understand how the Jews 'have been able to retain their individuality till the present day' ([1955f]:136–37). . . . Freud himself appears to be resisting the solution to this problem."[131] Geller goes on to locate the source of Freud's resistance in the *Leitfossil* of *Moses and Monotheism*: circumcision. The very act that enables the resistance (*Widerstand*) of the Jewish People, the mark of repression/sublimation that releases the "uncanny secretion" is that which feminizes the Jewish man: "After the *Leitfossil* circumcision is unearthed, this analysis reconstructs the traumatic knowledge [Santner's 'cursed knowledge'], which Freud seeks to repress, of a source of the anti-Semitism jeopardizing his situation as a Jew: in the Central European cultural imagination, male Jews are identified with men without penises, that is, with women, thereby problematizing sexual difference in a society in which individual identity and social cohesion are determined by the sexual division of labor."[132] At the site of the penis, the overdetermined mark of gendered and "racial" anomaly, circumcision concentrates for Freud the "castration"—political and sexual—of the male Jew, the Jew as female (penisless), queer (perverse and passive), and homeless (in Diaspora). All of these motifs come together in Jewissance, as I shall now try to show by expanding the opening that Geller's work has furnished.

The sexual and political themes, first concatenated in "My Son the Myops," come together in one stunningly overdetermined moment of *Moses and Monotheism*. Immediately after his discourse on the great man as Aryan father, Freud produces the following utterance:

Why the people of Israel, however, clung more and more submissively to their God the worse they were treated by him—that is a problem which for the moment we must leave on one side. It may encourage us to enquire whether the religion of Moses brought the people nothing else besides an enhancement of their self-esteem owing to their consciousness of having been chosen. And indeed another factor can easily be found. That religion also brought the Jews a far grander conception of God, or, as we might put it more modestly, the conception of a grander God. Anyone who believed in this God had some kind of share in his greatness, might feel exalted himself. For an unbeliever this is not entirely self-evident; but we may perhaps make it easier to understand if we point to the sense of superiority felt by a Briton in a foreign country which has been made insecure owing to an insurrection—a feeling that is completely absent in a citizen of any small continental

131. Geller, "Paleontological View," 50–51.
132. Geller, "Paleontological View," 52.

state. For the Briton counts on the fact that his Government will send along
a warship if a hair of his head is hurt, and that the rebels understand that
very well—whereas the small state possesses no warship at all. Thus, pride
in the greatness of the British Empire has a root as well in the consciousness
of the greater security—the protection—enjoyed by the individual Briton.
This may resemble the conception of a grand God.[133]

This bizarre analogy provides the climactic moment in Freud's attempted appropriation of the sublime phallus for Jews, and it renders
crystal clear what the political background for that attempt is. The Jew
is the epitome of the citizen of the small state with no warships, indeed
"he" is not a citizen of any state at all. Freud is arguing that the Jews'
"grander [more sublime] conception of God," their sublimation (masculinization) of physicality and desire, the vaunted "advance in *Geistigkeit*," provides them with an alternative asset for the warships and state
power that they do not possess. At this point it is obvious that the
Zionism of Freud's contemporary, Theodor Herzl, was another—more
direct and more responsive to new and emerging paradigms of the masculine, namely, "Muscular Christianity"—answer to this same Jewish
question. Where Freud sought for Jews a compensation for the lack of
imperial power, Herzl pursued imperial power itself (see next chapter).
It is immediately in the next paragraph after this encomium to imperial
power that Freud invokes the prohibition against making images of
God as a sign of the "triumph of *Geistigkeit* over sensuality, or strictly
speaking, an instinctual renunciation." These are the characteristics encoded as sublime, male, and Protestant in Freud's cultural world. In the
next paragraphs Freud writes of "our children, adults who are neurotic,
and primitive peoples," and of the succession of the matriarchal social
order by the patriarchal one. The connections between these expressions are clear, but it is vital to remember that it was the Jews who were
branded as neurotic, primitive, sensual, and female in fin de siècle central Europe.

We can now see Freud's claims for the "superiority" of the Jews in a
different light. Key to my interpretation is the recoding of "submissive"
from feminine to masculine within the space of this passage. By reading
the "inclination to intellectual interests" as a product of the demateri-
alization or sublimation of God, Freud accomplished another brilliant
defensive move. What has been stigmatized as the femaleness of the
Jewish male, both his circumcision and his devotion to the interior, "fe-

133. Freud, *Moses*, 112.

male" pursuits of study, actually marks him as more masculine than the Greek, who in his very muscularity is less restrained, less able to "renounce instincts," and thus paradoxically less "male"—than the Jew.[134] Jewish carnality, adherence to a law characterized by its passionate attachment to blood and flesh and thus described by antisemites, in this case Hegel, as feminine is transvalued by Freud into a very masculinist *Geistigkeit* or denial of the body itself. The very binary oppositions of maleness and femaleness, renunciation and submission, civilization and oppression have been destabilized in Freud's text. This instability has to do, in part at least, with the vacillating "racial" positioning of the fin de siècle Jew.

Freud remained ambivalent about the civilizing mission of colonialism almost to the very end, and his ambivalence is marked by a series of equivocations in his writing. In 1908 he described female neurosis as being the product of libidinal renunciation occasioned by civilization: "Anyone who is able to penetrate the determinants of nervous illness will soon become convinced that its increase in our society arises from the intensification of sexual restrictions,"[135] and even: "The cure for nervous illness arising from marriage would be marital unfaithfulness."[136] In this text, then, the primitive is written as the healthy libido unrepressed by civilization—Gauguin's Tahiti. At the same time, however, a parallel and opposite tectonic movement takes place in Freud's writing. As Marianna Torgovnick has remarked, in a text published in 1915, "Thoughts for the Times on Life and Death," Freud fathomed the deleterious aspects of civilization but still claimed that "the great ruling powers among the white nations" should, in fact, rule over the others in order to "civilize" them.[137] Nineteen thirteen saw the publication of *Totem and Taboo,* which concerns itself with "some points of agreement between the mental lives of savages and neurotics."[138] In the

---

134. Freud, *Moses,* 115 and especially 116. It is symptomatic that when Freud writes of the legendary founding of rabbinic Judaism in R. Yohanan ben Zakkai's escape from besieged Jerusalem, he mentions only the "masculine" pursuit of intellectuality that it presaged and not the notoriously "feminine" mode of the escape through trickery, in a coffin (124).

135. Freud, *"Civilized" Sexual Morality,* 194.

136. Freud, *"Civilized" Sexual Morality,* 195; see also discussion in Gay, *Tender Passion,* 351.

137. Torgovnick, *Gone,* 197.

138. Freud, *Totem.* Freud is certainly aware that "savages" hedge sexual life with prohibitions and taboos, as he explicitly writes in the first chapter of *Totem.* I think, nevertheless, that he not infrequently imagines the "primitive" as a space of unrepressed libido, as in Gauguin and Douanier Rousseau.

late 1920s, when *Civilization and its Discontents* was being written, civilization, with its demanded instinctual renunciations, was seen as the source of neuroses,[139] and Freud could write that "civilization behaves towards sexuality as a people or a stratum of its population does which has subjected another one to its exploitation."[140]

The negative evaluation of the civilizing mission in this last comment supports the hypothesis that Freud's ambivalence about repression versus sublimation parallels and opens up to the uncertainties of his political situation. Freud's critique of civilization (and male domination) goes hand in hand with his understanding of the evils of colonialism itself, and his sanction of colonialism accompanies his self-contradicting championing of renunciation and sublimation as male virtues. In other words, Freud as the object of racism—and particularly one that configures him as "female"—finds it perhaps easier as well to identify with women than he does later on when it is crucial that he ally himself with the male. In the earlier text, the female incapacity for intellectual thought is a social product caused by repression by male civilization of the sexual instinct in girls of modern society, while in the later text this incapacity is a sign of primitivity. In 1908 Freud contests Moebius's view that "women's physiological feeble-mindedness [Freud's scare quotes]" is caused by an opposition between sexuality and intellectuality, and he argues that "the undoubted intellectual inferiority of so many women can rather be traced back to the inhibition of thought necessitated by sexual suppression";[141] but by the late 1930s his views seem more similar to Moebius's. This conflict is an index of the ambivalent, middle-man position of the Jew as both object and subject of the racism of the civilizing mission, as we will see in the following anecdote.

An early disciple of Freud's and the founder of psychoanalysis in India, G. Bose once sent Freud a depiction of an English gentleman, remarking that he imagined that was how Freud himself appeared. Freud responded that Bose had not paid attention to certain "racial" differences between him and the English, which of course can only be a reference to his Jewishness.[142] As this wonderful anecdote suggests, Freud's origins as *Ostjude* constantly crossed his aspirations as a bourgeois European. He was both the object and the subject of racism at the same

---

139. Freud, *Civilization*, 87, 97, esp. 139.
140. Freud, *Civilization*, 57.
141. Freud, *"Civilized" Sexual Morality*, 199.
142. Seshadri-Crooks, "Primitive," 185, 211 n. 19.

time. Seen from the perspective of the colonized, Freud might look like a white man; from his own perspective, as from that of the dominating Christian white, he was a Jew, every bit as racially marked as the Indian. In the racist imaginary of the late nineteenth century, in fact, Jews were most often designated mulattos. The best denotation, then, for the "race" of the European Jew seems to be off-white.[143]

Two modalities of reading the "race" of Freud's discourse have emerged in recent years: one—the "colonial"—would read this passage, and by extension Freud's other "ethnological" comments and texts, as being about "black" men and thus as having been produced by a "white" man.[144] The other would read "white" and "black" here as barely disguised ciphers for Aryan and Jew.[145] In the first Freud is the colonizer; in the second, the colonized.

These disparate ways of reading Freud on race are not, in fact, mutually exclusive, but two equally crucial aspects of the peculiar racial situation of the European Jew, who is "white"—but not quite. Jews are not white/not quite in Homi Bhabha's felicitous formulation for other colonial subjects. Freud was at once the Other and the metropolitan, the "Semite" among "Aryans" and also the Jew desperately constructing his own whiteness through an othering of the colonized blacks.[146] The results of this double condition are virtually indistinguishable in Freud's texts, because Jews were a genuinely racialized Other (just as much as African-Americans are in the United States) and, paradoxically, because of his identification with his own oppressors. For Freud, "the repugnance of the Aryan for the Semite" was *not* an instance of "the narcissism of minor differences" but rather an instance parallel to that of the "white races for the coloured;" it contrasts with the narcissism of the minor difference.[147] I mean that Jewishness functioned racially in Austro-Germany substantially as "blackness" does in the United States. The "one drop" theory was operative for Jewishness. For instance, a typical antisemite of Freud's time stated: "Jewishness is like

<hr/>

143. Interestingly enough, a similar situation seems to obtain for the Irish. As Enda Duffy remarks, "[I]t was inevitable that the Irish would be seen to occupy an ambivalent middle ground between the 'master' and the 'dark' races" (*Subaltern Ulysses,* 42–43).

144. Bhabha, *Location,* 89; Kazanjian, "Notarizing," 103–5.

145. Gilman, *Jew's,* 175; *Freud,* 21.

146. For analogous processes in American culture, see Rogin, "Blackface"; Gilman, "Dangerous Liaisons."

147. Freud, *Group,* 101; contra Gilman, *Case,* 21, 22, and passim. To be sure, in *Civilization,* 114, it appears as if Freud is giving hostility to Jews as an example of "the narcissism of minor differences," but careful reading shows that this is not necessarily the case. See also Pellegrini, "*Without* You."

a concentrated dye; a minute quantity suffices to give a specific character—or at least, some traces of it—to an incomparably greater mass."[148]
Another representative nineteenth-century savant refers to "the African
character of the Jew," while Houston Stewart Chamberlain, Wagner's
son-in-law and Hitler's hero, wrote that the Jews are a mongrel race
that had interbred with Africans.[149] The Jew was the mulatto, quite literally, as W.E.B. Du Bois found out one night in Slovenia when a taxi
driver took him to the Jewish ghetto (see Plate 11).[150]

Seshadri-Crooks writes that "Freud had certainly assumed an implicit identity for the analyst as a white European man,"[151] an assertion
with which I can only agree. I would interpret this very sentence, however, in a sense perhaps unintended by its author but which nevertheless
resides within the syntax, reading it as: Freud had certainly assumed
[put on] an identity [mask] for the analyst [himself: a not quite white,
"Hottentot," Jewish sissy] as a white European *man.*[152]

Freud, however, remains forever equivocal about this, as one can easily see by his dual comments within the space of a page about "more
and more instinctual renunciations" as leading "in doctrine and precept
at least—[to] ethical heights which had remained inaccessible to the
other peoples of antiquity," but these very same renunciations "possess
the characteristic of obsessional reaction-formations."[153] Moreover, we
can locate this fault line in his psychodynamic theory itself at the site
of the ambiguity surrounding the term "sublimation" vis-à-vis reaction
formation, aim-inhibition, and repression. J. Laplanche and J. B. Pontalis note somewhat dryly that in Freud's writings "there are only the
vaguest hints of dividing lines between sublimation" and repression,
obsession, and aim-inhibition, but "the capacity to sublimate is an essential factor in successful treatment."[154] Since obsession and repression
are part of what there is to be treated in a successful treatment, the cure
and the disease become hard to distinguish. This famous moment of

148. Quoted in Gilman, *Jew's,* 175.
149. Freud had read Chamberlain (Gilman, *Freud,* 236). For extensive documentation of the "blackness" of Jews, see Gilman, *Jewish Self-Hatred,* 172–75; Gilman, *Case,*
19–21. For a fascinating explanation of the functions of such discourse, see Cheyette,
"Neither Black."
150. Gilroy, *Black Atlantic,* 212.
151. Seshadri-Crooks, "Primitive," 194.
152. "Hottentot" is a reference to the *Ostjuden,* the "black" Jews, who spoke a language that one converted German Jew referred to as "Hottentot."
153. Freud, *Moses,* 134–35. Cf. the somewhat similar reading of another aporia in
Freud's text by Geller, "Paleontological View," 62.
154. Laplanche and Pontalis, *Language,* 433.

JUDEN UM 1818.

Plate 11.   The "African Character" of the Jew. This antisemitic German cartoon was published anonymously in 1818. (Courtesy of the Leo Baeck Institute, New York.)

incoherence in the dynamic theory is the product of the pervasive ambivalences I have been exploring as products of Freud's fin de siècle sexual/political situation, indeed, almost emblematic of a liminality that Freud manifests.

Seen in this light, Freud's apparent, if ambivalent, rapport with the civilizing mission, as well as his acceptance of the bromide that ontogeny recapitulates phylogeny, is a much more complex political move than it might first appear to be, for the "primitives" to which he addresses himself are as much Jewish primitives—indeed, first and foremost Jewish primitives, primitives within—and only secondarily the contemporary objects of the civilizing mission of colonialism.[155] Freud's apparently guileless use of the phrase "a state within a state" as a metaphor for "pathological phenomena"[156] is telling here, since, of course, that phrase was coined for women and Jews, the twin primitive Others within the German state.[157] Freud had apparently, almost against his will, internalized the antisemitic ideology that Jews were a people both out of time and out of place. Other Jews in his milieu had also incorporated such views, most notably the western European Zionists of Herzl's movement (see next chapter).

Although Freud was not, certainly by 1939, a Zionist in the sense of being a supporter of Jewish settlement in Palestine and the founding of a Jewish state there, his interpretation of Jewish history was exactly the same as the Zionist interpretation—ancient glory followed by thousands of years of degradation producing moral, spiritual, and esthetic distortions in the oppressed people. The "high" religion of the Egyptian Moses, the purely spiritual monotheism, was the production of a "fortunate period of established possession"; that is, "[i]n Egypt, so far as we can understand, monotheism grew up as a by-product of imperialism," but as the Jewish people underwent the trials and sufferings of the Diaspora, "their god became harsh and severe, and, as it were, wrapped in gloom . . . they increased their own sense of guilt in order to stifle their doubts of God." Freud explicitly echoes the best of German Prot-

---

155. If my reading begins to sound somewhat like Cuddihy, this is not entirely accidental. Although my own interpretation of the *Ostjude*, as well as my evaluation of Weber, could not be more different from Cuddihy's, there are some ways in which our interpretations converge, at least insofar as we both see Freud's discomfort with the *Ostjude* as a component of self as a motive force in aspects—different ones for Cuddihy than for me—of his writing. Cuddihy's reading whereby the *Ostjude* is not only a part of Freud or of the Jews but of everyone cannot be dismissed either. See also D. Boyarin, *Épater*.

156. Freud, *Moses*, 76.

157. Geller, "Paleontological View," 56.

estant Bible scholarship: "Institutions such as the ritual ordinances, which date unmistakably from later times, are given out as Mosaic commandments with the plain intention of lending them authority." The great ideals of the true Mosaic religion remained dormant within the people, but the priests with their "ceremonials" became increasingly the dominant force.[158]

Freud went beyond most of his contemporaries, however, by actually splitting Moses and thus Judaism into two different antithetical and antagonistic groups with two different Moseses and two different religious traditions. The "true" Moses, the Egyptian one, is remarkably like the ideal Protestant. Freud's Moses fantasies and dreams provide important backing for this thesis. When he dreams he is on a mountain looking yearningly at "the Promised Land," it is not, however, the Land of Israel, but Rome, like Hannibal at Lake Trasimeno,[159] and this is emblematic of the metamorphosis of the man Moses at his hands. In the early essay on the *Moses* of Michelangelo, Freud discovers that Moses is not about to throw down the tablets of the Law, but is in fact checking that impulse and that, therefore, Michelangelo has "added something new and more than human to the figure of Moses; so that the giant frame with its tremendous physical power becomes only a concrete expression of the highest mental achievement that is possible in a man, that of struggling successfully against an inward passion for the sake of a cause to which he has devoted himself."[160] Moses is now the very model of a masculine spirituality and renunciation, as well as a "manly" aggressiveness: "in contrast to the meditative king, he was energetic and passionate."[161]

The other Moses, the second Moses was, on the other hand, all too Jewish, and the religion that he founded was obsessed with "neurotic" ritual observances and not with "sublime abstractions." "Everything in the [Egyptian] Mosaic god that deserved admiration was quite beyond

158. Freud, *Moses*, 64, 65. Cf. the description by Manuel of German Reform Judaism: "Reform Judaism, which had distanced itself from traditional rabbinism, owed something to the Christian idealization of ancient Judaism, the object having molded itself to fit the image in the mind of the beholder" (Manuel, *Broken Staff*, 263). Manuel points out that Herder had described biblical religion as "sublime" (264). Manuel also refers to the Christian tradition dating back to the thirteenth century which admired "the Mosaic law but despised the legalistic accretions of the Talmudists" (266–67). Freud is not far from such views, and that is the point.

159. Freud, *Interpretation*, 194; cf. Masson, *Complete Letters*, 285.

160. Freud, *Moses of Michelangelo*, 233. See B. Goldstein, *Reinscribing*, 76.

161. Freud, *Moses*, 60.

the comprehension of the primitive masses."[162] On Freud's own theory that such ancient fault lines reappear in later splits within a people, could we not read this as a covert, perhaps unconscious, representation of the distinction between German Jews and their embarrassingly primitive relatives, the *Ostjuden*.[163] Such a "family romance" was not unprecedented among Viennese Jews of Freud's generation. Theodor Herzl went so far as to write explicitly that the *Ostjude* was of a different "race" from the "evolved" German Jew. Freud's account of how the ideas of the original Moses, "the idea of a single god, as well as the rejection of magically effective ceremonial and the stress upon ethical demands made in his name,"[164] were suppressed but reappeared hundreds of years later would be an allegory of the reappearance of such "high" ideas of religion among the German Jews after centuries of their abeyance among the *Ostjuden*. As one of Freud's Bnai Brith lodge brothers couched it: "We Jews . . . are not constrained by dogma. In his inner being the Jew, the true Jew, feels only one eternal guide, one lawgiver, one law, and that is morality."[165] Gilman appropriately glosses this: "This image of the Jews as following only 'natural law,' rather than the complicated rules and rituals of traditional Judaism, imagines them as the ultimate rationalists, at one with God and nature."[166] Hiding behind the second, "too Jewish," ritualist Moses is none other than Mauschel, "little Moses" (or "Ikey"), the malicious name that German antisemites, both Jewish and gentile, applied to East European Jews. Mauschel is obsessed with his primitive, atavistic, and irrational rituals. If the first Moses is Moses Mendelssohn, the second is Mauschel. Indeed, one might almost wish to rename the work *Mauschel and Monotheism*.

The crisis of the early 1930s so heightened this strain that it gave way finally in a "personality split" within Moses and likewise the Jewish People: *Moses and Monotheism*.[167] Each of the "religious" categories

---

162. Freud, *Moses*, 63.
163. Freud, *Moses*, 38; Gilman, *Jewish Self-Hatred*, 99.
164. Freud, *Moses*, 66.
165. Ludwig Braun, 1926, quoted in Gilman, *Case*, 75.
166. Gilman, *Jewish Self-Hatred*.
167. Torgovnick shrewdly sees the same split in the 1930 preface to the new edition of *Totem*, not associating it, however, with *Moses*. The difference between my reading and Torgovnick's is that where she sees a rather simple contrast between the way that the Jew is portrayed by the antisemite and Freud's attempt to counter it, I see much more equivocation within Freud himself. Torgovnick does not cite the very early valorization of the "primitive" in *Civilized Sexual Morality* and thus misses an opportunity to see a

which Freud projects is, like Rome, split and doubled. Judaism is not identical with itself, and neither is Christianity. The split between the "queer effeminate" *Ostjude* and the "straight male modern" Jew,[168] between Mauschel and Mendelssohn, seems to be repeated in a split between the Austrian Catholic and the German Protestant as well, suggesting further Freud's complicated identifications of self and other—all within. Another way of saying this would be that the evolutionary narrative is from Catholic to Protestant Christian—and from Catholic to Protestant Jew (with some temporary devolutions along the way). "Maimonides is, within Medieval Judaism, the revealing mark of Protestantism" wrote Hermann Cohen,[169] and Freud's description of the religion of sublime abstraction is surely much more like that of Moses Maimonides—and Hermann Cohen—than like that of the biblical Moses.

It is clear now which border, which frontier it was that Freud desired to cross in the "Myops" dream with which this chapter began. It is the border between Jews and gentiles. When he has crossed it—by escaping to England, however—he has lost something. As Bram Dijkstra has perceptively written, "The truly psychotic, rather than merely neurotic, idealization of a supremely evolved white male and the concomitant assumption that somehow all others were 'degenerate' had, as Freud was writing [*Civilization and Its Discontents*], begun to reap its most evil harvest. Even the most casual reader of the theoretical disquisitions of the later nineteenth-century exponents of the science of man must at once perceive the intimate correlation between their evolutionist conclusions and the scientific justification of patterns of 'inherent' superiority and inferiority in the relations between the sexes, various races, and the different classes in society."[170] The ambivalence in Freud's disposition vis-à-vis civilization and the primitive is generated by the ambiguity of his position as "white male." Freud as the Jew, the "black," the unacknowledged (by him) object of the racist discourse of evolution, sees well the horror of colonial domination, but when Freud iden-

---

layer of identification with the "primitive" Eastern Jew long before "the pressure of Nazism" (Torgovnick, *Gone*, 201). Otto Rank was more consistent than Freud. For him the "essence of Judaism" was in its avoidance of repression and its "stress on primitive sexuality," which was a positively marked term for Rank (Rank, "Essence"; also see discussion in Gilman, *Case*, 176).

168. Brenkman, *Straight Male*.
169. Quoted in Derrida, "Interpretations," 53, 65.
170. Dijkstra, *Idols*, 160.

tifies himself with the "white man," then he perceives the great virtues
of the civilizing mission.

This tension was always present, but it resolves itself most definitely in the gap between *Civilization and Its Discontents* and *Moses
and Monotheism*. While still in the killing field of the "evil harvest,"
Freud perceives the violence of civilization. Safe, however, among the
"great[est] ruling power among the white nations," in *Moses and Monotheism* Freud ruminates that it is the "primitive" who has not (yet) undertaken renunciation of libidinal strivings who is most similar to the
neurotic and the female, and renunciation thus has become a sign of
greater psychic health. Now the "Jew" has to be demonstrably on the
side of civilization.[171] Read this way, these texts form almost an uncanny inchoate preliminary draft for the *Dialectic of Enlightenment*.[172]
Far from proposing this as a sign of bad faith on Freud's (or Adorno
and Horkheimer's) part, I suggest that the off-whiteness of the Jew is
productive of a kind of insight, all the more powerful for its being disguised in the texts. This disguise is not, on this reading, mystification
but "persecution and the art of writing." This aporia, or set of aporias,
in the Freudian text is best read as built into the heart of modernity, and
the personal in Freud is, therefore, political in ways only adumbrated in
previous contexts. Freud's ambivalence, his bitextuality, finally is a kind
of knowledge.

With this I come back to the astonishing Freudian passage quoted
earlier, the one in which the aggressive feelings of the Wolf Man toward
his sister "were meant to efface the memory of an event which later
on seemed offensive to the patient's masculine self-esteem, and they
reached this end by putting an imaginary and desirable converse in the
place of the historical truth. . . . *These phantasies, therefore, corresponded exactly to the legends by means of which a nation that has become great and proud tries to conceal the insignificance and failure of
its beginnings.*"[173] In this passage, it could be said, Freud has included
an entire theory of the nexus between the personal and the political, an

---

171. These two orientations of the Jew for Freud almost mirror the differential relations of nineteenth-century German and British anthropology toward Jews, as described
by Efron, *Defenders*, 35–36.

172. For readings of this text appropriate to this context, see J. Boyarin, *Storm*, 108–
10, and Harpham, "So . . . What *Is*?" 532. For a different analogy between Freud and
Adorno, see Gilman, "Otto," 108, and Stieg, "Kafka," 196.

173. Freud, *From the History*, 20, emphasis added.

entire theory of the way that masculinism produces violence directed toward women (and gay men, as implied through the whole context of "passivity" as shameful) as well as nationalist violence directed toward others. Both are the products, according to Freud, of a defensive reversal meant to restore self-esteem to a male person who has perceived himself as feminized, and both have deadly effects. Although Freud doesn't come right out and say it, the sociopolitical context of a period within which "passivity" was considered the deepest source of shame for a man, the period of the "rise of heterosexuality," would be conducive to the greatest masculinist/nationalist violence. If Freud had been able to perceive the operations of this psychic process in his own work, he would have been even greater than he was, but under the conditions of oppression within which he suffered, it is perhaps understandable that he wasn't. It can be said fairly that here, as in other places, it is Freud himself who provides the knowledge that enables critique—of Freud!

CHAPTER VII

The Colonial Drag

Zionism, Gender, and Mimicry

IF HE IS A BOY, HE MUST BE A STALWART ZIONIST

After Sabina Spielrein, Jung's patient and mistress, having abandoned her dream of bearing a Jewish "Siegfried" to Jung, had informed him that she was pregnant by her Jewish husband, Freud wrote her: "I am, as you know, cured of the last shred of my predilection for the Aryan cause, and would like to take it that *if the child turned out to be a boy he will develop into a stalwart Zionist, and if a girl, she will speak for herself.* He or she must be dark in any case, no more towheads. Let us banish all these will-o'-the-wisps."[1] The "racial" aspects of Freud's prayer for the child are obvious, but the gender encoding is more mysterious.[2] The Zionist is gendered male for Freud.[3] Why?

---

1. Quoted in Yerushalmi, *Freud's,* 12–13. We can get some sense of the meaning of these loaded cultural terms for Freud by comparing the affect expressed by a contemporary German Jew, Theodor Lessing, while a young man in the 1890s: "How would I survive in this Aryan world of joyful muscular Siegfrieds with their healthy and crude ideals of strength and blood? I considered myself the offspring of the most disgusting mercenary marriage. I hated both parents and the graves of my ancestors" (letter to his friend, Ludwig Klages, quoted in Baron, "Theodor," 328).

2. Yerushalmi completely misses the gendered aspect of this wish. Gilman goes so far as to erase this point, arguing that "Freud did not articulate the difference in terms of gender—the imagined Jewish 'boy' can become a Zionist, a Jewish nationalist, and the Jewish 'girl' (Spielrein's daughter Renate) 'will speak for herself'" (Gilman, *Freud,* 33). But Freud articulates the difference precisely in terms of gender, as Gilman himself seems to have noticed earlier (Gilman, *Jew's,* 195). Although he expresses somewhat parallel ambitions for the male Jewish infant and the female one, after all "speaking for oneself" is simply not the same as being a Zionist.

3. Interestingly enough, this is not so for Lessing (see note 1), for whom "his analysis of feminism served as the prototype of his rationale for Zionism" (Baron, "Theodor,"

For Freud (*at the time that he wrote this letter*),[4] Zionism is coded male because it is essentially about masculinity. The Spielrein letter was written explicitly in reaction to Freud's break with and acrimonious feelings toward Jung's antisemitic tendencies, as Yerushalmi has made clear. Jung had unambiguously ventilated the European topos of Jewish male "effeminacy."[5] Another way of saying this would be that "Zionism" had for Freud at this point in his life the same function that oedipality had for him at other nodes. Both signify a masculinizing of the allegedly feminized—queer—Jewish male. As in the case of his rela-

---

329). However, even this "feminist Zionist" believed that "only the abolition of political, socio-economic, and personal inequalities between the sexes would allow women, as well as men, to be truly themselves," and that being "truly themselves" would mean, once more, that women would not have to work in factories or business (331). Similarly, "Zionism for Jews, like feminism for women, offered its supporters the chance to discover their real identity, rather than always having to react to the hardships and expectations imposed on them by a hostile environment," and thus they would also, like women, abandon their "keen intellectuality," which had evolved only "to compensate for their 'history of dependence and suffering' " (332). Lessing's associations between Jews and women are thus ultimately very different from those of Weininger or even the Zionist Nordau, even though in the end his Zionism, like his feminism, calls for a "normalization" of gender roles into the properly male and the properly female. As Baron remarks, "Lessing's idiosyncratic Zionism provided him with a positive Jewish alter ego, which was as much German as Jewish in inspiration" (336).

Let this note nevertheless serve as a first caution that even my most trenchant comments upon and interpretations of Herzlian Zionism could be countered by referring to other Zionisms. There were even movements calling themselves Zionism that would today be called *antizionism,* such as those that called for a completely secular binational state in Palestine for Jews and Palestinians together, the stated program of the left wing of the Palestine Liberation Organization, as well as of Israeli Jewish antizionists in Matzpen, among whose number I count myself! Moreover, even on the matter of Jewish culture, as Aschheim points out, this story is not as univocal as it might seem. A later generation of German-speaking Zionists became quite enamored of that which they called "*Jüdischkeit,*" that is, *Yiddishkayt,* thus signaling as well their growing admiration for *Ostjuden.* The older generation of German Zionists found this development quite mystifying (Aschheim, *Brothers,* 100–120)! See also Mendes-Flohr, *Divided,* 77–132, for a fascinating discussion of a fin de siècle version of Jewish Orientalism that romanticized the Ostjude. To be sure, such idealizing moves are often enough the "flip side" of contempt, as Said has shown, as have, of course, many feminists. It nevertheless remains the case that this movement provided for an increasing pull toward a revival of specifically Jewish cultural forms in the generation following Herzl's demise and an appeal to the Eastern Jew as preserver of genuine vitality and "roots" for a Jewish cultural revival. Martin Buber, who was one of the central figures in the most progressive form of Zionism, the Brith Shalom movement, was also pivotal in this "return to the East," and his Hasidic writings are undoubtedly to be considered part of this cultural move (85). It is, I think, quite significant that (at least according to Mendes-Flohr himself) the most significant positive responses to Buber's Hasidic works came from non- and anti-Zionists, from Rathenau to Lukács and even Ernst Bloch (96–109). I am gratefull to David Myers for pointing me to Mendes-Flohr's important essay.

4. Freud's affect about Zionism was ever changing, as shown by in McGrath, *Freud's,* 313–17.

5. Gilman, *Freud,* 31.

tions with Fliess (discussed in chapter 5), as well as in his letter to Spiel-rein, disavowed homoeroticism and Zionism are correlated. Freud was quite frank about his homoerotic feelings toward Jung, having written Jones about a faint in Jung's presence that it had to do with "some unruly homosexual feeling,"[6] and interpreting this faint in terms of the "negative Oedipus complex."[7] Giving up the "Aryan" cause consists then of the "overcoming" of "unruly" desire for the "Aryan" Jung.

When the child Freud heard from his father of his "passivity" in the face of antisemitic intimidation, his response was to fantasize about being Hannibal, whose brave father swore him to seek revenge for his "Semitic" people against the Roman oppressors. Indeed, Moses seems almost to be merged with Hannibal in Freud's mind. Moreover, one can add the not insignificant point that even Freud's "Semitic" hero Hannibal was hardly Jewish. From a traditional Jewish point of view, he was every bit as "pagan" in both religion and cultural identity as his Roman adversaries. As Bluma Goldstein has so keenly written: "And with what better model to wage battle against such antagonism and antisemitism than with a Semitic warrior! But with a Semitic warrior who is not a Jew?"[8] Freud's fantasies of Hannibal the Semite and Massena the allegedly Jewish war hero, and ultimately of Moses the Egyptian prince who founds the Jewish people, represents a wish to remain Jewish in name but be entirely transformed in such a way that the Jewishness would be invisible.

The "Jewish" heroes, whether of the Bible or modernity, are all transformed into mimics of gentile heroes. This point could use some further expansion, because as it stands it sounds both essentialist— "War heroes could not possibly be *really* Jewish"—and counterfactual. What, after all, about Samson and the other biblical warriors? My point is not to deny that there was ever a Jewish martial tradition, nor to assert that being violent is un-Jewish, which would be at best a nonstrategic essentialism. As it developed historically, however, Diaspora Jewish culture had little interest in Samson, and its Moses was a scholar. I have remarked elsewhere the sharp antagonism of the Rabbis to the "heroes" of Masada (the Rabbis called them "hooligans") and their extreme ambivalence about Jewish military figures like Bar Kochba. Even the Maccabees were deprived of their status as military heroes in the

6. Jones, *Young Freud*, 348.
7. Blum, "Prototype," 155.
8. B. Goldstein, *Reinscribing*, 73.

Talmud.[9] Not surprisingly, they were the very type of the Jewish hero in the eyes of chivalric Europe. As Elias Bickerman has observed, "The Christian world, which had taken the Books of Maccabees into their Holy Scripture, meanwhile honored Judah Maccabee *as a paragon of knighthood.* Even today the statue of Judah may be seen in the principal market place of Nüremburg. His figure, along with those of eight other heroes (three pagans, three Jews, three Christians), decorates the Schöne Brunnen (1385), a masterpiece of the age of chivalry."[10]

It is highly significant, therefore, that as emancipated Jews became desperate to remake the Jewish male in the image of the Anglo-Saxon (in particular) as the ultimate white male of their world, they sought to discover such male models within something they could call Jewish— Hannibal, a transformed Moses; Massena, and ultimately the whole biblical tradition of sovereignty and war-making understood as the antithesis of the Diaspora Jewish wont for passivity. Jewish gymnastic groups, in mimicking the *Turnkunst* gymnastic movement founded by Ludwig Friedrich Jahn in Germany, took the names of Jewish warriors like Bar Kochba and Maccabee (both quite marginalized and often disparaged in rabbinic Jewish tradition) as their icons.[11] For the Zionist *Jugendstil* artist, E. M. Lilien, Herzl was Moses, as he created an image of Moses with the face of Herzl for the *Benei Brith* in Hamburg (see Plate 12).[12]

Zionism is thus for Freud a mode of repressing, of overcoming his Jewish homosexual effeminacy. Both this family romance—I am a direct descendant of the warrior Semites of old, not the child of passive, effeminate *Ostjuden*—and the Oedipus romance function in the same way to deny Freud's paternity as the son of the "impotent"—queer—

---

9. D. Boyarin, "Tricksters."

10. Bickerman, *From Ezra,* 134–35.

11. Berkowitz, *Zionist Culture,* 108. See also Mosse, *Image,* 40–55. For Judah Maccabee as the very image of the knight—in the gentile tradition!—Keen, *Chivalry,* 14.

12. On Lilien, the following comment of a contemporary seems to me particularly sharp: "[Lilien] is an outsider who was remote from Jewish organic art, failed to grasp the rhythm of the Jewish ornament and was ignorant of the Jewish letter ... *It is not without reason that he was so closely associated with the Bezalel Art School in Jerusalem, that he rejected the spirit of the people and embraced the Biblical, Zionist sentiment with all its superficialities and pseudo-romanticism*" (Ryback and Aronson, "Di Vegen"; trans. in Kampf, *Jewish Experience,* 29, emphasis added). However, as Bluma Goldstein has suggested to me in private conversation, the canonization of a "decadent" form of art as the art of Zionism suggests that the relation of Viennese ideals of honor to gender is more complicated than the simple equations of honor with "manliness" with which I am working here. She will be exploring these issues in future work, and my account will undoubtedly require further nuancing in the wake of hers.

Plate 12.   Moses with the Face of Herzl. E. M. Lilien's stained-glass window for the *Benei Brith* of Hamburg. (Courtesy of the Leo Baeck Institute, New York.)

Jew who picked up the hat that the gentile threw down, thus signifying his passivity in the face of the virile Aryan. "If he had to have a Jewish father, little Sigmund would at least have wanted him to be a man proud of his race, a bold warrior."[13]

Seen in this light, Zionism is truly the most profound sort of assimilationism, one in which Jews become like all the nations, that is, like Aryans (Oedipus), but remain Jews in name (and complexion): Bar Kochba, warrior Moses, and Maccabee; not Tancred (Herzl's *nom de mensur*) or Siegfried (a *Jugendstil* representation of whom appeared on the souvenir card of the Second Zionist Congress held in Basel in 1898).[14] Sabina Spielrein is not to give birth to a blonde Siegfried, but "if he is a boy he must be a stalwart Zionist." For Freud, it seems, it was not actually necessary to participate in the building of a Jewish National Home in order to solve the Jewish problem; merely being a "stalwart Zionist" was enough to transform the Jewish man from his state of effeminate degeneracy into the status of proper, that is—in spite of Freud's disclaimer—mock-"Aryan male."[15]

13. Robert, *From Oedipus*, 112.

14. Cf. also Enda Duffy, in whose reading of *Ulysses* we discover a Joyce who "exposes nationalism and other chauvinist ideologemes of 'imagined communities' chiefly as inheritances of the colonist regime of power-knowledge they condemn" (*Subaltern Ulysses*, 3; and esp. 33). Joyce's thematizations of Zionism in the book are highly germane. (I would like to thank Robert Alter who first redirected my attention to *Ulysses* with respect to my current project and thus helped generate another project, which I hope to bring to fruition.)

Note that formally retaining the name "Jew" while assimilating Jewishness to the forms of gentility is not inconsistent with assimilation *tout court,* which, as Paula Hyman has recently noted, involved for Jews generally adopting gentile cultural patterns while remaining Jewish in identity. Thus she argues that the fact that German Jewish women attended synagogue in greater numbers than did men at a certain period was a mode of assimilation for these women, because among their Protestant contemporaries similar patterns obtained (*Gender,* 25). In other words, since "true women" (the wives of "real men") went to church, true women who happened to be Jewish went to synagogue. Fanny Neuda's "A Word to the Noble Mothers and Women of Israel," published as an appendix to her *Stunden der Andacht,* provides an elegant exemplification of Hyman's thesis. The text is a plea for educating girls in Hebrew so that they will remain faithful to Judaism, but the values expressed and the theories of the roles of gender are those of the bourgeois and quite different from traditional Jewish ones. No Glikls here; the Jewish woman is expected to be the "angel in the house." This seems to be a perfect female analogue to the pursuit of a Jewish manliness on the part of assimilating men such as Herzl, and in both cases it is superficially cast (in good faith) as an intensification of Jewish identity! I am grateful to Helen Epstein for calling the last text to my attention.

15. For this seeming paradox inherent in the fact that the very site of assertion of cultural identity is as well the most intense locus of denial, one need only cite Herzl's comments on the writing of *The Jewish State:* "My only recreation was listening to Wagner's music in the evening, particularly to *Tannhäuser,* an opera which I attended as often

HERZL AND SELF-HATRED:
ZIONISM AS COLONIAL MIMICRY

I propose that Freud's reading of Zionism was not as idiosyncratic as it might at first glance appear. As has been shown more than once, Zionism was considered by many to be as much a cure for the disease of Jewish gendering as a solution to economic and political problems of the Jewish people.[16] Exemplary in this regard is Max Nordau, "the second great embodiment of early Zionism":[17] "Nordau's demand that the Jews reform their bodies was yet another attempt from within the Jewish community to adapt the underlying structure of anti-Semitic rhetoric and use its strong, political message for other ends. Nordau's call for a 'new muscle Jew' was based on the degeneration of the Jew 'in the narrow confines of the ghetto.' . . . Zionism demanded that the new muscle Jews have healthy bodies and healthy minds."[18] George Mosse had already succinctly written: "Zionists and assimilationists shared the same ideal of manliness,"[19] which in my reading results in an equivalence of Zionism and assimilation.

Given the contemporary gendering of muscularity, it is hardly surprising then to find Freud encoding Zionism as male, as virile,[20] and as the specific answer to Jung's antisemitic descriptions of Jewishness as effeminate. Freud, like Nordau, had, on this reading, internalized the negative and pathologizing interpretation of Jewish manhood of the antisemites and thus saw Zionism as the solution. To a not inconsiderable extent, the project of these Zionists (known as political Zionists) was to transform Jewish men into the type of male that they admired, namely, the ideal "Aryan" male. If the political project of Zionism was to be a nation like all other nations, on the level of reform of the Jewish psyche it was to be men like all other men. The Zionist catchphrase, ככל הגוים, "like all of the Nations," thus has a double meaning, since in its popular acceptance it would have meant rather "like all of the (male) gentiles." It was this aspect of Zionism, I propose, that appealed

---

as it was produced. Only on the evenings when there was no opera did I have any doubts as to the truth of my ideas" (Herzl, *Zionist Writings,* 17; see also Elon, *Herzl,* 3). I thank Jonathan Boyarin for reminding me of this reference.

16. Berkowitz, *Zionist Culture,* 18–19; cf. D. Biale, *Eros,* 176.
17. Berkowitz, *Zionist Culture,* 9; D. Biale, *Eros,* 178–79.
18. Gilman, *Freud,* 105.
19. Mosse, *Nationalism,* 42.
20. D. Biale, *Eros,* 176–77.

to Freud. By identifying himself with Moses, conquistador, Freud was remasculating himself, undoing the unmanning of his Jewishness, but remaining nominally and affectively Jewish, just like the Austrian Jewish men who created the Jewish gymnastic clubs, Maccabee and Bar Kochba. Berkowitz refers to the "Jewish gymnast's symbiosis of *Deutschtum, Judentum,* and liberalism," and remarks that this combination "was a critical transmitter of Zionist national culture."[21]

HERZL THE GERMAN

I am a German-speaking Jew from Hungary and can never be anything but a German. At present I am not recognized as a German. But that will come once we are over there.
                                                    —Theodor Herzl

Through Zionism Jews will again be able to love this Germany to which, despite everything, our hearts have clung.
                                                    —Theodor Herzl

I turn to the texts of Theodor Herzl, the "father of the Jewish State." Rereading these texts with the critical categories of postcolonial theory in mind will be productive of a dramatic new take on Herzlian Zionism.[22] Zionism is presented by its adherents as anti-assimilationism, a will to power in the face of oppression or as a nativism not entirely

21. Berkowitz, *Zionist Culture*, 108.
22. I will qualify the "Zionism" to which I refer here by the adjective "Herzlian," as there were and are different Zionisms. For all my disdain for Herzlian liberalism, religious Zionisms (that combine statism with religion, whether Orthodox or not—for example, blood and soil mysticism of the right and left) are even more problematic and, given the actual situation of the populations of Palestine and Israel today, more deleterious. It is a matter of controversy to what extent Herzl's ideas are actually carried out in the state of Israel. The best of them certainly are not. I try to indicate here some of the negative manifestations of Herzlian thought about Jewish history as they play themselves out in Israeli cultural performance. I would argue that much of the violence of contemporary Israeli cultural and political life is generated by inchoate anticolonial struggles on the part of Oriental and traditionalist Jews against the "civilizing mission" of the "Western" liberals, which unfortunately often enough (but not always) result in intensification of neocolonialism with respect to the Palestinians rather than in solidarity with their anticolonial struggle. The only variety of historical Zionism with which I can identify at all is that of Judah Magnes and the "Covenant of Peace" group, which did not seek Jewish political hegemony, a Jewish State, but quested rather for shared sovereignty together with Palestinians in a binational state. Today such a program is labeled antizionism, so I am an antizionist. For Buber's version of Zionism, see Simon, "Jewish Adult," 69–70.

unlike the negritude movement. The above passages, quoted from Herzl's diaries, need only be compared to the following statement by an exemplary assimilationist German Jew to show how mystified this picture is: "I have, and know no other, blood than German blood," wrote Walter Rathenau, "no other tribe, no other people than the German. Expel me from my German soil, I still remain German, nothing changes."[23] Herzl, with somewhat greater insight, had realized that only by leaving German soil and founding a Jewish State would he ever be truly German, but his identification with the Germans and desire to fully be one were the same as Rathenau's.[24] Zionism's opponents, however, see it as plain colonialism, a mere undiluted extension of European practices. My project is to describe how Zionism occupies a peculiar interstitial position to be understood as neither wholly nativist, in that there is only a partial assertion of difference, nor as a univocal tributary of colonialism.

It is crucial to understand the ideology of Jewish Emancipation as it was originally formulated by liberal European Christians. As opposed to racist antisemites who claimed that what was wrong with the Jews was biological and immutable, the "liberals" held that everything despicable about Jews in their eyes was a product of the material conditions within which Jews had to live and, especially, a result of the oppression that they suffered at the hands of Christians. A further cause of the degraded and decadent state of the Jews was their hanging on to a primitive and "Oriental" way of life. The solution to the "Jewish problem," according to a liberal like Christian Wilhelm Dohm, was for Jews to give up their primitive, "Oriental" distinctiveness and become "civilized."[25] Then they would show manly virtues and engage in such manly practices as dueling and soldiering, the civic duties and privileges of every citizen. Dohm's *Concerning the Amelioration of the Civil Status of the Jews* (1781) bears interesting analogies to Macaulay's "Minute on Indian Education," which set out infamously to produce a class of people, "Indian in blood and colour, but English in taste, in

23. Rathenau, letter.
24. To get a sense of how revolutionary Herzl's point was, we need to realize that remaining (becoming) fully German and leaving Germany were considered antithetical (mutually exclusive) options for German Jews—"*Nur zweierlei ist möglich: entweder: auswandern; oder: deutsch werden*" (either to emigrate or to remain German) (Ernst Lissauer, quoted in M. Goldstein, "German Jewry's," 246)—while Herzl held that only by leaving would German Jews become completely German!
25. Kornberg, *Theodor*, 16–19.

opinions, in morals, and in intellect."[26] *The "emancipation" of the Jews is thus functionally akin to a colonization.*

This view of the Jewish condition was completely taken over by Herzl, who was more than prepared to be a member of the class of those who would civilize the Jewish masses. In 1882 he was prepared to agree with all of the charges leveled against "the Jews" by the anti-semite Eugen Dühring, charges of crookedness, lack of ethical serious-ness, and parasitism. His only disagreement with Dühring was that while the former considered these to be biological characteristics of the Jews, Herzl considered them entirely the product of the Jewish environ-ment. For Herzl, the Talmud and all that it contained and produced was but "the product of an unnatural, imposed isolation from the main-stream of humanity, the pathetic consolation of distressed spirits."[27] There were other Jewish readings of the Jewish past: enlightened and learned Rabbis of Vienna considered Jewish culture in Europe the prod-uct of a fertile interchange between talmudic textuality and practices and the European culture as it developed around the Jews and as they contributed to it. Thus, "in emphasizing Judaism's Oriental character and foreignness to Europe, Herzl was closer to anti-Jewish polemi-cists."[28] For Herzl explicitly, as I have suggested above, and for Freud when we read between the lines, that which distinguishes Jews from gentiles is a deformation: "For Herzl, Jewish distinctiveness and dis-figurement were one and the same."[29]

Freud had expressed a desire in the "Myops" dream that his children would be educated in such a fashion that they would be able to freely cross the border into gentile society (see previous chapter). He stopped quite short, however, of desiring that they convert. He wished them, somehow, to remain loyal to some memory of Jewish identity, as long as it did not distinguish them in any way from gentiles. This was ulti-mately the solution that Herzl arrived at, the solution known as Zion-ism, but before getting there he had tried thought experiments with other means of turning Jews into gentiles and thus of having the Jews disappear as an independent cultural entity.

Herzl wrote in his diaries of his plan (of 1893!) to save the Jews via

26. Quoted in Bhabha, *Location,* 87.
27. Kornberg, *Theodor,* 20.
28. Kornberg, *Theodor,* 20.
29. Kornberg, *Theodor,* 24.

mass conversion. This remarkable and bizarre text will repay extended quotation:

> About two years ago I wanted to solve the Jewish Question, at least in Austria, with the help of the Catholic Church. I wished to gain access to the Pope ... and say to him: Help us against the antisemites and I will start a great movement for the free and honorable conversion of Jews to Christianity.
>
> Free and honorable by virtue of the fact that the leaders of this movement—myself in particular—would remain Jews and as such would propagate conversion to the faith of the majority. The conversion was to take place in broad daylight, Sundays at noon, in Saint Stephen's Cathedral, with festive processions and amidst the pealing of bells. Not in shame, as individuals have converted up to now, but with proud gestures. And because the Jewish leaders would remain Jews, escorting the people only to the threshold of the church and themselves staying outside, the whole performance was to be elevated by a touch of great candor.
>
> We, the steadfast men, would have constituted the last generation. We would still have adhered to the faith of our fathers. But we would have made Christians of our young sons before they reached the age of independent decision, after which conversion looks like an act of cowardice or careerism. ... I could see myself dealing with the Archbishop of Vienna; in imagination I stood before the Pope—both of them were very sorry that I wished to do no more than remain part of the last generation of Jews—and sent this slogan of mingling of the races flying across the world.[30]

This text reveals brilliantly fundamental and critically significant elements in Herzl's thought-world. The only problem with which he is concerned is the problem of Jewish honor and "acceptance," obviously not the problem of cultural survival. In the very text which becomes the foundation stone of Zionism, *The Jewish State,* Herzl indeed wrote, "I referred previously to our 'assimilation.' I do not for a moment wish to imply that I desire such an end. Our national character is too glorious in history and, in spite of every degradation, too noble to make its annihilation desirable." Upon such statements is the myth of a Herzlian conversion back to Judaism founded, but in the very next sentence, he writes: "Though perhaps we *could* succeed in vanishing without a trace into the surrounding peoples, if they would let us be for just two generations. But they will not let us be. ... *Only* pressure drives us back to our own; *only* hostility stamps us ever again as strangers."[31] To find a

---

30. Herzl, *Complete Diaries,* 7.

31. Herzl, *Jewish State,* 251. In his recent, smart book on assimilation, Barry Rubin explicitly opposes and objects to this offensive formulation but delicately does not indi-

way to preserve Jewish difference in a creative, vital manner was never in the program at all, not in the beginning nor at the end. The scheme was ever to find a way for Jews to assume their proper status as proud, manly, warlike people—just like everybody else. Herzl's most stirring statement: "We are one people," carries its immediate disavowal: "Our enemies have made us one whether we will or not." The suggestion is clear that if only allowed to, we would have disappeared long ago, and indeed Herzl says so explicitly.[32]

There is no more efficient mode of facilitating Jewish disappearance than actual conversion. As Kornberg shows, this "solution" to the Jewish problem had been a frequent one in the writings of assimilationist Jews who believed that "whatever differentiates men, also divides them." That being the case, the best solution would be for Jews to abandon that which differentiates them from other men, since Judaism was now "worn-out and out of date."[33] Herzl had adopted such notions as early as 1883, and he continues them here in his call for a "mingling of the races." In contrast to previous biographers of Herzl who considered this idea of his as the swan song of his assimilationism, Kornberg shows how it was preparation for his "Zionism." Herzl had come to the conclusion that antisemitism was essentially justified by the behavior of the Jews, especially of course the despised *Ostjuden,* and that only a radical act of self-transformation would win the esteem of Christendom for his degenerate compatriots. As we have seen, his only argument was with the modern versions of antisemitism that viewed the degradation of the Jews as a biological characteristic and therefore unchangeable. With classical Christian anti-Judaism, which considered the "Jewish problem" effectively a necessary product of Jewish refusal to accept Christ, he was apparently quite comfortable. The bold act of mass conversion, carried out in a decorous way, bravely and openly, was to be just such an act of Jewish self-transformation.

His curious notion that this project was somehow more "honorable" if the leaders remained Jewish is, in fact, of a piece with the whole affective and ideological endeavor, because the entire point of this drastic exercise would be sacrificed if the Jews were to appear cowardly, to ap-

cate who the author of it is: "Only assimilating Jews who no longer knew these self-affirming aspects could claim that external pressure alone prevented the Jews from disappearing" (Rubin, *Assimilation,* 6).

32. Herzl, *Jewish State,* 238.

33. Theodor Gomperz, quoted in Kornberg, *Theodor,* 115. On Gomperz, see Beller, "Otto," 94–96.

pear as if they were converting out of an "unmanly" and dishonorable fear or opportunism. By the leaders remaining faithful, and especially by enacting the conversion of children who have not yet reached the age of decision, somehow, it is imagined, any imputation of "cowardice or careerism" would be entirely avoided. We have here the very essence of Herzl's cultural fix. Kornberg considers Herzl's dual impulses toward assimilation and toward Jewish self-assertion as symptoms of extreme ambivalence. I would suggest rather that they are symptomatic of a double bind situation that he (and other colonials, *mutatis mutandis*) find themselves in without any easy breakout. The antisemitic charges against Jews that Herzl had internalized were of cowardice and opportunism, lack of principle in the face of external pressure. Kornberg himself documents such representations: "In one display of wit, a Viennese Jew claimed that it was his *Germanic* sense of loyalty and pride that prevented him from converting to Christianity," and another refers to baptism as Jewish nonsense.[34] By not converting, the Jew converts; but by converting he remains Jewish!

No wonder Herzl manifests a paradox. The dual impulses to transform Jews into gentiles and to be self-assertive in the face of antisemitism are thus both parts of the same answer to the same problem, one that leaves Jews damned if they do and damned if they don't. Conversion, which is by definition not self-assertion, would seem to be a sign of just such cowardice and careerism, while self-assertion without conversion would lead to a continuation of the same kind of antisemitic pressure that had led to the degradation in the first place. The problem was how to find a mode of becoming indistinguishable from gentiles without appearing cowardly. Herzl's initial solution was for the leaders to convert the simple people and children, while they themselves remained tenaciously Jewish and presumably suffered the consequences bravely. The ultimate solution, however, was to be Zionism.

In 1894, again according to Herzl's own account, Jewish difference was for him only a negative and unwilled condition, imposed on Jews by antisemites: "I understand what anti-Semitism is about. We Jews have maintained ourself, even if through no *fault* of our own, as a foreign body among the various nations. In the ghetto we have taken on a number of anti-social qualities. Our character has been corrupted by oppression, and it must be restored through some other kind of pressure. . . . All these sufferings rendered us ugly and transformed our

---

34. Kornberg, *Theodor*, 119, emphasis in original.

character which had in earlier times been proud and magnificent. After all, we once were *men* who knew how to defend the state in time of war."[35] The maintenance of a separate Jewish cultural life is something that Herzl could refer to as a "fault." And some kind of "pressure" would be necessary to undo Jewish difference, which, for Herzl is only "corruption" and "anti-social qualities." By 1894, Herzl had become convinced that this "other kind of pressure" could not be conversion — not, however, because he had undergone a transformation and "returned to his People," but because Christian friends of the Jews had responded extremely negatively to the suggestion. The notion of what constituted a proud and magnificent *Volk* never changed. The tension here is palpable; once more, we are faced with the paradox that the very definitions of what constituted regaining *Jewish* honor for Herzl involved a virtual transformation into Germans. Such tensions are what we have found in Freud and are to be found in Spinoza as well, who in a fascinating passage, writes: "The mark of circumcision is also, I think, of great importance in this connexion; so much so that in my view it alone will preserve the Jewish people for all time; indeed, did not the principles of their religion make them effeminate [*effeminarent*] I should be convinced that some day when the opportunity arises . . . they will erect their state once more [*suum imperium erectūros*], and that God will chose them afresh."[36] What a double bind! That which preserves the Jewish people is that which has "emasculated" them and prevents them from erecting their state. The association, however, of statehood with manliness is ineluctable.

Otto Weininger was to write: "Citizenship is an un-Jewish thing, and there has never been and never will be a true Jewish State. . . . The true conception of the State is foreign to the Jew, because he, like the woman, is wanting in personality, his failure to grasp the idea of true society is due to his lack of a free intelligible ego. Like women, Jews tend to adhere together."[37] Statehood would show, then, that Weininger was wrong, that Jews were not "like the woman." With ideas like this

35. Herzl, *Complete Diaries*, 9–10, emphasis added. As Michael Berkowitz points out, much of the enthusiasm of Jews for World War I, on both sides, had to do with the opportunities that it provided to demonstrate their manliness and thus win honor in the *Männerbund*. At that time, many Western Jews still imagined that Jews could "earn respect and acceptance through changing their own attitudes and behavior" and becoming "real men" (Berkowitz, *Western Jewry*, chapter 1).

36. Geller, "Paleontological View," 59, citing Spinoza; see also J. Boyarin and D. Boyarin, "Self-Exposure."

37. Weininger, *Sex*, 307–8.

blowing in the wind, no wonder the Zionist Herzl did not have his own son circumcised. No wonder also that Freud, in search of a Jewish masculinity, an antidote to circumcision and its uncanniness, finds the erection of a state.

In 1894 Herzl wrote *Das neue Ghetto*.[38] Much of the plot turns around a cultural motive with which Herzl, like many other Austro-Hungarian Jews of his time, was obsessed: the duel. The protagonist, a thinly disguised representation of himself, has provoked a gentile cavalry officer and then refused to duel him, because he was preoccupied at the time with a dying father. This incident had taken place five years before the opening of the play. To a gentile friend who dismisses the importance of the event, he says: "I haven't been able to forget it. Not I—you see, I'm a Jew. You and your kind can take that kind of thing in stride. When you, Franz Wurzlechner, settle such a run-in peaceably, that makes you a solid clear-headed chap. Me—me, Jacob Samuel—it makes a coward."[39] An even more unsettling moment is provided by a scene in which the same Franz Wurzlechner has come to "break up" with his former best friend, because the latter has married into a too-Jewish (in our parlance) family, and "It's you—you've changed. Your environment is different—the company you keep. I don't belong there—with these Rheinbergs, Wassersteins, the whole lot of them— they rub me the wrong way. And since your marriage I'm likely to run into them at any time in your home—there's no escaping them. It's not your fault—they're your people." Samuel's response is to understand, thank his "friend" for his frankness, and detail what he had learned from him over the years: "I learned big things and little—inflections, gestures, how to bow without being obsequious, how to stand up without seeming defiant—all sorts of things."[40] Jacob goes on to provide the usual Herzlian litany: Of course, you're right, we are despicable, but it's all your fault. There we have it, the perfect representation of the Austrian Jew, admiring and adapting gentile mores, and then hurt when it doesn't work, when it's not enough—in short, Theodor Herzl.

Wurzlechner is an allegory of liberal Austrian society which had at first encouraged Jewish Emancipation and now, in the 1890s, was becoming antisemitic again. In Jacob's response, although it is a full year

38. The text that I cite here is the slightly abridged version published in Lewisohn, *Theodor*.
39. Herzl, *New Ghetto*, 163.
40. Herzl, *New Ghetto*, 168, 169.

before his "conversion," Herzl already reveals the affect—both pretty
and ugly—that will be the motor for his Zionism: "Even if you had
given me a choice between you and Wasserstein [an extremely unattractive Jewish speculator, that is, a sort of *Ostjude* who even *Mauschels*,
speaks with a Yiddish accent][41]—well I've already made it. My place is
with Wasserstein, rich or poor. I can reproach him no more than I can
praise you. You each stand where history has placed you."[42] This highly
equivocal identification with Wasserstein is exactly what will reappear
a year later as: "We are one people. Our enemies have made us one
whether we will or not" in the Zionist manifesto. Moreover, it is this
most contemptible Wasserstein, the Eastern Jew who paradoxically
"carries the germs of Jewish redemption,"[43] just as Herzl was to realize
that Russian Jewry was the key to his Zionist plans. Not only Jacob
Samuel but other characters as well are made to voice sentiments that
would reappear in *The Jewish State* as Herzl's own. Thus Herzl has the
rabbi in the play opine: "Antisemitism isn't all bad. As the movement
gains force, I observe a return to religion. Antisemitism is a warning to
us to stand together, not to abandon the God of our fathers, as many
have done."[44] How far is this from Herzl's idea in his Zionist tract that
Jews have remained Jews only because of antisemitism? The major difference is that the rabbi considers the result to have been desirable,
while Herzl is at best ambivalent.

Following the "breakup" with Wurzlechner, Jacob Samuel reaches
for other ways to break out of the "new ghetto." His first turn is to
support the striking workers in a coal mine in which his wealthy
brother-in-law is investing.[45] This move in the play parallels Herzl's second great scheme for achieving Jewish honor (and thus "acceptance"
and disappearance), the plan for mass Jewish conversion to socialism.
Kornberg writes: "In unpublished notes, he [Herzl] called socialism the
answer to antisemitism in German, and baptism the answer in Austria,
evidence that he was thinking more of the method and style of Jewish
action, rather than of its ideological content."[46] Even more to the point,
"socialism" was for Herzl more an issue of the expression of *ressentiment* than anything else. Jews and the workers were both oppressed;

41. Gilman, *Jewish Self-Hatred.*
42. Herzl, *New Ghetto,* 169.
43. Kornberg, *Theodor,* 138.
44. Herzl, *New Ghetto,* 164–65.
45. Herzl, *New Ghetto,* 178.
46. Kornberg, *Theodor,* 122.

they would make common cause in promoting violence against the state. Herzl had seen the dignity that the oppressed workers achieved through their radical activity and devoutly wished for Jews to achieve that same self-transformation into proud fighters for a cause—almost any cause at all would do. If Jews were not to be allowed to defend the state, well then they could attack it. "In proposing that Jews turn to socialism he mentioned, indifferent to their goals, parties reformist in action and revolutionary in rhetoric, like the Austrian and German Social Democrats, and terrorist groups like the violent wing of French anarchism."[47]

Although Herzl himself was *not* a socialist (at the same time that he was advocating Jewish conversion to socialism in Germany, he was attacking the program of socialism itself), he was, it seems, from the characterization of Wasserstein in the play, and even Rheinberg, Jacob Samuel's relatively decent brother-in-law, as genuinely disgusted with parvenu Jewish capitalism as was Marx.[48] The difference between them is that where Marx was genuinely motivated by the plight of the workers, for Herzl it seems to have been ultimately the vulgarity of the Jews and the way that it prevented their full acceptance by the gentile elites that disturbed him.[49] Herzl, in a letter, described Jews as "harmless, contemptible fellow human beings, not to say fellow citizens, lacking honor and thus bent on profit, become crafty through prolonged oppression."[50]

The case that I am trying to build is that for Herzl (as for Freud in another key), it was primarily passivity that was the blemish that caused the degradation and degeneration. The very "Slavic" workers who in the play come to see Jacob and express their anger at the terrible

47. Kornberg, *Theodor*, 122.
48. The novel *Debit and Credit* by Gustav Freytag makes an illuminating parallel to Herzl's play. Many of the same stock figures, including the "good" Jew, appear in the antisemitic text as well. For discussion, see Mosse, "Image," 222–24.
49. Cuddihy's claim that all Jewish socialism is a bourgeois Jewish response to the problem of the uncouth Eastern Jew (Cuddihy, *Ordeal,* 5) fits Herzl much better than it does Marx. Herzl did, however, have a genuine concern for the safety of miners, as shown by his plan that all mines would be nationalized in the state of the Jews, in order that "mine workers should not be subject to an entrepreneur's parsimony. The State will not economize on safety measures" (Herzl, *Complete Diaries,* 162). Second, he also manifested a genuine liberalism in his proposal that the Jewish State would enshrine the seven-hour working day even on its flag. My argument is not that Herzl was some sort of reactionary but that he was a liberal—like John Stuart Mill, for example. Given the state of contemporary Israeli society, even a liberal colonialist vision would be preferable, but that is Cold Comfort Kibbutz, in my view. See also Elon, *Herzl,* 38, 118.
50. Quoted in Kornberg, *Theodor*, 124.

conditions in which they labor, can thus almost be read as a screen for the *Ostjuden* whom radical *activity* would transform into dignified, masculine human beings. Carl Schorske has discovered a key issue when he points to Herzl's association of radical politics and sexuality. In a feuilleton, Herzl had written of the anarchist Ravachol: "The common murderer rushes to the brothel with his loot. Ravachol has discovered another kind of lust: the voluptuousness of a great idea and martyr-dom,"[51] and Schorske sees that Herzl descries the same "voluptuous-ness" in socialist action that he had seen in the anarchist leader, the very same transformation from degraded passivity into virile activity.[52] Since the main—if not the only—meaning of the activity was activity itself and the masculinity that it conferred, it hardly mattered at all whether it was socialism, anarchism, or finally colonialism that composed the content, for it was the violence that was pivotal. Almost any "respect-able" violence that Jews would turn to would restore their dignity and honor, their masculinity, an almost ideal type of *goyim naches*.

This harsh interpretation can be verified by a closer reading of the play. The historical parable of Moses of Mainz, related by the rabbi at a crucial plot-turn in the play forms the central trope and motive force from thence till the end. Jacob Samuel, like Herzl and the assimilated Jews of Austria, has been rebuffed in his attempt to win simple accep-tance from his friend, the aristocratic gentile, Franz Wurzlechner. And, we will remember, he had related his avoidance of a duel with the arro-gant Count Von Schramm. Although Franz pooh-poohs this "cowardice" as grounds for shame, it is soon after that he renounces his friendship with the now "too-Jewish" Jacob, claiming that it is the association with the capitalists, Wasserstein and Rheinberg, that disturbs him.

In Act III, after Jacob has heard from the miners of their plight, gone there, supported their strike, and then witnessed a terrible mine col-lapse, he intends to confront his brother-in-law who has invested in the mine. At first we would think that it is genuine leftist sentiment that moves Jacob, as he describes his horror of the scene of destruction:

> Indescribable, beyond words. When I got there, they were just bringing up the bodies. Outside the pit entrance the women stood weeping and moaning. Some of them never said a word. I could hardly look at them. I tell you, I'll remember the scene as long as I live. Everything black in black, as though in mourning. The tattered clothes, all black with coal dust, and a sharp au-

51. From the *Neue Freie Presse* of April 29, 1892, quoted by Elon, *Herzl*, 105.
52. Schorske, *Fin-de-Siècle Vienna*, 154.

tumn breeze making the thin bodies shiver under the rags. . . . And the children. . . . They'll ride down just like their fathers who were being brought up—they'll push the iron trolleys before they're in their teens, for forty-five kreuzer a day. . . . Later on, when they become pickmen, they'll lie on their sides in the holes, hacking at the seam in the dark. One slip with the lamp, and the firedamp comes crashing about their ears. This time it was the water. It was a holocaust! . . . Yet tomorrow, they'll go down again. If they don't they'll just starve to death up above.[53]

In response, the rabbi recounts the story of Moses of Mainz as a cautionary tale. In 5143 (1383 C.E.), a certain Moses ben Abraham, while studying the Talmud, hears a cry of distress from outside the walls of the ghetto. He goes out to help the gentile in distress. "When he failed to return, his mother grew more and more anxious until at last she went after him. She too did not return. The next morning Moses was found stabbed to death just outside the open gate of the Ghetto. By his side sat his mother, an unearthly smile on her lips. She had gone mad."[54] Jacob's response to this moral tale of caution, this plea for Jews to stay within the ghetto, is "I say my heart goes out to Moses of Mainz, that I am proud of him. All of us should take him as an example. The cry for help is sometimes genuine." The rabbi replies, "But we are too weak," and Jacob's final word is, "What merit is there when the strong show compassion?"

Our expectation after this impassioned speech of radical indignation and Jacob's response to the "parable" is that the resolution of the play will be indeed a socialist one, that the play would end with a glorious vision of workers and new Jews arising together to create a brave new world. The way out of the ghetto is through class solidarity between subaltern Jews and subaltern gentiles (Slavs and workers). That, however, is not Herzl's enterprise. Not only have the workers been harmed through the capitalists' manipulations but so has the "old money" been attacked. The hereditary owner of the mine, the same Count Von Schramm, has also been done out of his inheritance. Jacob has come not to convince his brother-in-law to support the workers and ameliorate their conditions but to convince him to make good the losses to the Count for the sake of the honor of the Jews, of course. The brother-in-law cannot, even had he wanted to, because he has sold short and the real parvenu capitalist, Wasserstein, the *Ostjude,* has cornered the stock.

53. Herzl, *New Ghetto,* 182.
54. Herzl, *New Ghetto,* 183.

When Schramm comes in to demand financial satisfaction from Rheinberg, who has left, Jacob decides to defend his brother-in-law. His motives are unclear, since a few minutes earlier he had been condemning him. He attacks Schramm in the very terms that Rheinberg had proposed, namely, that it was his own incompetence in "playing the market" that had defeated him, and, moreover: "While you indulged your aristocratic pastimes, your slaves drudged for you underground"[55]—in other words the "socialist" theme *redivivus*. The following exchange is astonishing:

> JACOB: I've seen them with my own eyes. I've seen the widows too, and the orphans, who must go hungry now, because their fathers died for the Honorable Count Von Schramm! I don't think you even attended the funeral!
> SCHRAMM: I know you did. I have it on good authority.
> JACOB: I was there.
> SCHRAMM: Yes, for the strike too! It was because the miners refused to go down that the water backed up. At first I didn't understand what you were after. What's the Jew up to, I asked myself?
> JACOB: The Jew was doing his Christian duty.[56]

Of course, Schramm does not believe in Jacob's honor and accuses him of simply having been in league with his brother-in-law to make sure that the bottom fell out of the mine stock that the brother-in-law had sold short. Schramm calls Jacob a "dirty Jew" and says that, once more, as he had before, Jacob will "crawl." However, this time is different. Jacob slaps him in the face. Jacob is certain that Schramm will challenge him to a duel, and the rabbi intones as the curtain falls, "Like Moses of Mainz!" Were Jacob going out to fight for the workers, the simile would make sense to me. The Rabbi would be saying "Don't worry about the goyim; don't save them," and Herzl-Jacob would be responding, "No, the Jew must be a man with common human *Mitleid und Ehre* [compassion and honor]." As it is, with Jacob only going out to fight a duel, the semblance which Jacob and the rabbi—and Herzl— see entirely escapes me. There is no one in distress who is to be saved here but only a point of honor that must be rescued with violence. This is where Herzl's energy lies. "Socialism" has nothing to do with *Mitleid* but only with *Männlichkeit* [manliness].

The denouement confirms this. In the fourth act the duel finally

55. Herzl, *New Ghetto*, 187.
56. Herzl, *New Ghetto*, 188.

takes place. Jacob Samuel has become a Jewish Siegfried.[57] Wurzlechner, reconciled with his friend, has brought the dying man home.

JACOB: Where is Franz?

WURZLECHNER: (Moves to his side.) Here I am.

JACOB: Thank you. . . . Franz! I want to stay here . . . with my books. Remember what I wanted? . . . Fellowship!

DR. BICHLER: Don't talk so much.

JACOB: (Caresses Franz's hand.) Good old Franz! . . . Tell the Rabbi . . . like Moses of Mainz. (Mumbles.) And by the side of the body sat his mother, an unearthly smile on her lips. (Lapses into unconsciousness.) . . .

JACOB: (Comes to.) Tell the Rabbi!

WURZLECHNER: What does he want the Rabbi for? The last sacraments?

WASSERSTEIN: No, we Jews die without sacraments. . . .

JACOB: (Cries out weakly.) Father! Mother!

HERR SAMUEL: Kobi, here we are.

JACOB: Help me up! . . . (Takes his mother's hand and kisses it.) Forgive me this sorrow, Mother. . . . (Kisses his father's hand.) *You can understand, Father! You're a man!* . . . (Raises his voice.) O Jews, my brethren, they won't let you live again— until. . . . I want to—get—out! (Louder.) Out—of—the— Ghetto![58]

Just as for Freud, it is the duel that restores the Jew's honor and gets him out of the ghetto, not his willingness to take risks for the sake of downtrodden others. Gender is encoded right on the surface of this scene as well. The father will understand because he is a man, not a fearful, female Jew; he too would understand that his son has performed his "Christian duty" by engaging in a duel to the death with someone who has insulted him and his people. In the draft of the play, the continuation of the sentence, broken off after "until" is "until you have learned how to die."[59] It was a commonplace of antisemites that Jews did not know how to die with honor.[60] The contempt that Zionists in Palestine had for the Jews killed by the Nazis (and for survivors) in concentration camps is, I put forth, a direct descendant of this antisemitic representation, but those who died in the hopeless Warsaw Ghetto "Rebellion" were glorified as "New Jews," as the Polish branch of the "Palmach," the Zionist shock troops[61] (see Plate 13). They had "learned

57. Kornberg, *Theodor*, 171.
58. Herzl, *New Ghetto*, 192–93, emphasis added; some acting instructions deleted.
59. Quoted in Kornberg, *Theodor*, 171.
60. Mosse, *Nationalism*, 149–50.
61. One of the most harrowing examples of evidence of this antisemitic contempt

Plate 13.   The Ghetto Warrior and the Fighter for Freedom. In the Palmach Haggada, 1948, the weapons-bearer becomes the righteous son. (Collection of the author.)

to die." Over and over again, Zionist writers of the 1940s wrote in
near-fascist terms of the "beautiful death" of the Warsaw rebels and the
"ugly death" of the martyrs of the camps. This represents identification
with the oppressor in one of its most naked and obvious forms, and it
has its effects in imitation of that oppressor as well.[62]

The New Ghetto was written only one year before *The Jewish State*
was conceived, and if we do not accept the myth of a sudden and total
conversion of Pauline proportions, then the two texts must be seen in
their contiguity. Contrary to later Zionist myths, Herzl himself wrote
that the play was "the young fruit of *The Jewish State*."[63] We have seen,
moreover, how compatible the two texts are. The play does also represent, no doubt, the psychic damage that Jews suffer through assimilation and, moreover, does so in terms that are not entirely different from
the terms of Frantz Fanon's *Black Skins, White Masks*.[64] Kornberg has
phrased it well: "Embracing the material culture, they had internalized
its Jewish stereotypes. Assimilation had bred Jewish self-contempt and
an idealization of gentiles, persuaded them that Jewishness carried a
taint of materialism and cowardice, and robbed them of self-respect.
For this reason, Jews themselves had to alter the terms of gentile acceptance."[65]

Repeatedly in the play, Herzl identifies the very attempt to become
one with the gentiles as yet another source of Jewish servility. After his
rebuff by Wurzlechner, Jacob realizes that his friendship toward the
gentile had been based on servility, not civility, on gratitude at being
thrown a crumb of acceptance. My point, however, is that this is not a
new insight of Herzl's but yet another rendition of the conversion para-

---

that Israelis had for the "passive victims" of the Nazis is the slang term "soap" to refer
to the refugees, reflecting the incorporation of antisemitic ideology into the Zionist imaginary. For an important critical reflection of this social reality in Israeli fiction, see Kaniuk,
Adam, 132.

62. Zerubavel writes: "The Zionist suppression of positive aspects of exilic life to
promote the centrality of the people-land bond was reinforced by its denial of centuries
of Palestinian life in that land. This double denial made it easier to reshape the period of
Exile as a temporary regression between the two national periods, metaphorically sus-
pending time and space in order to appropriate both into the Zionist commemorative
narrative. Ironically, the recovery of the nation's roots in the ancient past implied playing
down its roots in Exile as well as the renunciation of the Palestinians' roots in the same
land." Zerubavel, *Recovered*, 22. See also Raz-Krokotzkin, "Exile"; and Zertal, "Sacrificed," especially the chilling quotations on 35.

63. Herzl, *Complete Diaries*, 2, 612.

64. I am not the first who has sensed some affinity between Fanon and Herzl; see
Elon, *Herzl*, 140.

65. Kornberg, *Theodor*, 131.

dox: how to become like them without being servile, ingratiating, and false. But not only is it the case that this problematic as explored in *The New Ghetto* is exactly the same one that plagued Herzl at the time of the conversion scheme, it remains as well the problem that his Zionism sets out to solve. Herzlian Zionism is the ultimate project for an honorable conversion of the Jews to Christianity, understood as it always was for Herzl as not a religion, but as *Kultur* itself, as civilization. When Herzl argued to the Grand Duke of Baden that Zionism was an extension of German *Kultur*,[66] this was not, I fear, for diplomatic effect. The only models that Herzl can mobilize for the very alteration "of the terms of gentile acceptance" still involve mimesis of gentile patterns of honor, that is, masculinity.

In this respect I quite dissent from Kornberg who seems to read Wasserstein as the hero of the play and the play as revealing that "the seeds of Jewish transformation existed in the Jewish character itself."[67] It seems to me that, at best, the *Ostjuden*, the Wassersteins, are to be admiring supporters and beneficiaries of Herzl's transformation of the Jewish character. I am convinced that when Herzl has Wasserstein say, "Yes, I buy and I sell—everything revolves around money. But there is something else too—honor," this is almost Tartuffian and hardly an attempt to "underline Wasserstein's noble side."[68] Wasserstein supports whatever is winning, and when "honor" seems to be successful, then it is honor that he shall have too. It is true, as we have seen, that Jacob expresses solidarity with the not unredeemable Wasserstein—a solidarity borne, however, of the fact that gentiles simply will not *let him* differentiate himself from the *Ostjude*. That indeed Herzl had truly understood by 1894. But this solidarity results in yet another version of the civilizing mission, directed this time by Western Jews at Eastern Jews.[69]

The problem continues to be for Herzl that the Jews have been released too precipitously and too late from the ghetto and are unable to

---

66. Elon, *Herzl*, 266.
67. Kornberg, *Theodor*, 145.
68. Pace Kornberg, *Theodor*, 147.
69. The leader of the German Reform movement, Avraham Geiger wrote: "We can term as 'of universal Jewish concern' only whatever goes on among those Jews who reside among the civilized nations, particularly in Germany, and who will later be emulated and followed by those who now are still among the uneducated" (quoted in Aschheim, *Brothers*, 17). As Aschheim makes clear, this attitude was by no means limited to the non-Orthodox. My overall point then is not that Herzl was somehow differentiated from most German-speaking Jews in his colonialism toward the *Ostjude* but that, pace Zionist mythology, he was hardly at all different at the end of the day. See also Mosse, "Image," 226.

fully assimilate. Their mimicry is too palpable and too pathetic.[70] Herzl had not here escaped the stereotype and self-contempt of the assimilated Jew, and never would. What he did eventually discover was a way for Jews to assimilate, while escaping from the painful need to seek gentile acceptance on a day-to-day basis, by rediscovering Jewish "honor," not merely by stripping off the distorting effects of antisemitism in Europe—which was not going to happen so easily—but by going somewhere else.[71] Actual return to the biblical glory days of Jewish independence—and imperialism—it was this that would cure the Jews of Jewishness, for Jewishness remained despised. Zionism is then only a logical extension of the liberal Dohm's solution to the Jewish problem. If Jews had indeed been courageous, warlike, manly, and patriotic in the "golden age" of the biblical kingdom, then the solution is to restore that kingdom itself, a Camelot in the desert, or rather, Vienna on the Mediterranean. At the end of the first draft of the play, the transformed Jacob reminds Wasserstein of a Maccabee.[72] We have already seen the assimilationist meaning of that appellation. It is merely a code word for *Judentum* converted into *Deutschtum,* almost identical to Freud's converted *Judentum.*

Herzlian Zionism, I suggest, is dueling carried on by other means, yet another desperate attempt to win Jewish honor and cultural disappearance as a deformed alterity by "doing our Christian duty." In fact, Zionism didn't quite replace dueling for Herzl. In his diary entry for June 9, 1895, Herzl wrote of his Zionist state, "I need dueling in order to have real officers and to impart a tone of French refinement to good society."[73] He did, however, allow for a possibility that in certain circumstances, instead of a duel, the "dueling tribunal" would decree something that he called a "secret verdict," because, after all: "Since only men of honor can fight a duel, the loser in any case would be the state, and for a long time to come it will need every able-bodied man. Therefore these duelers will be sent out on dangerous missions which the state happens to require. It may be cholera vaccination or at other

70. On Jewish mimicry, see Geller, "Mice," particularly with reference to Herzl. Geller, however, maintains the position that Herzl eventually dropped the mimicry solution to the Jewish Question, whereas I am arguing that he merely perfected it.

71. I have subsequently seen that David Biale had made substantially the same point. Of Herzl he has written: "When he became a convert to Jewish nationalism, he envisioned creating a European-style state for the Jews outside of Europe. *The goal remained the same: to abolish Jewish uniqueness*" (*Power,* 132, emphasis added).

72. Quoted in Kornberg, *Theodor,* 146.

73. Herzl, *Complete Diaries,* 1, 58.

times the fighting of a national enemy. *In this way the risk of death from the duel will be retained.*"[74] The contempt that traditional Jewry—including many in "assimilated" Vienna and Berlin, such as Arthur Schnitzler and Stefan Zweig—would have manifested for such senseless adoration of the risk of death is palpable.[75] Even for acculturated Jews as they were, such nonsense was still *goyim naches.*

Many of these same Jews understood the affective basis of Herzl's Zionism in contempt for Jews as well. Fifteen years after the production of *The New Ghetto,* Arthur Schnitzler has a Jewish character in his novel *The Road to the Open* say: "I myself have only succeeded up to the present in making the acquaintance of one genuine antisemite. I'm afraid I am bound to admit . . . that it was a well known Zionist leader."[76] Herzl was indeed an antisemite, as were many Viennese Jews of the fin de siècle.[77] He adopted all of the most vicious stereotypes of Jew hatred but employed an almost classic psychological move, splitting, in order to separate himself from them. There were two kinds of Jews in the world. The "true Jews," the manly, honorable, dueling, fighting Jacob Samuels, were the Zionists. The others were the tribe of *Mauschel,* crooked, "low and repugnant," frightened, unresponsive to beauty, passive, queer, effeminate, the very embodiment of Otto Weininger's, Fichte's—dubbed "Eisenmenger the second" by a Jewish contemporary[78]—and Wagner's description of what Jews were. Note the struc-

---

74. Herzl, *Complete Diaries,* 1, 58, emphasis added; see also the rich discussion in Kornberg, *Theodor,* 66–71.

75. Herzl, *Complete Diaries,* 1, 58, 69. Obviously, cholera vaccinating and even warmaking under certain circumstances are not negative activities; it is the encoding of them as of value not so much for themselves but as signifiers of manliness, like dueling, that I am pointing to here. Cholera vaccinating is produced by Herzl as only a poor substitute for dueling, borne of unfortunate necessity to keep valiant young men alive given their shortage in the Jewish polity.

76. Quoted in Kornberg, *Theodor,* 154. See also above, 238 n. 60.

77. My point, obviously, is not that Herzl was unusual in his self-hatred—indeed the phenomenon was so well known as to merit a name—but only that his Zionism was a manifestation of this self-hatred and not an antithesis to it. Zionist writers consistently obscure this point by such circumlocutions as: "Some of his [Kraus's] diatribes against Jewish scribes and businessmen echoed those of Herzl's, but in his hateful bitterness Kraus sounded like a precursor of Nazi propaganda" (Elon, *Herzl,* 306)—and Herzl's *Mauschel* doesn't sound like such a precursor? Sander Gilman's *Jewish Self-Hatred* is the classic study of this cultural practice which, I suggest, is typical of the colonial situation. Michael Berkowitz emphasizes that in the Zionist literature of the 1920s, it was the traditional Jews of Jerusalem, "not the Arabs, whom the Zionists presented as the most burdensome obstacle to the flowering of their plan, and whom they treated to their harshest invective" (Berkowitz, *Western Jewry,* chapter 5).

78. Rose, *Wagner,* 8.

tural homology between Herzl's theory of a split in the Jewish people and the double-Moses theory of Freud discussed in the previous chapter.

Herzl was by no means sui generis in this strange combination of self-assertion and self-hatred. Lawrence Baron had already pointed to a similar case of a very prominent German Jew slightly younger than Herzl, Theodor Lessing, who was both a "thinker whose *völkisch* critique of modern society paved the way for Nazi ideology" and a Jew who "advocated Zionism as an antidote for the self-hatred which wracked assimilated German Jews like himself who had internalised the antisemitic attitudes of their host society." Baron remarks that historians have divided Lessing into an early and a later one, the former a Jewish self-hater and the latter (after the shock of World War I) a Jewish patriot. This is analogous (although Baron does not mark the analogy) with Herzl's supposed "conversion" to Zionism: "Yet Lessing's derogatory characterisations of European Jewry reflected the same ideological criteria he used to justify his Zionism. Indeed, he dated his entry into the Zionist movement back to 1900, which was a decade before he penned his most derisive articles about Jews, namely, his descriptive sketches of the Galician Jews he met on his travels. . . . Lessing never saw any discrepancy between his commitment to Zionism and his disparagement of assimilated and unassimilated Jews alike. . . . The exposure of the degeneration of Jews who were either demoralised or coopted by their host societies was part of his broader attack on the material foundations of modern civilization. By highlighting the corruption of Diaspora Jewry, Lessing also demonstrated the need for its regeneration in a Jewish State. . . . Ashamed of his fellow Jews and, unconsciously, of himself, Lessing managed to retain a sense of honour by projecting his romantic ideals on to a future generation of Jews who would build a model organic community which respected the value of both humanity and nature."[79] In this description, Lessing reminds us of both Herzl and Nordau, so we can see that such ideation was not at all uncommon in the moment that founded political Zionism.[80]

---

79. Baron, "Theodor," 323–24.
80. Incidentally, I am not insensible to the charge that my own work has a similar structure in reverse. After all, I am also sharply critical of the way that contemporary Jews live their politics and also hark to a utopian notion of a future Jewish community, and, indeed, I am frequently tarred with the brush of self-hatred. That is, of course, not how I experience myself. Ultimately, I suppose it is not the form but the content of the utopian dream that will have to pass critique, a European "Aryan" set of romantic ideals or a historical critique and opposition to them as the summum bonum of Jewish exis-

Herzl himself realized the complicity of his plan with that of the anti-semites. Both, after all, wanted to rid Europe of the Jews: "The anti-Semites will become our most dependable friends, the anti-Semitic countries our allies."[81] Fichte had already written: "As to giving them civil rights, I see no way other than that of some night cutting off their heads and attaching in their place others in which there is not a single Jewish idea. To protect ourselves from them I see no means other than to conquer for them their promised land and to pack them off there."[82] Within Europe, Fichte thought, the Jews presented a serious obstacle to "brotherhood," and indeed at the 1878 International Conference on Demography, "The Russian delegate, starting from the proposition that a 'certain race tended to multiply faster than others' and thus threatened the numerical dominance of the native populations of its host countries, had urged 'its deportation en masse [laughter] to Jerusalem in order to restore the ancient kingdom of the Jews.'"[83] The kaiser wrote in the margins of his Swiss consul's report on the first Zionist Congress: "I am all in favor of the *kikes* going to Palestine. The sooner they take off the better."[84] Herzl was capable of worrying that the gentiles left behind in Europe might, *quel horreur,* undergo a *Verjudung* (Jewification) after the Jews left, and thus he mobilized one of the most vicious of all antisemitic terms.[85]

Even more appalling, in his essay, "Mauschel," Herzl wrote that this Jewish essence had been produced racially through an admixture: "The irreconcilable, inexplicable antitheses make it seem as though at some dark moment in our history some inferior human material got into our unfortunate people and blended with it. . . . Race! As if the *Jew* and

---

tence. And, of course, my own recreation of this critique and opposition draws as much on my own cultural needs as Lessing's (or Herzl's) drew on theirs.

81. Herzl, *Complete Diaries,* 84.

82. Quoted in Rose, *Wagner,* 9.

83. Quoted in J. Goldstein, "Wandering Jew," 528–29.

84. Elon, *Herzl,* 245. This "support" for Zionism became a virtual topos of the most virulent of European antisemites. Thus the Nazi ideologue Hans F. K. Günther "concluded that Zionism was the one way to secure the future of Judaism, for only it could provide a means for Jews to turn their backs on the 'modern spirit' and 'individualism' and to emphasize family and *Volk,* eugenics and rural life" (Hyams, "Weininger," 160). While it would be worse than scurrilous to condemn Zionism because it was supported by the worst of racists, it is nevertheless instructive that many Zionist representations of the ills of European Jewish life and their cure are exactly identical to those of *völkisch* thinkers. In other words, without ascribing either anti-Jewish or other racism to Zionists necessarily, the fundamental value system—blood and soil—seems to be convergent with that which produced fascism.

85. Herzl, *Complete Diaries,* 178–79; see Aschheim, "Jew."

Mauschel were of the same race."[86] This notorious antisemitic remark is the exact equivalent of Houston Chamberlain's charge that the Jewish race had an "admixture of negro blood," and thus doubly racist in import.[87] The title of Herzl's vulgar antisemitic screed says it all. "Mauschel"—Little Moses—is the German antisemitic equivalent of "*kike*" or "Ikey," and Herzl opens his piece by stating, "Ikey is an antizionist." Mauschel, the *Ostjude,* who is not—even "racially"—a true Jew is an antizionist.[88] Only a Zionist could be a Jew.

In fantasizing that this is how Jews could gain power over their oppressors, Herzl seems to have engaged in the same kind of psychological self-delusion that was Freud's in his interpretation of his dream of "The Man with the Yellow Beard." In this dream, Freud, who is worried about being denied a professorship for antisemitic reasons, imagines his two Jewish colleagues, who had already been denied such appointments, as respectively stupid and crooked. He thus dissociates himself from them, and imagines that he is not like "those" Jews with yellow beards (read *Ostjuden*). Freud writes in his interpretation, "It began to dawn on me that my dream had carried me back from the dreary present to the cheerful hopes of the days of the 'Burger' Ministry [when a Jewish boy could hope to be a minister], and that the wish it had done its best to fulfill was one dating back to those times. In mishandling my two learned and eminent colleagues because they were Jews . . . I was behaving as though I were the Minister, I had put myself in the Minister's place. Turning the tables on his excellency with a vengeance! He had refused to appoint me professor extraordinarius and I had retaliated in the dream by slipping into his shoes."[89] In her very sensitive

---

86. Herzl, *Zionist Writings,* 165; see Gilman, *Jewish Self-Hatred,* 238. Herzl was by no means the only German-speaking Jew who held such views (Aschheim, *Brothers,* 46–47). My point is obviously not, then, that Herzl invented this racism but that his "Zionism" did not cure it or even significantly ameliorate it. For the background of the notion that there are two Jewish races, see Efron, *Defenders,* 24–27.

87. Chamberlain, *Foundations,* 387, cited in Geller, "Mice." Note that the Kaiser made no such inner-Jewish racial distinctions. Mosse's claim that "Jews never directed the weapon of racism at others in order to facilitate their own acceptance into society" (*Nationalism,* 42) is at least partially falsified by this moment in Herzl. Western Jews did sometimes direct the weapon of racism at *Ostjuden* for this purpose.

88. The remarkable thing is that Herzl could also produce exactly opposite sentiments as well. After meeting actual Russian Jews for the first time at the First Zionist Congress in Basel (1897), he wrote: "How ashamed we felt, we who had thought that we were superior to them. Even more impressive was that they possess an inner integrity that most European Jews have lost. They feel like national Jews but without narrow and intolerant conceit" (Elon, *Herzl,* 246). *Mauschel,* however, was written quite a bit later than these sensitive lines.

89. Freud, *Interpretation.*

reading of this text, Barbara Breitman argues that Freud is only half
aware of what he is saying here. Far from a mere wish fulfillment to be
a minister and thus to triumph over the antisemitic minister by "step-
ping into his shoes," what Freud enacts here is identification with the
aggressor. His triumph is not so much over the antisemite but over
other Jews through "becoming the perpetrator of anti-Semitism in his
own psyche."[90] In "Mauschel," Herzl commits the same act with even
less self-awareness (and self-critique) than Freud here manifests, triumphing over antisemitism by becoming the perpetrator of antisemitism.

Herzl even ends the essay with a threat (characteristically alluding to
Wilhelm Tell): "Zionism's second arrow is aimed at Mauschel's heart."
In fact, this vicious sentence (in both senses of the word) was carried
out in the refusal of Zionist leaders in Jewish Palestine to engage in
rescue operations of European Jews during the Nazi genocide unless
these would contribute to the creation of the "New Jew" and the state.
Ben-Gurion infamously wrote in 1938 after *Kristallnacht:* "If I knew
that I could save all of the [Jewish] children of Germany by moving
them to England, or only half of them by moving them to the Land of
Israel, I would choose the second."[91]

The point of this exercise is not, of course, to condemn Herzl or
Freud as individual Jewish antisemites, or self-haters, but rather to argue that such views of Jews by themselves, while clearly not the only
ones available, were enormously widespread particularly among Viennese Jews of their generation. Like Freud, Herzl too is a Weiningerian
figure, suggesting the very widespread nature of Weininger's affect
among such Jews. Indeed, I would go so far as to suggest that Weininger
has been used as a scapegoat to draw off the poison of Jewish antisemitism and concentrate it on the goat who was driven off the cliff. As
Jenny Sharpe has written, it is not "useful to demand from authors
what was historically impossible for them to represent."[92] Sander Gilman's *The Jew's Body,* with its repeated demonstrations of Jewish doctors who believed that the Jewish foot, the Jewish nose, the Jewish psyche, the Jewish libido were deformed, is enough to argue this case. The
reason for focusing on Freud and Herzl is to argue that these affects
were crucial in the formation of two of the most fateful movements of
modern times, psychoanalysis and Zionism—both founded on Berg-

90. Breitman, "Lifting Up," 104–5.
91. Quoted in Tamir, "March."
92. Sharpe, *Allegories,* 29.

gasse, Vienna (Herzl at Berggasse 6, Freud at 19), in the mid 1890s.
Antisemitism was real, ubiquitous, and deadly, and each of these figures in his own way was searching for a way out from a terrible plight.
Moreover, internalization of both the stereotype created by the dominant culture and that culture's evaluation is a common phenomenon
among dominated minorities—if not an inescapable one.[93]

I am not so arrogant as to presume to know how I would have re-
acted to being a Jewish student in a university of which the official policy of the student government was: "Every son of a Jewish mother,
every human being in whose veins flows Jewish blood, is from the day
of his birth without honor and void of all the more refined emotions.
He cannot differentiate between what is dirty and what is clean. He is
ethically subhuman. Friendly intercourse with a Jew is therefore dishonorable; any association with him has to be avoided. It is impossible to insult a Jew; a Jew cannot therefore demand satisfaction for any
suffered insult."[94] To be sure, I might have responded as Herzl did, assimilating the negative stereotype and desiring only to escape it, but
Schnitzler, for instance, who was obviously subject to exactly the same
discourse, did not. If from the vantage point of my world, I find Freud's,
and especially Herzl's, solutions disastrously flawed in their political effects—on women, gay men, Jews, and Palestinians (multiply intersecting categories, of course)—this is not because I consider myself ethically superior to them. The question that I ask is not: "Were Freud and
Herzl good men?" but rather: "What can be learned from their 'mis-
takes' that can help us now?" It is clear—to me—that a solution to
the "Jewish problem" whose bedrock is a repudiation of Jewish male
"femininity" will not provide a useful answer.

OF MIMICRY AND MENSUR

Blond, moustached, dapper, the perfect lady-killer, Herzl's
ideal of masculinity.

　　　　　　　　　　　　—Amos Elon

I have argued that Zionism had for Freud replaced Greekness ("the
Aryan cause") as the means to manliness, honor, and civility. For Herzl,
it was conversion to Christianity, radical politics, and dueling—another

93. Mosse, Nationalism, 106-7.
94. Quoted in Schnitzler, My Youth, 128.

variety of the Aryan/Teutonic cause[95]—that Zionism replaced as the means to Jewish masculinity, to Jewish assimilation. If, in other national movements, "manliness" is made to serve nationalism, for Herzl nationalism was an instrument in the search for manliness. Peter Loewenberg has captured this Herzlian countenance perfectly. Remarking that Herzl referred to Jews in the derogatory terms of the virulent antisemite Heinrich von Treitschke, and that he envisioned these "pants-peddling boys" transformed into knights, Loewenberg writes:

> This expressed a deliberate effort to forge a new heroic national character (or to recapture a mythical biblical racial character), create a flag and accessory symbols that would be honored and would win "respect in the eyes of the world." This fantasy of a nation peopled by proud militant "new men" is, in Herzl's case, what Anna Freud has defined as "identification with the aggressor." He shares with anti-Semites a negative stereotype of the Jew. Herzl's contempt for "pants-peddling boys" is an admission of hatred of the Jews of the ghetto—and of the self. . . . *In this sense Herzl was a Jewish anti-Semite.* . . . For the learned, humiliated, sensitive Jew of the ghetto, he would substitute the rigorous, heroic, healthy farmer in his own land. Yiddish, the language of suffering, would be replaced by any cultured language. *The exclusive nationalism of Europe which rejects Jews would be replaced by a chauvinistic nationalism of Zion.* The values of the dominant majority are internalized and via reaction formation would become the ego ideal of the persecuted minority.[96]

Herzl, then, is an almost perfect example of that condition of the colonial subject so brilliantly anatomized in Frantz Fanon's *Black Skins, White Masks;* a book about Herzl and his compatriots could be called, *Black Pates, Blonde Wigs.*

We can now read the symbolic significance of Herzl's early determination that the Jewish State must be founded in Africa or South America. These were the privileged sites for colonialist performances of male gendering. My suggestion is that Herzlian Zionism imagined itself as colonialism because such a representation was pivotal to the entire project of becoming "white men."[97] What greater Christian duty could

95. Elon, *Herzl*, 53.
96. Loewenberg, "Theodor," 120–21, emphasis added.
97. See Cheyette, "Neither Black," 34, in which a Victorian novel is cited that explicitly identifies the "whiteness" of a particular (half) Jewish character with his being a "born colonial at heart"! This gives us a new way of reading Herzl's notorious inability to "see" the Palestinians, for as Sir Herman Merivale wrote in his 1839 lectures on colonialism, "The modern colonizing imagination conceives of its dependencies as a *territory,* never as a *people*" (Bhabha, *Location,* 97).

there be in the late nineteenth century than carrying on the civilizing mission, exporting manliness to the Eastern Jews and to darkest Palestine? Emblematic perhaps of this tendency was Herzl's plan to transform the wonder-working, mystical shaman, the Hassidic Rebbe of Sadigora into the Bishop of Haifa. Herzlian Zionism is thus itself the civilizing mission, first and foremost directed by Jews at other Jews and then at whatever natives happen to be there, if indeed, these natives are noticed at all. Herzl spun out his fantasies of a Jewish "colony" without reference whatever to where it would be—the Argentine, Uganda, or Palestine—and thus without reference as well to the native natives of this no-place. The only natives to whom he imagined directing his civilizing mission were those "Hottentot" *Ostjuden,* whom, as we have already seen, were read by him as constituting another "race." Like a Macaulay who could consider "a single shelf of a good European library worth the whole native literature of India and Arabia,"[98] Herzl has nothing but disdain for the two-thousand-year-old tradition of postbiblical Jewish literature and culture; the Bible and Goethe are more than worth the whole literature of the Jewish Diaspora. Let it be said right here, however, that the failure to recognize the possibility and then the very existence of already existing natives in the place where the Jewish colony was to be founded did not mitigate its destructiveness with reference to those natives but exacerbated it.

After finally meeting eastern European Jews, "formed by both modern European culture and their Jewish heritage,"[99] Herzl writes, "But we had always imagined them dependent on our intellectual help and guidance. . . . They are not Caliban but Prospero."[100] Herzl has then found some East European fellow Prosperos, but the Calibans of the world remain just that, whether Jewish or gentile. The Jews, as Zionists, constitute themselves both as natives and as colonizers. Indeed, it is through mimicry of colonization that the Zionists seek to escape the stigma of Jewish difference. If, one can almost hear Herzl thinking, being civilized means colonizing, then we too will be colonizers. If our choice is between being Caliban or Prospero, then Prospero we shall be.[101] Among the first acts of his foundation of Zionism was the estab-

98. Quoted in Sharpe, *Allegories,* 21.

99. Kornberg, *Theodor,* 221.

100. Herzl, *Zionist Writings,* 153.

101. David Myers has recently captured something of this paradox for a very special context, the foundation of Jewish scholarship in Palestine. He writes, "The European continent whence the Jerusalem scholars emigrated was never a fully comfortable home; it

lishment of "The Jewish Company"—under that name and in London.
Herzl had finally found a way for the Jews to become Europeans; they
would have a little colony of their own.

HERZL'S MIRROR

Preemancipation Jewishness in eastern Europe (and traditional Jewish identity in general)—it could be argued—was formed via an abjection of the *goy*, as Ivan, a creature stereotyped as violent, aggressive,
coarse, drunk, and given to such nonsense as dueling, seeking honor in
war, and falling in romantic "love"—all referred to as *goyim naches*.
For those Jews, it was abjection of "manliness"—itself, of course, a
stereotype—that produced their identity. In the colonial/postcolonial
moment, the stereotyped other becomes the object of desire, of introjec-
tion rather than abjection, and it is the stereotyped self that is abjected.
Freud and Herzl imitated the discourse of colonization itself as a prop—in
both the theatrical and architectural senses—for their newfound Jewish
masculinity: "If he is a boy he must be a stalwart Zionist."
    The Zionist slogan that accompanied foundation of their move-
ment—or better accompanied foundation of the state—"The Jewish
People reentered history,"[102] is testimony to this interpretation of Zionism. If the Jewish people have reentered history because of Zionism,
then, the implication is clear, previously they were a people without history, they were natives, Africans, "Hottentots." That Africans are a
people without history was a virtual commonplace of colonialism. This
was indeed explicitly the way that western European Jews experienced
their East European compatriots. Gilman evokes this moment: "In the
eyes of the formerly Yiddish-speaking convert [who had described the
Hebrew words in Yiddish as so deformed as to appear 'Hottentot'!],
Yiddish moved from being a language of a 'nation within nations' to a
language of the 'barbarian.' But for the Jew, convert or not, these bar-

---

produced a split cultural personality quite similar to that which colonized scholars in a
colonial setting have developed. And yet, for Jewish scholars the Continent was a more
natural habitat than Palestine, which they perceived as foreign, alien, and 'primitive'—full
of exotic allure, as well as elemental dangers. Inverting their own experiences, the re-
turners to Zion came as scholarly colonizers, intent on establishing an outpost of Wissenschaft in the new-old land" (*Re-inventing*, 10; the allusion to Herzl in the last phrase is
exactly apposite of course). In general, Myers's new book is a noteworthy analysis of
modern Jewish historiography under the sign of postcolonial and subaltern studies. It was
published just as I was completing final revision on this manuscript.
    102. Myers, *Re-inventing*.

barians must be localized, like the Hottentot, in some remote geographic place to separate them from the image of the German Jew. Their locus is the East."[103] This trope, I claim, finally provided Herzl with the solution to his dilemma, how to make the Jews be like "everybody" else. He had tried having them become Christians, duelers, socialists.[104] All of these had failed. Now the solution was at hand: Make the Jews into colonists, and then they will turn white! Zionism is thus the ultimate version of that practice dubbed colonial mimicry by Homi Bhabha.[105]

At the outset of his essay entitled, "Of Mimicry and Men: The Ambivalence of Colonial Discourse," Bhabha reproduces the following quotation by Sir Edward Cust: "It is out of season to question at this time of day, the original policy of conferring on every colony of the British Empire a mimic representation of the British Constitution. But if the creature so endowed has sometimes forgotten its real significance and under the fancied importance of speakers and maces, and all the paraphernalia and ceremonies of the imperial legislature, has dared to defy the mother country, she has to thank herself for the folly of conferring such privileges on a condition of society that has no earthly claim to so exalted a position."

Ultimately, however, the joke is on the colonized, for precisely what the British were exporting was mimic representations of the British Constitution; the French, mimic representations of the land of the "rights of man." This colonial project, like imperialist business, required native "compradors." This was the role that Herzl chose for the Jews: in Uganda, the Argentine, or even Palestine, the Jews were to turn into people "English in tastes, in opinions, in morals and in intellect." But they would go even further, exceeding the intentions of their British patrons, just like those mimic men with maces and parliaments, and actually turn white in blood and color as well. There is thus an ambivalence at the very site of such mimicry, just as there is at the site of that other

---

103. Gilman, *Jewish Self-Hatred*, 99. It should be noted that "Hottentot" is almost proverbial for subhuman in the seventeenth and following centuries (Bracken, "Philosophy," 247).

104. As Amos Elon has written: " 'Nowadays one must be blond,' Herzl wrote in a revealing little note found among his papers from that time. Was this irony? The evidence suggests that he may have meant it in all earnestness, manifesting in one short, casual line all the tortured convulsions of a sensitive secularized Jew's search for identity. One good way for a dark-haired Jew to appear blond, figuratively speaking, was to be active in one of the prestigious dueling fraternities" (Elon, *Herzl*, 54).

105. Bhabha, "Of Mimicry"; "Sly Civility"; now Bhabha, *Location*, 85–102.

form of mimicry, conversion to Christianity. Bhabha constantly points to the ways that the most apparent complicity with the colonizer turns into resistance.[106] However, it is also true that the seemingly most forceful resistance can turn into the most efficient complicity with the cultural project of the colonizer when the colonized becomes just like him, sometimes even more than "he" is himself; this is what we need in order to understand Zionism.[107] The Socialist co-commander of the Warsaw Revolt, the antizionist Marek Edelman, who remains in Poland as a Diaspora Jewish (Yiddish) nationalist and member of Solidarity, saw this very clearly: "This was a revolt!? The whole point was not to let them slaughter you when your turn came. The whole point was to choose your method of dying. All of humanity had already agreed that dying with a weapon in the hand is more beautiful than without a weapon. So we surrendered to that consensus." The notion that dying with a weapon is more beautiful and honorable than dying without one is a surrender of Jewish difference to a "universal," masculinist consensus.[108] The Zionist leaders decided that Edelman was insane and silenced his voice.[109] As late as 1981, his book could not find a publisher in Israel and had to be privately printed.

Bhabha writes that "what I have called mimicry is not the familiar

106. See also Bhabha, "Signs"; now *Location*, 102–22.

107. Romans such as Virgil and Lucan admired those of their enemies who fought and died bravely — "like Romans" — but King Telesphorus, who preferred to live in prison because "while there's life there's hope," was branded an effeminate coward (Barton, *Sorrows*, 30). According to Roman law, soldiers were ordained to vanquish or to die (Barton, "Moment"). In this context it is worthwhile at least to ask if the obsession with the refusal of the so-called ultraorthodox to participate in the army in Israel is not related to the antisemitic insistence that the Jews' inability (or unwillingness) to serve in the German army rendered them ineligible for full integration in the nation-state (Efron, *Defenders*, 30). This remained paradoxically the case even after World War I, when Jews served in the German army in a proportion far higher than their proportion of the population.

108. Quoted in Zertal, "Sacrificed," 38, emphasis added; see also Warschawski, "On the Three Sins." As the case of Edelman makes clear, this surrender was hardly unique to Zionists; revolutionary Jewish socialists (to whom I feel much more allegiance) were also caught up in the same imagery of "dignity" and "manliness." For excellent discussion, see Breines, *Tough Jews*, 131–32: "'At stake are our lives,' the Bundist, Chaim Helfand, concluded, 'and still more our honor and human dignity. We must not allow ourselves to be rounded up and slaughtered like oxen.'" Once more, I emphasize, it is not the first stake, life, that would put this utterance in conflict with the Rabbis but the second, the "still more." For the Rabbis, it is the one who kills *without any hope of saving his or her own life* who has surrendered human dignity and become like an animal.

109. At the Polish commemoration of the fiftieth anniversary of the revolt, Edelman was invited to speak. The Israeli Prime Minister, however, did not wish to appear on the same platform with him and so informed the Polish government, who, to their credit, did not give in. In the end, both the Israeli and the antizionist appeared together (Zertal, "Sacrificed").

exercise of *dependent* colonial relations through narcissistic identification so that, as Fanon has observed, the black man stops being an ac-
tional person for only the white man can represent his self-esteem."[110]
For Fanon then mimicry is that which deprives the colonized subject of
any claim to self, while for Bhabha it is the parodic performativity that
deconstructs the very discourse of European civilization, in the way that
Judith Butler argues that butch/femme deconstructs the discourse of
gender.[111] I am proposing that these two meanings of mimicry are two
sides of the same coin, two moves in an inexorable oscillation or dialectic. Ambivalence cuts both ways. Bhabha focuses on—indeed uncov-
ers—the former part of this dialectic, while I focus on the latter, perhaps more familiar, aspect of mimicry; he on the systole (the syntonic),
and I on the dystole. If Bhabha has produced an account of how the
discourse of colonialism is disarticulated at the very point of its articulation, a parallel account of the disarticulation of the discourse of resistance, national liberation, at *its* point of articulation must also be
assayed. And that disarticulation consists of a rearticulation of the
"civilizing mission" in a moment that forgets its own mimicry.[112]
Herzl's famous passion, shared with many German Jews, to achieve the
honor of the dueling scar, the *Schmisse,*[113] the notorious *Mensur,* is, in
this sense, a mimicry of inscription of active, phallic, violent, gentile
masculinity on the literal body, to replace the inscription of passive Jewish femininity on that same body.[114] His ultimate remedy, however, was
to lead to the inscription of this maleness on the body of Palestine—and
Palestinians.[115]

Herzl's Zionism, I argue controversially, is *almost, but not quite* co-

110. Bhabha, *Location,* 88.
111. Butler, *Gender.*
112. See now the very similar point made in Fuss, "Interior Colonies," 24–25.
113. M. Goldstein, "German Jewry's," 241; Gay, *Cultivation,* 11.
114. As Jay Geller points out in an extraordinary reading of Kafka's 1917 story, "A
Report to an Academy," his allegorized assimilated Jew, Red Peter, an ape aping humanness, has a scar on his cheek and one on his thigh. Geller associates the lower scar with
circumcision but I think misses the association of the upper one with the mensur. Although Geller's focus in that context is elsewhere, this point only strengthens Geller's
overall reading of the text (Geller, "Of Mice").
115. The discourse of gender of the actual Zionist movement and its eventual practices of oppression both with regard to gender and with respect to the Palestinians are
much more complex than any account of Herzl, for all his being "the father/prophet of
Zionism," could possibly envision. I hope someday to return to this project in the form
of a book to be entitled: *Mentsh and Supermentsh in Jewish Palestine.* My colleague
Michael Gluzman is currently working along these lines on a project entitled *The Zionist
Body: Representations of the Body in Modern Hebrew Literature.* For the nonce, his article "Body" is available.

lonialism. There are too many "striking features" that "betray its col-
ored [Jewish] descent."[116] Zionism was not to produce wealth for a
mother country. Just trying to figure out what might be the mother
country of Zionism immediately reveals the problem. This is why Herzl
had to "adopt" Britain as mother country.[117] Zionism, moreover, was
anything but the instrument of an attempt to spread "Jewish culture"
or Judaism to other peoples. And yet, Zionism in its discursive forms
and practices is very *similar* to colonialism. The plan was not for Jewish
Palestine to *be* a colony but for it to *have* colonies. When Herzl was
offered Uganda for Jewish settlement, his notion was that it would be
"a miniature England in reverse," that is, first the colony and then the
"Mother Country."[118] We can now reread Herzl's fear of a Jewification
of Europe upon the Jews' departure. Herzl's Zionism as an assertion of
partial difference was intended, as we have seen, to allow the true German essence of the German Jew to appear. The logic of such Zionism
is that if we can prove our manliness to the Germans by becoming colonizers, then they will see that we are the same. The ambivalence of Zionism thus comes to the fore most sharply in Herzl's fear of *Verjudung*
of Europe. On one hand, as I have said, this involves an infamous antisemitic stereotype. On the other hand, there is acknowledgment in this
fear that Germans may lose their Germanness in the absence of the
Other against whom hegemonic identity is constructed. So, if the Jews
were to leave Germany, the Germans would have to acknowledge the
integral Germanness of the Jews, but it also means that they become
vulnerable to losing their identity, thus making the Zionists the true
Germans. The insight on Herzl's part is that hegemonic identity can
only be constructed in the mirror of the other, and thus the necessity
for colonialism. As François Hartog has written of quite another time
and place: "How must the Athenians, who so insistently claimed to be
of autochthonous birth, have represented this alien figure [the Scythian]
whose whole being consisted in having no attachment to any place? It

116. Bhabha, *Location*, 89. For a fascinating parallel discussion of the "not
white/not quite" syndrome in Jewish decolonization, see Geller, "Mice."
    117. In this sense, it is difficult to fit Israel into a class that includes such "former"
white settler colonies as Australia, New Zealand, and Canada (Williams and Chrisman,
Colonial Discourse, 4). The fact that Zionist theory and practice cannot be easily classified does not in any way constitute an apologetic for the effects of Zionism, and little is
gained politically for the Palestinian people by simply categorizing Israel as a "white settler state."
    118. Letter to Nordau, cited in Elon, *Herzl*, 375.

is not hard to foresee that the discourse of autochthony was bound to reflect on the representation of nomadism and that the Athenian, that imaginary autochthonous being, had need of an equally imaginary nomad."[119]

As much as it is a reterritorialization of Jewishness, then, Herzlian Zionism is a deterritorialization of Germanness. Thus Jewish nationalists are really ardent Germanists, a rather peculiar trajectory wherein one ends up believing that by having a colony one can claim a nation, thus "a miniature England in reverse."[120]

This is masquerade colonialism, parodic mimesis of colonialism, Jews in colonialist drag.[121] Jewish "women" dressed up like "men." Indeed, the total destruction of Jewish difference that the liberal Zionist Herzl envisioned is the very point of such mimesis. By spreading *Bildung* to *Mauschel,* Herzl and his compatriots would reconfigure themselves as gentile men.

This should not be read as a trivialization of the disastrous effects of this discourse, especially with respect to its primary victims, the Palestinians. Zionism, at the same time that it subverts itself as discourse, shores itself up even more frantically with the pseudo-agency of the M16 rifle and racist legislation. Colonial mimicry in many of its practices can be a bloody business. The violence of Jewish hegemony in Palestine is a particularly egregious version (because of the transplantation in space) of the violence of national hegemony over separate ethnicities in many parts of the postcolonial world, since that also frequently materializes as the violent political domination of one particular tribe over others.

Herzl's colonialism, however, was not intended to be of the violent kind. He was, as I have said, the ultimate mimic of British liberalism, not of rapine and plunder; a John Stuart Mill, not a Cortez or a Sala-

---

119. Hartog, *Mirror,* 11; see also J. Boyarin, *Palestine,* "Introduction."

120. Seshadri-Crooks, letter.

121. The mimicry of the figures that Bhabha cites, from both sides of the imperialist power structure, "alienates the modality and normality of those dominant discourses in which they emerge" (Bhabha, *Location,* 88). Like Macaulay's interpreters, the Zionists "are the parodists of history. Despite their intentions and invocations they inscribe the colonial text erratically, eccentrically across a body politic that refuses to be representative, in a narrative that refuses to be representational. The desire to emerge as 'authentic' through mimicry—through a process of writing and repetition—is the final irony of partial representation" (88). But the parodists too often do not see for themselves how their mimicry disarticulates the colonialist text, and thus they find themselves trapped within the imaginary of its articulation.

zar.[122] Answering a Palestinian leader who had written him with great sympathy for the cause of a Jewish State but had pointed out that Palestine was unfortunately already inhabited, Herzl wrote: "You see another difficulty in the existence of a non-Jewish population in Palestine. But who wishes to remove them from there? Their well-being and individual wealth will increase through the importation of ours. Do you believe that an Arab who owns land in Palestine, or a house worth three or four thousand francs, will be sorry to see their value rise five- and tenfold? But this would most certainly happen with the coming of the Jews. And this is what one must bring the natives to comprehend."[123]

In his novel, Herzl imagined a German Jewish doctor setting up an eye clinic in Jerusalem and defeating trachoma for all of the Middle East.[124] In a speech in London on June 26, 1899, Herzl actually referred to Zionism as a "burden that the Jews were assuming for the wretched and poor of all mankind."[125]

For the Freud of the Spielrein letter and *Moses and Monotheism,* and Herzl, it was the discourse of colonialism itself that caught them. The very inappropriateness of Jewish mimicry, that very ridiculousness that Herzl perceived finally in such mimic behavior as conversion, in the end tragically eluded him in regard to "manliness": dueling, defending the "homeland," and white-settler-state-making.

POSTSCRIPT

Having contended that Herzl's "decolonization" of the Jews consisted of a neocolonialism, I now must acknowledge how my discourse is implicated in that of Herzl. I am also in search of a Jewish political subject who will find a place in modernity. As a Jew, like other people who do not unproblematically "belong" in Metropolis, I find modernity a dilemma. We are always in a "derivative discourse." The very struggle against colonialism, homophobia, and sexism that my project is born of is structurally identical with Herzl's struggle for "manliness" and its signifiers—colonialism, homophobia, and sexism—in the sense that it

---

122. As such, there are versions of Zionist practice that are considerably more vicious than Herzl's "liberalism," including some that are murderously assertive of Jewish difference. Liberalism has worse alternatives. As Biale points out, "In an ironic way, Herzl was perhaps the originator of the idea of a 'binational' state in Palestine" (*Power,* 135).

123. Quoted in Elon, *Herzl,* 312.

124. Herzl, *Old-Newland,* 110-11.

125. Elon, *Herzl,* 312.

is also informed by the values and ideals of the larger culture within which I find myself living as a Jew. I could not disavow Zionism as a Jewish practice without involving myself in an invidious and artificial essentialism cum triumphalism. Zionism is, it must be conceded, as "authentic" a practice of being Jewish as any other, and it is, moreover, what most—not all—Jews who identify strongly as Jews are doing now. It is one possible realization of the Jewish cultural code within a given set of historical and material conditions. It is there that I hope to intervene, because although people do not make the conditions within which they live, they can with a will change them.

George Mosse has recently pointed out how ubiquitous the challenge of manliness was for "outsiders" in modern Europe: "Modern masculinity needed the countertype, and those stigmatized as countertypes either attempted to imitate the ideal type or defined themselves in opposition to the dominant stereotype. Either way, escape was difficult." If most of modern Jewry has adopted until now the first strategy, I am calling for a turnabout to the second as ethically superior, but I do not imagine that thereby I have "escaped."[126] Zionism cannot be undone and history cannot be changed, but the future may be, and a first step, in my view, would be an attempt to recover and revalue the conditions and historical resources of a Jewish culture within which masculinity was *Edelkayt*.

Escape is indeed difficult. Paradoxically, much of the possibility of my own Jewish cultural continuance—including the absolutely critical ability to read Hebrew—is a product of the very Zionist entity that I struggle against. Spivak has articulated this dilemma as "saying an 'impossible "no" to a structure, which one critiques, yet inhabits intimately.'"[127]

Looking for a way of remaining Jewish, of preserving Jewish memory and being what I consider a politically moral human being, I (re)-construct moments and models in the Jewish past that seem to make this possible. This is not intended as a fantasized restoration of an ideal or idealized Jewish past, neither of the Talmud nor of eastern Europe before the *ḥurban* of the Nazis, but the critical deliverance of cultural materials and practices from that past and their resiting in a different

---

126. Mosse, *Image,* 13. For a longer discussion of this issue with respect to Freud and Fanon, see my essay "What Does a Jew Want?; or, the Political Meaning of the Phallus," forthcoming in *Discourse.*

127. Quoted in Prakash, "Postcolonial Criticism," 11.

modernity. The crisis of Jewish identity bears important comparison to the sometimes seemingly intractable dilemmas faced by all people caught in the syncopated arhythmicalities of modernity which are the subject of postcolonial cultural studies.

In the final chapter of this book, I wish to articulate my reading of the life of a modern Jew who did much better than either Freud or Herzl in negotiating being Jewish and being modern, in reclaiming and not disowning the differences of traditional Jewish gendering, one who was committed equally to the continued maintenance of Jewish traditional life, religion, and practice and to a militant feminist critique of that tradition, and who was committed to Jewish identity and to specieswide solidarity with equal passion. And so I come back to one who has been present through much of the text: my hero, Bertha Pappenheim.

CHAPTER VIII

Retelling the Story of O.

Or, Bertha Pappenheim, My Hero

O

Tell me all about Anna... —*Finnegan's Wake*

THE MYSTERY OF ANNA O.

It is a story that has become one of the founding myths of modernity. I quote the canonical account of Ernest Jones:

> From December 1880 to June 1882 Breuer treated what has become recognized as a classical case of hysteria, that of Frl. Anna O. The patient was an unusually intelligent girl of twenty-one, who developed a museum of symptoms in connection with her father's fatal illness. Among them were paralysis of three limbs with contractures and anesthesias, severe and complicated disturbances of sight and speech, inability to take food, and a distressing nervous cough which was the occasion of Breuer being called in. . . . She soon got into the habit of relating to him the disagreeable events of the day, including terrifying hallucinations, after which she felt relief. On one occasion she related the details of the first appearance of a particular symptom and, to Breuer's great astonishment, this resulted in its complete disappearance. Perceiving the value of doing so, the patient continued with one symptom after another, terming the procedure "the talking cure" or "chimney sweeping." Incidentally, at that time she could speak only English, having forgotten her mother tongue, German, and when asked to read aloud from an Italian or French book would do so swiftly and fluently—in English.[1]

The story has, in the canonical version, rather a sensational end. Josef Breuer became more involved with his young and beautiful patient, but, of course, did not recognize his "countertransference." One

---

1. Jones, *Young Freud*, 223–25.

day he arrived at the house to find Anna in the throes of a pseudocyesis, a false pregnancy. She exclaimed, "Now Dr. B.'s baby is coming!"[2] And Breuer, supposedly quite an inhibited person, ran from the house, took his wife on a second honeymoon and conceived their daughter, a daughter whom Jones does not fail to misinform us, committed suicide sixty years later in New York.[3] This information was gleaned by Jones from the account in the *Studies in Hysteria* and in various later Freudian papers. What Jones revealed for the first time, however, in his 1953 publication was that Anna O. was Bertha Pappenheim, the first social worker in Germany (Frankfurt-am-Main), founder of the German Jewish feminist movement and a militant feminist activist, translator of Mary Wollstonecraft, and highly prominent in the protests against "white slavery" and for women's education.

As her biographer, Lucy Freeman, has put it, "Perhaps the greatest mystery of all in the story of Anna O. is how the hysterical young woman Breuer thought better off dead and out of her misery could turn into a charming, powerful personality whose achievements were respected throughout Europe."[4] Previous interpreters of Anna O.'s transformation into Bertha Pappenheim have been notorious for either considering her feminist work a *continuation* of her illness, as have psychiatric antifeminists, or, more sympathetically, arguing that after and because she was cured of her hysteria, she became an effective powerful woman. Hélène Cixous has interpreted hysteria *as* feminist resistance.[5] I argue that for Anna O., Cixous's model of hysteria as feminism is completely compelling, which is, let me emphasize, the opposite of the claim that feminism is hysteria. "The hysteric, reported to be incurable, sometimes—and more and more often—took the role of a resistant heroine: the one whom psychoanalytic treatment would never be able to *reduce*."[6] If the story of Dora, another of Freud's patients, is the story of

2. I wish to make clear that I am not asserting the accuracy of any of the details of this history. Specifically, the false pregnancy (pseudocyesis) has been recently disputed by Christopher Reeves ("Breuer"). I am grateful to Muriel Dimen for this reference.
3. She actually killed herself in Vienna on the verge of the Nazi onslaught. There is, accordingly, no dark mystery there. For a much more reliable account of these events, see now Hirschmüller, *Life,* 98–116. She was also born before the alleged pseudocyesis. For further interesting discussion, see Appignanesi and Forrester, *Freud's,* 83–86.
4. Freeman, *Story,* 211.
5. Cixous and Clément, *Newly Born,* 4.
6. Cixous and Clément, *Newly Born,* 9. Cixous's reading of Freud's relation to the hysteric is that it is adversarial. Although Flaubert and Michelet are dubbed by her the most "feminine" of men, her third source of knowledge about sorceresses and hysterics, Freud, is seemingly the most masculine. In chapter 5 above, I have directly contested that reading, putting Freud quite explicitly into the Flaubertian line of male hysterics. Cixous's

a negated rebellion,[7] Anna O.'s is the story of a consummated one, signified via her woman-identification and refusal of marriage.[8]

In a curiously heterosexist account, Ann Jackowitz remarks that
"Pappenheim distrusted men who, unlike women, put their selfish interests first. She allowed no men on her board of directors and felt compelled to maintain a separatist attitude. She insisted that her attack on
men was not individual; *yet intimacy with men was beyond her.*" Jackowitz is, moreover, so stunned when one of Pappenheim's relatives refers
to Pappenheim as nothing but a lesbian that she reports that she felt "as
if someone stabbed me in the chest."[9] There is also a luscious moment
in one of Pappenheim's letters from Saloniki in 1911:

> The Jewish women of Saloniki are said to be especially beautiful. The most
> beautiful one I saw here, maybe the most beautiful Jewish woman I ever saw,
> perhaps the most beautiful alive, I found today in a brothel. What a pity,
> such a strong human flower, born in such an environment, to such a fate. I
> understand that a man will risk all for such a woman, yet I can't understand
> this twenty-year-old who thus sells the best, the most beautiful she owns, her
> body—in this way. Does she not have a soul? It is true, she cannot write,
> cannot read . . . it is ten o'clock; I'll stop for today. I'll go to sleep. Maybe I'll
> dream of beautiful Jolanthe; I can't forget her since I saw her today. . . . [10]

Almost as if she realized what she had revealed here, Pappenheim
writes on the morrow, "Of course I did not dream of Jolanthe." There
is accordingly some justification for considering Bertha Pappenheim a
foremother of lesbian separatist feminism!

---

explanation of why Freud abandoned the hysteric and mine are thus precise opposites as
well. For an elegant explanation of why sorcery (and hysteria) should be the particular
province of women and marginal, oppressed groups of men, see J. C. Scott, *Domination,*
141–42.

7. Ramas, "Freud's."

8. Appignanesi and Forrester produce a remarkable, and for me deeply moving, different end to Dora's story. Noting that she had become in later years a distinguished
contract bridge player and teacher, and that her partner was none other than Frau Zellenka (Frau K.), the love object of her early years, they suggest that "it is as if, across the
years, they had finally dispensed with the superfluous men who had previously been their
partners in their complex social games and contracts, yet they had retained their love of
those games whose skill lies in the secret of mutual understanding of open yet coded com-
munications within and across a foursome. Ida, adept at keeping her hand secret, also
knew when and how to play it. Freud might well have been impressed by Ida's fidelity to
her friend Frau Zellenka; it certainly would have reinforced in him his belated conviction
that Ida's secret love for her had been the deepest current in her mental life" (Appignanesi
and Forrester, *Freud's,* 167). It took her longer, but Dora also found her way to resist
heterosexuality!

9. Jackowitz, "Anna," 271, emphasis added; 269.

10. Edinger, *Bertha,* 38–39.

I propose that it is plausible to assume that her symptoms were a manifestation of passionate anger, an anger that later found more useful itineraries of expression than hallucinations, paralysis, and aphasia.[11] This is exactly contrary to a frequently held view that described her success as having happened *in spite* of her "illness," such as that of Albrecht Hirschmüller who writes, "The fact that she became such an impressive personality and achieved what she did despite these handicaps is for the measure of this woman's unique stature."[12] Given the potent effectiveness of Pappenheim's later life as a feminist, her case of hysteria seems a much stronger one with which to support a reading of hysteria as itself feminist protest than the case of Ida Bauer, the famous Dora, who has attracted so much more attention. Surprisingly little has been written about Anna O. from this point of view.[13] In a real sense, it is Bertha Pappenheim whose case confirms the argument that hysteria is inchoate feminism, because in her case the feminism became tangible and effective. Cixous writes that hysteria is both radical and conservative at the same time: "Antiestablishment because the symptoms—the attacks—revolt and shake up the public, the group, the men, the others, to whom they are exhibited," but "*conservative* because . . . every hysteric ends up inuring others to her symptoms, and the family closes around her again, whether she is curable or incurable."[14] This judgment, I suggest, is possible only because Cixous ignores the case of Anna O./Bertha Pappenheim: "To pass over into the act, making the transition to actions, moving to the inscription of the Symbolic in the Real, and hence producing real structural transformations, is the only possible gesture of departure from sorcery and hysteria. We are not there yet."[15] But Pappenheim was. Her political militance was a successful conversion of her "hysterical" rebellion.[16] The task of this chapter will be to hypothesize what made this possible.

One of the great clues to the mystery of this story is what took place between June 7, 1882, the date of Anna O.'s last session with Breuer in

---

11. For an extraordinarily cogent and lucid account of the process of "discovering that one has been angry," that is, and not guilty or depressed, see Scheman, *Engenderings*, 24–30.

12. Hirschmüller, *Life,* 126.

13. Hunter, "Hysteria," is the prime exception.

14. Cixous and Clément, *Newly Born,* 5.

15. Cixous and Clément, *Newly Born,* 10.

16. It is of course possible that Cixous herself would not consider this "conversion" a success, for there are ways in which the hysteric is threatening to the very symbolic itself that no political radical can touch. This question goes to the very heart of dilemmas in feminist theory, and it is not the place of this text to engage it.

Vienna and the appearance of Bertha Pappenheim as a strong, active young woman in Frankfurt in 1888,[17] followed by her growth into one of the most militant and effective feminist leaders of her time. One thing seems established: at the end of Breuer's treatment, Pappenheim was not yet "well."[18] She was admitted to Robert Binswanger's sanatorium a month later, a "fact" for which there is ample documentation.[19] If the "talking cure" didn't cure Anna O., then it seems plausible that the causes Breuer suggested for her hysteria were also not definitive.

Much has been written about Bertha Pappenheim; almost no one, it seems, has investigated in any nuanced way the place of Jewishness in her formation, her "illness," and her eventual spectacular career as a feminist activist.[20] Marion Kaplan has remarked that in Pappenheim's own time, feminists rejoiced in her feminist activity but were hostile to her Orthodox Judaism; the Orthodox were delighted with her activities on behalf of Orthodox Jewish learning and continuity, but were dismayed, for the most part, by her feminism. The same could be said for the reception of Bertha Pappenheim into the scholarly and critical tradition. She has been analyzed by analysts, celebrated by feminists, but hardly noticed by Orthodox Jews, or *as* an Orthodox Jew, at all. In her own unpublished imaginary obituary for the *Israelite,* an Orthodox publication, she wrote of herself, "She was often antagonistic—but did not defy her origins."[21] Naomi Shepherd explicitly writes that "Pappenheim respected and observed Jewish traditions, but she was certainly not an orthodox Jewess."[22] In my view, this is to surrender the field of Orthodoxy to the most socially conservative elements within Judaism. If Pappenheim observed Jewish tradition, as she clearly did, then she is

---

17. Freeman, *Story,* 207.

18. Hirschmüller attempts to explain how Breuer might have honestly thought that he had cured her of the psychological elements of her disease in spite of the fact that he clearly knew that she was quite "sick" years later (Hirschmüller, *Life,* 116). The attempt is laudable if unfortunately not quite convincing, since as late as 1887, hallucinations were among Pappenheim's symptoms.

19. See documents in Hirschmüller, *Life,* 276–312.

20. An exception is the paper of John Spiegel ("Anna"). Spiegel, however, plays fast and loose with historical facts. On what basis, for instance, does he declare that "she was not particularly gifted in intelligence or appearance" (57)? I find, moreover, his mode of expression, with its notion of a "Jewish Princess" syndrome, distasteful and misogynist in tone, in spite of his express support for Pappenheim's feminism. Reformulated, however, some of his thesis is similar to mine. A much more positive exception is Marion Kaplan, who also has anticipated other aspects of my interpretation in her fine essay ("Anna"). Thus, in contrast to Spiegel, Kaplan writes that "women who could *not* cope with the obvious injustices of their lot were psychologically 'healthier' " (105).

21. Edinger, *Bertha,* 99.

22. Shepherd, *Price,* 229.

Orthodox, and Orthodoxy has been redefined by her feminist militance. By describing Pappenheim—almost against her will, as it were—as having left "Orthodox" Judaism, these feminist writers willy-nilly repeat the very same gesture of exclusion that her Orthodox antifeminist opponents wished to achieve. *They exclude both the woman and the feminist from Judaism, and once more write Jewish culture and society as solely and normatively male.*

In 1928, on the twenty-fifth anniversary of the girls' club she had founded, she wrote with pride that "The Girls' Club carried through from its beginning everything according to strict Jewish dietary laws."[23] She did not, tendentious accounts to the contrary, abandon a commitment to and identification with traditional Judaism, but operated as a radical reformer *within* that culture and its institutions. After apparent early, inner, rebellion, Pappenheim remained a devout Jew in later life.[24]

A TALE OF TWO CITIES

Lucy Freeman considers Pappenheim's hysteria to have been the product of frustration at being denied education, a denial that she insists was a product of something that she refers to as "Orthodox civil law." It is not the case, however, that Orthodox Jewish women were kept illiterate or ignorant.[25] This is a mistake that Ellen Jensen makes as well.[26] True, they were denied access to the type of learning most valued by the cultural system, talmudic studies, but it is a gross category error to equate this disenfranchisement with an "old Jewish rule that women should learn nothing."[27] As Paula Hyman states clearly, "Women in traditional east European Jewish society were neither ignorant nor illiterate."[28] Most could read Yiddish;[29] Pappenheim translated the masterpiece of Yiddish women's devotional literature, the *Tzena Rena,* into German, as well as another early Yiddish religious classic, the *Maase-Buch,* a

23. Edinger, *Bertha,* 72.
24. Hirschmüller, *Life,* 121; M. Kaplan, "Sisterhood," 243; M. Kaplan, *Making,* 211.
25. Stampfer, "Gender," provides important correctives to this commonly held misconception.
26. Jensen, "Anna," 279.
27. Jensen, "Anna." When Pappenheim writes these words in her essay on the Jewish woman (Edinger, *Bertha,* 78), she is certainly referring to *Lernen,* the practice of talmudic study as a religious devotion, not to education in general, as I have argued in chapter 4.
28. Hyman, *Gender,* 54.
29. Parush, "Readers," 9.

text that was known as "the Yiddish Gemora [Talmud]" because it contained so much of the content of that central canonical work, and
which was extensively studied by women. The explicit intention of this
widely circulated book was that women (and men) would be able "for
every situation" to "give a law to be carried out in practice applicable
to the case."[30] As Chava Weissler remarks: "Readers of this literature
could gain familiarity not only with the content of traditional sources,
but also with the way in which traditional Jewish exegesis makes use of
sources and structures an argument."[31] A fair number of women could
read Hebrew as well.[32] In 1840, Rabbi Elijah Rogoler, an important
Lithuanian Orthodox leader, boasted of his younger sister that she "is
not only beautiful but knows grammar and how to write Hebrew, Polish and German perfectly, and also has a knowledge of Russian."[33] By
the second half of the nineteenth century many East European Jewish
women, even from very traditionalist circles, were educated in secular
culture as well and in fact educationally much advanced over their
brothers and husbands, who were learned only in Hebrew and talmudic

30. Quoted in Weissler, "Religion," 82.
31. Weissler, "Religion," 83.
32. Weinreich, *History,* 270; contrast Parush, "Readers," 16. My own great-grandmother was a prodigy who knew the entire Bible by heart. It was only Talmud she was
denied, not Hebrew learning in general. She is still memorialized in the "ultra" orthodox
Telshe Yeshiva as a paragon of the learned woman. The women of that community, originally from Lithuania, have always been famous for their learning—in everything but Talmud. I do not say this in order to excuse or apologize for the gender discrimination but
to emphasize how inadequate are the explanations for Anna O.'s frustration that have
been given until now. Pollock also emphasizes the evidence for Pappenheim's Jewish
learning, which was apparently acquired from private tutors (Pollock, "Glückel," 220).
Naomi Seidman cites the great critic and historian of Jewish literature, Dov Sadan, as
having written that early female Hebrew writers were all the only daughters of learned
fathers who chose to teach Torah to their daughters in the absence of a son, and she
mentions the very important Devora Baron in that connection (Seidman, "Marriage,"
252). Seidman notes two discrepancies, however. First of all, Baron, whose father had
taught her, had a son as well, and Baron's brother was apparently sympathetic and helpful
in her learning. Second, Sadan emphasizes that each of these fathers must have had "modern ideas which would allow him to go through with it [teaching his daughters Torah],"
while Baron's father seems not to have had modern ideas, certainly not feminist ones, as
Seidman clearly points out. What she fails to conclude explicitly from this, however, is
that the pattern of encouraging at least particularly bright daughters to learn some (or
occasionally a lot) of Torah may not have been so unusual and "modern" as the official
tradition would have us believe, and even the official tradition knows of the daughters of
Rashi who had no brothers and who were learned in Talmud and even put on phylacter-
ies. Baron's case demonstrates, however, that this kind of learning did very little to ameliorate the bitterness of these daughters at their second-class existence in traditional Jewish life.
33. Stampfer, "Gender," 69; on this figure, see Etkes, *Lita.*

lore and knew nothing of European languages and literatures and practical disciplines such as arithmetic.[34]

In fact, these women were often much more acculturated to "modernity" than their husbands and brothers, which ultimately caused a crisis[35] that was resolved in part by the widespread development of Orthodox Jewish educational institutions for girls, beginning in the second half of the nineteenth century, as well as the promotion of talmudic learning for women by the leading German Orthodox rabbi, Azriel Hildesheimer. This was a movement that Pappenheim was very active in as well. Freeman's explanation, moreover, is contradicted by the abundant evidence that Bertha Pappenheim was in fact highly educated from girlhood. Freud himself had written of her, "The patient had been a young girl of unusual education."[36] The fact that in her aphasia Pappenheim produced speech in a veritable Babel of fluent French, Italian, and English—no German—certainly supports this point as well.[37] She was fluent in all of these languages, as well as in Hebrew and Yiddish, and must have been, therefore, quite well-read in them. Her allusions to authors in her hysterical speech uphold this as well. Her knowledge of Shakespeare impressed Breuer, as Dianne Hunter has noted, and "she baffled her family and servants with discourses in languages they did not understand and astonished her doctors by producing a rapid, fluent extemporaneous English translation of any text in French or Italian that she was asked to read aloud."[38]

There is need for a much more detailed and nuanced account of the sources of Pappenheim's anger than the caricatured and misleading allegations that claimed an alleged Jewish mandate kept girls ignorant. It was not knowledge that women as a class were prevented from obtaining in this society, so much as the power and symbolic capital that went with a very particular mode of cultural competence. In chapter 4, I have argued that this prohibition was the central modality of the mainte-

34. Parush, "Readers," 7; "Women."
35. Parush, "Women."
36. Freud, *Autobiographical Study,* 20.
37. Diane Price Herndl offers the improbable postulate of "a simultaneous, overnight fluency in English, French and Italian (which she had known previously, but not fluently)" ("Writing," 65). This implausible account has the effect of further downplaying the obvious evidence supplied by polylingualism that Pappenheim had been given access to an excellent education, as far as it could go, given the larger social system within which she lived.
38. Hunter, "Hysteria," 469.

nance of male hegemony and sex-right within rabbinic societies, and nothing I am saying here dims or eclipses that critique.[39] The bourgeois ideology, however, disenfranchised women even more by insisting that their *only* functions were to be decorative and reproductive, while earlier, more traditional Jewish cultures stipulated a wide range of important public, economic activity for women.[40]

Pappenheim complains that she had not had a "down-to-earth education," that is, the kind of education that girls from early modern (pre-embourgeoisement) Jewish families would have had. There is compelling evidence that Pappenheim was extremely frustrated as a girl by the kind of life that she was expected to lead and by some deprivation in the educational sphere which she refers to as "defective intellectual [*geistig*] nourishment."[41] However, her description of the useless life that she was expected to lead is nothing like the life of the traditional Jewish girl and wife: "riding, going for walks, tea parties, visits to the theatre and to concerts, handwork, producing 'those countless pointless, insipid trivia which ... prove so alarmingly durable because of their uselessness.' "[42] Breuer wrote that she had a powerful intellect that was being denied solid food *since leaving school,* but noted as well "the contrast between the refined education she had received and the monotonous home life she led."[43] Her anger had less to do with a fictitious Orthodox Jewish insistence on women's ignorance than with the fact

39. Weissler brings this out elegantly. In the very passage that I have quoted above in this chapter, in which she proposes that the Yiddish women's religious literature gave women access not only to content but also to the method of rabbinic thinking, she also writes that "there is an elite deciding what it is appropriate for the 'folk' [i.e., women and ignorant men] to know" ("Religion," 83). This parallels and underlines my analysis of rabbinic culture as paternalistic in structure.

40. Hyman, *Gender,* 67. Contrast this to the unsupported statement made by Anne Steinmann ("Anna") that "the single-identity female role of Anna O.'s ultratraditional culture should not be confused with the fused double identity of family orientation and self-achieving of pre-Industrial Revolution females." That "fused double identity" is *precisely* what marked "ultratraditional" Jewish culture as well! The "single-identity female role" was an innovation of the bourgeois reign of heterosexuality and not of traditional Jewish culture (see Mosse, *Image,* 54–55). Even in Germany, eastern European Jewish women comprised a share of the Jewish female workforce greater than their proportion of the Jewish population and worked, moreover, in traditional "male" occupations in industry (M. Kaplan, *Making,* 5). It was, accordingly, not the so-called ultratraditionalism of Anna O.'s family but their embourgeoisement that enforced the single-identity female role.

41. Quoted in Jensen, "Anna," 277. Jensen translates *geistig* as spiritual here, which is clearly not appropriate.

42. Quoted in Hirschmüller, *Life,* 100.

43. Ellenberger, "Story," 267.

that Viennese society disallowed higher and professional education for women.[44]

It was the law of the Austrian university, and not any alleged Jewish practice, that prevented her from entering that institution.[45] Hannah Decker has eloquently described the contrast in educational opportunities for Ida Bauer (Dora) and her brother in Vienna one generation later: "*Gymnasium* was only for boys ten to eighteen years of age, so there was no question of Dora's attending one. The difference in the secondary education available to boys and girls at the turn of the century is instructive. . . . The difference between Dora's and Otto's educa-

44. Where do these scholars suppose that Pappenheim could have gotten formal education, were she not part of an orthodox Jewish family? At Barnard perhaps—founded, incidentally by German Jewish women (to be sure, not orthodox ones)? Given that Bertha Pappenheim's situation as the daughter of an orthodox Jewish home was no worse than that of her nonorthodox and non-Jewish sisters in late nineteenth-century Vienna (and indeed may very well have been "better"), harping on the deleterious effects of Judaism on the part of several authors is itself symptomatic. Even Appignanesi and Forrester, generally so careful, write that Bertha Pappenheim was "deprived by both family traditions and state restrictions of a secular secondary education" (*Freud's*, 73), not paying attention to the simple fact that there were no institutions, owing to those "state restrictions," at which such an education could be sought for women. There is, moreover, as we shall see below, little reason to imagine that traditional Jewish families would have had religious reason to deprive their daughters of *secular* secondary education. Iris Parush has sharply contested "studies dealing with the history of Jewish education [that] dismiss the question of women's education with a short discussion that finds the education of women being neglected, the women themselves withering away in their ignorance," in part by carefully distinguishing between Jewish education and the education of Jews (Parush, "Politics"). Jewish women had little Jewish education but much other education, as Shaul Stampfer has also pointed out (Stampfer, "Gender"). I do not agree, however, with his apologetic conclusions, and Pappenheim, of course, was bitterly angry at the deprivation in religious education, as we saw in chapter 4 above. For the record, let me state clearly that Naomi Shepherd, whose work came to my attention after this book was complete, gets this "right" (Shepherd, *Price*, 209), but unfortunately also repeats the strange idea that the reason that Bertha's brother went to university while she didn't was because the family was Orthodox (215).

45. Ellenberger, "Story," 272. It is astonishing how many authors have not paid attention to this simple fact. Thus Rosenbaum ("Anna," 16) also claims that "her brother had been encouraged to study at the University of Vienna and go on to study law while she had to settle for a Catholic secondary school." Perhaps, he also expected her parents to send her to Barnard or Radcliffe. Jackowitz writes deceptively, describing Pappenheim's upbringing as "one typical of the Jewish middle class, in which being born a daughter meant being excluded from an independent or professional life. Attendance at the university was forbidden" (Jackowitz, "Anna," 258). One would easily conclude from these sentences that "attendance at the university was forbidden by Jews," which is patently not the case; it was forbidden by the Austrian laws. Similarly, in her play, *Frauenrecht*, it is Austrian law and custom that Pappenheim depicts and deplores, not Jewish law, contra Freeman. For the law in question in that play that gives a husband unrestricted power over his wife's property, see Decker, *Freud*, 81. This law was a specific target of the Austrian feminist movement at the time that Pappenheim was writing her play, so it is simply mischievous to insist that her protest in this play was against Judaism.

tion had academic, social, and psychological significance. At the turn of
the century, the graduate of a *Gymnasium* was a member of an elite
group. . . . What a sharp contrast between Otto at nineteen, looking to
the future and possessing the abilities to pursue his goals, and Dora at
eighteen, dominated by her illness and despairing of life."[46] The Bauers,
in contrast to the Pappenheims, were anything but Orthodox. They observed almost nothing of traditional Jewish life. Bertha Pappenheim's
deprivation and sense of injustice compared to the fate of her brother
had nothing, therefore, to do especially with her Orthodox Jewish environment but was endemic to Vienna. As Donald Bloch has remarked,
"Hapsburg Vienna was notable for the extent to which it defined sexuality and sex roles differently for males and for females."[47] To put it into
my terms, Vienna was particularly affected by the triumphant rise of
heterosexuality in the nineteenth century.

Pappenheim wrote a spirited denunciation of the life of bourgeois
Viennese girls who were expected to pass the time and waste their lives
in trivial pursuits.[48] It is thus possible already to infer at this point that
the pattern of life that Pappenheim protested in that tract was little different from that of girls from any Viennese bourgeois household; there
was nothing essentially or peculiarly Jewish about it. Pappenheim herself, who had no inhibitions about critiquing and exposing the demerits
of either Judaism or Jewish culture, entitled her polemical tract: "Zur
Erziehung der weiblichen Jugend in den höheren Ständen" ("On the
Upbringing of Female Youth in the Upper Classes").[49]

The fact that Pappenheim's aphasia took the form of, among other
things, a total inability or unwillingness to speak German suggests a
cultural protest as well.[50] As Henri F. Ellenberger acutely remarks: "Ob-

46. Decker, *Freud,* 57–58.
47. D. A. Bloch, "Family," 148.
48. Hirschmüller, *Life,* 100.
49. The quotation from this text that Marion Kaplan reproduces bears out the gen-
erality of her target: "Until now, an axiom of proper education was to keep girls from
knowing anything that occurred beyond the confines of their homes. They studied history
from books which were 'rewritten for girls' but they remained cut off from the enormous
demands of daily life. They do not understand the relationship of poverty, sickness and
crime. To them, poverty is a street beggar or a scene in a play, sickness is disgusting, and
crime is a sin" (quoted in M. Kaplan, *Jewish Feminist Movement,* 41). This simply does
not reflect anything special, or anything at all representative, of Jewish women's lives, but
is characteristic of the Viennese *haut bourgeoisie,* Jewish as well as Christian. Helene
Lange, Christian founder of the German feminist movement describes her life as a *höhere
Töchter* in nearly identical terms.
50. Hunter, "Hysteria," 468.

viously Bertha Pappenheim had nothing in common with the 'sweet girl' (*das süsse Mädel*) of Schnitzler's theatricals and novels."[51] Is it possible to imagine that it was her Jewish culture that produced this gap? Steven Beller has pointed to some important evidence that the Jewish Viennese bourgeoisie invested *more* not less in daughters' education: "The different attitude of the Jewish bourgeois . . . was evident when the daughters of the two groups went to the same school, the *Beamten-töchterschule*, which Käthe Leichter attended. She describes the way in which the bureaucrats' daughters were intentionally kept childlike and brought up to be above all well-ordered, as their fathers had to be, their exercise books as spotlessly clean as officials' documents. The Jewish girls, though totally assimilated, were quite different . . . [with] a completely different attitude toward culture, the officials' daughters reading girls' books, the Jewish girls reading Wilde and Schnitzler."[52] Leichter herself wrote: "With my friends I discussed 'last things [ultimate meaning],' shared with them my experiences from books, poetry, nature and music. With the officials' daughters I played mother and child."[53] Anna O.'s deprivation was not produced by her Jewishness but by Viennese bourgeois society. Sidney Bolkosky traces the peculiar and extreme conditions of family life in Vienna to its condition as long-term "bureaucratic center of the Habsburg *Hausmacht*," and writes, "This original function of the city was a lasting one that permeated all aspects of life there. The concomitant indifferent, nonfeeling and unsympathetic relationships have historically called for avoiding motherliness. This is not to say that women could not be both mature and loved, mothers and lovers. It *is* to say that they were rarely perceived that way by men, and that the values of Viennese society militated against the individuation of women."[54]

Pappenheim is often, particularly in Lucy Freeman's biography, portrayed as the enemy of a benighted monolithic "Orthodoxy" that was totally indifferent (or worse) to women.[55] There are two apparent sources for such a (mis)interpretation of Pappenheim. One is surely her

51. Ellenberger, "Story," 272.
52. Beller, *Vienna*, 186. See also the important statistics in Rozenblitt, *Jews*, 121, which also suggest that Jews sent their daughters to whatever schools were available in numbers far higher than their proportion of the population.
53. Steiner, *Käthe*, 309; quoted in Beller, *Vienna*, 186.
54. Bolkosky, "Alpha," 145.
55. Incidentally, Freeman's characterizations of what she chooses to call "Orthodox civil law" are often enough simply misinformed.

extensive activity protesting the Jewish involvement in the procurement
of Jewish girls for prostitution and the inability, or unwillingness, of
most Rabbis to stop this. There is no doubting that Jewish "white slavery" was a scandal;[56] the suggestion by Freeman that it is somehow allowed, or even mandated, by "Orthodox Jewish civil law," however, is
monstrous.[57] Of course, Freeman's was not Pappenheim's own opinion.
It is a projection on the part of her biographer who is so virulently hostile to traditional Jewish culture that she cannot distinguish between a
smear and the truth.[58] Pappenheim herself writes of the chief Rabbi of
Istanbul that he "does not know enough" about the traffic in Jewish

56. In 1897, according to the Russian census, the ratio of prostitutes to the population of women was higher among Jews (forty-four in one hundred thousand) than in any
other single ethnic group (D. Biale, *Eros,* 163).

57. She was not totally lacking in rabbinical support for her feminist activities. The
most prominent German orthodox rabbi of her day, the famous Rabbi Nehemiah Nobel
of Frankfurt, was an ally of her struggles for greater women's equality within orthodoxy,
and she compared him to Rabbi Gershom of Mayence who had banned polygamy in the
German Jewish community nearly a millennium earlier (Edinger, *Bertha,* 81). Most rabbis
were unsympathetic to her feminism, and the record of orthodox Judaism is hardly to be
vindicated on that score. The reaction of the chief rabbi of Budapest to Pappenheim's
request that he support the struggle against the abduction of young Jewish girls and their
sale into forced prostitution makes chilling reading. In her reports to her followers, appropriately named *Sysyphus-Arbeit,* she writes that "he said, without a quiver of his eye-
lids: 'I am not interested in this matter'" (Pappenheim, *Sisyphus-Arbeit,* 12; partial English translation in Edinger, 38). Pappenheim contemptuously dismisses him as a "theater
Rabbi" (13).

Once more, while this point does not in any way exonerate or excuse the indifference
of most other rabbis or the ways that social conditions produced through Jewish practice
(such as the inability of abandoned women to remarry) may have exacerbated the problem, it does suggest that the tendentious picture drawn by (Jewish) scholars implacably
hostile to Jewish tradition has to be corrected. It is astonishing to me that such writers
can record that the Catholic and Protestant feminist movements received some clerical
support, while Pappenheim had no allies among the rabbis at all, when the documents
clearly indicate that two of the most important rabbis of Europe, Nobel in the West and
the Alexanderer in the East, were in some ways her allies. What percentage, it may be
asked, of the German Christian clergy were feminists? It is perhaps not inapposite to note
that Dora Edinger's biased account was published in English by a Reform congregation,
although we should be extremely grateful to her for gathering and publishing the documents that contradict her own synthesis.

58. It seems, however, to have been a topos of slanders by assimilated Jews against
"the orthodox" that they sold their daughters into prostitution and that such sale was
mandated by Jewish law. See Harrowitz's illuminating discussions of Lombroso in this
regard (Harrowitz, "Lombroso," 117–18, and "Weininger," 83). Of Lombroso, Harrowitz
writes: "At best, we can regard this [the claim that Jewish law warrants the sale of daughters into prostitution] as a confusion between different biblical laws regarding the legislation of slaves and marriage contracts. At worst, it is a deliberate misreading and misinter-
pretation of the story of biblical Jews, designed to link them to cults of prostitution and
to infer a connection between pernicious antisemitic stereotypes and biblical paradigms,
as if the stereotype of Jew-as-profiteer is already imbedded in these first biblical Jews and
thus an inseparable part of what is Jewish" (85).

girls going on underneath his nose, and that he cannot close the synagogue maintained by the pimps, "because everybody here is afraid of
them."[59] The picture is not one in which the rabbis cause the scandal but
one in which cowardice, and in some cases indifference, prevents them
from doing anything about it, while a brave woman could—and did.

My aim is not to defend the record of the rabbis—most of whom
were indeed reactionary and antifeminist—but rather to reclaim Bertha
Pappenheim as a devout, feminist, radical Jew. At the end of her life, she
translated the *Tzena Rena* into German from Yiddish. This is hardly
consistent with the picture that Freeman projects (in the full technical
sense of this term) of a woman who believes that all religions are oppressive to women but Judaism is the worst. To argue that Pappenheim
was dedicated to feminist reform for all women and that she did not
single out Judaism as particularly villainous is not to deny in any way
the critique of Orthodox Judaism and its oppression of women that she
undertook. It is to challenge a reification of Judaism that she herself was
very active in combating as well. Thus, even when Pappenheim is protesting bitterly the hair-covering of the married Jewish woman, she is
careful to note that it is a general East European custom, not confined
to Jews.[60]

Pappenheim fought vigorously to have the evil of Jewish traffic in
Jewish girls exposed in the world. Among her opponents on this issue
were many Orthodox rabbis with whom she thus contended strenuously. She would not, however, have made the mistake of thinking that
they opposed her efforts because they (or traditional Judaism) in any
way condoned such practices or were indifferent to them, but knew that
those Rabbis were afraid that antisemites would make use of such
knowledge to further harm Jews as a whole. And, indeed, to her horror,
the Nazis did later exploit Pappenheim's writings, distorting them into
an accusation that Jews trafficked in Christian girls. However, to echo
Pappenheim herself, it is important not to let explanation be made into
excuse. I do not think she was wrong and the rabbis were right—racists
will always find a way and Jews fighting against Jewish evil frequently
enhance the Jewish reputation among people of good will—only that it
is an error to conclude from this engagement that Pappenheim rejected
Judaism or blamed it *particularly* for women's oppression, as does

59. Edinger, *Bertha*, 39.
60. Edinger, *Bertha*, 86.

Hunter[61] in the wake perhaps of Freeman. It is thus highly deceptive when Dora Edinger writes that "prostitution and illegitimacy" are "connected with the legal status of women who still lived under Jewish civil law."[62] Pappenheim, in a text anthologized by Edinger herself, writes that it is the *relaxation* of adherence to Judaism that has led to the immorality, not the adherence![63] She over and over again emphasizes that the Jewish communities have no power over the procurers.

The other source of misreading Pappenheim as an opponent of Jewish traditional life is the vigor of her protest against depriving women of the opportunity to study Torah and Talmud, a protest already discussed in chapter 4. As we have seen there, the very terms of Pappenheim's protest indicate, however, that her concern was to ensure the continuation of Jewish traditional life and learning, even Orthodoxy, not to end them.

Pappenheim realized the positive aspect of traditional Jewish women's access to practical knowledge and economic power, but at the same time she was furious at the second-class status of Jewish women within Jewish society and the deprivation inherent in their exclusion from valued religious knowledge that was the province of men. What she proposed, I think, reading her essay "The Jewish Woman" closely, was the reconstruction of an "Orthodox" Jewish life that would maintain the positive and powerful aspects of traditional Jewish women's life—that is, against embourgeoisement—at the same time that it fought their disenfranchisement in the religious sphere and the "inferior position [of] a daughter in an Orthodox Jewish home." As we have seen in chapter 4, Pappenheim's aim here was to *radically* reform and enhance Orthodox Jewish religious life through the enlivening access of women to its vital heart, Torah study. She emphasizes, moreover, that it was "strictly Orthodox" people who sent their girls to the Baron Hirsch schools, in which secular learning was offered for Jews. Boys were generally prevented from attending these schools. However, she also clearly recognizes that the combination of access to secular learning and German language, via Yiddish, together with the dearth of Jewish learning was leading to "the influence of German language and German culture, but

61. Hunter, "Hysteria," 477.
62. Edinger, *Bertha*, 17. Contrast Shepherd (*Price*, 13), who clearly elucidates that it was the breakdown of Jewish communal institutions and tradition, *not their survival*—as well as grinding poverty—that produced the scandal of Jewish prostitution.
63. Edinger, *Bertha*, 48.

at the same time among the women less interest in Jewish consciousness, often in favor of the new national consciousness."[64] Bertha Pappenheim's fight was not against traditional Judaism but for its radical
reform.[65]

PAPPENHEIM'S COMPLAINT

Pappenheim's complaint is not that she was denied all education and
kept ignorant but that she was denied practical education and preparation for some sort of concrete and useful activity, while her brother
trained to be a lawyer. On her own account, it was "a down-to-earth"
education that she envied, not the spiritual pursuits of rabbis,[66] much as
she protested the inferior position of women with respect to Jewish
learning as well. As I have emphasized, she was certainly outraged by
the inferior social position of women and girls in historical traditional
Judaism—this was crucial to her feminist work—but the factors that
produced her "hysteria" had much more to do with Victorian Vienna
than with traditional Judaism. In fact, at the same time, in eastern Europe Jewish women were gaining more and more access to practical
secular education of various types because the communities had not

64. Edinger, *Bertha,* 79. The German original has *Geist* where I have substituted
"culture" for Dora Edinger's "spirituality." Pappenheim is clearly referring to that combination of German intellectuality and literary life marked by love of Goethe, Kant, and
Schiller, and not to anything that in English would be referred to as "spirituality." This
becomes particularly clear when she claims that "the Jewish Women's Federation has remained for 30 years consistently Jewish in faith and spiritually [*sic*] German" (80), an
obvious oxymoron. She means, of course, Jewish in faith and culturally German. The
same conclusion is obvious when *Geist* is glossed by her as "the influence of philosophy,
art and romance in literature" (87).
65. Freeman claims (and Jensen repeats, probably relying on Freeman) that Jewish
religious law forbids the support of illegitimate Jewish children who would be given out
to be raised as Christians, which is simple poppycock. Illegitimate children, that is children born to an unmarried woman, have no disability whatever from the point of view
of religious law—I am, of course, not making a judgment here on what actual social
practice was—and are not even called *mamzerim,* the Hebrew term usually but mislead-
ingly translated "bastards." Children born to adulterous unions are *mamzerim* and suffer
many religious disabilities, including being forbidden to marry anyone but another of
their same status. This is a famous scandal of Judaism, protested already in the Talmud,
but it does not result, in any sense, in an interdiction on economic support or even education for such unfortunates. Many advertisements in the Yiddish press of *mamzerim*
seeking mates testify to the fact that they were kept within the Jewish fold. Indeed, one
such "bastard" became in the nineteenth century a famous Talmud scholar and the head
of a major Yeshiva! In general, as David Biale points out, "enlighteners," like all colonizers with "civilizing missions," were at pains to portray traditional "orthodoxy" as un-
bending and unchanging when, in fact, there were various reform movements active
within "orthodoxy" in the nineteenth century (*Eros,* 163–64).
66. Jensen, "Anna," 277; Edinger, *Bertha,* 89.

adopted the value systems of western Europe, and the symbolically more valorized talmudic study was reserved for boys while girls were allowed, and even encouraged, to pursue nonreligious intellectual vocations. Just for example, an official report published in Warsaw in 1828 claims that "the school for girls of the Mosaic faith is in no wise inferior to the best of the general elementary schools."[67] This was consistent with the well-established social norm within which Jewish women were ideally the breadwinners for their scholarly husbands.[68] The Yiddish writer known as Shomer notes, "Daughters were taught the language of the country and all the know-how requisite to trade, the better to manage the affairs of home and commerce."[69] As Marion Kaplan remarks: "Even in the 1890s [most German Jews] had grandmothers or mothers who had been partners in family enterprises, or had supported their families themselves. These women had maintained the authority which went along with their contributions as helpmates and partners, and younger couples noticed the esteem in which older women were still held."[70]

Among East European Jews and more traditional rural German Jews, the older patterns still held. This pattern, of course, involves both liberatory or empowering aspects, as well as distinctly oppressive ones. David Biale has caught both of these in his description of the revolt against traditional Jewish marriage and gender roles on the part of the so-called enlighteners of the nineteenth century: "The maskilim [enlighteners] envisioned a family in which the position of women was at once better and worse than in the traditional family or, at least, in their image of the traditional family. While they experienced their mothers-in-law and, to a lesser extent, their wives as powerful and domineering, they imagined an ideal family in which power implicitly lay in the hands of the husband. Their revolt against the traditional family was a

67. Quoted in Parush, "Politics."

68. "The phenomenon of women breadwinners was not an innovation of Jewish society in the nineteenth century, but, as the historian Jacob Katz wrote, this phenomenon became the rule at that time"; and also: "It was precisely the traditional patterns, customs and life style of Jewish society, which continued well into the nineteenth century, that created the conditions which permitted certain sectors of the female society to serve as 'agents' of change, and to accelerate the processes of modernization" (Parush, "Women"; see also her "Politics").

69. Quoted in Parush, "Women." At the same time, he records as well the bitter protests of his mother at women's estate in Jewish society: "My mother in all the days of her long life bitterly resented the meagerness of her youthful education and cordially despised the three special duties even if she did, in a manner of speaking, observe them" (quoted in Stampfer, "Gender," 75).

70. M. Kaplan, *Making*, 52.

revolt against a perceived matriarchal family. If the wife was to be lib-erated from the yoke of traditional marriage, she must also be divorced from the power that women were thought to wield in the old system. While the maskilim directed their polemics against a specifically Jewish system of marriage and family, their goal was the same as that of other nineteenth-century advocates of domesticity—upholding such values as privacy and chastity. Their solution to what they saw as the promiscuity and sexual dysfunction of traditional Jewish society was the imposition of bourgeois constraints upon desire."[71]

While Biale is obviously correct in his skepticism with regard to the amount of real power that women held in this traditional society, we must also be sensitive to the stores of autonomy, power, and fulfillment that productive economic activity purchased for them and the erosion of such satisfactions that occurred as they were reduced to "angels in the house" by enlighteners of various types, including the Viennese bour-geois Orthodox.[72] With regard to medieval Jewish women of France and Germany, Biale writes, "In fact, women in the French and German Jewish communities of the High Middle Ages appear to have enjoyed rather astonishing freedom, probably a result of their active role in business and other public professions. Women may have also demanded a greater liturgical role, for lively debates were carried on in legal circles about the place of women in the synagogue and in talmudic study."[73] For instance, it is only in this chronotope of Jewish history that in some communities women were counted for the minyan, the public quorum for prayer. Louis Finkelstein proposes that this increased religious par-

71. D. Biale, *Eros,* 161.

72. To a certain extent, this is true of European societies in general (Pateman, *Sexual Contract,* 90). What is interesting are the ways that traditional Jewish society, as oppres-sive of women as it was, also supported willy-nilly resistance to the *embourgeoisement* that was overtaking western Europe. The fact that male Jewish culture allowed for this resistance for its own purposes, which had nothing to do with the "liberation of women," does not undo its resistant and subversive power vis-à-vis the rise of heterosexuality. When Jewish women *do* appear in and to the dominant culture, they may appear as mon-sters because they are then read in a different sex-gender coding. According to historian Paula Hyman, the "Jewish Mother" is an internal stereotype that refers to these differ-ences in gender coding between immigrant Jewish and American families and the tensions that these differences produced (*Gender,* 156–60). From the point of view of European *Kultur,* the female Jew is not a man but a monstrous parody of a man—a monster or, later, a lesbian (Gilman, "Salome"). Thomas Luxon reminds me here of John Knox's "Monstrous Regiment of Women" as an account of viraginized women, such as tradi-tional Jewish women would have appeared to be from the perspective of the romantic-become-bourgeois European formation.

73. D. Biale, *Eros,* 74; Marcus, "Mothers."

ticipation—which he calls a "movement toward 'women's rights,'" and which included authorities who permitted women to act as judges in religious courts, be counted for a quorum for grace, and be called to the Torah, as well as shifts toward equality in marriage and divorce laws—"had its origin and compelling force largely in the fact that women began to occupy a prominent position in the economic world."[74]

It follows then that the reduction of women's economic power, prominence, and independence in the nineteenth century constitutes the conditions for a retrenchment of women's power in the religious and social sphere as well. According to Biale, the "enlighteners desired marriages based on companionship in which bourgeois respectability would substitute for traditional chastity and in which women would be placed firmly within the confines of the home"[75] where they had not been enclosed heretofore. As Kaplan's study emphasizes, the paradigm that Pappenheim so strenuously protests in her tract on women's education, the expectation of women that they be decorative "ladies of leisure," was a relatively new bourgeois innovation among German-speaking Jews as well. And Paula Hyman has noted, "The vast majority of Jewish women in nineteenth- and early-twentieth-century eastern Europe grew to maturity in a society that did not facilitate the division between the public and domestic realms that was essential for the emergence of the middle-class lady."[76] Thus, had Pappenheim's family been more traditional in their life patterns and less *embourgeoisée*, there is reason to believe that she might have been less frustrated. Her later adoption of Glikl as role model and ego-ideal certainly supports this position as well.

Pappenheim's feminist essay "The Jewish Woman" bears out these observations. She opens with a clear analysis and statement that the reason for the general abandonment of Judaism by Jewish women owes to their traditional lack of access to Torah-learning. Pappenheim notes, however, glimmers of hope for women in their access to Yiddish as well as "precisely the lack of interest in what women and girls were learning," which "brought a slow and in the beginning not noticeable movement into Jewish womanhood." For her, the Yiddish literature, "the woman's German" as opposed to both Hebrew and standard German,

74. Finkelstein, *Jewish Self-Government*, 378–79.
75. D. Biale, *Eros*, 162.
76. Hyman, *Gender*, 66–67.

was to be the vehicle of a cultural revolution, whereby Jews would remain warm, active Jews and still become a part of German cultural
life.[77] Her translations of its classics into standard German were not,
then, a sideshow accompanying her major cultural and feminist projects
for a reconstruction of traditional Jewish life with women at the center.
They form, rather, a feminist answer to Moses Mendelssohn's translation of the Bible from Hebrew into Judeo-German. Pappenheim thus
records the existence of women's creativity and religious power in traditional Jewish culture, alongside of the "official" story of an all-male
tradition being produced only in Hebrew.[78] This Yiddish religious tradition was, for all its secondary status, an avenue of Jewish learning for
women in the past that produced "the true Glückel" and a source of
female (even protofeminist) power.

That others recognized this role for the old Yiddish women's literature as well is made clear by the "enlightened" author of the first secular Yiddish literature, A. M. Dik, who averred of his own writing that
"I wrote for the benefit of our women whose eyes look only into a
Taytsh-khumesh [the very women's Bible that Pappenheim translated]
written in a language of stammerers which includes unseemly passages
that should never be read by pious women and maidens. Not so my stories written as they are in a fine style, full of ethical teaching, free of
any words of eroticism and blemish and they instruct the women to
walk in the paths of righteousness and to turn away from all evil."[79]

Startlingly, it is the traditional, "Orthodox" women's literature
which is tainted by "words of eroticism and blemish." As Biale makes
clear, the function of writing such as Dik's was to further the embourgeoisement of young Jewish women, their "protection" from desire and
confinement within the private sphere of domesticity.

Yiddish writers of the "Enlightenment" as well sought to reconfigure
female Jews as European "women." A "utopian" description by Dik of
"a Jewish society purged of all dross" includes the following reverie of
a "redeemed Jewish womanhood": "I never see any women of the better classes in the shops and trading places, and obviously no young girls,
save for the market women who sell pastries, fruit, vegetables, and fish,
and young girls who sit with boxes of trinkets and bric-a-brac. . . . Neither do I see any Jewish tradeswomen milling around the inns and both-

77. Pappenheim, *Jewish Woman.*
78. Seidman, "Marriage."
79. Quoted in D. Biale, *Eros,* 167.

ering all the travelers with accounts of their merchandise."[80] Dik rejects earlier traditional culture as providing *too much latitude for women*, while the modernizing, enlightening process would fetter them more successfully. As David Roskies has described his view, Dik believed "that naturally vain and frivolous, their innate shortcomings were given free rein by Polish rulers who for centuries had encouraged the women to go against nature and take over the Jewish economy. . . . While the men needed to spend less time in the synagogue Study-House to assume a more vigorous entrepreneurial role, the women needed to model themselves on the biblical woman of valor (Prov. 31:10–31), becoming good housewives and devoted mothers."[81] Among the ironies of this position is, of course, the fact that that very "woman of valor" is described in the biblical text as economically active, in contact with the "outside" world, and dominant—"She made a cloth and sold it to a Canaanite"—while her husband sits "in the gates" with the men discussing Torah![82]

Dik had written: "For fifty years ago, the custom was wide-spread in Lite [the Jewish name for greater Lithuania, including today's Latvia and Beloruss], that wives supported their husbands. The grooms were idlers, and *were therefore called by the names of their wives and mothers-in-law. . . .* And thus [the matchmakers] would praise each bride that she is big and strong and able to support a husband, and therefore it is no wonder that until this very day we find in the little villages men who are called by the names of their wives: Avramel, Sarah Hanah's; Reb Yudel, Recha's; Reb Chaim, Gitke-Toibes, and the like."[83]

Dik, in his utopian vision, completely ignores the fact that the Jewish women of his time who have "taken over" the Jewish economy are acting in accord with Jewish traditional patterns, and he desires to replace that model of Jewish womanhood with that of the "angel in the house." Such was (at least some) Jewish "Enlightenment."[84] Dik's program for modernization of Jewish society thus would have comprised what is for us the decidedly dystopian production of a class of cloistered, idle bour-

80. A. M. Dik, "The Utopia of a Maskil," quoted in Parush, "Readers," 15.
81. Roskies, *Bridge*, 93.
82. Cantor, *Jewish Women*, 110.
83. Dik, *Rabbi*, 133. I am grateful to Naomi Seidman for pointing me to this text. This is my translation from Sadan's rendering of the Yiddish into Hebrew.
84. I do not deny a genuine feminist impulse in the writings of some of the "Enlighteners" but suspect that, in general, it was their desire to attack traditional culture that motivated them, like any colonial compradors, more than their zeal for the benefit of women.

geois women and girls, for the presence of middle-class women in public spaces had become unacceptable in "modern, enlightened" circles.[85]
"Because their female ideal was fragile and vulnerable, *maskilim* perceived the skills typical of petty commerce, when practiced by women,
as a particular assault on the image of the Jewish community as a
whole."[86] This embourgeoisement was the regime that caused Anna
O.'s great suffering. While Ibsen was protesting Nora's condition, the
"Enlighteners" among the Jews were holding her up as an ideal for a
Jewish society "purged of all dross"! All of these were in direct opposition to Bertha Pappenheim's program for Jewish modernization
*through a radical reclamation and enhancement of the traditional eco-
nomic and social power of Jewish women* and of Yiddish—of exactly
what the other modernizers (including many Zionists) were reading as
the *"no longer acceptable* ways of Jewish women."[87] Max Nordau,
eventually the second in command of the Zionist movement, even produced a novel, *The Right to Love,* intended explicitly as a refutation of
Ibsen's *Doll's House.*[88]

Dik wished to neutralize the traditional economic power of European Jewish women and, moreover, to negate the cultural power of the
older female literary tradition which was a source, it would seem from
Pappenheim's report, of feminist resistance from within. The following
report of a nineteenth-century Galician woman, from a Yiddish memoir, reveals the extent to which this was valid: "Bubbe Leah well remembered the days and nights up in the attic. While Zeide Moishel
consorted with the Hasidim until late, Bubbe Leah would sit in the hidden nooks up in the women's section of the synagogue rocking the
cradle of her eldest son and reading the books of legends [those that
Pappenheim was translating!]. How many hours of comfort did she ex-

85. I am puzzled by Parush's statement that "the fact that Dik envisages the enlightened society of the future in such staunchly traditional terms is not without irony." As far
as I can see, the patterns that Dik is inveighing *against* were the traditional ones; the
"Enlightenment" that he envisaged was simply embourgeoisement and was congruent
with contemporary movements within European culture, for which John Fout ("Moral")
provides a good account.
86. Hyman, *Gender,* 70.
87. In this light, her decision to translate the *Tsenerene,* the Yiddish "Women's Bible" may be poignantly contrasted to Zionist and "Enlightenment" contempt for this text
(Seidman, "Marriage," 310–12). Cf. also Chava Weissler who writes: "Ashkenazic Judaism itself offered multiple possibilities for the cultural construction of gender, possibilities
which can still be explored and reclaimed" ("Religion," 94).
88. Mosse, "Introduction," 22.

perience by virtue of these stories in Yiddish. The slight volumes of legends protected this lonely woman and produced great desire in her heart. *Bubbe Leah would gaze upon her only daughter, Tante Itke, and secretly hope that she, this Tante Itke, would win at the game that her mother had lost.*"[89]

We see here clearly the double role that the Yiddish women's religious literature played: On one hand, it "protected and comforted" the lonely Rabbi's wife who would have loved to be a part of the study community of the Hasidim of which her husband was the leader, but on the other hand, it produced "great desire in her heart" that the daughter, at least, would be able to enter such a community, "would win at the game that her mother had lost." The Yiddish literature, intended to comfort women and keep them, as it were, in their place, was thus the incitement for a feminist impulse within the heart of the most traditional of Jewish communities. Pappenheim certainly understood well the roles of Yiddish and Hebrew in antithetical politics of Jewish modernization. Where she sought continuity with family and tradition, together with radical reform from within and synthesis with the "best" of European culture, the "Enlighteners" and the Zionists sought a complete break with tradition and the reconstruction of the Jewish collective as a separate (but equal) modern nation. She identified Yiddish, and particularly the literature known as Women's German, as the avenue for both of her programs, both feminist and cultural reconstruction. She fathomed the analogy between the emancipation of women and Jews, because "while each group sought to fit into the dominant society, each had acquired a consciousness of its unique qualities which it deserved to retain."[90] The Zionists revived Hebrew "by tapping into a strong distaste for the disempowered *galut* [Diaspora] existence that was often consciously or unconsciously perceived as having emasculated or feminized the Jewish collective; this distaste reflected itself, above all, in the rejection of the *mameloshn* ['mama language,' or Yiddish] that both expressed and was the product of the objectionable Eastern European past."[91]

Pappenheim perceived that by seeing the Jewish collective as "feminized," Zionists were effectively writing out the women entirely, be-

89. Trunk, *Polin*, 224, emphasis added.
90. M. Kaplan, *Jewish Feminist Movement*, 200.
91. Seidman, "Marriage," 277.

cause Jewish women were anything but feminized.[92] "I found in the unknown Jewish woman of diaspora Judaism the ability to perform great
tasks,"[93] but "Zionists, (not Zionism)—in their first pronouncements
considered all those women's duties which I consider absolutely necessary as negligible."[94] Zionism was, after all, explicitly designed to produce a Jewish version of the *Männerbund*, a culture of Muscle-Jews.[95]
Her objections to Zionism were thus founded on the ways that gender
traversed the whole project:[96] its rejection of the family and cultural
continuity, its intentional uprooting of children from parents in order
to produce "New Jews," and together with these, its adoption as one of
its primary "task[s] the suppression of the Yiddish language with all its
feminine associations."[97] Zionism and Hebrew were projects of the
masculinist "same," while traditionalism, Yiddish (Women's German),
and feminism were undertakings of difference.

Pappenheim's critique was both consciousness-raising and redemptive at the same time. On one hand, she was recovering a tradition of
women's spirituality and women's literature, as well as women's public
economic and social activity that had been largely lost to the bourgeois
German-speaking Jews of her time and which had led to a situation in
which for the Jewish woman of the present Judaism had become a dead
letter. On the other hand, she was also strenuously indicting the traditional practice—maintained in eastern Europe—that had kept women
from full participation in Jewish learning. In this she had a younger
counterpart, and eventual associate, in Sore Shenirer, daughter of a
Cracow Hassidic family, who as a young girl struggled against the limi-
tations on education for women, divorced, and continued studying. Interestingly enough, it was after hearing a sermon in Vienna at the Orthodox Stumper Gasse Synagogue calling for the betterment of Jewish
women's education that Shenirer became fired with the idea of radically reforming Jewish women's lives by founding a chain of Orthodox

92. Seidman is particularly sharp on the explicit marginalization of the female in the
project of revival of the "masculine" tongue, Hebrew, in Palestine ("Marriage," 272–80).

93. Edinger, *Bertha*, 79.

94. Edinger, *Bertha*, 81. Her "not Zionism" I take to mean that it is not necessary to
the project of national revival that it disregard women's oppression or women's power;
but these were pandemic among actual Zionists. At other places, she explicitly designs
herself an "old active enemy of the [Zionist] movement" (Edinger, *Bertha*, 99).

95. Berkowitz, *Zionist Culture*, 19; Nordau, "*Muskeljudentum.*"

96. Edinger, *Bertha*, 81–82.

97. M. Kaplan, *Jewish Feminist Movement*, 48–49.

Jewish women's schools. Because this sermon was delivered in 1914, after fifteen years of Pappenheim's work for radical reform of women's education in Judaism, we cannot rule out the possibility that it was her consciousness-raising efforts that had ultimately led to this very sermon.

In any case, Sore Shenirer's analysis was identical to that of Pappenheim. Jewish women were leaving the fold because of their enforced ignorance of Jewish tradition.[98] As Irena Klepfisz has put it, "Both a radical and a traditionalist, she wanted to work *with* the Orthodox community and not against it."[99] With the encouragement of her brother, a rabbi, she went to visit a major Hassidic figure, the Belzer Rebbe who strongly supported her, and she then founded the Bes Yakov movement in Cracow, which by the beginning of World War II had more than forty thousand students in 250 girls' schools throughout central and eastern Europe.[100] Like Pappenheim, Shenirer's "commitment to preserving traditional *yiddishkayt* was intimately connected to her devotion to the Yiddish language."[101] Bertha Pappenheim's last public activity was to take a trip to Cracow for a meeting of the Board of Trustees of the Bes Yakov movement.

I find Pappenheim is a precursor of one strand of contemporary feminist thought that insists on the significance of female resistance in the past and not exclusively on the efficacy of male domination. She thus anticipates the point made by Naomi Seidman, when the latter writes critically of Max Weinreich's description of the marginalization of Yiddish and the Jewish woman in "traditional Jewish society": "My argument with Weinreich here is double: first, there must be some way to discuss the hierarchy of values in traditional Jewish life that does not reduce it to the perspective of the male intellectual sphere. Certainly there were areas and moments where women were central, where the 'primacy' of men must have been felt as rather remote. In these places (the market, the 'women's section' of the synagogue), Yiddish and women were primary."[102] It is crucial in critiquing Jewish androcen-

98. Hyman, *Gender,* 59.

99. Klepfisz, *"Di Mames,"* 20. Klepfisz's excellent article gives short biographies of several powerful modern Jewish woman radicals, both traditionalists and decidedly anti-traditionalists.

100. Weissman, *"Bais."*

101. Klepfisz, *"Di Mames,"* 20.

102. Seidman, *"Marriage,"* 80.

trism (as all others) to retain a sense of outrage at the oppression and domination without losing sight of the locations within which women had real power in the society as well. Otherwise, as Seidman perceives, we simply reproduce the cultural caste system once more. Pappenheim, it would seem, already saw this point.

The hysteric grew into the feminist, because being a feminist "cured" the hysteric. But what enabled the transformation from one—clearly most painful and not to be romanticized—form of protest to another?[103] Part of the answer to the mystery has been suggested by Freeman, who writes, "In Vienna, Bertha Pappenheim had been a nobody, just a 'girl,' not allowed to go to a university. . . . But in Frankfurt she became a 'somebody.' "[104] I propose, therefore, the following hypothesis: The difference between the conditions of life for Jewish women in Vienna and Frankfurt was one of the factors that made it possible for Anna O. to become Bertha Pappenheim. Strong, at least circumstantial, evidence for this hypothesis can be gleaned from the fact that after stays in Karlsruhe in which she took nursing courses, a visit to Vienna in 1883 brought on a relapse of her hysteria such that she committed herself to a psychiatric sanatorium on three separate occasions for several months each between that year and 1887. After her move with her mother to Frankfurt in 1888, there is no further record of psychiatric disturbance. Pappenheim's contemporaries also remarked the specificity to Vienna of her confinement to a useless life of leisure and the reversal with the

103. I am trying to make clear here that by reading a political protest in Bertha Pappenheim's condition, I am not doing her the posthumous injury of making light of her suffering. It has sometimes seemed as if those who would read the illnesses of both female hysterics and Daniel Schreber as political thereby suppress the suffering that they underwent. However, I feel that *palaeodiagnosis*, the medical treatment of long-dead people like Anna O., is a nearly useless procedure, an opinion which has the support of at least one expert historian of medicine: "Psychiatric case histories, even such comprehensive accounts as Breuer's, should not be assimilated to timeless pathological or anatomical descriptions. We are not free to wrench symptoms and diagnosis from their own temporal and sociocultural contexts. The question of 'correct' diagnosis (or of 'correct' treatment indeed!) is hardly fruitful. The interpretation of this case, as of others, is stamped with the thought schemata of a given period, as well as being influenced by current institutional conditions. The identification and description of categories appropriate to a particular time would be a most difficult task" (Hirschmüller, *Life*, 132). My interest as a cultural analyst and critic is to use the material in a venture to reconstruct as much of the temporal and sociocultural context and the thought schemata of the time, not to diagnose someone who can no longer be helped (but whose memory might be hurt) by such a procedure. If I write "illness" with scare quotes, then, this is not to make light of Pappenheim's suffering but to emphasize what I take to be the environmental causes of that suffering. Cf. the very significant remarks of Tania Modleski on romanticized anorexia (Modleski, *Feminism*, 110).

104. Freeman, *Story*, 249; see also Appignanesi and Forrester, *Freud's*, 78.

Plate 14.   Bertha Pappenheim at Approximately the Time She Was Anna O.
Untitled, ca. 1890, artist unknown (Dora Edinger?). (Courtesy of the Leo
Baeck Institute, New York.)

move to Frankfurt (see Plate 14). She became the housemother in an
orphanage for Jewish girls, an occupation virtually impossible to imagine for the bourgeois girl, the *höhere Tochter* in Vienna. One of her later
charges wrote of her earliest time in Frankfurt: "This period meant a
complete revolution in her life . . . with total renunciation of her former
habits—she was very spoiled in Vienna and lived the life of a *höhere*

Tochter—she did justice to the many demands which this new sphere of activity imposed on her."[105]

In Vienna, even when she was sick Anna O. displayed, according to Breuer, an ability to take care of others, thus signaling on many accounts her predisposition for her later activities. We must, however, draw a distinction between the private sphere of home-care for the invalid and the public sphere of both social work and political action that Pappenheim later engaged in. Indeed, the distinction between private and public and the ways that this binary functioned in women's lives is crucial to understanding Anna O.'s metamorphosis. Frankfurt had developed a tradition of Jewish women's public social activism, which Vienna apparently lacked.[106]

Pappenheim herself later writes of the "necessity to adjust the *Mizwah* (religious commandment)—to help your neighbor in changing times—from overblown philanthropy and blind, senseless spending of money to sensible and conscientious action [i.e., politics]. *The congregation of Frankfort-on-the-Main fifty years ago offered a rich and challenging place for such an effort.*"[107] There was also a strong current of Jewish feminist activity in Frankfurt at the time and Pappenheim remarks explicitly that the participants were both "orthodox and liberal."[108]

It was in Frankfurt that she was able, therefore, to take the position as housemother in a Jewish orphanage, an option that had been unavailable to her in Vienna, and that proved to be her doing. From that position she moved on to the directorship of the orphanage and thence to her feminist political and social activities. *Post hoc ergo propter hoc* seems a not unreasonable deduction under the circumstances. Moving to Frankfurt was, then, one of the most important elements in her cure.[109]

Aside from her tale of two cities, her discovery of Jewish and non-Jewish female role models, such as Mary Wollstonecraft and Glikl of Hameln—both of whose works she translated—was clearly a significant factor in her self-reconstruction. Her intellectual cousin, Anna Etlinger in Karlsruhe, strongly encouraged her own literary endeav-

---

105. Quoted in M. Kaplan, *Jewish Feminist Movement*, 42.
106. Edinger, "Bertha," 182.
107. Edinger, *Bertha*, 80, emphasis added; see also Hyman, *Gender*, 30.
108. Edinger, *Bertha*, 14.
109. I am encouraged to discover that this point has been adumbrated but not developed by Karpe ("Rescue," 24). In specific, Karpe does not even mention the differences of Jewish life between the two places as relevant but just "cultural climate and sociological conditions."

ors,[110] and soon after the move to Frankfurt, her first book, *Little Stories for Children,* was published.[111]

This book and its sequel were literary renditions of what Breuer had referred to earlier when he wrote: "This girl who was bubbling over with intellectual vitality led an extremely monotonous existence in her puritanically-minded family. She embellished her life in a manner which probably influenced her decisively in the direction of her illness, by indulging in systematic daydreaming, which she described as her 'private theater.'" It is not at all incidental that her first book was published anonymously, that her succeeding works were published under the male pseudonym, Paul Berthold, and that only a decade later did she publish under her own name.[112] Her publication itself marks the progression from the private to the public. Thus we have two parallel structures of development in the metamorphosis of Anna O. into Bertha Pappenheim, and both involve the move from a *private* theater to a *public* one, from a theater of inner reverie and hysterical performance to a public arena of literary production[113] and militant feminist activism, from self-punishment to punishment of the male power structures that oppressed her and other women, especially Jewish women.

As Decker has expressed it in the case of Dora: "Since women often could not be overtly assertive in Victorian life, they could be passively aggressive. Hysteria gave them indirect power, which they used quite well. Hysterical women could leave relatives, friends, and doctors baffled, annoyed, angry—and impotent either to understand the situation or do anything about it. The angrier others became toward the hysterical female patient, the more she responded in the only way she could, indirectly, with intractable symptoms and increased manipulation of those close to her.... Yet in striking out against a world she did not like, Dora ultimately lashed out most cruelly against herself." Luckier than most, Bertha Pappenheim was to discover direct power, which she used to much purpose. I categorically reject pathologizing interpretations of Pappenheim's later life that seek to diagnose her political life as illness. This is the importance, rather, of diagnosing "illness" as political speech, without denying the very real suffering of the hysteric. In contrast to Dora, Pappenheim discovered the power that Dora's

---

110. Hirschmüller, *Life,* 115.
111. Hirschmüller dates this publication between 1888 and 1890.
112. Hirschmüller, *Life,* 117.
113. Herndl, "Writing."

brother, the Austrian Marxist leader, had found in political life: "Through
socialism, Otto had a socially approved outlet for venting complaint,
outrage, and rebellion. He could move beyond directing his feeling and
behavior solely toward family members and instead direct his emotions
toward symbolic objects."[114] Decker writes of Dora that "her resort to
hysteria indicated that Dora was not an overt rebel."[115] Bertha Pappenheim became an overt rebel, as had Otto Bauer, and thus reclaimed herself from the expedient of hysteria, and she, unlike Bauer, did this with
the explicit intention of preserving Jewish life, not of surmounting it.
The move from private to public, from Viennese Victorian "angel in the
house" to political fighter, is what enabled that transformation.

    Like Freud and Herzl, Bertha Pappenheim was, in part, a trans-
planted Eastern Jew; her father was born in Pressburg (now Bratislava)
in Slovakia. Her mother was the daughter of a wealthy Frankfurt Jewish family. Pappenheim grew up, like them, in Vienna during a cultural
moment in which heterosexuality was being invented, and Jewish men
and women were being interpellated into its regime. Ann Pellegrini has
sharply focused on this cultural nexus as it impinged on one aspect of
Freud's theories. Her analysis is, however, illuminating for my purposes
as well. She proposes "a structural analogy between the more dominant
household role played by Jewish women in Eastern Europe (as opposed
to the 'angel in the house model' of Victorian, Christian womanhood),
on the one hand, and the masculinization of early childhood femininity,
on the other. The achievement of properly passive and vaginal female
sexuality would then be structurally analogous to the 'westernization'
of Jewish household dynamics, in which the male assumes the normative and Christianized role of head of household, and the female recedes
to the background." And "in Freud's subterranean geography of Jewishness, gender, and race, East is to West as phallic women are to angels
in the house. . . . In Freud's own 'case history,' East was to West as his
Galician mother, Amalie Nathanson Freud, was to his German wife,
Martha Bernays Freud."[116] Thus if, as Samuel Slipp writes, "in patriarchal Victorian society, women were deprived of an individual identity

114. Decker, *Freud*, 71. I find even this formulation of Decker's somewhat reductive
and psychologistic, a judgment that I repeat anent her statement that, "in those cases
where a girl's growing-up years had been satisfactory and she had, on the whole, received
equitable and considerate treatment within the family, she could sublimate whatever
grievances she had and injustices she had observed in charity work. This is what Anna O.
had done, and it eventually led to a career. Not surprisingly, she never married" (233).
115. Decker, *Freud*, 106.
116. Pellegrini, "*Without* You."

and needed to achieve a sense of self by identifying with the social and economic successes of their husbands,"[117] this would have led to massive conflict between the gender performances of traditional Jews and those of Victorian Vienna. As Ernst Simon cleverly put it, "In this patriarchal home the mother ruled: she possessed the greatest fund of energy and vision."[118]

A typical (if satirically theatrical) description of an East European couple can be found in the autobiography of an anonymous Maskil, cited by Iris Parush:

> True, my uncle would sit in my aunt's shop, but it would have been better if he hadn't. He was ignorant in the language of the land and he feared every gentile, man or woman. He sat crouching over a book; customers did not approach him and he did not approach them. "Margolit [his wife] will be right here" he would console them. My aunt was the mistress of house and shop. It was she who managed the business and journeyed to the trade fairs in Moscow and St. Petersburg. It was she who rounded up the money to purchase wares and settle accounts. Though he, the lord and master, wrote the letters and signed the accounts, it was not only with her knowledge and by her orders that he did so but indeed in her very name: "Margolit, wife of Shamai Aharoni."[119]

Parush, for her part, sagely remarks that "so comical a description is obviously open to charges of exaggeration. Yet it is hard to cast doubt on the social practice that it reflects vis-à-vis the division of roles in the family, a practice that reinforced the image of the vigorous woman and the passive man" (Women).

A fascinating piece of evidence for this has been adduced by Chava Weissler, who shows that in the Yiddish women's versions of midrashic compilations, the "Patriarchs" are presented as passive recipients of God's blessings, the "Matriarchs" as active intercessors with God. As she remarks, "The [classic] midrashic material, in the aggregate, certainly does not portray the patriarchs as passive, in contrast to active matriarchs. Yet this text, by selecting among midrashic motifs, puts together a picture that gives that impression,"[120] thus suggesting that it is the cultural model of gender of the Ashkenazi editors that has dictated the selection. Shaul Stampfer also remarks of nineteenth-century East

117. Slipp, *Freudian*, 7.
118. Simon, "Sigmund," 272.
119. Ben-Hillel Hacohen, *Kevar*, 20–22.
120. Weissler, "Religion," 92.

European Jews: "Even the concepts of beauty were different. The ideal man was the retiring, pale, delicate Talmudist with sensitive hands and long white fingers, while the ideal woman was an active, even aggressive, full-bodied woman with multiple chins."[121] As Hyman has succinctly phrased it: "The strong, capable working woman was the dominant cultural ideal, in contrast to the ideal of woman as the creator of a domestic haven (or heaven) that prevailed in the bourgeois West."[122] This, at any rate, was hardly a "woman deprived of an individual identity" who "needed to achieve a sense of self by identifying with the social and economic successes of her husband." My only addition would be to remark once more that the religious sphere did deprive Jewish women of individual and intellectual identity.

Such a gendered pattern was bound to appear queer to Germanized Jews (and to the bourgeoisie in general).[123] Within late nineteenth-century German culture, as John Fout has emphasized, manliness was defined as (among other things) having a career and supporting one's family economically. Anthropologist David Gilmore considers this to be a near universal definition of manhood, writing: "To be a man, in most of the societies we have looked at, one must impregnate women, protect dependents from danger, and provision kith and kin. So although there may be no 'Universal Male,' we may perhaps speak of a 'Ubiquitous Male' based on these criteria of performance. We might call this quasi-global personage something like 'Man-the-Impregnator-Protector-Provider.'"[124] Historian of sexuality Vern Bullough goes even further, promoting this to a universal definition of manliness: "Though what constitutes manhood has varying definitions according to a society or culture or time period, the most simplistic way of defining it is as a triad: impregnating women, protecting dependents, and serving as provider to one's family."[125]

It is not surprising then that European Jews upset the nineteenth-century gender order, for this triad patently did not define manhood for traditional Ashkenazic Jewish society, within which, whatever the dis-

121. Stampfer, "Gender," 72.

122. Hyman, *Gender*, 68; see also Glenn, *Daughters*, 14.

123. An piquant sidelight to this point is the fact that Leopold von Sacher-Masoch, a Polish non-Jew who rather favored dominant women, frequently had Jewish women as his heroines. One of his stories was about the wife of a Talmud scholar, who was "born to rule" and—dressed in furs. On this, see the illuminating article by D. Biale, "Masochism," 313–14.

124. Gilmore, *Manhood*, 223.

125. Bullough, "On Being," 34.

abilities and disenfranchisements of their status, women assumed responsibility for families of dependents, including their scholar-husbands who neither "protected" nor provided for them, but *did,* of course, impregnate them—quite frequently.[126] Within the context of the dominant fiction of European culture, for a man, being supported by a woman would certainly have been encoded, then, as effeminizing, while having a career rendered a woman a viraginized monster. George Mosse has powerfully argued that women who did not fulfill the womanly ideal were dangerous because of the ways that they threatened to expose "real manliness" as a fabrication, and that this would have real social, economic, and political consequences.[127] As John Fout writes: "Women did not have careers because if they worked at all, it was argued, it was merely to supplement the efforts of their men. It was often reiterated, for example, that it was wrong for women to want access to men's work. By claiming the rewards of work as the sole domain of men, the moral purity movement sought to limit as long as possible any new opportunities for women to expand areas of women's work. The moralists wanted to maintain the strict gender polarization and gender-specific features of most paid employment. The male moral purity movement understood all too well the remarkable power that came with the male role."[128] But Jewish women had traditionally held at least *that* kind of remarkable power, thus bringing the bourgeois paradigm and the traditional Jewish one into sharp dissonance.[129]

In her early life, Pappenheim lived in the Jewish "ghetto" of Leopoldstadt, which was by then quite full of Galician immigrants. A difference between the family environments of Pappenheim, on one hand, and of Freud and Herzl, on the other, is that she was raised in a quite traditional but highly acculturated Orthodox Jewish home, while theirs were equally acculturated but respectively quite and thoroughly estranged from Jewish traditional life. Thus, where the two male figures devoted themselves to escaping the difference of Jewish gender, Pappenheim was engaged in enhancing its usable aspects and radically transforming its deleterious mien. In 1934, she writes extensively in protest against the Zionist and other youth movements, which al-

126. I suspect it is a far less universal pattern than Gilmore or Bullough imagines. For the comparatively recent stabilization of this definition even within Euro-American society, see Seecombe, "Patriarchy."
127. Mosse, *Image,* 12.
128. Fout, "Moral," 21.
129. Parush, "Women."

though they provide enrichment of girls' lives, "tear the pre-adolescent and adolescent young people out of their families in which they should be firmly rooted for the future, because religious ties during girlhood through education and custom should surround the whole religious existence."[130] As Naomi Seidman observes, for Zionists "Hebrew was not just a language, it was also a reorganization of traditional family structures, a recovery program for wounded Jewish masculinity and a corrective to *the no longer acceptable ways of Jewish women.*"[131] As I have elaborated above, these "no longer acceptable ways" involved those sources of economic and thus social autonomy and power that traditional Jewish culture did make, willy-nilly, available for women. This authority is symbolized in part by the fact, pointed out by a scandalized Aizik Meir Dik in the above-quoted passage, that men were frequently called by the names of their wives or mothers-in-law. Such names remain Jewish surnames until this day: Perles (belonging to Perl), Taubes, and so on. In other words, at least Western Zionism was an instrument of the colonization of Jewish culture in this respect as well.[132]

Glikl of Hameln provided Bertha Pappenheim with several vital constituents for the creation of a traditionally Jewish, feminist identity. She was an author who, apparently like Anna O., wrote "for fear of falling into melancholia."[133] Pappenheim, to be sure, emphasizes the exceptional nature of Glikl's literary career[134] and protests the fact that it was essentially private in nature, written as it was for her family, a fact that provides further evidence for my claim that the binary of private/public was a central dynamic in Pappenheim's social psychic life. Pappenheim wanted to go beyond Glikl to full, active cultural participation for Jewish women in public religious and literary life. At the same time, however, she claims Glikl as a model for her own and other Jewish women's lives. Pappenheim writes explicitly that Glikl "represents the German-Jewish culture of her day"[135] at the same time that she protests that Glikl did not influence that culture. In other words, once again we find

---

130. Edinger, *Bertha*, 90.

131. Seidman, "Marriage," 280, emphasis added.

132. To be sure, other Zionisms offered for a moment more radical gender options as well. These were quickly closed off, however, once male Jewish machismo became the main goal (D. Biale, *Eros*), and even on the most radical of kibbutzim women became quite quickly the cooks and nurturers, men the farmers and workers.

133. Pollock, "Glückel," 218–19.

134. Glikl herself, however, writes of a sister who also produced "a wonderful will," that is, an ethical will or moral tract written for her children.

135. Edinger, *Bertha,* 77.

the dual move of her resistance to the terms of a bourgeois civilization that would deprive Jewish culture of significance and value for women, at the same time that she pursues a militant critique of that society's treatment of women. Pappenheim sought to enhance the valuable aspects of traditional Judaism and surmount the injurious ones.

I am not suggesting that all early modern Jewish women had lives like Glikl's; not all were as talented or as fortunate in family and marriage as she. But I am claiming that her life was well within the parameters of what could be expected and hoped for in many traditional Jewish societies. Bertha Pappenheim protested against Jewish societies that did not live up to this ideal and she sought to reconstruct them as well as herself in its image. As Pappenheim resisted embourgeoisement, heterosexualization, and thus the confinement of fin de siècle Viennese women and became more like Glikl of Hameln, she became more powerful and left her affliction behind. I hypothesize that "her solid, rugged, masculine appearance,"[136] was not an idiosyncrasy but a cultural characteristic (see Plate 15). Bertha Pappenheim, like Sigmund Freud and Theodor Herzl, was caught in the crisis of Jewish gender at the fin de siècle, a crisis that was both part of a general European moment as well as a specific moment in Jewish modernization, one particularly acute in Vienna. In not insignificant ways, her life and personality paralleled theirs: she had the passion, the nearly obsessive quality, and the power to inspire a "cult of personality," as well as impatience with those who disagreed with her. The difference is that Pappenheim's practice was dedicated to the continuation of Jewish culture as an independent alterity, while Freud's and Herzl's were dedicated to its disappearance. For Pappenheim, Judaism—for all of her bitter critique—was syntonic; for Freud and Herzl, dystonic. They were devastated by the construction of Jews as differently gendered; Pappenheim owned this difference.[137] They adopted made-up pseudo models—Hannibal, Massena, and Tancred (see previous chapter)—and an imaginary Egyptian Moses; she had a "real" Jewish role model.

In a heuristically suggestive analysis, Frederick Bram has already

136. Edinger, *Bertha*, 77, quoting from a memoir.
137. One cannot ignore the fact that in the general economy of gender in Euro-American culture, "butch" seems almost always valued over "femme." This would argue that viraginizing women are more acceptable than feminizing men; thus the Jewish female is ultimately more assimilable as such than the Jewish male, at least on the psychosexual level. Men and women will boast of having a "tomboy" daughter; how many (even feminists) will boast of having a "sissy" son?

Plate 15.   Bust of Bertha Pappenheim Illustrating Her Strong "Masculine" Appearance. Untitled, n.d., Fred J. Kormis. (Courtesy of the Leo Baeck Institute, New York.)

proposed that issues of gender identification are crucial for understanding Anna O. and her transformation into Bertha Pappenheim.[138] Pappenheim's mother had, on more than one occasion, been described as "dragonlike," a description that suggests to me that she was a powerful personality. Recha Goldschmidt Pappenheim was, I imagine, more like her "ancestress" Glikl—whose legal name, for the government, was Goldschmidt[139]—in certain crucial ways than she was like the "angels in the house" of bourgeois fin de siècle Vienna. That's why she was called "dragonlike," a description very similar to descriptions of Freud's (Galician) mother as well. I wish to suggest that this was at least as much a cultural characteristic as an individual idiosyncrasy. These women did not fit the mold of proper bourgeois females. As Martin Freud wrote explicitly of his grandmother: "She was a typical Jewess of Ashkenasi origin. She was not what one would call a lady, had a lively temper and was impatient, self-willed, sharp-witted and highly intelligent."[140] Recha Goldschmidt Pappenheim was also apparently "not what one would call a lady," and that undoubtedly recommended her as a role model in the eyes of her daughter, but, equally undoubtedly, promoted massive role model conflicts between the historical family pattern for women and that of the circumambient bourgeois society of which the Pappenheims aspired (like nearly all Jews of the place, time, and class) to be full members.

Bram thinks that in the young Bertha this led to learning "to deprecate womanhood and the role of women." From this he concludes that "Anna, a brilliant youngster 'bubbling with intellectual vitality' found refuge only in the more prideful masculinity of her father." Quite naturally, he derives from this premise that she identified first with her father, then with Breuer, both of whom "abandoned" her, which made her sick. In order to be cured she had to "come to terms with her mother. . . . She became *like* her mother, which proved the lesser of the evils, and having thus decided the immense problem of *who* she was going to be, she was then able to carry on a useful life—although with the incorporated discouragement of the mother remaining a burden throughout her years."[141]

There is almost no evidence for the aspects of this interpretation that

138. Bram, "Gift."

139. N. Z. Davis, *Women*, 8. She was not an actual ancestress, for Recha Goldschmidt was the descendant of a sister of Glikl's husband (215).

140. Martin Freud, quoted in Appignanesi and Forrester, *Freud's*, 14.

141. Bram, "Gift," 57.

in effect blame Recha Pappenheim for her daughter's condition; however, there is something very useful in this account for all that. I would
rewrite it in the following fashion: Pappenheim suffered in her youth
from extreme conflicts in role models, since her mother was a very powerful and active woman but all of the sociocultural expectations and
stereotypes that surrounded her were of women's passivity and idleness.
Pappenheim sought to identify herself with or win acceptance, therefore, from the male figures in her life. This, however, left her furious at
those very authority figures.[142] When she found ways of identifying as
a strong, active female, she was able to "introject" her mother as a positive role model. As evidence for her identification with her mother, I
would adduce the fact that when she died, she was buried according to
her request next to her mother in Frankfurt and not her father in Vienna; this was a long-term plan recorded in *Yahrzeit* (memorial) prayers
she wrote in honor of her mother.[143]

It seems that one of the most compelling moments in the transformation that enabled this incorporation of the mother was the discovery of
Glikl of Hameln as an ancestress, an event which took place sometime
in the second half of the 1890s.[144] Breuer reports that Anna was completely irreligious, although she kept traditional Jewish law for her father's sake at the time Breuer treated her, and, as Ellenberger remarks,
"One would wish to know how and when she returned to the faith of
her ancestors and became the ardent religious personality of the later
years."[145] The answer is to be found once more in the discovery of positive, active, female Jewish role models who functioned in public and
were not confined to the "private theater." The most important of these
was Glikl. When Bertha Pappenheim discovers a Jewish woman whom
she admires, she refers to her as "the true living Glückel" (see above),
thus expressing her conception that Glikl is not a single individual but
an ideal type of Jewish woman, the powerful, articulate, vibrant, active
woman, the very antithesis of a Victorian "angel in the house."

In a brilliant lecture delivered just as this book goes to press, Bluma

142. Richard Karpe, writing in *The Psychoanalytic Quarterly* several years before
Bram published his paper, clearly remarks the aspects of anger at male oppressors (my
term) in Pappenheim's "illness" ("Rescue," 9). On the other hand, Karpe's picture of
Pappenheim as feminist is hardly free of antifeminist stereotypes.
143. Edinger, *Bertha*, 97.
144. See, however, above, n. 139. The first edition of the Yiddish original of the text
was published by David Kauffman in 1896. Pappenheim's German translation of Glikl's
memoirs was published in 1910.
145. Ellenberger, "Story," 278.

Goldstein has revealed another vitally important aspect of Glikl's text: its explicit thematization of female political agency and female solidarity. Glikl retells the stories of two Jewish women whose husbands had disappeared, leaving them "anchored women" not permitted to remarry, nor given the status of widows. In Glikl's version of these historical narratives, as opposed to the male-authored version, the neighbor of one of these women, a certain Rebecca, took matters into her hands and proved that the husband had been murdered, thus freeing the wife. Another woman in the same situation was empowered and inspired through this action to do the same. In Goldstein's analysis, the story is made into a paradigm through its thematization of its empowering effect on the second woman.[146] We can easily imagine that Pappenheim, in turn, took this as a parable and as an inspiration for her own exercise of female power and solidarity with respect to very similar issues of the liberation of women within the religious community. Glikl thus provides a model for a feminist resistance from a position of wholehearted identification with Jewish Orthodoxy. It is certainly highly significant that when she had a portrait painted, Pappenheim dressed in the clothing that Glikl would have worn, including the hair covering of the traditional Jewish woman (see Plate 16).[147]

JEWISH MALE EFFEMINISM: AN EPILOGUE

If the dilemmas posed by gentle Jews (victimization) and
tough Jews (brutalization) are to be resolved, an important
first step will be critically to work through and ultimately
beyond the male assumptions of present thinking.[148]

—Paul Breines

It is probably clear by now that if for Bertha Pappenheim, Glikl of Hameln was an ego-ideal, then Bertha Pappenheim is such for me: she

146. B. Goldstein, "Doubly Exiled."

147. The original has been lost. Fortunately, it has been twice published: once in the original calendar of the Jüdischer Frauenbund, and once in the *Blätter* of that organization for 4 April 1932 (Edinger, *Bertha,* 101). The reproduction here is taken from the copy of the *Blätter* in the collection of the Leo Baeck Institute, New York. The portrait is reproduced on the cover of a new edition of Glikl, published in 1979 in Darmstadt by the Verlag Darmstdäter Blätter as if it were a portrait of Glikl herself and nowhere identified in the book as a portrait of Pappenheim. I am not sure whether Pappenheim would have been pleased or not at this total erasure of the border between her and her "ego-ideal."

148. Breines, *Tough Jews,* 39.

Plate 16.　Bertha Pappenheim in Her Portrait as Glikl. (Courtesy of the Leo Baeck Institute, New York.)

is the Jew who "got it right," who figured out how to combine—however tensely—militant feminist protest and demand for radical change within Judaism with a continued commitment to the existence of vibrant, full traditional Jewish life and personal commitment to continuing the practice of Halakha. I would have my portrait painted while wearing Bertha Pappenheim's clothes.[149] She seems to have been able to negotiate the minefield between critique and defense of Jewish culture, between polemic and apologetic, that seems so formidable and yet so imperative. She is also the Jew who, moreover, combined her passionate concern for "her own People" and her devotion to their way of life with activity on behalf of all oppressed women everywhere, in concert with efforts by other women.[150]

This has finally revealed itself to be a book about identification—and cross-gendered identification at that. What I ask—at the risk of a final violation and abandonment of academic decorum—is: Is it a fluke that the Jew that I identify with is . . . a Jewess? And especially: Is it accidental that in describing myself, the two most prominent attributes would be Jew and feminist? Is some kind of gender-crossed identification, in short, constitutive of Jewishness, one that Freud and Herzl were eager to escape and Pappenheim embraced (an embrace that includes the bitingly critical aspects of her attachment to Judaism)?

Marjorie Garber has written: "It is the *Jewish woman* who gelds or castrates her own father; as with James Joyce's Bella Cohen—or, indeed with the stereotypical 'Jewish American Princesses' of macho-Jewish writers like Roth and Mailer—the fantasized Jewish woman crosses over into the space of 'masculinity' which is put in question by the ambivalent cultural status of the Jewish man."[151] This is a stunning insight, tossed out in a parenthetical remark by Garber. I am going to introduce some critical complications into the explanation, however, because there seems at first glance to be some circularity in Garber's narrative. Who is doing what to whom? Is the "Jewish woman" gelding her father, or is the ambivalent cultural space already occupied by her

---

149. See Fradenburg, "Pleasures," 377, for a concise and rich discussion of the implications of such identifications and their sexual and gendered collations.

150. "The social work that grew roots in the religious topsoil of Frankfurt Am Main would not have found resonance beyond the boundaries of the city, had it not found stimulation and support from the German women's movement at large. Out of this fusion of German cultural elements with Jewish cultural heritage grew an intellectual substance that gained the greatest momentum, both for the German women's movement as well as for Jewish life" (Pappenheim, "Jewish Woman").

151. Garber, *Vested Interests,* 229.

father virilizing her? And from whose point of view are "gelding" and "masculinity" being projected? These are obviously cultural constructions, so whose "ambivalent cultural space" is it anyway? There is strong evidence, however, that just as Jewish men were perceived as feminized—and queer—by European gentile culture, Jewish women were perceived as virilized, indeed as viragos.[152]

As Ann Pellegrini has written, "The hyperbolic femininity of the *belle juive* conceals her 'real' nature: a perverse masculinity."[153] Sexual categories are racialized ones: Jewish men are femminized and Jewish women phallicized. Pellegrini has shown how Jewish heroines, such as Judith, were "taken up into the anti-Semitic stereotype of the Jewess as deadly seductress."[154] Rather than a one-sided perception of Jewish men as feminized or of Jewish women as viraginized, can we not begin to conceive of the structure of Jewish gender as being differently configured, as being resistant to the increasingly rigidifying patterns of gender that the European regimes of romantic love and heterosexuality were enforcing more and more vigorously in the nineteenth century? This is not on my part—any more than it was on the part of my "ego-ideal"— an attempt to simply valorize prebourgeois Jewish society as better for women than modernity is. Such a reactionary apologetic mode would thoroughly cross my purpose of forging a feminist Jewish strategy within a set of complicated and conflicted loyalties and desires. This book is rather an endeavor at writing a different history of the present, so as to make possible a catachresis, a certain mode of existence that is different from what is happening now that calls itself traditional Judaism. One of the things I find in this archive and in Jewish "cross-gendering" is a genealogy for male Jewish feminism.

The male panic that so characterizes European life at the end of the nineteenth century was deeply connected with Judeophobia as well. Jews threatened the heterosexual, bourgeois order of gender in some profound way.[155] It is no accident that Otto Weininger's work evoked such profound response, nor that Daniel Schreber imagined himself as woman and as Jew.[156] The antisemitic and homophobic movements of

152. This suggests a further possibility for thought, namely, that just as Freud's narrative of progression from more feminine to more masculine on the part of men is an allegory of escape from *Ostjudische* gender-trouble, his myth of little girls who are little boys who develop femininity might be the same. See also Pellegrini, *Performance*, 49–50.
153. Pellegrini, *Performance*, 70.
154. Pellegrini, *Performance*, 70.
155. Mosse, *Nationalism*, 151–52.
156. Geller, "Unmanning."

fin de siècle Austro-Germany were strongly connected. Antifeminism was antisemitic as well.[157] Hannah Decker has emphasized this connection, citing the declaration of the chairman of the German League against Women's Emancipation who wrote: "The modern feminist movement is, like Social Democracy, an international, foreign body in our national life. Both movements are, considering the great participation of the Jewish element, international in origin, and fight, with equal fanaticism against all fundamentals of the people's life."[158] The leader of the right-wing Austrian antisemitic political movement, Georg von Schönerer had written: "In general, it is unoccupied women who devote themselves to the idiocy of female suffrage, women who have failed in their calling as women or who have no wish to answer it—and Jewesses. They naturally get the support of all the old women of the male sex and of all 'feminists,' that is, those men who are no men."[159] "Men who are no men" are the partners of women who are no women,[160] and "Jewesses" are prominent in that latter category, just as male Jews were prominent in the former.[161]

Feminists are here, paradoxically enough, male Jews, *identified with women*. The political is very personal indeed. I suggest, very diffidently, that vestiges of a different gendering persist in the socialization of many male Jews even today,[162] and that far from being accidental that a Jewish man would identify himself with a female, feminist leader, this is the inchoate, tacit, working out of a cultural difference, a very fragile one to be sure and one, moreover, that once recognized requires both care-

157. Volkov, "Antisemitism," 31–35.

158. Quoted in Decker, *Freud*, 199.

159. Quoted in Pulzer, "Rise," 222. According to Gunther d'Alquen, the chief editorial writer for Himmler's *Das Schwarzer Korps*, National Socialism had ended the Jewish domination of art, saving it from its "embrace by homosexuals and 'manly women'" (Mosse, *Nationalism*, 163).

160. Note how similar this set of ideas is to Weininger's basic concept of womanish men attracted to viraginous women who together will form a perfect couple (Weininger, *Sex*, 80). 'Twas ever so: "*Viragines* are the feminine counterpart to *cinaedi*" (Brooten, *Early Christian*, II.B.1).

161. Geller, "Blood," 30. Paul Rose comments that while Wagner was dependent on Heine for the theme of *The Flying Dutchman*, "what vitiated Heine as either a poetic or a revolutionary model for Wagner was his Jewish irony. The earnest Wagner could never understand—or forgive—this quintessential quality in Heine. Heine's Flying Dutchman certainly placed before Wagner the ideal of redemption by means of woman's love, but the poet's flippantly ironic ending of his piece must have perplexed the young Wagner—Heine's moral is that women should beware of Flying Dutchmen!" (*Wagner*, 33). In light of the above text, is it not possible that there is something else in Heine's ending (its implicit "feminism," or at any rate sympathy with women) that annoyed Wagner and led him eventually to disavow the connection with the Jewish poet?

162. Brod, *Mensch*.

ful nurturing and close guarding from the dangers of becoming *mere* appropriation—all identification comprises some appropriation—what Tania Modleski has called "feminism without women."[163]

This is a book about male identification with women, a collective one in the cultural history of male Jews but also my own. I say this to lend authority to my work and also to take authority away from it. The authority that I wish to lend it is the authority of my commitment, and the authority that I wish to deprive it of is the authority of "objective" science. Jewish scholarship, known until now as the "Science of Judaism," *Wissenschaft des Judentums,* has pretended to a disinterestedness, to an objectivity, even as it has been always intimately involved in one political agenda or another, either apologetic defense of Judaism or polemic attacks upon it or on one of its historical forms. Even scholars who have genuinely, sincerely imagined that they are seeking only "the historical truth" can be shown, with the hindsight of other times, to have been pursuing an agenda all the more palpable for its having been occluded.

I freely acknowledge (without claiming to be transparent even to myself) that I seek interested knowledge. I am a sort of orthodoxymoron, a male feminist Orthodox Jew, and my interest is in the perpetuation of Judaism through an internal process of feminist reformation. By calling myself "Orthodox," I am making two statements: first, that I am committed to the compelling character of Jewish practice for Jews and to the principle that such praxis cannot be changed simply by fiat; and second, that I believe it is within the current community of Jews who call themselves "Orthodox," many of whom live their lives in daily and consistent study and practice of Jewish life, that the most likely future for continued Jewish alterity is to be found, so it is there that radical change must ultimately happen. In short, rather than proclaiming a solution or resting place, as perhaps it will inevitably be heard, my use of "Orthodox" is intended to augur the *radically* unfinished (and utopian) nature of my personal, scholarly, political, cultural, religious project— and not to declare my identification with or cast aspersions on any institution of contemporary Jewry. I am no happier in (and with) the institutions of contemporary Judaism that call themselves Orthodox than with any other ones.

By constructing a model of rabbinic Judaism as a tensive culture within which issues of gender and sexuality were being contested and

163. Modleski, *Feminism.*

for which possibilities were progressively shut down within later Jewish history, I am hoping to reposition Judaism as a culture in the present day as well—not as a culture that is hostile to women's fullest participation and fulfillment, nor as a culture that is "homophobic," but as one that is open to organic change in its practices regarding these issues, because its fullest, deepest understandings of humanness and Jewish community will require such changes, given our contemporary social and cultural situations. It is in this sense that Pappenheim cried out that Jewish women were to "learn nothing"—not that they were to be ignorant, as she has been misunderstood to say, but that they were not to be part of the community of Torah-learning, the Bes Hamidrash. If women and men feminists and lesbigay people learn Torah, the very Torah that they learn will change itself.[164] This utopian hope is based on an understanding of Torah, not as text or institution, but as the practice of living Jewish communities of study and interaction with the text.[165]

We know virtually nothing of the actual lives of Jews (men and women) in the talmudic period, while we know quite a bit about such actual lives in modernity; and if we do not know whether (or to what extent) women were or felt oppressed within Jewish culture in late antiquity,[166] we do certainly know that women—including many who remained "Orthodox"—felt, that is, *were*, woefully oppressed by the system of exclusions and domination that obtained in modern traditional Jewish society.[167] There are two simultaneous propositions that must be kept in mind: first, that this textual practice known as rabbinic Judaism has given rise (certainly in modern times) to oppressive social formations vis-à-vis gender and sexuality; and second, that such oppressive social structures are not the only logically possible ones that could arise from this particular set of texts and significations, nor necessarily the only ones that have existed in the past. Nor is it a matter of separating

164. This perspective is very close to that articulated by Rachel Biale over ten years ago (*Women*, 266), and I think that this formulation at least partially addresses some of the questions that Laura Levitt has recently posed to it (Levitt, *Reconfiguring*, 57).

165. J. Boyarin, "Voices."

166. All that I mean by this is that, since anthropologists have amply demonstrated frequent systematic differences between male and female conceptual schemata and symbolic systems in many cultures, we cannot assume that we know anything about the women of talmudic times to whose voices we have virtually no access, except by reading against the grain of the Talmud and related literature.

167. Another potentially very rich resource for the actual lives and even voices of Jewish women would be the medieval Mediterranean communities that produced the archives in the Cairo Geniza (Goitein, *Family*). This is such a rich lode of material, however, and its scope is so far from the focus of this book on Europe, that it will have to wait for another project.

out "good" moments from "bad" ones. The very articulations that support gender domination are those that empower an alternative construction of gender and power. Much more fine-grained analysis of the rabbinic systems of domination of women (whether or not we assume their actual "reality" as other than signifying practices) seemingly will advance our understanding and redemptive critique enormously.

In other words, two forms of critical work need to be engaged at the same time. One is directed at a critique of traditional Jewish culture and gender practice, while the other mobilizes aspects of that practice in order to demystify dominant ideologies of gender within the larger cultural and social context. One argues for the potential and necessity for radical change within traditional Judaism, while the other argues that that traditional culture has something to offer in the effort to produce radical change within the culture of "the West." Without the former the latter is an ethical impossibility. This will explain the double-movement of my work, at once critical and recuperative of traditional Judaism. Although the entire project is redemptive critique, readers will have been aware that at certain moments (in certain chapters or sections) one or another of these modes, redemption or critique, is dominant. For instance, in chapter 3, in the course of presenting one of the originary texts of construction of the rabbinic, counter-manly male ideal, I began also to consider some of the negative effects of the construction of Jewish male gender through a self-femminization, and especially the manner within which this produced an almost structural exigency to keep women away from the study of Torah, with all of the devastating effects that that exclusion has had. However, I discern within this text itself a nascent internal critique of the social effects of homotopia. That rudimentary internal critique encourages me to carry further the critique, as one from within the culture.

My work is a defense of the Rabbis even as it is a claim that contemporary traditional Jewish culture needs to find resources for radical change with respect to gender and sexuality. I hope to accomplish this through a radical rereading of the existing tradition and texts rather than an attack upon them. It should be said, however, that this is a peculiar sort of apologetic, if only because I imagine that many, if not most, if not nearly all, of the current community who define themselves as inheritors of the classical rabbinic tradition will be appalled by it. What seems to be at work here is a complicated play of competing claims for realness, both informed, however, in different ways by "modernity" and "Enlightenment." If I am not willing to claim some sort of nativist authenticity (the really real) for my dissenting reading, neither am I willing to grant really realness to the regnant interpretations—patriarchal, homophobic—of rabbinic Jewish culture. The trick is to take a position that does not deny or sweep under the rug, and thus perpetuate, the reality, the authenticity, historical and hermeneutical, of that with which I cannot live in a traditional Jewish culture, while not conceding the field of tradition, of authenticity to that version alone—a trick that feels sometimes a bit like walking a tightrope over the Grand Canyon. Common apologetics and much feminist critique seem to fall easily into one version or another of a positivist assumption of what Judaism really is, either to reify or to reject. In a sense then this highly idiosyncratic (but not, I hope, wild) reading of talmudic culture is intended as a work, not so much of reconstruction, as of recovering materials for an altogether new and different construction of a Jewish past and everyone's future. Tradition, as Bertha Pappenheim understood and enacted it, is precisely the critical recovery of the past that we make for the redemption of the future.[168]

168. I venture to hope that readers will feel the spirit of Walter Benjamin hovering here.

Works Cited

Abrahams, Beth-Zion, trans. and ed. *Memoirs* [Glückel of Hameln: Life 1646–1724]. Introd. by Beth-Zion Abrahams. New York: Thomas Yoseloff, 1963.

Alter, Robert. "Freud's Jewish Problem." *Commentary.* January 1992.

Anzieu, Didier. *Freud's Self-Analysis.* Trans. Peter Graham. Preface by M. Masud and R. Khan. Paris: 1975. Reprint, Madison, Conn.: International UP, 1986.

Appignanesi, Lisa, and John Forrester. *Freud's Women.* New York: Basic, 1992.

Arens, Katherine. "Characterology: Weininger and Austrian Popular Science." In *Jews & Gender: Responses to Otto Weininger,* ed. Nancy A. Harrowitz and Barbara Hyams. Philadelphia: Temple UP, 1995. 121–39.

Aschheim, Steven E. *Brothers and Strangers: The East European Jew in German and German Jewish Consciousness, 1800–1923.* Madison: U of Wisconsin P, 1982.

——. " 'The Jew Within': The Myth of 'Judaization' in Germany." *The Jewish Response to German Culture from the Enlightenment to the Second World War,* ed. Jehuda Reinharz and Walter Schatzberg. Hanover, N.H.: UP of New England, 1985. 266–93.

Bakhtin, Mikhail. *Rabelais and His World.* Trans. Hélène Iswolsky. Bloomington, Ind.: Indiana UP, 1984.

Baldwin, P. M. "Liberalism, Nationalism, and Degeneration: The Case of Max Nordau." *Central European History* 13 (1980): 90–120.

Baron, Lawrence. "Theodor Lessing: Between Jewish Self-Hatred and Zionism." *Leo Baeck Institute Yearbook* (1981): 323–40.

Barratt, Barnaby B., and Barrie Ruth Straus. "Toward Postmodern Masculinities." *American Imago* 51.1 (1994): 37–67.

Barton, Carlin A. "All Things Beseem the Victor: Paradoxes of Masculinity in Early Imperial Rome." In *Gender Rhetorics,* ed. Richard Trexler. Albany: SUNY, 1994. 83–92.

————. "The 'Moment of Truth' in Ancient Rome: Honor and Embodiment in a Contest Culture." Unpublished essay. Berkeley, 1995.

————. "Savage Miracles: The Redemption of Lost Honor in Roman Society and the Sacrament of the Gladiator and the Martyr." *Representations* 45 (Winter 1994): 41–71.

————. *The Sorrows of the Ancient Romans: The Gladiator and the Monster.* Princeton, N.J.: Princeton UP, 1993.

Baskin, Judith R. "Rabbinic Judaism and the Creation of Woman." *Shofar* 14.1 (1995): 66–71.

Bataille, Georges. *Eroticism.* Trans. Mary Dalwood. 1957. Reprint, London: Marion Boyars, 1987.

Beller, Steven. "Herzl, Wagner, and the Ironies of 'True Emancipation.' " In *Tainted Greatness: Antisemitism and Cultural Heroes,* ed. Nancy A. Harrowitz. Themes in the History of Philosophy. Philadelphia: Temple UP, 1994. 127–55.

————. "Otto Weininger as Liberal?" In *Jews & Gender: Responses to Otto Weininger,* ed. Nancy A. Harrowitz and Barbara Hyams. Philadelphia: Temple UP, 1995. 91–101.

————. *Vienna and the Jews, 1867–1938: A Cultural History.* Cambridge: Cambridge UP, 1989.

Ben-Amos, Dan, and Jerome R. Mintz, trans. and eds. *In Praise of the Baal Shem Tov [Shivḥei Ha-Besht].* In *The Earliest Collection of Legends about the Founder of Hasidism.* Bloomington: Indiana UP, 1970.

Ben-Hillel Hacohen, Mordekhai, ed. *Kevar.* Warsaw: Shtibel, 1923.

Benjamin, Jessica. *The Bonds of Love: Psychoanalysis, Feminism, and the Problem of Domination.* New York: Pantheon Books, 1988.

Bergmann, Martin S. "Moses and the Evolution of Freud's Jewish Identity." *The Israel Annals of Psychiatry and Related Disciplines* 14 (1976): 3–26.

Beritela, Gerard F. "The Wish That Dares Not Speak Its Name: Homoerotic Longing in Freud's 'Myops' Dream." Unpublished paper. Syracuse University, 1993.

Berkowitz, Michael. *Western Jewry and the Zionist Project, 1914–1933.* Cambridge: Cambridge UP, 1996.

————. *Zionist Culture and West European Jewry Before the First World War.* Cambridge: Cambridge UP, 1993.

Berman, Marshall. *All That Is Solid Melts Into Air: The Experience of Modernity.* 1982. Reprint, New York: Penguin Books, 1988.

Bernstein, Michael Andre. *Foregone Conclusions.* Contraversions: Critical Studies in Jewish Literature, Culture, and Society. Berkeley and Los Angeles: U of California P, 1994.

Bersani, Leo. "Foucault, Freud, Fantasy, and Power." *GLQ* 2.1–2 (1995): 11–33.

————. *The Freudian Body: Psychoanalysis and Art.* New York: Columbia UP, 1986.

————. "Is the Rectum a Grave?" In *AIDS: Cultural Analysis / Cultural Activism.* Cambridge: MIT P, 1988. 197–222.

Bhabha, Homi K. *The Location of Culture.* London: Routledge, 1994.

———. "Of Mimicry and Men: The Ambivalence of Colonial Discourse." *October* 28 (1984): 125–33.

———. "Signs Taken for Wonders: Questions of Ambivalence and Authority under a Tree Outside Delhi, May 1817." *Critical Inquiry* 12.1 (1985): 144–65.

———. "Sly Civility." *October* 34 (1985).

Biale, David. *Eros and the Jews: From Biblical Israel to Contemporary America.* New York: Basic, 1992.

———. "Masochism and Philosemitism: The Strange Case of Leopold von Sacher-Masoch." *Journal of Contemporary History* 17 (1982): 305–23.

———. *Power and Powerlessness in Jewish History.* New York: Schocken, 1986.

Biale, Rachel. *Women and Jewish Law: An Exploration of Women's Issues in Halakhic Sources.* New York: Schocken, 1984.

Bickerman, Elias. *From Ezra to the Last of the Maccabees.* New York: Schocken, 1962.

Biller, Peter. "Views of Jews from Paris around 1300: Christian or Scientific." *Studies in Church History* 29 (1992): 187–207.

Bloch, Donald A. "The Family Therapy of Anna O.: Other Times, Other Paradigms." In *Anna O.: Fourteen Contemporary Reinterpretations,* ed. Max Rosenbaum and Melvin Muroff. New York: Free, 1984. 141–48.

Bloch, R. Howard. *Medieval Misogyny and the Invention of Western Romantic Love.* Chicago: U of Chicago P, 1991.

Blum, H. P. "The Prototype of Preoedipal Reconstruction." In *Freud and His Self-Analysis,* ed. M. Kanzer and J. Glenn. New York: Jason Aronson, 1979. 143–63.

Bolkosky, Sidney. "The Alpha and Omega of Psychoanalysis: Reflections on Anna O. and Freud's Vienna." *Psychoanalytical Review* 69 (1982).

Borch-Jacobsen, Mikkel. "The Oedipus Problem in Freud and Lacan." Trans. Douglas Brick. *Critical Inquiry* 20.2 (1994): 267–82.

Boyarin, Daniel. "Are There Any Jews in the 'History of Sexuality'?" *Journal of the History of Sexuality* 5.3 (1995): 333–55.

———. *Carnal Israel: Reading Sex in Talmudic Culture.* The New Historicism: Studies in Cultural Poetics. Berkeley and Los Angeles: U of California P, 1993.

———. "*Épater L'Embourgeoisement:* Freud, Gender, and the (De)Colonized Psyche." diacritics 24.1 (1994): 17–42.

———. "The Eye in the Torah: Ocular Desire in Midrashic Hermeneutic." *Critical Inquiry* 16 (1990): 532–50.

———. "The Great Fat Massacre: Sex, Death and the Grotesque Body in the Talmud." In *People of the Body: Jews and Judaism from an Embodied Perspective,* ed. Howard Eilberg-Schwartz. Albany: SUNY, 1992. 69–102.

———. *Intertextuality and the Reading of Midrash.* Bloomington: Indiana UP, 1990.

———. "Language Inscribed by History on the Bodies of Living Beings: Midrash and Martyrdom." *Representations* 25 (Winter 1989): 139–51.

———. "Paul and the Genealogy of Gender." *Representations* 41 (1993): 1–33.

———. *A Radical Jew: Paul and the Politics of Identity.* Contraversions: Criti-

cal Studies in Jewish Literature, Culture, and Society. Berkeley and Los Angeles: U of California P, 1994.

———. " 'This We Know to Be the Carnal Israel': Circumcision and the Erotic
Life of God and Israel." *Critical Inquiry* 18.2 (1992): 474–506.

———. "Tricksters, Martyrs, and Appeasers: 'Hidden Transcripts' and the Diaspora Arts of Resistance." In *Jews and Other Differences: The New Jewish
Cultural Studies*, ed. Jonathan Boyarin and Daniel Boyarin. Minneapolis: U
of Minnesota P, in press.

Boyarin, Daniel, and Jonathan Boyarin. "Diaspora: Generation and the Ground
of Jewish Identity." *Critical Inquiry* 19.4 (1993): 693–725.

Boyarin, Jonathan. "The Other Within and the Other Without." In *Storm from
Paradise: The Politics of Jewish Memory*. Minneapolis: U of Minnesota P,
1992. 77–98.

———. *Palestine and Jewish History: Criticism at the Borders of Ethnography*.
Minneapolis: U of Minnesota P, in press.

———. *Storm from Paradise: The Politics of Jewish Memory*. Minneapolis: U
of Minnesota P, 1992.

———. "Voices around the Text: The Ethnography of Reading at Mesivta Tif-
ereth Jerusalem." In *The Ethnography of Reading*, ed. Jonathan Boyarin.
Berkeley and Los Angeles: U of California P, 1993. 212–37.

Boyarin, Jonathan, and Daniel Boyarin. "Self-Exposure as Theory: The Double
Mark of the Male Jew." In *Rhetorics of Self-Making*, ed. Debbora Battaglia.
Berkeley and Los Angeles: U of California P, 1995. 16–42.

Bracken, Henry. "Philosophy and Racism." *Philosophia* 8.2–3 (1978).

Bram, Frederick M. "The Gift of Anna O." *British Journal of Medical Psychology* 38 (1965): 53–58.

Brandes, Stanley. *Metaphors of Masculinity: Sex and Status in Andalusian Folklore*. Philadelphia: U of Pennsylvania P, 1980.

Breines, Paul. *Tough Jews: Political Fantasies and the Moral Dilemma of American Jewry*. New York: Basic, 1990.

Breitman, Barbara. "Lifting up the Shadow of Anti-semitism: Jewish Masculinity in a New Light." In *A Mensch among Men: Explorations in Jewish Masculinity*, ed. and introd. by Harry Brod. Foreword by Letty Cottin Pogrebin.
Freedom, Calif.: Crossing, 1988. 101–17.

Brenkman, John. *Straight Male Modern: A Cultural Critique of Psychoanalysis*.
New York: Routledge, 1993.

Brennan, Teresa. *The Interpretation of the Flesh: Freud and Femininity*. New
York: Routledge, 1992.

Breuer, Josef, and Sigmund Freud. *Studies on Hysteria; The Definitive Edition*.
Trans. and ed. James Strachey. Trans. Anna Freud. New York: Basic, n.d. (=
SE II).

Briggs, Sheila. "Images of Women and Jews in Nineteenth- and Twentieth-Cen-
tury German Theology." In *Immaculate and Powerful: The Female in Sacred
Image and Reality*, ed. Clarissa W. Atkinson, Constance H. Buchanan, and
Margaret R. Miles. Boston: Beacon, 1985. 226–59.

Brod, Harry, ed. *A Mensch among Men: Explorations in Jewish Masculinity*, introd. by Harry Brod. Foreword by Letty Cottin Pogrebin. Freedom, Calif.: Crossing, 1988.

Brooten, Bernadette J. *Love Between Women: Early Christian Responses to Female Homoeroticism and Their Historical Context.* Chicago: U of Chicago P, 1996.

——. *Women as Leaders in the Early Synagogue: Inscriptional Evidence and Background Issues.* Brown Judaica Studies, vol. 36. Chico, Calif.: Scholars', 1982.

Brude-Firnau. "A Scientific Image of Woman? The Influence of Otto Weininger's *Sex and Character* on the German Novel." Trans. Barbara Hyams and Bianca Philippi. In *Jews & Gender: Responses to Otto Weininger,* ed. Nancy A. Harrowitz and Barbara Hyams. Philadelphia: Temple UP, 1995. 171–82.

Bullough, Vern L. "On Being a Male in the Middle Ages." In *Medieval Masculinities,* ed. Clare A. Lees. Medieval Cultures, vol. 7. Minneapolis: U of Minnesota P, 1994. 31–45.

Burrus, Virginia. "Fecund Fathers: Heresy, the Grotesque, and Male Generativity in Gregory of Nyssa's *Contra Eunomium.*" Unpublished paper. Madison, N.J., 1994.

——. Letter to author. 1995.

——. *The Making of a Heretic: Gender, Authority, and the Priscillianist Controversy.* Transformations of the Ancient World. Berkeley and Los Angeles: U of California P, 1995.

——. "The Male Ascetic in Female Space: Alienated Strategies of Self-Definition in the Writings of Sulpicius Severus." Paper presented at SBL / AAR. 1992.

——. "Reading Agnes: The Rhetoric of Gender in Ambrose and Prudentius." *Journal of Early Christian Studies* 3.1 (1995): 25–46.

Bush, Larry. "To Be or not to Be Larry Bush." In *A Mensch among Men: Explorations in Jewish Masculinity,* ed. and introd. by Harry Brod. Foreword by Letty Cottin Pogrebin. Freedom, Calif.: Crossing, 1988. 30–36.

Butler, Judith. *Gender Trouble: Feminism and the Subversion of Identity.* Thinking Gender. London: Routledge, 1990.

Bynum, Caroline Walker. *Jesus as Mother: Studies in the Spirituality of the High Middle Ages.* Berkeley and Los Angeles: U of California P, 1982.

Caldwell, Sarah Lee. *Begotten not Made: Male Metaphors of Procreative Power.* Master's thesis, University of California at Berkeley, 1987.

Cantor, Aviva. *Jewish Women / Jewish Men: The Legacy of Patriarchy in Jewish Life.* San Francisco: HarperSanFrancisco, 1995.

Castelli, Elizabeth A. " 'I Will Make Mary Male': Pieties of the Body and Gender Transformation of Christian Women in Late Antiquity." In *Body Guards: The Cultural Politics of Ambiguity,* ed. Julia Epstein and Kristina Straub. New York: Routledge, 1991. 29–49.

Chamberlain, Houston Stewart. *Foundations of the Nineteenth Century.* Trans. John Lees. Eng. orig. 1910; Germ. orig. 1899. Reprint, New York: Howard Fertig, 1968.

Cheung, King-Kok. "The Woman Warrior versus the Chinaman Pacific: Must a Chinese American Critic Choose Between Feminism and Heroism?" In

Conflicts in Feminism, ed. Marianne Hirsch and Evelyn Fox Keller. New York: Routledge, 1990. 234-51.

Cheyette, Bryan. "Neither Black nor White: The Figure of 'the Jew' in Imperial British Literature." In *The Jew in the Text: Modernity and the Politics of Identity,* ed. Linda Nochin and Tamar Garb. London: Thames and Hudson, 1995. 31-41.

Chodorow, Nancy J. *Femininities, Masculinities, Sexualities: Freud and Beyond.* The Blazer lectures for 1990. Lexington, Ky.: U of Kentucky P, 1994.

Cixous, Hélène, and Catherine Clément. *The Newly Born Woman.* Trans. Betsy Wing. Minneapolis: U of Minnesota P, 1986.

Cohen, Ed. *Talk on the Wilde Side: Towards a Genealogy of Male Sexualities.* New York: Routledge, 1993.

Cohen, Shaye J. D. "Menstruants and the Sacred in Judaism and Christianity." In *Ancient History, Women's History,* ed. Sarah Pomeroy. Chapel Hill: U of North Carolina P, 1991. 273-99.

Connell, Robert W. *Masculinities.* Berkeley and New York: U of California P, 1995.

Cooper, Kate. *The Virgin and the Bride.* Cambridge, Mass.: Harvard UP, 1996.

Craft, Christopher. *Another Kind of Love: Male Homosexual Desire in English Discourse, 1850-1920.* The New Historicism: Studies in Cultural Poetics. Berkeley and Los Angeles: U of California P, 1995.

Crews, Frederick. "The Unknown Freud." *The New York Review of Books* XL.19 (1993): 55-66.

Cuddihy, John Murray. *The Ordeal of Civility: Freud, Marx, Lévi-Strauss and the Jewish Struggle with Modernity.* Boston: Beacon, 1987.

Dahan, Gilbert. *Les Intellectuels chrétiens et les juifs au moyen age.* Paris: Le Cerf, 1990.

Davidson, Arnold. "Sex and the Emergence of Sexuality." In *Forms of Desire: Sexual Orientation and the Social Constructionist Controversy,* ed. Edward Stein. New York: Routledge, 1992. 89-132.

Davis, Natalie Zemon. *Women on the Margins: Three Seventeenth-Century Lives.* Cambridge, Mass.: Harvard UP, Belknap P, 1995.

Davis, Russell H. *Freud's Concept of Passivity.* Psychological Issues. Madison, Conn.: International UP, 1993.

Dean, Tim. "On the Eve of a Queer Future." *Raritan:* 116-34.

Decker, Hannah S. *Freud, Dora, and Vienna, 1900.* New York: Free, 1991.

DeJean, Joan. "Sex and Philology: Sappho and the Rise of German Nationalism." *Representations* 27 (Summer 1989): 148-71.

Dellamora, Richard. *Masculine Desire: The Sexual Politics of Victorian Aestheticism.* Chapel Hill: U of North Carolina P, 1990.

Delphy, Christine. *Close to Home: A Materialist Analysis of Women's Oppression.* Trans. and ed. Diane Leonard. Amherst: U of Massachusetts P, 1984.

Derrida, Jacques. "Interpretations at War: Kant, the Jew, the German." *New Literary History* 22.1 (1991): 39-96.

Deutsch, Helene. "The Significance of Masochism in the Mental Life of Women." In *Essential Papers on Masochism,* ed. Margaret Ann Fitzpatrick Hanly. New York: New York UP, 1995. 411-22.

Dijkstra, Bram. *Idols of Perversity: Fantasies of Feminine Evil in Fin-de-Siècle Culture*. New York: Oxford UP, 1986.

Dik, Aizik Meir. *Rabbi Shemaiah the Blesser of the Festivals*. Trans. and ed. Dov Sadan. Sifriat Dorot. Jerusalem: Bialik Institute, 1967.

Dinshaw, Carolyn. "A Kiss Is Just a Kiss: Heterosexuality and Its Consolations in *Sir Gawain and the Green Knight*." *diacritics* 24.2–3 (1994): 205–26.

Douglas, Mary. *Purity and Danger: An Analysis of Concepts of Pollution and Taboo*. 1969. Reprint, London: Routledge and Kegan Paul, 1978.

Dover, K. J. *Greek Homosexuality*. Cambridge, Mass.: Harvard UP, 1989.

Downing, Christine. *Myths and Mysteries of Same-Sex Love*. New York: Continuum, 1990.

Duffy, Enda. *The Subaltern Ulysses*. Minneapolis: U of Minnesota P, 1994.

Edelman, Lee. "Redeeming the Phallus: Wallace Stevens, Frank Lentricchia, and the Politics of (Hetero)sexuality." In *Engendering Men*, ed. Joseph A. Boone and Michael Cadden. New York: Routledge, 1990. 36–52.

Edinger, Dora. "Bertha Pappenheim (1859–1936): A German-Jewish Feminist." *Jewish Social Studies* XX.3 (1958): 180–86.

———. *Bertha Pappenheim: Freud's Anna O*. Highland Park, Ill.: Congregation Solel, 1968.

Edwards, Catherine. *The Politics of Immorality in Ancient Rome*. Cambridge: Cambridge UP, 1993.

Edwards, Tim. *Erotics & Politics: Gay Male Sexuality, Masculinity, and Feminism*. Critical Studies on Men and Masculinities, vol. 5. London: Routledge, 1994.

Efron, John. *Defenders of the Race: Jewish Doctors & Race Science in Fin-de-Siècle Europe*. New Haven: Yale UP, 1994.

Eilberg-Schwartz, Howard. *God's Phallus and Other Problems for Men and Monotheism*. Boston: Beacon, 1994.

———. *The Savage in Judaism: An Anthropology of Israelite Religion and Ancient Judaism*. Bloomington: Indiana UP, 1990.

Ellenberger, Henri F. *The Discovery of the Unconscious: The History and Evolution of Dynamic Psychiatry*. New York: Basic, 1970.

———. "The Story of 'Anna O': A Critical Review with New Data." *Journal of the History of the Behavioral Sciences* 8 (1972): 267–79.

Ellenson, David. "German Orthodoxy, Jewish Law, and the Uses of Kant." In *Between Traditional and Culture: The Dialectics of Modern Jewish Religion and Identity*. Atlanta: Scholars, 1994. 15–26.

Elon, Amos. *Herzl*. New York: Schocken, 1986.

Epstein, Boruch. *Mekor Boruch: My Memoirs from the Previous Generation*. 4 vols. Vilna, Lithuania: Rom, 1928.

Erikson, Erik H. "The Dream Specimen of Psychoanalysis." *Journal of the American Psychoanalytic Association* 2 (1954): 5–56.

Esterson, Allen. *Seductive Mirage: An Exploration of the Work of Sigmund Freud*. Chicago, Ill.: Open Court, 1993.

Estrich, Susan. *Real Rape: How the Legal System Victimizes Women Who Say No*. Cambridge, Mass.: Harvard UP, 1987.

Etkes, Immanuel. *Lita Biyerushalayim: The Scholarly Elite in Lithuania and the*

Prushim of Jerusalem as Reflected in the Writings of Shmuel of Kelme (in Hebrew). Jerusalem: Yad Izhak Ben-Zvi, 1991.

——. "Marriage and Study among the Lithuanian *Lomdim* in the Nineteenth Century." In *The Jewish Family*, ed. David Kraemer. New York: Oxford UP, 1989. 153–78.

Evans, Martha Noel. "Hysteria and the Seduction of Theory." In *Seduction & Theory: Readings of Gender, Representation, and Rhetoric*, ed. Dianne Hunter. Urbana: U of Illinois P, 1989. 73–85.

Fanon, Frantz. *Black Skin, White Masks*. Trans. Charles Lam Markmann. Paris, 1952. Reprint, New York: Grove Weidenfeld, Evergreen P, 1967.

Feldman, Yael S. " 'And Rebecca Loved Jacob,' but Freud Did Not." In *Freud and Forbidden Knowledge*, ed. Peter L. Rudnytsky and Ellen Handler Spitz. New York: New York UP, 1994. 7–25.

Finkelstein, Louis. *Jewish Self-Government in the Middle Ages*. Philadelphia: Jewish Publication Society, 1924.

Fish, Stanley. "Withholding the Missing Portion: Psychoanalysis and Rhetoric." In *Doing What Comes Naturally: Change, Rhetoric, and the Practice of Theory in Literary and Legal Studies*. Post-Contemporary Interventions. Durham, N.C.: Duke UP, 1989. 525–54.

Fletcher, Anthony. *Gender, Sex & Subordination in England 1500–1800*. New Haven: Yale UP, 1995.

Fonrobert, Charlotte. *Women's Bodies, Women's Blood: Politics of Gender in Rabbinic Literature*. Diss. Graduate Theological Union. 1995.

Foucault, Michel. *The Care of the Self*. Trans. Robert Hurley. New York: Vintage–Random House, 1986. Vol. 3 of *The History of Sexuality*. Paris: Galliamard, 1984.

——. "The Subject and Power." *Michel Foucault: Beyond Structuralism and Hermeneutics*. Afterword by Hubert Dreyfus and Paul Rabinow. Chicago: U of Chicago P, 1983. 208–26.

Fout, John C. "The Moral Purity Movement in Wilhelmine Germany and the Attempt to Regulate Male Behavior." *Journal of Men's Studies* 1.1 (1992): 5–31.

——. "Sexual Politics in Wilhelmine German: The Male Gender Crisis, Moral Purity, and Homophobia." *Journal of the History of Sexuality* 2.3 (1992): 388–421.

Fox, Alan. *Beyond Contract: Work, Power and Trust Relations*. London: Faber and Faber, 1974.

Fradenburg, Louise O. "The Pleasures of History." Introd. with Carla Freccero. *GLQ* 1.4 (1995): 371–84.

Freeman, Lucy. *The Story of Anna O*. New York: Walker and Company, 1972.

Freud, Sigmund. *Analysis of a Phobia in a Five-year-old Boy*. Vol. 10, *The Standard Edition of the Complete Psychological Works of Sigmund Freud*, ed. and trans. James Strachey and Anna Freud. 1909. Reprint, London: The Hogarth, 1955. 3–149.

——. *An Autobiographical Study*. Vol. 20, *The Standard Edition of the Complete Psychological Works of Sigmund Freud*, ed. and trans. James Strachey and Anna Freud. 1925. Reprint, London: The Hogarth, 1955. 3–74.

———. *Civilization and Its Discontents*. Vol. 21, *The Standard Edition of the Complete Psychological Works of Sigmund Freud*, ed. and trans. James Strachey and Anna Freud. 1930. Reprint, London: The Hogarth, 1955. 59–145.

———. *"Civilized" Sexual Morality and Modern Nervous Illness*. Vol. 9, *The Standard Edition of the Complete Psychological Works of Sigmund Freud*, ed. and trans. James Strachey and Anna Freud. 1908. Reprint, London: The Hogarth, 1955. 179–204.

———. *The Economic Problem of Masochism*. Vol. 19, *The Standard Edition of the Complete Psychological Works of Sigmund Freud*, ed. and trans. James Strachey and Anna Freud. 1924. Reprint, London: The Hogarth, 1955. 157–72.

———. *From the History of an Infantile Neurosis*. Vol. 17, *The Standard Edition of the Complete Psychological Works of Sigmund Freud*, ed. and trans. James Strachey and Anna Freud. 1918. Reprint, London: The Hogarth, 1955. 3–123.

———. *Group Psychology and the Analysis of the Ego*. Vol. 18, *The Standard Edition of the Complete Psychological Works of Sigmund Freud*, ed. and trans. James Strachey and Anna Freud. 1921. Reprint, London: The Hogarth, 1955. 67–143.

———. *The Interpretation of Dreams* (First Part). Vol. 4, *The Standard Edition of the Complete Psychological Works of Sigmund Freud*, ed. and trans. James Strachey and Anna Freud. 1900. Reprint, London: The Hogarth, 1955. 1–338.

———. *The Interpretation of Dreams* (Second Part). Vol. 5, *The Standard Edition of the Complete Psychological Works of Sigmund Freud*, ed. and trans. James Strachey and Anna Freud. 1900–01. Reprint, London: The Hogarth, 1955. 339–627.

———. *Leonardo Da Vinci and a Memory of His Childhood*. Vol. 11, *The Standard Edition of the Complete Psychological Works of Sigmund Freud*, ed. and trans. James Strachey and Anna Freud. 1910. Reprint, London: The Hogarth, 1955. 59–137.

———. *Letters of Sigmund Freud*, selected and edited by Ernst L. Freud; translated by Tania Stern and James Stern. Introd. by Steven Marcus. New York: Basic, 1960.

———. *Moses and Monotheism: Three Essays*. Vol. 23, *The Standard Edition of the Complete Psychological Works of Sigmund Freud*, ed. and trans. James Strachey and Anna Freud. 1939. Reprint, London: The Hogarth, 1955. 3–137.

———. *The Moses of Michelangelo*. Vol. 13, *The Standard Edition of the Complete Psychological Works of Sigmund Freud*, ed. and trans. James Strachey and Anna Freud. 1914. Reprint, London: The Hogarth, 1955. 211–36.

———. *Psycho-analytic Notes on an Autobiographical Account of a Case of Paranoia [Dementia Paranoides]*. Vol. 12, *The Standard Edition of the Complete Psychological Works of Sigmund Freud*, ed. and trans. James Strachey and Anna Freud. 1911. Reprint, London: The Hogarth, 1955. 3–79.

———. *Sexuality in the Aetiology of the Neuroses*. Vol. 3, *The Standard Edition of the Complete Psychological Works of Sigmund Freud*, ed. and trans.

James Strachey and Anna Freud. 1898. Reprint, London: The Hogarth, 1955. 261–85.

———. "Three Essays on the Theory of Sexuality." In *Freud on Women: A Reader,* ed. Elisabeth Young-Bruehl. New York: W. W. Norton, 1990. 89–145.

———. *Totem and Taboo.* Vol. 13, *The Standard Edition of the Complete Psychological Works of Sigmund Freud,* ed. and trans. James Strachey and Anna Freud. 1913. Reprint, London: The Hogarth, 1955. 3–149.

———. *The "Uncanny."* Vol. 17, *The Standard Edition of the Complete Psychological Works of Sigmund Freud,* ed. and trans. James Strachey and Anna Freud. 1919. Reprint, London: The Hogarth, 1955. 217–56.

Freud, Sigmund, and Karl Abraham. *A Psychoanalytic Dialogue: The Letters of Sigmund Freud and Karl Abraham.* Ed. and trans. H. C. Abraham; ed. Ernst Freud; trans. B. Marsh. New York: Basic, 1965.

Freud, Sigmund, and Josef Breuer. *Studies on Hysteria; The Definitive Edition.* Trans. and ed. James Strachey. Trans. Anna Freud. New York: Basic, n.d. (= SE II).

Freud, Sigmund, and Sándor Ferenczi. *1908–1914.* Vol. 1, *The Correspondence of Sigmund Freud and Sándor Ferenczi,* edited by Eva Brabant and Patrizia Giampieri-Deutsch; transcribed by Ingeborg Meyer-Palmedo; translated by Peter T. Hoffer. Introd. André Haynal. Cambridge: Harvard UP, Belknap P, 1993.

Frieden, Ken. *Freud's Dream of Interpretation.* SUNY Series in Modern Jewish Literature and Culture. Foreword by Harold Bloom. Albany: SUNY, 1989.

Friedman, Mordechai A. *The Jewish Marriage in Palestine: A Cairo Geniza Study.* 2 vols. New York: The Jewish Theological Seminary of America, 1980.

Friedman, Shamma. "Literary Development and Historicity in the Aggadic Narrative of the Babylonian Talmud: A Study Based upon B.M. 83b–86a." In *Community and Culture: Essays in Jewish Studies in Honor of the 90th Anniversary of Gratz College,* ed. Nahum W. Waldman. Philadelphia: Gratz College, 1985. 67–80.

Fuss, Diana. "Interior Colonies: Frantz Fanon and the Politics of Identification." *diacritics* 24.2–3 (1994): 20–42.

Gallagher, Catherine. "George Eliot and *Daniel Deronda*: The Prostitute and the Jewish Question." In *The New Historicism Reader,* ed. H. Aram Veeser. New York: Routledge, 1994. 124–40.

Garber, Marjorie. *Vested Interests: Cross-Dressing & Cultural Anxiety.* New York: Routledge, 1992.

———. *Vice-versa: Bisexuality and the Eroticism of Everyday Life.* New York: Simon & Schuster, 1995.

Garner, Shirley Nelson. "Freud and Fliess: Homophobia and Seduction." In *Seduction & Theory: Readings of Gender, Representation, and Rhetoric,* ed. Dianne Hunter. Urbana: U of Illinois P, 1989. 86–109.

Gay, Peter. *The Cultivation of Hatred.* Vol. 3, *The Bourgeois Experience: Victoria to Freud.* New York: Norton, 1993.

———. *The Tender Passion.* Vol. 2, *The Bourgeois Experience: Victoria to Freud.* New York: Oxford UP, 1986.

Geller, Jay. "Blood Sin: Syphilis and the Construction of Jewish Identity." *Faultline* 1 (1992): 21–48.

———. "Freud v. Freud: Freud's Reading of Daniel Paul Schreber's *Denkwürdigkeiten Eines Nervenkranten.*" In *Reading Freud's Reading,* ed. Sander L. Gilman, Jutta Birmele, Jay Geller, and Valerie D. Greenberg. Literature and Psychoanalysis. New York: New York UP, 1994. 180–210.

———. " 'Glance at the Nose': Freud's Inscription of Jewish Difference." *American Imago* 49.4 (1992): 427–44.

———. "(G)nos(e)ology: The Cultural Construction of the Other." In *People of the Body: Jews and Judaism from an Embodied Perspective,* ed. Howard Eilberg-Schwartz. Albany: SUNY, 1992. 243–82.

———. "Of Mice and Mensa: Anti-Semitism and the Jewish Genius." *Centennial Review* (1995).

———. "A Paleontological View of Freud's Study of Religion: Unearthing the *Leitfossil* Circumcision." *Modern Judaism* 13 (1993): 49–70.

———. "The Unmanning of the Wandering Jew." *American Imago* 49.2 (1992): 227–62.

Gilman, Sander L. *The Case of Sigmund Freud: Medicine and Identity at the Fin de Siècle.* Baltimore: Johns Hopkins UP, 1993.

———. "Dangerous Liaisons." *Transitions* 64 (1994): 41–52.

———. *Freud, Race, and Gender.* Princeton: Princeton UP, 1993.

———. "The Image of the Hysteric." In *Hysteria beyond Freud,* ed. Sander L. Gilman et al. Berkeley and Los Angeles: U of California P, 1993. 345–452.

———. *Jewish Self-Hatred: Anti-Semitism and the Hidden Language of the Jews.* Baltimore: Johns Hopkins UP, 1986.

———. *The Jew's Body.* London: Routledge, 1991.

———. "Karl Kraus's Oscar Wilde: Race, Sex, and Difference." In *Inscribing the Other.* Lincoln: U of Nebraska P, 1991. 173–90.

———. "Otto Weininger and Sigmund Freud: Race and Gender in the Shaping of Psychoanalysis." In *Jews & Gender: Responses to Otto Weininger,* ed. Nancy A. Harrowitz and Barbara Hyams. Philadelphia: Temple UP, 1995. 103–20.

———. "Salome, Syphilis, Sarah Bernhardt and the 'Modern Jewess'" *German Quarterly* 66 (1993): 195–211.

———. "Sigmund Freud and the Sexologists: A Second Reading." In *Reading Freud's Reading,* ed. Sander L. Gilman, Jutta Birmele, Jay Geller, and Valerie D. Greenberg. Literature and Psychoanalysis. New York: New York UP, 1994. 47–76.

———. "The Struggle of Psychiatry with Psychoanalysis: Who Won?" *Critical Inquiry* 13.2 (1987): 293–313.

Gilmore, David D. *Manhood in the Making: Cultural Concepts of Masculinity.* New Haven: Yale UP, 1990.

Gilroy, Paul. *The Black Atlantic: Modernity and Double Consciousness.* Cambridge, Mass.: Harvard UP, 1993.

Ginzburg, S. M., and P. S. Marek. *Yiddish Folksongs in Russia*. Edited, annotated and introduced by Dov Noy. Ramat Gan: Bar-Ilan UP, n.d.

Gleason, Maud W. *Making Men: Sophists and Self-Presentation in Ancient Rome*. Princeton: Princeton UP, 1995.

Glenn, Susan. *Daughters of the Shtetl: Life and Labor in the Immigrant Generation*. Ithaca: Cornell UP, 1990.

Gluzman, Michael. "The Body as Text, Virility as Language: On the Language of the Body in *The Book of Internal Grammar*." *Siman Keriah*, in press.

Goitein, Shlomo D. *The Family*. Vol. 3, *A Mediterranean Society*. 5 vols. Berkeley and Los Angeles: U of California P, 1978.

Goldberg, Hillel. *Israel Salanter: Text, Structure, Idea: The Ethics and Theology of an Early Psychologist of the Unconscious*. New York: Ktav Publishing House, 1982.

Goldhill, Simon. *Foucault's Virginity: Ancient Erotic Fiction and the History of Sexuality*. The Stanford Memorial Lectures. Cambridge: Cambridge UP, 1995.

Goldstein, Bluma. "Doubly Exiled in Germany: Deserted Wives in Glikl Hameln's *Memoirs* and Solomon Maimon's *Autobiography*." Paper presented at a memorial meeting for Amos Funkenstein. Berkeley, 1996.

———. *Reinscribing Moses: Heine, Kafka, Freud, and Schoenberg in a European Wilderness*. Cambridge, Mass.: Harvard UP, 1992.

Goldstein, Jan. "The Wandering Jew and the Problem of Psychiatric Anti-Semitism in Fin-de-Siècle France." *Journal of Contemporary History* 20 (1985): 521–51.

Goldstein, Moritz. "German Jewry's Dilemma: The Study of a Provocative Essay." *Leo Baeck Institute Yearbook* II (1957): 236–54.

Goldstein, Rebecca. *Strange Attractors: Stories*. New York: Viking, 1993.

Gottfried, Barbara. "What *Do* Men Want, Dr. Roth?" In *A Mensch among Men: Explorations in Jewish Masculinity*, ed. and introd. by Harry Brod. Foreword by Letty Cottin Pogrebin. Freedom, Calif.: Crossing, 1988. 37–52.

Goux, Jean-Joseph. *Symbolic Economies: After Marx and Freud*. Trans. Jennifer Curtis Cage. Ithaca: Cornell UP, 1990.

Graetz, Naomi. "Rejection: A Rabbinic Response to Wife Beating." In *Gender and Judaism: The Transformation of Tradition*, ed. T. M. Rudavsky. New York: New York UP, 1995. 13–23.

Gravdal, Kathryn. *Ravishing Maidens: Writing Rape in Medieval French Literature and Law*. Philadelphia: U of Pennsylvania P, 1991.

Greenberg, David F. *The Construction of Homosexuality*. Chicago: U of Chicago P, 1988.

Grinstein, Alexander. *Sigmund Freud's Dreams*. New York: International UP, 1980.

Grossman, Avraham. "Violence against Women in Medieval Mediterranean Jewish Society." In *A View Into the Lives of Women in Jewish Societies: Collected Essays*, ed. Yael Atzmon. Jerusalem: The Zalman Shazar Center for Jewish History, 1995. 183–208.

Guha, Ranajit. "Dominance without Hegemony and Its Historiography." In *Subaltern Studies VI,* ed. Ranajit Guha. Delhi: Oxford UP, 1989. 210–309.

Ha῾am, Achad. "The Transvaluation of Values (1898)." In *Zionism Reconsidered,* ed. Michael Selzer. New York: The Macmillan Company, 1970. 157–74.

Haberman, Clyde. "Israeli Seizures of Arab-Owned Land Set Off Storm." *New York Times,* May 6, 1995, 4.

Hake, Sabine. "*Saxa Loquuntur:* Freud's Archaeology of the Text." *Boundary 2* 20.1 (1993): 146–73.

Hall, David. "Epispasm and the Dating of Ancient Jewish Writings." *Journal for the Study of Pseudepigrapha* 2 (1988): 71–86.

Hall, Donald E. "Muscular Christianity: Reading and Writing the Male Social Body." In *Muscular Christianity: Embodying the Victorian Age,* ed. Donald E. Hall. Cambridge Studies in Nineteenth-Century Literature and Culture 2. Cambridge: Cambridge UP, 1994. 3–13.

Halperin, David M. "One Hundred Years of Homosexuality." Review of *Die Griechische Knabenliebe,* by Harald Patzer. *diacritics* 16.2 (1986): 34–45.

——. *One Hundred Years of Homosexuality, and Other Essays on Greek Love.* New York: Routledge, 1990.

——. *Saint Foucault: Towards a Gay Hagiography.* Oxford: Oxford UP, 1995.

Harpham, Geoffrey Galt. "So . . . What *Is* Enlightenment? An Inquisition into Modernity." *Critical Inquiry* 20.3 (1994): 524–56.

Harrison, Verna E. F. "A Gender Reversal in Gregory of Nyssa's First Homily on the Song of Songs." Paper presented at Eleventh International Conference on Patristic Studies, Oxford, 19–24 August 1991. *Studia Patristica,* in press.

——. "Male and Female in Cappadocian Theology." *Journal of Theological Studies* 41.2 (1990): 441–71.

——. "Receptacle Imagery in St. Gregory of Nyssa's Anthropology." *Studia Patristica* 22 (1989): 23–27.

Harrowitz, Nancy A. "Lombroso and the Logic of Intolerance." In *Tainted Greatness: Antisemitism and Cultural Heroes,* ed. Nancy A. Harrowitz. Themes in the History of Philosophy. Philadelphia: Temple UP, 1994. 109–26.

——. "Weininger and Lombroso: A Question of Influence." *Jews & Gender: Responses to Otto Weininger,* ed. Nancy A. Harrowitz and Barbara Hyams. Philadelphia: Temple UP, 1995. 73–90.

Hartog, François. *The Mirror of Herodotus: The Representation of the Other in the Writing of History.* Trans. Janet Lloyd. The New Historicism. Berkeley and Los Angeles: U of California P, 1988.

Hauptman, Judith. "Traditional Jewish Texts, Wife-Beating, and the Patriarchal Construction of Jewish Marriage." Unpublished paper. New York, 1995.

——. "Women and Inheritance in Rabbinic Texts: Identifying Elements of a Critical Feminist Impulse." Paper presented at Annenberg Institute. Philadelphia, 1991.

Heller, Peter. "A Quarrel over Bisexuality." In *The Turn of the Century: German Literature and Art, 1890–1915,* ed. Gerald Chapple and Hans H. Schulte. Modern German Studies, vol. 5. Bonn: Bouvier, 1981. 87–116.

Herndl, Diane Price. "The Writing Cure: Charlotte Perkins Gilman, Anna O., and 'Hysterical' Writing." *NWSA Journal* 1.1 (1988): 52–74.

Hertz, Neil. "Dora's Secrets, Freud's Techniques." *diacritics* 13 (1983): 65–76.

Herzl, Theodor. *The Complete Diaries of Theodor Herzl.* Ed. Raphael Patai. Trans. Harry Zohn. New York: Herzl, 1960.

———. "The Jewish State." In *Theodor Herzl: A Portrait for This Age,* ed. Ludwig Lewisohn. Cleveland: The World Publishing Company, 1955. 233–303.

———. "Mauschel." *Selected Writings of Theodor Herzl.* 1897. Reprint, Tel Aviv: M. Neuman, n.d. 176–80.

———. *The New Ghetto: A Play in Four Acts.* In *Theodor Herzl: A Portrait for This Age,* ed. Ludwig Lewisohn. Cleveland: The World Publishing Company, 1955. 152–93.

———. *Old-Newland (Altneuland).* Trans. Lotte Levensohn. New York: Bloch Publishing Company, 1941.

———. *Zionist Writings: Essays and Addresses.* Trans. Harry Zohn. New York: Herzl, 1973.

Hirschmüller, Albrecht. *The Life and Work of Josef Breuer.* Bern, 1978. New York: New York UP, 1989.

Hoberman, John M. "German-Jewish Ideas about Courage at the *Fin de Siècle.*" Paper presented at MLA. San Diego, 1994. Photocopy.

———. "Otto Weininger and the Critique of Jewish Masculinity." In *Jews & Gender: Responses to Otto Weininger,* ed. Nancy A. Harrowitz and Barbara Hyams. Philadelphia: Temple UP, 1995. 141–53.

Holt, Robert R. "Freud's Parental Identifications as a Source of Some Contradictions within Psychoanalysis." In *Freud and the History of Psychoanalysis,* ed. Toby Gelfand and John Kerr. Hillsdale, N.J.: The Analytic, 1992. 1–28.

Hunt, Margaret. "Wife Beating, Domesticity, and Women's Independence in Eighteenth-Century London." *Gender and History* 4 (1992).

Hunter, Dianne. "Hysteria, Psychoanalysis, and Feminism: The Case of Anna O." *Feminist Studies* 9 (1983): 465–88.

Hyams, Barbara. "Weininger and Nazi Ideology." In *Jews & Gender: Responses to Otto Weininger,* ed. Nancy A. Harrowitz and Barbara Hyams. Philadelphia: Temple UP, 1995. 155–68.

Hyman, Paula E. *Gender and Assimilation in Modern Jewish History: The Roles and Representation of Women.* The Samuel & Althea Stroum Lectures in Jewish Studies. Seattle: U of Washington P, 1995.

Ilan, Tal. *Jewish Women in Greco-Roman Palestine.* Texte und Studien zum Antiken Judentum. Tübingen: J. C. B. Mohr (Paul Siebeck), 1995.

Irigaray, Luce. *This Sex Which Is Not One.* Trans. Catherine Porter and Carolyn Burke. Ithaca: Cornell UP, 1985.

Jackowitz, Ann H. "Anna O., Bertha Pappenheim, and Me." In *Between Women,* ed. Carol Ascher, Louise de Salvo, and Sarah Ruddick. Boston: Beacon, 1983.

Jardine, Alice A. *Gynesis: Configurations of Woman and Modernity.* Ithaca: Cornell UP, 1985.

Jensen, Ellen. "Anna O: A Study of Her Later Life." *Psychoanalytic Quarterly* 39 (1970): 269–93.

Johnson, Barbara. "The Frame of Reference: Poe, Lacan, Derrida." In *The Purloined Poe,* ed. John P. Muller and William J. Richards. Baltimore: Johns Hopkins UP, 1987. 213–51.

Jones, Ernest. *The Life and Work of Sigmund Freud: The Years of Maturity.* New York: Basic, 1955.

———. "The Madonna's Conception through the Ear." In *Essays in Applied Psychoanalysis,* vol. 2. London: The Hogarth, 1951. 266–357.

———. *The Young Freud. The Life and Work of Sigmund Freud.* New York: Basic, 1953.

Joshel, Sandra R. "Female Desire and the Discourse of Empire: Tacitus's Messalina." *Signs* 21.1 (1995): 50–82.

Joyce, James. *Ulysses.* 1914. New York: Random House, 1961.

Kalmin, Richard. *Sages, Stories, Authors, and Editors in Rabbinic Babylonia.* Brown Judaica Studies, vol. 300. Atlanta: Scholars, 1994.

Kaminsky, Marc. "Discourse and Self-Formation: The Concept of *Mentsh* in Modern Yiddish Culture." *American Journal of Psychoanalysis* 54.4 (1994): 293–316.

———. Letter to author. 1994.

Kampf, Avram. *Jewish Experience in the Art of the Twentieth Century.* South Hadley, Mass.: Bergin & Garvey, 1984.

Kaniuk, Yoram. *Adam Resurrected.* New York: Atheneum, 1971.

Kaplan, Marion A. "Anna O. and Bertha Pappenheim: An Historical Perspective." In *Anna O.: Fourteen Contemporary Reinterpretations,* ed. Max Rosenbaum and Melvin Muroff. New York: Free, 1984. 101–17.

———. *The Jewish Feminist Movement in Germany: The Campaigns of the Jüdischer Frauenbund, 1904–1938.* Westport, Conn.: Greenwood, 1979.

———. *The Making of the Jewish Middle Class: Women, Family, and Identity in Imperial Germany.* New York: Oxford UP, 1991.

———. "Sisterhood under Siege: Feminism and Antisemitism in Germany, 1904–38." In *The Jewish Response to German Culture from the Enlightenment to the Second World War,* ed. Jehuda Reinharz and Walter Schatzberg. Hanover, N.H.: UP of New England, 1985. 242–65.

Karpe, Richard. "The Rescue Complex: Anna O's Final Identity." *Psychoanalytic Quarterly* 30 (1961): 1–27.

Katz, Jacob. *Tradition and Crisis.* Trans. Bernard Cooperman. New York: Schocken, 1993.

Katz, Jonathan Ned. *The Invention of Heterosexuality.* Foreword by Gore Vidal. Afterword by Lisa Duggan. New York: Dutton, 1995.

Kazanjian, David. "Notarizing Knowledge: Paranoia and Civility in Freud and Lacan." *Qui Parle: Literature, Philosophy, Visual Arts, History* 7.1 (1993): 102–39.

Keen, Maurice. *Chivalry.* New Haven: Yale UP, 1984.

Kinney, Clare R. "The (Dis)embodied Hero and the Signs of Manhood in *Sir*

Gawain and the Green Knight." In *Medieval Masculinities,* ed. Clare A. Lees. Medieval Cultures 7. Minneapolis: U of Minnesota P, 1994. 47–57.

Klein, Dennis B. *Jewish Origins of the Psychoanalytic Movement.* Chicago: U of Chicago P, 1985.

Klepfisz, Irena. "*Di Mames, Dos Loshn* / The Mothers, the Language: Feminism, *Yiddishkayt,* and the Politics of Memory." *Bridges: A Journal for Jewish Feminists and Our Friends* 4.1 (1994): 12–47.

Koestenbaum, Wayne. *Double Talk: The Erotics of Male Literary Collaboration.* New York: Routledge, 1989.

Kofman, Sarah. *The Enigma of Woman.* Trans. Catherine Porter. Ithaca: Cornell UP, 1985.

Kohut, Heinz. *The Restoration of the Self.* Madison, Conn.: International UP, 1977.

Kopelson, Kevin. *Love's Litany: The Writing of Modern Homoerotics.* Stanford: Stanford UP, 1994.

Kornberg, Jacques. *Theodor Herzl: From Assimilation to Zionism.* Jewish Literature and Culture. Bloomington: Indiana UP, 1993.

Die Körperliche Renaissance der Juden: Festschrift zum 10 Jährigen des "Bar Kochba" Berlin. Berlin, 1909.

Kris, Ernst. *The Origins of Psychoanalysis.* New York: Basic, 1954.

Kritzman, Lawrence D., ed. *Michel Foucault: Politics, Philosophy, Culture. Interviews and Other Writings, 1977–1984.* New York: Routledge, 1988.

Lacan, Jacques. "The Meaning of the Phallus." In *Feminine Sexuality: Jacques Lacan and the École Freudienne,* ed. Juliet Mitchell. Ed. and trans. Jacqueline Rose. New York: Norton, 1985. 74–85.

———. *The Psychoses, 1955–1956.* Ed. Jacques-Alain Miller. Trans. and ed. Russel Grigg. In *The Seminar of Jacques Lacan: Book III.* New York: W. W. Norton, 1993.

Lacoue-Labarthe, Philippe, and Jean-Luc Nancy. "The Unconscious Is Destructured Like an Affect: Part I of 'The Jewish People Do not Dream.'" *Stanford Literary Review* 6.2 (1989): 191–209.

Lane, Frederick M. "The Genital Envy Complex: A Case of a Man with a Fantasied Vulva." In *The Psychology of Men: New Psychoanalytic Perspectives,* ed. Gerald I. Fogel, Frederick M. Lane, and Robert S. Liebert. New York: Basic, 1986. 131–51.

Laplanche, J., and J. B. Pontalis. *The Language of Psycho-Analysis.* Trans. Donald Nicholson-Smith. Introd. by Daniel Lagache. New York: W. W. Norton, 1973.

Lefkovitz, Lori. "Coats and Tales: Joseph Stories and Myths of Jewish Masculinity." In *A Mensch among Men: Explorations in Jewish Masculinity,* ed. and introd. by Harry Brod. Foreword by Letty Cottin Pogrebin. Freedom, Calif.: Crossing, 1988. 19–29.

Lentricchia, Frank. "Patriarchy against Itself: The Young Manhood of Wallace Stevens." *Critical Inquiry* (1987).

Le Rider, Jacques. *Modernity and Crises of Identity: Culture and Society in Fin-de-Siècle Vienna.* Trans. Rosemary Morris. New York: Continuum, 1993.

———. "The 'Otto Weininger Case' Revisited." In *Jews & Gender: Responses*

to Otto Weininger, ed. Nancy A. Harrowitz and Barbara Hyams. Philadelphia: Temple UP, 1995. 21–33.

Lerner, Gerda. *The Creation of Patriarchy.* New York: Oxford UP, 1986.

Levine, Lee I. *The Rabbinic Class of Roman Palestine in Late Antiquity.* New
York: Jewish Theological Seminary of America, 1989.

Levitt, Laura Sharon. *Reconfiguring Home: Jewish Feminist Identity/ies.* Ph.D.
Diss. Emory U. 1993. Microfilm.

Lewisohn, Ludwig, ed. *Theodor Herzl: A Portrait for This Age.* Pref. by David
Ben-Gurion. Introd. by Ludwig Lewisohn. Cleveland: World Publishing
Company, 1955.

Lloyd, Genevieve. *The Man of Reason: "Male" and "Female" in Western Philosophy.* 2d Ed. Minneapolis: U of Minnesota P, 1993.

Loewenberg, Peter. "A Hidden Zionist Theme in Freud's My Son the Myops
Dream." *Journal of the History of Ideas* 31 (1970): 29–32.

———. "Theodor Herzl: Nationalism and Politics." In *Decoding the Past: The
Psychohistorical Approach.* 1969. Berkeley and Los Angeles: U of California
P, 1985. 101–35.

Loraux, Nicole. *The Experiences of Tiresias: The Feminine and the Greek Man.*
Princeton: Princeton UP, 1995.

Lowenthal, Marvin, trans. *The Memoirs of Glückl of Hameln.* New York:
Schocken, 1977.

Luxon, Thomas J. Letter to author. 1995.

Lyotard, Jean-François. "Figure forclose. ler janvier 1969." *L'écrit du temps* 5
(1984): 65–105.

McGrath, William J. *Freud's Discovery of Psychoanalysis: The Politics of Hysteria.* Ithaca: Cornell UP, 1986.

McNamara, Jo Ann. "The *Herrenfrage:* The Restructuring of the Gender System, *1050–1150.*" In *Medieval Masculinities,* ed. Clare A. Lees. Medieval
Cultures 7. Minneapolis: U of Minnesota P, 1994. 3–30.

Magnes, Shulamit S. "Pauline Wengeroff and the Voice of Jewish Modernity."
In *Gender and Judaism: The Transformation of Tradition,* ed. T. M.
Rudavsky. New York: New York UP, 1995. 181–90.

Mahony, Patrick L. *Cries of the Wolf Man.* History of Psychoanalysis, mono-
graph 1. New York: International UP, 1984.

Major, Rene. "Revolution of Hysteria." *International Journal of Psycho-analysis* 55 (1974).

Manuel, Frank E. *The Broken Staff: Judaism through Christian Eyes.* Cambridge, Mass.: Harvard UP, 1992.

Marcus, Ivan. "Mothers, Martyrs, and Moneymakers: Some Jewish Women in
Medieval Europe." *Conservative Judaism* (Spring 1986).

Martin, Dale B. *Slavery as Salvation: The Metaphor of Slavery in Pauline Christianity.* New Haven: Yale UP, 1990.

Mass, Lawrence D. *Confessions of a Jewish Wagnerite: Being Gay and Jewish in
America.* Foreword by Gottfried Wagner. Cassell Lesbian and Gay Studies.
London & New York: Cassell, 1994.

Masson, Jeffrey Moussaieff. *The Assault on Truth: Freud's Suppression of the
Seduction Theory.* Harmmondsworth, Middlesex, England: Penguin, 1985.

———, ed. and trans. *The Complete Letters of Sigmund Freud to Wilhelm Fliess, 1887-1904*. Cambridge, Mass.: Harvard UP, Belknap P, 1985.

Mendes-Flohr, Paul. *Divided Passions: Jewish Intellectuals and the Experience of Modernity*. The Culture of Jewish Modernity. Detroit: Wayne State UP, 1991.

Metzger, Mendel. *La Haggada enluminée: Étude iconographique et stylistique des manuscrits enluminés et décorés de la haggada du XIIIe au XVIe siècle*. Pref. by René Crozet. *Études sur le Judaïsme médiéval*. Leiden: E. J. Brill, 1973.

Milbank, John. *Theology & Social Theory: Beyond Secular Reason*. Oxford: Blackwell, 1990.

Miller, D. A. "Anal Rope." In *Inside / Out: Lesbian Theories, Gay Theories*, ed. Diana Fuss. New York: Routledge, 1991. 119-41.

———. "*Cage Aux Folles*: Sensation and Gender in Wilkie Collins's *The Woman in White*." *Representations* 14 (Spring 1986).

Miller, Justin. "Interpretation of Freud's Jewishness, 1924-1974." *Journal of the History of the Behavioral Sciences* 17 (1981): 357-74.

Miller, Patricia Cox. "The Devil's Gateway: An Eros of Difference in the Dreams of Perpetua." *Dreaming* 2.1 (1992): 45-63.

Mirrer, Louise. "Representing 'Other' Men: Muslims, Jews, and Masculine Ideals in Medieval Castilian Epic and Ballad." In *Medieval Masculinities*, ed. Clare A. Lees. Medieval Cultures 7. Minneapolis: U of Minnesota P, 1994. 169-86.

Mitchell, Juliet. *Psychoanalysis and Feminism*. New York: Vintage-Random House, 1974.

Modleski, Tania. *Feminism without Women: Culture and Criticism in a "Postfeminist" Age*. New York: Routledge, 1991.

Moeller, Robert G. "The Homosexual Man Is a 'Man,' the Homosexual Woman Is a 'Woman': Sex, Society, and the Law in Postwar West Germany." *Journal of the History of Sexuality* 4.3 (1994): 395-429.

Montrelay, Michèle. "Why Did You Tell Me I Love Mommy and That's Why I'm Frightened When I Love You." *American Imago* 51.2 (1994): 213-27.

Mopsik, Charles. "The Body of Engenderment in the Hebrew Bible, the Rabbinic Tradition and the Kabbalah." In *Fragments for a History of the Human Body*, vol. 1, ed. Michel Feher et al. New York: Zone Books, 1989. 48-73.

Morgan, Robin. "The Politics of Sado-Maschochist Fantasies." In *Against Sadomasochism: A Radical Feminist Analysis*, ed. Robin Ruth Linden et al. San Francisco: Frog in the Well, 1982. 109-23.

Mosse, George L. *The Image of Man: The Creation of Modern Masculinity*. New York: Oxford UP, 1996.

———. "The Image of the Jew in German Popular Culture: Felix Dahn and Gustav Freytag." *Leo Baeck Institute Yearbook* II (1957): 218-27.

———. Introduction to *Degeneration*, by Max Nordau. 1968. Reprint, Lincoln, Neb.: U of Nebraska P, 1993. xiii-xxxvi.

———. *Nationalism and Sexuality: Middle-Class Morality and Sexual Norms in Modern Europe*. Madison: U of Wisconsin P, 1985.

Myers, David N. *Re-inventing the Jewish Past: European Jewish Intellectuals and the Zionist Return to History.* Studies in Jewish History. New York: Oxford UP, 1995.

Neuda, Fanny. *Stunden der Andacht: Ein Gebet und Erbauungsbuch für Israels Frauen und Jungfrauen.* Prague: Verlag von Wolf Pascheles, 1862.

Nietzsche, Friedrich. In *On the Genealogy of Morality,* ed. Keith Ansell-Pearson. Trans. Carol Diethe. Cambridge Texts in the History of Political Thought. Cambridge: Cambridge UP, 1994.

Nordau, Max. *Degeneration.* Introd. by George L. Mosse. Lincoln: U of Nebraska P, 1968.

———. "*Muskeljudentum.*" In *The Jew in the Modern World: A Documentary History,* ed. Paul R. Mendes-Flohr and Jehuda Reinharz. New York: Oxford UP, 1980. 434–35.

Olender, Maurice. *The Languages of Paradise: Race, Religion, and Philology in the Nineteenth Century.* Trans. Arthur Goldhammer. Cambridge, Mass.: Harvard UP, 1992.

Olyan, Saul. "Lying with a Male the Lying Down of a Woman: The Meaning and Significance of Leviticus 18:22 and 20:13." *Journal of the History of Sexuality* 5.2 (1994).

O'Neill, John. "Law and Gynesis: Freud V. Schreber." In *Shadow of Spirit: Postmodernism and Religion,* ed. Philippa Berry and Andrew Wernick. New York: Routledge, 1992. 238–49.

Pappenheim, Bertha. "The Jewish Woman." In *Bertha Pappenheim, Leben und Schriften,* ed. Dora Edinger. Trans. Renata Stein. Frankfurt am Main: Ner-Tamid Publishers, 1963.

———. *Sisyphus-Arbeit: Reisebriefe aus den Jahren 1911 und 1912.* Leipzig: Verlag Paul E. Linder, 1924.

Pardes, Ilana. *Countertraditions in the Bible: A Feminist Approach.* Cambridge, Mass.: Harvard UP, 1992.

Parry, Benita. "Problems in Current Theories of Colonial Discourse." *Oxford Literary Review* 9 (1987): 27–58.

Parush, Iris. "The Politics of Literacy: Women and Foreign Languages in Jewish Society of Nineteenth-Century Eastern Europe." *Modern Judaism,* in press.

———. "Readers in Cameo: Women Readers in Jewish Society in Nineteenth-Century Eastern Europe." *Prooftexts* 14.1 (1994): 1–24.

———. "Women Readers as Agents for Social Change: The Case of East European Jewish Society in the Nineteenth Century." *Gender and History,* in press.

Pateman, Carole. *The Disorder of Women: Democracy, Feminism, and Political Theory.* Stanford: Stanford UP, 1989.

———. *The Sexual Contract.* Stanford: Stanford UP, 1988.

Pellegrini, Ann. *Performance Anxieties: Staging Psychoanalysis, Staging Race.* New York: Routledge, in press.

———. "*Without* You *I'm Nothing:* Performing Race, Gender, and Jewish Bodies." In *Jews and Other Differences: The New Jewish Cultural Studies,* ed. Jonathan Boyarin and Daniel Boyarin. Minneapolis: U of Minnesota P, in press.

Perkins, Judith. *The Suffering Self: Pain and Narrative Representation in the Early Christian Era*. London: Routledge, 1995.

Peskowitz, Miriam. "Engendering Jewish Religious History." *Shofar* 14.1 (1995): 8–34.

———. "Imagining the Rabbis: Daniel Boyarin and 'Israel's' Carnality." *Religious Studies Review* 21.4: 285–90.

Pollock, George H. "Glückel von Hameln: Bertha Pappenheim's Idealized Ancestor." *American Imago* 28.3 (1971): 216–27.

Prakash, Gyan. "Postcolonial Criticism and Indian Historiography." *Social Text* 31/32 (1992): 8–19.

Prasad, Madhava. "A Theory of Third World Literature." *Social Text* 31/32 (1992): 57–98.

Proust, Marcel. *Sodom and Gomorrah*. Trans. C. K. Scott Moncrieff and Terence Kilmartin. Revised by D. J. Enright. In Search of Lost Time. New York: The Modern Library, 1993.

Pulzer, Peter G. J. *The Rise of Political Anti-Semitism in Germany and Austria*. New York: John Wiley & Sons, 1964.

Ramas, Maria. "Freud's Dora, Dora's Hysteria: The Negation of a Woman's Rebellion." *Feminist Studies* 6.3 (1980): 472–510.

Rank, Otto. "The Essence of Judaism (1905)." In *Jewish Origins of the Psychoanalytic Movement*. ed Dennis B. Klein. Chicago: U of Chicago P, 1985.

Rathenau, Walter. "Letter of 23 January 1916 to Wilhelm Schwaner." In *Schriften,* ed. Arnold Harttung. Berlin: Berlin Verlag, 1965. 114.

Raz-Krakotzkin, Amnon. "Exile within Sovereignty: Toward a Critique of the 'Negation of Exile' in Israeli Culture." *Theory and Criticism: An Israeli Forum* 4 (1993): 23–56; 184–86 (English summary).

Reeves, Christopher. "Breuer, Freud, and the Case of Anna O: A Re-examination." *Journal of Child Psychotherapy* 8 (1982): 203–13.

Reik, Theodor. *Masochism in Modern Man*. Trans. Margaret H. Beigel and Gertrud M. Kurth. New York: Farrar & Reinhart, 1941.

Reinhard, Kenneth. "Freud, My Neighbor." *Lacan's Catholic Science,* special issue of *American Imago,* ed. Daniel Boyarin. In press.

———. "Kant with Sade, Lacan with Levinas." *Modern Language Notes* 110.4 (1995).

Reynolds, Kimberley, and Nicola Humble. *Victorian Heroines: Representations of Femininity in Nineteenth-Century Literature and Art*. New York: New York UP, 1993.

Richlin, Amy. *The Garden of Priapus: Sexuality & Aggression in Roman Humor*. New York: Oxford UP, 1992.

Riemer, Jack, and Nathaniel Stampfer. *So That Your Values Live On—Ethical Wills and How to Prepare Them*. Woodstock, Vt.: Jewish Lights Publishing, 1991.

Robert, Marthe. *From Oedipus to Moses: Freud's Jewish Identity*. Trans. Ralph Manheim. Garden City, N.Y.: Anchor Press, 1976.

Robinson, Paul. *Freud and His Critics*. Berkeley and Los Angeles: U of California P, 1993.

Rogin, Michael. "Blackface, White Noise: The Jewish Jazz Singer Finds His Voice." *Critical Inquiry* 18 (1992): 417–53.

Roith, Estelle. *The Riddle of Freud: Jewish Influences on His Theory of Female Sexuality.* The New Library of Psychoanalysis. London: Tavistock Publications, 1987.

Roper, Lyndal. *Oedipus and the Devil: Witchcraft, Religion, and Sexuality in Early Modern Europe.* New York: Routledge, 1994.

Rose, Paul Lawrence. *Wagner: Race and Revolution.* New Haven: Yale UP, 1992.

Rosenbaum, Max. "Anna O. (Bertha Pappenheim): Her History." In *Anna O.: Fourteen Contemporary Reinterpretations,* ed. Max Rosenbaum and Melvin Muroff. New York: Free, 1984. 1–25.

Rosenfeld, Abraham, trans. and ed. *The Authorised Selichot for the Whole Year According to the Rite in Use among Hebrew Congregations in the Commonwealth and in Central Europe.* 1956. Reprint, New York: Judaica, 1978.

Roskies, David G. *Against the Apocalypse: Responses to Catastrophe in Modern Jewish Culture.* Cambridge, Mass.: Harvard UP, 1984.

———. *A Bridge of Longing: The Lost Art of Yiddish Storytelling.* Cambridge, Mass.: Harvard UP, 1995.

Rosman, Moshe. *Founder of Hasidism: A Quest for the Historical Baᶜal Shem Tov.* Contraversions: Critical Studies in Jewish Literature, Culture, and Society. Berkeley and Los Angeles: U of California P, 1996.

Rothenberg, Rabbi Meᶜir. *Responsa.* Prague: N.p., 1893.

Rotman, Yuval. *The Attitude of the Church to Castration and Eunuchs in the Period of the Later Roman Empire.* Master's thesis, Tel Aviv University, 1995.

Rousselle, Aline. "Parole et inspiration: Le travail de la voix dans le monde romain." *History and Philosophy of the Life Sciences* 5 (1983): 129–57.

Roy, Parama. *Indian Traffic: Subjects in Motion in British India.* Berkeley and Los Angeles: U of California P, in press.

Rozenblit, Marsha. *The Jews of Vienna, 1867–1914: Assimilation and Community.* Albany: SUNY, 1983.

Rubin, Barry. *Assimilation and Its Discontents.* New York: Times Books, 1995.

Ryback, Issachar, and Boris Aronson. "Di Vegen fun der Yiddisher Malerei." *Oifgang.* Kiev: Kulturlige, 1919.

Sacher-Masoch, Leopold von. "Venus in Furs." *Masochism.* New York: Zone Books, 1991. 143–293.

Santner, Eric. Letter to author. 1995.

———. *My Own Private Germany: Daniel Paul Schreber's Secret History of Modernity.* Princeton: Princeton UP, 1996.

Satlow, Michael L. " 'They Abused Him Like a Woman': Homoeroticism, Gender Blurring, and the Rabbis in Late Antiquity." *Journal of the History of Sexuality* 5.1 (1994): 1–25.

———. " 'Wasted Seed,' the History of a Rabbinic Idea." *Hebrew Union College Annual* LXV (1994): 137–75.

Scheman, Naomi. *Engenderings: Constructions of Knowledge, Authority, and Privilege.* Thinking Gender. New York: Routledge, 1993.

Schnitzler, Arthur. *My Youth in Vienna.* Trans. Catherine Hutter. New York: Holt, Rinehart, and Winston, 1970.

Schorske, Carl. *Fin-de-Siècle Vienna: Politics and Culture.* New York: Knopf, 1980.

Schur, Max. *Freud Living and Dying.* New York: International UP, 1972.

——. "Some Additional 'Day Residues' of 'the Specimen Dream of Psychoanalysis.'" *Freud and His Self-Analysis,* ed. M. Kanzer and J. Glenn. New York: Jason Aronson, 1979. 95–120.

Schürer, Emile. *History of the Jews in the Time of Jesus.*

Scott, James C. *Domination and the Arts of Resistance: Hidden Transcripts.* New Haven: Yale UP, 1990.

Scott, Joan Wallach. *Gender and the Politics of History.* Gender and Culture. New York: Columbia UP, 1988.

Sedgwick, Eve Kosofsky. *Between Men: English Literature and Male Homosocial Desire.* New York: Columbia UP, 1985.

——. *Epistemology of the Closet.* Berkeley and Los Angeles: U of California P, 1990.

Seeberg, Reinhold. "Antisemitismus, Judentum und Kirche." *Zum Verstandnis der gegenwartigen Krisis in der europaischen Geisteskultur.* Leipzig: A. Deichert, 1923.

Seecombe, Wally. "Patriarchy Stabilized: The Construction of the Male Breadwinner Wage Norm in Nineteenth-Century Britain." *Social History* 2 (1986): 53–75.

Seidman, Naomi S. *"A Marriage Made in Heaven"?: The Sexual Politics of Hebrew-Yiddish Diglossia.* Ph.D. Diss., University of California at Berkeley. 1993. Photocopy.

Senelick, Laurence. "The Homosexual as Villain and Victim in Fin-de-Siècle Drama." *Journal of the History of Sexuality* 4.2 (1993): 201–29.

Seshadri-Crooks, Kalpana. Letter to author. 1994.

——. "The Primitive as Analyst." *Cultural Critique* 28 (Fall 1994): 175–218.

Sharpe, Jenny. *Allegories of Empire: The Figure of Woman in the Colonial Text.* Minneapolis: U of Minnesota P, 1993.

——. "The Unspeakable Limits of Rape: Colonial Violence and Counterinsurgency." *Genders* 10 (Spring 1991).

Shaw, Brent D. Letter to author. 1995.

——. "The Passion of Perpetua." *Past & Present* 139 (May 1993): 3–45.

Shechter, Solomon, ed. *Aboth de Rabbi Nathan.* Vienna, 1887. Reprint, New York: Philipp Feldheim, 1967.

Shepherd, Naomi. *A Price below Rubies: Jewish Women as Rebels & Radicals.* Cambridge, Mass.: Harvard UP, 1993.

Showalter, Elaine. "Hysteria, Feminism, and Gender." In *Hysteria beyond Freud,* ed. Sander L. Gilman et al. Berkeley and Los Angeles: U of California P, 1993. 286–344.

——. *Sexual Anarchy: Gender and Culture at the Fin de Siècle.* New York: Penguin Books, 1990.

Siegel, Carole. *Male Masochism: Modern Revisions of the Story of Love.* Bloomington: Indiana UP, 1995.

Silverman, Kaja. *Male Subjectivity at the Margins.* New York: Routledge, 1992.

Simon, Ernst. "Jewish Adult Education in Nazi Germany as Spiritual Resistance." *Leo Baeck Institute Year Book.* London: Leo Baeck Institute, 1956. 68–104.

————. "Sigmund Freud the Jew." *Leo Baeck Institute Year Book.* London: Leo Baeck Institute, 1957. 270–305.

Sinfield, Alan. *The Wilde Century: Effeminacy, Oscar Wilde, and the Queer Moment.* Between Men, between Women. New York: Columbia UP, 1994.

Slipp, Samuel. *The Freudian Mystique: Freud, Women, and Feminism.* New York: New York UP, 1993.

Smith, Paul. "Eastwood Bound." In *Constructing Masculinity,* ed. Maurice Berger, Brian Wallis, and Simon Watson. New York: Routledge, 1995. 77–97.

Socher, Abe. "A Magus from the East; or, Maimon at the Margins of the Public Sphere." Unpublished paper. Berkeley, 1995. Photocopy.

Somerville, Siobhan. "Scientific Racism and the Emergence of the Homosexual Body." *Journal of the History of Sexuality* 5.2 (1994): 243–66.

Spiegel, John P. "Anna O. (Bertha Pappenheim): Her History." In *Anna O.: Fourteen Contemporary Reinterpretations,* ed. Max Rosenbaum and Melvin Muroff. New York: Free, 1984. 52–58.

Spitzer, Leo. *Lives in between: Assimilation and Marginality in Austria, Brazil, and West Africa, 1780–1945.* Studies in Comparative World History. Cambridge: Cambridge UP, 1989.

Sprengnether, Madelon. *The Spectral Mother: Freud, Feminism, and Psychoanalysis.* Ithaca: Cornell UP, 1990.

Stampfer, Shaul. "Gender Differentiation and Education of the Jewish Woman in Nineteenth-Century Eastern Europe." *Polin: A Journal of Polish Jewish Studies* 7 (1992): 63–87.

Steakley, James D. *The Homosexual Emancipation Movement in Germany.* New York: Arno, 1975.

Stein, Ruth. Letter to author. 1993.

Steiner, Herbert, ed. *Käthe Leichter: Leben und Werk.* Vienna, 1973.

Steinmann, Anne. "Anna O.: Female, 1880–1882; Bertha Pappenheim: Female, 1980–1982." In *Anna O.: Fourteen Contemporary Reinterpretations,* ed. Max Rosenbaum and Melvin Muroff. New York: Free, 1984. 118–31.

Stewart, Larry. "Freud before Oedipus." *Journal of the History of Biology* 9 (1976): 215–28.

Stieg, Gerald. "Kafka and Weininger." Trans. Barbara Hyams. In *Jews & Gender: Responses to Otto Weininger,* ed. Nancy A. Harrowitz and Barbara Hyams. Philadelphia: Temple UP, 1995. 195–206.

Stoltenberg, John. *Refusing to Be a Man: Essays on Sex and Justice.* New York: Meridian Books, 1989.

Tamir, Joseph. "The March of the Coopted Historians." *Ha'aretz,* May 20 1994, B9.

Theweleit, Klaus. *Male Fantasies: Volume 1: Women Floods Bodies History.*

Trans. Stephen Conway, Erica Carter, and Chris Turner. Foreword by Barbara Ehrenreich. Theory and History of Literature. Minneapolis: U of Minnesota P, 1987.

Thomas, Kendall. "Corpus Juris (Hetero)sexualis: Doctrine, Discourse, and Desire in *Bowers v. Hardwick.*" *GLQ: A Journal of Lesbian and Gay Studies* 1.1 (1993): 33–51.

Torgovnick, Marianna. *Gone Primitive: Savage Intellects, Modern Lives.* Chicago: U of Chicago P, 1990.

Trunk, Yehiel Yeshayahu. *Polin: Memories and Portraits.* Trans. Ezra Fleischer. Jerusalem, n.p., 1962.

Van Herik, Judith. *Freud on Femininity and Faith.* Berkeley and Los Angeles: U of California P, 1982.

Veith, Ilsa. *Hysteria: The History of a Disease.* Chicago: U of Chicago P, 1965.

Veyne, Paul. "Homosexuality in Ancient Rome." In *Western Sexuality: Practice and Precept in Past and Present Times,* ed. Philippe Ariès and André Béjin. Oxford: Oxford UP, 1985. 26–35.

Vilna, Eliahu, and Vilna Gaon. *Commentary on the Book of Proverbs.* Warsaw, n.p., 1837.

Volkov, Shulamit. "Antisemitism as a Cultural Code—Reflections on the History and Historiography of Antisemitism in Imperial Germany." *Leo Baeck Institute Yearbook* 23 (1978): 25–46.

Walton, Jean. "Re-placing Race in (white) Psychoanalytic Discourse: Founding Narratives of Feminism." *Critical Inquiry* 21.4 (1995): 775–804.

Warner, Marina. *Joan of Arc: The Image of Female Heroism.* New York: Vintage, 1982.

Warschawski, Michael. "On the Three Sins of Tel Aviv: Misappropriating the Mantle of the Slain." *News from Within* XI.6 (1995): 26–29.

Weininger, Otto. *Sex and Character.* (Originally published as *Geschlecht und Charakter.*) 6th ed. G. P. Putnam's Sons, 1906. Reprint, New York: AMS, 1975.

Weinreich, Max. *The History of the Yiddish Language.* Trans. Shlomo Noble and Joshua Fishman. Chicago: U of Chicago P, 1980.

Weissler, Chava. "For Women and for Men Who Are Like Women." *Journal of Feminist Studies in Religion* 5 (1989): 7–24.

———. "The Religion of Traditional Ashkenazic Women: Some Methodological Issues." *Association for Jewish Studies Review* 12.1 (1987): 73–94.

———. "Women in Paradise." *Tikkun* 2.2 (1987): 43–46; 117–20.

———. "Women's Studies and Women's Prayers: Reconstructing the Religious History of Ashkenazic Women." *Jewish Social Studies* New Series 1 (Winter 1995): 28–47.

Weissman, Deborah. "*Bais Yaakov:* A Historical Model for Jewish Feminists." In *The Jewish Woman: New Perspectives,* ed. Elizabeth Koltun. New York: Schocken, 1976.

Wiedemann, Thomas. *Emperors and Gladiators.* New York: Routledge, 1992.

Wilde, Oscar. *The Importance of Being Earnest.* New York: Dover Publications, 1990.

Williams, Patrick, and Laura Chrisman, eds. *Colonial Discourse and Postcolo-*

nial Theory: A Reader. Introd. by Patrick Williams and Laura Chrisman. New York: Columbia UP, 1994.

Winkler, John. *The Constraints of Desire: The Anthropology of Sex and Gender in Ancient Greece.* London: Routledge, 1989.

Wittels, Fritz. *Sigmund Freud: His Personality, His Teaching, and His School.* London: Allen and Unwin, 1924.

Yerushalmi, Yosef Hayim. *Freud's Moses: Judaism Terminable and Interminable.* New Haven: Yale UP, 1991.

Zertal, Idith. "The Sacrificed and the Sanctified: The Construction of a National Martyrology." *Zemanim* 12.48 (1994): 26–45.

Zerubavel, Yael. *Recovered Roots: Collective Memory and the Making of Israeli National Tradition.* Chicago: U of Chicago P, 1995.

Index

๛

Abraham, Karl, 40
Achilles Tatius, 7
Adorno, Theodor, 269
Agnes, St., 21–22
Allen, Grant, 3
Allen, Woody, 241
Ambrose, St., 109
Anality: and creation, 204–5
Anna O. *See* Pappenheim, Bertha
Antisemitism: and castration complex, 232–44; and circumcision, 239–41; and colonialism, 261–65; and Freud, 299–300; and homophobia, 215–16, 241–42, 253–54; Jewish, 237–39; and misogyny, 241–42; and Nazism, 237, 245–46; and Zionism, 286, 297–98
Anzieu, Didier, 202n. 49, 206–7, 223n. 10, 242n. 75
Aryans: and Jews, 250–51
Assimilation: and Judaism, 222, 248; and Zionism, 277

Bakhtin, Mikhail, 92–93
Baron, Lawrence, 271n. 1, 272n. 3, 297
Barratt, Barnaby, 243–44
Barton, Carlin, xi, 6n. 15, 83n. 8, 96n. 34, 100n. 43, 103n. 49, 115n. 81, 129n. 4, 306n. 107
Baskin, Judith, xxii, 25n. 76, 28
Bataille, Georges, 124
Batya, Reina, 172–80, 181

Bauer, Ida, 316, 322, 323, 341–42
Beethoven, Ludwig van, 255
Beller, Steven, 74–75, 238n. 60, 282n. 33, 324
Ben-Gurion, David, 300
Benjamin, Jessica, 114, 115nn. 78,80; 121n. 96, 236
Benjamin, Walter, 359n. 168
Bergmann, Martin, 34–35
Beritela, Gerard, 203, 226, 227–28
Bersani, Leo, 14n. 39, 96n. 33, 106n. 56, 114, 122, 125
Bhabha, Homi, x, 262, 280n. 26, 302n. 97, 305–8
Biale, David, x, 24–25, 43n. 28, 49nn. 50,52; 51n. 62, 57nn. 69,71; 59n. 76, 61n. 80, 62 n, 67n. 92, 139n. 32, 153n. 9, 160n. 26, 165nn. 40,41; 277nn. 16,17,20; 295n. 71, 310n. 122, 325n. 56, 328n. 65, 329–30, 331, 332, 344n. 123, 346n. 132
Bickerman, Elias, 274
Bildung: and Judaism, 229; and Zionism, 309. See also *Kultur*
Biller, Peter, 210
Binswanger, Robert, 317
Bloch, Donald, 323
Bloch, R. Howard, 43n. 26, 46n. 42, 48, 75, 132n. 13
Bolkosky, Sidney, 324
Bordieu, Pierre, 151
Bose, G., 261

Boyarin, Daniel, xxn. 15, 10n. 30, 38n.
    15, 43n. 27, 45n. 38, 48n. 48, 68
    n, 87n. 17, 89n. 21, 92n. 26, 93n.
    30, 100-101n. 45, 111n. 71, 115n.
    82, 132n. 14, 139n. 32, 147n. 59,
    152nn. 5,8; 170,n. 55, 216n. 108,
    239n. 66, 240n. 67, 250n. 100,
    252n. 110, 253n. 116, 258, 273n.
    9, 284n. 36
Boyarin, Jonathan, x, 74n. 108, 87n.
    17, 233n. 42, 239n. 66, 252n. 110,
    253n. 116, 269n. 172, 277n. 15,
    284n. 36, 309n. 119, 357n. 165
Bram, Frederick, 347, 349
Brandes, Stanley, 97n. 37
Bray, Alan, 18
Breines, Paul, xi, xxi, 79n. 122, 212n.
    88, 246, 306n. 108, 351
Breitman, Barbara, 19n. 60, 148-49,
    299-300
Brenkman, John, 191n. 6, 196n. 23,
    205n. 62, 215n. 101, 236-37, 268n.
    168
Breuer, Josef, 207, 313-14, 316-17,
    320, 321, 340-41, 349, 350
Briggs, Sheila, 11, 48n. 47
Brod, Harry, xiii-xiv, 355n. 162
Brooten, Bernadette, 5, 156,n. 17,
    355n. 160
Buber, Martin, xxiii, 278n. 22
Bullough, Vern, 26n. 79, 63n. 83, 344
Burrus, Virginia, xi, 6, 20-22, 109-10,
    121n. 96, 144n. 53, 145-46, 150,
    161
Bush, Larry, 15, 17
Butler, Judith, xviin. 5, 113, 193n. 11,
    307
Byron, Lord, 75

Caldwell, Sarah, 84, 121-22n. 96
Calvin, John, 166,n. 44
Cantor, Aviva, 11, 59n. 77, 144n. 53,
    150n. 66, 153n. 9, 184, 333n. 82
Carnal Israel (D. Boyarin), 10n. 30,
    43n. 27, 45n. 38, 48n. 48, 67n. 94,
    132n. 14, 147n. 59, 152nn. 5,8;
    170n. 55
Castration complex: and antisemitism,
    232-44; and femminization, 9; and
    gender, 242-44; and Judaism, 231-
    44; and phallus, 10, 236n. 52. See
    also Freud, Sigmund; Little Hans;
    Oedipus
Catullus, 140
Cecci d'Ascoli, 210
Chamberlain, Houston Stewart, 263,
    299

Chanson de Roland, 129
Charcot, Jean Martin, 194, 209, 210
Chrétien de Troyes, 169
Christianity: and gender, 6, 21-23, 25-
    26, 107-111; and homophobia, 208-
    9; and Judaism, 74, 108, 115, 253,
    279; and masculinity, 64, 145-46;
    and Rome, 228-29; and Zionism,
    282-83. See also Jesus Christ
Circumcision: and antisemitism, 239-
    40; and castration complex, 232-33,
    240-41
Civilization and its Discontents (Freud),
    261, 268, 269
Cixous, Hélène, 213n. 96, 314, 316
Cockburn, Cynthia, 154
Cohen, Hermann, 251, 252n. 110, 268
Colonialism: and antisemitism, 261-65;
    and Jews, xvii; and Zionism, 278-312
Cooper, Arnold, 119, 177n. 69
Craft, Christopher, 2n. 4, 3n. 7, 18,
    170n. 54, 219n. 123, 228n. 30
Cuddihy, John Murray, 37n. 11, 39-42,
    44-47, 49-51, 75, 265n. 155, 287n.
    49
Cust, Sir Edward, 305

Davis, Natalie Zemon, x, 55n. 67, 159-
    60, 162n. 31, 349
Decker, Hannah, 322-23, 341, 355
Delphy, Christine, xvin. 2, 122, 155,
    162n. 31, 167n. 46, 171n. 56, 193
Den Haag, Ernest van, 44-45, 46
Derrida, Jacques, 251, 268n. 169
Deutsch, Helene, 82
Dijkstra, Bram, 42n. 23, 45n. 36, 46,
    50, 73n. 104, 76n. 117, 77n. 118,
    79, 138, 268
Dik, A. M., 332-34, 346
Dohm, Christian Wilhelm, 279, 295
Donne, John, 42
Dora. See Bauer, Ida
Dreyfus, Alfred, 222
Du Bois, W. E. B., 263
Du Maurier, Daphne, 41
Dühring, Eugen, 279-80
Dworkin, Andrea, 122

Eckstein, Emma, 213-14
Edelman, Marek, 306
Edinger, Dora, 180n. 72, 182n. 76,
    315n. 10, 317n. 21, 318nn. 23,27;
    325n. 57, 326-27, 328n. 66, 336nn.
    93,94,96; 340nn. 106,107,108;
    346n. 130, 135, 347n. 136, 350n.
    143, 351n. 147
Edwards, Catherine, 95n. 33, 121n. 96,

130n. 8, 136n. 22, 137nn. 27, 28; 138n. 29, 139n. 34, 140, 141, 142n. 48

Eilberg-Schwartz, Howard, 206n. 64; 212n. 88, 216n. 108, 217n. 111, 252–53, 254

Elijah, 94, 97

Ellenberger, Henri, 321n. 43, 322n. 45, 323–24, 350

Ellis, Havelock, 2, 6, 42n. 25, 118–19, 169–70

Elon, Amos, 74n. 108, 276n. 15, 287n. 49, 288n. 51, 293n. 64, 294n. 66, 296n. 77, 301, 305n. 104, 308n. 118, 310nn. 123,125

Enlightenment: Jewish, xvii–xviiin. 6, 332–33, 335, 358–59. *See also* Modernity

Entmannung: and femininity, 216–20

Erikson, Erik, 202

Estrich, Susan, 19n. 59, 177

Etlinger, Anna, 340

Euclid, xv

Euripides, 22

Evans, Martha, 190–91

Fanon, Frantz, 239, 248, 293, 302, 307, 311n. 126

Femininity: and *Entmannung*, 216–20; and gender, 82–86, 118; and homophobia, 354–55; and homosexuality, 245; and masculinity, xx–xxi, 90–92, 110–11, 121, 123–24, 191–92; and phallus, 96–97

Feminism: and heterosexuality, 17–19; and hysteria, 314–17, 337–42; and Judaism, xviii–xix, xx–xxi, 172–85, 171, 317–59; and Zionism, 334–36

Femminization: and castration, 9; and heterosexuality, 151; Jewish, 4–5, 10, 11–12, 23, 26, 81-86, 92, 142, 211–12, 240, 242, 358; and masculinity, 102–103

Ferenczi, Sandor, 206, 218

Fichte, Johann Gottlieb, 296, 298

Finkelstein, Louis, 330–31

Fliess, Wilhelm, 194, 196, 197, 200, 201–8, 209, 211, 214, 218–19, 224–25, 226, 228, 273

Foreplay: and Judaism, 41–42

Foucault, Michel, xix, xx, 14, 16n. 48, 24, 26n. 77, 85n. 12, 109n. 64, 122, 216n. 108

Fout, John, 189, 209n. 75, 215, 229, 254n. 118, 334n. 85, 344, 355

Francis of Assisi, St., 25, 108

Freeman, Lucy, 314, 318, 322n. 45, 324–25, 326, 328n. 65, 338n. 104

Freud, Sigmund, 9–10, 14n. 39, 28, 33–36, 38–42, 46n. 40, 47, 52, 73n. 103, 77n. 118, 102n. 48, 106, 114, 115n. 78, 116n. 84, 119, 138, 149, 189–220, 221–70, 280, 284, 291, 295, 296, 304, 310, 311n. 126, 312, 314–15, 320,n. 36, 354n. 152; and antisemitism, 299–301; and homosexuality, 194–95, 196–220; and Judaism, 208–16, 342, 345, 347, 353; and Zionism, 271–77

Freud, Martin, 349

Frick, Wilhelm, 216

Garber, Marjorie, 4n. 10, 5n. 11, 6n. 16, 38n. 13, 143n. 50, 202n. 47, 211n. 84, 212–13n. 92, 215n. 104

Garner, Shirley, 191n. 7, 202, 206, 212n. 90

Gauguin, Paul, 260

Geller, Jay, x, xviin. 5, 107n. 57, 121n. 94, 138n. 30, 202n. 45, 203, 204nn. 54,56; 211n. 84, 216–18, 228n. 29, 233nn. 40,42; 335n. 51, 240n. 71, 252n. 108, 258, 263n. 153, 265n. 157, 266n. 158, 284n. 36, 294n. 70, 299n. 87, 307n. 114, 308n. 116, 355n. 161

Gender: and anxiety, 136–37; and bourgeoisie, 343–45; and castration complex, 242–50; and Christianity, 6, 21–23, 25–26, 107–111; and culture, 199; and desire, 105–106; and femininity, 82–86, 118; and God, 9; and Greece, 7–8, 9–10; and hysteria, 190–201; and Judaism, ix–x, xiii–xiv, xv–xvi, xvii–xxiv, 8–9, 10, 13, 25–28, 151–54, 343–51, 347, 353–59; and phallus, xiv, 111–17, 120, 121, 148–50; and rabbinic culture, 157–84; and Rome, 5–6, 21–22, 86–98, 120–21; and Talmud, ix–x, 179, 153–56; and Torah, 151–54, 153–56, 257, 258. *See also* Femininity; Femminization; Masculinity; Queerness; Sexuality

George, Stefan, 79

Gilmore, David, 344

Gilman, Sander, 210n. 83, 211n. 85, 213, 214–15, 238–39, 241–42, 246, 250n. 97, 252n. 112, 254n. 118, 255n. 123, 262nn. 145,146,147; 263nn. 148,149; 267, 268n. 167, 269n. 172, 271n. 2, 272n. 5, 277n. 18, 286n. 41, 296n. 77, 299n. 86, 300, 304–5, 330n. 72

Gleason, Maud, 130nn. 6,7,8; 135n.
  21, 140n. 39, 141nn. 44,45; 147n.
  58, 151, 152
Glikl of Hameln, 28, 44, 52–55, 159–60,
  177, 181–83, 162n. 31, 340, 346–52
God: and gender, 9; and Judaism, 245,
  257–59; and masochism, 114–15
Goethe, Johann von, 227, 249, 255,
  328n. 64
Goldstein, Bluma, 229n. 31, 266n. 160,
  273, 274n. 12, 350–51
Gottfried, Barbara, 98
Goux, Jean-Joseph, 252
Grasse, J. G., 75
Grau, Rudolph, 245
Gravdal, Kathryn, 42n. 25, 44n. 33,
  92n. 27, 129, 133n. 16, 134n. 17,
  169
"Great man": and Judaism, 254–55
Grinstein, Alexander, 223n. 10, 227
Grossman, Avraham, 162–64, 167n. 49
Gutmann, Moses, 214

Hall, Donald, 19, 37n. 12
Halperin, David, xix, xx, 14, 85n. 12,
  135, 137n. 26, 142n. 48, 212
Hamilcar, 39
HaNagid, Samuel, 24–25
Hannibal, 39n. 17, 226–27, 242, 250,
  273, 274, 347
Harrison, Verna, 145, 147n. 58
Hartog, François, 308–9
Hauptman, Judith, x, xxii, 28, 163,
  165n. 42, 172n. 60
Heath, Stephen, 19
Hegel, G. W. F., 160, 250–51, 252n.
  108, 260
Heine, Heinrich, 75, 127, 355n. 161
Heller, Peter, 202, 205n. 60, 212n. 90,
  218n. 117, 227n. 19
Herzl, Theodor, 25, 28, 73–80, 221–26,
  238n. 60, 241n. 71, 249n. 93, 259,
  265, 267, 274, 275, 342, 345, 347,
  353; as antisemite, 276–312. See also
  Zionism
Heterosexuality: and feminism, 17–19;
  and femminization, 151; and homosexuality, 15–17, 119, 212; as institution, 14–15; and Judaism, 13–23, 28,
  323, 342. See also Sexuality
Hildesheimer, Azriel, 320
Hirsch, Marianne, 124
Hirschfeld, Magnus, 209n. 76, 213n.
  92, 215
Hirschmüller, Albert, 316–17, 318n.
  24, 321n. 42, 323n. 48, 338n. 103,
  341nn. 110,111,112

Hitler, Adolf, 263. See also Nazism
Hoberman, John, 39n. 15, 43, 44n. 29,
  233, 238n. 60, 254n. 121
Homer, 7n. 21, 135
Homophobia: and antisemitism, 215–
  16, 241–42, 253–54; and Christianity, 208–9; and femininity, 354–55;
  and misogyny, 17–18; and Nazism,
  216; and patriarchy, 17–18
Homosexuality: and femininity, 245;
  and Freud, 194–5, 196–220, 228–31;
  and heterosexuality, 15–17, 119, 212;
  and Judaism, 209–16, 226–27, 229–
  31; and masculinity, xix–xx, 222. See
  also Sexuality
Horkheimer, Max, 269
Horney, Karen, 237–38n. 59, 242
Hunter, Dianne, 320
Hyman, Paula, xviii, 5n. 10, 173n. 63,
  248, 276n. 14, 318–19, 321n. 40,
  330n. 72, 331, 334n. 86, 337n. 98,
  344
Hysteria: and feminism, 314–17, 337–
  42; and gender, 190–201

Ibsen, Henrik, 334
Interpretation of Dreams, The (Freud),
  33–36, 196, 205, 206, 221–22, 223n.
  10, 227, 299–300

Jackowitz, Ann, 315, 322n. 45
Jensen, Ellen, 318, 321n. 41, 328nn. 65,
  66
Jesus Christ, 22, 113n. 74, 225. See also
  Christianity
Jewish State, The (Herzl), 73n. 106, 76,
  281, 286, 293
Jewissance, xxiii, 256–58
Jones, Ernest, 194–95, 207, 218n.
  115, 227n. 23, 228n. 30, 273n. 6,
  313–14
Joseph: and Jewish sexuality, 58
Joyce, James, 38, 108, 110n. 67, 118–
  19, 276n. 14, 313, 353
Jung, Carl, 4n. 10, 194n. 16, 228n. 30,
  271–72, 277

Kafka, Franz, 221, 231, 237, 307n. 114
Kaminsky, Marc, x, 36–37, 39nn.
  15,16; 67n. 91
Kampen, Natalie, 79n. 122, 162n. 31
Kant, Immanuel, 250–52, 256, 257,
  328n. 64. See also Sublime, the
Kaplan, Marion, 50n. 54, 160n. 29,
  182, 317, 318n. 24, 321n. 40, 323n.
  49, 329, 331, 335n. 90, 336n. 97,
  340n. 105

Katz, Jacob, 164 n. 40
Kinney, Clare, 8
Klepfisz, Irena, 337
Koestenbaum, Wayne, 17–18, 132 n. 13, 202 n. 47, 204 n. 55, 213 n. 93
Kohut, Heinz, 123
Kornberg, Jacques, 225–26, 238, 246 n. 60, 279 n. 26, 280 nn. 27,28,29; 282–83, 286, 287 n. 50, 291 nn. 57,59; 293, 294, 295 n. 72, 296 nn. 74,76, 303 n. 99
Krafft-Ebing, Richard von, 119
Krauss, Shmuel, xxiii, 247
Krestin, Lazar, 35, 71
Kris, Ernest, 202, 189 n. 2
Kultur: and Judaism, 224, 246–47, 293–94. See also Bildung

Lacan, Jacques, 8–10, 131 n. 10, 243 n. 77, 252
Lane, Frederick, 2–3
Laplanche, J., 263
Lefkowitz, Lori, xx, 19 n. 62
Leichter, Käthe, 324
Leonardo da Vinci, 205 n. 61, 219 n. 120, 255
Lessing, Theodor, 271 n. 1, 271–72 n. 3, 297
Levine, Molly, 140, 156 n. 17
Levitt, Laura, x, xvii, xxii, 28, 156, 171, 357 n. 164
Lilien, E. M., 274, 275
Little Hans, 231–54. See also Castration complex; Freud, Sigmund
Lloyd, Genevieve, 251, 253 n. 117
Loewenberg, Peter, 222 n. 6, 302
Loraux, Nicole, 118
Lord, Audre, 25
Luxon, Thomas, x, 42, 120, 228, 330 n. 72

Macaulay, Thomas, 279, 303, 309 n. 121
Maccabee, Judah, 273, 274
MacKinnon, Catherine, 122
Mailer, Norman, 353
Maimonides, Moses, 163–64, 168 n. 51, 268
Marcus Aurelius, 142–43
Martial, 140
Marx, Karl, 50, 287
Masculinity: and Christianity, 145–46; and effeminacy, 97; and femininity, xx–xxi, 90–92, 110–11, 191–92; and femminization, 102–103; and homosexuality, xix–xx, 222; Jewish, 1–6, 10–12, 37–38, 55–67, 68–73, 76–80,

142, 221–70, 277, 343–46, 354; and Nazism, 79; and phallus, 82, 84–85, 90–91, 101, 121, 123–25, 138–39, 142; and Rome, 12, 103, 139–43; and state, 284; and Talmud, 81–126, 127–50; and Zionism, 11, 88, 221–31, 271–312, 336, 345–46
Massena, 273, 274, 347
Masson, Jeffrey, 189 n. 3, 190, 194 n. 17, 195 nn. 19,20; 197 n. 28, 198 n. 32, 199 n. 35, 201 nn. 40,44; 202 nn. 48,50; 204 n. 57, 213 nn. 93,94; 214 nn. 97,98; 221, 226 n. 17, 228 n. 30, 229 n. 31, 266 n. 159
McGrath, William 34 n. 4, 207–8, 221, 222 n. 6, 227, 272 n. 4
Mendelssohn, Moses, xviii n. 6, 267, 268, 332
Michelangelo, 266
Milbank, John, 31
Misogyny: and antisemitism, 241–42; and castration complex, 232–33, 236; and homophobia, 17–18. See also Masculinity
Modernity: and Judaism, 43, 50, 310–12, 320, 333–34, 358–59. See also Enlightenment
Modleski, Tania, xviii–xix, 18 n. 57, 102 n. 48, 103 n. 49, 149, 338 n. 103, 356
Moebius (Jean Giraud), 261
Mopsik, Charles, 48
Morgan, Robin, 83, 104, 113 n. 73, 149
Moses and Monotheism (Freud), 222, 231, 235 n. 50, 244–70, 310
Moses, 182, 225, 239, 273, 274, 275, 277, 296, 347
Mosse, George, 3 n. 8, 4 n. 9, 5 n. 13, 8, 36 nn. 6,7; 38 n. 13, 52, 77 n. 118, 96 n. 33, 103 n. 50, 210 n. 80, 212 n. 91, 212–13 n. 92, 215 n. 99, 216 n. 107, 277, 291 n. 60, 294 n. 69, 299 n. 87, 301 n. 93, 311, 321 n. 40, 334 n. 88, 345, 354 n. 155
Muscle-Jews, 76–77, 336. See also Nordau, Max

Nazism: and antisemitism, 237, 245–46; and homophobia, 216; and Judaism, 253–54, 326, 354–55; and masculinity, 79; and Zionism, 291, 297. See also Hitler, Adolf
New Ghetto, The (Herzl), 74 n. 110, 75, 221, 223, 225–26, 284–96
Nietzsche, Friedrich, 85–86, 103, 161, 209 n. 76
Nordau, Max, 37 n. 12, 75 n. 114, 76–

Nordau, Max (*continued*)
  77, 239n. 65, 241n. 71, 272n. 3,
  277, 297, 308n. 118, 334, 336n. 95.
  See also Muscle-Jews

O'Neill, John, 122, 219–20
Oedipus, 39, 189–96, 199–201, 208,
  211, 212n. 90, 215, 216, 217n. 111,
  218, 219–20, 241, 242, 250, 274. *See
  also* Castration complex; Freud
Oppenheim, Moritz, 56
Orthodox Judaism, xv, xvi, xxiii,
  356–59
Ovid, 139, 140

Pappenheim, Bertha, xii, xxiii–xxiv, 28–
  29, 40, 49n. 49, 172–73, 180–84,
  238n. 60, 312, 313–59
Parsons, Talcott, 50
Parush, Iris, xxii, 37n. 9, 72n. 102,
  318n. 29, 319n. 32, 320nn. 34,35;
  322n. 44, 329nn. 67,68,69; 333n.
  80, 334n. 85, 343, 345n. 129
Pateman, Carol, 26n. 77, 90–91, 152,
  154, 156n. 17, 158n. 18, 160n. 28,
  160–61, 330n. 72
Paul, St., 108n. 60, 109
Pellegrini, Ann, x, 39n. 17, 238n. 60,
  250n. 97, 262n. 147, 342, 354
Penis: and phallus, 8–10, 48n. 48, 108
Perkins, Judith, 6–7, 24, 59n. 75, 82
Perpetua, 21
Peskowitz, Miriam, x, xxii, 1–2, 8, 28,
  153n. 8
Phallus: and castration complex, 10,
  236n. 52; and femininity, 96–97; and
  femminization, 242; and gender, xiv,
  111–17, 120, 121, 148–50; and Juda-
  ism, 239; and masculinity, 82, 84–85,
  90–91, 101, 123–25, 138–39, 142;
  and penis, 8–10, 48n. 48, 108. *See
  also* Oedipus
Philo, 253
Pilcz, Alexander, 214–15
Plato, 90, 131, 203n. 52
Pontalis, J. B., 263
Powers of Diaspora (Boyarin and
  Boyarin), 87n. 17
Protestantism: and Judaism, xviii, 46–
  47, 246–48
Proust, Marcel, 215, 222n. 7, 229n. 32
Prudentius, 21–22, 109
Psychoanalysis. *See* Freud, Sigmund

Queer Nation, 29
Queerness: Jewishness as, 212, 214–15
Queer theory, 13–14

Rank, Otto, 235, 268n. 167
Rashi, 42–43, 51, 141, 319n. 32
Rathenau, Walter, 279
Reik, Theodor, 47, 100, 106n. 55, 107,
  108, 113
Renan, Ernst, 251
Richlin, Amy, xi, 86, 97, 110n. 67, 130
  n. 8, 139–40
Roith, Estelle, 46n. 39, 47, 72n. 103, 75
Rome: and Christianity, 228–29; and
  gender, 5–6, 21–22, 86–98, 120–21;
  and masculinity, 12, 103, 139–43
Rose, Paul, 51, 75, 296n. 77, 298n. 82,
  355n. 161
Rosenzweig, Franz, xxiii
Roskies, David, 70 n, 79n. 122, 333
Rosman, Moshe, 56–58
Roth, Philip, 98, 241, 353
Rousseau, Jean-Jacques, 26n. 77, 251
Ruskin, John, 3, 6

Salanter, Israel, 52
Santner, Eric, x, 84–85, 251, 255–56,
  257
Satlow, Michael, 9n. 28, 12, 14, 15, 19–
  20n. 62
Schachter, Zalman, xv
Schnitzler, Arthur, 238n. 60, 295–96,
  301n. 94, 323, 324
Schönerer, Georg von, 355
Schorske, Carl, 288
Schreber, Daniel Paul, 102n. 48, 106n.
  56, 110n. 68, 114, 121, 122, 138n.
  30, 206, 216–20, 228n. 30, 249n.
  94, 255–56, 338n. 103, 354
Schürer, Emile, 112n. 72
Schur, Max, 207–8, 214n. 97
Scott, J. C., 95n. 33, 156, 172, 240,
  315n. 6
Sedgwick, Eve Kosofsky, xvi n, 16n. 47,
  118, 131nn. 9,12; 132n. 13, 136n.
  24, 209n. 76, 219n. 123, 227
Seeberg, Reinhold, 245–46
Seidman, Naomi, x, xviin. 6, 37n. 9,
  151, 173n. 62, 319n. 32, 332n. 78,
  333n. 83, 334n. 87, 335n. 91, 336n.
  92, 337, 346n. 131
Seneca, 142
Seshadri-Crooks, Kalpana, x, 239,
  248n. 90, 261n. 142, 263, 309n. 120
Sexuality: and bourgeoisie, 329–31; his-
  tory of, 189–90; and Judaism, 45–46,
  48; and Talmud, 170–71. *See also*
  Gender; Homosexuality; Heterosexuality
Shakespeare, William, 320
Shapiro, Susan, xxii, 234n. 47

Sharpe, Jenny, xviin. 5, 300, 303n. 98
Shaw, Brent, xi, 8n. 21, 21n. 65, 21n. 67, 142-43
Shenirer, Sore, 336
Shepherd, Naomi, 160n. 29, 172n. 60, 317, 322n. 44, 327n. 62
Shomer, 329
Showalter, Elaine, 73n. 104, 76n. 117, 117n. 85, 191n. 5, 192-93, 203n. 52, 212n. 90, 215nn. 102,103
Sidney, Phillip, 42
Siegel, Carole, 2, 42n. 25, 108, 116n. 84, 118-19, 170n. 53
Silverman, Kaja, 2n. 2, 6n. 15, 119, 124, 136-37n. 24
Simon, Ernst, 34n. 2, 74n. 107, 238n. 62, 278n. 22, 343
Slipp, Samuel, 201, 342
Smith, Paul, 82-83, 113n. 73, 119
Socialism: and Jews, 287-88
Spencer, Herbert, 50
Spielrein, Sabina, 271-72, 276, 310
Spiess, Camille, 3
Spillers, Hortense, 193
Spinoza, Baruch, 284
Spitzer, Leo, 72
Spivak, Gayatri, 311
Sprengnether, Madelon, 38n. 15, 39n. 17, 199n. 7, 192, 199-200, 213-14, 245
Stampfer, Shaul, 67n. 90, 174n. 66, 183n. 78, 318n. 25, 319n. 33, 322n. 44, 329n. 69, 343-44
Stein, Ruth, x, 114
Stewart, Larry, 209
Stieg, Gerald, 237, 269n. 172
Stites, Richard, 160n. 29
Stoecker, Adolf, 215, 253-54
Stoker, Bram, 41, 77n. 118
Stoltenberg, John, 11n. 35, 123
Strachey, James, 194-95
Straus, Barrie Ruth, 243-44
Streisand, Barbra, 143
Studies in Hysteria (Freud), 190, 198n. 33, 314
Sublime, the: and Judaism, 251-53. See also Kant, Immanuel
Suetonius, 139
Sulpicius, 145-46
Sydenham, Thomas, 211

Talmud, ix, xv-xvii, 23-29, 43, 48, 60-61, 65, 69, 80; and gender, 179, 153-56, and marriage, 44-45; and mascu-

linity, 81-126, 127-50; and maso-chism, 112-13; and sexuality, 171; and women, 327; and Zionism, 280
Theweleit, Klaus, 79
Thomas, Kendall, 219
Torah: and gender, xxii, 151-56, 357, 358; and masculinity, 59, 63, 68, 143-45; and women, 327
Torgovnick, Marianna, 229n. 32, 260, 267-68n. 167
Totem and Taboo (Freud), 260
Treitschke, Heinrich von, 302
Trunk, Yehiel Yeshayahu, 69-72, 78, 335n. 89

"Uncanny, The" (Freud), 234-35

Verdi, Giuseppe, 33
Violence: sexual, 162-69

Wagner, Richard, 73-80, 257, 263, 276 n. 15, 296, 355n. 161
Weininger, Otto, 4-5n. 10, 43, 50, 212, 232, 233-34, 236, 237-38, 239, 242, 251, 257, 272n. 3, 284, 296, 300, 325n. 58, 354, 355n. 160
Weinreich, Max, 319n. 32, 337
Weissler, Chava, xxin. 17, 26n. 78, 36n. 7, 162n. 31, 173nn. 61,64; 183n. 81, 319, 321n. 39, 334, 343
Wilde, Oscar, 44n. 34, 151, 212, 222, 324
Wittels, Fritz, 234
Wolf Man, the, 196, 199-200, 201, 204, 244-45, 249, 269-70
Wollstonecraft, Mary, 160, 314, 340

Yerushalmi, Yosef, 271nn. 1,2; 272
Yiddish: literary tradition in, 182-83

Zerubavel, Yael, 88, 93n. 30, 293n. 62
Zionism: and antisemitism, 286, 297-98; and assimilation, 277; and Christianity, 282-83; and colonialism, 278-312; European allegory of, 75; and feminism, 334-46; and Freud, 271-77; and masculinity, 11, 88, 221-31, 271-312, 336, 345-46; and Nazism, 281, 297; and Ostjuden, 267, and Talmud, 280. See also Herzl, Theodor
Zionist Writings (Herzl), 73n. 106
Zweig, Arnold, 239, 242
Zweig, Stefan, 296